Administrative Office Management

Tenth Edition

Norman F. Kallaus

The University of Iowa
Iowa City, Iowa

B. Lewis Keeling

Professor Emeritus
Bucks County Community College
Newtown, Pennsylvania

GE40JA
PUBLISHED BY
SOUTH-WESTERN PUBLISHING CO.
CINCINNATI, OH   DALLAS, TX   LIVERMORE, CA

Acquisitions Editor: Karen Schneiter
Developmental Editor: Jeanne R. Busemeyer
Production Editor: Sharon L. Smith
Photo Researcher: Diana L. Fears

ISBN: 0-538-70195-1

3 4 5 6 7 Ki 6 5 4 3

Printed in the United States of America

Kallaus, Norman Francis
    Administrative office management / Norman F. Kallaus, B. Lewis
Keeling. -- 10th ed.
        p.   cm.
    Includes bibliographical references and index.
    ISBN 0-538-70195-1
    1. Office management.   I. Keeling, B. Lewis (Billy Lewis)
II. Title.
HF5547.K43   1991
651.3--dc20   89-62809
                                                                       CIP

Preface

In each of its ten editions spanning seven decades, *Administrative Office Management* has carefully documented the problems and solutions of an expanding office world. It began with the First Edition in the depression years of the 1930s and continued on during the hectic war years, culminating in the present edition. In the Tenth Edition, like its predecessors, we explain *past* office problems, relate them to *current* office conditions, and explain how to ensure *future* effectiveness in office operations.

New thinking has emerged to redefine the office. Instead of a place where clerical work is performed, now we view the office more broadly as the *information function* as well as the *information center*—a place where information-related operations occur. The pace of change in information technology, so swift and universal in the 1970s and 1980s, has accelerated even more in the 1990s. This means that our students preparing for business careers, as well as workers on the job seeking positions in management, need to be on the "cutting edge" of technology and human relations to maximize the use of information tools and procedures in their work.

In the Tenth Edition we follow the same logical organization plan as its predecessor, but with substantial updating and strengthening of content. However, we emphasize the overriding importance of *people* more strongly than in any of the previous editions. It is people who make decisions, and who plan, organize, direct, and control the administrative process. In other words, *it is people who manage*. And, since *all* employees have some of these decision-making responsibilities, all employees, to some degree, manage, even if it's only their own individual work assignments.

We have broadened Part 1 in scope to introduce students to the fundamentals of effective management. These fundamentals include basic principles of management, problem solving, systems, and communications needed to administer the office function. Part 2 stresses people and their role in using the tools of information technology required in the battle to increase productivity. In Part 3 we highlight the main concepts needed to understand the services used by successful office administrators—computers, text/word processing, telecommunications, records management, microimage and reprographic systems, and the space, furniture, equipment, and environment required to use these services. Part 4 provides a "control" setting that explains how office managers evaluate the productivity of their office systems and the "bottom-line" importance of living within their budgets.

To update and further strengthen its coverage of the field, we have provided these new features in the Tenth Edition:

1. A personal, more informal writing style that is in line with our greater emphasis on people.
2. An expanded set of chapters on general management principles in Part 1 that includes basic systems concepts.

3. A discussion of the latest human relations issues, such as the need for cost-effective employee benefits programs, drug and alcohol abuse, and AIDS in the workplace.
4. A condensed discussion of unions and an integration of this material into a human resources problems setting.
5. New concepts in information technology that include (a) broadening word processing to include text management; (b) developing a new "umbrella" function, information distribution, that includes telecommunication and mailing systems; (c) redirecting the area of micrographics into the broader field of microimage systems; and (d) an integration of automated services in the modern office.
6. Profiles of real-world managers who describe their current job descriptions, answer the authors' questions about the managers' methods of solving pressing human and technology problems in the office, and provide personal information on their education and work experience. These profiles, which are located in most of the chapters, are termed, "Dialog on the Firing Line," and are designed to give students practical information from those managers and supervisors presently employed on the job (that is, on the "firing line").

Throughout the Tenth Edition, our emphasis is on systems. This emphasis aids students in understanding the *interaction* of the main elements in the process of administrative office management. Also, the systems "way" of thinking helps students to apply the concepts involved in discussing the questions posed and in solving the case problems presented at the end of each chapter. Thus, we have provided a strong management-based background so that students may assume responsibilities later as members of the management team.

The Tenth Edition of *Administrative Office Management* represents our combined teaching, research, and consulting experience. This experience has been strengthened materially by the valuable contributions of the following persons:

Joseph V. Arn
University of Central Arkansas

Julia Bradley
Administrative Management Society
Trevose, Pennsylvania

Anna M. Burford
Middle Tennessee State University

Olive D. Church
University of Wyoming

Sherry Crone
Dimension 11 Limited
Regina, Saskatchewan, Canada

Eleanor Davidson
Nassau Community College

Michael F. Emig
The Wyatt Company
Washington, DC

J. Claude Ferguson, Jr.
Andersen Consulting
Philadelphia, Pennsylvania

Howard Freedman
Tredegar Industries, Inc.
Richmond, Virginia

Mary Giovannini
Northeast Missouri State University

Marty Hanson
Black Hawk College
Moline, Illinois

David B. Henry
Wm. B. Reily & Co., Inc.
New Orleans, Louisiana

Thomas M. Hestwood
MCI Communications Corporation
Washington, DC

Larry B. Hill
San Jacinto College Central

Marilyn Joyce
The Joyce Institute
Seattle, Washington

Alice Karsjen
The Principal Financial Group
Des Moines, Iowa

Joan P. Klubnik
Transamerica Occidental Life Insurance
Company
Los Angeles, California

Karen Lee Kothenbeutel
Southwest Missouri State University

Richard Kozitka
The Quaker Oats Company
Chicago, Illinois

David M. Maksymovich
Educational Testing Service
Princeton, New Jersey

Joyce P. Moseley
Trident Technical College
Charleston, South Carolina

Patty Nelson
Intel Corporation
Hillsboro, Oregon

Gladys D. Oldham
Winston-Salem State University

Raymond E. Polchow
Muskingum Area Technical College
Zanesville, Ohio

Donald Porter
CIGNA Corporation
Philadelphia, Pennsylvania

Jennie D. Prant
Trenton State College

Jeanette J. Purdy
Mercer County Community College
Trenton, New Jersey

Barbara J. Railsback
Washburn University of Topeka

Richard S. Sabo
The Lincoln Electric Company
Cleveland, Ohio

Ron Schlattman
University of Wisconsin-Eau Claire

Richard A. Wueste
State University of New York at Stony Brook

In addition, office managers; students; colleagues, including users of earlier editions of the textbook; and a highly competent editorial staff have contributed many useful suggestions. The result is a book that has two primary uses: (1) as a textbook in the classroom, and (2) as a valuable reference source on the job.

Good luck in your study of administrative office management, and much success as you start (or continue) your work in the office!

N. F. K.
B. L. K.

Brief Contents

Part Four

Controlling Administrative Services 644

Contents

Part Three

Managing Administrative Services   362

Part Four

Controlling Administrative Services   **644**

PART 1

Basic Concepts in Administrative Office Management

1

Administrative Office Management in the Information Age

GOALS FOR THIS CHAPTER

After completing this chapter, you should be able to:

1. Define the functions of management and indicate the managerial levels at which these functions may be carried out.
2. Define the functions of administrative office management and describe some of the typical office activities that may be performed in each of the functional areas.
3. Show how the information-handling responsibilities of the administrative office manager may vary according to the size of the organization.
4. Identify the skills and competencies needed by administrative office managers.
5. Describe the goals of the Administrative Management Society and its Certified Administrative Manager program.
6. Identify briefly the major characteristics of, and contributors to, each of the following schools of management thought: classical, behavioral, management science, and systems.

Welcome to your study of Administrative Office Management! As you learn more about this field, we are sure you will agree that it is one of the most essential and satisfying professions in business. At the same time, however, this profession can be one of the most frustrating. You will see that managing other people differs greatly from doing the work yourself. For the first time, you will be faced with an entirely different set of duties and responsibilities. As a manager, you will begin to use more of your conceptual and human skills, and, as a result, your managerial skills and competencies will grow. These are just a few of the topics you will be exploring in this opening chapter. However, before undertaking an in-depth study of this subject, let's examine each of the words in the name *Administrative Office Management* in order to learn more about the complex nature of this field.

Administrative is related to the word *administration*, which describes the performance of, or carrying out of, assigned duties. The word "administration" is also used to refer to a group of persons who execute these duties, such as the governing board of your school or the top-level executives of a corporation. We shall soon see that administration is essential in every aspect of business operations.

Office is a term used by many to refer to the *place* where business affairs are carried on, such as a credit office or a lawyer's office. Others may use the word "office" when referring to the *people* working in that location. For example, we may hear, "The employment office left work Monday at 3:30." Today, we commonly look upon the office as a *function*, where interdependent systems of technology, procedures, and people are at work to manage one of the firm's most vital resources—*information*. In these offices, the focus is not on the "high-tech" machines and equipment used but on the *systems* within which both the technology and the workers function to create that product—information—at the lowest possible cost.

Management is the art or skill used by administrators in the process of blending together the *six M's*—Manpower, Materials, Money, Methods, Machines, and Morale—in order to set and achieve the goals of the organization. The word "management" is also commonly used when referring to the *group of persons*, such as top management, who collectively direct or manage the organization. In the process of blending the six M's, those in charge of the organization—the managers—are greatly involved with directing people and coordinating the use of economic resources.

Before putting all three of these words together and learning about this exciting field of administrative office management, let's examine the duties or functions of management in general.

THE FUNCTIONS OF MANAGEMENT

Any form of group endeavor (an **organization**), whether it is a social club, a governmental unit, an educational institution, or a business firm, requires leadership and direction at various levels in order to realize its goals. To achieve its goals as an organization, a firm must be well managed. Thus, the functions of **management** involve the planning, organizing, and controlling of all resources and the leading or directing of people to attain the goals of a productive, unified organization.

The functions of management are performed by persons called **managers** at several levels in any organization, from the president to a supervisor. The titles held by managers vary considerably depending upon the nature of the work assigned, the responsibilities delegated to the position, and the type and size of organization. Usually, managerial levels are divided as shown in Figure 1–1.

THE FUNCTIONS OF ADMINISTRATIVE OFFICE MANAGEMENT

What has been said about management in general also applies to those responsible for managing the office and for making decisions that concern the day-to-day operations of the office. (Such decisions often are called **operational decisions** or *administrative decisions*.) **Administrative office management** is the process of planning, organizing, and controlling all the *information-related activities* and of leading or directing people to attain the objectives of the organization.

Traditionally, the administrative office management functions were limited to basic clerical services and to office personnel. However, with the passage of time came an accompanying increase in government regulations, a larger and more diverse work force, a growing economy, and the development of new information technologies, such as the computer. All of these factors brought about an *information revolution*—an increased demand for more information in order to make intelligent decisions at greatly accelerated rates. Management began to rely more upon office personnel and well-designed work systems as the new technology created greater information-processing power. The "one-department office" concept gradually gave way to a broader, company-wide information management concept in which the administrative office manager became responsible for the expanding, vital areas of work in the information age.

THE ADMINISTRATIVE OFFICE MANAGER

The person who heads up the company-wide information management function may have one of several titles, such as administrative

Figure 1–1
Managerial
Levels,
Titles, and
Responsibil-
ities

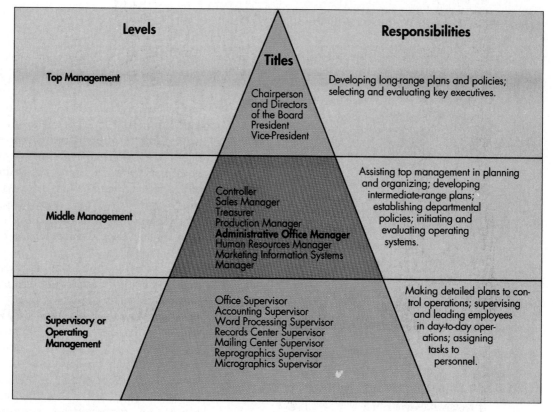

Figure 1–1
Managerial Levels, Titles, and Responsibilities

office manager; office manager; manager, administrative services; information manager; manager, information services; manager of office services; and administrative manager. Throughout this textbook, the person responsible for planning, organizing, and controlling the information-processing activities and for leading people in attaining the organization's objectives is called the **administrative office manager** or *office manager*. Because of the high frequency with which these two titles are used, they are often abbreviated—AOM or OM—just as CEO is commonly used for chief executive officer.

Responsibilities of the AOM

We shall present the scope and responsibilities of the AOM by first identifying and then analyzing each of the managerial functions as they apply to office activities. The logical sequence of these functions and their related activities is outlined in Figure 1–2.

Although similarities exist in the job content of OMs, no two have exactly the same job responsibilities. In a small firm, we often find that the OM is an accountant who also has been assigned the added supervision of correspondence, mailing, filing, and other general administrative services. In another firm, we may find the OM assuming the additional responsibility of human resources manager or credit manager with miscellaneous supervisory activities. In still another company, we may find that the OM is an office services executive who supervises support services that meet the needs of users in all office divisions. Such support services include mailing, records management, word

Figure 1-2
Managerial
Functions
and Related
Office
Activities

Managerial Functions	Office Activities
Planning: analyzing relevant information from both the past and the present and assessing probable developments of the future so a course of action—the *plan*—may be determined that will enable the firm to meet its stated goals.	*Developing policies and objectives for the various information-processing services,* such as communications, records management, mailing, and reprographics or copymaking; procuring a suitable office site; equipping the work areas with modern, functional office furniture, machines, and equipment; staffing the office with qualified employees so the work will flow smoothly and quickly.
Organizing: bringing together all economic resources (the work, the workplace, the information, and the workers) to form a controllable (manageable) unit—the *organization*—to accomplish specific objectives.	*Applying basic principles of office organization in determining the working relationships among employees,* who are equipped with the best physical facilities and work flows, to achieve the maximum productivity.
Leading: motivating and directing the workers so the objectives of the organization will be successfully achieved.	*Directing and supervising effectively the office activities;* adopting and implementing workable personnel policies that maintain a desirable level of morale; training, orienting, counseling, promoting, and compensating office personnel; providing static-free communication lines between employees and employer.
Controlling: ensuring that operating results conform as closely as possible to the plans made for the organization.	*Developing, installing, and improving administrative office systems and procedures* to be followed when completing each major phase of office work; supervising the procurement, preparation, and use of office forms and other supplies; measuring the work done and setting standards for its accomplishment; reducing the costs of administrative services; preparing budgets, reports, and office manuals as means whereby costs are reduced and controlled.

processing, messenger service, communications, copymaking, and office security and maintenance.

The differences in responsibilities assigned to AOMs are due to several factors, the most important of which is the size of the organization. Many large banks, for example, employ several thousand office workers; and major insurance companies employ 10,000 or more. Naturally, in such organizations where the collection and

production of information constitute the main responsibilities of the office staff, the volume of service activities is so great that their supervision and direction under an AOM are necessary. The job description in Figure 1-3 lists the typical responsibilities that may be assigned to a manager of administrative services in large and medium-size organizations. In small organizations, factory workers may be the primary source of business activity; hence, the office force is

Figure 1-3
Job Descrip-
tion Showing
Responsibili-
ties of Man-
ager, Admin-
istrative
Services

Manager, Administrative Services
1. Supervises administrative services such as word processing, telecommunications, records storage and retrieval, printing and/or duplicating, mailing, reception, and messenger.
2. Secures office supplies, furniture, and equipment and contracts for maintenance and repairs of office equipment.
3. Controls interoffice communications and maintains local, in-house, and 800-number directories.
4. Conducts special studies to determine equipment performance and costs and meets with sales representatives to evaluate new equipment.
5. Coordinates with operating departments to establish new and to modify existing administrative office systems.
6. Supervises the orientation and training of office employees.

not so large. In such firms, the office service activities may be supervised directly by an accountant, the controller, the treasurer, the credit manager, or the human resources manager (formerly called the personnel manager).

In this section, we shall briefly examine three very challenging areas in which AOMs have great responsibilities: the information cycle, the management information system, and office automation. Each of these areas of responsibility will be discussed in more detail in later chapters.

The Information Cycle

AOMs have a company-wide responsibility for managing the **information cycle**: the collecting, processing, storing, retrieving, and distributing of information for internal and external use. Each of these sequential phases of the information cycle is shown in Figure 1-4. Administrative office management is looked upon as a process of converting information into action. Information is viewed by organizations as a critical economic resource—an asset that is as valuable as any physical property owned, such as a building or machines and equip-

ment. AOMs are aware that the competitive positions of their companies depend on their abilities to produce timely and reliable information and to use that information productively. Like all other resources, information must be managed.

At all levels of management, there is a growing interest in improving the quality of decision making. To do so, decisions must be made upon the basis of relevant, accurate, and timely information. To provide information that meets these qualifications, management information systems have been developed.

Management Information Systems

A **management information system (MIS)** is an organizational process designed to supply timely information to managers for use in drawing conclusions, making predictions, recommending courses of action, and, in some cases, making decisions in order to take action. Thus, an MIS is directly tied into the productivity of any business enterprise.

At the heart of an MIS is the computer, which performs many of the functions that make up the information cycle. For example, the computer is used for collecting, processing, and storing business information;

Figure 1-4
The Infor-
mation Cycle

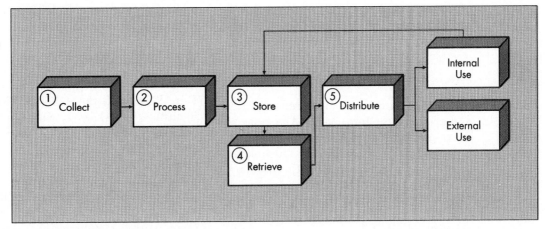

and when the need arises, the computer retrieves information to assist in decision making. The computer also aids managers in formulating plans for the future based upon an analysis of the contents of its extensive historical files.

The raw or unprocessed data collected for an MIS may be obtained from many sources within and outside the organization: personal contacts with workers, management, vendors, and suppliers; incoming mail;

Computers play a key role in providing and processing information used by AOMs.

information systems operating by means of services provided by the telephone industry; and analyses of the firm's systems, procedures, and files.

In an MIS, not all the activities in the information cycle are performed by automated machines, because the MIS is controlled by people. People play an active part in each step in decision making as well as in developing solutions to all types of problems.

In large companies, such as banks, financial services firms, airlines, and insurance firms, we may find a management specialist with the title **information manager** or *chief information officer (CIO)*, who has responsibility for all information-handling activities. In addition to having expertise in managing administrative services, the information manager has some of the training and experience required of a systems analyst, a data processing manager, and a communication specialist. Such broad experience and education are required to understand and to manage the information-related activities in the organization.

AOMs have always been managers of facts and information. They have had the responsibility for developing and maintaining good systems, efficient personnel, and reliable equipment. With the advent of office automation, as discussed next, the AOM's sphere of responsibility has been further extended throughout the company.

Office Automation

Of all the changes that occurred in offices as we entered the Information Age, none has more dramatically affected the AOM's responsibilities than office automation. According to John Naisbitt, writing in *Megatrends*, the official transition of the United States from an industrial economy into an information economy occurred in 1956. For the first time in our history, white-collar workers in technical, managerial, and clerical positions outnumbered blue-collar workers; *for the first time most of us were working with information rather than producing goods*.[1]

As we saw earlier, all organizations are faced with the challenge of developing high-quality yet cost-effective information systems. Office automation offers the most promising approach for meeting this need. **Office automation (OA)** is an MIS process that aims to maximize the productivity of managing information through the integration of skilled personnel, powerful technology, and sophisticated systems. The components of OA—people, technology, and systems—make up an interdependent team, none of which stands alone or apart from the rest.

Before the trend toward OA within an information society began in the 1950s, most offices were collections of independent entities such as *a* telephone system, *a* duplicating system, *a* data processing system, and *a* work force. Today, however, OA views these same entities as essential components of the information system—all *interrelated*,

all *interdependent*, and all *interconnected* by telecommunication systems.

Skills of the AOM

In the *Dialog on the Firing Line* on page 9, Don Porter of the CIGNA Corporation identifies those skills a person should develop for a successful career in the field of administrative office management. Throughout this textbook, we enter into similar dialogs with managers and supervisors who are skilled in solving problems that arise in the office. These individuals are "on the firing line" every workday—taking aim at problems and hitting the target by finding solutions that will be mutually agreeable to them, their subordinates, and their organizations.

We agree with Porter that the AOM must be a skillful innovator—a creative manager—to administer the changes occurring in an organization's information-handling activities. We have classified the types of skills needed by creative managers as (1) conceptual, (2) human, and (3) technical and briefly discuss each one below.

Conceptual Skill

Conceptual skill is the ability to use existing knowledge in order to acquire additional knowledge. One example of conceptual skill is the ability to view an entity as a whole and see how a change in one of its parts affects all other parts or functions. Thus, the AOM is using conceptual skill when viewing the firm's management information system as a whole to see how a change in one information-handling activity has its effects upon other activities.

Let's say that you are evaluating the need to install an automated system for storing company records. In making a decision, you are displaying your conceptual skills as you question, explore, and probe to see how such a change will affect all other phases of the information cycle, especially the processing and locating or retrieving of records.

[1]Jack Gordon, "Desk Jobs: Marketing the Information Age," *Training* (December, 1987), pp. 37–43.

Dialog on the Firing Line

DONALD W. PORTER
Vice-President, Operations & Employee Services
Human Resources & Services Company
CIGNA Corporation
Philadelphia, Pennsylvania

BA, Franklin & Marshall College
Reporting to the Executive Vice-President for Human Resources and Services, Porter is responsible for the corporation function of payroll/personnel information processing and reporting; benefits administration; relocation; and human resource systems development and maintenance. For the human resources function, Porter has responsibility for financial planning and the reengineering/quality/productivity functions.

QUESTION: For a few minutes, Don, think about career success in the field of administrative office management. What skills should a person develop? What are some of the changes facing tomorrow's manager?

RESPONSE: The basic managerial functions of planning, organizing, leading, and controlling continue to be the foundation of the successful administrative office manager. However, there are a number of changes that are imperative for the successful manager of the future to be prepared to deal with. These include:

- *Innovation.* The manager of tomorrow must constantly seek opportunities for innovation and change, not for the sake of change but to improve productivity and therefore the competitive position of the organization. Along with this need is the ability to assess valid ventures and to manage change effectively within the organization.
- *Logical Thinking.* The complexity of much of our information processing requires that the manager be able to examine a process in a very logical fashion. This requires breaking the current process into component pieces and perhaps reassembling them in a very different form (reengineering).
- *Technology Familiarity.* I do not believe a manager can be successful without a basic conversant knowledge of today's technology and a commitment to stay abreast of the changes as they evolve. I do not suggest that a manager be able to program and operate a computer. A manager should, however, be aware of the kinds of support that technology can afford and be conversant with these capabilities. Thus, the needs of the organization can be expressed in ways that supporting groups, such as systems, can deliver the technology support that will advance the manager's purpose.
- *Information Management.* Managers seem to be either information rich or information poor. The latter is usually a matter of too much data—data that address no specific purpose. The effective manager (information rich) selectively decides and uses only that data critical to making the key decisions.
- *Diversity of Work Force.* We are no longer dealing solely with a work force comprised of full-time people working from 8:00 a.m. to 4:00 p.m., five days a week. While this group continues to be a major part of our work force, we are now managing people on a matrix arrangement for projects, shared work schedules, and flexible work arrangements. The effective office manager must be able to manage this diversity and, in fact, plan and use the diversity as an advantage.

Human Skill

Human skill is the ability to use knowledge and understanding of people as they interact with others. Such knowledge and understanding enable the AOM to identify, comprehend, and solve human problems. To do so, the AOM must be aware of the attitudes and beliefs held by individuals and groups and understand how these attitudes affect the workers' attempts to attain their goals. As a result, the AOM is able to sense the workers' needs and drives, to empathize with various lifestyles, to lead a group of workers, to work effectively as a member of the team, and to obtain cooperation from all team members.

Human skills are exhibited daily by AOMs in leading and directing subordinates and in their interrelationships with peers and superiors. As an example, let's say that you are appointed to serve as head of a labor-management committee that is investigating a change in work schedules. In this role, you are exhibiting human skills by being sensitive to the feelings and needs of others and by creating an environment in which workers freely express themselves and offer suggestions for improvement.

Technical Skill

Technical skill is the ability to understand a specific function, with its specialized knowledge, and to use efficiently the tools and techniques related to that function or activity.

As an example of the use of technical skill, assume that you are updating the salary compensation plan for your office personnel. To develop a fair compensation plan, you must know how to undertake a salary survey and be informed of current government regulations that affect the payment of wages and salaries. Some of the methods used to adjust salaries may require that you have expertise in charting current and proposed salary rates or in using mathematical techniques to determine salary rates and ranges.

Throughout this textbook, you will be aided in learning more about each of the three skills needed by AOMs. In particular, your skills will be sharpened by solving the case problems at the end of each chapter. Also, you will have additional opportunity to improve your management skills while you work in your chosen career. Thus, by means of academic courses and on-the-job training, you increase your competency as an office manager. In the next section, we will examine those competencies that are needed for effective office administration.

Competencies Needed by the AOM

Studies have been undertaken in which office managers, directors of human resources, and instructors of office management were asked to identify those competencies needed by office administrators. The findings of these research studies are summarized in Figure 1–5, which classifies the relative importance of the competencies in the training of office administrators.

Each of the competencies classified in Figure 1–5 as *vital* and *essential* is an example of conceptual or human skill. At the middle management level where we may find the AOM, fewer technical skills are required, because persons at these levels do not need to have in-depth technical know-how. This statement is supported by the labeling of technical skills as *important* but not vital or essential competencies. As we move down the organization ladder, however, we find that midlevel technical supervisors and entry-level managers need more specialized technical skills than conceptual skills.

In another study designed to identify those concepts necessary for office managers to succeed in their positions, we see that the ability to apply technology is essential while a person is climbing the promotional ladder

Figure 1-5
Competencies Needed by the Administrative Office Manager

COMPETENCIES NEEDED FOR OFFICE ADMINISTRATION		
Vital	**Essential**	*Important*
Communicating	Controlling Decision making Directing Human relations Planning Problem solving Staffing Supervision	Records management Data processing Word/information processing Telecommunications Office planning, layout, and design

Source: Dolores D. Gioffre, "What Research Says about Competencies Needed for Office Administration," Research Summary #11-1, 1984, Gamma Beta Chapter, Delta Pi Epsilon, Trenton State College.

to an office manager position. However, once there, the emphasis placed upon concepts essential for success changes. At the office manager level, the top three concepts essential to successful office administration are: having a good attitude, being dependable, and delegating (and outlining) responsibilities. (Interestingly, the findings of the study also indicate that technology should be considered in office management curriculums but should not be the emphasis in such courses of study.)[2]

Careers in Administrative Office Management

What opportunities for professional development are there in the field of administrative office management? To answer this important question, let's take a look at some of the possible career paths that you may follow. As you have seen earlier, the job titles, job content, and responsibilities of the positions in administrative office management vary, mainly due to differences in the size of organizations.

In small firms, you may find that as the office manager, you are often responsible for functions such as accounting and human resources in addition to your company's administrative support services. As the OM in one of these firms, you may have been employed originally as an accountant or credit manager. However, with the passage of time, you were delegated additional responsibilities, with the result that your job grew into one that included the management of all office services. In other instances, you might have first held an information-related job such as word processing operator, records clerk, or administrative assistant. Then, as you gained more experience, sharpened your skills, and expanded your competencies, you were promoted to a supervisory post and later to the OM position. Thus, we see that small firms usually offer no clear-cut path of promotion to the position of OM that we generally find in larger organizations.

In a large firm, depending upon your education and experience, you might have been employed initially as a word processing operator, systems analyst, payroll clerk, or executive secretary. As you gained experience on the job and demonstrated your managerial skills and competencies, you were promoted to a supervisory position in one of the firm's departments, such as

[2]Marcia L. James, "Technology: What Should Be the Emphasis?" *Office Systems Research Journal* (Spring, 1988), Vol. 6, No. 2, pp. 15–21.

administrative services, accounting, or the records center. Based upon the career paths or career tracks maintained by your firm, the next stage of your career development may be a middle management post, such as administrative office manager, controller, or manager of human resources. Your company's management training and development program may show that next you will be assigned to a senior executive (a *mentor*), who will help you groom yourself for promotion to a top-management position, such as vice president of information systems or chief information officer. (Training and development programs for supervisors and middle managers are further discussed in Chapter 8.)

You will find that the salaries paid office managers, like other middle managers, vary a great deal, depending on factors such as type and size of business, geographic location, and responsibilities assigned the position. For example, let's take a look at the results of two salary surveys:

> In 1989, the Administrative Management Society reported an *average* annual salary of $36,600 for administrative/office services managers. Managers working in banks and insurance, finance, utility, transportation, and communication companies earned the highest average salaries ($39,500 to $41,000). The lowest salaries, averaging $32,400, were paid managers in education, government, and nonprofit organizations. Companies in the West paid the highest salaries, while the lowest paid managers were found in the West Central region.[3]
>
> The 1988 salary survey conducted by *Training* magazine found the *average* salary paid nontraining managers (personnel managers and managers not assigned responsibility for training) was $43,954. This study found the highest

salaries in the Pacific area, while the lowest were in the Northeast. By size of firm, companies with fewer than 500 employees paid the lowest average salary ($41,549); the highest salaries ($47,433) were found in firms with 500 to 2,499 employees. Companies with 2,500 or more employees paid less, $46,386.[4]

The information above, although somewhat dated, may be of help to you in learning about the amount of salary that managers command. However, as we will see in Chapter 10, the results of any salary survey must be accepted with caution. If you are comparing a salary offered you by a prospective employer with the results of a recent survey, you must examine more than merely the two job titles. For example, are the job responsibilities of the two positions comparable? Are the companies under consideration of similar size? in the same recruiting area? in the same industry? with similar operations?

Professional Organizations for the AOM

Your skills and competencies as an AOM are further strengthened by membership and active participation in various professional organizations. You may wish to become associated with one or more organizations, such as the Data Processing Management Association (DPMA), Association of Information Systems Professionals (AISP), the Association of Records Managers and Administrators (ARMA), the Society for Advancement of Management (SAM), the Association for Systems Management, and the Administrative Management Society (AMS).

---

[3]*1989 Management Salaries Report*, Administrative Management Society (Trevose, PA: 1989), pp. 8–11.

[4]Beverly Geber, "*Training*'s 1988 Salary Survey," *Training* (November, 1988), pp. 29–38.

About 11,000 persons whose work is related to administrative office management comprise the membership of the Administrative Management Society. This organization, consisting of more than 135 chapters in the United States and Canada, is concerned with enhancing and promoting the common professional goals of persons involved or interested in management. AMS has furthered the careers of thousands of management professionals by providing for the:

1. Professional development of its members.
2. Exchange of technical knowledge.
3. Development of interdisciplinary awareness.
4. Open exchange of management information.
5. Development of individual careers.

As a means of recognizing managers as "professionals," AMS sponsors the **Certified Administrative Manager (C.A.M.)** program. To achieve the C.A.M. designation and to gain membership in the Academy of Certified Administrative Managers, you must meet the following five program standards:

1. Have at least three years of management experience.
2. Possess high standards of personal and professional conduct.
3. Exhibit leadership ability.
4. Have made a contribution to administrative management effectiveness.
5. Pass the C.A.M. examinations covering five content areas (management concepts, personnel management, finance, administrative services, and information systems) and the case study analysis.

This certification program is further evidence of the broadening scope and important responsibilities of the manager in today's office.

Like today's C.A.M. who might walk through a museum of natural history to learn more about the evolutionary process, we are going to take a short tour through the museum of management thought to learn about the evolution of management theory and principles. In the following closing section of this chapter, we are going back to the time of the Industrial Revolution to examine some of the differing philosophies of management that laid the foundation for contributions being made today by professional managers, educators, and other practitioners in the Information Age.

SCHOOLS OF MANAGEMENT THOUGHT

We find that, because of their differing personal philosophies, office managers follow different lines of thinking in managing the information function. For example, some OMs view the management process primarily as the *science* of managing—knowing what the principles are and how they should work. Others look upon management mainly as an *art*—knowing when, how, and why to apply a given principle in a particular situation. As in the question, "Which came first—the chicken or the egg?" no precise answer is available for resolving the question of whether management is a science or an art.

Science and art are two sides of the same management coin, and it would be pointless to support an approach based solely on either science or art. In their decision-making processes, OMs use the scientific method of problem solving (discussed later in this chapter and in Chapter 3); but the skill and the ability of OMs as they employ this method represent the art side of the coin. As a science, the study of management develops many basic assumptions upon which decisions are based and presents proven theories that make up the basis of management education. However, many successful OMs are unable to spell out these theories even though, as a result of their "practicing management," they use the theories. Plans must be scientifically developed; but their implementation may be disastrous if the art of management, which involves working with and through people to accomplish the aims of the plans, is not practiced. Although the science of management can be predicted in many of its aspects, no one has scientifically determined how people will conform as they become emotionally involved in those plans.

The efficient office reflects a *perceptive* or *intuitive* manager—one who by training, experience, and intuition has sensed the need for improvement and has taken steps to make necessary changes. Managers who know or perceive, as a result of their *intuition*, are much in demand at all managerial levels because by their training and experience they have proven themselves able to direct people effectively toward the firm's objectives. As we shall see in Chapter 3, highly intuitive managers form the most innovative and creative pool of talent in their organizations. These persons are the **intrapreneurs**—those managers who create innovation of any kind *within their organizations.*[5] Unfortunately, however, many of us are not gifted with such powerful intuition. Therefore, we turn to education to learn about the conceptual, human, and technical skills required to manage the firm's economic and human resources.

Over the years, various functions in the management process have been identified and attempts have been made to classify the approaches used by management theorists and practitioners. In this discussion, the divergent streams of management thought are divided into four schools—classical, behavioral, management science, and systems. Each school of thought emphasizes a somewhat different approach to management and draws separate, though related, conclusions as to the most significant factors in the management process. These differing conclusions have become basic to the management process and over the years have been looked upon as principles of management, which are presented in the following chapter. Although as students of administrative office management, you may not find the specific answers you desire in the literature of these schools, you will discover established principles that will serve as guidelines for any actions you take and as aids in better understanding the information management concept.

The Classical School

In the eighteenth and early nineteenth centuries, the Industrial Revolution brought about the mass production of goods and created the modern industrial organization. The new companies with their great potential for production were little understood, and the need for knowledge about the management of such firms soon became apparent. Hence, it is not surprising that the early approaches to the study of management concerned themselves with the major characteristic of the newly formed businesses—production. The early theorists emphasized the essential nature of management and its relationship to the production process.

Intertwined in the development of classical management theory were two views toward the management of work and of organizations—scientific management and total entity management. These views and several of the leaders who followed them are briefly discussed in the following paragraphs.

---

[5]Weston H. Agor, "Nurturing Executive Intrapreneurship with a Brain-Skill Management Program," *Business Horizons* (May-June, 1988), pp. 12–15. Also in this same issue, pp. 16–21, see W. Jack Duncan *et al.*, "Intrapreneurship and the Reinvention of the Corporation."

Scientific Management

Scientific management was developed to solve two major problems: how to increase the output of the average worker and how to improve the efficiency of management. Scientific management has been called doing that which is most logical; that is, using common sense to make decisions. What is required in scientific management, however, is a higher order of common sense involving the careful definition of problems and the development of plausible solutions. The **scientific method of problem solving**, which characterizes scientific management, involves the use of logical, systematic steps to develop effective solutions to problems. These steps are explained fully in Chapter 3.

Frederick W. Taylor

Taylor is looked upon as the father of scientific management. In the 1880s, using his engineering background, Taylor studied work standards and the relationship of output to wages. His emphasis was on management at the shop level rather than on general management, and he was concerned mainly with the efficiency of workers and managers in actual production.

Taylor considered each worker to be a separate economic man motivated by financial needs. He believed that workers tended to restrict their output because of their fear of displacement. To minimize this fear, Taylor suggested that workers be educated to understand that their economic salvation lay in producing more units of work at a lower cost. The effectiveness of his argument could be proved to workers by placing them on a piecework system; and

thus by producing more, they would earn more. Underlying Taylor's entire approach to scientific management was the conviction that there is *one best way* of doing everything, whether it be using a shovel or filing a piece of paper.[6]

Taylor saw several new functions emerge for managers: the replacement of rule-of-thumb methods with scientific determination of each element of a person's job; the scientific selection and training of workers; the need for cooperation between management and labor to accomplish work in accordance with the scientific method; and a more equal division of responsibility between managers and workers, with managers planning and organizing the work.

Frank and Lillian Gilbreth

In the early 1900s, the husband-and-wife team of Frank and Lillian Gilbreth furthered the development of scientific management thought. The Gilbreths invented devices and introduced techniques to aid workers in developing their fullest potential through training, tools, environment, and work methods. Among their accomplishments were the use of motion pictures to study and improve motion sequences, development of charts and diagrams to record work-process and

---

[6]Frederick W. Taylor, *The Principles of Scientific Management* (New York: Harper & Bros., 1911).

work-flow patterns, exploration into the area of worker fatigue and its effect on health and productivity, and application of principles of management and motion study to self-management.

Max Weber

Weber (pronounced Vāber) was a German sociologist who developed the concept of an ideal model or pure form of organizational design. The label **bureaucracy** is used to describe Weber's pure form of organization, which is formal, impersonal, and governed by rules rather than by people. Weber's bureaucratic model was identified by features such as:

1. A clear-cut division of labor in which complex jobs are broken down into simple, repetitive operations, with each specialized operation being performed by one worker.
2. A well-defined hierarchy with a fixed chain of command.
3. A system of abstract rules for controlling operations.
4. Administrative acts, decisions, and rules recorded in writing to provide permanent files.
5. Employment and promotion based on technical qualifications.
6. Employee protection against arbitrary dismissal.

Weber made great contributions to the understanding of organization structure and management. However, we would expect to find very few features of his pure form of bureaucracy in today's well-managed offices.

William H. Leffingwell

Leffingwell, looked upon as the father of office management, was credited with applying the principles of scientific management to office work. His book, *Scientific Office Management*, published in 1917, was the forerunner of all modern studies in office management.

Leffingwell developed the Five Principles of Effective Work. Since these principles are related to the proper management of *all* work, they may be easily applied to the office, as shown below:

1. *Plan the work.* Any OM must plan what work must be done; how, when, and where it must be done; and how fast it can be done.
2. *Schedule the work.* By recognizing a total office plan of organization and product development, the OM can coordinate the efforts of all workers, machines, and information to formulate a proper work schedule to agree with the plan.
3. *Execute the work.* Proper operating systems and procedures, record-keeping practices, and methods for executing the work must be developed. The work must be done skillfully, accurately, rapidly, and without unnecessary effort and delay.
4. *Measure the work.* With the effective development of measurements, standards, and layouts for getting the work done, it must then be measured as to quantity, quality, the workers' potential, and past records.
5. *Reward the worker.* Perhaps of most importance, the OM must select, train,

motivate, compensate, and promote employees to keep their interests and those of the firm at an optimum level.

Total Entity Management

The followers of the total entity management school of thought emphasized an *overall* approach to the administrative problems of management. Thus, they searched for effective means of directing the business firm as a whole, or as an entity.

Henri Fayol

In his book, *General and Industrial Management,*[7] Fayol presented his concept of the universal nature of management, developed the first comprehensive theory of management, and stressed the need for teaching management in schools and colleges.

Fayol was the first management author to state a series of management principles that would provide guidelines for successful coordination. He looked upon the elements of management as its functions—planning, organizing, commanding, coordinating, and controlling. In his writings, he stressed over and over that these elements apply not only to business but also *universally* to political, religious, philanthropic, military, and other undertakings. His thesis was that since all enterprises require management, the formulation of a theory of management is necessary to provide for the effective teaching of management.

Mary Parker Follett

Follett was a political philosopher, social reform critic, and creative problem solver in the field of motivation and the group processes in industry. Her work spanned the gap between Taylor's scientific management and the new social psychology of the 1920s that promoted better human relations in industry, a first concern of modern management.

Follett called for a revolutionary new concept of association. This concept was found in her one principle, which stated that *group organization* was to be the new method in politics, the basis for the future industrial system, and the foundation of international order. In her penetrating study of human relations, Follett was perhaps the first to promote what she termed "togetherness" and "group thinking."

Many of the later developments in management thought were anticipated by Follett: the application of behavioral science to problems of organization; the constructive uses of conflict; the psychology of power; the nature of horizontal communications; and, above all, the social responsibilities of management.

The early classicists emphasized the structure and the formal relationships in business firms but did not ignore the human element. They developed an extensive body of knowledge and logically related concepts, many of which form the basis for the

---

[7]Henri Fayol, *General and Industrial Management* (New York: Pitman Publishing Corporation, 1949, translated from French; originally published in 1916).

organization of this book and, more specifically, the discussion of managerial principles in Chapter 2.

The Behavioral School

Scientific management is still used as the basis for solving business problems, but coupled with it is an even greater concern for the human element. Today there is a clear-cut recognition that, as workers, we are interested in more than money. We have social, psychological, and physiological needs that are of great importance to us as well as to the person who is our supervisor or manager.

Having become interested in the human element within the organization, managers began to conceive two main approaches that placed increased emphasis upon the members of the organization. The early approach to worker behavior—the **human relations approach**—calls attention to the importance of the individual within the organization. The modern approach to worker behavior—the **behavioral science approach**—cuts across the fields of psychology, sociology, and anthropology to emphasize interpersonal relations and democratic actions on the part of workers.

Human Relations Approach to Worker Behavior

In the 1920s and 1930s, the idea emerged that people are important considerations in management since objectives are set and achieved by individuals. Representative of this early approach to the development of human relations is Elton Mayo, whose Hawthorne experiments are briefly discussed below.

Elton Mayo

The human relations approach was stimulated by a group of researchers from Harvard University who conducted studies from 1927 to 1932 among a group of women workers at the Hawthorne plant of Western Electric in Chicago.[8] The research team, headed by Elton Mayo, a Harvard University professor, was formed to study the effects of the physical environment upon worker productivity.

The Hawthorne Experiments. In one of the Hawthorne experiments, Mayo's research team examined changes in the amount of light available in the working area. The results were confusing at first. When the lighting was increased, output rose; on the other hand, when the lighting was decreased, output still rose. An analysis of this and other such puzzling results showed that the workers were highly motivated not only by the amount of light provided but rather by their feelings of importance that resulted from their participation in the study. It mattered to them that they were really making a contribution to company operations.

The research team also examined other effects of change in the workers' environ-

[8]See Elton Mayo, *The Human Problems of an Industrial Civilization* (Cambridge: Harvard University, 1933), and F. J. Roethlisberger and William J. Dickson, *Management and the Worker* (Cambridge: Harvard University Press, 1939).

ment. They varied the working conditions such as rest periods, hot lunches, and working hours; used interviews to determine attitudes; and analyzed the social organization among workers. During the studies, it was found that changes in the work environment had little long-term effect upon worker productivity. The explanation offered was that the workers were made to feel like more than just cogs in machines and that management realized their importance. Since management had asked for their opinions on working conditions, the workers felt that their relationships with management were no longer impersonal. The workers felt they had achieved status and some degree of respect. The Hawthorne experiments proved that the road to more effective worker effort lay in recognizing the emotional as well as the physical well-being of the employees, explaining to them the reasons for management decisions, and making them aware that management appreciated the importance of their work.

The Hawthorne study placed new emphasis upon the social, psychological, and physiological factors in the study of work. As a result of this concern with human relations, the study of management took a new direction—the behavioral science approach.

The Behavioral Science Approach to Worker Behavior

Early theories of behavior tended to explain all behavior on the basis of a single need, such as the need to assert one's ego. Modern behaviorists typically list several needs ranging from three (physical, social, and egoistic) to 15 in number. Managers cannot *see* their own human needs or those of their workers but must *infer* their pattern from

a study of human behavior. Therefore, it is expected that there will be different theories about human needs, as explained below.

Abraham Maslow

One classification of human needs came from Abraham Maslow, a psychologist who developed a theory of human motivation.[9] At the core of his theory is the concept that we are motivated by fulfilling a hierarchy of needs. The hierarchy of needs shows that as our lower-level needs are satisfied, they are no longer motivating factors. At this time, our higher-level needs become dominant. A need at one level does not have to be completely satisfied before the next need emerges, however. Since very few of us ever fully realize the fulfillment of our higher-level needs, there is always a basis for motivation. (The hierarchy of needs is illustrated and further discussed in Chapter 7.)

The AOM must recognize that the needs pattern of each worker is different and should not assume that a single approach can be used to motivate all workers toward the accomplishment of the organizational objectives. Further, AOMs should be aware that well-satisfied needs do not motivate. After obtaining a reasonable satisfaction of their needs, workers will be stimulated to direct their actions toward satisfying higher-level needs.

[9]Abraham Maslow, *Motivation and Personality* (New York: Harper Bros., 1954).

Douglas McGregor

The nature of people, with all their apparent contradictory feelings and emotions, has long puzzled philosophers. Some see us as having a capacity for tenderness, sympathy, and love, with little need for external regulation. Others see us as having tendencies toward cruelty, hate, and destruction, with the need for close control and regimentation for the good of society. These contradictory thoughts suggest that people may have a *dual nature*. The concept of a dual nature was introduced into management theory by Douglas McGregor, who explored the human side of organizations and defined the traditional and the current views of worker behavior.[10] These views, which McGregor labeled Theory X and Theory Y, are explained in Part 2.

William Ouchi

During the past decade, American managers have become very interested in the Japanese management system and its techniques for increasing productivity. Managers in the United States are aware that the Japanese have high quality standards and realize that the Japanese believe high quality to be the key to increased productivity and greater profits. The attitude of Japanese management toward work and

workers is contained in Theory Z. "Theory Z management" is a term coined by Professor William Ouchi, who spent years researching Japanese companies and examining American companies with Theory Z management styles.[11] The nature of Theory Z management is explored further in the next part of this book.

Frederick Herzberg

The research conducted by Frederick Herzberg and his associates at the Psychological Service in Pittsburgh resulted in the **motivation-hygiene theory.**[12] According to this theory, we work in an environment wherein the following two kinds of factors are present:

1. **Motivators,** which result from experiences that create positive attitudes toward work and arise from the job content itself. Examples are those incidents associated with the feelings of self-improvement, recognition, achievement, and desire for and acceptance of greater responsibility.
2. **Hygienic** (or maintenance) **factors,** which are related to productivity on the job but are peripheral to the job itself. Examples are pay, working conditions (such as heating, lighting, and ventilation), company policy, and quality of supervision.

Herzberg found that when, as workers, we feel the hygienic factors are inadequate, they function as *dissatisfiers*. On the other hand,

---

[10]Douglas McGregor, *The Human Side of Enterprise* (New York: McGraw-Hill, Inc., 1960), pp. 33–57.

[11]William G. Ouchi, *Theory Z: How American Business Can Meet the Japanese Challenge* (Reading, MA: Addison-Wesley, 1981).

[12]Frederick Herzberg, Bernard Mausner, and Barbara B. Snyderman, *The Motivation to Work*, 2d ed. (New York: John Wiley & Sons, 1959). See also Frederick Herzberg, *Work and the Nature of Man* (Cleveland: World Publishing Company, 1966).

American managers continue to study the Japanese management system and to experiment with some of its techniques.

when the hygienic factors *are* present, they do not necessarily motivate us to greater productivity; instead, they make it possible for the motivators to function.

The motivation-hygiene theory is discussed further in Part 2, along with other motivational approaches such as job enrichment, participative management, management by objectives, goal setting, and expectancy theory.

The Management Science School

The **management science school**, also known as the *operations research* or *mathematical approach*, makes use of engineering and mathematical skills to solve complex decision-making problems. Simply stated, **decision making** is the making of a conscious choice between two or more alternative courses of action. While this definition is readily understandable, the selection of such courses of action—that is, how a decision is made—is more complex. We do know, however, that *sound* decision making depends on the accuracy and timeliness of the relevant information upon which the decisions are based.

Management science, aided by the advances in mathematics and computer technology, can be applied to many business problems, such as how to conserve energy and effectively use natural and human resources. Managers are able to collect volumes of data to perform precise mathematical calculations and analyses as substitutions for their intuition. Examples of the mathematical techniques for making decisions include (a) *work sampling*, where a number of random samples are taken in order to supply information for use in setting work standards and (b) *waiting-line theory*, in which a study is made of the behavior of persons waiting in line, such as customers lining up at a bank teller's window. Many mathematical techniques of decision making use higher-level mathematics and depend on the rapid calculating ability and accuracy of the computer.

Students of administrative office management are encouraged to understand the scientific approaches to decision making since quantitative tools and techniques may be used by practicing managers in conjunction with their own personal judgment and intuition.

The Systems School

In most modern approaches to the study of the management process, the systems concept is used as a means of describing the total organization. A **system** is a group of parts that are interrelated in such a manner that they form a unified whole and work together to attain a definite objective. An organization may be viewed as a system made up of the following interrelated parts:[13]

1. The *individual*—who, with his or her own personality, is the fundamental unit of the organizational system.
2. The *formal organization*—how the individuals and the work they do are

---

[13]Henry L. Sisk and J. Clifton Williams, *Management & Organization*, 4th ed. (Cincinnati: South-Western Publishing Co., 1981), pp. 33–34.

arranged. As indicated in the next chapter, this arrangement is often depicted by means of a formal organization chart.

3. The *informal organization*—those informal groupings and lines of communication that arise out of work situations but that are not shown on the company's organization chart.

4. The *roles*—assumed by individuals as a result of their positions and functions in the organization. For example, office supervisors are often "caught up in the middle" in their roles as linking pins between their superiors and their subordinates.

5. The *physical setting*—refers to the concept of seeking the optimum relationship between the physiological factors required for effective work and the psychological factors that explain how workers react to that environment. Ergonomics, the science that brings together the physiological and the psychological factors in a study of the work environment, is discussed in a later chapter.

As developed in detail later in the text, systems are given boundaries for the purpose of analysis. However, there are no systems that are completely independent of others. For example, when the activities of office management are viewed as a system, many environmental factors must be taken into consideration. When OMs plan, they must take into account such external matters as technology, social forces, laws, and regulations. When OMs work with others in designing an organizational system to help their people perform, they cannot help but be influenced by the patterns of behavior that people bring to their jobs from a variety of external influences. Thus, perceptive OMs see their problems and operations as a network of interrelated elements having daily interactions with environments inside and outside their organizations.

SUMMARY

1. The sweeping developments in computer technology have brought about marked changes in the offices of the Information Age. Today, emphasis in office operations focuses upon computer systems and the information contained in the records and forms produced by those systems. Administrative office managers are no longer merely "keepers of the books" but, instead, managers of systems within which both the technology and the workers function to create information at the lowest possible cost.

2. Although no two AOMs have exactly the same duties and responsibilities, they represent the major party in the operation of the information cycle—collecting, processing, storing, retrieving, and distributing information. AOMs often are assigned responsibility for developing, implementing, and supervising the firm's management information system. In addition, many organizations have delegated to the AOM full responsibility for office automation. Thus, by shouldering these responsibilities, the AOM often becomes the chief information officer of the company.

3. Today's AOMs must be creative persons with conceptual, human, and technical skills. By means of formal courses, on-the-job training, and active membership in professional organizations, AOMs are able to improve their skills so that the competencies needed for effective office administration are at their peak.

4. As a student of administrative office management, you can profit greatly from

the experiences of management theorists and practitioners of the past and the present. By studying and evaluating the principles and practices of management that have emerged from followers of the classical school, the behavioral school, the management science school, and the systems school, you gain insight into theories and practices that will aid you in better understanding and working in today's changing offices.

GLOSSARY

Administrative office management—the process of planning, organizing, and controlling all of the information-related activities and of leading people to attain the objectives of the organization.

Administrative office manager (AOM)—the person responsible for planning, organizing, and controlling the information-processing activities and for leading people in attaining the objectives of the organization; known by several other titles, such as office manager (OM).

Behavioral school—a group of theorists who emphasize the social and psychological needs of people within the organization.

Behavioral science approach—an approach followed in the management process that emphasizes interpersonal relations and democratic actions on the part of workers.

Bureaucracy—a model of organizational design that is formal, impersonal, and governed by rules.

Certified Administrative Manager (C.A.M.)—a person holding professional certification from the Administrative Management Society.

Classical school—an early group of theorists who emphasized the essential nature of management and its relationship to the production process.

Conceptual skill—the ability to use existing knowledge in order to acquire additional knowledge.

Controlling—a function of management which ensures that operating results conform as closely as possible to the plans made for the organization.

Decision making—the process of consciously choosing between two or more alternative courses of action.

Human relations approach—a behavioral approach followed in the management process that calls attention to the importance of the individual within the system.

Human skill—the ability to use knowledge and understanding of people as they interact with others.

Hygienic factor—a component (such as pay or working conditions) related to productivity on the job but peripheral to the job itself.

Information cycle—the collecting, processing, storing, retrieving, and distributing of information for internal and external use.

Information manager—the person responsible for the information-handling activities of an organization; also known as the *chief information officer (CIO).*

Intrapreneurs—those managers who create innovation of any kind *within their organization.*

Leading—a function of management in which workers are motivated and directed so that the objectives of the organization will be successfully achieved.

Management—the process of planning, organizing, and controlling all the resources and of leading or directing people to attain the goal of a productive, unified organization.

Management information system (MIS)—an organizational process designed to supply timely information to managers for use in drawing conclusions, making predictions, recommending courses of action, and making decisions in order to take action.

Management science school—those writers who emphasize the use of engineering and mathematical skills to solve complex decision-making problems; also known as the *operations research* or *mathematical approach.*

Manager—the person who performs the functions of management: planning, organizing, leading, and controlling.

Motivation-hygiene theory—a theory of motivation that examines the effects of hygienic and motivator factors upon people in a work environment.

Motivator—a factor (such as the feeling of self-improvement or recognition) that creates positive attitudes toward work.

Office automation (OA)—an MIS approach that aims to maximize the productivity of managing information through the integration of skilled personnel, powerful technology, and sophisticated systems.

Operational decisions—those decisions that are concerned with day-to-day operations of the office; also known as *administrative decisions.*

Organization—any form of group endeavor.

Organizing—a function of management that brings together all economic resources (the work, workplace, information, and workers) to form a controllable (manageable) unit—the organization—to accomplish specific objectives.

Planning—a function of management that analyzes relevant information from the past and the present and assesses probable developments of the future so that a course of action—the plan—may be determined that will enable the firm to meet its stated goals.

Scientific management—the approach toward the management of work and of organizations characterized by the scientific method of problem solving.

Scientific method of problem solving—a tool of scientific management that uses logical, systematic steps to develop effective solutions to problems.

System—a group of parts that are interrelated in such a manner that they form a unified whole and work together to attain a definite objective.

Technical skill—the ability to understand a specific function, with its specialized knowledges, and to use efficiently the tools and techniques related to that function or activity.

Total entity management—an approach toward the management of work and of organizations characterized by the search for effective means of directing the business firm as a whole, or as an entity.

FOR YOUR REVIEW

1. List the six M's that must be blended through the management process in order to ensure business success.

2. How may administrative office management be defined?

3. What is meant by the statement that no two office managers have exactly the same job responsibilities?

4. a. Define each of the four functions of management.
   b. What office activities are related to each of these functions?

5. List the several phases of the information cycle in their proper sequence.

6. Describe the major characteristics of a management information system.

7. What are the three interdependent components of office automation?

8. a. Describe the three types of skills needed by AOMs.
   b. How are the competencies needed by AOMs related to these three skills?

9. What are the requirements for achieving the C.A.M. designation?

10. Explain the statement: "The efficient office reflects a perceptive or intuitive manager."

11. What are the distinguishing features of the classical school of management thought?

12. What were the major contributions made by Taylor, the father of scientific management?

13. a. Why is Leffingwell looked upon as the father of office management?
    b. What are Leffingwell's five principles of effective work?

14. In what way are Fayol's concepts of management related to total entity management?

15. What were the major contributions made by Mayo and his research team to the development of the behavioral school of management thought?

16. What are the implications of Maslow's theory of motivation for today's administrative office manager?

17. How are motivator factors and hygienic factors related to Herzberg's motivation theory?

18. Explain how the management science approach aids in the decision-making process.

19. Describe the five parts that make up an organization when it is viewed as a system.

FOR YOUR DISCUSSION

1. Some companies, mainly banks, financial services, airlines, and insurance, have created a brand-new position for a new breed of manager: the *chief information officer (CIO)*. The position often requires the CIO to bridge the gap between the nontechnical people on the board of directors and the heads of the management information systems. Generally, CIOs concentrate on long-term strategy and planning and report directly to a high-ranking executive, such as the chief executive officer or chairperson. If your firm were planning to create a new position for CIO, in which functional areas of your company would you search for CIO candidates? Which of the three skills—conceptual, human, technical— would you rank highest in your search for a CIO candidate? Why?

2. With the continuing advances in office automation and the computer's takeover of routine work, what changes do you see occurring among office workers and their supervisors in large companies, such as those in the banking and insurance industries?

3. An office worker in one of the major computer manufacturing firms was asked to describe the qualifications required of a good office manager. The worker's answer indicated, among other things, that the person must be a self-starter, a highly motivated individual with the ability to see what is needed, and the capacity to make plans and follow through. The worker concluded the answer by saying that if the right person is in the job, he or she will take orders from the situation. What is meant by "the situation"? Do these statements apply equally well to all middle managers, including the office manager? If the right office manager is in the job, how is he or she able to take orders from the situation?

4. Let's say that you have been assigned the responsibility for designing a management training and development program for office managers. What skills and competencies would you consider to be most important to teach in your program?

5. During the past several years, many articles have appeared that stress the importance of intuition in management decision making. Some schools of business are experimenting with courses dealing with the development of intuitive management skills. How do you account for this rather sudden interest in intuition as a tool of management?

6. In an address before a human resources conference, Frederick Herzberg spoke of how we believe in "holy technology" but we have ended up with a "passionless" society. Later, during an interview, Herzberg spoke more about the passionless society when he observed that people today are in the Information Age; they are dealing with cerebral jobs and with abstractions such as finance and information—things that cannot be touched, things that cannot be felt.[14] Do you agree that today's mental laborers or knowledge-workers have given rise to a passionless society?

7. Since the dawn of management, the concept of a total information system has been an ever-present dream. Today, however, instead of being a means for better decisions, information has often become an end product, with the computer turning out more information than a manager can use. Comment upon the validity of these statements.

8. A top-ranking executive with more than 50 years' experience in the business world made the following statements in an article dealing with management theories and styles:[15]
   a. Like fads and fashions, business theories tend to come and go. They are the talk of the town one year, gone and forgotten the next.
   b. The trouble with these neat theories, however, is that no company I know of is run in strict accordance with either Theory X or Theory Y.
   c. I do not envision a future in which American working men and women will turn to the Japanese style of corporate paternalism, starting each working day singing songs in praise of General Motors, ITT, or any of the old component parts of the Bell System.
   d. No Theory X, Y, or Z will give us simple answers to complex problems.

   Let us accept that these statements are fairly typical of those made by men and women at the helm of today's business organizations in America. Why, then, should you as students of administrative office management be expected to learn about the various management theories and styles of yesterday and today?

---

[14]Hermine Zagat Levine, "Highlights of AMA's 57th Annual Human Resources Conference, Part I," *Personnel* (September, 1986), pp. 19–27.
[15]Harold S. Geneen, "Theory G," *United* (November, 1984), pp. 60–68.

SOLVING CASE PROBLEMS

Good office managers are good problem solvers. Therefore, at the end of each chapter in this textbook, two case problems are presented so you will be able to gain experience in problem solving as you work individually or in small groups. The case problems play a vital part in learning about the process of administrative office management—its theories, principles, and practices. However, effective problem solving requires proper instruction in the techniques of problem solving. Before you are introduced to these techniques in Chapter 3, you will want to know exactly what this subject, administrative office management, is all about. Also, you will want to be introduced to workable principles of management prior to tackling a full-fledged case problem. Therefore, the first two chapters of this textbook have been designed to provide you with background knowledge that will be of benefit to you in solving your first case problems in Chapter 3.

At this time, you will examine two relatively short case problems with the purpose of aiding you in developing a proper attitude toward problem solving. After you have studied each of the case problems, answer the questions that follow. Later, after you have studied Chapter 3, your instructor may wish you to return to one or both of these case problems and engage in more intensive problem solving.

Case 1-1 Developing a Problem-Solving Attitude—A

One Friday in early December, Ann Busse and Jeanne Meyer, computer operators for the Normandy Company, were discussing their plans to spend Mardi Gras in Rio de Janeiro. Busse said that their hotel reservations had been made and that she was now waiting for flight confirmations. Excitedly, Meyer commented: "I'm sure glad we saved those five days of vacation time this year. That gives us three whole weeks in sunny Rio next February!"

As Busse and Meyer left work that day, they noted that their supervisor, Marty Ansell, was still at his desk, checking time sheets for the week. "Guess we'd better clear our vacation plans with Marty," Busse said to Meyer. The conversation continued:

Meyer: Marty, Ann and I've decided to take the last week in February and the first two weeks in March for our vacation time next year. You'll remember that we still have five days due us for this year.

Ansell: (flustered at being interrupted in his work) I remember. Go ahead with your plans. Just give me a note to remind me of your vacation dates. See you Monday—have a good weekend!

On Monday afternoon, after Ansell had read the note indicating Busse and Meyer's vacation dates, he broke into their work to say: "Hey, you two! You know you can't carry your vacation time over from year to year. You've got to use up all of those five days before the end of this month!"

Busse: (stunned) But, Marty, you can't do that to us. On Friday you told us to go ahead with our plans. Don't you remember? We've made our hotel reservations and Saturday we paid for the airline tickets. If we cancel our flight plans now, we'll be faced with a penalty of something like 25 percent.

Ansell: Guess I wasn't thinking too clearly Friday. I sympathize with you; I really do. But, look here in the employee handbook. See? It says that all vacation time must be taken during the calendar year. Employees cannot accumulate vacation time from year to year.

1. In a few words, what is the real problem in this case?

2. Did Busse make any mistakes? If so, what is the nature of the mistakes?

3. Did Meyer make any mistakes? If so, what is the nature of the mistakes?

4. Did Ansell make any mistakes? If so, what is the nature of the mistakes?

Case 1-2 Developing a Problem-Solving Attitude—B

You are an office supervisor in a wholesale stamp and coin company that has been experiencing a sharp increase in sales volume. Today you receive the letter shown on page 29 from one of your valued customers, Shaw Stamps, Inc.

1. What is the real problem or problems involved in this case? Can you identify clearly the specific nature of the problem?

2. Which individuals are causing the problems? Explain.

3. As the office supervisor, what key questions would you raise of the individuals whom you believe are causing the problems?

Shaw Stamps, Inc.
2759 Roberstson Avenue
Cincinnati, OH 45212-3386
Phone: (513)555-4800

July 20, 19--

Ladies and Gentlemen:

On June 8, I received an insured package containing 500 (five
hundred) No. 1341, $1 Airlift mint stamps from your company. I
refused to accept the shipment since my order of May 28 was for
only 50 (fifty) No. 1341 stamps. I called Larry Hernandez in
your Order Department, and he assured me that the error would be
corrected at once. On June 12, I received your invoice for 500
No. 1341 stamps @ $3 each, which represented the incorrect
shipment. I paid no attention to this bill since I assumed that
the whole matter would be corrected "at once" by Hernandez.

The following weeks were a "nightmare," as you will see when you
read what happened:

1. On June 20 I called Hernandez again and asked why I still had
    not received my correct shipment. I tried to make the point
    that I had several customers who were waiting for this
    particular stamp. Hernandez said that he had requested a
    verification of my order from the Shipping Department and he
    had no idea why I had not yet received the correct shipment.
    He then promised to expedite matters by canceling my old
    order and resubmitting a new order, which would be processed
    on your newly installed computer.

2. On July 10 I received a past-due notice for the 500 No. 1341
    stamps. Right away I telephoned Berta Anolak of your Billing
    Department. She told me that all invoice adjustments had to
    originate with Mark Sharon in the warehouse, since he is the
    only person authorized to enter data pertaining to
    adjustments.

3. Later on July 10, I called Sharon and found that in order to
    have my account corrected, I would have to contact Vera
    Newton in the Shipping Department.

4. When I called Newton, I was told she was on vacation. Her
    replacement was unable to find any information about either
    order!

5. On July 5 I received my correct order for 50 No. 1341 stamps.

6. On July 19 I received an invoice for the 50 No. 1341 stamps
    and a second past-due notice for the 500 No. 1341 stamps.
    With the notice came your computerized form letter telling me
    that because of my unpaid bill, your company was commencing
    legal action.

Sincerely,

Tom Shaw

Tom Shaw

2

Principles of Administrative Office Management

GOALS FOR THIS CHAPTER

After completing this chapter, you should be able to:

1. Discuss the nature and purpose of theory in the study of administrative office management.
2. State and describe briefly each of the eight basic principles of management as applied to the office.
3. Show how the organization chart is an important tool for the administrative office manager.
4. Describe each of the following forms of organization: the formal organization, especially the line, functional, line and staff, committee, and matrix forms; and the informal organization.
5. Prepare an organization chart for the commonly used line-and-staff form of organization.
6. Distinguish between centralization and decentralization of managerial authority and note the difference between decentralized authority and physical decentralization in the office.
7. Identify the main characteristics of the five styles of leadership that may be displayed by administrative office managers.

The word **principles** is widely used in educational circles. It refers to broad, general statements that are considered to be true and that accurately reflect real-world conditions in all walks of life. Thus, you will find principles of conduct, principles of sociology, principles of accounting, and principles of management, to name a few. Over the years, new principles are developed, and old principles are questioned and, in some cases, changed or discarded if they no longer serve useful purposes.

Principles are based on long-term observation and verification of events by practitioners, such as managers and other professional persons specializing in the field. In other situations, principles are developed by scientists and related researchers in university settings. In both cases, once the principles have been tested (that is, checked for being true and for representing reality), they are useful in predicting what will happen when real-world conditions similar to those used in the testing situation are found.

When sets of principles are grouped into a general framework that explains the basic relationships among them, a **theory** is created. Thus, the set of principles included in this chapter are classified and grouped into a managerial framework and can be thought of as **management theory**. By applying these principles under carefully controlled conditions, you should be able to predict accurately the outcomes of management operations. In this way, theory can be put to practical use by the administrative office manager.

Since administrative office management is a specialized field of study, administrative office managers need a solid understanding of the principles of management. These principles serve as the backbone of all decisions made in the office—decisions concerning planning, organizing, and controlling administrative office operations and leading office workers to accomplish the goals of the organization.

In this chapter, you will first examine the basic principles that apply to any specialized area of management, such as administrative office management. Next, you will study the forms of organization in which the principles and styles are applied and a major related issue—whether to centralize or decentralize office operations. The chapter closes with an examination of the role of leadership in the effective office and those leadership styles commonly observed.

BASIC PRINCIPLES OF MANAGEMENT

From your introduction to administrative office management in Chapter 1, it should be clear that management is a complex process. In order to manage the office with minimum physical and mental effort, and at the lowest possible cost, the AOM has to consider many persons. Within a corporation, these persons include stockholders, the board of directors, managers and supervisors, and workers. In less complex, small firms, such as proprietorships and partnerships, the manager-owners, supervisors, and workers need to be considered. Outside each firm, customers, suppliers, the government, and many others must also receive the attention of management in the organization of their firms.

Each business firm designs its own structure as a means of organizing the various resources needed to meet its goals. However, a good structure does not guarantee sound organizational health. In the words of Peter F. Drucker, "The test of a healthy business is not the beauty, clarity, or perfection of its organization structure. *It is the performance of people.*"[1] On the job, managers and workers apply management principles using various **techniques** (ways of doing assigned

tasks) needed for completing work. Figure 2–1 outlines the main principles associated with good management along with examples of practical application techniques used by managers and workers. The effectiveness of these principles is measured by the performance of people in achieving desired results, which is the ultimate test of good management.

PRINCIPLE 1

Define Objectives

The objectives of an organization and all of its divisions must be clearly defined and understood.

An **objective** is a desired goal. Objectives range from broad, general statements about an overall organization to specific, narrow statements about a department or an employee's activities. For example, company-wide objectives are commonly stated in this way:

- To earn a fair return on investment for our stockholders.

When management principles are applied properly, employees and managers work together effectively to meet the goals of the organization.

[1]Peter F. Drucker, *Management: Tasks, Responsibilities, Practices* (New York: Harper & Row Publishers, Inc., 1974), p. 602.

Figure 2–1
Management
Principles
and Tech-
niques for
Applying
Principles

Summary of Management Principles	Techniques Used in Applying Management Principles
1. Objectives clearly defined and understood	**Develop** and explain policies, objectives, and budgets to workers in meetings and organization manuals.
2. Responsibility for proper organization of work	**Analyze** functional needs of the organization and create a sound organization structure including an organization chart in line with the objectives.
3. Unity of functions	**Emphasize** in meetings and group projects the interrelationships among the functional areas in the firm.
4. Use of specialization	**Assign** work to persons with highest levels of aptitude, interest, work experience, and education.
5. Delegation of authority	**Schedule** meetings involving managers, supervisors, and workers to clarify the responsibilities assigned to each level.
6. Unity of command	**Explain** flow of authority to workers and identify the person from whom they must take orders.
7. Span of control	**Study** the work being performed by workers and the organization chart to determine how many persons report to each supervisor; expand amount of participative decision making.
8. Centralization or decentralization of managerial authority	**Centralize** all highly complex or technical responsibilities, such as the computer system, in one location. **Decentralize** all simpler responsibilities, such as copying systems, in each department.

- To improve our share of the market.
- To provide the best possible service to our customers.

More specific objectives, which are easier to understand and to measure, may be stated as:

- To increase the productivity of word processing operators by 10 percent during the current year (department goal).
- To reduce by 15 percent the costs of operating the mailing center (department goal).
- To improve attendance on the job (individual worker's goal).

Often objectives are established as part of the planning process for one- and five-year periods. As conditions require, such objectives are revised on a regular basis in order to adjust to major unexpected changes. For example, objectives may be altered because of reduced earnings from sales or an increase in the prime interest rate.

In progressive firms, top management is responsible for setting quantifiable (measurable), attainable objectives and then directing the organization toward meeting these objectives. This popular and effective management technique—management by objectives—is explained in Chapter 7.

For each of the organization's objectives, a **policy**—a broad guideline for operating the organization—should be developed. A common policy in most firms stresses the continual need to maximize profits in a just, reasonable manner. As a result, the corresponding objective of such a business firm would be to earn the highest possible profits by increasing sales, an objective that, in turn, determines how the operations of the sales department are carried out. A related objective of the manufacturing division is to produce the right amount of goods at the lowest cost to fill the increased sales orders. A main objective of the administrative office management function is to coordinate and communicate the information activities of each of the organization's main divisions so that unit costs of production may be reduced and productivity increased. Here, administrative office management provides a support service for all other functions. Several techniques used to achieve Principle 1 are outlined in Figure 2–1.

PRINCIPLE 2

Accept Responsibility

Responsibility for organizing work exists with managers at all levels, beginning with top management and extending to first-line supervisors.

Responsibility is the obligation and accountability for properly performing work that is assigned. At the top level, the chief executive officer must determine the major work functions and the responsibilities for organizing each division that is responsible for performing assigned work. At this same level, the company's long-range plans and objectives are formulated. Sound organization is necessary if these plans and objectives are to be achieved. Thus, top management must identify and accept the many responsibilities that accompany such high-level work.

In the same way, each succeeding level of management—from middle management to first-line supervision—must accept an appropriate amount of responsibility. In order to do so, each level should first:

1. Identify its major objectives.
2. Determine the activities necessary to attain these objectives.
3. Develop the most logical pattern of organization to carry out its activities and to meet the needs of its workers. A technique for applying this point is summarized in Figure 2–1.
4. Assign responsibility to workers for the accomplishment of these objectives. Where similar but not identical assignments are given to several individuals, the similarities and differences should be carefully explained to prevent misunderstanding.
5. Establish proper communication channels among all responsible parties to unify efforts and to develop team spirit.

These same steps are used at every level of management throughout the company. The only difference in their use lies within the scope of authority and responsibility of the job and the supervision of detailed work. **Authority** is the right to command, to give orders, and the power to make decisions. Figure 2–2 shows that as you move up the levels in the company, there is more authority and responsibility but less supervision of detailed work. As you move down, the reverse is true.

PRINCIPLE 3

Unify Functions

All organizations are composed of various functions that must be effectively integrated so they can work together as a unit to achieve their major objectives.

As discussed in Chapter 1, an organization may be thought of as a system. Thus, each

Figure 2-2
Comparing
Authority
and Respon-
sibility with
Supervision
of Detailed
Work

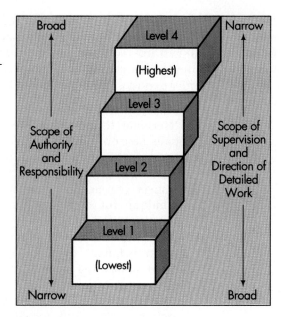

of the four major functions of a business organization—production, marketing, finance, and personnel or human resources administration—may be regarded as a subsystem or subdivision. Since these subsystems are interrelated, the effectiveness of any one functional subsystem depends on, as well as affects, the operations of the other three. Each of these subsystems, in turn, must be considered in relation to the other parts of the system. For example, a subsystem may need to be expanded or reduced in size in order to satisfy the overall objectives of the business. An effective technique for emphasizing such interrelationships—and thereby applying Principle 3—is shown in Figure 2-1.

The unity-of-functions principle requires that:

1. The various organizational functions identified earlier be in *proper balance* in keeping with the importance of their contributions to meeting the firm's objectives. For example, if a firm's objectives require increased sales of 8 percent, then production capacity must be expanded accordingly. Also, enough funds must be made available to purchase additional equip-

ment; and the number of workers needed for the new production volume must be recruited, oriented, trained, and supervised.

2. A reasonable amount of *stability* in personnel be maintained. This allows an organization anticipating a lengthy decline in sales income to provide for a stable work force by cutting back the number of hours each office employee works during the week.

3. *Flexibility* be ensured to meet seasonal or economic changes. As an example, in many offices the workers are trained to perform more than one kind of job so that during rush periods the workers may be transferred from job to job as the need arises. Flexibility also means providing for the possibility of growth and expansion in order to adjust easily to future needs of the firm. As explained in a later chapter, an AOM effectively adjusts either to expansion or contraction of office operations by installing furniture, equipment, and lighting systems that can be quickly and inexpensively moved about.

The successful administrative office system provides support service activities for every functional area in the organization. These activities are so closely interrelated that none can be considered without considering their effect upon the others. For example, the services offered by word processing must be related to the needs of the persons writing letters, to records management, to the mailing function, and to office supervision. Also, the activities of the human resources function must relate to each of the activities just mentioned. And the managers of other functions, such as production and marketing, must work with the AOM, because in various ways their activities are interdependent. Similarly, as the office organization expands by adding more supervisors and administrative assistants, all must work together as a unit or team under the direction of the AOM. This integration of functions must be constantly kept in mind because it improves productivity and reduces the cost of the work. The result is an increase in the efficiency of the information function, which is a major objective of the AOM.

PRINCIPLE 4

Utilize Specialization

An organization should utilize specialization to achieve efficiency. The more specialized the work assigned to individuals within the limits of human tolerance, the greater the opportunity for efficient performance.

A **specialist** is a person who masters or becomes expert at doing a certain type of work. Usually such expertise comes from extended periods of training, good work experience, or some combination of the two.

Specialization has made possible much of our economic and social progress. Workers with expert skills can be found everywhere—welders on the automotive assembly lines, chefs in restaurants, sales agents in the insurance industry, and full-time records clerks and computer programmers in offices. When people specialize, the quality of their work is higher; they are usually more accurate and adaptable; they learn new tasks faster; and they can accomplish more work in a given time period. Hence, such workers are more productive than workers without specialized skills.

Specialization, however, can be overdone. When the work becomes too narrow in scope or too repetitive, workers may become bored; and the quality and quantity of the work may suffer. To solve this common problem, several personnel techniques, such as job enlargement and job enrichment discussed in Chapter 7, are used. Another useful technique for applying Principle 4 is listed in Figure 2–1, on page 32. Stated simply, this means that managers should concentrate on management work while

clerical personnel specialize in support services, accountants focus on accounting duties, and salespersons handle their selling responsibilities.

PRINCIPLE 5

Delegate Authority

Authority must be delegated to individuals in the organization in keeping with the responsibility assigned them so that they can be held accountable for performing their duties properly.

Delegation is the process of entrusting work to employees at lower levels who are qualified to accept responsibility for doing the work. We should think of delegation as a three-part process that involves (1) *assigning responsibility* to complete a task, which ranges from preparing a report to keeping the morale of the work force at a high level; (2) *granting authority* to the subordinate for doing the job, such as the department manager's power to hire and fire; and (3) *creating accountability*, which is the subordinate's obligation to carry out the task assigned by the manager. When work is delegated to others, the results to be accomplished should be mutually understood by the delegator—a manager or supervisor—and the subordinate. (A common technique for achieving such understanding is summarized in Figure 2–1, page 32.) In order for delegation to work well, there must be a clear-cut flow of authority from the top to the bottom of the organization. If this can be accomplished, functions can be carried out effectively, and duplication and overlapping of work assignments can be minimized. As a result, management goals can be achieved.

A common complaint in many firms is that managers and supervisors fail to delegate authority. As pointed out in Chapter 7, some supervisors never learn to delegate; instead, they insist on handling many work details themselves. Also, in many cases, managers assign their assistants responsibilities but little or no authority.

To manage their departments successfully, office supervisors must delegate authority properly. As a minimum, they should delegate enough authority to get the work done, to allow their key workers to take initiative, and to keep work flowing in their absence. Of course, the people to whom authority and responsibility are delegated must be willing to accept their obligations and be competent in those areas for which they are being held accountable.

PRINCIPLE 6

Report to One Supervisor

Each employee should receive orders from, and be responsible to, only one supervisor.

Reporting to one supervisor is frequently called the principle of **unity of command**. When employees receive orders from more than one supervisor, they often fail to work efficiently because they do not know from whom they should receive orders or what work should be done first. When two supervisors share the responsibility for one department, one supervisor may not know where his or her authority stops and the other's begins. The result may be confusion among workers and a breakdown in morale and discipline. By reporting to one supervisor only, which is the main theme of the principle of unity of command, workers should know exactly what work is expected of them and supervisors should know exactly who reports to them. An interpersonal exchange of such information is a useful technique for ensuring that necessary information is received. (See Figure 2–1, page 32.)

Each office employee should report directly to the one individual named as the primary supervisor on a specific job or project. In one firm, the AOM may report to the controller because of the conditions existing in that company; in another firm where administrative services are mainly sales oriented, the OM may report to the vice-president of sales. Who reports to whom depends on the organization structure, the objectives, and existing conditions within each company. With today's emphasis on task forces and project teams, many middle managers and staff personnel often report to several superiors—one with primary authority and others with secondary authority. (This arrangement is discussed later in this chapter.)

PRINCIPLE 7

Limit Span of Control

For effective supervision and leadership, the number of employees reporting to one supervisor should be limited to a manageable number.

Span of control, also known as the *span of management*, refers to the number of employees who are directly supervised by one person. There is no preset number that rigidly defines the span of control since each situation must be carefully evaluated by considering the following factors:

1. The capacity and skill of the manager or supervisor and the workers reporting to such supervisory personnel.
2. The type of direction and control exercised over the employees, together with the freedom extended to the employees in making decisions.
3. The stable or changing nature of the work processes.
4. The technical nature of the work.
5. The amount of time that the manager or supervisor spends on nonsupervisory work.
6. The size of the organization.
7. The number of interpersonal relationships existing in each work setting.

When the span of control is narrow, a great opportunity exists for close supervision and regimentation. In such cases, the number of levels or layers in the organization is usually great, which creates a tall pyramid-shaped structure, as shown in Figure 2–3A. To illustrate this point, prior to deregulation, the American Telephone and Telegraph Company (AT&T) had 17 levels of management. After deregulation forced a reorganization and cutback in the number of management levels, AT&T's communications with its far-flung customers improved. As the span is broadened, the degree of freedom for the employee becomes greater because the organization has fewer levels, as shown in Figure 2–3B. The heavy lines in each chart show the **chain of command**, which is the means of transmitting authority from the top level (the chief executive officer) through successive levels of management to the workers at the lowest operative level.

Early management theorists stated emphatically that the span of control at the top level should be no more than five or six persons whose work is closely related. Other management authorities consider 12 to 15 workers to be the maximum span at the lower levels in the organization. However, in firms that have company-wide computerized information systems, many workers at the same level often perform the same or very

Figure 2–3B
Broad Span of Control (two levels)

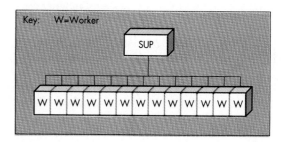

similar kinds of work. Thus, it becomes possible through internal control systems to increase the number of persons being supervised by one individual. Many large, high-technology firms, such as the Ford Motor Company and the Xerox Corporation, are reducing the number of their organization levels by eliminating large numbers of middle managers. This process, which is called *downsizing*, has the effect of widening the spans of control of senior managers, which results in "leaner" and "flatter" organization structures.[2] A basic technique used to control the number of persons reporting to each supervisor is summarized in Figure 2–1.

By studying the organization chart, as discussed later in this chapter, it is possible to avoid an excessively tall pyramid-shaped structure, which usually means too many levels of command. To encourage independence and self-control among workers, the overly long chain of command can be shortened by decreasing the number of supervisory levels. Also, it is possible to avoid overtaxing the mental and physical capacities of supervisors if the span of control is not too broad.

Figure 2–3A
Narrow Span
of Control
(five levels)

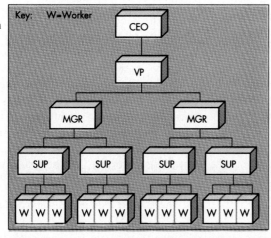

[2]Lynda M. Applegate, James I. Cash, Jr., and D. Quinn Mills, "Information Technology and Tomorrow's Manager," *Harvard Business Review* (November-December, 1988), p. 128.

■ *PRINCIPLE 8*

Centralize or Decentralize Managerial Authority

Wherever possible, centralize managerial authority and responsibility for all highly complex or technical functions in one location and decentralize the responsibility for all simpler functions throughout the organization.

The word *center* is widely used today in our society. Typically, you will find the computer center, the learning resources center (or library), and the audiovisual center on college campuses. In most large communities, you will also find the medical center (hospital), the financial center (representing banking and lending institutions), and the shopping center. In each case, certain specialized functions are located in one place; that is, the functions are *centralized*. In a similar way, managerial authority may be centralized in an organization.

In organizations with **centralized authority**, similar functions are carried out in one place; and decisions tend to be made at or near the top of the organization. This is true of large corporate computerized information systems as well as the payroll function. If, on the other hand, much authority is delegated to lower levels in the organization, **decentralized authority** exists. In a firm with decentralized authority, usually fewer levels of management are found and the prevailing philosophy is that decisions should be made at the lowest levels possible. Figure 2–1 shows a typical management practice—to decentralize within each department the authority and responsibility for operating and maintaining the less complex copiers.

FORMS OF ORGANIZATION

A basic responsibility of management is the development of an effective organization structure. The term **organization structure** refers to the arrangement of functions—the framework—that must be constructed in order to achieve the organization's goals. The best structure is the simplest one that will do the job. The simpler the structure, the easier the organization of work will be understood by all office workers. With a simple form of organization, the inter-relationships among the workers will become clearer, and there will be fewer problems.

To create a simple form of organization in the office, the key activities or functions needed to produce the desired results must be provided. Thus, in designing a sound organization structure, the OM serves as an architect who must keep in mind the basic purposes for which the office exists. One critical set of problems to avoid in organizing the office is known as **Parkinson's Law**, a condition that exists at times in all companies. C. Northcote Parkinson, who originated this "law," found that the following serious problems can be expected in firms that lack good organization structures:

1. Work expands to fill the time available for its completion with little regard for the volume or usefulness of the tasks to be carried out.
2. Work expands to fit the organization that is designed to perform that work.
3. Each unit in an organization tends to build up its importance by expanding the number of its personnel.[3]

When these conditions are found, too many workers are employed in useless red tape, which brings about inefficiency and excessive costs.

Organization structures are usually planned on a functional basis; that is, according to the basic functions of business—production, marketing, finance, and human resources. Within each of the groupings, the functions may be further subdivided. As

---

[3]C. Northcote Parkinson, *Parkinson's Law* (Boston: Houghton-Mifflin Company, 1957).

noted in Chapter 1, the administrative services function, which includes the office, may be a subgroup under finance or under another major function, general administration. In addition to examining the functionally planned formal organization in this section, you will learn about the informal organization that is found worldwide in all sizes and types of firms.

Formal Organization

The plan of organization pictured on an organization chart is called the **formal organization**. A formal organization is designed to plan work, to fix responsibility, to supervise work, and to measure results. To understand the nature of the formal organization, a knowledge of departmentation, organization charts, and various types of formal organization must be mastered. The formal organization must also recognize the existence of, and work alongside, the informal organization in the firm.

Departmentation

The process of intentionally organizing work into distinct areas is called **departmentation**. Most frequently, we find this arrangement based on functional lines with a separate department for each of the main functions, such as sales, production, and finance. Service departments may also be organized for managing the work in word processing, public relations, and research and development. Although each of the areas is most often called a department, some firms prefer the term "division"; others use "section" or "branch." For example, there may be a purchasing department in one firm while in another company the same function is called a purchasing division. In other firms, the use of each term may imply a hierarchy of organization. For example, reading from the top of an organization chart to the bottom, a vice-president may head a division, a manager may head each of the several

departments in the division, and a supervisor may be in charge of each of the sections in each department. This type of structure is commonly found in government organizations and in many large corporations. Effective AOMs develop and maintain up-to-date organization charts for reasons noted in the following paragraphs.

Charting the Formal Organization

An **organization chart** is a graphic picture of the functional units in a firm showing how they are tied together along the principal lines of authority. Such charts, as illustrated in this chapter, are management tools that indicate the flow of work, the span of control, and the major responsibilities for work in each functional area or department. In order to keep charts simple and easy to understand, unnecessary detail should be avoided; and, if needed, several charts may be prepared to give a complete guide to a company's organization.

No matter how well organized the firm, people must understand the structure in order to make the organization plan work. In this respect, charts help workers understand basic reporting relationships, which is important in developing teamwork and in reducing buck-passing and duplication of work effort. Having available an up-to-date chart helps the AOM in identifying lines of decision-making authority which, in turn, can help to disclose inconsistencies and overly complex work assignments. Then, too, charts are especially useful for managers in the orientation of new personnel since charts tie together the entire organization structure.

Having a chart available, however, is no assurance that good organization exists. Since they show only the present structure, with little regard for the future, many charts quickly become obsolete; and when they are not updated, charts become relatively useless to managers. Most charts are criticized because they show only the formal relationships within a firm and not *how much authority* has been granted at any one point in the structure. Most charts also ignore informal relationships, which are discussed in a later section.

Figure 2–4 presents ten suggestions for preparing organization charts. These suggestions are not hard-and-fast rules, because charts should be modified when the occasion demands. Often organization charts are housed in the **organization manual**. This manual explains in narrative form the organization, duties, and responsibilities of the departments and all other functional areas of the firm. Charts for each of the main forms of organization are shown in the following section.

Figure 2–4
Suggestions for Preparing an Organization Chart[4]

1. Identify the chart fully showing the name of the company, date of preparation, and title of person or name of department responsible for preparation. If the chart is for one division of the company only, include such information as part of the title.

2. Starting at the top of the organization structure, identify the major functions (divisions, departments, and so on) and then the secondary functions to be charted.

3. Use rectangular boxes to show either an organizational unit or a person. Several executives functioning as a committee occupy one box.

4. The vertical placement of the boxes shows relative positions in the organizational hierarchy; however, due to space limitations, line units are frequently shown one level below staff units. (See Figure 2–7.)

5. Any given horizontal row of boxes should be of the same size and should include only those positions having the same organizational rank.

6. Use vertical and horizontal solid lines to show the flow of line authority; use dotted lines to show functional and staff authority.

7. Lines of authority enter at the top center of a box and leave at the bottom center; they do not run through the box. Exception: the line of authority to a staff assistant or an assistant-to may enter the center of one side of the box. (See Figure 2–7.)

8. The title of each position should be placed in the box. The title should be descriptive and show function. For example, vice-president is not sufficient as it does not show function. The functional area, e.g., manufacturing, should be included even though it is not a part of the official title. Titles should be consistent; if necessary, revise titles so they are both consistent and descriptive.

9. Include the name of the person currently holding the position unless personnel turnover is so great that revision of the chart is burdensome.

10. Keep the chart as simple as possible; include a legend if necessary to explain any special notations. When preparing a separate chart for an organizational unit, include the superior to whom the unit reports and the date the chart was approved.

[4]Adapted from J. Clifton Williams, Andrew J. DuBrin, and Henry L. Sisk, *Management and Organization*, 5th ed. (Cincinnati: South-Western Publishing Co., 1985), p. 283.

Types of Formal Organizations

Through the years many types of formal organizations have evolved based upon the specific needs of management. Those organization structures available to the AOM are described briefly in this section.

Line Organization. The earliest and simplest form of organization structure is the **line organization**, also known as the *scalar* or *military* type. In a line organization, authority is passed down from top management to middle managers in charge of particular activities and from them down to supervisors who are directly in charge of workers at the operative level. As shown in Figure 2–5 below, authority flows in an unbroken line—the *chain of command*—from the president to the individual office worker.

The line organization is simple and easy to understand. In a line organization, the division of authority and responsibility and the corresponding duties to be performed are clearly identified. In turn, the performance of duties can be easily traced to a worker and to the person supervising that worker. In the line organization, decision making is completed with a minimum of red tape, thus enabling action to be taken quickly. On the other hand, each supervisor is responsible for a wide variety of duties and may not be expert in all these areas. Usually there is little coordination among departments because each department is concerned chiefly with its own work. Thus, specialization at the supervisory level may be lacking.

As each succeeding level of organization is examined, we find that the variety of duties performed often overloads middle managers and supervisors. As a result, they are unable to deal with all matters requiring their personal attention.

The line form of organization is found in government agencies, in military organizations, and in small business firms. However,

Figure 2–5
Partial Line Organization in Administrative Office Management

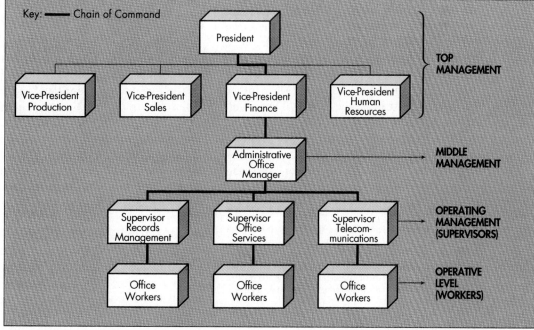

Key: ———— Chain of Command

President

Vice-President Production | Vice-President Sales | Vice-President Finance | Vice-President Human Resources

TOP MANAGEMENT

Administrative Office Manager

MIDDLE MANAGEMENT

Supervisor Records Management | Supervisor Office Services | Supervisor Telecommunications

OPERATING MANAGEMENT (SUPERVISORS)

Office Workers | Office Workers | Office Workers

OPERATIVE LEVEL (WORKERS)

few business offices follow a "pure" line organization, although some phases of work in large firms may follow a line-organization plan.

Functional Organization. The concept of **functional organization** was originally developed by Frederick W. Taylor to provide for specialized skills at the supervisory level in the plant. To handle the mental and physical aspects of production, a clerical force consisting of a time and cost clerk, an instruction card clerk, an order of work and route clerk, and a shop disciplinarian was provided.[5] The objective of the functional organization was to provide specialists at the supervisory level who would be in charge of the work related to their specialties in departments other than their own.

When applied to an office, the functional organization might appear as shown in Figure 2–6 on page 43. Instead of having one large general office to carry out administrative work for the firm, four divisions, each headed by a vice-president, are provided; and in each division a staff of office workers is maintained. Notice that each of the main functions has line authority (the solid lines) over the office staff. At the same time, the office staff in each division is supervised by a specialist in employee training, with the dotted lines in Figure 2–6 representing the functional authority. (Many other specialties exist in larger firms.) Thus, each of the office workers has two supervisors, with the exception of the Employee Training area, where line authority exists between the Employee Training Supervisor and the office staff. Such a "two-boss" arrangement represents a violation of the unity-of-command principle cited earlier in this chapter. At the same time, however, such a structure may be defended on the basis of its being an application of the principle of specialization also discussed earlier.

In the functional form of organization, each supervisor devotes time to only one phase of work. Such specialization provides for increased efficiency because the workers are given expert and skilled supervisory attention. However, with the development of so many kinds of independent specialists, confusion can result due to overlapping of authority and a lack of fixed lines of responsibility. As a result, the functional form lends itself to "buck-passing." Since the workers must report to two or more supervisors, conflicting instructions are often given, which results in friction. Because of all its disadvantages, a "pure" functional organization, like the line form, is rarely found in business today. As we see in the following paragraphs, however, the workable principles of the line form and the functional form have been brought together in the commonly used line-and-staff form of organization.

Line-and-Staff Organization. In a **line-and-staff organization**, policies and practices at the top management level are carried out on a *line* plan. Further down the line of authority and responsibility, the work is carried out on a functional basis, department by department. The *staff* feature emerges when a group of experts assist management as advisers to all the various departments. In many organizations, the AOM is a line officer who is responsible for certain business activities but acts as a staff specialist offering expert advice to many other functional departments requiring administrative services, such as records management, word processing, and reprographics.

---

[5]Taylor's contributions to the classical school of management thought are described in Chapter 1. From 1880 through 1890, Taylor formulated fundamental principles, called duties of management, that challenged the traditional methods of management. See Frederick W. Taylor, *Scientific Management* (New York: Harper & Bros., 1947).

Figure 2-6
Partial
Organization
Chart Show-
ing Func-
tional Organ-
ization
Structure

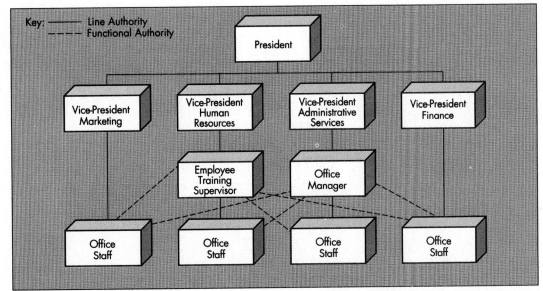

As shown in the partial line-and-staff organization chart in Figure 2-7 on page 44, a clear-cut flow of authority and responsibility exists from the top to the bottom of the organization. Operating efficiency through specialization is achieved because middle managers, such as the AOM, directly control the employees under them and are held responsible for specific activities. Supervisors, such as the head of administrative services, report through the AOM to the controller. The supervisors, however, are not burdened with all the varied duties that they would have under the line form of organization. The personnel in the staff positions shown in Figure 2-7 (internal auditing, systems and procedures, personnel, budgets, and reports) act as advisers and provide services for line managers throughout the organization. (In Figure 2-7, only the relationship of the staff positions to the controller is illustrated by the dotted lines.)

An **assistant-to**, or *administrative assistant*, serving as a personal assistant to his or her chief, is often found in many firms. The assistant-to the president, as shown in Figure 2-7, is a form of staff authority whose duties vary widely from one firm to another and may vary from time to time within the same company. No specific line authority is associated with the position since authority is granted only for the completion of each individual assignment. Assistants-to do not act in their own behalf; rather, they act as personal representatives of their supervisors.

Staff managers usually have the necessary line authority to supervise their own departments, but their basic responsibilities are to provide expert advice and to render services for the line managers. Traditionally, staff managers do not give orders directly to line personnel outside the staff managers' departments, nor do they ordinarily have the authority to put their recommendations into action. *The authority and responsibility for executing operations rest with the line managers.*

Today, however, as a result of the increased complexity of business operations and the development of new concepts in

Figure 2-7
Partial Line-
and-Staff
Organization

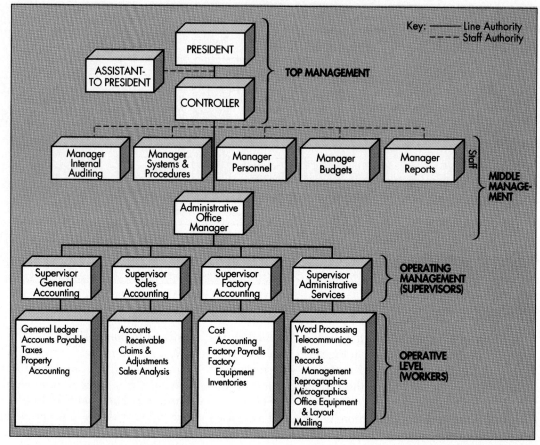

technology and the behavioral sciences, we find the traditional distinction between line and staff has become blurred in many firms. Danger arises when specialists are added to the staff without any clear understanding of how their activities interact with those of the line personnel. Disagreements arise and friction occurs when staff departments usurp line authority and exert this authority over individuals and departments in line positions. Line managers, in turn, may hesitate to accept accountability and may abdicate their authority. We should not forget, however, that line managers are users of the services rendered by staff personnel, whose job is to make the line operations more productive at lower costs.

Alternatives to the line-and-staff concept, which by its very nature may create problems with interpersonal relationships, are presented in the following sections.

Committee Organization. With the growth of larger and more complex organizations, the need for interaction and coordination among personnel at all levels has increased. To meet this need, the **committee organization** provides a structure where authority and responsibility are jointly held by a group of individuals rather than by a single manager. The committee form of organization is usually employed in conjunction with, or as a modification of, the regular line-and-staff structure.

Sometimes committee organization is expanded by the addition of a second level known as a *management council*, which enables as many of the supervisors as possible to participate in decision making. The management council can be effective in handling specific problems pertaining to individual departments and in helping to sponsor new ideas and theories for consideration by top management.

Other types of committee organization are:

1. *Work groups*—formed by various executives and their subordinates to obtain coordination among the primary functions of the firm.
2. *Task forces*—consisting of representatives of several functions to handle interdepartmental problems.
3. *Staff groups*—whose primary purpose is to integrate a basic management activity, such as planning within the firm.
4. *Labor-management committees*— whose objective is to find solutions to labor problems before the union contract expires.
5. *Codetermination*—where employees participate in decision making at upper-management levels, sometimes being appointed to the board of directors.
6. *Matrix organization*—a relatively new form of structure whose popularity is growing, as discussed below.

Advantages of Committee Organization. Those favoring group decision making point out the following advantages of committee organization:

1. People often accept a group decision rather than the dictates of one person.
2. Members of the group actively participate in their interactions. This provides better teamwork, and supervisors think of their organization more as a cohesive unit than in terms of their own individual departments.

3. Broader understandings of the decision are developed because the group examines the overall conduct of the organization, discusses problems that affect more than one unit of the company's organization, and sees the reasoning behind a particular course of action selected.
4. Plans developed by the group may be executed more easily because all members participate in pooling their knowledge and experience to develop the plans.

Disadvantages of Committee Organization. Others who have served on committees and experienced group decision making point out the following negative features of this form of organization:

1. The group is slower in reaching decisions than is one person, although admittedly snap judgments are eliminated.
2. No one individual is fully responsible for any decisions made by the group since the majority rules. As a result, compromise decisions that may not be of the best quality are often made.
3. Group meetings consume much valuable time, and group members often do little more during a meeting than display ignorance and exchange prejudices. Too often the committee is faced with time-consuming problems that should be handled by individual executives.

Matrix Organization. Matrix organization, sometimes called *project organization*, combines both vertical authority relationships and horizontal or diagonal work relationships in order to deal with complex work projects. The objective of matrix organization is to obtain a higher degree of coordination than can be obtained in the conventional organization structures discussed earlier. Work is organized around several ongoing projects rather than around the specialized departments or functional areas found in the line or the line-and-staff organizations.

As you can see in the simple form of matrix organization in Figure 2–8, four functional managers, with their vertical authority relationships, are positioned along the vertical axes. The managers of the three projects are placed along the horizontal axes. The functional managers and the project managers have dual authority over those working in the matrix unit. At the top of the matrix, or grid, is the president or the chief executive officer, who is responsible for balancing the power between the dual orientations—the functional managers and the project managers. Each work group on the matrix (represented by a square) is held uniquely accountable to two supervisors— one functional manager in the department where the employee regularly works and one special project manager who uses the employee's services for a varying period of time. Thus, the matrix organization form seemingly violates the principle of unity of command, discussed on page 36. Because of

the conflicts that may occur when personnel have two supervisors, matrix organizations are difficult to manage. Each matrix manager appears to have overlapping, and often conflicting, roles of authority and responsibility.

Along with being complicated to manage, the matrix organization is faced with added pressures to share its human resources. For example, in Figure 2–8, assume that the manager of Project A is responsible for installing and operating a new management information system. At various stages of the project manager's work, team members are drawn upon from the functional areas as needed. This allows the project manager to obtain expertise from systems and procedures analysts, computer center personnel, financial analysts, and administrative services support personnel as well as advice from outside vendors of forms, equipment, and furniture. When the project is completed, the personnel are returned to their various de-

Figure 2–8
Matrix
Organization

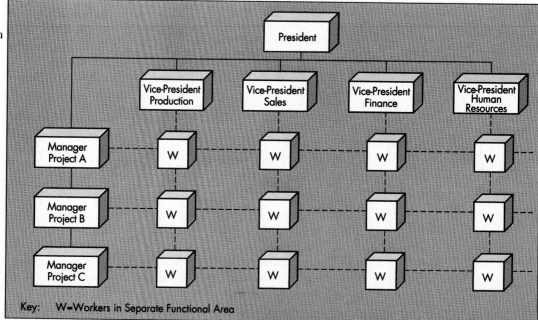

Key: W=Workers in Separate Functional Area

partments or cost centers for assignment to new projects.

Matrix organization designs have been adopted by large domestic corporations, multinational companies, government agencies, and hospitals and health agencies. These firms have found that more than one kind of orientation is needed to manage their matrix organizations. For example, outside pressures may require an insurance company to respond simultaneously to one orientation—its product line competition (i.e., life, fire, marine, automobile)—as well as to another orientation—area differences (i.e., urban vs. rural or West vs. East). When responding to two or more environments, an increased amount of information must be collected and processed in the matrix. With so much information to be processed in a matrix organization, the decision-making process is often delegated to lower levels in the organization. In such case, decisions are made at levels where the relevant knowledge needed to process the information resides, and the upper levels of the matrix organization do not become overloaded with day-to-day operational decisions. Here the span of control of the chief executive officer can be broadened because he or she is freed from daily decision making, which is now handled at lower levels in the matrix.

Informal Organization

The **informal** or *unwritten* **organization** refers to the many interpersonal relationships that do not appear on the formal organization plan, the organization chart. An informal organization develops over time to meet the human needs of the workers, such as the need for recognition and socialization, which are not explicitly provided in the formal organization plan.

The typical informal organization is composed of two or more persons who, by design or chance, develop mutually useful interaction concerning personal and job-related matters. For example, during work breaks, group assignments, or regular routine work activities, a closeness develops among certain individuals because of common interests and problems that are not resolved in any other way. Such people may extend their job associations to after-hour activities in the community including participation in professional meetings related to their work in which the employees "talk shop." Thus, ample opportunity is provided for people to air their attitudes and feelings, an important psychological outlet for the healthy employee.

One of the most important values of the informal organization is its capability for efficiently sending and receiving communications in the office. The term **grapevine**, which is discussed in Chapter 5, describes the informal oral communication network that helps employees learn more about what is happening in the organization and how they, in turn, might be affected by it. Often such an informal channel is more effective than the formal line in passing information, obtaining feedback, solving problems, and revising procedures. The dotted lines in Figure 2–9 represent a common type of informal organization that exists alongside the formal organization (represented by solid lines in Figure 2–9) within one department. Similar patterns of informal activities are commonly found between departments.

Because the informal organization is ever-changing and in many cases is undefined, we find that it is often abused. A common example of abuse is the "buddy system" in which workers find "opportunities" to work together even though no such work assignments have been made. Also, workers may agree informally not to comply with official changes in policies and procedures.

The perceptive OM knows that the informal organization complements the

Figure 2-9
Partial
Organization
of an Office
Management
Department—
Formal and
Informal
Organization

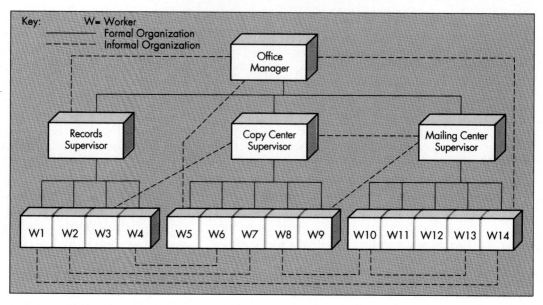

formal plan. In fact, no company can exist without these interactions of people at all levels. Rather than try to eliminate the informal organization, the effective manager will observe carefully the typical interactions of his or her office staff in order to identify such informal groups. The OM can then work closely with such groups who will feel an added sense of belonging and, ultimately, job satisfaction, even though their names do not appear on the company's organization chart

CENTRALIZING/DECENTRALIZING MANAGERIAL AUTHORITY

One of the basic organizational decisions that managers make relates to the question, "Shall we centralize or decentralize our operations?" This topic, which appears as Principle 8 on page 38, usually involves two basic issues: (1) centralizing or decentralizing the firm's functions, such as computer systems, sales, and human resources departments; and (2) centralizing or decentralizing the location in which the company's operations are performed.

If a large firm with 50 departments sets up a human resources department that does all the hiring and firing of workers for all departments, we have an example of *functional centralization*. On the other hand, if each department is permitted to do its own hiring and firing of workers, we have an example of *functional decentralization*.

If this same firm has 15 branch offices located throughout the United States and each branch is permitted its own human resources, sales, finance, and production units, the firm practices *geographic decentralization*. When the firm locates all its operating units in one place, it uses *geographic centralization* in its organization plan. The answer, then, to the question asked at the beginning of this section depends on a thorough study of the benefits of both centralization and decentralization.

Benefits of Centralization

A firm with centralized authority may realize the following benefits: (1) actions taken are in strict accord with policies, (2) there is a reduction in the risk of errors made by subordinates who lack either information or ability, (3) the skills of specialized experts are utilized, and (4) close control may be exercised over operations. As a rule, an organization that is still in the hands of its original owner is likely to retain a centralized form of authority.

Benefits of Decentralization

Firms having decentralized authority often cite the following benefits: (1) decisions are more speedily made; (2) action can be taken on the spot as needed without consulting higher levels of management; (3) decisions can be adapted to local conditions, such as in branch offices; (4) subordinates to whom authority and responsibility have been delegated show a great deal of interest and enthusiasm in their work; and (5) top-level executives can better utilize their time by setting policies as well as planning and organizing the firm's goals.

Generally the degree of centralization depends upon factors such as the nature, size, and complexity of the business; its products and markets; the extent of automated operations; and the managerial styles and skills of those involved. Large, diversified, and mature companies tend to benefit from the advantages of both centralized and decentralized authorities.

Centralization of Office Operations

Office work is made up of a wide range of services, such as telecommunications, word processing, mailing, records management, micrographics, reprographics, and accounting. Under a capable AOM, centralizing the management of information and the administration of office services fixes responsibility, lessens the duplication of machines and equipment, permits effective supervision, and balances the distribution of the work load. Thus, the bulk of office activities is often centralized under a

capable, experienced, and well-trained AOM, who delegates to assistants the authority and responsibility for supervising the various decentralized support services. Many large firms install word processing centers that use the latest and most effective dictating and transcribing equipment. Also, filing, mailing, and reprographics departments may be established. These support services, each under the direction and control of a subordinate who is accountable to the AOM, can be provided at minimum cost and with expert supervision. In addition, in large companies some decentralized office work is often performed by administrative assistants, executive secretaries, and others who maintain their own personal or confidential files.

An example of centralization found in some firms is the **satellite administrative services center** or *substation*. The substation is a compact workstation that handles information processing and general office activities that are usually scattered throughout a number of offices. The administrative services substation, under centralized direction and control, links together workstations that are in close proximity to the users of the office services.

A newly established substation may be organized to supply a minimum number of local administrative services, such as mail, stationery supplies, and fast copies, in a defined area that serves operations in close proximity. As the substation proves successful in meeting the needs of the users, additional services may be provided in a sort of building-block plan. Ideally, each of the substations is linked with one another, with the central services unit, and with the computer center.

Physical Decentralization of Office Operations

The decentralization of authority should not be confused with the **physical decentralization** or *geographic dispersion* of a company's management or of any office operations. In large organizations, the home-office managers may be geographically separated from the division or branch managers. If desired, the delegation of authority can be limited, however. Under such conditions, the firm is highly centralized even though the activities of the organization are decentralized geographically.

When a firm maintains plants and offices in several locations, many of the information-processing activities and administrative services are often decentralized to permit more efficient operations. As a result, a certain amount of duplication of supervision and investment in equipment occurs. Often, we find that the administrative support services are decentralized because of branch offices in many locations. However, as a result of improved telecommunication systems, the accounting operations may be centralized in one location, such as the home office. Centralizing the accounting function is not only less costly but also more efficient. The work is done more accurately; and by means of more timely reports, management can make better use of the accounting and statistical information.

The operation of branch offices varies with different firms. In many firms, the branch office is a sales office under the direction of a branch sales manager who is provided as much clerical and accounting assistance as necessary. Under this arrangement, the AOM in the home office provides little guidance and control except, perhaps, to issue manuals or instruction sheets for office procedures developed by the home office. The rest of the work is ordinarily directed by the branch sales manager.

Some branches are established on a somewhat independent basis, with each branch acting as a separate unit. In such a branch, the OM is assigned the same duties and responsibilities as any other OM. In some firms, too, there is a greater volume of office work than in others. For example, in life

insurance companies, banks, and brokerage firms, the amount of information processing is much greater than in manufacturing or retail organizations. With all the foregoing thoughts in mind, you can see that the question of centralized versus decentralized authority tends to become an individual problem to be solved by each firm.

LEADERSHIP STYLES OF THE ADMINISTRATIVE OFFICE MANAGER

The success with which the AOM applies the principles of management discussed earlier depends largely upon effective leadership. **Leadership** is a purely human process of influencing people to work willingly and enthusiastically to attain organizational objectives. When a consistent pattern of behavior is found in a leader, a **leadership style** is said to exist.

As Figure 2–10 shows, there is a wide range of leadership styles, each involving managers and workers to varying degrees in the decision-making process. Leadership styles are styles of management that bring forth either cooperation or resistance from subordinates. Research has shown that there is no one best leadership style, although for many decades it was believed that all great leaders possessed certain traits. A widely held view is that leaders have high intelligence, broad social interests and maturity, strong motivation to accomplish, and great respect for, and interest in, people. However, important research on leadership goes beyond identifying personal leadership traits to emphasize (1) the *tasks to be performed* (that is, the work to be completed), and (2) the *human relationships in the workplace*. Illustrating this last school of research is the work of Fred E. Fiedler, whose **contingency theory of leader effectiveness** is widely recognized. Fiedler's studies suggest that the situation confronting the leader and the workers determines the style of leadership that will be successful in

Figure 2–10
Leadership
Styles

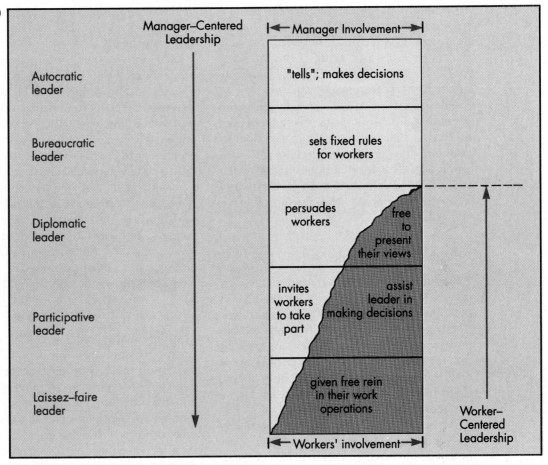

the firm. More specifically, Fiedler has found that leadership style is contingent upon a combination of three factors: leader-worker relations, task structure (how the work is organized), and leader position power. Fiedler observed that in very good or very bad situations (where production levels are very good or very bad and human relationships are highly satisfactory or highly unsatisfactory), a leader who is very production (work or task) oriented will be more successful than a people-oriented leader. In situations of medium difficulty (that is, where the production levels and human relationships are moderately satisfactory), then the people-oriented (human) leader will be the most effective. However, Fiedler noted that in most work situations, there will be some favorable and some unfavorable factors; hence, most situations call for a more people-oriented leader.[6]

The best style of leadership for an OM, which may be a mix of several styles, depends on the following factors: (1) the manager's personality; (2) the kind of workers reporting to the OM, especially their

[6]Leadership studies completed over the past 50 years have centered on (1) personal traits and characteristics that distinguish leaders from nonleaders, (2) behaviors thought to be associated with effective leaders, and (3) the latest research dealing with contingencies among the leader, followers, and the situation. For an especially clear discussion of research resolving these three studies, see Robert Albanese, *Management* (Cincinnati: South-Western Publishing Co., 1988), Chapter 14.

expectations and their willingness to assume responsibility; (3) the type of work performed; (4) the philosophies and leadership styles prevailing at the top level of the company; and (5) the particular situation or problem being explored.

The effective OM will carefully study the strengths and weaknesses of each of the leadership styles discussed in this section. In addition, the people with whom the OM works as well as the conditions under which the work is performed must be examined in order to choose the most effective leadership style.

Autocratic Leadership Style

An **autocratic leader**, or authoritarian leader, rules with unlimited authority. This is the OM who "tells" rather than "sells" or "consults." The autocratic OM keeps the bulk of the power and influence in the decision-making process to himself or herself. Thus, the autocrat's subordinates are provided little, if any, motivation to engage in problem solving or in decision making at their levels.

When decisions must be made quickly, such as during emergencies, the "telling" style of leadership is effective and efficient. Such a style is workable when dealing with office employees who do not seek freedom of action on their jobs and who are very secure working under close supervision. On the other hand, this style of management emphasizes one-way communication; there is little, if any, feedback from the office workers. As a result, misunderstanding may occur often and result in costly mistakes and wasteful office practices.

Bureaucratic Leadership Style

The **bureaucratic leader** sets and follows fixed rules; a hierarchy of authority; and narrow, rigid, formal routines. The OM viewed as a bureaucrat "tells" the office workers what to do. The bases for the OM's orders are the policies, procedures, and rules of the organization rather than the force of the leader's personality, as is true of the autocratic leader.

Office workers who report to a bureaucratic OM understand that the firm's policies and procedures will be consistently interpreted for them and that the OM will be fair and impartial. However, the bureaucratic style is marked by inflexibility when exceptions to the rules must be made to meet the needs of a particular situation. Also, when situations arise that are not covered by a policy or a rule or when the rules may be ambiguous, the workers may become annoyed and frustrated because they do not know what to do. Consequently, office workers may become resentful and resist later attempts by the OM to lead them.

Diplomatic Leadership Style

The **diplomatic leader** is skillful in helping people to solve their problems or to meet the needs of a particular situation. This manager is expert in employing tact and conciliation and rarely arouses hostility among the workers. The diplomatic OM, who prefers "selling" rather than "telling" people, manages by persuasion and individual motivation. The office workers are usually provided some freedom to react, to question, to discuss, and even to present arguments that support their views.

The diplomatic OM gains the cooperation and enthusiasm of his or her subordinates by taking time to give them explanations and reasons for particular procedures to be followed. When this style of leadership fails to sell the workers on the "why" of decisions that have been made, a diplomatic manager must resort to giving orders ("telling"). As a result, the workers may then see the diplomat's style as hypocritical and weak.

Participative Leadership Style

The **participative leader** openly invites the workers to join in and take part in making decisions, setting policies, and analyzing methods of operation. Some participative OMs are democratic and let their workers know in advance that the group's decision, usually arrived at by consensus or majority vote, will be binding.

When office workers are given the freedom to participate and help form a plan of action, they tend to support it and strive harder to make the plan work. The participative OM, in turn, benefits by obtaining the best information, ideas, and experiences from the subordinates. As a result, better worker attitudes are created and productivity increases. The office workers are encouraged to develop, grow, and rise in the organization; and they have a feeling of personal satisfaction and accomplishment. On the other hand, because of the time spent in meetings between the OM and the workers, participative leadership can be time-consuming; and some OMs may use this style as a means of avoiding responsibility. Further, if the workers' ideas and recommendations are consistently rejected or ignored as a result of the OM's misuse of the participative style, a breakdown of managerial control may occur.

Free-Rein Leadership Style

The **free-rein leader** sets goals and develops clear guidelines for subordinates who then operate freely with no further direction unless they ask for help. However, the free-rein or *laissez-faire* ("hands-off") OM does not abandon all control since the manager is ultimately accountable for the actions (or lack of actions) of the office employees. The free-rein OM delegates to the greatest extent in an effort to motivate the office workers to their fullest. However, the free-rein style can be disastrous for the manager if the workers are not qualified to accept the responsibilities and authority delegated.

As indicated earlier, there is no one best leadership style for an OM. In the various forms of organization discussed in this chapter, OMs may effectively use characteristics of each managerial style. Such managers are flexible in deciding what style of leadership is needed to solve the existing problems.

SUMMARY

1. In their daily activities, AOMs must rely greatly upon basic principles of management. These principles are designed to provide a healthy organizational climate in which human resources are effectively used to produce results. As we observed in this chapter, these principles pertain to the objectives of the organization, scope and assignment of responsibilities, unity of functions, use of specialization, delegation of authority and responsibility, unity of command, span of control, and centralization or decentralization of managerial authority.

2. Although the line and the functional forms of organization are rarely found in a pure state in today's offices, the workable features of these two forms are effectively blended in the commonly found line-and-staff organization. In large organizations, various kinds of committee organizations and the relatively new matrix form are used in conjunction with the line-and-staff plan. Within any one of these organization forms, office employees group themselves into informal relationships that must be recognized, understood, and effectively used by the OM. However, only the formal relationships, span of control, and lines of authority and responsibility are graphically displayed on the organization chart.

3. The AOM may be in an organization where the authority is centralized or decentralized. More often, however, today's organizations combine the positive features of both centralized and decentralized authority, whether the organization is housed in one building or geographically dispersed throughout the United States and abroad.

4. In putting the management principles to work, OMs select a style of leadership that mirrors their individual personalities, philosophies, and behavioral traits. Some OMs may exhibit an autocratic, bureaucratic, diplomatic, participative, or free-rein style; other OMs may adopt a managerial style that represents a mix of the best features of the several styles.

GLOSSARY

Accountability—a subordinate's obligation to carry out the task assigned by the manager.

Assistant-to—a personal assistant with staff authority whose administrative duties vary widely, depending upon responsibilities assigned.

Authority—the right to command, to give orders, and the power to make decisions.

Autocratic leader—one who rules with unlimited authority; an authoritarian.

Bureaucratic leader—one who sets and follows fixed rules; a hierarchy of authority; and narrow, rigid, formal routines.

Centralized authority—similar functions are carried out in one place.

Chain of command—the means of transmitting authority from the top (the chief executive officer) through successive levels of management to the workers at the lowest operative level.

Committee organization—an organization structure where authority and responsibility are jointly held by a group of individuals rather than by a single manager.

Contingency theory of leadership effectiveness—the situation confronting the leader and the workers determines the style of leadership that will be successful in the firm.

Decentralized authority—the delegation of considerable authority to many lower levels in the organization.

Delegation—the process of entrusting work to employees at lower levels who are qualified to accept the responsibility for doing the work.

Departmentation—the process of intentionally organizing work into distinct areas.

Diplomatic leader—one who is skillful in helping people solve their problems; prefers "selling" rather than "telling."

Formal organization—the plan of organization graphically pictured on an organization chart.

Free-rein leader—one who sets goals and develops guidelines for subordinates and then lets them operate freely with no further direction unless the subordinates ask for help.

Functional organization—an organization structure that provides specialists at the supervisory level who are in charge of work related to their specialties in departments other than their own.

Grapevine—an informal oral communication network within an organization.

Informal organization—those interpersonal relationships and self-groupings of employees that do not appear on the organization chart; also known as *unwritten organization*.

Leadership—the human process of influencing people to work willingly and enthusiastically to attain organizational objectives.

Leadership style—a consistent pattern of behavior found in a leader.

Line-and-staff organization—an organization structure that combines features of the line and the functional organization forms; line personnel have the power to act and to command, and specialized staff personnel serve as advisers.

Line organization—an organization structure where authority is passed down in an unbroken chain of command from top management through middle managers and supervisors to workers at the operative level; also known as the *scalar* or *military type*.

Management theory—a set of principles that are classified and grouped into a managerial framework to predict accurately the outcomes of management operations.

Matrix organization—an organization structure that combines both vertical authority relationships and horizontal or diagonal work relationships in order to deal with complex work projects; also known as *project organization*.

Objective—a desired goal, sometimes considered a target or aim.

Organization chart—a graphic picture of the functional units in a firm showing principal lines of authority.

Organization manual—a book that describes the organization, duties, and responsibilities of the firm's departments and all other functional areas of the firm.

Organization structure—the arrangement of functions—the framework —that must be constructed to achieve the organization's goals.

Parkinson's Law—a concept that explains the expansion of work to fill the time available for its completion with little regard for the volume or usefulness of the tasks to be carried out; the expansion of work to fit the organization designed to perform that work; and the tendency for each unit to build up its importance by expanding the number of personnel.

Participative leader—one who openly invites workers to join in and take part in decision making, setting policy, and analyzing methods of operation.

Physical decentralization—the geographic separation of home-office managers from the division or branch managers; also known as *geographic dispersion*.

Policy—a broad guideline for operating the organization.

Principle—a broad general statement widely considered to be true.

Responsibility—the obligation and accountability for properly performing work that is assigned.

Satellite administrative services center—a compact workstation that handles information processing and general office activities for users of the office services; also known as a *substation*.

Span of control—the number of employees who are directly supervised by one person; also known as *span of management*.

Specialist—a person who masters or becomes expert in doing a certain type of work.

Technique—a way of doing an assigned task, or a method of accomplishing work.

Theory—a set of principles that are grouped into a general framework that explains basic relationships among the principles.

Unity of command—each employee receives orders from, and is responsible to, only one supervisor.

FOR YOUR REVIEW

1. What is the relationship between theory and principle as used in management studies?

2. Of what value are principles of management to the administrative office manager?

3. What are the main characteristics of objectives?

4. For what reasons are policies developed by a business firm?

5. What steps should be taken by each level of management as it approaches its organizational responsibility?

6. Distinguish between authority and responsibility.

7. a. Explain how a business organization may be looked upon as a system.
   b. With which principle of management is such a comparison related? Explain.

8. What conditions must be met in the organization for the principle of unity of functions to operate effectively?

9. Explain the role of specialization in designing an organization structure.

10. Why should an office worker receive orders from and be responsible to only one supervisor?

11. What factors limit the office manager's span of control?

12. How does an organization chart serve as an important tool of management to the administrative office manager?

13. What are the advantages and disadvantages of the line form of organization?

14. Explain why the functional form of organization lends itself to "buck-passing."

15. a. Describe briefly the line-and-staff form of organization.
    b. In this form of organization, is the position of office manager ordinarily classified as line or staff?

16. What advantages and disadvantages are associated with the committee organization?

17. Explain the operation of a matrix organization as it functions in undertaking a new project—relocating the home office from the center of the city to the suburbs.

18. a. What is informal organization?
    b. What are some of the abuses to which an informal organization is exposed?

19. List the benefits of centralization and decentralization of organizations.

20. Upon what factors does the degree of centralization in organizations depend?

21. How would a centralized office operation differ from a decentralized office operation?

22. Define the five leadership styles frequently found in organizations.

23. Contrast the characteristics of the autocratic leadership style with those of the participative leadership style.

FOR YOUR DISCUSSION

1. You have just been hired as administrative assistant to May Olcott, office manager of Barber's Medical Services Company. In your orientation, Olcott gave you the briefest introduction to your new organization by saying:

> We have a friendly group of people here. Besides you, there's Liz, my secretary; Bill Snakenberg, who supervises our accounting section; Martha Gomez, who's in charge of sales and who's ably assisted by Troy Carter; Leslie Kingsley, our financial section head; Karen Gilchrist, records manager; and Bill Neal, our new word processing chief. I believe that's all the supervisors. Oh, by the way, each has a private secretary and an assistant-to (you know what that is, I'm sure). I believe we total approximately 45 staff members in all. Get to know them as soon as you can, for it will help you to learn your job here more quickly.

   This too-limited orientation leaves you overwhelmed. You recall your management studies and the emphasis placed on charting the organization and wonder what steps you should take to, as the saying goes, "get a handle" on your new job and the role it plays in the organization.

   Using the charting suggestions in Figure 2–4, prepare a chart of your new organization. Indicate what additional information is needed to complete your "picture" of your firm and how you plan to get this information.

2. Jennifer Li, supervisor of the records management center, has tried on several occasions during the past three months to make improvements in her office's filing and retrieval methods. Whenever she suggests changes to her superior, however, her recommendations are ignored or Li is stymied by remarks such as, "It has always been done this way. Your suggestions have been tried before without success." Li feels these are not satisfactory answers and would like to bypass her superior and go to a higher level of authority for approval of her ideas. Discuss how you feel Li's problem should be resolved.

3. Computers link the corporate headquarters of many companies with their branch offices to provide "instant information" on such vital matters as sales, inventories, and production data. To the administrative office manager, this information made possible by the computer actually improves the centralized authority and control over all key business functions. Discuss how this improvement in centralized authority and control over business functions is brought about.

4. Over the years as needed, the Fontaine Company has added new administrative services units, such as records management and word processing, in the firm's main office in Indianapolis. Each of these units is headed by a well-qualified manager who is responsible for all such service activities in the main office and who, in turn, reports to the administrative services director. Next year the firm plans to expand its operations to the South Bend, Evansville, and Muncie areas within the state; and, if the new branch plan works out satisfactorily, there will be branch offices set up in each of the adjacent states. As the manager of the centralized administrative services department in Indianapolis, you wonder what plans should be made, or what discussions should take place, regarding the need for continued centralization of these activities or possibly the need to decentralize this work. Prepare a list of important questions that should be asked in a forthcoming planning meeting.

5. Explain the significance of the following statement made by a practical-minded student of administrative office management: "All this theory about management is unnecessary. What I really need is a lot of facts about how to run an office."

6. It has been observed that the fundamental problem with organizations today is the absence of the employees' all-important feelings of belonging to a worthwhile enterprise where they can grow and contribute and where they can feel they are part of a cause to which they can dedicate their talents and energies. What is your reaction to this concept of motivation? How do you account for this feeling on the part of many of today's workers?

7. "The delegation of decision making, which is sometimes known as decentralization, is a current fad. Many apparently believe that all problems would dissolve if only the boss would delegate and decentralize." What are your reactions to these comments made by the chairperson of the board of a large insurance company?

8. Rita Garcia, manager of corporate records for an electronics company, finds herself involved in many operational details even though she does everything necessary to delegate responsibility. In spite of defining authority, delegating to competent people, spelling out the delegation, keeping control, and coaching, she is still burdened with a mass of detailed work. What reasons can you advance for Garcia's over-involvement in details of her daily work?

SOLVING CASE PROBLEMS

The following two case problems will help you prepare for the problem-solving activities that commence at the end of Chapter 3. Before studying these case problems, you may wish to review the comments given on page 27.

Case 2-1 Developing a Problem-Solving Attitude—A

For 12 years, Jeff Phillips served as supervisor of the accounts payable section of his firm, a large office supplies manufacturer in the Midwest. Phillips took great pains to see that all details of the invoices to be paid were checked twice by his accounting clerks; and unknown to his clerks, Phillips manually checked 10 to 15 percent of their work that he was required to initial for approval. Other aspects of his supervisory style seemed unique. For example, he insisted that all employees keep neat desk areas (which he monitored each week). Also, from 8:50 to 9:10 A.M. each day, Phillips positioned himself near the entrance to the office in order to check on the punctuality of his workers because he insisted that each be on time—to arrive as well as to depart from work every day. None of the five clerks objected to Phillips' supervisory style. In fact, he was very popular with the group, because he kept records of their birthdays and other important anniversaries in order to remember them in some special way; and he seemed to be very sympathetic to their personal needs for time off from work when the occasion demanded it.

Phillips' section had an excellent record of productivity. Largely for this reason he was chosen to "move up" to the position of office manager. In this position, Phillips would be responsible for five sections, each headed by a supervisor who, in turn, was responsible for the work of eight to ten persons, depending on the section involved. A total of 48 persons now report to the office manager.

As he starts his new job, Phillips has a good talk with himself in which he looks back approvingly at the success of his work as accounts payable supervisor. Thus, he believes he can effectively manage the entire office using the very same leadership style.

1. What important problem(s) would you anticipate in this case?

2. Considering Phillips' work history, how would you expect him to delegate work? Does it appear that he applied equally well all the principles of management found on page 32?

3. How would you classify Phillips' leadership style? Do you feel that his past leadership style will be effective in his relationship with his new subordinates? Explain.

Case 2-2 Developing a Problem-Solving Attitude—B

The Osaka Company, a manufacturer of computer hardware, has expanded steadily over the past 20 years and recently has received several large orders from the government for small computers. The expansion of the office activities has taken place under three vice-presidents, each of whom is in charge of one of the main functions of manufacturing, marketing, and finance. However, no one person in the company has been assigned responsibility for administrative office services.

The three functional vice-presidents maintain their own records storage, secretarial, mailing, and reproduction departments. Supervisors are in charge of the functional activities under each of the vice-presidents. Part of the organization chart indicates that in the manufacturing area supervisors are in charge of purchasing, receiving, storing, accounts payable, factory payroll, cost accounting, and shipping. Under the heading of marketing, supervisors are in charge of sales, advertising, credit, and accounts receivable. Under the direction of the vice-president in charge of finance, there are supervisors of financial accounting, taxes, government reports, and office payroll.

Many of these supervisors have been shifted into supervisory positions with little knowledge of systems or methods. The supervisors find it difficult to complete the work because of inefficiency, lack of knowledge, and needless duplication of records and work. Office equipment is ordered periodically and placed where it is thought it will be used later.

The president of the company, T. J. Osaka, has recently been overwhelmed by the difficulty of obtaining information needed to manage the firm. Whenever information is needed, several different sources must be contacted; and much time is wasted locating the information. Osaka is also beginning to notice idle equipment in the offices and delays in the preparation of important operating reports.

Osaka has recently had a conference with the three vice-presidents in charge of manufacturing, marketing, and finance and has indicated his dissatisfaction. The three executives feel they cannot change any of their work routines or give up any of their personnel.

1. What major problem areas do you see in this case?

2. Are there any principles of management being violated by the officers of the company? Explain.

3. Under which form of organization is the company presently operating? Do you find any evidence of decentralized managerial authority? Explain.

3

Solving Problems in the Office

GOALS FOR THIS CHAPTER

After completing this chapter, you should be able to:

1. Explain the relationships among problem solving, decision making, and choice making.
2. Define *problem* and explain each of the steps in the problem-solving process.
3. Explain the concept of productivity and its dependence on adequate problem solving in the office.
4. List the main factors in the problem-solving environment and their interrelationships.
5. Outline the steps in the problem-solving process and the essential features of each.
6. Discuss the typical barriers to problem solving found in each of these basic problem areas in the office: (a) human, (b) systems, and (c) economic.
7. Illustrate how the problem-solving process can be applied to various types of problems in the office.

As we pass through life, a bewildering number of problems surround us. As students, we face *financial* problems (how to earn or borrow enough money to pay our tuition, how to pay for our room and board, and how to keep our automobiles in good operating condition). We face *career* problems (what profession to enter, how to get a good job when the competition for jobs is very keen, and how to perform well in job interviews). And we face *personal* problems (how to get by on four hours' sleep each night, how to find time for jogging each day and still have time for work and study, and how to be socially accepted by our peers). The list of problems facing us is, indeed, endless.

The same situation faces the management of organizations. As we have seen in the first two chapters, management is a complex process with many organizational functions to coordinate. At the very core of the management process is problem solving, which requires that managers (1) identify problems to be solved, and (2) delegate the solving of problems to the most qualified individuals. Usually these are the people who will need as little information, time, and money as possible to make the best decisions.

As we see in Figure 3–1, problem solving, decision making, and choice making are closely related. *Problem solving*, the broadest of the three concepts, is the process of recognizing or identifying a discrepancy (or gap) between an actual and a desired state of affairs and then taking action to resolve the discrepancy (that is, to close the gap).

Decision making, on the other hand, includes those problem-solving activities that range from the recognition of a problem through the actual choice of a preferred solution. Thus, decision making in its broadest context is a central part of the problem-solving process. The third activity—and the narrowest in scope—shown in Figure 3–1 is *choice making*, which represents the process of evaluating and selecting among alternatives available for solving a

Figure 3-1

Activities Involved in Problem Solving, Decision Making, and Choice Making

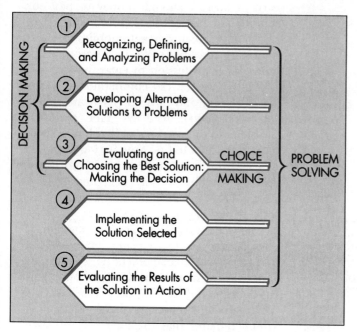

In the last quarter of the twentieth century, which has been characterized by unsettling changes in the world economy, the management profession has focused on the topic of productivity as its primary objective. Because of the widespread need to understand problems so that managers can become better problem solvers, this chapter discusses in detail the entire problem-solving process. Included are an explanation of the manager's responsibilities for problem solving; a discussion of the concept of productivity as an important problem in the office; guidelines for solving human, economic, and systems problems; and a summary of common problem areas to which the OM must be alert.

To tie together this discussion of the problem-solving process, a detailed illustration of a case problem is provided. Both the general thinking involved in problem diagnosis and the specific work required to analyze and solve a problem are discussed. This presentation should be especially useful in completing the end-of-chapter assignments in this textbook and the related assignments provided by your instructor. More important, however, the material in this chapter should have practical value for solving problems in your life, both on and off the job.

problem.[1] Much of the remainder of this chapter is built upon a correct understanding of these three terms and a clear appreciation of the basic universal problem facing each organizational manager: *finding an effective way to meet the organization's objectives.*

The management process has a special role to play in the office, which is responsible for managing the information needs of the firm. In this complex age of increasing international competition, great concern for human needs, and the availability of more efficient ways of automating office work, many serious problems face office managers. In a real-world sense, these challenges represent problems to be solved based on reliable information and sound decision making.

PROBLEM SOLVING: THE BASIC MANAGERIAL RESPONSIBILITY

All employees—whether managers, supervisors, or subordinates—are judged on the basis of their ability to identify and to solve problems. In fact, each of the managerial functions of planning, organizing, leading, and controlling may be regarded in a broad way as a *problem* area. The manager is responsible for solving many basic functional problems, such as the following:

1. Setting the right objectives.
2. Organizing the employees, equipment, and space to meet these objectives.

[1]George P. Huber, *Managerial Decision Making* (Chicago: Scott, Foresman and Company, 1980), p. 8.

3. Directing and supervising the work force in a productive manner.
4. Putting into place controls over systems and procedures to ensure that high levels of productivity are maintained.

Problem solving is a managerial skill. It involves an understanding of the nature and types of responsibilities facing managers. Further, problem solving requires a person's ability to tie together organizational goals with the abilities to plan, organize, and use the many resources needed to meet those goals. In turn, these problem-solving skills must be coordinated among people and departments, which requires the ability to understand, communicate, and cooperate with people. Without these various abilities and the skill to use them to produce workable solutions, managers cannot solve problems.

Typically, AOMs as middle-level managers face operating problems that put into action the policies made by top management. Such problems generally fall into two categories: (1) *routine*, or programmed, *problems* that are well structured and that occur regularly with the operation of the business; and (2) *nonroutine*, or unprogrammed, *problems* that are unique and that require creative solutions. Typical routine problems are the reordering of office supplies and the recruiting of productive office employees. Common nonroutine problems include setting up a new branch office, converting from a manual to a computerized filing system, selecting appropriate software, and dealing with an unexpected drop in office productivity. All types of managers—whether they are problem avoiders, problem solvers, or problem seekers who routinely search for problems to solve—can benefit from a study of the problem-solving process, which begins by defining the concept of *problem*.

Definitions of *Problem*

To understand the concept of *problem*, which has both general and specific

meanings, the following common definitions of the term are provided:

1. In a specific sense, a **problem** is a *question to be answered*. Examples of such a question are:

   How can the accuracy of word processing operators be improved?
   How well is management communicating to the employees?
   In what departments can office operating costs be trimmed?

2. In a general, academic sense, a problem is considered as the difference between *what is* (the present condition) and *what should be* (the goal). In a similar way, a problem may be considered as the difference between *that which is known* and *that which is unknown but desired*. (See Figure 3-2, which shows in very general form a broad definition of a problem.) Examples of this broad view of a problem are:

   The difference between the actual number of letters produced in the office and the standards (or quotas) of production set by the OM.
   The difference between the present turnover of office employees in the firm (a known fact) and the turnover of this group in competing firms (unknown but desired information).

Most people regard Definition 1—a question to be answered—as simple and easy to use. For this reason, problem statements such as those found in Definition 2 are often revised into question forms. For instance, the

Figure 3-2
A General Definition of a Problem

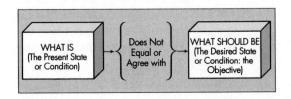

first example for Definition 2 can easily be changed into a question such as:

> What is the difference between the number of letters produced in the office and the number expected of average typists or word processing operators?

The individual typist and records clerk, respectively, involved may also state the problem to be solved in a more personal question form:

> How many more letters must I type in order to meet my quota?
> How much faster must I file correspondence to be considered an above-average records clerk?

Such problem-questions can be answered by obtaining production records and by comparing these amounts with the standards set by the office manager. The difference between the two amounts represents the *extent of the problem*. A much more difficult problem to solve—again stated in question form—is, "How can the office manager motivate the word processors to increase their production in order to meet their work quotas with accuracy?" or, "How can the OM be certain that the standards set for the workers are fair?"

Office problems usually fall into two categories. The first category involves the destruction, removal, or containment of *something present but not desired*, such as absenteeism, noise, inaccurate word processing and accounting work, or poor morale. The second category of office problem involves acquiring *something not present but desired*. Examples of this category of problem are making friends, achieving a high performance rating as an office supervisor, or receiving a promotion in rank and a large increase in salary. All of the problems identified in this textbook fall into one or the other of these two problem categories, as do all the problems in present-day offices.

Practical office managers consider problems as present or anticipated sources of dissatisfaction for which more desirable alternatives exist. If managers are faced with a number of undesirable circumstances *over which they have no control*, such as the high cost of acquiring badly needed space, then no problem exists. Such circumstances are a part of the external environment of the firm. Managers should not waste their time on conditions they cannot change.

Problem Solving and Productivity

Problems in the office have a direct bearing on the *quantity* and the *quality* of work produced by the office staff. For this reason, office productivity has become a major factor in the economic struggle against inflation and the mounting costs of office operations.

Productivity refers to the ratio between the resources (inputs) used by a business firm (hours of labor, capital, machinery and equipment, raw materials such as information, and energy) and what the same business firm realizes from using those resources. Or, as economists define it, productivity is the net wealth created after subtracting the inputs (those resources mentioned above) and throughputs (the activities required to process work) from the outputs or final results.

The office productivity concept is illustrated in Figure 3–3. It defines the productive office as one in which the value of the output produced outweighs the costs of the inputs and the costs of the throughputs, or processing activities.

Within the past few decades, the activities of office personnel have shifted dramatically from manual clerical work to computer processing and related automation services. With this shift have come higher salaries, which raise the costs of office operations unless there are more than corresponding

Figure 3-3
The Office Productivity Concept

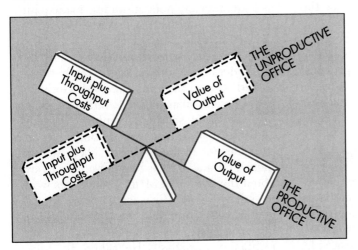

increases in the output of the workers. At the same time, space and energy costs have skyrocketed and more government regulations have been imposed, which also increase the amount of paperwork and office costs.

Measuring the output of an office staff is difficult because much of the work is mental and hence intangible in nature. However, most surveys show that the output of each labor hour in the office has declined as the cost of that labor increases. *This means that office workers produce less while earning higher salaries.* To a lesser extent, this situation exists in the factory, where prices for goods and services must be raised to cover the increasing costs of production. If, however, productivity levels can be improved—that is, if more units of work can be produced in a given period of time relative to the prices of resources in the economy— then productivity will have increased. This in turn will lower labor costs and, before long, will also lower the prices asked for products and services.

The administrative office manager alone has little control over some resources used in the office. For example, energy costs are set outside the firm; prices of furniture and equipment are also set by the manufacturers and vendors; and salaries of some office workers are directly influenced by prevailing rates in the community. However, the OM has the power to solve low productivity problems within the office and thus exert a positive effect on the costs of producing goods and services in the firm.

To assist OMs, major efforts are needed to improve productivity. One outstanding example of such a national effort is provided by the **Japan Productivity Center**, which was created in 1955. The Center offers many services to Japanese businesses and citizens with the aim of improving productivity throughout their country. In the United States, many not-for-profit centers have been created to study productivity and the quality of work life. The most prestigious is the **American Productivity Center (APC)**, in Houston, Texas, which is funded by many blue-ribbon American firms. The APC engages in research on productivity improvement and distributes information on its findings through short courses and publications.

In one landmark study, the APC investigated the problems of white-collar productivity, a major concern of AOMs. In this recent nationwide study, 1,000 office workers and managers from 122 firms were asked to answer the question, "How can white-collar productivity be increased without sacrificing the quality of work life?"[2]

---

[2]The reader is referred to the full study, *White-Collar Productivity: The National Challenge* compiled by the American Productivity Center and sponsored by Steelcase, Inc., Grand Rapids, MI, 49501. Other useful information on productivity is available in James L. Riggs and Glenn H. Felix, *Productivity by Objectives* (Englewood Cliffs: Prentice-Hall, Inc., 1983), and in Robert N. Lehrer, *White Collar Productivity* (New York: McGraw-Hill Book Co., 1982).

While the findings of this study are noteworthy, space limitations prevent their being included. What is more important for this chapter, however, is the set of conclusions drawn by the APC before starting the study. Figure 3-4 outlines the main conclusions drawn by the APC along with the principal features of each. Such a list offers useful guidelines for the AOM who is studying productivity problems in the office.

THE PROBLEM-SOLVING PROCESS

Solving problems is a universal occupation. On and off the job, we face small and large problems; personal and social problems; and cultural, economic, and political problems, many of which are interrelated. For example, experienced workers agree that office politics account for many personal problems on the job, some of which can be traced to conditions in the home. And problems with achieving high levels of clarity in composing written communications may stem from a lack of interest, poor attitudes, inadequate skills, or a combination of these factors on the part of office employees.

Usually problems do not "arrive" at the OM's desk in a prearranged, ready-to-be-solved form. Instead, the OM finds an unorganized, unarranged, conflicting situation involving sensitive employee feelings and information that may be both relevant or irrelevant to the problem. There will be factual data as well as biased points of view about the ways that office procedures work or fail to work. Because of such typical conditions surrounding most problems, it is important that a systematic, logical, and unbiased approach be taken to solve problems. With such an approach, the best and fairest thinking is brought to bear on a problem and thus ensures that the most appropriate solution will result.

Figure 3-4
Conclusions
Drawn in the
APC Study
of White-
Collar
Productivity

Conclusions Drawn about White-Collar Productivity	Main Factors Considered in the Conclusion
1. Productivity improvement depends on the integration of people, tools, and places.	Human resource development, automated office systems, and environmental design.
2. Work means more than titles. It is the nature of the work that is important.	Interdependence of people, the routine or variation in the work, and the extent to which the work involves information.
3. Improved productivity means better delivery of products and services.	Quality of output that results from coordinating the work of managers, supervisors, and subordinates is more important than individual efficiency.
4. Productivity results from a balance between efficiency and effectiveness.	Effectiveness centered on such factors as timeliness and quality of services provided; efficiency centered on cost reduction.
5. Productivity relates to the quality of work life.	Work satisfaction depends upon office surroundings, and job performance depends on how the workers feel at the end of the workday.

Source: *White-Collar Productivity: The National Challenge*, compiled by the American Productivity Center and sponsored by Steelcase, Inc.

Dialog on the Firing Line

RICHARD A. WUESTE

Assistant Vice-President for Institutional Services
State University of New York at Stony Brook
Stony Brook, New York

AB, Ripon College
JD, University of Chicago

In his current position as Assistant Vice-President for Institutional Services at the State University of New York at Stony Brook, Richard Wueste is responsible for auxiliary services (including the bookstore, travel center, campus bus services, facilities management, the University Club, and supervision of commercial development), central services (including automotive garages, mail, property control, recycling services, woodcrafting services, and central receiving), graphic support services, and purchasing and stores. Mr. Wueste is also an instructor at the university's Harriman School of Policy and Management and a member of the board of directors of the university's auxiliary service corporation.

QUESTION: What method have you found most effective in solving problems among your staff and why is the method so effective?

RESPONSE: The first step is to open lines of communication before problems arise. Information sharing must be nurtured, not just vertically, but horizontally between peers who sit in different reporting hierarchies.

The second step is to foster a sense of teamwork in the unit. Everyone works together. Everyone helps. Public mistakes make us look bad, so problems must be resolved in-house. And when confronting a problem, the solution is what matters. Assigning blame must never be allowed to waste our time. Disagreements will occur. Talented people will often have differences of opinion, but our respect for each other requires us to approach conflict reasonably. At the very least, we must agree to disagree amicably and move on.

The manager must present these ideas as part of his/her management philosophy. Then he/she must serve his/her employees by encouraging them to adopt this approach and rewarding those who do. Most important, the manager must lead by example. Actions give meaning to the words.

On the surface, it appears that there are many different types and forms of problems; however, in reality only the specific situations in which they occur are different. Thus, the general characteristics of most problems are very similar. For example, too high a cost of producing copies of reports for a department over a one-year period has many of the same general characteristics as the problem of too little space available for comfortable, efficient work performance in the office. Both situations, when carefully studied, show that the *present conditions* fail to meet the *conditions desired* and that the problem solver must determine the extent of the differences between the present and desired states. Once this has been accomplished, some specific means of removing the barriers between these conditions can be found.

Simply, the *process* of solving problems remains the same for these two situations as well as for all other problem-solving situations. First, we must understand the nature of the problem before that understanding can be turned into action as details about the specific problem are clarified. Thus, a common, systematic approach to solving problems is required, bearing in mind the total environment within which problems occur and the frequent difficulties we face in solving problems. Each of these topics is discussed in this section along with some basic guides to solving all types of problems.

The Problem-Solving Environment

The *problem-solving environment* includes the conditions surrounding the problem and the specific factors directly involved in its solution. Some of these factors can be controlled by the AOM and others cannot. The principal features of this environment are discussed below.

Cultural Backgrounds

Because all of us must solve problems, our cultural backgrounds play important roles in

problem solving. Persons born and reared in rural areas often develop values very different from those of people living in metropolitan areas. Ethnic groups with widely differing backgrounds bring widely different attitudes and values to the workplace. To illustrate, U.S. business firms and governmental agencies as well as colleges and universities are seeking to develop closer working ties with their counterparts in the Middle East and in the Orient. Students of intercultural communication point out the widely differing values held by the people in these cultural areas—values relating to the home and family, to their elders, to their religious convictions, and to their concepts of fairness and equity in the workplace. For example, conducting an office interview with a Japanese executive calls for the American participant to understand the many cultural differences existing between the two nations. Failure to observe some of the important interview protocols (who enters the room first, the time and nature of the handshake, and the times of arrival and departure) can quickly make such an interview ineffective and the interviewer considered uncaring or even insulting.

Human Attitudes

Our cultural backgrounds are responsible for developing the attitudes that each of us workers and managers brings to our jobs. Included in this important problem-solving factor are attitudes of workers toward themselves; attitudes toward other workers, including superiors and subordinates; and attitudes toward the work. Attitudes are complex mental outlooks that are developed and strengthened through the years and, as a result, are difficult to change.

One of the most common—and serious—human attitudes in problem solving is a resistance to change. Studies show that resisting change is almost instinctive—that doing things differently upsets comfortable ways of thinking and of doing work. Too, change involves risks, especially the risk of failure. The following comments, often made in problem-solving situations in the office, illustrate this resistance-to-change attitude:

- That's a great idea for some firms, but not for us.
- We've never done it that way.
- It just won't work.
- We haven't the time now to consider that idea.
- The budget won't permit it.
- We're not quite ready for such an idea yet.
- Not a bad idea, but our office is different.
- That's too academic; we're practical-minded here.
- That idea involves too much paperwork.
- It's against company policy.
- We're too small (or too big) for that.
- Let's form a committee to study the idea.

Generally the use of such expressions represents an excuse to veto an idea and procrastinate or even avoid action that would lead to changes in personnel, work organization, or work procedures in the office. Such negative attitudes effectively stop progress because they are serious barriers to problem solving. On the other hand, positive attitudes stemming from open minds that are willing to consider suggestions for change will lead to improved productivity, which is vital to all office functions. The section entitled *Creative Ability*, page 71, discusses positive attitudes in more detail.

Other aspects of human nature cause barriers to effective problem solving. Included in such a list are the following human traits:

1. We have very limited memories with a capacity to use only a few pieces of information at a time.
2. Of the information we retain, we can process only a limited amount of information simultaneously since people are basically serial processors of information (item 1, then item 2, then item 3, rather than all three items being processed at one time).
3. Unlike computers, we have limited computational ability and care about the outcomes of our problem solving.
4. We are greatly influenced by the group to which we belong and often make decisions that we think the group would look upon favorably. Similarly, we as problem solvers are strongly influenced by the organizational environment. Thus, if the organization rewards cautious decisions, the OM's decisions might well be cautious ones, playing it safe.
5. As problem solvers and decision makers, we must often act under considerable stress, which makes it difficult to make decisions in a rational manner.[3]

Basic Elements of the Problem

Before a problem can be defined in clear form, let alone solved, all the basic elements of the problem must be identified. These elements are the *factors* required in stating what the problem (or the condition requiring improvement) is.

The principal elements causing problems in the office are (1) *personnel*, including the decision maker responsible for solving the problem; (2) *space* in which the office work is done; (3) *machines and equipment*; (4) *time* required for completing the work; (5) *systems and procedures* needed to perform the work; and (6) *other resources*, including *capital*, the *psychophysiological environment*, and the *information* available for performing the work. An understanding of these elements as well as a knowledge of the present state, the desired state, and related factors is needed to solve office problems effectively.

[3]Ramon J. Aldag and Timothy M. Stearns, *Management* (Cincinnati: South-Western Publishing Co., 1987), pp. 586–588.

The Present State

As mentioned earlier in the definition of *problem*, a problem to be solved can be viewed as a state or condition that requires improvement (as in the case of an existing system, a procedure, or a worker's attitude). Or, the problem may require obtaining valid information on a subject about which information is lacking. Common examples of the *present state*, that is, the current office problems, are:

1. Low morale of key office workers.
2. Unequal distribution of work within the office.
3. Difficulties in accessing records requested from the electronic files.
4. Workers bored by so-called dull paper-filing tasks.
5. Too much work for the size of the staff.
6. Failure of the staff to work at a reasonable pace, leading to lower-than-expected productivity.
7. Inability of supervisors to delegate tasks.
8. Little or no measurement of office work and, hence, problems in compensating workers for their contributions to the work done.
9. Overemphasis on the values of office automation and at the same time underemphasis on the human factors in an automated setting.
10. Lack of coordination by the office manager regarding the various functions under his or her jurisdiction.

Each of these conditions is considered as a problem when it is compared with the desired state discussed in the next section.

The Desired State

Usually, the *desired state* or condition of an office operation is described in the objectives, goals, or expected outcomes statements toward which all office work is directed. (The planning function, which includes setting organizational objectives, was discussed at length in Chapter 2, pages 31–33.) Examples of general objectives are as follows:

1. Increasing productivity.
2. Reducing office expenses.
3. Decreasing absenteeism.

To be useful, such general objectives must be converted into more specific objectives against which the office work can be measured. For example, an AOM along with the office supervisors may convert the general objectives discussed earlier into the following specific goals:

1. Increasing production of correspondence by 10 percent without a corresponding increase in personnel.
2. Reducing office overtime expenses by 25 percent.
3. Decreasing absenteeism in the clerical staff by 5 percent.

If, for example, an AOM has set a specific objective of reducing departmental telephone expenses by 15 percent, a problem will exist if at the end of the period such expenses have *increased* by 8 percent. The present state would then exceed the desired state by 23 percent. This is the amount representing the difference between the *present state* (an increase of 8 percent) and what is desired (a decrease of 15 percent). Such a problem can be considered as solved when this difference is reduced to zero.

Some personnel problems, such as personality conflicts and low morale, do not lend themselves to solutions stated in quantitative terms. This is true because neither the present state of personnel nor the desired state is easily measured, which accounts for much of the AOM's difficulty in solving human problems.

Controllable and Uncontrollable Factors

When buying an automobile, we can control such items as the make and model to buy, which accessories to choose, and what financing plan to select. Such factors may be either quantitative, such as the number of doors or cylinders, or qualitative, such as the type of seat covering. OMs, too, have control over many factors operating in their environments, such as which workers are hired, to whom work is delegated, what procedures to design for performing the work, what makes and models of machines to buy, and whether or not to purchase service agreements on these machines.

In many cases, however, some of the factors may *not* be controllable by the OM. Some firms have policies requiring that all office machines be placed under service agreements or that such machines be purchased exclusively from one vendor. Working hours that are specified by top management and over which the OM has no control may also affect the office personnel and contribute to office problems. Closely related to these uncontrollable factors are limitations that are imposed on the office function. For example, the size of the budget for salaries may limit how many new staff members are hired to help reduce a steady backlog of work or how much renovation of badly needed space is permitted. Too, when top management allows three full workdays for the preparation of a major report that realistically requires one week, a time "bind" exists that must be carefully managed if the work is to be completed on schedule.

Problem-Solving Abilities

The problem solver needs both knowledge of the problem and a broad background concerning its causes. In addition, an effective problem solver needs three types of human abilities: creative, logical, and intuitive, which are discussed in this section.

Creative Ability

Creativity is an inborn trait that is not restricted to the artist. On the contrary, creativity exists in every worker and is considered to be an absolute requirement for the innovative manager and the office staff. The creative office worker is one who can develop useful ideas for solving problems. Such a person is able to suggest many alternate options as possible answers for the problem in question. And when creative individuals work together, each helping to add to the fund of new ideas, one worker can often "hitchhike" on the others' ideas, which enriches the whole problem-solving process.

Managers use various techniques to develop creativity in their workers. One technique is **brainstorming**, in which a problem-solving group creates dozens of ideas in a few minutes. (Fifty ideas in five minutes is not an uncommon number during a brainstorming session.) Brainstorming requires that four rules be followed:

1. Defer judgments; that is, initially the group does not stop to decide whether the ideas are worthwhile or not.
2. Freewheel or "hang loose" without concern for the ideas of others.
3. Do not wait for an idea to come but rather develop another idea out of the last one given (the so-called hitchhiking process).
4. Aim for a quantity of ideas as a goal; it can be decided in a later evaluation session which ideas are valuable and which are not.

The main idea behind brainstorming is the more ideas gathered, the greater the opportunity for good ideas. Brainstorming is especially useful in generating alternate solutions in problem solving, such as when your class works on a solution to this problem:

> In our high-rise office building, a man comes to work each morning. He boards the elevator, presses the 10th floor button, gets out, and walks to his office on the 15th floor. At closing time, he boards the elevator on the 15th floor, pushes the ground floor (lobby) button,

rides to the lobby, and gets out. What is the man up to?[4]

Another technique for stimulating ideas is the **idea quota**, in which a fixed number of ideas is required in a stated period of time, thus forcing extreme concentration by employees. To use this technique in a department meeting, you as a manager may ask each of the employees to write down:

- Five ways to reduce proofreading errors, in one minute.
- Six ways to improve spelling awareness in correspondence, in two minutes.
- Seven ways to make performance appraisal procedures more useful, in three minutes.

A third technique, **forced relationship**, requires problem solvers to consider in a new way something that is already known. Familiar topics are everywhere if the workers only take time to see them in a new light. For example, a group of workers is given the following question: "What would be the result if you were to combine an office desk with a four-drawer file?" In answering this question, the workers are forced to see a new relationship (a desk connected *to a* file cabinet) made up of familiar items (a desk *and* a file cabinet). From an intensive study of such relationships, alternate points of view are developed that, in turn, become alternate solutions to the problem.[5]

Creativity can be learned if a steady, determined effort is made. However, creativity is blocked by the fear of making mistakes; the fear of being criticized; the fear of being "alone" (a person with a new, controversial idea is a minority of one); the fear of disturbing traditions; the fear of losing the security of comfortable old habits; and the fear of losing the respect of the group. Such fears block progress, misdirect our energies, and keep us from taking action necessary to develop new ideas. Thus, fear stifles the spirit of creativity needed for successful problem solving. However, as long as managers can motivate workers to want to develop new ideas, positive attitudes can be built—attitudes that go a long way toward creating useful alternatives from which effective problem solutions can be chosen.

Logical Ability

Creativity and logic work together in the difficult task of problem solving. The effective use of logic requires us to collect relevant, current facts; to use them in an orderly, unbiased way; and to reason in a systematic, analytical manner with an open mind to solve the problem at hand. The logical person does not have preconceived ideas that impede a fair answer to the problem question. Rather, such a person uses the mind to weigh carefully all information; to get as much assistance as possible from competent, unbiased persons; and to use such information while working toward a fair solution. For example, the creative employee might develop a number of artistic ideas for making the office area more attractive in appearance. On the other hand, the logical worker would compare the cost of such recommendations with the available budget and would come to the conclusion that most of the ideas are too expensive to implement. Perhaps the most common current example of logical ability in problem solving is found in programming a computer, which is discussed later in the text.

---

[4]Harvey J. Brightman, *Problem Solving: A Logical and Creative Approach* (Atlanta: Business Publishing Division, Georgia State University, 1980), p. 84.

[5]There is a large body of literature available on developing creativity and understanding its role in decision making. At the outset, you should consider the many contributions of Alex F. Osborn, *the* pioneer in developing creative thinking, and the growing list of publications from the Center for Creative Leadership, 5000 Laurinda Drive, Greensboro, NC 27402. For an excellent discussion of many useful techniques for generating and evaluating ideas, see Arthur B. VanGundy, *Techniques of Structured Problem Solving*, 2d ed. (New York: Van Nostrand Reinhold Company, 1988), Chapters 4–7.

Intuitive Ability

While the literature on business problem solving has historically emphasized creative and logical abilities, we find that a third ability—*intuitive ability*—is stressed by experienced managers. As the name suggests, intuitive ability is made up of intuition, the emotional feelings and judgment that managers develop based on long years of experience using work methods that have worked well or poorly for them. When managers say, "I have a gut feeling (or reaction) as to what will likely work for us," they are using their intuitive ability. Intuitive thinkers use hunch, a "sixth sense," and unspoken or unverbalized messages (discussed as nonverbal communications in Chapter 5). By using fewer people to make decisions than the logical, systematic problem solvers, intuitive thinkers can move quickly to consider more simplified solutions than other types of problem solvers. In doing so, however, such intuitive thinkers run the risk of ignoring and failing to consider all aspects of a problem. Managers, including AOMs, use creative and logical abilities to solve problems, but frequently they fall back on their intuition about what seems right and wrong in a decision-making situation, especially when time is limited.[6]

Basic Steps in Problem Solving

Generally people solve problems in one of two ways: People with considerable common sense, much work experience, and a good feel for the situation often solve simple problems in an *informal*, intuitive way without specifically considering the steps outlined in this chapter. Other people, however, may use a more *formal* approach to problem solving, especially if the problems are unusually complex or of long

duration. This latter approach is emphasized in this section and outlined in Figure 3–5. It shows in logical, sequential order the steps required to *state* (define and analyze) the problem and then to *solve* it, an approach that is especially useful in problem solving. Each step in this process is discussed briefly in this section. Later in the chapter, all steps are combined in a case that illustrates the complete problem-solving cycle in action.

▌ STEP 1

Recognizing the Problem

To be solved, problems must first be recognized, which is not as easy as it seems. Too often, we mistake problems for **symptoms**, which are signs indicating that a problem may exist. An ailing patient, for example, may complain of a lack of appetite, which in turn seems to be responsible for weight loss. Yet the physician, who is trained to differentiate between problems and symptoms, recognizes these "problems" as symptoms of the real problem, cancer, and accordingly takes steps to treat the real problem.

In an office, a common symptom may be high turnover of personnel. This can be traced to a condition of low morale, which may lead to the more basic problem, the manager's inability to lead and delegate. Poor productivity may be a symptom of inefficient work flow, which may then be traced to the root problem of overcrowded working conditions. Typical sources of problems are the personal dissatisfactions of employees, poor working conditions, insufficient compensation for workers, and inefficient work methods.

▌ STEP 2

Defining the Problem

Answering the question, "What is the problem?" requires that we first carefully

---

[6]One of the most valuable sources of information on the value of intuition in management is Weston H. Agor. One of his useful publications is "Unlocking Your Intuition," *Management World* (May, 1985), pp. 9-10.

Figure 3-5
Steps in the
Problem-
Solving
Process

STATING THE PROBLEM		SOLVING THE PROBLEM	
Step Number	Process Steps	Step Number	Process Steps
1	Recognizing the problem	5	Developing alternate solutions to the problem
2	Defining the problem	6	Choosing the best solution
3	Collecting relevant information	7	Implementing the solution
4	Analyzing relevant information	8	Evaluating the results

define the problem. At the outset, each of us as a problem solver brings to the situation insight that comes from the sum total of our experiences to that moment. From available information, we then seek to determine the goals that were given to the worker or department and the apparent reasons for not achieving those goals. Thus, *defining* means *deciding* what the main issues of the problem are and clarifying the differences between the major goals and the actual operating results. The use of relevant information, then, is very important in defining the problem. In haste, some problem solvers mistakenly assume that the difficulties found in the office are obvious and define themselves; therefore, the definition phase is bypassed, which usually results in inadequate solutions. For this reason, the axiom "The problem well defined is half solved" is good advice.

STEP 3

Collecting Relevant Information[7]

While this step in the problem-solving process is listed as Step 3 in Figure 3-5,

[7]In the computer systems field, two terms—data and information—are commonly used. In this context, *data* refers to alphabetic and numeric characters that serve as the raw material to be processed into its finished form, *information*. In this chapter, however, information is used in a broad, generic sense that includes data.

actually the collection of relevant information is not limited to just this step. Information is collected throughout the problem-solving cycle.

If we are to be efficient information collectors, we must be good questioners who leave no stone unturned in seeking useful information to solve the problem. To assist in the process of data collection, you will find this simple questioning framework to be invaluable:

1. WHAT is the real problem, and what are the principal components or elements including symptoms making up the problem?
2. WHERE did the problem occur? WHY did it occur there?
3. WHEN did the problem occur? WHY did it occur at that time?
4. HOW did the problem occur? WHY did it occur in that way?
5. To WHOM did the problem occur? WHY did it occur to him or her (or them)?
6. WHO should make the final decision for solving the problem?

No easy set of guidelines is available for collecting information. Rather, a thorough knowledge of the problem and its setting, plus good judgment, will point the way to gathering information.

STEP 4

Analyzing Relevant Information

After the information has been gathered, we are able to analyze the main aspects of the problem, piecing together as much information as possible to ensure a true picture of the situation. In the process of analysis, many complex mental activities are involved, during which time the majority of our real learning about the problem takes place.

To analyze a problem means to examine each element and its relationship to the other elements and to the whole problem; to discover interrelationships and patterns in the work operations; to compare the problem with other situations; and to sort, sequence, or order the problem. In general, to analyze a problem means to search for insight within the problem, similar to the way an X ray provides an "insight" into the human body.

An illustration of analytical thinking about an office problem shows how questioning, further questioning, and comparing of processes are necessary. For example, suppose a male office supervisor in the purchasing department has suddenly started coming in late for work and has been harassed by his peers; and the work of his entire section continues to decline. The supervisor has been an efficient worker for the past ten years. He has an employed wife and three teenage children.

To analyze this problem would require answering such questions as:

1. What is the real problem? What are only symptoms?
2. Who can help me solve this problem?
3. Who are the supervisor's closest associates?
4. What is the total scope of the supervisor's responsibilities?
5. Which factors in the problem can be controlled and which cannot?
6. How does the supervisor's personal life relate to his work on the job?
7. What does the supervisor himself have to say about the problem? Does he have a reasonable explanation for it?
8. What are the viewpoints of the supervisor's associates (peers and subordinates)?
9. How extensive or important does the problem seem? Is there agreement about its severity?

By asking such questions during the analysis stage, answers will be obtained that are useful in developing solutions to the problem. Usually time is limited; no problem solver has sufficient time but must set deadlines by which time the solution must be determined.

STEP 5

Developing Alternate Solutions to the Problem

This is the creative phase of the problem-solving process. At this time, a useful set of **hypotheses** or alternate solutions for eliminating the problem is developed. This phase involves finding better ways or means for reaching goals, developing useful options, and uncovering possible choices, thus providing various possibilities for action. For example, an insurance office manager faced the problem of insufficient staff to handle a greatly enlarged work load. The three key alternate solutions brainstormed by the problem-solving group were: (1) hire three well-qualified workers, (2) use the present staff to work overtime on a regular basis, and (3) use temporary help, such as personnel from Kelly Services or Manpower, Inc. Frequently, a **decision tree**, as shown in Figure 3–6, is used to chart the alternate courses of action for solving the problem and some of the probable consequences stemming from each course of action.

In one office work-flow problem, analysis showed that many conditions blocked the smooth flow of work. When the office group sought to solve this problem, they used the

Figure 3-6
A Decision
Tree Show-
ing Alternate
Solutions to a
Problem

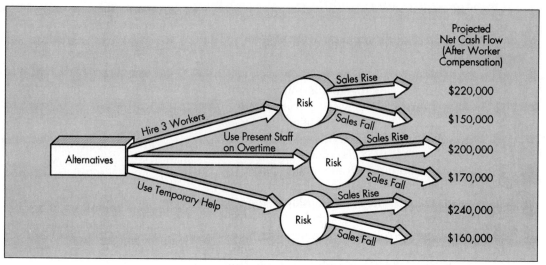

following questions to develop possible solutions to the problem:

1. *Elimination*: What procedures, forms and reports, and office positions can be eliminated?
2. *Rearrangement*: Can the work, the job assignments, or the office layout be rearranged or resequenced? If so, how?
3. *Modification*: What new form, shape, or "twist" can the work procedures take? Can more work be assigned to some employees and less to others? Can more or less work be included in the procedures altogether?
4. *Substitution*: Can certain workers be substituted for others or machines substituted for workers?
5. *Combination*: Can certain procedures, such as those for creating forms and other paperwork, or the responsibilities of certain workers, be combined?
6. *Enlargement*: What work/workers should be added? Should more time be given for completing work? Can files be placed in higher, longer, or deeper cabinets?
7. *Reduction*: What work/workers should be subtracted? Should less time be allocated for completing work? Can the quantity

of files be reduced and still provide adequate information?

Using the adage, "Two heads are better than one," managers have found that small groups of people with common interests, backgrounds, and motivations can create more solutions to problems than persons working alone. The main advantages cited for using groups, rather than an individual, in decision making include (1) more information and knowledge are available; (2) more alternatives are likely to be generated, (3) more acceptance of the final decision is likely, (4) improved communication of the decision may occur, and (5) more accurate decisions generally result. On the other hand, the group process typically takes longer than individuals making decisions, so it is costlier. Often, too, groups may compromise, which makes their actions indecisive and hence ineffective. Many times one person dominates the group; and in other cases, Groupthink sets in. **Groupthink** occurs when the group's desire for consensus and cohesiveness overcomes its desire to reach the best possible decisions. In such cases, the group may arrive at decisions that are not in the best interest of the group or the organization.

In the office, we know that a group of office supervisors and their workers can be very useful to the AOM in developing solutions to the problems of improving working conditions. Quality circles, which are discussed in Chapter 22, illustrate an effective method for solving problems by groups. But it is usually the AOM who makes the final decision—which alternative to choose and why.

STEP 6

Choosing the Best Solution (Making the Decision)

For various reasons, experience tells us that one of the several alternatives developed in Step 5 will usually be considered better than the others. Typical reasons why we decide to choose one solution over the others are as follows:

1. It takes less time.
2. It will be more effective.
3. It will be preferred by employees (or by management).
4. It will result in greater productivity.
5. Intuition tells me it's the thing to do.
6. It will help to reduce operating costs.

In times of continuing inflation and rising costs, this last reason provides a powerful argument for solving problems in the office. In any case, the solution chosen should be a realistic one.

STEP 7

Implementing the Solution

Implementing means putting the selected solution to work. By the time we reach this stage, all the replanning, reorganizing, and other necessary work have been completed. If the problem involves the selection of a new computer for the office, implementing is the step in which the computer is installed and put into operation. If the decision involves the hiring of a new administrative assistant, implementing is the step in which the new worker appears for work, is oriented to the job, and begins work on the job.

STEP 8

Evaluating the Results

After the problem solution has been put into operation for a reasonable period of time, the results of such operations are evaluated by the OM. In the evaluation process, two factors are considered: (1) *quantity* (how much work is produced) and (2) *quality* (how satisfactory or how convenient is the new operation). The sum of the two factors (quantity and quality) represents the total value of the solution measured against the objectives to be met. As a result of putting a new problem solution into operation, were the employees more productive? Did the costs of operating the office decrease? Was there a more satisfactory level of morale?

Evaluating involves many complex studies: self-criticism of a group's solution, reviewing present work processes in order to do better in the future, and objectively rating how well the solution removes or decreases the seriousness of the problem. Also, an evaluation may show some unforeseen benefits or some negative side effects that are minor in nature. Or, it may show that the solution was not satisfactory. In the last case, the entire problem-solving process must be repeated, beginning with the definition step.

COMMON PROBLEMS IN ADMINISTRATIVE OFFICE MANAGEMENT

The problem-solving process discussed in this chapter is a **general problem-solving model**, which means it is useful for solving all types of office problems. While all office problems ultimately affect productivity, we know from experience that each problem has certain features that must be recognized if an acceptable solution is to be found. For this reason, you need to understand the common types of office problems and the typical barriers to problem solving that constitute a major portion of the discussion in this textbook. Figure 3-7 outlines the major types of problems encountered by the AOM and the main barriers to solving each type of problem.

Human Problems

Human problems comprise the first and most important set of problems facing the AOM. Such problems deal with individual perceptions (often defined as a person's view of the world and his or her fears of failure in it); attitudes and biases that have evolved during our years of human development; motivation and interest in our jobs; fears that many of us have of being laid off or losing the respect of supervisors and co-workers;

and personal skills, such as the effective use of time and the ability to organize, write, and speak effectively. Supervisors and managers also face these problems and additional ones common to the level of their work. Such problems include their inability to set priorities and delegate work, failure to assume assigned responsibilities, reluctance to discipline employees, limited views of their spheres of work, and lack of vision regarding future needs of their units.

The number of human problems is limitless, and each age seems to extend the numbers even further. For example, the computer age overloads the human mind with information. (Specialists in psychology estimate that the mind can hold only about seven "pieces" of information in its short-term memory.) And the advancing use of many forms of information technology in the office creates many special human problems concerning the need to (1) design satisfying jobs, (2) protect the privacy of employee information, (3) ensure that jobs will con-

Figure 3-7
Major Problems in the Office and Barriers to Their Solution

	Type of Problem and Barriers to Its Solution	Examples of Barriers
	1. Human Barrier: Subjective, intangible, emotional human nature	Misperceptions Negative attitudes Attitudes of personnel Interpersonal conflict
	2. Systems Barrier: Inability to achieve higher levels of productivity	Poor working conditions Inefficient use of machines Weak procedures Inadequate training
	3. Economic Barrier: Poor use of available funds and other resources	Poor use of time by office workers Theft of company property Failure to develop a sense of cost cutting

tinue, (4) provide retraining if necessary, and (5) resolve power struggles among leaders in office automation.[8]

Human problems must be resolved first since people are responsible for all aspects of the office operation. Figure 3–7 illustrates this point clearly, for it shows that human problems become barriers in solving other types of problems in the office. If human problems are allowed to continue, solutions to other problems will be largely meaningless. The major difficulty in dealing with human problems is our subjective, intangible, and emotional nature. This many-sided human quality makes problem solving more difficult because the achievement of objectives is harder to measure. Consequently, the qualities of trust, fair-mindedness, patience, good judgment, and common sense are basic qualifications for persons responsible for solving human problems.

Systems Problems

A second major category of office problems deals with the many facets of systems that are set up to accomplish the assigned work. Examples of this type of problem are overly expensive costs of machine operations; frequent machine breakdown; poor working conditions, including cramped work areas, too little light, and the ineffective operation of air conditioners; inadequate training and inefficient procedures for performing the work; poorly designed forms for recording information; disorganized files; and lack of good control over all phases of the office operation.

Systems problems are much more objective and measurable than human problems. As a result, we can solve systems problems in a more straightforward manner. However, the solutions to such problems still depend on an understanding of the problem and acceptance of the solutions by people, as implied in Figure 3–7.

Economic Problems

Money is doubtless the basic means by which all organizations—profit and not-for-profit—continue to operate; and the misuse of money is a common economic barrier, as shown in Figure 3–7. Office workers face a host of problems rooted in practical economics, including high energy costs in the office, too much time required to do assigned work (remember that "time is money"), lowered productivity, theft of company property, and exceeded office budgets. The typical economic problem we find in offices is that too much money is being spent for the resulting amount of output. Economic problems can be stated in tangible terms (hours of work to be saved or numbers of forms to be eliminated), but the solution to cutting costs still depends on the attitudes and interests of the office staff and the effectiveness of the supervisor and manager in leading the group toward such a goal.

EFFECTIVE PROBLEM SOLVING: A CASE ILLUSTRATION

Most real-life problems faced by the AOM are complex. These problems are composed of many facts, details, and relationships that take time and considerable study to understand. In this textbook, problems are presented in case form. For solving these

[8]The Administrative Management Society Foundation has conducted extensive research investigations into the problems facing AOMs. The results of such studies have been published in a four-part series, *Managing the Office—1990s and Beyond*, available from the Administrative Management Society, Trevose, PA 19090. Titles of the four studies are as follows: Part One: "The Office Revolution: 'Managing Tomorrow's Workforce'"; Part Two: "The Office Environment: Automation's Impact on Tomorrow's Workplace"; Part Three: "The Office Technologies: Tomorrow's Tools for Automation Success"; and Part Four: "Strategies for Office Automation: Planning for Success in the Office of 1990."

case problems, you should follow these suggestions:

1. Question what is going on—or what has happened—and attempt to determine why the problem occurred.
2. Carefully identify each of the individuals involved and study their backgrounds, work assignments, and motivations.
3. Search for the underlying causes of the problem. Also, make an effort to determine what could have been done to prevent the problem from occurring.
4. Suggest procedures that might be used to prevent a recurrence of the problem.

The following practical case shows the relationships between each of the elements in a problem and how the steps in the problem-solving process are used. The case also provides a brief example of a memo report that summarizes the results of the solution to the case problem.

Basic Elements of the Case Problem

In this section each of the basic elements in the case is discussed so that sufficient background is provided to help you understand the problem and the solution recommended.

The Firm

Hometown Realtors is a small firm whose only service is selling real estate (private homes, commercial establishments, farms, and acreages). Located in a medium-size midwestern city, the firm has long been a member of the local multiple-listing association of realtors that has 15 member firms. In this association, each member firm is automatically informed of, and has an opportunity to sell, the property listings of all other member firms. On the average, the Hometown Realtors office maintains listings of more than 300 homes, over 100 commercial firms, and 60 to 70 farms and acreages.

The Office Staff

The Hometown office staff consists of three persons: two salespersons (the owner-manager, Randi Allen, and a part-time person, both of whom are paid from commissions on sales) and a full-time secretary. The secretary coordinates the schedules and appointments of the sales staff but does no actual sales work. The part-time salesperson receives 50 percent of the 7 percent commission charged for selling property, a rate agreed upon by all association members. In such a small-office setting, there is little opportunity for work specialization; thus, each of the workers gets involved in all phases of the operation. This may account for the main source of difficulty—that is, the real problem: *the files on real estate listings are not kept up-to-date and therefore are not immediately available to salespersons and customers.*

Main Factors to Be Considered

The following factors—some controllable and others uncontrollable—relate directly to the problem. Each is discussed briefly in this section.

Controllable Factors. With better management, Allen, as owner-manager, believes she could have a reasonable amount of control over most of the following factors:

1. Customers call or come into the office and ask for a certain type of house (ranch style, three-bedroom, brick construction) or ask for a listing of all houses in the $75,000–$100,000 price range in the northeast section of the city. Because Hometown Realtors does not file listings by type of house or price, the office staff has trouble identifying such houses quickly. This situation causes the most difficulty during the busy season (April through August), but it occurs five to ten times daily throughout the year.

2. Much time is required to match all the interests of customers with available properties.

3. Each of the listings is recorded on a multiple-listing association form, filed by property location, and cross-referenced by owner name. Within the association, each real estate firm sets up its own record classification system from the copy of the listing that is provided several times a week by the association coordinator.

4. In the Hometown Realtors office, one set of records for each type of listing is filed in a three-ring notebook. The owner often works from her home and needs a complete set of listings there also. The office space (30 feet by 28 feet) can accommodate additional files and is large enough that each staff member has a workstation (desk) with a telephone. This arrangement permits consultation with customers but often causes simultaneous needs for the listings file.

5. Because of the frequent changes in listings, a backlog of unfiled listings is a constant problem. These listings include new properties on the market as well as listings to be deleted because of sales or because the listing time has expired. (Both conditions are largely uncontrollable.)

Uncontrollable Factors. In contrast to the factors discussed in the preceding section, the following factors are largely beyond the control of the Hometown Realtors office staff:

1. Customers call in asking about listings; but they do not furnish their names, thereby robbing the firm of follow-up for future sales. Many, in fact, refuse to give their names when asked.

2. Some customers want to buy property but cannot do so until they sell their home or business, thereby using as a down payment on the new property the equity held in the property to be sold.

Objectives of the Hometown Realtors Office

The office staff has become frustrated by the obsolete-listings problem and the effect it has had on their ability to provide efficient services. As a beginning step in solving the problem cited, they have decided to clarify the objectives the records system should meet so that the office can provide good service to its customers. The objectives are listed as follows:

1. To provide ready access to any listing of the multiple-listing service from which information is requested by customers. This information includes price range; property location; type of home; type of commercial business; and farm information that includes size, type of soil, and records of crop yields.

2. To match quickly the real estate interests of potential customers with the available listings.

3. To increase the number of sales and listings without adding to the costs of operating the office or adding to the staff.

Limitations

The achievement of these objectives is not automatic because of typical limitations that are placed on the staff. For example, little time is presently available to revise the records system; and the present office employees would not have the expertise to do so if time permitted. Too, all records must be available at all times in the office. Therefore, the files cannot be taken out of the office to be studied in order to create a new filing system. Further, the office budget does not permit the acquisition of an automated records retrieval system, but Allen has made $1,000 available to improve office operations.

Key Questions to Be Answered

The problem with the records system as well as the objectives and limitations of the office require careful study by the Hometown Realtors office staff. Before starting this study and solving the problem, they have identified these questions that need to be answered:

1. What record systems changes can be made in order that the listings file will be up-to-date at all times and available to all the office staff when needed?
2. How can the retrieval of information be speeded up so the listing information requested by customers will be immediately accessible?
3. To what extent can the multiple-listing association assist its members in improving their filing systems? Can all of the association member offices be connected by computers through the telephone system?
4. Can a simplified version of a computer system be utilized by the Hometown Realtors office, as well as by other members of the association? Or is it possible to make sufficient changes in the present manual system so the records system will function more efficiently?
5. What time and cost considerations are involved in any changes made? Will the benefits anticipated from such changes more than offset the costs of making changes in the system?

Possible Solutions

After dealing with the records problems outlined in this case and considering the questions stated above, the three members of the Hometown staff met on several occasions to search for solutions to the problems cited. The work sheet, shown in Figure 3–8, was used to separate relevant facts from irrelevant facts and also to identify possible causes of, and solutions to, the problem. Two possible solutions to the problem emerged:

1. Install small computer terminals on a trial basis in all multiple-listing association member offices that are connected by telephone line to a service bureau. Thus, responsibility for the technical operations of the computer network could be provided by a service bureau for a modest monthly fee. All listings could be entered into the terminals from each office and thus would be immediately available to all salespersons. If the terminals were portable, Allen could carry one with her and also operate it from her home simply by connecting it to her telephone.
2. Revise the present filing system, maintaining at least two copies of notebooks for each type of listing. The future filing tasks could be simplified if the multiple-listing association agreed on a classification scheme for all listings and then marked all new listings and listings to be removed from the file by classification code for easy storage in the appropriate file.

In order to communicate the results of the complete problem-solving process, some type of report was considered necessary. Figure 3–9 on page 84 illustrates the format and a portion of the content of a short, informal report. Longer, more formal written reports may also be used along with an oral presentation defending the recommendations made. Chapter 5 expands upon the subject of such communication, as used by the AOM.

Figure 3–8
A Problem
Solver's
Work Sheet

STEP 1—SPECIFY THE PROBLEM

	Relevant Facts	Irrelevant Facts
What is it?	No adequate category of listings. Listings difficult to find in categories requested by customers. Changes in listings so frequent that the office file is never up-to-date.	One salesperson works part time. Salespersons are paid from sales commissions while the secretary is paid from profits of the firm.
Where is it?	Records problems occur at the real estate office and at the residence of the owner-manager.	Size of the office space (30 feet by 28 feet).
When does it occur?	Five to ten times daily during busy periods.	Time of day.
How extensive is it?	Retrieval of records and matching customer interests with listings occur daily for each salesperson and for all association member offices.	

STEP 2—ANALYSIS OF RELEVANT INFORMATION

1. There is no central source of all listings arranged by most-requested categories.
2. Multiple-listing association has not developed a standard classification of listings.
3. Each worker needs access to total file of listings concurrent with other workers.
4. Files of listings are never up-to-date because of delay in categorizing and the time needed to make additions and cancellations to the listings each week.

STEP 3—DETERMINE MOST LIKELY CAUSE OF PROBLEM

1. No approved standardized classification for listings.
2. No efficient filing/retrieval system in association member offices.
3. No set of priorities in the office, such as completing all listing file updates by the end of each workday.

STEP 4—LIST POSSIBLE SOLUTIONS

1. Ask association to develop and approve a standard classification scheme for all listings. Revise the Hometown office files using this classification plan. Provide one copy of all listings to each Hometown office staff member. Require that all new/canceled listings be posted by the end of the day received.
2. Consider an association-promoted system of automating all listings on a terminal installed in each member office. Updating could be done centrally, but the updated files would be immediately available to all association members via their local terminals.

Figure 3–9
A Short,
Informal
Memoran-
dum Report

HR
Hometown Realtors

To: Brad H. Thompson
President, Multiple-Listing Association

From: Randi Allen   RA
Manager, Hometown Realtors

Date: October 17, 19--

Subject: Suggestions for Improving the Multiple-Listings Files

During each of the last four association meetings, discussion has centered on the problems association members are having with the maintenance of the listings files. Providing ready access to the information in these files has become a critical problem, calling for immediate study. I am reporting the results of a study of the problem in the Hometown Realtors office. You may find this information useful in the offices of other association members.

Purpose

The purpose of our study was to pinpoint the main operating problems in our office as they relate to (1) keeping the listings files up to date and (2) providing ready access to listings information on a concurrent basis for all three members of our staff. We believe that a further objective of our study was to provide assistance to other association members who have indicated they are having the same types of problems.

Summary and Recommendations

Many times each day our office receives requests for listings information but cannot quickly locate the information because the files are not up to date. Usually the main drawback to immediate filing is the lack of standard classification. Our staff suggests that such a classification scheme be developed by the association to furnish uniform codes to speed up the maintenance of the listings files. Since access to such files is concurrently required by each staff member, the association should furnish multiple copies of each listing. At the end of each workday, all updates of listings should be completed.

Much busywork regarding listings files is encountered. If funds are available, a feasibility study should be conducted to determine if an association-funded minicomputer could handle listings. Thus, all changes to the files could be handled centrally as soon as they occur; and all association member offices equipped with terminals linked to the computer would have the benefit of this uniform classification and would have immediate, concurrent access to the file.

Discussion of the Problem

Hometown Realtors continues to have problems keeping its listings files up to date. Presently we receive only one complete copy, and several times daily our staff members need the files at the same time. Retrieval of records is slow, especially when many offerings are needed as alternative suggestions to customers who indicate specific buying interests. We are losing customers and income in the process. Further, we feel that the association has a responsibility to help its members improve their method of operation.

SUMMARY
1. Since problem solving is the most basic responsibility of managers, the ability to solve problems effectively is an important skill for AOMs. To such managers, a clear-cut definition of *problem* and its relationship to productivity is basic.
2. To understand the complex nature of problem solving, the principal features of the environment surrounding the problems must be identified. These features include the cultural background of the workers and their attitudes, the present state as compared with the desired state (with the extent of the problem defined being the difference between the two states), and other factors, some of which can be controlled. Creative, logical, and intuitive skills are required by the problem solver, who must also understand the basic steps in the total problem-solving cycle.
3. Common office problems are divided into three categories: human, systems, and economic. The latter two categories typically offer more objective bases for developing solutions to problems than the subjective nature of human problems.

GLOSSARY
American Productivity Center (APC)—a not-for-profit privately funded organization whose primary objective is to develop practical programs for improving productivity and the quality of work life.

Brainstorming—an idea-developing technique used by small groups in the problem-solving process.

Creativity—an inborn trait or aptitude for developing ideas for solving problems.

Decision tree—a chart used to show the alternate courses of action in problem solving and some of the consequences stemming from each course of action.

Forced relationship—a technique that requires problem solvers to consider familiar topics in new ways.

General problem-solving model—a framework for solving problems that has general use in the solution of all types of problems.

Groupthink—a situation that occurs when a group's desire for consensus and cohesiveness overcomes its desire to reach the best possible decisions.

Hypotheses—alternate solutions to a problem.

Idea quota—a technique for forcing a fixed number of new ideas in a stated period of time.

Japan Productivity Center—a major Japanese organization that offers services in improving productivity to Japanese businesses and citizens.

Problem—a question to be answered; the difference between a state or condition that exists and the state or condition that is desired.

Productivity—the ratio between the resources used by a business firm and what the same business firm realizes from using those resources.

Symptoms—the signs or conditions that indicate the existence of a problem.

FOR YOUR REVIEW

1. What differences in meaning exist among the terms *problem solving*, *decision making*, and *choice making*?

2. Define *problem* in two ways, and identify two types of problems that face administrative office managers.

3. How is office productivity affected by the status of problem solving in the firm?

4. In what general ways does the productive office differ from the unproductive office?

5. Discuss the purpose of the American Productivity Center.

6. List the main assumptions made by the American Productivity Center in its national study of white-collar productivity.

7. Even though each problem has many characteristics that are unique, is it possible that a common approach can be used to solve all office problems? Explain.

8. Why is a knowledge of the cultural background of problem solvers an important part of the problem-solving environment?

9. What roles do the present state and the desired state play in solving problems?

10. Identify controllable and uncontrollable factors in solving office problems. How important is the latter group to the office manager since he or she has no influence over them?

11. Compare the functions of creativity, logic, and intuition in the problem-solving process.

12. List the steps required to solve problems by the formal approach. How does such an approach differ from the informal, intuitive approach?

13. How does the process of analysis relate to defining the problem to be solved?

14. Outline the steps involved in the questioning framework used to collect information in the problem-solving process.

15. Why are human problems more difficult to solve than other types of problems in the office?

16. Cite several common systems problems. Are these problems related in any way to human problems? Explain.

17. Are economic problems in the office separate and distinct from human and systems problems, or are they closely interrelated? Discuss.

FOR YOUR DISCUSSION

1. On an office wall poster, you read the following widely distributed message:

> We have met the enemy and it is us.
>
> *Pogo*

Brainstorm the relevance of this quotation to problem solving.

2. To emphasize the importance of alternatives in developing solutions to problems, your instructor asks you to list, in three minutes, the following:
   a. One word that expresses the same meaning (in this case, one alternative) for each of these terms: white, yes, alive, north, pass, and laugh.

    b. Five words that have more than one degree (or gradation) of meaning (that is, several alternatives), such as tall, thin, and pretty.

3. A practical-minded business executive spoke to a college class in administrative office management and asserted flatly that "Problem-solving as discussed in management textbooks is a lot of poppycock; problem-solving, when you get down to brass tacks, is mainly hunch and good intuition. It's having a 'feel' for the situation." What is your reaction to this comment?

4. Outline the main considerations in defining the following types of office problems:
   a. The poor productivity of file clerks.
   b. Frequent, unexplained absences of an office supervisor.
   c. Repeated instances where office operating costs exceed the budget provided.
   d. Inability of the office manager to delegate work to the support staff.

5. On several occasions during the four years you have served as an administrative assistant, you have made reasonable suggestions for improving the office operations in your firm. On each occasion, your supervisor, Marian McNally, has indicated the idea has been tried before and did not work; therefore, "It won't work now." After analyzing the situation, you are sure the main reason for the failure of these ideas is that the supervisor did not think of them herself. What steps can be taken to change this situation so McNally will be more open to change and so the efficiency of the office can be improved?

6. Everyone is creative, but some people are more so. That idea was recently mentioned by a visitor to your campus. To prove this point—that each member of your class is creative—you are asked to do the following:
   a. List ten other uses for a metal paper clip.
   b. Suggest how waste paper can be "reclaimed" for use in the office without spending any money.
   c. Recommend a way of using the shavings that accumulate in the pencil sharpeners in an office.
   d. Discuss ways of using personal accessories on office desks (photographs, plants, and the like) that will provide a uniformly attractive appearance for the entire office area.
   e. Assume your stapler has other uses. List five.
   f. Find a way of retrieving books from the top shelf of a seven-foot bookcase without the use of a ladder or step stool.

7. The German philosopher Friedrich Nietzsche once commented on creativity and problem solving in this way: "The surest way to corrupt a youth is to teach him to hold in higher esteem those who think alike than those who think differently." How does this statement, made many years ago, apply to present-day AOM students?

8. Your instructor has given you a sheet with nine dots arranged in the form of a square, as follows:

$$\begin{matrix} \bullet & \bullet & \bullet \\ \bullet & \bullet & \bullet \\ \bullet & \bullet & \bullet \end{matrix}$$

You are asked to place a pencil on one of the dots and draw four straight lines without lifting the pencil so that all nine dots are covered by the lines. Complete this assignment and indicate how this miniproject is useful to managerial problem solvers.

SOLVING CASE PROBLEMS

In each of the preceding chapters, you had an opportunity to study case problems in order to identify problems and appreciate their complexities. That introduction will now assist you in effectively dealing with the heart of the problem-solving process—*developing the solution.*

At this point in your study of administrative office management, it will be helpful if you:

1. Review the components of the problem-solving attitude you developed in studying the cases in Chapters 1 and 2.

2. Reexamine the guidelines for solving problems in Chapter 3, especially the section *Basic Steps in Problem Solving*, which begins on page 73. Once you understand the logical flow of thought outlined in these guidelines, you are ready to begin problem solving in earnest. You may now wish to return to the cases in Chapters 1 and 2, this time to apply systematically the problem-solving principles in order to solve one or more of the cases. You are then prepared to solve the problems in Chapter 3 and the remainder of the cases in this textbook.

In order that you may retain a sound, problem-solving attitude and become adept in applying the principles of problem solving, you should periodically review the contents of Chapter 3. Doing so will assist you in becoming an effective problem solver throughout the course and in later life.

Case 3-1 Developing Logical Thinking

After returning from a one-week seminar on problem solving, your office manager, Peter Day, has instituted a set of training sessions for the entire office staff. The major objective of these sessions is to improve problem-solving skills and ultimately office productivity.

The theme of the first session is "Developing Logical Thinking." Day feels that this skill is more basic than any other to problem solving in the age of automation. In his session, Day stresses the importance of listening, recording facts accurately, thinking clearly, and noting key relationships among the facts so that the facts "work" for the problem solver in developing the solution to the problem.

Day then challenges your group with this problem, which requires a logical answer to the question, "Who holds what office job?"

1. Jim is married to the supervisor's sister.

2. Diana and Joe sometimes play bridge with the accountant.

3. The office manager is engaged to a member of Diana's family.

4. Joe and Cynthia are both older than the CEO.

5. Cynthia and the personnel director are both married.

6. Norm and the accountant both have red hair.

7. Jim and the personnel director were both born in Richmond.

8. Norm is a distant cousin of both the personnel director and the CEO.

9. Diana, Joe, and the supervisor belong to the same country club.

10. Cynthia and the supervisor both have two children.

Using the formal problem-solving process discussed in this chapter,

1. Discuss the logical nature of the problem and possible approaches for its solution.

2. What do you feel is the best method for solving this type of problem?

3. Outline a solution to this problem that shows both a logical approach to problem solving and a set of correct answers to the main question, "Who holds what office job?" Also comment briefly on the values of this type of mental exercise.

Case 3-2 Assessing the Potential of a Minority Employee

Shortly after migrating to the United States from Honduras six months ago, Carlotta Sanchez joined your sales office staff. Her duties involve typing correspondence and reports and serving as a backup person for the receptionist to assist in handling the many customers coming to the office. Sanchez has excellent writing skills stemming from seven years of English language study in her homeland; however, owing to lack of practice, her oral language skills are not yet well developed. This has created problems, because the longer she is on the job the more she is expected to answer the telephone and help in receiving customers, which requires making introductions and giving extensive oral instructions and directions. Coupled with this problem is Sanchez's personality. Although she is very pleasant and well liked, she is unusually shy, making her reluctant to speak out and gain the speaking experience she needs. As time goes on, her typing work improves, but she has "gone into a shell," as the supervisor, Barbara Parker, mentions.

Parker has discussed the problem with you, her assistant, and the other office supervisors, who feel that Sanchez is making progress and that in time she will overcome the language barrier. Parker, on the other hand, does not agree, indicating that she is strongly considering terminating Sanchez's employment because of her inability to perform the job for which she was hired. Only because of a physical handicap (Sanchez lost the use of one leg in a childhood accident) has Parker delayed making a decision earlier.

Using the problem-solving process outlined in this chapter,

1. Define the problem and constraints. Determine the controllable and uncontrollable factors important to its solution.

2. What sources would you consult before making a decision? Why?

3. What alternate solutions would you recommend to Parker?

Prepare your solution in a short informal (memo) report such as the one illustrated in Figure 3-9 on page 84.

4

Administrative Office Systems

GOALS FOR THIS CHAPTER

After completing this chapter, you should be able to:

1. Explain the nature and purpose of administrative office systems in the modern organization.
2. Identify the basic systems concepts and explain their value in understanding administrative office systems.
3. Discuss the steps involved in conducting systems studies and the relationship of such studies to the management and problem-solving processes.
4. Describe the basic role of the human system in the office.
5. Compare the various methods of organizing the systems function and the advantages and disadvantages of each method.

With the continuing growth of information technologies based upon systems thinking, use of the term *system* has increased to the point where it has become a central concept in general management and administrative office studies. In all areas of society, references are frequently made to systems—to circulatory and nervous systems in medicine; to free enterprise and socialistic systems in government; and, as discussed throughout this textbook, to accounting, communication, word processing, and computer systems in business and industry. From a personal standpoint, too, the efficient worker is often labeled as having a good system for performing work or as being *system*atic by nature.

Chapter 1 has shown us that the systems school of management was introduced as the latest in a series of major viewpoints regarding the nature of the management process. At that point, the systems concept was introduced from an *organization-wide* perspective and is usually called a *management information system (MIS)*. In this chapter, on the other hand, the concept of system is defined in a more *specific, work-related* manner. With this latter thought in mind, the word *system* refers to a *set* of *related elements* that are *linked together* according to a *plan* for achieving a specific *objective*. However, all levels of systems share the same basic components shown in italics in this definition; each system depends on the proper coordination and operation of all its elements in order to achieve its assigned goals.

The information function is carried out through **administrative office systems (AOS).**[1] These specialized systems are responsible for planning, organizing, oper-

---

[1]To communicate more effectively with the reader, the term *administrative office systems* is represented by the initials *AOS*. This practice is consistent with the use of *AOM* and *OM* to represent the terms *administrative office manager* and *office manager*, respectively, throughout this textbook.

ating, and controlling all phases of the information cycle in order to meet the main systems objective—*to provide appropriate information and service for management's use in making decisions.* Increasingly greater impetus has been given to AOS with the expanding use of the computer and related automated information processes.

All sizes and types of firms depend on AOS. For this reason, managers and their employees must understand systems concepts in order to perform their jobs efficiently. This chapter identifies the major AOS and discusses basic concepts needed to create, operate, and evaluate systems. Special attention is devoted to the human factor in making each system function properly. The specific techniques by which personnel analyze, operate, and evaluate AOS are covered in Part 4.

THE ADMINISTRATIVE OFFICE SYSTEMS FUNCTION

The work to be accomplished in an organization must, through effective leadership, be carefully planned, organized, and controlled. Each department manager is in effect an administrator who must apply Leffingwell's Principles of Effective Work, which were discussed in Chapter 1. In systems terms, this requires making decisions on *what* work is to be done; *how* it is to be done; *who* will do the work; *when* the work will be done; and after the work has been completed, determining *how well* the work has been done. To the extent that the effective performance of the work depends largely on the use of information, *each department manager is also an information manager.*

The key elements in the AOS function discussed earlier are shown in systems terms in Figure 4-1. This figure emphasizes the primary role of *personnel* in managing, supervising, and doing the work. Such work must be done through the use of *physical*

resources, such as office furniture, machines and supplies, and the space necessary for housing these resources and personnel. *Data* must be available for processing into information using efficient *methods* (manual, mechanical, and automated) for completing the work. And *media,* such as forms and related records for storing, retrieving, and using data must be provided. All of these elements are regulated by a set of *controls*—policies, rules, objectives, procedures, computer programs for processing the data, and various evaluation techniques—to ensure that the system achieves its *goals.* And as we know, *all systems depend completely on adequate financial support to ensure their effective operations.*

Major Administrative Office Systems

In all business organizations, we find the major administrative functions of purchasing, sales, production, finance, accounting, and human resources. In addition, we usually see a separate administrative function that handles the general-office services. Even so, each of the major-function departments may have added to its regular responsibilities a certain amount of administrative operations so that each department manager is in effect an information manager, as stated earlier. For example, a large production department may handle some of its own personnel and purchasing responsibilities even though separate human resources and purchasing departments exist. If a decentralized plan is in operation, each department also maintains its own correspondence and record systems, which may be controlled by the department manager. Or the maintenance of correspondence and records may be placed under the central responsibility of the administrative office manager. Figure 4-2 illustrates a firm's main systems and **subsystems,** which are lower-level subdivisions of systems that are responsible for accom-

Figure 4-1
Key Elements in Administrative Office Systems

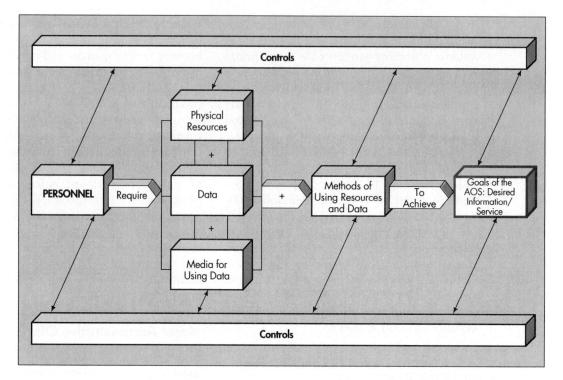

plishing specialized functions of the total system (the firm). Note, however, that any subsystem has all the same systems features as its "parent."

In the operation of each department, the manager develops a number of procedures for completing the work. A **procedure** is a planned sequence of operations for handling recurring transactions uniformly and consistently. For example, in a purchasing system, various procedures are set up to complete the required work in each of the subsystems. To request a desired machine, an office worker must obtain the necessary information to place the order, fill out a purchase requisition form, compute the total cost of the desired item, obtain the approval of the requesting department head, and forward the requisition to the purchasing department head for final approval.

For each step within the procedure, we note that a method is required to accomplish that phase of the work. A **method**, as shown in Figure 4-1, represents a manual, mechanical, or automated means by which each procedural step is performed. Continuing with the previous example, in a purchasing system the department head may use one of several methods of obtaining or transmitting information. The manager may talk in person to an employee, write a letter to a distant vendor, or use a telephone or facsimile transmission to expedite the shipment of a rush order. The nature of the system's needs, the skills and preferences of the workers, and the cost and availability of the equipment determine the various methods used in each system.

Objectives of Administrative Office Systems

"If you don't know where you're going, any road will take you there." As organizations

Figure 4-2
Major Systems and Subsystems in a Business Firm

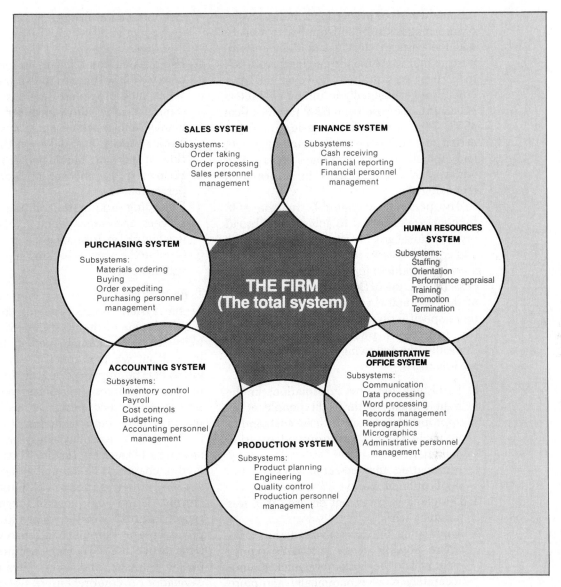

SALES SYSTEM
Subsystems:
   Order taking
   Order processing
   Sales personnel
     management

FINANCE SYSTEM
Subsystems:
   Cash receiving
   Financial reporting
   Financial personnel
     management

HUMAN RESOURCES SYSTEM
Subsystems:
   Staffing
   Orientation
   Performance appraisal
   Training
   Promotion
   Termination

PURCHASING SYSTEM
Subsystems:
   Materials ordering
   Buying
   Order expediting
   Purchasing personnel
     management

THE FIRM
(The total system)

ADMINISTRATIVE OFFICE SYSTEM
Subsystems:
   Communication
   Data processing
   Word processing
   Records management
   Reprographics
   Micrographics
   Administrative personnel
     management

ACCOUNTING SYSTEM
Subsystems:
   Inventory control
   Payroll
   Cost controls
   Budgeting
   Accounting personnel
     management

PRODUCTION SYSTEM
Subsystems:
   Product planning
   Engineering
   Quality control
   Production personnel
     management

grow larger and more complex, so does their need for considering "where they are going"; that is, deciding on the *objectives* of their administrative office systems. In such a complex environment, new information technologies are available to provide more powerful methods of automating office work, which causes an increasingly greater dependence on the AOM or the systems staff to plan and coordinate the work. With the

costs of labor and employee benefits accounting for as much as 75 percent of all office costs, productivity is a critical issue as these costs continue to escalate while the output of labor continues to decline.

Ironically, the opposite is true of technology. As new information technology emerges, the efficiency of automated machines goes up while machine costs go down. For example, from 1960 to 1980, the estimated costs of processing a million cycles of information dropped from $40 to 4 cents; and the costs of storing a million units of information for a month declined from $64 to $1.80. At the same time, however, the labor costs to enter manually a million characters of information rose from $302 to more than $650. This trend of increasing machine efficiency and decreasing machine prices and operating costs continues because of widespread improvements in information technology.[2]

The personnel responsible for the AOS function are expected to achieve this broad organizational goal: *to plan, design, operate, and control systems that result in the highest levels of productivity at the lowest possible cost.* In turn, the office manager or the head of the AOS unit is responsible for achieving more specific objectives that include all of the important phases of the system. Typically, the following tangible objectives are identified:

1. Furnishing the best information, in the right format, to the right people at an appropriate time, at the least cost, and in the right amount so improved decision making results.
2. Eliminating unnecessary work or the duplication of work.
3. Designing systems that ensure safer, less fatiguing work.
4. Automating the repetitive, routine tasks where possible when automatic equipment will do the work more quickly, more accurately, more economically, and more reliably. Such a system should be as flexible as possible to meet the users' present requirements and still be able to accommodate changes in future requirements without the need for major systems revisions.
5. Establishing an efficient, uniform procedure to follow for each similar transaction. When such procedures are based upon a standard time allowance for identical manual and machine operations, wasted motion, errors, and delays in the smooth flow of work are eliminated or reduced.
6. Fixing responsibility for satisfactory work performance.
7. Providing adequate training for employees and supervisors to ensure top-level work performance.
8. Gaining the acceptance and support of all systems users.

Because such objectives relate to all phases of the system, many systems studies are required. One of the most basic is the **feasibility study**, a planning method that seeks to find out whether specific systems operations can be improved and if the addition of new resources (machines, equipment, personnel) is economically justified for making these improvements. (The steps followed in a feasibility study are outlined in Figure 4–3 and are further discussed later in this chapter.) These and other systems studies cover paperwork management (forms design and control, records and reports control, correspondence studies, and procedures development and analysis), work flow, work measurement, equipment and personnel usage, and work scheduling and evaluation. A comprehensive systems study of such magnitude requires high-level skills and broad work experience of the office manager, for it not only affects all the technical work processes but also, more important, the basic attitudes of people toward themselves, their supervisors, and their work. To be effective, a systems study must promote change toward better working conditions and more efficient work performance through a concentrated, analytical approach to problem solving. Such an on-

---

[2]Herbert F. Schantz, "OCR Adds to Productivity in Data-Entry Applications," *The Office* (February, 1983), p. 42. The continued trend in the reduction of computing costs over time is confirmed in an article, "Is the Computer Business Maturing?" *Business Week* (March 6, 1989), p. 70.

Figure 4–3
Steps in
Making a
Feasibility
Study

Steps in Making a Feasibility Study

1. *Define the nature and scope of the problem as well as the objectives to be achieved by the study.* Examples of such objectives include (a) reducing administrative office costs, (b) speeding up processing operations, (c) increasing the productivity of present personnel or equipment, (d) developing management information for more efficient and effective operations, (e) introducing new management methods, (f) determining the relative merits of various types of systems or equipment, and (g) attaining greater prestige and a more progressive image.

2. *Gather data on current operations.* Through personal interviews and mail questionnaires, find answers to such questions as:
   a. What information is available and what additional information is needed? What documents (forms, correspondence, and reports) are received, from what sources, and how often? What files are kept to support operations?
   b. What personnel are involved in the operations and what are their assignments and skill levels?
   c. What machines and equipment are used in the system, for what purpose, and for how long?
   d. What output is required of the system, and how is such output evaluated?
   e. What are the time and cost requirements for completing an operations cycle? (Note direct or tangible costs, such as personnel, equipment, and floor space, and indirect or intangible costs, such as customer dissatisfaction and employee morale.)

3. *Analyze the data collected.* Study work/data flows including space assignments; the unique characteristics of managerial, supervisory, and work personnel as well as the equipment used; the number of hours worked in a week on each assignment; and the costs and benefits of performing systems operations.

4. *Develop an approach for solving the problem.* Include factual information that logically defends the approach. Examples of such information include documenting how to eliminate personnel, equipment, time, space, or paperwork; balanced facts on the costs and benefits of the present system as well as reasonable methods for improving the system.

5. *Present the completed feasibility study to management for their consideration and action.*

going search for improved office operations eliminates the weakness found in many offices—because a job has always been done a certain way, that way is still satisfactory.

The systems objectives outlined in this section serve as the foundation for the discussion of systems studies later in this chapter. In essence, *each objective is directed toward finding the best way to perform each office job.*

Systems Problems

As we know, each office manager must be realistic about the operation and effectiveness of the AOS in the organization. If each of the objectives discussed earlier were consistently attained, there would be no systems problems. In the real world, however, such is not the case. Hence, it is important that the principal systems

Systems study is an ongoing process that involves human and nonhuman resources.

problems be identified so that the office staff can take steps toward achieving their solution.

In general, AOS problems may be classified and illustrated as shown in Figure 4-4. Each of these problems is typical of the difficulties encountered by office managers as well as many other managers in general. Such problems can be solved or reduced in intensity if the proper problem-solving attitude is present. The power of positive thinking plays an important role in this phase of the office manager's work.

BASIC SYSTEMS CONCEPTS

If you are to understand the nature and purpose of systems in all areas of management—but especially in AOS—you must be able to identify several basic systems concepts. These concepts are (1) the general systems model that explains the overall operation of any system; (2) the organization of systems within the firm; and (3) the various systems levels that we find in operation, ranging from

Figure 4-4 Administrative Office Systems Problems and Examples	Types of Problems	Examples
	1. Organizational	High costs, low productivity levels, excessive waste, decreasing profits, poor organization structure.
	2. Managerial	Ineffective delegation of work, difficulties in assigning responsibility, infrequent interaction with workers, inappropriate or unknown goals, poor organization, failure or inability to lead.
	3. Personnel	Poor motivation, tardiness and absenteeism, low morale, and increasingly serious interpersonal problems on the job.
	4. Information systems	Poor use of space, inefficient work flow, poorly designed forms, lack of control over records creation and disposition, lack of knowledge about information needs of the firm, failure to control costs, poor selection of equipment, poor use and care of equipment, inability to identify and measure production levels, late completion of work, and excessive overtime work.

the completely manual to the most automated type of system.

In the discussion of systems in this textbook, emphasis is placed on general systems and the needs of the small office for improving its system. This type of basic systems thinking will simplify your efforts in learning about all types of systems—from the manual systems that still play important roles in modern offices to the automated systems discussed in the remaining parts of this textbook.

The General Systems Model

As you learned earlier, models are used to an increasing degree in problem solving and management planning. In one sense, a model represents an *ideal* form of operation, such as a model office or a model worker. More commonly in systems work, a **model** explains in simplified, *general* form the complex interrelationships and activities of an organization or its parts. Thus, the model is free of the many specific details that would prevent an easy understanding of the total or overall system.

To study AOS, a **general systems model** is used to represent a broad explanation of the system (or any of its subsystems) to which more concrete details can be added as needed. Figure 4–5 outlines the principal phases of a system arranged in the sequential order in which each phase functions. Throughout the use of this model, the AOM and other managers can more readily

Figure 4–5
The General
Systems
Model

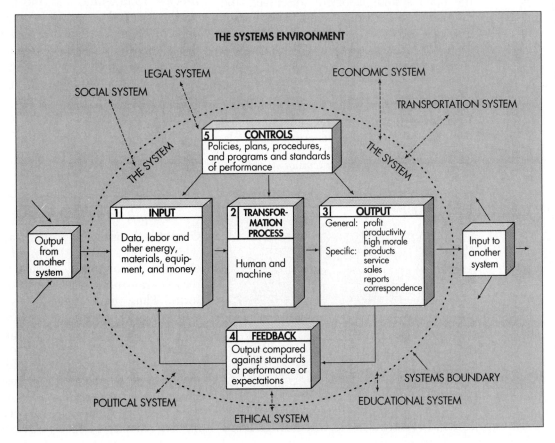

understand the changes that occur within their systems as each system continues its operations.

Systems are usually divided into two classes: open systems and closed systems. An **open system** interacts with its environment, as we see in Figure 4–5, in order to attain its goals. A business firm is an open system, because it is affected by many factors, such as tax laws, its competition, and the quality of its workers. A **closed system**, on the other hand, operates as a self-regulating unit; hence, it does not interact with its environment. A traffic light that works without outside influence (ignoring its electricity source) is an example of a closed system. For all practical purposes, AOMs deal only with open systems in the business firm. In this section, each of the phases of the open system is briefly discussed and numbered to correspond with the numbers in Figure 4–5.

SYSTEMS PHASE 1

Input

Input is the first phase of any system in which data, labor and other energy, materials,

Are these businesses open systems or closed systems?

equipment, and money are received from another system. Examples of input are raw materials introduced into a manufacturing operation, the arrival of the morning mail, the skill of a word processing operator needed to produce a letter, or telephone calls coming into the office. (As discussed in a later paragraph, feedback also furnishes information that becomes input for further operations of the system.) Other examples of input are shown in Figure 4–6.

SYSTEMS PHASE 2

Transformation Process

That phase of the system that changes or transforms input into a desired form is called **transformation process**, often shortened to *process*. (Sometimes, too, this phase of the system is called *processor* because a worker or a machine combined with an efficient procedure is involved.) Common examples of transformation processing activities dealing with information are classifying, sorting, storing, retrieving, and computing; additional examples frequently found in other types of systems are shown in Figure 4–6.

SYSTEMS PHASE 3

Output

Output is the ultimate goal of a system, that which results after the input has been changed in some way during the second phase—transformation process—to a desired form. Thus, unprocessed sales data (the system's input) are converted (transformed) into a finished sales report (the system's output) by certain processing procedures. In so doing, the process phase adds value to the input, which makes it more useful to the firm. Common examples of output in the AOS are correspondence, reports, accounting statements, budgets, advertising bro-

Figure 4–6
Common
Systems
Examples

COMMON SYSTEMS	SYSTEMS PHASES				
	1 Input	2 Trans-formation Process	3 Output	4 Feedback	5 Controls
A. Production system	Raw materials Labor Energy Blueprints	Assembling Construction Welding	Automobile Box of cereal Telephone service	Customer evaluation of product or service	Policies Procedures Plans Federal Communi- cations Commission
B. Sales system	Sales data Feedback (complaints from customers)	Classifying Sorting Storing Billing Filling orders	Invoices to customers Sales reports	The results of comparing sales with sales quotas	Policies Procedures Plans Competition
C. College student (human system)	Money Attitudes Abilities Food Rumor Class lectures	Advising Studying Testing Using the brain as a processor	Course grades Changed attitudes Knowledge College degree	Employer evaluation of graduates Graduates' reactions to courses	Parents Social customs Finances Laws

chures, and invoices. More general forms of output in other types of systems are listed in Figure 4–6.

SYSTEMS PHASE 4

Feedback

In the AOS, **feedback** is the regulating force that compares the system's output (*what was produced*) with the standards of performance set for the system (*what should have been produced*). Notice how this feedback definition compares with the definition of *problem* in Chapter 3. Thus, if the actual output levels are lower than the levels desired, a message is "fed back" to the input phase of the system specifying how the next operating cycle of the system involving all five systems phases must be modified in

order to attain its goals. Several types of feedback are shown in Figure 4–6.

SYSTEMS PHASE 5

Control

While the previous four systems phases usually function in 1, 2, 3, 4 sequential order, the control phase operates in a different manner. **Control** is the systems phase that dictates what can and cannot be done in each of the other phases of the AOS. As a result, controls are placed over the input phase, the transformation process phase, the output phase, and the feedback phase. Examples of control inside the firm include plans, procedures, programs, and standards of employee performance. The dotted lines in Figure 4–5 represent the **systems boundary**, which defines the scope or limits of an open system and at the same time separates a system from its environment. (If the dotted lines were replaced by a solid line, a closed system would be illustrated.) Outside the firm (that is, outside the dotted lines shown in Figure 4–5) is the *systems environment*, which sets up controls that affect the operations of the firm. Government (legal) regulations on taxes, working conditions, and labor relations, as well as the economic, political, social, transportation, educational, and ethical systems in existence, impose controls that affect the behavior of any firm and the people within it. (See Figure 4–6.)

The Systems Model in Action

A sales system illustrates each of the phases in the systems model. As input, the sales orders coming into a firm are classified, sorted, and computed; and the customers are properly billed—all transformation processing activities. The results of such activities typically appear in two forms of output: formal sales reports as well as invoices or notices sent to customers regarding the amounts owed. At the end of a sales period, such as every three months, the sales quota (the standard of performance) set for each salesperson is compared with the actual sales made by each member of the sales staff. If the sales quota has not been met, corrective action in the form of more intensive sales efforts is "fed back" into the system as new input for the next sales period; that is, for the next cycle of the sales system's operation. If the quota has been met, no such corrective action is needed. In the same way, the sales department's file copies of sales invoices feed back information for use in the preparation of customers' bills and for documentation purposes in the accounts receivable department. A copy of the customer's bill becomes input to the customer's accounts payable system.

Examples of several common systems are shown in Figure 4–6. The third example illustrates the human being as a system with the brain as the main processing agent to process the information received as input through the five senses. This example qualifies as a system because it includes all the elements found in the general systems model.

Systems Structure

Because of the complex set of management information needs, an equally complex set of AOM systems is required. Thus, a *systems structure*, or systems hierarchy, somewhat related to the structure appearing on an organization chart, evolves as the form of organization for providing a wide variety of systems services to the firm. Several of the most important systems relationships in this structure are discussed in this section.

Total System–Subsystems Relationships

As we see in Figure 4–2, various key systems are needed to meet the goals of any firm. When all of these systems are combined into a **total system**, they form a company-wide information network. In this respect, we note that the physician regards the human body as a total system made up of many major systems. Each of these main systems is, in turn, divided into a number of subsystems. The communication system operates in a similar manner as a subsystem of the broader AOS just as the cardiac, or heart, system acts as a subsystem of the broader cardiovascular system in the human body. However, all three levels of system—total, major, and subsystem—have the same general makeup and follow the same operating phases outlined in Figure 4–6.

Each system is related to the other systems and in a sense "leans" on the others in order that the total system can fulfill its mission. In a business firm, for example, the human resources system is responsible for hiring workers, the production system is responsible for assigning the workers their duties, and the accounting system is responsible for paying the workers. In an interdependent manner, these systems and their subsystems support the main objective of the firm—to sell at a profit the products or services made available by the firm.

Information Systems

The information function defined in Chapter 1 operates through a system that controls the many activities making up the *information cycle* (collecting, processing, storing, retrieving, and distributing information). Thus, management typically considers each of its major systems as an **information system** and the total set of such systems as a *management information system*. At the heart of such a system is the computer, which performs many of the functions making up the information cycle. For example, the computer is used for collecting, processing, and storing business information; and when the need arises, it retrieves information to assist in decision making. The computer also aids managers in formulating plans for the future based upon an analysis of the contents of its extensive historical files.

Database

A **database** is a central master file containing company-wide information from the major systems of the firm. Or, on a smaller scale, we find departments setting up databases that consolidate their own automated records. The ideal database represents a total collection of information from such areas as accounting, engineering, marketing, human resources, production, and research and development in one large computerized library. It also provides organization-wide access to the master file via computer terminals. Information to be used in the database is "captured" and stored only once. As a result, total file space is reduced since duplicate files, previously maintained by individual departments, can be eliminated. Because transactions come into the system

at one point only, updating of files is facilitated.

The database concept becomes possible with the use of large computers or with small computers linked together to provide additional storage power. However, in most firms or departments within firms, only portions of the files are automated. Many departments or individuals within departments are reluctant to release certain information to a centralized unit responsible for maintaining the database because they fear unauthorized access to the files or accidental destruction or removal of the stored information.

Systems Levels

Systems may be classified in terms of processing power and thus in terms of the degree of automation involved. In this section, we note three levels of systems: (1) manual, (2) mechanical (sometimes called electromechanical), and (3) computer.

Manual Systems

With all the emphasis given to computers in today's society, we naturally find it difficult to remember the millions of manual systems still in existence. However, we have only to study the commonplace manual system sketched in Figure 4–7 to realize there are many systems in which manual or hand processing of information is clearly preferable.

In a **manual system**, *the earliest and still most prevalent type of system*, the human being is the data processor. We can illustrate such a system by considering the preparation of paychecks in small firms, such as restaurants, woodworking shops, or service garages. In such firms with manual payroll systems, the person preparing the payroll receives input data through the senses, usually the eyes and ears, from the information appearing on time cards or time sheets and related oral communications. The data

Figure 4–7
A Common Office Workplace Illustrating a Manual System

are then sent via the nervous system to the brain for storage, with the brain acting as the control unit. The brain may also act as a processing unit by performing such processing operations as arithmetic calculations; storing these results; comparing one number or word with others (as in the case of proofreading); and finally producing output such as paychecks, payroll registers, and tax reports. Output in the manual system is provided by the set of instructions or "program" stored in the payroll clerk's brain or perhaps contained in a procedures manual.

In the earliest manual systems, all tools for processing data (pencils and pens) and the journals and ledgers for storing information were operated by hand. Under such a system, information appears in a human-readable form and changes or corrections are easily made. Such manual methods may be quickly

adapted to various working conditions and to the exercise of judgment in making decisions from the data. However, we find certain weaknesses in manual systems. The human mind is subject to fatigue and boredom, which frequently cause from 5 to 10 percent error in computations and related clerical tasks. Too, our minds are slow in performing arithmetic calculations and, because of the impact of emotions, we may have difficulty applying the rules of logic. The final output in a manual system can be no better than our human conditions—both psychological and physical—will permit.

Mechanical Systems

For most of the past century, simple machines have assisted in the operation of the manual system. For many of us, simple machines such as typewriters, adding and calculating machines, dictation and transcribing machines, and the telephone have become handy office tools, with each performing a single processing function. Compared with performing all office work by hand, such machines offer great speed and accuracy; but at the same time, their use is limited to the skill, experience, and control of human beings.

A higher-level **mechanical system** incorporates the use of punched-card equipment for reading and processing the data stored in the cards. Punched-card records served for many decades as the mainstay of information processing by machine. Later, as the computer age dawned, punched cards became important input documents for automated systems. However, because such systems are too slow and costly for processing information in today's high-speed processing world, punched-card systems have greatly diminished in number and importance. However, we still find punched-card records often used for time cards, invoices, and other common applications that can be linked to the computer.

Computer Systems

The **computer system**, familiar by name to most of us, is made up of a group of interconnected machines, including the computer, that process data at the speed of light and that perform many other information-handling functions. Unlike earlier machines, the computer is able to store in its internal "memory" both the data to be processed and the instructions (or **program**) to process the data. A computer system depends upon a code, or machine language, for representing data within the machine. Alphabetic and numeric data appearing on source documents in typewritten or handwritten form must, as a rule, be recorded in coded form on diskettes, magnetic tape, punched paper tape, punched cards, or some other input medium.

After this initial recording, the coded data and the instructions for their processing are fed into the computer, where they are stored in the form of magnetic codes for use in the computer's processing system. Computations are performed, and summaries and various types of output reports are prepared according to the stored instructions. Processed data appear on the terminal screen for later storage or are printed out of the computer on punched cards, magnetic tape, magnetic disk, or business documents (such as invoices, reports, paychecks, journals, and ledgers). We know from observation that the computer system also uses many manual systems whenever the systems functions cannot be performed by machines. Examples are the human functions, such as customer relations, keyboarding of information, proofreading source documents, solving human relations problems, and making decisions from data based on intuition, judgment, and common sense. Hence, *we must not forget that people serve*

as the main control element in this highest level of system as in other levels of systems.

CONDUCTING SYSTEMS STUDIES

Generally we call the process of improving systems a **systems study**. Other names used are systems analysis, systems and procedures analysis, methods analysis, systems engineering, or work simplification. Whatever the label used, a systems study is closely related to the processes of management and problem solving discussed earlier in Part 1. In fact, senior managers, looking back on long, successful business careers, describe success in management in terms of satisfactory problem solving and the ability to make sound decisions. Thus, *we can conclude that effective office management is solving problems that occur in the systems and procedures of the office.*

The staff in charge of AOS must be alert to internal problems throughout the systems as well as to those problems that involve the external environment (the business community and the customers or clients). A well-planned program of systems studies should be developed by the staff unit that specializes in systems work. Of special importance in such a program is the mental attitude of the analyst. Systems studies require of the analyst a keen, analytical skill and an objective viewpoint that sets aside preconceived ideas about the area of study and which places personal considerations in the background. For these reasons, each problem must be carefully defined, clear-cut objectives formulated, and the systems approach to problem solving carefully followed. In this section, each of the required steps in the systems study cycle is discussed briefly. Typical areas of application in AOS are then treated in the following section of this chapter.

The Systems Approach

In this age of systems, we still use widely the scientific method for solving office problems discussed in Chapter 3. This problem-solving technique centers on the careful definition of a problem and the development of reasonable solutions to the problem. Since the primary objective of systems analysis is problem solving, analysts have taken the scientific method, adapted it to their needs, and called it the **systems approach** to problem solving. When they use the systems approach, analysts apply the scientific method in addition to these unique systems steps:

1. *Identifying the work problem and all its components, noting the interrelationships of all parts and how each contributes to the total work system.* Frequently this all-components approach is called "seeing the big picture." Systems studies are far more concerned with interrelationships in the work system than were the early scientific management problem-solving studies.
2. *Clarifying the objectives for which the system is designed.* Systems analysts emphasize the great need for developing and writing objectives or unit goals so all workers involved understand what is expected of them.
3. *Noting the effect of* **synergism** *in the system.* (This term describes the fact that interrelated parts produce a total effect greater than the sum of each of the parts working independently. An example would be a symphony orchestra playing in concert or a successful football team playing on the field.) What this means in the office is that more can be accomplished through creativity and teamwork than through working as individuals.
4. *Considering all problems from a systems point of view,* that is, considering the input, transformation processing, output, feedback, and control factors involved in any problem.

The effect of any proposed changes in AOS must be weighed carefully because of the large or long-term investment involved. By working together to improve AOS, the office staff has reinforced again and again a basic systems concept—*interrelatedness.* Usually one change in a system, no matter how small, results in a series of other changes. An office manager may purchase an expensive machine only to realize later that it cannot handle the load for which it was designed and requires considerably more worker retraining, maintenance costs, and space than were considered at the outset. Such a disaster might have been foreseen if a feasibility study had been made prior to the purchase.

This and other types of organizational studies use the steps in the systems study cycle discussed in the next section.

The Systems Study Cycle

As we saw earlier, systems studies are problem-solving activities designed to improve productivity in the office. The conduct of such studies involves the **systems study cycle**, a set of sequential, problem-solving steps required to improve the systems function.

Typically a systems study begins whenever a recurring problem of some importance is recognized by the information user. Usually such a study covers three major steps: (1) analysis of the present system; (2) design of a new or improved system; and (3) installation of the improved system.

To put these *general* steps into action, several *specific* activities are performed. Six of these activities, as outlined in Figure 4–8, are discussed in this section.

Figure 4–8
Steps in the Systems Study Cycle

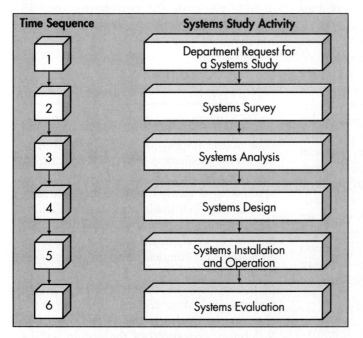

Time Sequence	Systems Study Activity
1	Department Request for a Systems Study
2	Systems Survey
3	Systems Analysis
4	Systems Design
5	Systems Installation and Operation
6	Systems Evaluation

STEP 1

Department Request for a Systems Study

Recognizing that a systems problem may be the cause of reduced productivity, a department head may request that a systems study be conducted. The systems staff (or the office manager) may then conduct a feasibility study to determine the probable value of such a study. During this time, the problem is redefined and objectives (such as lowering costs, improving the data flow, strengthening operating controls, improving customer relations, or automating a phase of the office system) are established. The study is broken down into major phases (personnel, equipment, space layout, and procedures), and a timetable is developed for completing each phase of the study.

STEP 2

Systems Survey

After the department request for a systems study has been approved by the systems unit or the office manager, data must be collected concerning all aspects of the problem. During this phase of a study, it is important to explain to the employees in the department involved why the study is being done and what data are needed from them. The facts are recorded on questionnaires, preferably during personal interviews. Frequently charts, such as the organization charts and charts for showing work flow, space utilization, worker motions, work sequence, and travel time involved, are used to pinpoint the task assignments of all workers involved. Experienced analysts may visit other companies having similar information needs and get advice from systems specialists and equipment vendors having expertise in solving the type of problem under study.

STEP 3

Systems Analysis

One of the most important phases in the systems study involves the analysis of the data collected. During this phase, the analyst considers the objectives of the system and notes the special causes, effects, and interrelationships of problems and systems elements. Often the analyst discusses the facts collected with members of the department under study in order that the accuracy of the data may be determined and the possible solutions to the problems may be explained.

STEP 4

Systems Design

Based upon the information obtained during the systems analysis, a new system is designed (or a proposal for revising an existing system is developed). Such a design proposal is usually a joint effort stemming from suggestions of the department personnel involved and managers who understand the nature of the problem. The proposal must consider possible effects on (1) employees (whether anyone will be laid off, how much retraining will be required, or what interdepartmental transfers may be suggested by the study); (2) profits (how the proposed system may affect salaries, space, material and supplies, overhead costs, cost of capital, and profits earned on capital invested as well as on equipment required); (3) work schedules; and (4) customer service. While no set rule for answering these kinds of questions is available, we find that experienced analysts frequently use a checklist covering each of the many elements of systems studies in their systems-design efforts.[3]

STEP 5

Systems Installation and Operation

Good planning and persuasion are required to sell a department staff on making a change in their systems operation, because the jobs and personal security of the workers are at stake. An effective approach for selling the new system is for the analyst to work with department personnel during the entire study period, thereby gaining their confidence. The report presenting the proposal should be carefully prepared in clear-cut form and made available to all personnel concerned. Emphasis should be placed on the anticipated savings, advantages, and the expected results related to the profits to be realized. If a large-scale study is involved, sometimes

[3]Useful systems analysis and design checklists can be found in the systems analysis textbooks available in college and university libraries. Additional information on systems studies is available from the Association for Systems Management, 24587 Bagley Road, Cleveland, OH 44138.

parallel operations are conducted, which allows the old, scaled-down system to operate alongside the new system until all of the problems or "bugs" have been removed. At that time, the old system can be phased out.

STEP 6

Systems Evaluation

One of the important control activities in AOS is the evaluation of systems operations. Periodically the office manager studies systems to determine how effectively they are meeting their goals. Such studies include (1) appraising the performance of personnel, the use of equipment and space, and the allocation of financial resources and (2) determining the overall benefits and costs of the system. In addition, a full-fledged systems evaluation seeks to find out what changes should be made in the system so that future operations of the system will be more effective.

Typical Areas for Systems Studies

From long-term studies of office work, we find that the same general types of systems problems occur in most offices although the specific details of each differ. Thus, the systems steps discussed in the previous section are commonly followed in studying these typical problem areas:

1. *Work flow.* The study of work flow in the system involves the effective use of space as well as the flow and frequency of movement of the workers who transport information (paperwork) throughout the office. From such studies, wasted motion and needless backtracking of the work can be spotted. Thus, changes can be made in the office procedures to shorten the time required for completing the work, which results in higher productivity.

2. *Forms.* The records used in AOS are critical to the effective operations of the systems since all key transactions are usually recorded on business forms.

3. *Equipment use.* Throughout the office, many data and word processing activities are performed that use mechanical equipment. For example, sorting, keyboarding, calculating, and communicating tasks use machines to ensure efficient office operations. In a systems study, an analysis of the equipment needs and the comparative costs and advantages of the various methods of performing work (manual or machine) should be undertaken.

4. *Personnel use.* Before any system is analyzed, the role of personnel in the department under study should be given the highest priority; for the workers can "make or break" the system. Studying the use of personnel involves such areas as job analysis and evaluation, work incentives, motion economies, work distribution among employees, personnel policies, attitudes, training programs, and employee performance appraisal.

5. *Systems costs.* Systems studies focus strongly on the control of office costs, such as the costs of moving equipment and people, renovating costs (repainting, relocating telephones and electrical outlets), furniture costs, and the costs of converting the files to a new system and removing the current system.

After the costs of operating the present and proposed systems have been pinpointed, the benefits anticipated from the improved system should be determined. Some of the benefits may be measured in dollars. However, other benefits, such as better public relations, more prompt deliveries to customers, and higher employee morale, although not measurable in dollars, provide benefits that ultimately have a strong influence on the firm's profit picture.

THE HUMAN SYSTEM IN THE OFFICE

One overriding thought we must never forget: *People and their needs must receive first and last consideration in any systems study.* The success of an AOS program is closely tied to the effective participation and harmonious work relationships that exist between department personnel and the systems staff. The staff must rely on the managers of the departments under study to provide the knowledge and information for developing effective policies, procedures, and methods in the operating departments. On the other hand, the managers need the expertise of the systems personnel for analyzing the systems and developing new and improved designs.

The most important element in the office is the human system; that is, the expectations, behavior, and performance of the people responsible for the system. The office manager and the office staff represent the key input to any office job; and accordingly, this group has the greatest impact on the output of the office. Managers and their employees bring *individual inputs*, such as their skills, knowledge, motives, needs, attitudes, and values to any task. Similarly, collections of individuals bring *group inputs*, such as group cohesiveness, group norms and ideas, and group conduct regarding what is acceptable behavior, to their work. For example, office managers have a very positive effect on their staffs by the manner in which they direct the staffs. Similarly, a group of keyboard specialists in a word processing center, if unhappy with the type of supervision provided, may reduce their daily output of correspondence to show their dissatisfaction.

By understanding and applying the philosophies of the behavioral and the systems schools of management thought discussed in Chapter 1, effective managers consider employee goals and company goals in systems planning. Thus, job satisfaction

Dialog on the Firing Line

DAVID B. HENRY
Data Processing Manager
Wm. B. Reily & Co., Inc.
New Orleans, Louisiana

BBA, University of Mississippi
CDP (Certificate in Data Processing)
CSP (Certified Systems Professional)

As Data Processing Manager, David Henry manages an IBM 4381-23 computer installation with a staff of 16 for Wm. B. Reily & Co., a food manufacturer and service company. Computer applications for which he is responsible include all accounting functions, route accounting, communications through handheld computers, exception reporting, graphics, customer analysis, financial analysis, online data entry, and inquiry.

QUESTION: What characteristics of people are most essential to the operation of an effective business system? Please comment briefly on how these characteristics can be developed in greater numbers of people.

RESPONSE: The operation of an effective business system requires a number of characteristics of the people involved in the operation. First, each person must be versatile. In other words, if one stumbles, another must be ready to step in and perform the task without delay. This must be done without regard to status or ego. Each task must be completed for the good of the whole, not because the job description says it must be done.

Second, fear of failure must not be a factor. Experience is the best teacher. One learns best by making mistakes, correcting them, and moving on to the next step. It is easy enough to tell someone to "Save" work before turning off the PC, but until that person has lost everything he or she has done for the last eight hours, it does not sink in.

Third, use the "Y" theory of management. People respond best if they are made to feel a part of the organization. This also has a byproduct of weeding out those who just do not fit in with the others. They will sense the peer pressure that they are not carrying their weight. Most of the time they will quit on their own, thus avoiding a tense firing situation.

Fourth, delegate. One person cannot be everywhere at the same time. To delegate authority is to overlap functions thereby saving the corresponding time. Remember, however, responsibility cannot be delegated. Just like in the navy, the captain may delegate to another the authority to steer the ship, but he is still responsible for where the ship goes.

If one can develop these four characteristics, effective business systems will automatically follow.

for the worker and profit making for the firm are basic, compatible objectives of effective AOS.

ORGANIZING THE SYSTEMS FUNCTION

The most common approaches for organizing the systems function are:

1. Employing a firm of management consultants or systems analysts to make special studies of AOS, procedures, and methods.
2. Developing in the large firm an internal staff of systems analysts whose services are available to the entire organization.
3. Assigning responsibility for systems improvement in the small firm to the office manager.

The organizational approach used for studying and improving systems is determined by the size of the office, the skills of the staff, and the attitude of management toward this phase of work. Whatever the subdivision of office work may be, the office manager must realize that the analysis of AOS requires the support and approval of top management if new or improved systems are to be successfully installed and operated.

The program of systems studies must be recognized not only by top management, but also by the company as a whole. The entire company must participate in recognizing, defining, analyzing, and solving systems problems and in implementing the recommended changes that are aimed at increasing company profits. Through the issuance of company regulations or instructions, proposals for systems improvement must be "sold" to the employees. In this way employees will understand that in most instances they will not lose their jobs, that their skills and abilities will be used more effectively, and that they will not receive less pay.

Use of Outside Consultants

A number of consulting firms engage in systems analysis. Many firms specialize in general systems analysis, which involves layout, equipment and personnel use, and interdepartmental information flows. Others specialize in the study of office automation, word processing, and communications. Consultants are hired in much the same way a company hires auditors or lawyers to provide expert advice.

Outside consultants bring certain advantages to a firm. Such consultants:

1. Provide special counsel and offer new ideas because of their experience with other firms.
2. Are outsiders and thus can study the client's systems with an objectivity that the internal consultant does not possess.
3. Often carry more weight than an internal consultant who may have become a part of the firm's political network.

On the other hand, the use of outside consultants creates certain disadvantages for the firm, such as:

1. The consultant's lack of familiarity with the firm, especially its strong informal organization, discussed in Chapter 2.
2. The relatively high cost of consultants' services.
3. The negative reaction of many workers to the so-called efficiency expert, as a person who may eliminate many jobs within the firm and who may not care about the best interests of individual workers.

As a rule, the *advantages* of using outside consultants may be considered as *disadvantages* of using internal consultants. Similarly, the *disadvantages* of using outside consultants can be translated into *advantages* of using internal consultants, as discussed in the remaining paragraphs of this chapter.

The Systems Function in Large Firms

Large firms with highly specialized staffs find the use of an internal systems staff a necessity as the systems become more complex. If the firm is especially large with many branches, such as General Electric Company and the Ford Motor Company, a centralized systems staff may be set up to coordinate the work of the decentralized staffs, which can deal more effectively with the systems found in each division. On the other hand, firms that are served by a corporate staff in one central location view the organization as an entity and maintain adequate systems service for each of the individual departments. In either case, systems personnel should meet the standards set by the Certified Systems Professional (CSP) program to ensure high quality of AOS work. However, even after granting CSP status to a candidate, the certifying agency requires recertification every three years.[4]

There is no set rule that dictates the size of an internal systems staff. Some corporate managers estimate that an adequate systems staff is 1 percent of the office personnel employed by the firm. Others believe that there should be one analyst for approximately every 200 office workers. The size of the systems staff should be determined by the results expected of its work—ensuring high productivity in the organization by supplying management with better information and at the same time producing sufficient savings to justify its existence.

To ensure that a company-wide perspective is maintained, in most firms the systems staff reports to a high-level administrator, such as the president, an administrative vice-president, the controller, or the treasurer. Regardless of its organizational placement, the systems staff should be available to all departments in the firm for assistance in improving working conditions and levels of work performance.

The Systems Function in Small Firms

In the typical small firm, we find that the office manager is *the* specialist in information management. Thus, the OM is responsible for systems work since the main goal of systems work is the improvement of information flow. To fulfill this responsibility, the office manager must possess these attributes of an effective systems analyst: a logical, probing, perceptive mind; an inventive, imaginative, creative nature; sound judgment; and a thorough understanding of the firm and its information needs. As a part-time analyst, the office manager offers an inexpensive means of systems improvement that can be used by small as well as large offices. Also, the office manager is usually more familiar with the work than anyone else. On the other hand, he or she may be so busy with routine duties that the systems work may be neglected. On occasion, too, the employees reporting to the office manager may resent the office manager's efforts more than those of a separate staff unit or an independent consulting firm.

For the enterprising office manager who handles the bulk of the firm's systems duties, considerable assistance is available at little or no cost. Memberships in such organizations as the Association for Systems Management (ASM), the Administrative Management Society (AMS), and the Association of Records Managers and Administrators (ARMA) give office managers access to worthwhile meetings, conventions, and useful publications dealing with systems

---

[4]The CSP program is sponsored by 14 associations and administered by the Institute for Certification of Computer Professionals (ICCP), 2200 East Devon Avenue, Des Plaines, IL 60018. To receive certification, candidates must meet personal requirements as well as receive satisfactory scores on examinations covering five broad areas: (1) environment of systems, (2) project management, (3) systems analysis, (4) systems design and implementation, and (5) tools and technology.

subjects. Additional advice can be obtained from many firms, such as the Standard Register Company and Moore Business Forms, Inc., that specialize in the design and control of business forms. Also, representatives of office machine and equipment manufacturers, including IBM, Unisys, and the 3M Company, will aid in the design or adaptation of systems to their equipment. Through contact with such firms, many office managers are able to adapt the systems used by other firms and thereby improve their own office productivity.

SUMMARY

1. Administrative office systems (AOS) are organized in business firms to meet the information needs of those organizations. Each system contains these common elements: people; physical resources, such as machines, space, and equipment; data; methods for completing the work; media, such as forms and records; and controls for ensuring that these elements are properly regulated to meet the system's goals. General models of systems have been created to describe the sequential phases of a system's operation: input, transformation process, output, feedback, and control.

2. Systems work is performed at all levels of an organization. Although most recognition is given to computer systems, two other levels of systems are found: manual and mechanical in which manual labor is combined with electrical machines, such as copiers, calculators, and typewriters, to perform the required work.

3. Systems studies begin when a department head requests that the operations be studied because of plaguing problems. Following the approval of such a request, a logical set of "study" steps is followed. The system is surveyed, the data from such a survey analyzed, and a new system designed. Upon approval of the design, the new system is installed and later evaluated for its effectiveness. In all systems studies, the human factor is considered the most important element.

4. Large firms maintain their own internal staff of systems personnel, while small firms typically assign systems work to the office manager. Frequently, companies of all sizes obtain the services of outside consultants whose objectivity and broad experience offer many advantages for improving the systems function.

GLOSSARY

Administrative office systems (AOS)—specialized systems responsible for managing all phases of the information cycle.

Closed system—a type of system that operates as a self-regulating unit and thus does not interact with its environment.

Computer system—a group of interconnected machines, including the computer, that process data at the speed of light and in which the data and the instructions for processing the data are stored within the computer.

Control—that phase of the system that dictates what can and cannot be performed in each of the other phases of the AOS.

Database—a central master file containing company-wide information about a firm or department-wide information within a department.

Feasibility study—a systems planning method that seeks to find out whether systems operations can be improved and if the addition of new resources is economically justified for making such improvements.

Feedback—a systems phase that compares the system's output with set standards of performance.

General systems model—a broad explanation of a system in which more concrete details may be added as needed.

Information system—the major system for collecting, processing, storing, retrieving, and distributing information within a firm.

Input—the first phase of any system in which data, energy, or information are received from another system.

Manual system—the earliest and most prevalent type of system in which the human being functions as the data processor.

Mechanical system—the system in which many of the data are processed by electromechanical machines.

Method—the manual, mechanical, or automated means by which each procedural step is performed.

Model—a simplified, general explanation of the complex interrelationships and activities of an organization or its parts.

Open system—a type of system that interacts with its environment in order to attain its goals.

Output—the ultimate objective of a system that results after the input has been transformed into the desired results.

Procedure—a planned sequence of operations for handling recurring transactions uniformly and consistently.

Program—a set of instructions for processing data in a computer system.

Subsystem—a subdivision of a system that is responsible for accomplishing specialized functions of the total system.

Synergism—the overall effect created in a system whereby interrelated parts produce a total effect greater than the sum of each of the parts working independently.

Systems approach—a method of problem solving used by the systems analyst in which interrelationships in the work system are emphasized.

Systems boundary—that element of a system which defines its scope or limits and which separates a system from its environment.

Systems study—the process of improving systems; also known as *systems analysis, systems and procedures analysis, methods analysis, systems engineering,* or *work simplification.*

Systems study cycle—a set of sequential, problem-solving steps required to improve the systems function.

Total system—a company-wide information network composed of a large number of major systems.

Transformation process—a phase of the administrative office system that changes inputs into outputs; also known as *process.*

FOR YOUR REVIEW

1. Explain the nature and purpose of an administrative office system.

2. Why is it necessary for administrative office managers to understand fully the function of administrative office systems in their organizations?

3. What are the main elements in an administrative office system? Cite several of the main administrative office systems in which these elements operate.

4. Explain the relationship that exists among a system, a procedure, and a method.

5. What are the principal objectives of administrative office systems?

6. Identify several of the most important problems found in administrative office systems.

7. Why are models used in the study of administrative office systems?

8. Describe the purpose of each of the following phases of an administrative office system: input, transformation process, output, feedback, and control.

9. Describe the advantages of a database. How practical is such a concept for present-day business firms?

10. Identify each of the systems levels (classified in terms of processing power) and show the interrelationships that exist among these levels.

11. What uses are made of manual systems in this age of automation?

12. Besides its great processing power and speed, how does a computer system differ from earlier machine systems?

13. What is the systems approach? How does it differ from the use of the scientific method in the solution of administrative problems?

14. List the principal steps in the systems study cycle, and indicate why the office manager should be familiar with these systems analysis responsibilities.

15. Identify the principal costs incurred in designing and operating an administrative office system. What benefits to the organization can be cited to compensate for these costs?

16. Why is the human factor considered the key to the effective operation of any system?

17. Compare the use of systems consultants with the development of an internal staff of systems analysts as a means of studying the administrative office systems of a firm.

18. What role can the office manager play in handling the systems responsibilities of the small office?

FOR YOUR DISCUSSION

1. Recently your class toured a large new office building occupied by the Ajax Corporation. In the systems department of the firm, the following two slogans were framed and hung on the wall of each workstation:
   a. There is nothing quite so useless as doing with great efficiency something that should not be done at all.
   b. Where am I going? How do I get there? How do I know when I've arrived?

   Explain why systems personnel would find these two slogans relevant to their work.

2. Explain in detail the nature and purpose of an administrative office system, using your office management class as an example. What limitations and strengths does your class system possess in helping you to arrive at a full understanding of a system?

3. Because the work of data-entry operators and file clerks is tangible, such work can be efficiently designed and measured in an administrative office system. On the other hand, the work of supervising and managing these employees is intangible and thus difficult to measure. Because of these differences in the type and level of work in an administrative office system, how can a systems analyst design an effective system which assures that both types of worker will make an equitable contribution?

4. The president of the Barry Appliances Corporation agreed to hire a systems analyst on a full-time basis as long as twice the analyst's annual salary of $40,000 could be saved for the firm each year as a result of systems analysis. During the first three years, the systems savings amounted to $80,000, $85,000, and $82,500, respectively; but during the fourth year, the savings fell to $37,500. The analyst was aware of the conditions under which the hiring took place; and since the annual savings for the fourth year did not exceed the salary provided, the analyst was dropped from the staff. Discuss the pros and cons of this hiring-firing policy from a managerial point of view.

5. Following is a list of common office machines:
   a. Typewriter.
   b. Hand-held electronic calculator.
   c. Copier.
   d. Postal scale.
   e. Telephone voice-recording device.

   What information-cycle functions does each of these machines provide in the administrative office system?

6. The *total* administrative office system of the Kerry Manufacturing Company includes these main systems for accomplishing the goals of the firm:
   a. Purchasing of raw materials and semifinished goods.
   b. Receiving purchased items.
   c. Sales.
   d. Production (manufacturing of the firm's products for sale).
   e. Collection (receipt) of sales revenues.
   f. Billing (invoicing) customers.
   g. Delivery of products sold.

   Using the systems approach, define the purpose of each main system and identify the principal subsystems likely to be found in each main system. Then arrange each system and its subsystems in a logical sequence that reflects the order of each in the total system's operations. The use of a modified organization chart would help to show the interrelationships that exist among the main systems in the firm.

7. You have been asked to help an office manager, Richard Ames, decide on the better method of handling systems-improvement projects in his office—using outside consultants or assigning this responsibility to an assistant office manager on a continuing basis. What approach would you recommend be taken to resolve this problem? What aspects of the problem are mainly objective in nature, and what aspects seem mainly subjective? How should Ames proceed?

8. Your office management class is planning to take an "observation tour"—visiting legal, medical, and city government offices in your community. Since the main intent of these

visits is to *observe* common systems in action, what type of guidelines should be given the students before undertaking this visit?

9. Figure 4-4, page 96, outlines four types of systems problems and provides examples of each. What differences in *method* of problem solving would you recommend if you were responsible for solving both the personnel and information systems problems shown in this figure? (Note: You are not asked to solve the problems.)

SOLVING CASE PROBLEMS

Case 4-1 Identifying Systems Concepts in a College Registration System

After a class discussion of the main concepts found in administrative office systems, your instructor asks you to observe the operating procedures of a "real-world" organization in order to understand better the functions of office systems. As a practical and timely way of completing this assignment, you have selected the registration system of your college as you are about to complete your registration for five three-hour courses for your next and last semester in college.

After obtaining the *apparent* approval of your adviser, you take the required registration form to the registrar's office to complete your computerized registration. The terminal operator (T/O) takes your form, keyboards the information into the terminal, and obtains feedback information on the terminal screen. Shortly thereafter, this conversation takes place:

T/O:　I'm sorry, but Tax Accounting 425 and Computer Analysis 402 are both closed.

You:　But these are required courses for my major; and if I don't complete these courses by the end of next semester, I'll have to stay in school an additional semester. Isn't there anything I can do—maybe put my name on a waiting list?

T/O:　I'm sorry. All I do here is operate the terminal and tell you whether you are registered or not. The registrar has told me to tell students with this problem to contact their department advisers or check with the heads of the departments concerned. Of course, if you want to go higher, you can always appeal your case to the dean of the college. Maybe the department heads will waive the course requirements for you. By the way, I just noticed that your adviser failed to initial the five courses listed on your schedule, so they aren't officially approved. You'll have to get these initialed before I can complete your registration on the computer.

Feeling frustrated and angry, you leave the registrar's office.

Based upon this conversation, answer the following questions:

1. What is the systems structure (from total system to subsystems) involved in this administrative office system?

2. What specific controls are built into such a system? Using as a guide the general systems model shown on page 97, construct a registration systems model that includes all the phases of this open system.

3. How are human beings and human relationships an integral part of the system(s) issues raised here?

Case 4–2 Organizing the Systems Function in a Small Firm

During the past ten years, the office staff of the Palmer Company, a small service business with one central office location, has increased from 15 to 50. With this rapid growth in the office staff, however, there has been no corresponding increase in the number of office supervisors; and the administrative office systems have become unworkable. The president has announced plans to decentralize the company operations by opening three branches in nearby suburbs and transferring some of the home-office staff to these new offices.

As office manager in charge of all 50 office workers, you have repeatedly complained to the president about the need for a small internal systems unit to study the overall efficiency of the firm's systems on a continuing basis. The president has tentatively agreed to set up a small systems department to coordinate the work of the home office and branch office operations under the new decentralized plan, pending a report from you on how to handle the organization of the systems unit.

On the basis of this information, prepare a report to the president in which you suggest answers to these questions:

1. Who should be in charge of the systems department?

2. Who and how many should staff the department?

3. How should the costs of operating the systems be justified?

4. How should the functions of the home-office and the branch-office systems be coordinated?

5. How should a priority list of systems studies be developed?

6. What steps should be taken in order to obtain acceptance of the new systems program?

5

Communication in the Office

GOALS FOR THIS CHAPTER

After completing this chapter, you should be able to:

1. Describe the communication process and the purposes for which communication is transmitted.
2. Explain how formal and informal communication networks are used in the organization.
3. Describe each of the flows of communication and the channels that are used to transmit messages in these flows.
4. Identify the major barriers to communication that the administrative office manager may encounter.
5. Explain the importance of the different kinds of nonverbal communication in the messages transmitted and received by office managers and supervisors.
6. Summarize the several principles to be followed in effective report writing.

The word **communication** is derived from the Latin word *communis*, which means "common." In an organization, communication describes the process by which managers establish a degree of "commonness" (that is, common understanding) with employees and the public. As such, communication is the process by which information and human attitudes are exchanged with others. Simply stated, communication is the "glue" that holds business together. When communication breaks down, an organization invariably goes into decline; for without communication, the managerial functions of planning, organizing, leading, and controlling cannot be performed.

This chapter begins with a discussion of the communication process upon which all effective office administration depends. Next, communication networks, which represent the flow of communication as it ties together all persons in the firm, are described. Later, we shall point out the barriers to effective communication and make suggestions for their elimination. Finally, principles of effective report writing are identified to assist AOMs in coordinating their overall communication responsibilities in the firm.

THE COMMUNICATION PROCESS

In this section, we shall use a communication model to explain the manner in which communication occurs in the office. Understanding this concept of communication (often referred to as "communication theory") will assist you in designing and operating effective office communication systems.

The Communication Process Model

The **communication process** is the transmission of a message from one person (the *sender*) to another person (the *receiver*). (In automated systems, the sender may be

Dialog on the Firing Line

THOMAS M. HESTWOOD
Senior Manager, Corporate Compensation
MCI Communications Corporation
Washington, DC

BA in Business Administration, Geneva College
MA in Industrial Relations, University of Minnesota

Prior to joining MCI, Thomas Hestwood held management positions in compensation and employee relations with Mellon Bank Corporation in Pittsburgh and before that with Norwest and Control Data Corporations in Minneapolis. Mr. Hestwood has made numerous presentations to professional groups and is the author of articles in *Compensation Review, Personnel Journal*, and *Human Resources Planning*.

QUESTION: Let's say you are meeting with an office manager who has been assigned responsibility for creating a new policy on drug and alcohol abuse for the company policy manual. What recommendations have you for the office manager who is commencing to undertake the task?

RESPONSE: Policy development can be particularly difficult when the policy involves a legally and employee-sensitive area such as alcohol and drug abuse. Nevertheless, these difficulties can be managed if the appropriate process is followed. The following steps are suggested:

1. Policy development
2. Policy communication
3. Policy evaluation

To develop the policy, the office manager must research the issue and determine its scope and content. For example, will the policy be a mere statement of conduct or will it include drug testing? If drug testing is included, will testing be preemployment, during employment, or both? The office manager will want to discuss these issues with top management to see how they fit with management's employee relations philosophy. If there is a union, some of these issues may have to be negotiated. The office manager will not want to venture very far in this area without the advice of a knowledgeable attorney.

Policy communication requires an analysis of the best ways to inform and educate policy recipients. Training is essential for communicating any complex policy and should cover the following points:

- The purpose of the policy.
- Responsibilities of managers, employees, and human resources staff.
- Circumstances in which the policy applies.
- Consequences of not adhering to the policy.
- Possible deviations.
- Related policies for reference.
- Availability of ongoing help.

The price of ignoring training is poorly educated managers and the misapplication or the nonapplication of the policy.

Evaluation ensures that the policy appropriately meets the needs of the organization. The policy can be assessed by monitoring the number and type of people seeking assistance (maintaining confidentiality of the identities of those involved) and by conducting a special survey of a sample of managers in various parts of the organization regarding issues that arise in application. An employee attitude survey can also be useful.

Ultimately, there is no "right way" to implement policies. Sensitivity to the culture and climate of the organization and close coordination of all parties affected by the policy are the key requirements.

a terminal operator and the receiver, a computer. Other aspects of technical communication systems are found in Chapters 16 and 21.) As you see in Figure 5-1, the process begins when the sender's senses (sight, hearing, touch), experiences, skills, attitudes, and emotional needs are combined with information to form an idea. The idea (or ideas) generated will become the content of the *message*. The idea is encoded, or organized, into a series of symbols (words, numbers, etc.) that are used for transmitting the message to the receiver through a selected *channel*. At the receiving end, the receiver decodes, or interprets, the message and takes action (or nonaction) as revealed by the feedback. *Feedback mechanisms* are used to send another message from the receiver to the sender saying that the original message has been received and understood. Below, we shall take a look at a very common feedback mechanism—the question-and-answer session at the end of a meeting.

To see how the communication process operates in a typical office situation, let's sit in on a monthly department meeting. Christie Blake, supervisor of accounts receivable (the *sender*), has talked (the *channel*) about the new procedure (the *message*) to her workers (the *receivers*) for processing customers' accounts. Following her presentation, Blake answers several of the workers' questions (the *feedback*) and discusses with them how their present billing methods will be affected by the change. With accurate feedback, Blake is able to make an objective and realistic evaluation of her presentation and to detect any potential problems that may affect the implementation of the new procedure.

Verbal Communication

In the communication process, the most basic form of communication is verbal. **Verbal communication** consists of words—spoken

Figure 5-1
A Model of the Communication Process

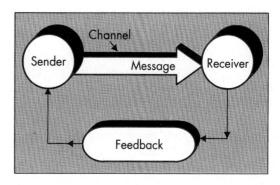

or written. This form of communication is discussed in this section.

In spoken communication, usually called **oral communication**, your tone of voice or emotional state influences the message as significantly as the words you use. In the office, oral communication consists of one-to-one conversations, conferences and meetings of all kinds, telephone conversations, and messages transmitted through public address systems, television, radio, and film. Equally important in oral communication is the emotional state of the listeners, because their reception and understanding of the message are greatly influenced by their preconceived opinions, personal relationship with the speaker, and general outlook toward the organization.

When very important messages are involved, the sender often avoids oral communication and, instead, relies upon **written communication**. Examples of written communication transmitted in the office are the letters, reports, memos, invoices, and paychecks that may be handwritten or printed out on a typewriter, word processor, or computer. When using written communication to transmit messages, the AOM has tangible evidence of what the employees have been asked to do. Also, since the messages can be stored permanently, the AOM is able to refer to them as needed in order to evaluate the actions taken by workers.

Purposes of Communication

The purposes for which oral and written communication are transmitted in the office and some of the media commonly used for their transmission are presented in Figure 5-2. Messages such as those listed in this figure may be transmitted through formal or informal communication networks, which are described in the following section.

COMMUNICATION NETWORKS

A **communication network** is the pattern of channels used to communicate messages to and from, or among, a group of people. These networks may be classified as formal or informal.

Formal Communication Network

The formal communication network is based on the chain of command and its lines of authority from the top of the organization down. The formal communication network

Figure 5-2
Purposes of
Communica-
tion and
Commonly
Used Media

Purpose of Communication	Communication Media
1. To inform	1-1 Interoffice memo announcing a meeting 1-2 Telephone call in which a customer is quoted a price and shipping date for goods ordered 1-3 Insert for employee handbook explaining a new benefit
2. To persuade	2-1 Personal conversation in which a co-worker is requested to serve as a volunteer in a fund-raising drive 2-2 Sales letter announcing a fall clearance of merchandise 2-3 Report to management on the need to purchase new word processors
3. To evaluate	3-1 Performance appraisal records 3-2 Quality control report summarizing the output of word processing center 3-3 Budget performance report that compares amounts budgeted with expenses incurred
4. To instruct	4-1 Instruction manual for operating a personal computer 4-2 Directions given orally to co-workers for reconciling a bank statement 4-3 Instructions given by vendor to mail room personnel on proper use of postage meter machine
5. To meet human and cultural needs	5-1 "Small talk" ("Hello, how are you today?" "Have a good weekend?" "Are you free to bowl tonight?") before, during, and after business hours 5-2 Informal note inviting workers to participate in the annual Christmas caroling 5-3 Announcement of free World Series tickets to be given as incentive to improve attendance record

is shown on the organization chart in Figure 5-3. In this formal network, messages are transmitted up and down the structure through the channels identified with heavy lines.

The formal communication network is used to transmit official messages, policies, procedures, directives, and job instructions. For example, in Figure 5-3, a new directive pertaining to hours of work would flow from the vice-president, administrative services, to each manager and then to each supervisor, who might hold small group meetings to present the changes to the office workers. Although the formal network is used mainly for communicating downward in the organization, provision is usually made for

formal upward communication such as attitude surveys, grievances, suggestions, and performance appraisals.

As any office manager knows, office workers transmit many messages every day that do not flow through a formal network. Instead, the workers use an informal communication network that is mainly oral. Many of the messages transmitted informally are not vital to office operations since they do not affect the completion of work assignments. Often this information is referred to as "scuttlebutt" (so named after a drinking fountain aboard ship or at a naval

Figure 5-3
A Formal
Communica-
tion Network

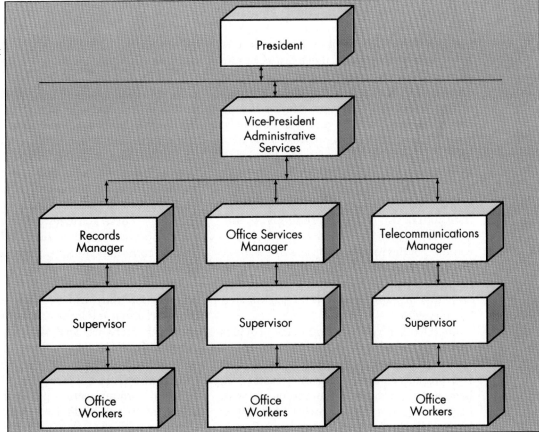

installation where the crew congregates to pass along rumors or gossip).

Much informal communication occurs when office employees socialize and pass along information that they believe their co-workers may not have. For example, consider the opportunities that workers have for informally communicating when they commute in carpools, work out together at a health center, or spend work breaks together. On occasions such as these, information is freely transmitted among workers at various levels in the organization. Those receiving the messages are in a position to transmit the information to others directly above or below them in the formal communication network. Thus, the effect of the informal communication network becomes very extensive, as evidenced by the operation of the grapevine.

The **grapevine** is an informal communication network in which messages are rapidly transmitted, usually orally on a one-to-one basis. Like a grapevine, the tendrils of the informal network wander in and out of the organization and attach themselves to any willing listener without regard to the formal organization structure and its channels. Rumors about company matters such as a proposed merger, relocation of the headquarters office, or a cutback in the work force are often spread by means of the grapevine. The effects of the messages transmitted can cripple productivity and seriously disturb the climate of the organization. For this reason, the grapevine is often viewed negatively by managers and employees since the messages transmitted are either groundless or have been distorted in some way.

On the other hand, the grapevine provides office managers with an excellent means of finding out what their subordinates think and feel. Workers associate informally on the job, have a natural desire to communicate with each other, and wish to be aware of the latest happenings in the firm. As a very informal means of quickly spreading information, the grapevine provides workers with a means of finding answers to their questions and aids in filling a communication void.

Office managers should accept the fact that the grapevine cannot be eliminated, even if it were desirable to do so. Instead, an attempt should be made to analyze and understand any rumors being circulated and then take positive steps to prevent their recurrence. OMs should be aware of the grapevine and "feed" accurate information only to those "leading grapes" or key employees who can be relied upon to transmit information without embellishment or distortion. As a result, OMs may find the grapevine working favorably for the firm. For example, the grapevine can clarify and publicize a company directive often in more understandable language and far more rapidly than the formal communication network.

The Communication Audit

An organization conducts a **communication audit** to evaluate how effectively and efficiently its communication system is working. In the audit, an inventory is taken of all the firm's communication activities, such as group meetings, hiring and exit interviews, company publications, bulletin boards, and supervisor-subordinate scheduled meetings. These activities are then analyzed and appraised to determine whether the firm's communication policies are being followed.

As part of its communication audit, the organization may use network analysis to study its formal and informal communication networks. **Network analysis** is a communication research technique that is used to find out where workers go to get their needed information. In network analysis, the informal communication patterns within an organization are studied to learn how they compare with the relationships expected if the formal communication network were used. Such studies aid OMs in evaluating the present formal network and adopting new policies and procedures that will better satisfy the needs of all workers.

THE FLOW OF COMMUNICATION

In the flow of communication, the office supervisor serves as a "linking pin," since he or she is the main person in the formal channel that links together the downward and upward communication. As shown in Figure 5–4, the office supervisor is a member of two groups in an organization. As a linking pin, the supervisor is the leader in his or her group of workers and a subordinate in the other group of middle managers to whom the supervisor is held accountable. As a person "caught up in the middle," the office supervisor must carefully select communication channels that will clearly transmit the messages to receivers whose feedback shows their clear understanding of the contents of the messages.

To be successful, communication must be two-way—*up* and *down* between supervisors and employees. The supervisor must take into account not only the upward and downward flows of communication in an organization but also the lateral and diagonal flows. Each of these four communication flows is discussed in this section.

Downward Communication

Downward communication flows vertically from the top of the organization to one or more levels below and carries the messages that translate top-management planning and decision making into orders that direct office employees. Much of the downward communication transmitted by OMs and their supervisors involves:

1. Informing employees of their job responsibilities.

Figure 5–4

The Office Supervisor As a Linking Pin in Downward and Upward Communication

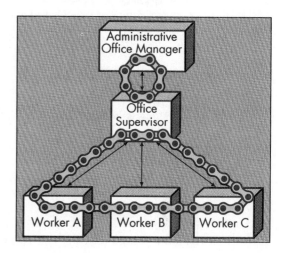

2. Enlisting the understanding and support of employees about management objectives and company goals.
3. Instructing employees on how to improve their productivity.
4. Relaying to employees the results of their job performance.

When communicating downward with employees, the key is *openness*. OMs should not be so formal that employees are afraid to approach them. To see if you, as an office manager or supervisor, are effectively communicating downward, answer each of the questions in Figure 5–5. If you can *honestly* check seven or eight Yeses, you are an exceptionally effective communicator!

Most messages are transmitted downward through several formal channels such as face-to-face meetings, conferences, and committees and in written materials. Although the use of more than one channel brings about a certain amount of repetition, a combination of oral and written communication channels ensures that information will be received and understood.

Figure 5-5
A Checklist
for Effective
Downward
Communi-
cation

	Yes	No
Study each question carefully, answer it honestly, and see how many "Yes" check marks you have. If you have fewer than 7 "Yes" check marks, you need to improve your downward communication skills.		
● Do I keep my subordinates informed about planned changes in company policies and procedures?	____	____
● When I am faced with problems that affect my workers and their productivity, do I freely consult with them?	____	____
● Are my workers aware of how I feel about their on-the-job problems?	____	____
● Do I initiate steps to become informed of my workers' personal interests?	____	____
● Am I familiar with and try to advance the career goals of my employees?	____	____
● Do I often have private talks with my subordinates?	____	____
● Do I try to squelch any unfounded rumors about company policies and practices?	____	____
● Do I hold meetings during which employees may freely raise questions?	____	____
● When I give an employee a directive, do I explain it and offer reasons for my decision?	____	____
● Do I plan and schedule performance appraisals so that my subordinates are not taken by surprise?	____	____

When deciding which channels of downward communication to use, the OM should consider the following factors:

1. *Speed of transmission.* Some channels provide faster transmission than others. For example, the OM can explain changes in company practice such as new work schedules more quickly at a group meeting than by announcing the new schedules in the company newspaper.

2. *Appropriateness to employee level.* The complex features of a firm's retirement plan may be adequately explained by means of a memo to all supervisors. However, to ensure that all workers understand how the retirement plan affects them individually, each supervisor may plan to hold question-and-answer sessions at small group meetings. The supervisors may decide to reinforce the discussion at the group meetings by inserting a question-and-answer column in each issue of the company newspaper.

3. *Perception of authority.* Office workers view some channels of downward communication as more authoritative than others. The president of the organization exercises more authority and has more power than the AOM. However, office workers may attach more importance and trust to the AOM's oral explanation of

changes in the salary compensation program than the president's announcement of the changes in a formal letter received at their homes.

4. *Nature of information to be transmitted—good news or bad news.* Most messages transmitted to office workers are likely to be viewed either positively or negatively. The favorable results of an employee appraisal and an accompanying salary increase are usually positively received by an office worker. Such good news is often transmitted by informal oral communication—a personal chat—between the employee and the immediate supervisor. On the other hand, bad news, such as a reduction in working hours because of a decline in sales, is often communicated in a group meeting. At the meeting, all employees' questions can be answered and future prospects for returning to a normal workweek schedule can be explored.

5. *Need for feedback.* When transmitting many kinds of messages, the AOM needs to find out to what extent the employees have understood and accepted the communication. For example, consider an AOM who is explaining to the supervisors the company's change in its year of operations for accounting purposes. The AOM must make sure by means of question-and-answer sessions that all supervisors clearly understand how their departmental operations will be affected and what steps must be taken to implement the changes. If, on the other hand, the office is shutting down at noon today because of inclement weather, the AOM's announcement over the public address system requires no feedback!

The factors above, which are considered when selecting channels for transmitting messages, are further described in the following examination of several channels of downward communication.

Meetings

Formal meetings with middle managers, supervisors, and workers should be regularly scheduled to convey the importance of keeping the lines of communication open. In small group meetings, two-way communication is facilitated; employees can ask questions, freely discuss information, and receive answers. Thus, feedback is immediately obtained. Office supervisors should also be urged to hold *informal* discussions with their employees. In such settings of mutual trust and respect, employees are more at ease and seem to relate their true feelings more freely. This approach has a very positive effect on the morale of employees; and at the same time, supervisors learn what the workers think and how they feel.

Company Publications

Company publications, such as newsletters and newspapers, are used to keep workers informed of the operations, plans, and changes in the firm. Also commonly found in company publications are good-news

Small group meetings allow open discussion and immediate feedback.

items such as promotions, retirements, hiring of new employees, births, weddings, and anniversaries. In addition, the publications describe off-work experiences of employees, announce cultural and recreational activities, and explain various safety and health practices.

Pamphlets, booklets, manuals, and posters are used to inform workers of changes in company policies and methods, new products or services, and future plans. Letters from the president or other officers of the company to the employee's home are especially effective when a new policy or procedure is to be installed or when a new product or service is being offered.

Bulletin Boards

Bulletin boards are used by nearly all organizations as a means of keeping employees informed. Bulletin boards may be used for posting rules and regulations; announcements of recreation and social events; safety records; job openings; attendance records; suggestion system awards; new product announcements; vacation schedules; lost and found notices; personal announcements of illness, births, weddings, and deaths; educational opportunities; and press releases. To be an effective communication channel, bulletin boards should be sufficient in number and properly located to attract the attention of all workers. The communications posted on the boards should be kept current, and both managers and workers should be encouraged to use the boards.

Upward Communication

Upward communication flows vertically from one level in the organization to one or more levels above. An effective flow of upward communication aids in motivating office workers to perform their jobs in the most efficient manner possible. The establishment of effective upward communication channels between the office supervisor and the employees is one of the most important and demanding problems of human relations affecting business offices. As offices become larger, the problem of maintaining adequate communication becomes more difficult. In many organizations, the problem of keeping the upward communication lines open and providing feedback is so important that attitude surveys (discussed in Chapter 7) are conducted periodically to find out how workers feel about their firm, its products or services, and its supervisors and managers.

Upward communication channels are used in the office mainly:

1. To provide the OM and supervisors with feedback indicating whether the messages transmitted downward have been received and understood.
2. To transmit information needed for higher-level decision making.
3. To pass along suggestions for systems improvements and changes in policies.
4. To give office employees an opportunity to ask questions, to make complaints, and to express satisfaction or dissatisfaction with the way office activities are being managed.

Generally you will find that the most effective channels for upward communication are the informal discussions that occur between you and your supervisor or manager. In these discussions, a major problem in communication is the unwillingness or inability of your supervisor to encourage feedback of your viewpoints and reactions. If supervisors or managers lack empathy, they are unable to put themselves in your position and see things through your eyes and mind. Or, the organization may have failed to provide managers and supervisors with an adequate understanding of the importance of communication and sufficient training in developing a high level of communication skill. Thus, upward communication is often haphazard and unreliable.

Another problem in upward communication is associated with the hierarchy found in most business organizations. For example, your supervisor or department head may stifle your complaints or block your reports of dissatisfaction. Some of the fault may be yours, especially when you tend to tell your superiors only what they want to hear. Or, your supervisor may be a poor listener and hear only what he or she wants to hear. As a result, the organization may attempt to minimize these problems by creating formal upward communication channels that flow around the immediate superior. This is true, for example, of employee suggestion systems and grievance-handling procedures, which are briefly described below.

Employee Suggestion Systems

An **employee suggestion system** is a channel of upward communication in which employees offer ideas that result in cost reduction and the elimination of inefficiency and waste. Suggestion systems are used as a means of building morale among office workers and of getting workers to think more seriously about their jobs.

Most employees are eligible to participate in the suggestion system. However, the officers of the company are usually excluded from participation. Supervisors ordinarily receive awards only for ideas not connected directly with their own departments or fields of activity. The disadvantage of having both workers and supervisors submit suggestions is that the workers and supervisors come into competition with one another. As a result, conflicts may arise. Also, the workers may think their ideas are being "stolen" by the supervisors.

Some companies pay a flat amount for each suggestion accepted. Other firms pay a percentage of the savings that result from implementing the suggestion. When determining the amount of the award, AOMs should consider whether the idea involves recurring or nonrecurring savings and the possibility that the idea may be later supplanted by another suggestion that would bring forth still greater savings.

Grievance-Handling Procedure

In unionized offices, we find that specific rules for handling grievances are provided within the union contract. In nonunion offices that do not have a formal arrangement for handling employee grievances, a definite procedure should be provided for their settlement. Having an established procedure for handling grievances facilitates the office workers' upward communication and improves their morale. Also, by having a grievance-handling procedure, the organization recognizes that complaints do exist in the office and that they should be considered a normal part of supervising office work.

Lateral Communication

Organizations often see the need for lateral (horizontal) communication as well as downward and upward communication. **Lateral communication** occurs among personnel at the same level. Provision for lateral communication is essential in order to coordinate the activities of co-workers and to facilitate their interactions as they perform their jobs.

For example, the job assignment of a worker in the records management department may require periodic consultation with a worker in office services. As shown by the heavy lines in Figure 5–6, the formal network requires that the records management employee communicate through the immediate supervisor to the records manager to the vice-president, administrative services, and then to the office services manager to the supervisor and finally to the co-worker in office services. For purposes of efficiency in practice, however, lateral communication, shown by the broken line in Figure 5–6, is

Figure 5-6
Lateral Communication
Between
Office
Workers in
Two
Departments

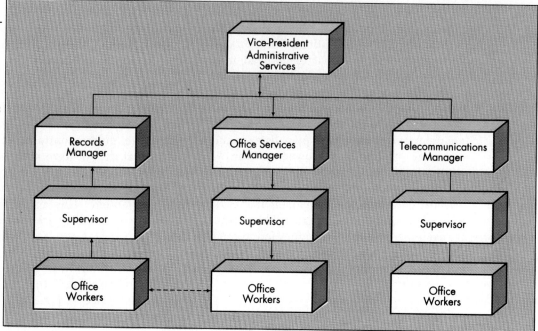

encouraged so long as it has been authorized by both supervisors.

Diagonal Communication

Diagonal communication occurs when employees communicate with other workers at higher or lower levels in the organization using communication networks other than those formally shown on the organization chart. For example, the broken lines in Figure 5-7 show a records manager who communicates diagonally with the vice-presidents of sales and human resources in addition to communicating upward with the vice-president of administrative services. Such diagonal communication regarding routine office operations is encouraged by most organizations to aid in efficiently solving problems involving two or more segments of the organization.

Both diagonal and lateral communication enables employees to plan jointly when establishing policies and procedures that affect several departments, to share information, and to resolve conflicts. Diagonal and lateral communication provides for the direct exchange of messages more quickly and with less distortion than when the senders and receivers are required to use formal upward and downward communication. Thus, the communication barriers described in the following section may be avoided.

BARRIERS TO EFFECTIVE COMMUNICATION

In any type of communication—downward, upward, lateral, or diagonal—there are inherent difficulties or barriers that we should recognize and overcome. A common breakdown in communication occurs when we, as senders, fail to transmit the message intended for those who should receive it. In

Figure 5-7
Diagonal
Communica-
tion Between
the Records
Manager and
Two Vice-
Presidents

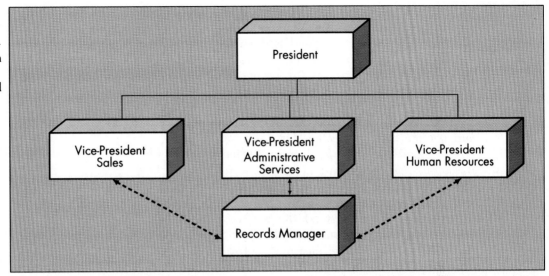

turn, many people for whom a message is intended either do not receive it or receive a distorted version. As a result, the effective operation of the communication system is hampered or blocked. This section examines several barriers to effective communication and points out ways to reduce communication breakdown.

BARRIER 1

Differences in Perception

Each office worker is unique and brings to the job a unique **perception**—a way of interpreting situations based on the individual's personal experiences. Thus, the employees' perceptions determine the manner in which they interpret whatever they see or hear. For example, Bob Cruz, a mail clerk, perceives his supervisor, Lauren Ford, as a "parent figure." Cruz may accept or reject most of what Ford says, depending upon Cruz's personal experiences at home. In Ford, Cruz may see his quiet, submissive mother and thus react with eagerness to please. On the other hand, Cruz may see in Ford's actions and words those of his loud, abusive father; as a result, Cruz may rebel against Ford's authority.

When office employees sense they have been "let down" by a former supervisor, they are likely to view the replacement with distrust. Often, because of their differing value systems, older office workers are unable to "tune in" on the younger workers' "wave length" and thus experience difficulty in communicating.

As an office manager, you must learn enough about each employee to know what meaning will be attached to your messages and what emotional overtones may be expected. Here, the key to effective, open communication is feedback. Means should be provided for the sender of the message to verify its receipt and understanding

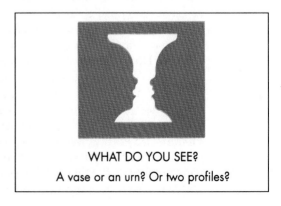

WHAT DO YOU SEE?
A vase or an urn? Or two profiles?

through some feedback process or two-way interaction. Although two-way communication is more time-consuming and not feasible for all kinds of messages, it is viewed as more accurate and more satisfying to the parties involved than one-way written communication.

Listening is probably the most important and yet the most neglected dimension of communication. By *listening*, office managers can learn much about how employees perceive the office environment and the emotional states they may be experiencing. To understand the worker's perceptions, the office manager should try to listen to the entire message before evaluating its contents. For example, Phil Minot, head of the computer center, informs his boss, Tom Garcia, that there is no way to meet the deadline for producing the year-end reports unless more help is made available. Garcia hears only the first part of the message—no way to meet the deadline—and quickly perceives how top management will react to the delay and its effect upon his performance. Here, Garcia seems more interested in immediately evaluating a part of the message than listening to the entire communication. Had Garcia listened to the whole story, without evaluation, he might have understood Minot's frame of reference and effectively worked with him in mutually solving the problem.

You know that there is a great difference between "hearing" and "listening." Most of us have the capacity to receive sounds—to *hear*—but how many of us really *listen* by "tuning in" and paying attention to those sounds? Do we listen intensely and absorb into our consciousness what the other person is saying? How many times in class or on the job have you "come to" with a start and asked yourself what the speaker said during the last several minutes? Have you experienced any major setbacks because you were not listening? Did the other person with whom you were conversing perceive that you

were hearing only the words? Have you recently taken inventory of your skill (or bad habits) regarding listening? Here are some guidelines for you to consider as you evaluate and sharpen your listening skill:

While I am listening:

1. I pay close attention by looking at the speaker. I do not daydream, doodle on my notepad, or shuffle papers.
2. I suspend judgment of the speaker and the message by being open-minded to differences of opinion.
3. I try to understand the speaker's purpose.
4. I separate facts from opinions.
5. I focus on the main points, evaluate carefully, and avoid jumping to conclusions.
6. I listen carefully before asking questions or offering comments.
7. I take notes at meetings and during my instructor's lectures, but I don't let note taking become a substitute for listening.

BARRIER 2

Differences in Semantics

Semantics is the study of word meanings and their effect upon human behavior. How often have you heard statements such as, "Don't worry about it; it's just a matter of semantics" or "The difficulty is that we have a problem in semantics"?

Since the meaning of words may be interpreted differently by the sender and the receiver, a barrier to communication may be created. Often there is no connection between the *symbol* (the word) and *what is being symbolized* (the meaning). Thus, a message may be received very differently

Bob is NOT WEALTHY, but he does earn a COMFORTABLE LIVING. What is his annual income? $25,000? $40,000? $50,000?

than was intended. For example, let's say you tell a worker, "Please *duplicate* this two-page report." Is the worker to *retype* the two pages? *reproduce* the report on an office copier? or prepare offset masters and *run copies* on the office duplicator? In selecting words, you must carefully consider the receiver of the message and the likely interpretation of the words being used.

BARRIER 3

Differences in Status

Status, or the level of individuals in the organization structure, influences the quality of communication. Differences in status create communication barriers since generally it is easier for persons of equal rank than for a superior and a subordinate to share information and their feelings.

When communicating downward, some managers believe that subordinates should not receive all information. Therefore, the managers "dilute" or "water down" the messages. In other cases, subordinates may be given information that is not relevant to their needs or is not received in time to be useful. The OM should make every effort to reduce any unnecessary dilution of

TOP MANAGEMENT
Next year we've got to downsize all operations by at least 15%.

MIDDLE MANAGEMENT
Next year we've got to reduce the number of office services personnel by about 1/6.

SUPERVISOR
Next year we've got to cut back a little.

WORKERS
What do I tell my mate?

downward communication so that subordinates receive as much timely information as possible.

In upward communication, subordinates often dilute messages by giving their superiors only partial information. Subordinates may also "color" or distort events in order to conceal news that may be unpleasant. The conscious manipulation of facts in order to distort events is called **slanting**. A subordinate often slants communication in order to appear competent in the eyes of the superior. For example, Charles Firth, an office supervisor, "toned down" one of his worker's cost-reduction suggestions in the publicity release for the company's newspaper. The newspaper article was slanted so that most credit for the savings would be attributed to Firth rather than to his subordinate. Firth felt that the cost-savings ideas should have originated with him because of his supervisory position. Thus, he did not want any communication "leaks" to reflect negatively upon his own performance.

At the highest status level in the organization, managers are often faced with information overload. **Information overload** is the communication of an excessive number of details about company operations and personnel activities. The computer, with its tremendous information-producing capability, adds greatly to the problem of information overload in many organizations. However, this same computer can be used in information-distribution systems that are designed to channel information only to those persons who need it. Thus, it is possible to provide information "on call" by means of terminals that are linked with computerized libraries to supply information on various subjects. Top-level managers must decide what information is really needed for decision making and how often that information must be updated. However, in their programs of reducing information overload, managers must make certain that all crucial messages get through.

BARRIER 4

Differences in Preconceived Judgment or Opinion (Bias)

Bias, or prejudice, is the highly personal judgment or opinion formed by an individual before the facts are known. Bias, like prejudice, is both a positive and a negative word. For example, as employees we may be biased *against* or biased *in favor of* a particular company executive, the color selected for the general offices, the dress code adopted by the company, etc. As we shall see, bias is a barrier in face-to-face communication as well as in written communication.

Bias may be found when an interviewer is obtaining background information from a job applicant. Often the interviewer, possibly subconsciously but because of bias, selects a person who has similar interests, hobbies, and personal experiences. **Stereotyping**, which is closely related to bias, is the formation of a commonly held mental picture of how people of a particular sex, religion, or race appear, think, feel, and act. Like bias, stereotyping is a barrier in face-to-face communication. For example, the sales manager loses the attention of some of

I know she'll make a good worker – she looks and acts just like my mother!

EMPLOYMENT MANAGER

the male and female sales force when at the monthly meeting reference is constantly being made to "My sales*men*." Or, consider the interviewer who is searching for a male to fill a middle management position with a starting salary of $50,000 and a female to fill the job of secretary at a salary of $16,000!

Bias is often created in written communication when the reader's perception of the message is tilted in one direction or another. Studies have been made that relate the appearance of the sender to the receiver's interpretation of oral and written communication. It has been found that the sender's picture greatly influences how the receiver evaluates the quality of the communication.

For example, with the insertion of the author's picture alongside this paragraph, he can expect the message to be interpreted differently by you, the reader, depending on how you are influenced by the picture. Some readers will be biased by the strength of character appearing in the lines of the face and attach much importance to the words; others may see in the picture a lack of sincerity and therefore attach little significance to the content of the message.

In written communication, readers are also greatly influenced by the different faces and styles of type that are used. For example, how did you react to the content of the preceding paragraphs, which are printed in a color other than black and which have been set in a typeface and type size that differ from those used in other parts of the book?

BARRIER 5

Differences in Organization Climate

Some organizations encourage workers to express their opinions openly and to participate in important decision-making activities. In these firms, the climate is one of mutual trust and respect between management and employees. As a result, even very controversial messages can be easily transmitted. On the other hand, some managers are authoritarian and discourage the participation of employees and their freedom of expression. As might be expected, the messages transmitted in these organizations are highly diluted and slanted. In both types of organizations, managers at all levels exert considerable influence on communication by the kind of climate they create.

BARRIER 6

Business Jargon

Oral and written communication often become ineffective because of the use of jargon. **Jargon** consists of technical terms and idioms that are peculiar to a special group or activity such as business. When the receivers of messages containing business jargon do not recognize and understand the terms, the messages become merely a collection of words that are confusing and unintelligible.

Here is a memo sent by a manager to the employees: *"It is anticipated that our forthcoming meeting will provide considerable opportunities to generate viable alternatives and sufficient interface for resolving the continuing conflict existent in our department. Group interaction should facilitate and expedite problem solutions."* By eliminating the jargon and words of many syllables, the manager could have sent the following memo, which would have been clearly understood by all workers: *"At our meeting we will discuss different ways for quickly solving the problems in our department."*

Spoken and written messages are also misunderstood if they contain words of many syllables or use long, complex sentences. *A loss in mental perception and acuity is less likely to transpire if the materials presented have no deficiencies in grammatical expression and structural cohesiveness that might contribute to a diminution of clarity.* See what we mean? This type of writing (or speaking) has been labeled "gobbledygook" and should be eliminated in all written and oral com-

munication. Through training and experience in plain talking and writing, you can convert the previous italicized sentence into something like this: *"Misunderstanding is less likely to occur when the materials presented are clear."*

Many organizations hire consultants to teach employees how to write and speak clearly. Some companies send their managers to one-day communication-improvement classes, while other firms bring in coaches for seminars that may last several days. These companies realize that messages loaded with jargon, somewhat like static in a radio broadcast, waste time and money and cause much vital information to wind up in the waste basket.

BARRIER 7

Poor Reading Skills

Some office workers have deficiencies in their reading skills and thus are unable to understand and take action on the messages received. Such deficiencies can be detected through tests, and reading-improvement programs may be conducted to improve the skill levels. With training, even good readers can learn to read faster and with greater comprehension. Many organizations encour-

age their employees to attend such training sessions as part of their communication-improvement program.

Other Barriers to Effective Communication

Other barriers that bring about a faulty transmission and reception of messages in the office include:

1. *Time pressure*, as evidenced by the overly busy office manager who does not have time to see all subordinates or talk with them as fully as might be desired. Subordinates, also working under time pressures, often do not take the time to read thoroughly the messages received.
2. *Noise*, such as telephones, operation of machines and equipment, and workers' conversations, especially in open areas where employees are trying to talk and hear each other.
3. *Physical distance* between the sender and the receiver, such as the several feet over which the office supervisor in a private office must loudly call to a secretary located in a nearby cubicle.

The interpersonal communication process discussed up to this point relies upon verbal (oral or written) symbols. However, in face-to-face communication, another kind of communication—nonverbal communication—is occurring at the same time as, or in place of, the spoken words. We shall explain this form of communication in the following section.

NONVERBAL COMMUNICATION

Probably the oldest human communication process, **nonverbal communication** consists of any information not spoken or written that is perceived by our senses. Thus, everything we see, touch, smell, taste, or hear that is not structured into a formal verbal message is considered nonverbal communication. Examples of nonverbal communication are the gestures, facial expressions, mannerisms, touching, tones of voice, body positions, uniforms, hairstyles, and other nonverbal stimuli used by the sender and the receiver. Since nonverbal communication may last only a fleeting moment, it cannot be easily remembered or written down for future recall like spoken words.

Several kinds of nonverbal communication and their importance to administrative office managers and supervisors are discussed in the next sections.

Body Language

Body language refers to our gestures, expressions, and body positions. This nonverbal form of communication conveys to us as senders and as receivers the attitudes and feelings of the other and is just as important to the communication process as the words being spoken. Body language may be consistent with the words we speak, or it may contradict our oral message. In the latter case, body language may become a more accurate expression of the situation and thus reduce the credibility of what we say.

For example, Wilma Harter, an office supervisor, is explaining a new departmental regulation to her work force. While casually reading the message, she shrugs her shoulders, lets a smirk appear on her face, and avoids any eye-to-eye contact with her workers. Although Harter's subordinates may hear what she is saying, it is unlikely they will pay much attention or take any favorable action regarding the newly issued rule. The workers have perceived the rule as one in which Harter has little faith and one she plans not to enforce. Thus, when transmitting oral communication, we must be very concerned with our body language and how it will be perceived by those receiving the message.

Research into the field of **kinesics**—the study of the relationship between body motions and communication—shows the importance of recognizing the emotional attitudes of people who are sending and receiving messages since these attitudes are often communicated nonverbally. Therefore, we should learn how to monitor nonverbal communication and act upon it to our advantage. For example, when trying to present an open attitude to our subordinates, we should guard against the use of any gesture, such as folding our arms across our chest, which may reveal a closed mind. We usually find it easy to portray attitudes that are considered to be positive. It is much less easy, however, to control those nonverbal signals that should be concealed.

Physical Space

The distance that we maintain with others is related to our feelings toward those persons, indicates something about the relationships, and determines the kind of communication that takes place. The study of **proxemics** examines how individuals use physical space in their interactions with others and how physical space influences behavior.[1] Proxemics has identified four basic zones of physical space—intimate, personal, social, and public—that are described in detail in Chapter 13.

An understanding of proxemics helps us in planning and controlling the territorial space in which communication occurs. For example, the AOM will find that the success of a small group meeting is affected by the amount of available space. When meeting in small offices or conference rooms, the employees tend to become more argumentative and more difficult to control. The small space also intensifies conflict.

Therefore, to hold a more efficient meeting and reduce potential conflict, the AOM should seat everyone around a large table in a spacious room.

Paralanguage

Paralanguage consists of those aspects of oral communication such as voice qualities and vocalizations that are free of words. Voice qualities include pitch, rhythm, resonance, and tempo; vocalizations are nonlanguage sounds such as laughing, whispering, and "nonwords" such as "uh-huh" and "uh-uh" (standing for yes and no, respectively).

Often more meaning is communicated by paralanguage than by the words we speak. Through training, we can learn to vary our voice qualities and vocalizations to convey a wide range of emotions such as enthusiasm, disappointment, sincerity, interest, or disinterest.

You have now seen how important verbal and nonverbal communication skills are in the problem-solving process, which was fully explained in Chapter 3. When tentative solutions to problems are developed and one is selected for use, discussion, persuasion, and acceptance occur, which involve both oral and written communication. One communication skill that is basic to all phases of work performance but especially important to the solution of office problems is the writing of reports. Report writing is the topic of this closing section of the chapter.

REPORT-WRITING PRINCIPLES

Reports are prepared to transmit many kinds of messages. For example, reports are written to reflect past, present, and future financial positions or operating results; to summarize the appraisal of employee performance; and to present details of productivity-improvement programs. Reports are used by AOMs to make decisions, since the facts and opinions included in the reports are sound bases for action. Each

---

[1]The term *proxemics* was introduced by Edward T. Hall, the noted anthropologist, who first systematically studied the human use of space. See Edward T. Hall, *The Hidden Dimension* (Garden City, NY: Doubleday, 1966).

report states problems and recommends solutions as discussed in Chapter 3.

The size and structure of the organization determine the type and frequency of reports. In a small company, monthly reports prepared from accounting records usually suffice to describe the firm's financial condition. As the company grows, however, we find that the work becomes more specialized and departments are provided with supervisory staff. Therefore, it becomes necessary to keep all levels of management informed by reports that are prepared more frequently. The following discussion provides a set of general principles that is useful for preparing all types of business reports.

PRINCIPLE OF SOUND PURPOSE

The report must have a sound and specific purpose that may be translated into effective business management by the decision maker.

The main reason for writing a report is to transmit information in the hope that action will be taken based on the conclusions reached in the report. Generally a report serves managers in two ways: (1) it forms the basis for a discussion of the facts and for recommendations, and (2) it serves as a historical record of that phase of the business activity.

Persons preparing reports for management must determine the minimum information requirements of each manager in relation to his or her needs in the decision-making process. Often managers may not know their needs exactly and may request more information in order "to play it safe." In turn, the managers become burdened with information overload, as discussed earlier in the chapter. Thus, those responsible for report preparation must make sure that they are meeting the needs, as opposed to the wants, of management.

PRINCIPLE OF EFFECTIVE ORGANIZATION

The report should be well planned and well organized.

Since business reports differ widely in content, their organization also varies. For example, a report of operations is usually an accounting report supported by financial statements and schedules. Other reports are statistical, while still others are surveys or investigations that present answers to specific questions. The organization of most reports includes these sections that are usually arranged in this order:

1. *Purpose*: The introduction states the reason for writing the report, the information it contains, and the method employed in collecting the data.
2. *Summary*: The summary contains the conclusions reached and the recommendations made. Many managers prefer the summary at the beginning of the report since placing it first saves them the time of reading the entire report. If necessary, they can examine the supporting details later.
3. *Problems and solution*: The body of the report consists of a logical development of the subject matter. For example, a report dealing with the retrieval of information from the files might show the present method and cost of manually retrieving documents, the average cost of each document retrieved, a description of the proposed automated method of retrieval, the expected costs under this method, the advantages and disadvantages of each method, case studies of firms using each method, and recommendations.
4. *Recommendations*: Whenever a report results in recommendations for action, the recommendations should be stated positively, clearly, and completely. They

may be stated in the form of a summary at the end of each section, or they may be part of the summary at the beginning of the report.

5. *Appendix*: Exhibits should be included whenever the narrative of the report needs more detailed explanation. Appendix items may be in the form of supporting letters, memorandums, charts, layouts, tabulations, or statistics.

A very long formal report may include additional sections, such as preliminary pages consisting of the title page, copyright page (if appropriate), foreword, acknowledgments, table of contents, and list of tables and charts; bibliography; and sometimes an index. A letter of transmittal (sometimes called a cover letter) should be attached to the report to inform the reader about the nature and purpose of the report.

PRINCIPLE OF BREVITY

The report should be kept as short as possible.

The old adage "If I had more time, I would have written less" applies to report writing. The reader's attention can be quickly captured by reducing or eliminating much introductory material.

Reports should be reasonably brief because (1) they are expensive to prepare; (2) long reports are complicated, are difficult to analyze, and usually indicate poor planning; (3) verbosity usually indicates too much emphasis on minor details or irrelevant matters; and (4) unnecessary length evokes criticism about efficiency.

PRINCIPLE OF CLARITY

Simple language should be used for easy understanding.

When writing reports, we should avoid long, involved sentences. We should select our words carefully so that our intended meaning is clearly communicated to our readers. New, technical terms that may create misunderstanding should be defined in order to eliminate communication "static," which may detract from the purpose of our message.

PRINCIPLE OF TIMELY SCHEDULING

Reports should be scheduled so they can be well prepared without undue burden on the staff.

The interval between compiling the data and completing the report should not be so long that the content is obsolete by the time it is presented. With the availability of personal computers, managers are greatly aided in the timely scheduling and preparing of business reports.

PRINCIPLE OF JUSTIFIED COST

The benefits received from the preparation and use of a report should exceed its cost.

With today's high-speed computer printers, many managers are flooded with useless reports that are sent out under the guise of useful information. Therefore, someone should be assigned the responsibility of evaluating the reporting needs of the firm to determine whether the cost of preparing and using the reports justifies their continuance. Such a study is aimed at determining the essential information needs of all managers, discontinuing any unneeded and questionable copies of reports, and revising reports to omit information not sufficiently useful to warrant the costs of collection and reporting. Definite procedures should be established and maintained for a cost-control study throughout the year so that the preparation of any new reports is properly authorized.

SUMMARY

1. Communication is a highly personal and emotional process. Business offices, like the individuals working in them, have their own unique personalities. What works in one office to communicate effectively may be only slightly effective or may fail in another office.

2. In many instances, the lack of good communication lies not in the network or channel selected but in the communicator—the sender of the message. The sender must transmit messages that are understood by the receiver so that desired action is taken as evidenced by feedback. Importantly, too, the sender must be concerned with the emotional reactions, attitudes, and feelings of those who receive the messages.

3. Communication is not a one-way street between the office manager and the employees, or vice versa. Successful communication flows not only downward and upward but also laterally and diagonally. In each of these flows, there is potential for a communication breakdown unless the sender is aware of barriers relating to perception, semantics, status, bias, organization climate, jargon, and the receiver's reading skills. The sender must also be concerned with nonverbal communication, such as body language, which is just as important to the oral and written communication processes as the spoken and written words.

4. Much of the written communication in offices is transmitted by formal reports, which are often used in decision making. Successful business reports have a sound purpose and are well planned and organized, brief, easily understood, timely scheduled, and cost justified.

GLOSSARY

Bias—the highly personal judgment or opinion formed by an individual before the facts are known; also called *prejudice*.

Body language—a person's gestures, expressions, and body positions.

Communication—the process by which information and human attitudes are exchanged with others.

Communication audit—an evaluation of the communication system to determine how effectively and efficiently it is working.

Communication network—the pattern of channels used to communicate messages to and from, or among, a group of people.

Communication process—the transmission of a message from one person (the sender) to another person (the receiver).

Diagonal communication—the transmission of messages to workers at higher or lower levels in the organization using communication networks other than those formally shown on the organization chart.

Downward communication—the transmission of messages that flow vertically from the top of the organization to one or more levels below in order to translate top-management planning and decision making into orders that direct office employees.

Employee suggestion system—a channel of upward communication in which employees offer ideas that result in cost reduction and the elimination of inefficiency and waste.

Grapevine—an informal communication network in which messages are rapidly transmitted, usually orally on a one-to-one basis.

Information overload—the communication of an excessive amount of details about company operations and personnel activities.

Jargon—those technical terms and idioms that are peculiar to a specific group or activity.

Kinesics—the study of the relationship between body motions and communication.

Lateral communication—the transmission of messages among personnel at the same level in the organization; also called *horizontal communication.*

Network analysis—a communication research technique used to find out where people go to get their needed information.

Nonverbal communication—any information not spoken or written that is perceived by one's senses.

Oral communication—that form of verbal communication which is spoken.

Paralanguage—those aspects of oral communication such as voice qualities and vocalizations that are free of words.

Perception—a way of interpreting situations based on the individual's personal experiences.

Proxemics—the study of how individuals use physical space in their interactions with others and how physical space influences behavior.

Semantics—the study of word meanings and their effect upon human behavior.

Slanting—the conscious manipulation of facts in order to distort events.

Stereotyping—the formation of a commonly held mental picture of how people of a particular sex, religion, or race appear, think, feel, and act.

Upward communication—the transmission of messages that flow vertically from one level in the organization to one or more levels above.

Verbal communication—the most basic form of communication, which consists of words—spoken or written.

Written communication—that form of verbal communication which consists of non-spoken words.

FOR YOUR REVIEW

1. Explain the operation of the communication process.

2. Why are written rather than spoken words recommended when important messages are to be transmitted?

3. Distinguish between the formal and the informal communication network.

4. How can an office manager effectively use the grapevine?

5. Explain how the office supervisor serves as a linking pin in the flow of communication.

6. What factors should be considered by the office manager when deciding which channel of downward communication to use?

7. What are the main uses of upward communication channels?

8. Why is there need for lateral and diagonal communication in the office?

9. How do differences in perception become barriers to effective communication?

10. When communicating upward, why do subordinates often slant their messages?

11. Explain how the climate of an organization may affect the communication process.

12. Since nonverbal communication cannot be easily remembered or written down, why is it important in the communication process?

13. What is the significance of proxemics to the communication process?

14. In what order do the sections of most business reports appear?

15. How can the office manager determine the cost effectiveness of reports produced in the organization?

FOR YOUR DISCUSSION

1. Why does downward communication frequently create more problems than communication between two co-workers on the same level?

2. The administrative manager for Court Health Care, Clay Radcliff, has created a communication climate so well liked by his subordinates that they drop into his office very often merely to chat. Radcliff does not want to react negatively to his workers and "turn them off," since he does not want to be avoided when they have information he needs. However, Radcliff is very much concerned about the amount of time being wasted every day in idle chitchat. What approach can you recommend he use to reduce the number of "drop-ins"?

3. Some authorities strongly advocate that managers should *never* use the grapevine to disseminate information. Do you agree with these authorities? Why? If you disagree with them, under what conditions could you effectively use the grapevine?

4. Carol Rosato prides herself on her supervisory abilities and often tells visitors and clients that she has "good communications" in the office. As a visitor receiving this message, explain what you think Rosato means by her statement.

5. William Tobin is the newly hired office manager of Los Gatos, Inc. Only 24 years old and relatively inexperienced, Tobin is aware of his number one deficiency—very weak oral communication skills. Do you believe Tobin can hope to function effectively with this deficiency? Explain.

SOLVING CASE PROBLEMS

Case 5-1 Hurrying Along the Meeting

At the monthly staff meeting held yesterday, Adam Coreaux, office manager for the Sax Company, learned that the proposed employee appraisal program had been approved. Under the revised program, all office workers who have been with the firm one year or longer will be conducting a self-appraisal along with the usual evaluation completed by their immediate supervisors. Newly hired employees and those with the company less than one year will undergo a quarterly appraisal. Since Coreaux was instrumental in developing the revised appraisal program, he is very familiar with its contents and the procedures to be followed.

Today Coreaux is chairing a meeting with all of his supervisors, who have been called together in his private office to hear about the new appraisal program. Coreaux opens the meeting by saying:

> This has been one big day for me—meetings all over the place. Come on in, Karen, we've just gotten underway. We're short a chair, so I hope you don't mind standing; this session will be a short one anyway. I wanted to get together with you to pass out this report on the revised appraisal procedures. I know you've heard me talk about it for the past eight months, so I'm sure it must be "old hat" to you by now. Well, look it over and get back to me if you have any questions. Now, let's hurry along to the next item on the agenda. . . .

Just as Coreaux disposed of the last item on the agenda, Karen Headley, supervisor of word processing, interrupted by asking: "Adam, could we go back to this appraisal report? Take a look on page 4 where you say. . . ." But at this point, Coreaux stood up, broke in on Headley's question, and exclaimed: "Karen, you've got to read the whole report before that early stuff makes any sense. I've got to go, pronto. Catch me later."

1. Evaluate Coreaux's ability to communicate downward at the meeting with the supervisors. What elements in the communication process did Coreaux ignore?

2. What barriers to effective communication were found at the meeting with the supervisors? How might Coreaux have prevented these barriers from occurring?

3. What is your reaction to Coreaux's written report in view of the comment he made to Headley?

Case 5-2 Writing More Clearly

Ruth O'Keeffe, vice-president of office services at Hanover Savings, believes that many of the reports prepared by her supervisors are so poorly written that the messages become garbled in transmission. As a result, those receiving the messages have difficulty in determining what action, if any, they are to take. O'Keeffe's beliefs are confirmed by samples of her supervisors' reports that have been collected and analyzed over the past six months. Some of the findings of O'Keeffe's audit are given below:

1. Words and phrases to be simplified. What short, simple words can the supervisors use instead?

   a. afford an opportunity
   b. prioritize
   c. voluminous
   d. consummate
   e. automatization

   f. interrogate
   g. utilization
   h. finalize
   i. profitwise
   j. substantial portion

2. A few "static-loaded" sentences. How can these sentences be revised to communicate more clearly by using simple words?
   a. The antiquated electronic calculator housed in my office is ineffectual for solving the sophisticated mathematical problems I encounter.
   b. It is imperative that all unwarranted absenteeism be adequately investigated so reminders can be promulgated to the parties at fault.
   c. The customer's dilatory actions precipitated the necessity for our loan people to respond with exiguous information.

3. Several sentences that will have more "punch" if they use the active rather than the passive form. How should each sentence be rewritten?
   a. The raw data are keyboarded by the CRT operators each Friday afternoon.
   b. All of our peripheral equipment is serviced regularly by the Arten Company.
   c. The new procedures were promulgated by Ms. Rosen and were explained later by her in a departmental meeting.
   d. The first-class mail is first sorted by David Tokes and then distributed by Matt Tyrone.

4. Ideas not expressed in parallel form. How can each sentence be rewritten to state the ideas in parallel form and yet communicate clearly?
   a. All of my workers have been given copies of the procedures for writing effective reports, for using the offset duplicator, and how to keep all of their operating manuals up-to-date.
   b. Specifically, Hazel Borge was employed to receive visitors to our company, to operate the PBX, to help out in opening the incoming mail, and a variety of other duties that might be assigned by her supervisor.
   c. In the motion study conducted yesterday, I observed Rachel Milstein input the information, verify the output manually, and a lot of extraneous activities such as answering the telephone and file the tapes.

Give O'Keeffe a helping hand by answering the questions she has raised in 1 through 4.

PART 2

Managing Human Resources

6

Recruiting and Orienting the Office Staff

GOALS FOR THIS CHAPTER

After completing this chapter, you should be able to:

1. Discuss the advantages and disadvantages of the sources of personnel that may be used by the administrative office manager in recruiting qualified office workers.
2. Describe a typical procedure used by small and large companies to select office personnel.
3. Classify and state the purposes of preemployment tests that may be used by the administrative office manager as supplemental tools in the employee recruitment process.
4. Describe an effective orientation program for newly employed office workers.
5. Describe briefly those government regulations that directly influence the employment process.

Human resources, the most valuable asset in the office, is the theme of this second part of the textbook. As we saw in Chapter 1, determining the needs for human resources is one of the major activities in the office management function of planning. After the needs have been determined, the required number of office personnel are recruited, selected, and oriented.

In many small and medium-size offices, recruiting and orienting office workers are major phases of the administrative office manager's job. In large offices, the responsibility for recruiting and orienting office personnel may be assigned to a specialist in the human resources department. Or the orientation may be combined with the initial training program under the jurisdiction of the training department or the AOM.

Regardless of who selects and orients office workers, every effort must be made to keep and promote qualified workers. For a fair day's work, an office employee must be paid a fair day's salary. Salary costs are at their highest level in history and represent an increasing percentage of the cost of products and services. Further, the cost of employee benefits (fringe benefits) is 37 cents of every payroll dollar. This means that in addition to regular pay, employers spend an average of $10,750 annually for benefits for each employee.[1] Another element that adds to increased staffing costs is the creating and processing of employee records. For example, great increases have been noted in federal, state, and local reporting requirements; equal opportunity compliance records; legally required insurance and compensation forms; performance analyses; and job evaluations. All of these record-keeping and forms-completion activities involve costly administrative labor time and thus create substantial charges against a firm's profits.

---

[1]*Employee Benefits, 1989 Edition*, Survey Data from Benefit Year 1988 (Washington: Chamber of Commerce of the United States, 1988), p. 5.

The costs of recruiting new office personnel have likewise increased. In 1987, to hire each office or clerical worker, employers spent an average of $961 (30% more than the previous year).[2] Thus, keeping employee turnover at its lowest level becomes one of the objectives of sound administrative office management. As we shall see in Chapter 12, turnover can be kept at a minimum by efficient selection and orientation processes,

adequate training, and payment of salaries that are in keeping with skills required and competitive market conditions.

As we see in Figure 6–1, recruiting, selecting, and retaining well-qualified employees for office positions involve knowing the sources of supply; interviewing and testing the applicants; maintaining personnel records, such as personnel requisitions and application forms, required by business and government; properly introducing the new office workers to their jobs; and keeping abreast of the government regulations and agency guidelines that affect employee recruitment. Each of these topics

[2]"For Your Information," *Personnel Journal* (November, 1988), p. 12. Data obtained from Employment Management Association (EMA) *Report of National Cost-per-Hire Data for 1987*.

Figure 6–1
Recruiting,
Selecting,
and Retaining Office
Personnel

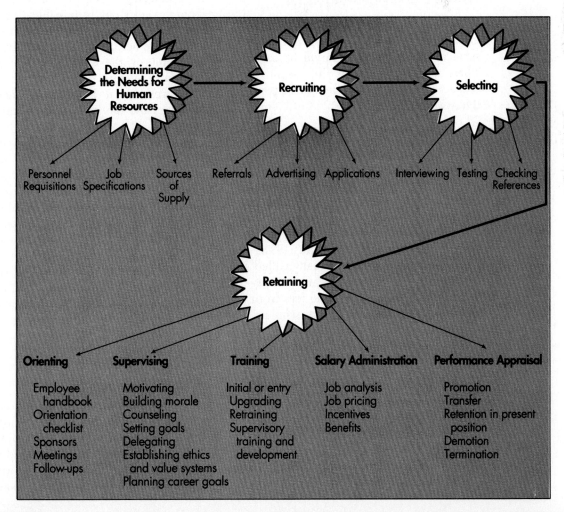

is discussed in this chapter. Supervising, training, appraising, promoting, and compensating office personnel are discussed in the following chapters.

SOURCES OF OFFICE WORKERS

The selection of the sources of office employees is based on these criteria: economy of time on the part of the employer by interviewing a minimum number of applicants; reduction of turnover as a result of careful screening by reliable sources; and creation of a work force that is cooperative, progressive, productive, and happy.

Employment Services and Private Employment Agencies

When recruiting office personnel, many employers make use of public employment services and private employment agencies. These organizations put an employer in contact with a selected number of prospective workers.

Public Employment Services

The largest **public employment service** is the United States Employment Service (USES), which is supervised by the Department of Labor. Each state has an employment service, sometimes called an employment commission or an employment security agency, which is affiliated with USES. The state placement service is usually called *Job Service*. Job Service, located in every metropolitan area, requires no fees from the job seekers or the employers who use its services.

Some of the services provided by Job Service include:

1. Locating qualified workers through a nationwide recruitment service.
2. Selecting qualified workers through valid interviewing and testing techniques.
3. Testing and counseling people about the fields of work for which their aptitudes and interests best suit them.

4. Providing guidance in solving problems of turnover and absenteeism.
5. Developing training courses to help alleviate existing shortages of qualified workers and meet expected needs for additional trained workers.
6. Aiding veterans by relating their service training to civilian job openings.
7. Developing special programs for recruiting older workers, the disabled, and members of minority groups.

Private Employment Agencies

Private employment agencies, also known as *placement firms*, charge a fee for their selection and placement services. This fee, depending upon local or state law, may range from a week's pay to possibly 15 percent of the employee's first-year pay. Practices vary as to whether the fee is paid by the job applicant or the employer. For example, when an executive recruiting agency is hired to search for a high-level executive or manager, the fee is commonly paid by the employer.

In selecting a private employment agency, the AOM should make sure that the agency is professionally qualified to do its job. The AOM can determine that an agency subscribes to professional and ethical standards by checking to see that the agency has membership in its state and national employment agency association. More information about the agency's standing and reputation in the community may be obtained from the Better Business Bureau, the chamber of commerce, and consumer protection bureaus.

Temporary Office Help Services

Temporary office help services "rent out" office workers for varying periods of time, such as a day, a week, several months, or longer. Temporary workers, an integral part of the labor force, have been used for years as emergency fill-ins to reduce work overloads during peak periods, to assist with special projects, and to fill in for vacationing employees. Today, however, with the growing need for technological specialists, we find companies using temporary workers as long-term employees, especially in word processing and computer operations. Among the nationally known temporary office help services are Accountemps, Kelly Services, Manpower, Inc., Olsten Corporation, and Western Temporary Services. Use of temporary office personnel has brought about significant savings for many firms and enabled them to lower labor costs without lowering their pay rates.

In using the services of temporary workers, the employer commonly pays a flat fee to the temporary office help service. The temporary employee is interviewed, trained, and paid by the service. The employee's bonding, social security records, tax deductions, accident and sickness insurance, and vacation, if earned, are all obligations of the service. The client-company realizes its savings in the areas of record-keeping costs, payroll taxes, workers' compensation, vacation and sick time, and use of the employee only when needed. Because of the tremendous increase in the cost of employee benefits, companies realize considerable savings by using temporary help.

The following guidelines are offered to the AOM who is considering the use of temporary office help:

1. Determine in advance the number of clerical hours needed in the department requiring help. Compare the cost of part-time help on the company's own payroll with the cost of using temporary helpers (sometimes called "temporaries" or "temps").
2. When seeking workers, provide the service with a current and complete job description for each position to be filled. Thus, if a payroll clerk is needed, the service will not refer a person who has the skills of only a data-entry clerk.

3. Have the work ready prior to the arrival of the temporary worker by planning complete step-by-step job instructions.
4. Make sure the permanent workers understand in advance that the temporary is being brought in for special needs only and not to complete their work. Ask the permanent workers to be helpful and cooperative in whatever way possible.
5. Make sure that the office equipment to be used is in good working order, supplies are on hand, and space is adequate for the temporary's needs.
6. Appoint one person to meet the temporary worker, to introduce the worker to others in the department, and to orient the worker to the locations of the lounge, the cafeteria, and the workstation.
7. Make sure the temporary understands the step-by-step job instructions.
8. If possible, employ the temporary a day in advance so he or she can become familiar with the duties of the person being relieved. Company practices regarding time for lunch and work breaks and procedures for handling personal incoming and outgoing calls should be reviewed.
9. If a temporary's work is not satisfactory, contact the service and explain the situation. Usually a temporary can be released after the first few hours, and the worker will be replaced by the service.
10. Review with the temporary the overall performance on each job so that ways may be discovered to do the job better and at a lower cost.

Employee Leasing Services

Some firms obtain employees from leasing companies that assign workers to the client firms under a contract to provide on-the-job services. In contrast to a temporary help service, an **employee leasing service** places

Dialog on the Firing Line

JOAN P. KLUBNIK
Career and Management Development Consultant for
    Information Systems
Transamerica Occidental Life Insurance Company
Los Angeles, California

EdD, University of California at Los Angeles

As Career and Management Development Consultant for
Transamerica Occidental Life Insurance Company's
Information Systems organization, Joan Klubnik is responsible for the career and management development
programs for data processing personnel. She also is
affiliated with the University of California, Irvine, serving
as the academic coordinator and networking instructor
for the Managerial Skills Certificate Program. Ms.
Klubnik has taught and consulted in the data processing
and career development fields and has published several
articles on the subject of employee training.

QUESTION: Tell us about the major features of the
orientation program you designed for your company.

RESPONSE: The New Employee Orientation
program for the Information Systems organization
of Transamerica Occidental Life Insurance Company is designed to:

- Provide new hires with information about the way
  we do business.
- Expose them to key personnel within our
  organization.
- Help them to more quickly and efficiently come
  up to speed in their new jobs.
- Provide information about how things operate so
  that it is easier to work with new hires because
  they better understand the operations.

Our orientation includes 25 key individuals who
present information about the operations for which
they are responsible. Each presenter provides an
overview of his or her area—what is done in the
area, and which programs/processes are critical to
operations. New hires are able to gain a sense of
the person—his or her style and priorities.

The 20-hour program is offered over a five-day
period. All new hires to our organization participate
in the program. Evaluations conducted periodically
since the program's inception five years ago identify
it as a major tool in our career management
program.

workers on a permanent, or fairly permanent, basis.

In a typical employee leasing arrangement, an employer discharges his or her workers (or certain groups of workers), who then are hired by the leasing service. The leasing service, in turn, prepares a leasing agreement and assigns the same employees back to their original employer. The original employer still determines who works for the firm, who receives how much compensation, who gets promotions, who gets time off, and who is discharged.

Some leasing services base their fees on a percentage of the client-firm's total payroll. The fee, which varies with the number of employees and their pay scale, may range from 3 to 10 percent of a company's total payroll. Other leasing services quote a flat annual fee, such as $500 to $1,000, depending upon the size of the client-firm.

Business firms enter into this type of "lease-back" arrangement in order to reduce the costs of administering their personnel function. The employee leasing service often offers full personnel administration services and provides employee benefits such as health and dental care insurance and pension plans. Thus, by leasing its employees, a small firm is better able to compete with a larger company in providing high-quality benefits. When it can offer a broader array of benefits, a small firm may often experience a higher morale level and a lower turnover rate. The leasing service is also responsible for computing the payroll and paying the employees, maintaining all payroll records, and preparing all employee-related reports.

Local Community Agencies

Sources of office personnel include the local community agencies operated by minority groups; veterans' organizations; churches; charitable organizations; fraternal lodges and clubs; trade associations; and institutions for rehabilitation of physically and mentally

disabled persons, drug addicts, and ex-prisoners. Generally such agencies refer only members of their own groups and do not charge the applicant or employer a fee for the services rendered.

Advertising

Before placing help-wanted advertisements, a careful study should be made of the most profitable form of advertising and the most appropriate medium. The type of position to be filled will influence the selection of a medium, and a little experimentation will show which is the most satisfactory. Care must be exercised when placing help-wanted advertisements to make sure the wording of the advertisements does not conflict with fair employment practices laws, which are discussed later in this chapter.

Many help-wanted advertisements include an "Equal Opportunity Employer" statement as one way of complying with fair employment practice laws.

One disadvantage of placing help-wanted advertisements in newspapers is that a large number of replies may be received, but time and resources permit only a few applicants to be interviewed. This method proves suitable, however, for the firm that has a human resources department adequately staffed to screen, interview, and test applicants.

Referrals

A firm often obtains qualified employees through **referrals** by present employees, company officers, and customers. Great care must be exercised when using such referrals, however. If a customer or an officer of the firm recommends a person who is not suitable or qualified for the job, it may cause the firm some embarrassment if the applicant is not hired or is not retained for any length of time.

Some firms encourage their workers to recommend friends as possible employees because it adds to the prestige of present employees and creates a good psychological effect. Firms may offer incentives, such as cash payments, United States savings bonds, and company merchandise, to be given for referrals after the newly employed worker has been on the job for a stipulated period of time.

Educational Institutions

Many large business firms send representatives to college and school campuses to interview students, such as you, about possible employment after graduation. If it is not possible to send representatives to college campuses, a firm may write to the placement office of the college, describe the types of job openings available, and ask you to submit your personal resumé (personal data sheet). Often, however, firms find it difficult to decide from your resumé whether or not to invite you to visit the company. In such cases, it may be less expensive to have a company recruiter visit the campus than to have you visit the company for interviewing.

Many private business schools maintain a placement service for their students, some of whom have had office experience. A number of high schools, vocational schools, junior colleges, community colleges, and universities cooperate with industry by setting up internship and cooperative work-study programs in which students attend school part-time and work part-time. Some companies sponsor summer-hire programs in which students work for the companies during the summer months of their junior and senior years. If the students' work proves satisfactory, they are asked to return the following summer at an appropriate salary increase. Such cooperative training programs develop many good trainees who later become full-time employees of the participating companies.

Other Sources of Office Employees

Additional recruiting sources include applicants who walk in from the street to apply for a position and applicants who have written unsolicited letters of application. Some manufacturers of office equipment have established training schools and placement agencies to supply their customers with well-trained, efficient operators of their equipment. Career conferences and job fairs are also used in recruiting office personnel. Finally, two other sources that should not be overlooked when recruiting new office workers are former employees who had good work records and previous job applicants who were not hired because there were no appropriate vacancies at the time of application.

PROCEDURES FOR SELECTING OFFICE WORKERS

You will find that the employee selection procedure in small offices is very simple compared to that in offices having large staffs. In small offices, an interview is usually all that is necessary, followed by a statement that within a few days you will be informed if you have been offered the position. In this way, no decision need be reached until a sufficient number of applicants have been interviewed. In large offices, however, the procedure becomes more formal and complex since the larger the office staff, the more necessary the record-keeping requirements become.

Federal, state, and local laws affecting the employment process have stimulated the need for complete and detailed records of job applicants and employees. For small and medium-size offices, the employment records should include, as a minimum, the application form and the record of employment. In a firm large enough to have a human resources department, additional forms become necessary in order to establish definite procedures and adequate control over employee selection.

Personnel Requisition Form

To many people, the application is probably the first and most important office employment record. Its use in large offices, however, is sometimes preceded by the **personnel requisition** prepared by a department head. This form specifies the number of persons required and the kind of work to be done. If job specifications have been prepared, they are studied in order to obtain specific information concerning the job requirements. This study is completed before any search for a job applicant begins. If a list of previous job applicants is kept on file, reference is made to this list so qualified persons may be notified for an interview. If no such list is kept, the sources previously mentioned are consulted.

Application Form

Probably the most frequently used form in the selection process is the **application form**. Careful use of application forms permits a preliminary screening of applicants for a position, thus saving the interviewer's time.

The information called for on an application form is usually grouped under the headings of personal information, education, business experience, references, and general remarks. In designing application forms, employers should request only data that are useful in predicting job-relevant behavior. Employers should not ask questions that may become the basis for charges of discrimination under the fair employment practices regulations. For example, questions that request your sex and religion are clearly inappropriate unless it can be

Application forms provide employers with concise, pertinent information about an applicant.

shown that they are bona fide ("good faith") occupational qualifications (discussed later in this chapter). Questions about age, race, marital status, and national origin are also unacceptable. Questions about intimate subjects, such as your sexual practices or personal characteristics, are doubly dangerous. These questions not only are illegal on the basis of their relevance to job requirements, but also represent an invasion of your privacy.

State departments of labor examine application forms to make sure they are prepared within the meaning of the law. Whenever there are inconsistencies between federal requirements and state laws, federal requirements may take precedence. For example, in many states the fair employment practices legislation makes it illegal to identify your race on your personnel record. However, federal agencies have found it useful to have this information to detect possible discrimination in a firm. The federal government may, therefore, request that certain companies maintain such records, with the stipulation that the information is not to be used for unfair discrimination.

The Interview

Let's say that you are interviewing a job applicant for the position of administrative assistant in your firm. By studying the jobseeker's application blank or personal resumé, you can select specific areas to discuss or to clarify during the interview. You should guard against arriving at hasty conclusions regarding the applicant's personality, intelligence, skills, abilities, and motivations. Instead, you should try to remain as objective as possible and resist drawing conclusions about the applicant until the interview is well under way and you have obtained enough evidence to justify your feelings.

During the interview, you can evaluate the applicant's personal appearance in relation to the job opening and to any dress codes (regulations) your firm may have established. In many firms, dress codes are flexible depending upon the job and the extent to which the jobholder meets the public. For example, your company may require its male employees to wear dress shirts, ties, and jackets if they meet and work with the public in the course of their workday. However, in some departments of your firm, such as the computer center, sports shirts without ties and jackets may be acceptable.

In arriving at an opinion about the applicant's suitability for the job opening, you should strive to preserve the applicant's sense of dignity and self-respect. At the close of the interview, the applicant should be able to leave with a positive feeling toward the company. For some job openings, a second interview may be scheduled in order to check impressions gained during the first meeting and to ensure that the applicant still displays interest in the position. During the second interview, senior members of the firm may be called upon to interview the applicant to make sure that the individual is well qualified for the position.

You can use several different kinds of interviews, or approaches, to obtain information from the job applicant about education, training, and experience. Three common types of interviews—direct, indirect, and patterned—are briefly described in Figure 6-2.

Record of Interview

The **record of interview** contains in an organized format all the information acquired during the interview. The record aids you, as an interviewer, in remembering all the facts and in making a thorough analysis regarding an applicant's employment. If the personal interview was favorable and there is a possibility of employment, you may

Figure 6–2
Three Common Types
of Interviews

DIRECT INTERVIEW

The interviewer asks job applicants direct questions related to their qualifications and ability to fill the job.

> ### Sample Questions Asked by Interviewer
> 1. What is your keyboarding rate?
> 2. What hours of work do you prefer? Why?
> 3. Do you like to work overtime?
> 4. Do you work better in a group or alone?
> 5. Do you like our work schedule? Why?

The interview is completed relatively quickly because a concise answer is required for each specific question. The direct interview is commonly used to screen applicants for routine office jobs.

The amount of information obtained during the interview is limited. Often no more is learned than specific "yes"or "no" answers, which may not provide enough information to make a hiring decision. Applicants may have pertinent information to pass along but are not given the opportunity to do so.

INDIRECT INTERVIEW

The interviewer asks open-ended questions in order to stimulate the applicants to talk about themselves. The questions asked are designed to solicit opinions and ideas from the applicants, to learn about their attitudes, and to obtain insight into their value systems.

> ### Sample Questions Asked by Interviewer
> 1. Why are you interested in obtaining a position in our company?
> 2. What are your long-range goals?
> 3. What are your plans for furthering your education?
> 4. What are your major strengths and weaknesses?
> 5. What is most important to you about your job?

By listening carefully, the interviewer learns much as the applicants elaborate on important points, such as why they left their former jobs. During this time, the interviewer sees how well the applicants demonstrate their qualifications and observes their self-expression, along with other factors such as manners, poise, and self-confidence.

The indirect interview is time-consuming and requires an able interviewer who is skilled at listening and observing, who can keep applicants from digressing too far from the subject at hand, and who can effectively interpret the answers.

PATTERNED INTERVIEW

Each interviewer uses a standard printed form or questionnaire containing specific key questions like the following:

> ### Sample Questions Asked by Interviewer
> 1. How may years experience do you have?
> 2. What languages do you speak fluently?
> 3. What weekly salary do you expect to receive when starting on this job?
> 4. What days or evenings during the week would you not be available for overtime work?
> 5. How soon will you be able to start work?

As the questions are asked during the interview, the interviewer records the applicant's answers. This type of interview is especially effective when many people are being screened to fill a number of jobs. Time is saved by obtaining the same type of information from all applicants so the responses may be compared. Also, more than one interviewer may be used at the same time, and the questionnaire answers can then be compared and reviewed by a senior executive, such as the human resources administrator.

schedule a follow-up interview during which you use the interview record.

Reference Checks and Letters of Recommendation

Many office managers find that the value of reference checks is limited since job applicants naturally list as references those persons who can be relied upon to provide positive comments. Persons giving reference information must guard against supplying information that may be looked upon as discriminatory or slanderous. For this reason, a former employer named as a reference may provide only information such as dates of employment, the person's job title, location of job site, and possibly the salary. Some employers require the permission from former employees before supplying such information. Thus, these employers are protected against the attack of having invaded the privacy of their former employees.

When checking references, a telephone call can be effective if, as an interviewer, you establish good rapport with the reference and ask carefully phrased questions. In the conversation, you should follow up on every hint or clue about the applicant's past work performance, or there is a risk of your accepting biased information. Telephone calls are an excellent means of checking references when time is of the essence and thorough information is essential.

Office managers find that letters of recommendation, like reference checks, are only fairly effective. First, as you might expect, job applicants name those persons who are likely to write favorable letters of recommendation. Second, fearful of potential lawsuits, many persons decline to give information to a prospective employer unless that information is favorable. As a result, letters of recommendation are often vague, noncommittal, or incredibly glowing. Finally, requests for information from the references supplied by the job applicant may not be answered.

Record of Employment

The **record of employment**, typically maintained in the human resources department of medium-sized and large companies, consists of the employee's personal resumé and a history of employment with the firm. In addition to providing personal data and other information usually found on the application, the record of employment is kept up-to-date by recording such information as the employee's absences, promotions, transfers, and salary increases. Much of the information kept on the record of employment is needed at the time of employee appraisal and also for preparing statistical reports required by government agencies.

Employment Records and Employee Privacy

Many workers are greatly concerned about threats to their personal privacy and thus question the use of the information kept in their employment files. At the federal level, the **Privacy Act of 1974** regulates the collection and use of personal data by the government. This act is designed to protect each citizen's right to privacy by permitting you to exercise some control over the information the government keeps about you. Some companies have voluntarily set up informal record-keeping procedures to meet the concern of workers about their personal privacy. These procedures attempt to discourage the misuse of information contained in employees' medical and insurance records, although they do provide for computer printouts of records for employee verification.

Some states have enacted laws relating to the keeping of employee records and the inspection rights of workers. For example, in Pennsylvania, all employees have the right to inspect their individual personnel files. Employers, however, may use the following guidelines when applying the law:

1. Employees may be required to inspect records on their own time.
2. Employees may be required to fill out a written form requesting access to their personnel files and stating either the purpose of the inspection or the specific records they want to see.
3. Employers may require that inspection of the files be done in the presence of a management-level employee.
4. Inspections may be limited to once a year for each employee, unless an employee has "reasonable cause" to inspect the file more than once.

The Pennsylvania law permits note-taking, but not copying of records. Employees are allowed to place in their files any counter-statements of disagreement with any of the material kept on file. However, inspection rights do not apply to criminal or grievance procedure records, letters of reference, medical records, or staff planning information.

PREEMPLOYMENT TESTING

The use of tests in selecting office workers is based upon these two principles:

1. Tests for selecting, placing, evaluating, and promoting office employees must be administered and interpreted in an unbiased, objective manner.
2. Tests are not exclusive devices but *supplemental* tools in the total assessment of personnel.

Testing practices that have a discriminatory effect upon job applicants are prohibited. As a result of the U.S. Supreme Court ruling in the *Griggs* v *Duke Power* case, "Any test must measure the person for the job, and not the person in the abstract."[3] The court decision was designed not to abolish job tests but, rather, to make sure the tests are "job-related." The word **test** is interpreted broadly to include any paper and pencil or performance measure used as a basis for any employment decision. Thus, included in the concept of testing are not only traditional kinds of tests but also personal history questions, scored application forms, scored interviews, and interviewers' rating scales.

All aspects of employee selection are open to examination for possible discriminatory personnel practices. Employers must be able to validate, or justify, any selection procedure that adversely affects members of any race, sex, or ethnic group by showing that the procedure is job-related. The validation procedures are contained in the *Uniform Guidelines on Employee Selection Procedures*, prepared by the U.S. Office of Personnel Management, the Department of Justice, the Equal Employment Opportunity Commission, and the Department of Labor. The guidelines apply to all aspects of the employee selection procedure used in making employment decisions—interviews, tests, reviews of experience or education from application forms, work samples, physical requirements, and evaluations of performance. The guidelines apply not only to hiring but also to other employment decisions such as promotion, demotion, retention, and selection for training or transfer.

Major Kinds of Preemployment Tests

The major kinds of preemployment tests are classified and briefly described in Figure 6–3.

---

[3]In 1971, the U. S. Supreme Court unanimously declared that practices that act to exclude applicant groups artificially because of race or other factors and that cannot be shown to bear a predictive relationship to job performance violate the law. Nothing in the ruling prevents employers from excluding minority members, but if they do, they must be able to demonstrate a substantial relationship between the test scores and critical job performance.

Figure 6–3
Types of
Preemploy-
ment Tests

Type of Test and Its Purpose	Examples of Published Tests*
1. **Intelligence tests**—designed to measure mental and reasoning ability.	Wonderlic Personnel Test Wechsler Adult Intelligence Scale Otis Self-Administering Test of Mental Ability SRA (Science Research Associates) Verbal Thurstone Test of Mental Alertness
2. **Aptitude tests**—designed to measure the ability to perform a particular kind of task (such as facility with numerical concepts) and to predict future performance on the job or in training.	Minnesota Assessment Battery Wolfe-Spence Programming Aptitude Test Fogel Word Processing Operator Test Systems Programming Aptitude Test Hay Clerical Test Battery
3. **Achievement tests**—designed to measure the degree of proficiency in a given type of work such as typewriting and related clerical skills.	SRA Typing Skills Test Typing Test for Business Seashore-Bennett Stenographic Proficiency Test Wolfe Programming Language Test: COBOL Office Skills Test
4. **Personality and psychological tests**—designed to measure abstract concepts such as aggressiveness, honesty, independence, conformity, and passivity.	Minnesota Multiphasic Personality Inventory Survey of Interpersonal Values Thurstone Temperament Schedule Jackson Personality Inventory Predictive Index California Personality Inventory
5. **Interest tests**—designed to identify a person's likes and dislikes to aid in career counseling.	Strong-Campbell Interest Inventory Kuder Preference Record Strong Vocational Interest Blank

* A directory of test publishers that gives a listing of tests, critical evaluations of the tests, and the names and addresses of the publishers is contained in Buros' *Mental Measurements Yearbook* series. The *Yearbook* series may be obtained from Gryphon Press, Highland Park, NY 08904, and in many public and university or college libraries.

Some professional testers maintain that a group (or battery) of tests is necessary in order to test the variety of abilities required for a specific job. Others feel that every job can be analyzed into certain basic skills and abilities that can be discovered by a single test.

Whether the testing program should be installed by someone within the company, such as the office manager, or handled by an outside professional organization depends upon the number of workers who must be hired from time to time. The cost of tests and trained personnel to administer and interpret the tests is more than some firms wish to spend. Large companies may purchase published tests, develop their own tests, or have them designed by a consulting firm of professional testers. Other firms experiment by using published tests and those of their own creation until they find a combination of testing practices and procedures that is valid and reliable. Whether a firm selects tests developed by test publishers or creates its own, the factors of reliability and validity should be considered.

Reliability

A test used in selecting office workers should have a high degree of **reliability**; that is, the test should measure *consistently* the items it is designed to measure. This means that the same general score can be expected if the test is given to the same person more than once. The publishers of reputable, standardized tests include within their instruction manuals information on the reliability of their tests.

Validity

A test has **validity** if it can be shown to serve the purpose for which it was intended. For example, the validity of an employment test depends on whether a score on the test accurately predicts a level of performance on the job. If the test accurately predicts performance at a particular level, the test is valid. If the test does not accurately predict performance at that level, the test is not valid. Tests that have been professionally constructed and can be shown to measure an important aspect of the job, such as typewriting and keyboarding tests, are usually accepted as valid.

Other Types of Preemployment Testing and Screening

In addition to using one or more of the preemployment tests described above, employers often test and screen job applicants with reference to drug and alcohol abuse, physical condition, criminal record, and honesty. Results from tests such as these enable employers to make hiring decisions aimed at decreasing absenteeism and tardiness, improving productivity, and decreasing accidents. To prevent discriminatory testing practices, however, federal and state laws limit what kind of information may be solicited in these types of screening. Thus, to avoid potential lawsuits, the person in charge of preemployment testing and screening must ask applicants only for information that is directly related to their ability to perform the job they seek.

Drug and Alcohol Abuse

The screening of job applicants for drug and alcohol use is not prohibited by federal law. Nor does federal legislation prohibit private employers from refusing to hire an applicant because of current drug and alcohol use. Generally the courts have ruled that a job seeker's right to privacy is second in importance to public safety. Thus, the courts usually permit the testing of job applicants for drugs and alcohol when the job opening is directly involved with public safety. Also, the courts generally grant employers more freedom to test job applicants than to test employees who are presently working for the company. However, several states have passed laws that limit the situations in which private employers may test job applicants and present employees for drug use. Because of rapidly changing legislation, those in charge of applicant-screening procedures should check their state and local laws.

Physical Condition

Many states have used the Vocational Rehabilitation Act, discussed earlier, as their model in passing laws that prohibit discrimination against handicapped persons. Under this federal law, people are classed as handicapped if they have a mental or physical condition that substantially affects their ability to perform one or more major "life activities" (caring for one's self, performing manual tasks, walking, seeing, hearing, speaking, learning, and working). The courts have held that obesity, suicidal tendencies, diabetes, and great sensitivity to tobacco smoke are examples of handicaps protected by federal or state law. Since state laws vary greatly in their definition of a handicapped person, the interviewer should ask questions about an applicant's physical condition only if the questions are job related and do not violate those laws that prohibit handicap discrimination.

Many state laws provide that Acquired Immune Deficiency Syndrome (AIDS), like other communicable diseases, is a physical handicap entitled to protection under anti-discrimination laws. Therefore, it could be illegal in many jurisdictions to ask job applicants whether they carry the AIDS anti-bodies and thus to screen them out of the firm's work force.

Criminal Record

The regulations issued by the Equal Employment Opportunity Commission prohibit an employer from asking a job applicant to disclose information about an arrest or detention that did not result in conviction. An employer may, however, ask the job applicant whether he or she has ever been *convicted* of a criminal offense. The courts have generally held, under Title VII of the Civil Rights Act, that asking questions about a job applicant's arrest record is discriminatory against minorities. Further, the courts find no evidence that past arrests tell the interviewer anything about how the applicant is likely to perform on the job. However, questions may be raised about pending indictments, since the answer could be relevant to job performance. For example, suppose a job seeker has been charged with the theft of a social security check from a neighbor's mailbox, a crime directly related to the job being applied for in the mailing room. When the job applicant has been charged with such a criminal offense, the interviewer may want to postpone a hiring decision until it is known that the applicant will be cleared of the charge.

In some states you as an employer are permitted to ask job applicants whether they have ever been convicted of a crime. However, you cannot follow a blanket policy of refusing to hire all persons who have ever been convicted. In evaluating applicants convicted of a crime, you should determine the severity of the crime, how long ago the applicant was convicted, evidence of rehabilitation, and the presence of any mitigating circumstances.

The **Fair Credit Reporting Act of 1968** governs the use of credit and investigative agencies that supply information about a person's character, general reputation, and life-style. You may use such reports (often referred to as investigative consumer reports) to verify the information provided by job applicants. When using *investigative consumer reports*, you must notify the applicant or the present employee in writing that you are requesting such a report. Also, you must notify the applicant or employee that he or she may request information from you about the nature and type of information sought. In the event you deny employment because of the consumer report information, you must inform the applicant that this was the reason or part of the reason for denying employment. Further, you must furnish the applicant with the name and address of the consumer reporting agency that made the report.

Honesty

The **Employee Polygraph Protection Act of 1988** bars *private* employers from requiring that most job applicants and current employees be given polygraph (lie detector) tests. Among those who may use polygraph testing are federal, state, and local governments and any political subdivision of a state or local government. Polygraph tests may be administered also for national defense or security reasons. In addition, polygraph testing is permitted in connection with investigations that involve theft at the workplace or other injury or loss to an employer's business.

Among the exemptions contained in the act is the preemployment testing of security guards and employees who will have direct access to controlled substances. Questions regarding religious, political, racial, and union beliefs, as well as questions relating to sexual behavior, are prohibited in the polygraph tests. Those giving the tests are required to present all questions to the examinee in writing before the test, and the examinee is entitled to review the results of any test and to terminate a test at any time.

ORIENTING THE OFFICE STAFF

Orientation refers to a carefully planned, systematic, and effective introduction of new workers to their jobs so they may start working with a minimum of delay, misunderstanding, and error. Orientation covers many topics such as those listed in Figure 6–4, which shows the contents of a typical handbook given to all new office employees. In addition to providing employees with essential information, the **employee handbook** aids in establishing a warm relationship between management and employees at the beginning of the employment experience.

The Orientation Checklist

Supplementing the employee handbook is the **orientation checklist**, which contains items that the supervisor should cover when introducing new employees to their jobs. The checklist is one of the most effective means of making sure that new employees are properly introduced to the firm and to their jobs.

The two-page checklist shown in Figure 6–5 on pages 163 and 164 provides for an orientation program extending over a period of eleven days. This carefully planned program leaves a lasting impression of the firm's interest in its workers and is very effective for "breaking in" new employees. Furthermore, using this checklist properly ensures a complete orientation in all the details of the firm's policies and procedures.

The Sponsor System

Many companies find the sponsor system to be an effective technique for orienting new office employees. Under the **sponsor system**, you, as a new employee, are assigned to a worker who acquaints you with the duties of the job and answers your questions. The sponsor system relieves a supervisor or department head of part of the orientation procedure. It also gives the sponsors an added sense of responsibility and participation and aids in their own self-improvement. The sponsor selected to orient you should have a job similar to the one you are assuming, a complete knowledge of company policies and department operations, a pleasant outgoing personality, an interest in people and their problems, and the desire to be a sponsor.

GOVERNMENT REGULATIONS AFFECTING THE EMPLOYMENT PROCESS

To solve today's problems of fair employment and at the same time to comply with relevant labor relations laws and company requirements, AOMs must thoroughly understand federal, state, and local regulations. The most important of these regulations affecting the employment process are described in this section.

Civil Rights Act of 1964

Nearly half of the pages contained in the Civil Rights Act of 1964 affect AOMs and their responsibilities for staffing the office. The act contains sections dealing with voting rights; prohibition of discrimination on the basis of race, color, religion, or national origin by hotels, restaurants, and certain other facilities; and the creation of new federal agencies. However, of most significance to the OM is Title VII, known as **Equal Employment Opportunity**. This section of

Figure 6–4
Contents
Page of an
Employee
Handbook

MANN'S ROBOTICS

CONTENTS...

Hours of Work	Gambling, Alcohol, and Drugs
Checking In and Out	on the Premises
Rest Periods	Smoking and Nonsmoking
Absences from Work	Areas
Compensation Plans	Receiving Personal Mail
Payroll Deductions	Personal Use of Telephone
Pay Period	Employee Grievances
Safety and Accident Prevention	Jury Duty
	Military Leave

Vacations	Profit-Sharing
Holidays	Pension and Retirement
Group Life Insurance	Suggestion Awards
Hospitalization and	Benefits Required by Law
Surgical Insurance	(FICA, unemployment
	compensation, workers'
	compensation, disability
	insurance, etc.)

Medical Facilities and Annual	Cafeteria
Physical Examinations	Robotics in the 21st Century—
Stock Purchases	our monthly magazine
Credit Union	Recreational Programs
Tuition Reimbursement	

Figure 6–5
Orientation
Checklist
(page 1)

Sample Orientation Checklist

FOR USE BY SUPERVISORS AS A GUIDE IN ORIENTING NEW EMPLOYEES

One of the most effective tools that can be used in orienting new workers is the orientation checklist. Its primary value lies in the fact that it spreads orientation over a number of days, giving the new employees a chance to absorb and digest the various facts, figures, rules, and policies they should know. With the use of a checklist like this one, the employer can be certain that the new workers are getting all the information about the company they need in order to do a good job. And it helps the supervisor present the information in a logical, orderly manner.

Supervisor _____   Date _____

For Employee_____   Dept. _____

BEFORE WORKER ARRIVES

Check when completed

_____ **1. Prepare Future Associates** (by individual or group conference) If
    a. The job is different
    b. The person is different
    c. Someone could have been promoted from within
_____ **2. Have Desk and Supplies Ready**
_____ **3. Alert Job Instructor**
_____ **4. Arrange for Luncheon Escort**
    Escort will explain location of employee lounge and other facilities (show employee)

FIRST DAY

_____ **1. Review the Job**
    a. Confidential aspects
    b. Stimulate job enthusiasm and satisfaction in a job well done
    c. Explain work in other sections (give copy of job description and organization manual)
      1. The way work originates
      2. Where it goes
      3. Relation of the job to other jobs in section
      4. Relation of the section to division
      5. Relation of the division to company
      6. Let employee know you are depending on him or her
      7. Give assurance employee will learn quickly
_____ **2. Explain Hours of Work** (give copy of company personnel manual)
    a. Starting and quitting time
    b. Hours per week
    c. Break periods
    d. Lunch period
_____ **3. Review Compensation**
    a. Amount
    b. When paid
    c. Cost of living allowance
    d. Mention deductions
      1. Income taxes (federal and state)
      2. Social security taxes
      3. Retirement (if applicable)
    e. If applicable, review company's retirement plan (give copy of retirement plan)
    f. Emphasize value of employee benefits paid by company
    g. Salaries must be kept confidential
    h. Explain thoroughly the electronic transfer of employee's net pay
    i. Right reserved to deduct for absence

Check when completed

_____ **4. Discuss Attendance Requirements and Records**
    a. Filling out time card (show card and demonstrate)
    b. Method of reporting tardiness (stress honor system)
    c. How and to whom absence is reported
    d. Stress punctuality
    e. Explain effect of good attendance and punctuality on employee's record
_____ **5. Has the Employee Any Questions?** (ask)
_____ **6. Explain Orientation Quiz**
    Voluntary; will be given if employee chooses at end of first 10 days
_____ **7. Introduce to Immediate Associates**
    In department and supervisors and others in related departments
_____ **8. Introduce to Workplace**
    a. Workplace to be in order as employee is expected to keep it
    b. Stress good housekeeping
_____ **9. Have Chair Adjusted**
_____ **10. Give Job Instruction** (use job breakdowns or manuals if available; have a trainer well prepared and temperamentally suited to teach)
    a. Prepare
    b. Tell
    c. Show
    d. Practice
    e. Check
    f. Explain what to do about any idle time
      1. Report to supervisor for more work
      2. Emphasize this is not a reflection on employee but responsibility of management
_____ **11. Discuss Work Instructions**
    a. Majority will come from supervisor
    b. Occasionally from department head
    c. Question any orders received from fellow workers—check with supervisor
    d. Stress that all instructions should be clearly understood
_____ **12. Explain Learning Aids**
    a. Examples of work (show employee)
    b. Job instruction breakdown, if available
    c. Special terms used, including abbreviations
_____ **13. Encourage Employee to Ask Questions**
    a. They aid in learning
    b. They help develop judgment
_____ **14. Explain Where to Store Work Overnight** (show)

Figure 6–5
Orientation
Checklist
(page 2)

SECOND DAY

Check when
completed

_____ 1. **Explain Performance Review** (show the form and illustrate with examples)
   a. Important to employee
   b. Raises depend upon work, attitude, length of service

_____ 2. **Explain Quality and Quantity of Work**
   a. Production standards, if any
   b. Importance of accuracy
   c. Quality before quantity
   d. Speed will come with experience

THIRD DAY

_____ 1. **Explain Telephone Technique if Employee Conducts Company Business on Telephone** (give copy of telephone company booklet)
   a. Speak clearly
   b. Give your name when answering
   c. Take messages in writing for those not present
   d. Deliver messages before you forget
   e. Find numbers in company directory

_____ 2. **Give Reasons for Rules, Policies, and Plans**
   a. To make cooperation easier
   b. To result in greater efficiency
   c. To avoid duplication of effort

_____ 3. **Explain Voluntary Disability Plan and Company's Group Insurance Plan** (give copy, if not already included in company manual)
   Sign up employee for group insurance

_____ 4. **Has Employee Any Questions?** (ask)

FOURTH DAY

_____ 1. **Give Employee Opportunity to Say How He or She Is Getting Along**

_____ 2. **Explain Use of Medical Facilities**

_____ 3. **Discuss Suggestion System** (show current scoreboard on bulletin board)
   a. How it encourages initiative and ideas
   b. How awards are made
   c. How to submit
   d. Should be well thought-out ideas
   e. Must sign suggestion form
   f. All suggestions are thoroughly considered

_____ 4. **Explain Messenger Service**
   a. Messengers work on regular schedule (show message carrier envelope and illustrate how to fill out)
   b. Don't expect special service
   c. Don't make a messenger of yourself

FIFTH DAY

_____ 1. **Discuss Personal Telephone Calls**
   a. Can be made during working hours if urgent
   b. Incoming calls only when urgent

_____ 2. **Explain Policy on Donations**
   a. No solicitors allowed in building
   b. Start no subscriptions for company without approval

_____ 3. **Discuss Departmental Policies that Are in Addition to (But Not in Conflict with) Overall Company Policy**

_____ 4. **Has the Employee Any Questions** (ask)

SIXTH DAY

Check when
completed

_____ 1. **Explain How to Get Additional Supplies**
   a. On requisition, on approval of department head
   b. Don't visit supply department
   c. Explain conservation of supplies

_____ 2. **Discuss Personal Mail**
   a. Best to have sent to home
   b. Deposit outgoing letter in box outside building (or in lobby)
   c. Company does not pay postage
   d. Can get stamps from cashier
   e. Do not write personal letters on company time

SEVENTH DAY

_____ 1. **Explain Change of Address**
   a. Company must have complete record
   b. Notify personnel department of changes
   c. Same for telephone number

_____ 2. **Explain Company Educational Program** (give copy of plan)

_____ 3. **Explain Company Security System**

EIGHTH DAY

_____ 1. **Explain the Employee's Association**
   a. Membership advantages
   b. Dues
   c. How collected

_____ 2. **Explain Company Library**
   a. Free to use it
   b. Where located

_____ 3. **Describe Company Magazine** (give copy of latest issue)

NINTH DAY

_____ 1. **Describe Vacation Plan** (show copy of schedules)
   a. Explain vacation system
   b. How length of vacation is determined
   c. The part seniority plays
   d. The part convenience to section plays
   e. Time selected must be approved by department head
   f. Subject to change for good of company

_____ 2. **Explain Company's Bulletin Boards**
   a. Do not post anything without approval
   b. Watch for current announcements

TENTH DAY

_____ 1. **Explain that Patience and Understanding are Important Qualities to Develop** (give examples)
   Employee will work with all types of persons as to age, training, education, experience, background

_____ 2. **Encourage Employee to Talk Things Over with Immediate Supervisor**

_____ 3. **Department Manager is Glad to Talk Things Over When Necessary with Knowledge of Immediate Supervisor**

_____ 4. **Administer Orientation Quiz** (get written answers)

_____ 5. **Review Employee's Public Relations Influence**

ELEVENTH DAY

_____ 1. **Review Quiz Results**

Employee's Orientation Completed: . . . .
Department Manager Signature

Instructions: Upon completion of this checklist, return it to personnel department for inclusion in employee's personnel file.

the act affects the hiring practices not only of business firms but also of unions and employment agencies and defines certain actions (or inactions) as unlawful employment practices. For the purposes of the **Civil Rights Act**, as amended in 1972, an employer is defined as a person who is engaged in an industry that affects interstate commerce and who has 15 or more workers. With the passage of the **Equal Employment Opportunity Act of 1972**, state and local governments became subject to the provisions against employment discrimination contained in the Civil Rights Act. The 1972 act also obligated the federal government to undertake all of its employment practices without discrimination.

As a result of the Civil Rights Act and its amendments and executive orders, if you, as an employer, refuse to hire job applicants because of their race, color, religion, national origin, or sex, your action is looked upon as an unlawful employment practice. It is also unlawful for you to discharge individuals or discriminate against them with respect to their compensation or any terms, conditions, or privileges of employment because of their race, color, religion, nationality, or sex. Further, you are prohibited from segregating or classifying employees for the reasons given above if doing so deprives them of employment opportunities or adversely affects their status as employees.

Bona Fide Occupational Qualifications

Employers are still permitted to hire and train persons on the basis of their race, religion, or sex when these are **bona fide occupational qualifications (BFOQ)** necessary to the normal operations of the business. Thus, if it can be shown that the sex of applicants for a job, such as modeling men's swimwear, would prevent them from performing successfully on the job (a BFOQ), this qualification may be used as a basis for recruiting job applicants. Also, for reasons of national or state security, information

about the applicant's national origin and creed may be a BFOQ. However, the task of demonstrating that a discriminatory requirement constitutes a BFOQ rests with the employer.

Employers may not place help-wanted advertisements that specify any preference, limitation, specification, or discrimination based on sex unless sex is a BFOQ. This provision has been interpreted to mean that the content of classified ads must be free of such preferences. For example, an ad stating, "WANTED: Young, attractive woman to be secretary to young male executive" directly violates Title VII. Also, the placement of ads in separate male and female columns is in violation of Title VII when sex is not an occupational qualification for the advertised job.

Employers may continue to apply different standards of compensation or different terms and conditions of employment provided such differences are not the result of an intention to discriminate on account of race, color, religion, national origin, or sex. Therefore, employers may set their hiring and work standards as high as they please, but they may not enforce them in a discriminatory manner.

Pregnancy Discrimination Act of 1978

The **Pregnancy Discrimination Act of 1978**, an amendment to the Civil Rights Act, makes it unlawful for an employer to fire or refuse to hire a woman because she is pregnant. Employers may not force the female employee to leave work at an arbitrarily established time if she is still willing and able to work. Further, all health care and disability benefits provided by the employer must be the same for pregnant employees as for sick or disabled employees. Employers are given the option of excluding from the benefits program any coverage for nontherapeutic abortions. However, if employers elect to exclude this condition, they are still required to furnish benefits for medical complications

The Pregnancy Discrimination Act protects the increasing number of mothers who elect to remain in the work force during pregnancy.

due to abortion, provided that medical benefits are also extended to other employees for non-job-related disabilities.

Equal Employment Opportunity Commission

Under the Civil Rights Act, the **Equal Employment Opportunity Commission (EEOC)** was created to enforce the law. The EEOC tries to obtain voluntary compliance with the law before a court action for an injunction is filed. The Commission may seek a temporary restraining order or other preliminary relief when a preliminary investigation determines that prompt action is needed to carry out the purposes of the act. If the Commission cannot reach an acceptable agreement with the party within 30 days, the Commission can file suit in a federal district court. However, where a state or local law forbids discriminatory practices, relief must first be sought under the state or local law before a complaint is filed with the Commission.

The EEOC may also institute court proceedings for an injunction if there is reason to believe that any person or group of persons is not complying with the law. The court may find that employers have intentionally engaged in an unlawful employment practice. In such cases, the court can order the employers to stop such practices, to reinstate employees, to pay back wages, and to take other appropriate action to eliminate existing discrimination and prevent its recurrence.

Affirmative Action and Executive Orders

Employers not subject to Title VII coverage discussed above may come within the scope of the Civil Rights Act by reason of a contract or subcontract involving federal funds. In a series of executive orders, the federal government has banned, in employment on government contracts, discrimination that is based on race, color, religion, national origin, or sex. More significantly, these orders have been held to require that contractors take affirmative action to ensure equal opportunity.

Affirmative Action

The concept of affirmative action was developed to clarify in a concrete, positive way what firms seeking to conduct business with the federal government must do to be equal opportunity employers. An **affirmative action plan** is a program designed to eliminate, limit, or prevent discriminatory treatment on the basis of race, ethnic group, and sex. Some plans are required by law, while others are developed voluntarily. Often the affirmative action plan is designed to remedy the effects of past discrimination and prevent its recurrence. Usually the plan involves an analysis of the use of the work force; the establishment of attainable results-oriented goals and timetables for recruiting, hiring, training, and promoting any under-represented classes; an explanation of the methods to be used to eliminate discrimination; and the establishment of responsibility for implementing the program.

Executive Orders

By means of **executive orders**, the executive branch of the federal government strives to require equal employment opportunities in firms doing business with the government. Executive Order 11246, the most significant of the presidential directives, requires equal employment opportunity and affirmative action by contractors and subcontractors having contracts with the federal government. Each contract amounting to $10,000 or more must contain an equal employment opportunity clause that is binding on the contractor or subcontractor for the life of the contract. The Office of Federal Contract Compliance Programs (OFCCP) of the U.S. Department of Labor is responsible for coordinating and overseeing the contract compliance program.

Nonconstruction contractors and subcontractors who have at least 50 employees and a contract exceeding $50,000 must establish affirmative action plans. The plans must include goals and timetables for the increased use of minority persons and women.

Other executive orders deal with age discrimination in the performance of federal government contracts, the offering of work to business enterprises owned by racial minority persons, and the creation of a national policy and program for women's business enterprises.

State and Local Fair Employment Practices Laws

The fair employment practices laws enacted by the states do not replace Title VII of the Civil Rights Act since the purpose of the federal law was to encourage the states to adopt such laws. Generally the state fair employment practices laws are aimed at employers, employment agencies, and unions. Employers are forbidden to discriminate in their hiring and firing practices, and unions and employment agencies are forbidden to aid or cause such discriminations.

Cities, too, have enacted ordinances that prohibit discriminatory practices in the employment process. One of the most comprehensive and enlightened laws of its kind is the Human Rights Law of the District of Columbia. This law covers discrimination by reason of race, color, religion, national origin, sex, age, marital status, personal appearance, sexual orientation, family responsibilities, physical handicap, matriculation (formal education completed), and political affiliation.

Age Discrimination in Employment Act of 1967

The purpose of the **Age Discrimination in Employment Act of 1967**, as amended, is to promote the employment of older persons based on ability rather than age, to prohibit arbitrary age discrimination in employment, and to help employers and workers find ways

Age discrimination is illegal, and it deprives employers of the talents and experiences of older workers.

of meeting problems arising from the impact of age on employment. The act covers employees of private business as well as federal, state, and local government employees other than elected officials and certain aides not covered by Civil Service.

The law, as amended, prohibits age discrimination by employers, employment agencies, and labor unions (those engaged in an industry affecting interstate commerce) against those individuals who are over the age of 40. Employees may not be forced to retire if they are otherwise capable of performing the duties of their jobs. However, exceptions are allowed for highly paid executive and top policy makers who would receive at least $44,000 in retirement benefits each year. Federal employees are permitted to work as long as they wish.

Under the law, as an employer of 20 or more persons, you are forbidden to discharge or refuse to hire any individual or to otherwise discriminate against any individual with respect to compensation, terms, conditions, or privileges of employment because the individual is over 40 years of age. You are also barred from using age as a basis for limiting, segregating, or classifying employees in any way that tends to deprive them of employment opportunities or otherwise affects their status as employees in a negative way.

Many businesses fail to make use of the talent available through older workers. Many older persons find themselves in positions to take seasonal and part-time work, and OMs should consider this source of labor when filling these jobs as well as those requiring full-time employees.

Vocational Rehabilitation Act of 1973

The **Vocational Rehabilitation Act of 1973** is designed to provide employment opportunities for qualified physically and mentally handicapped individuals and to eliminate employment discrimination based on physical or mental handicaps. Employers with federal contracts exceeding $2,500 have a legal duty, as stated in the act, to take affirmative action to provide adequate hiring, placement, and advancement opportunities for physically and mentally handicapped employees and applicants.

State laws and local ordinances have also been enacted to prohibit discrimination against the handicapped in employment. Nearly all employers are covered under these regulations.

Vietnam Era Veterans' Readjustment Assistance Act of 1974

Under the provisions of the **Vietnam Era Veterans' Readjustment Assistance Act of 1974**, employers with a federal government contract of $10,000 or more are required to take affirmative action to employ and advance in employment qualified veterans of the Vietnam era and disabled veterans of all wars. Employers are also required to list suitable employment openings with the appropriate local employment service, which will then give referral priority to veterans.

Immigration Reform and Control Act of 1986

Under the **Immigration Reform and Control Act of 1986**, employers are barred from hiring aliens who are unauthorized to work in the United States. The act requires *all* employers to verify the employment eligibility for all persons newly hired. To do this, the employer must examine the employee's work-eligibility documents (U.S. passport, certificate of naturalization, resident alien card with photo, birth certificate, Social Security card, driver's license, etc.) and complete an employment eligibility verification form to attest that the new employee's documents appear to be genuine.

Wage and Hour Regulations

The wages and salaries paid and the hours worked by office employees are regulated under federal law by a number of statutes. The Fair Labor Standards Act, commonly known as the Federal Wage-Hour Law, has broadest application for the AOM. The major provisions of this law concern minimum wages, overtime pay, restrictions upon the employment of children, and record-keeping requirements. Under the Equal Pay Act of 1963, an amendment to the Fair Labor Standards Act, an employer is forbidden to discriminate solely on the basis of sex in setting wage rates for men and women doing equal work under similar working conditions. These regulations, and others affecting the compensation practices of office managers, are discussed in detail in Chapter 10.

SUMMARY

1. In obtaining qualified office workers, AOMs select from the sources that will best meet the needs of their firms. Among those sources are public employment services, private employment agencies, temporary office help services, newspaper advertising, employee referrals, and on-campus recruitment.

2. As a result of federal, state, and local legislation that affects each phase of the employment process, the AOM must plan a definite procedure for selecting office workers. In this procedure, forms such as the personnel requisition, application, record of interview, and record of employment must be carefully worded to elicit the required employment information but at the same time not violate any legislation or guidelines that prohibit obtaining non-job-related information.

3. Valid and reliable preemployment tests and screening techniques, when properly used as part of the recruitment procedure, are an effective safeguard against unfair discrimination and aid the AOM in placing qualified personnel in jobs for which they are suited.

4. Through subordinates, especially first-line supervisors, the AOM is responsible for an orientation procedure that effectively introduces new office workers to their jobs. An orientation checklist is an aid in this procedure.

5. The AOM must ensure that each phase of the employee recruitment procedure complies with relevant laws, guidelines issued by enforcement agencies, and court decisions. To do so, the AOM must have a working knowledge of those regulations that affect each phase of the employment process from initial recruitment to retirement planning.

GLOSSARY

Achievement test—an employment test that measures the degree of proficiency in a given type of work.

Affirmative action plan—a program designed to eliminate, limit, or prevent discriminatory treatment on the basis of race, ethnic group, and sex.

Age Discrimination in Employment Act of 1967—a federal law that prohibits age discrimination against persons over the age of 40.

Application form—a personnel form on which the job applicant provides personal information, educational background, past experience, and references.

Aptitude test—an employment test that attempts to measure the ability to perform a particular kind of task and to predict future performance on the job or in training.

Bona fide occupational qualification (BFOQ)—a job qualification, such as race, sex, or religion, that in good faith is a job-related requirement necessary to the normal operations of the business.

Civil Rights Act of 1964—the federal law containing Title VII, "Equal Employment Opportunity," which, as amended, defines certain actions or inactions as unlawful employment practices as a result of discrimination on the basis of race, color, religion, national origin, or sex.

Direct interview—an interviewing technique in which job applicants are asked direct questions related to their qualifications and ability to fill the job.

Employee handbook—a communication medium that provides employees with essential information such as history of the firm, employment regulations and procedures, employee benefits, and employer-provided services.

Employee leasing service—an organization that assigns workers to client firms under contract to provide on-the-job services, usually on a permanent basis.

Employee Polygraph Protection Act of 1988—a federal law that bars private employers from requiring that most job applicants and current employees be given polygraph (lie detector) tests.

Equal Employment Opportunity—Title VII of the Civil Rights Act that affects the hiring practices of business firms, unions, and employment agencies and defines certain actions (or inactions) as unlawful employment practices.

Equal Employment Opportunity Act of 1972—a federal law that subjects state and local governments to provisions against employment discrimination contained in the Civil Rights Act.

Equal Employment Opportunity Commission (EEOC)—the regulatory body created by the Civil Rights Act to enforce the law.

Executive orders—the presidential directives that strive to require equal employment opportunities in firms doing business with the government.

Fair Credit Reporting Act of 1968—a federal law that governs the use of credit and investigative agencies that supply information about a person's character, general reputation, and mode of living.

Griggs v Duke Power—a U.S. Supreme Court case declaring that tests violate the law if they tend to exclude applicant groups artificially because of race or other factors and cannot be shown to bear a predictive relationship to job performance.

Immigration Reform and Control Act of 1986—a federal law that bars employers from hiring aliens who are unauthorized to work in the United States.

Indirect interview—an interviewing technique in which job applicants are stimulated to talk about themselves through the use of open-end questions.

Intelligence test—an employment test that measures mental and reasoning ability.

Interest test—an employment test, similar to an inventory of a person's likes and dislikes, that is generally used for career counseling.

Orientation—a carefully planned, systematic, and effective program that introduces new workers to their jobs so they may start working with a minimum of delay, misunderstanding, and error.

Orientation checklist—a tool of orientation containing items to be covered by the person who is introducing new employees to their firm and their jobs.

Patterned interview—an interviewing technique in which a standard printed form or questionnaire containing specific key questions is used by an interviewer to record the job applicants' responses.

Personality and psychological tests—employment tests designed to measure abstract concepts, such as aggressiveness, honesty, independence, conformity, and passivity.

Personnel requisition—a personnel form, originating in the department needing workers, that specifies the number of persons required and the kind of work to be done.

Pregnancy Discrimination Act of 1978—an amendment to the Civil Rights Act that states it is unlawful for employers to fire or refuse to hire a woman because she is pregnant.

Privacy Act of 1974—a federal law regulating the collection and use of personal data by the government.

Private employment agency—also known as a *placement firm*, a source of labor supply that charges a fee to either the job applicant or the employer.

Public employment service—a source of labor supply at the state level affiliated with the Department of Labor. No fee is charged to the job seeker or the employer. Also known as *Job Service*.

Record of employment—the personal resumé and history of applicant's employment with the firm.

Record of interview—a personnel form containing all the information acquired during the interview.

Referrals—a source of labor supply originating with present employees, company

officers, or customers who recommend a person for employment.

Reliability—the extent to which a test measures consistently whatever it measures; that is, the same general score can be expected if the test is given to the same person more than once.

Sponsor system—an orientation technique in which a new employee is assigned to a worker (the sponsor) who takes care of the new employee, acquaints him or her with the duties of the job, and answers questions.

Temporary office help service—a source of labor supply that provides temporary workers for varying time periods, with a flat fee being charged the employer.

Test—any paper and pencil or performance measure used as a basis for any employment decision.

Uniform Guidelines on Employee Selection Procedures—the regulations applying to all aspects of the employee selection procedure used in making employment decisions to make sure that Equal Employment Opportunity laws are not violated.

Validity—the extent to which a test serves the purpose for which it was intended.

Vietnam Era Veterans' Readjustment Assistance Act of 1974—a federal law requiring employers with government contracts of $10,000 or more to take affirmative action to employ and to advance in employment qualified veterans.

Vocational Rehabilitation Act of 1973—a federal law designed to provide employment opportunities for qualified physically and mentally handicapped individuals and to eliminate employment discrimination based on such handicaps.

FOR YOUR REVIEW

1. What are some of the services that Job Service offers administrative office managers who are recruiting office personnel?

2. What steps should the administrative office manager take to make sure that the private employment agency selected is professionally qualified?

3. In what ways does the use of temporary office workers bring about significant savings for employers?

4. In what ways may a small business benefit by obtaining its employees from an employee leasing service?

5. Briefly describe the main types of employment forms used in most large companies.

6. Why must special care be taken by employers in designing their application forms?

7. What are the advantages and disadvantages of using the direct interview when compared with the indirect interview?

8. Why do many managers place relatively little confidence in reference checks and letters of recommendation?

9. What two basic principles should guide the administrative office manager in using tests as an aid in selecting office workers?

10. Describe the major kinds of preemployment tests and state for what purpose each type is designed.

11. Distinguish between these two factors: test reliability and test validity.

12. What legal guidelines are available to employers who wish to test or screen job applicants for drug and alcohol abuse?

13. Explain how an orientation checklist is used in an orientation program.

14. What are the typical duties assigned a sponsor in the sponsor system of orienting new office workers?

15. What provision in the Civil Rights Act of 1964, as amended, has the most significance for the administrative office manager?

16. When may an employer hire a person on the basis of religion?

17. For what purposes does a company undertake the development of an affirmative action plan?

18. What are the major provisions of the Age Discrimination in Employment Act?

19. What protection is provided by law to prevent discrimination in the employment of the physically and mentally handicapped? of Vietnam era veterans?

FOR YOUR DISCUSSION

1. Consult your state's human relations commission, fair employment practices agency, or comparable organization to determine which of the following questions may legally be used on the application form:
   a. How long have you been a resident of this state?

    b. What is the birthplace of your parents?

    c. Have you ever been convicted of any crime?

    d. Do you regularly attend a house of worship?

    e. Is your spouse a naturalized or native-born citizen of the United States?

    f. How did you learn to speak and read Russian?

    g. May I have your photograph so I can attach it to your application?

    h. Who suggested that you apply for a position here?

2. During her interview Maria Jacobs, mother of two preschool children, was asked the following questions: Who would take care of your children when you're at work? What would happen if your children got sick? How does your husband feel about your taking business trips? Would your husband object to a male employee accompanying you on a business trip?

   How should Jacobs reply to each question? Is the interviewer on firm legal ground in requesting this information? Explain.

3. Before anyone is hired at the Webster Company, the human resources department has a handwriting analyst examine the job seeker's writing in order to develop a personality profile. Do you believe that handwriting analysis (graphology) is an indicator of personality? Can graphology be used to screen persons who have a drug or alcohol problem? What evidence can you offer to defend the validity of handwriting analysis?

4. Most people agree that good looks influence the choice of one's friends and mate. Do you believe that good looks affect the chances of a job applicant in obtaining an office position? As an interviewer, would you be swayed by the attractive appearance (or lack of attractive appearance) of an applicant when you make your hiring decision? Explain.

5. Jeff Kronski has just completed reproducing his two-page personal data sheet, which he plans to mail to several companies that have advertised job openings in the daily newspaper. After you read over Kronski's resumé, you ask, "Where is your cover letter?" Kronski replies that he does not plan to write a cover letter or letter of transmittal, because he would repeat in such a letter the personal data contained in his resumé. What suggestions have you for Kronski about the need for a cover letter? What are your recommendations for the contents of a cover letter?

6. As office manager of Excelsior Products, Inc., you plan to investigate whether employee leasing would be cost effective for your company. What factors should you consider as you weigh the pros and cons of employee leasing?

7. In a desperate moment three years ago, you misrepresented your educational background when you completed the application form at your present place of employment. Ever since, that little lie has been like a time bomb ticking away in your personnel file. Tomorrow you face an employee appraisal and a review of your qualifications for promotion. Today you are in a quandary. What should you do? Ask for your personnel file and delete the "padded" degree? Live with the lie and keep your mouth shut? Or what?

8. Friday afternoon Helen Powers, office supervisor of the Jackson Tire Company, called a local temporary help service and requested a payroll clerk for several days' work during the end-of-the-year rush. Monday morning Bob Kryder reported for work. After two days, Powers found that Kryder was a highly competent worker, got along well with his department head and co-workers, and took on responsibility as if he had been with

the firm for years and expected to be there for years to come. Toward the end of Kryder's first week a permanent vacancy occurred in the accounting department and Powers approached Kryder with a full-time job offer. She was pleased to find that Kryder liked the company and would like to become a full-time employee.

Was Powers unethical in approaching Kryder with an offer of full-time employment? What steps should Powers now take to obtain the services of Kryder on a full-time basis? What are the ethics and business practices involved in hiring a temporary worker on a permanent basis?

SOLVING CASE PROBLEMS

Case 6-1 Interviewing an Applicant Who Has the AIDS Virus

Two months ago Clint Hastings resigned his position as manager of office services for a leading advertising agency and since then has been searching for a new post. Just yesterday Hastings learned the results of a blood test he had undergone recently—AIDS positive.

Hastings is now seated before you, vice-president, administrative services, Hudson Manufacturing Company, in his first interview for the position of manager, office operations. As you learn more about Hastings and his qualifications, and begin to explore his reasons for leaving his former job, you are jolted when he interrupts to say:

> I want to be up front with you before we go any further in our talks. I just got the results
> of a blood test which confirms that I am infected with the AIDS virus.

1. Now that Hastings' disability has been put squarely "on the table," how will you proceed during the remainder of the interview?

2. Can your firm legally refuse to employ Hastings in view of his announced disability? Explain.

Case 6-2 Comparing Costs of Temporary Employees and Permanent Employees

As Sharon Madsen, supervisor of the word processing center, was scanning one of the journals she received in the morning's mail, her attention was drawn to an article dealing with the use of temporary office help. Two statements in particular attracted her attention as she began to think about the need to increase her staff in the center. One sentence indicated that generally a temporary worker is found to be less expensive than a permanent staffer when the costs of recruiting, training, insurance, vacation pay, and other company benefits for the full-time worker are added to the base salary. A second statement noted that studies had been conducted in which it was found that a $300-per-week employee may actually cost a company $425 each week when these factors are considered.

Madsen turns to you, her assistant, and asks you to undertake a cost study to find out if it really is less costly to employ temporary workers rather than add permanent workers to the payroll. For each word processing operator that Madsen needs in the center, the temporary help service has quoted a weekly fee of $365.

From Madsen and your firm's payroll department, you have obtained the following costs, which would be incurred if your company were to add new, permanent employees:

Weekly base salary, $260
FICA (7.65%)
Federal (.8%) and state (4.5%) unemployment insurance on the first $7,000 of salary paid
Disability insurance (.5%) and workers' compensation (.81%)
Vacations, holidays, sick time (10.7%)
Health insurance, pension plan, profit sharing, bonuses, incentives (15.8%)
Recruiting, hiring, record keeping, payroll costs, administrative paperwork (7.7%)

Prepare a report for Madsen in which you show:

1. A comparison of the costs of employing four temporary office workers and four new, permanent workers. The annual savings for your recommended source of office workers should be clearly set forth.

2. A list of intangible factors (those that cannot be equated to the dollar sign) to be considered when recruiting office workers under each of the two plans.

7

Supervising the Office Staff

GOALS FOR THIS CHAPTER

After completing this chapter, you should be able to:

1. Give examples of the office supervisor's responsibilities in the business organization.
2. Describe how discipline, counseling, and career goal planning are used by office supervisors in their human approach to supervision.
3. Explain the several theories of motivation and show how each helps office supervisors to understand better what motivates human behavior.
4. Explain how the ethics and value systems of office workers relate to effective supervision.

The organizational culture that is emerging in the Information Age as the result of automating office operations is challenging office supervisors to develop new skills and abilities. For example, we saw in Chapter 2 that one of the major changes is a flattening out of the classic pyramid-like organization structure, with more decision making being conducted at the supervisory or operating management level. This means that the people who can manage information most effectively are making more key decisions and judgments about administrative services and other internal operations such as marketing, shipping, and accounting. Thus, more power and authority are flowing downward from the top level of the organization to the supervisory level. In adapting to such changes, today's office supervisors strive to become proficient in using office technology and in achieving excellence as they accept new responsibilities for managing their human resources.

Up to this point in the text, we have been concerned mostly with *managers*, those members of an organization who plan, organize, lead, and control the work of others. As we saw in Figure 1–1 on page 4, managers at the top level of the organization include those commonly referred to as *executives* and *corporate officers*. Immediately below this level are the *middle managers*, such as the office manager, sales manager, and human resources manager. At the lowest level, we find the *first-line managers*, or *supervisors*, as they are usually called. These are the persons who directly supervise the *nonmanagement* employees in the organization. Although every person who has managerial responsibilities can be looked upon as a supervisor, the term *supervisor* is generally applied to the first level of managerial responsibility. It is from this point of view that we shall study the role of office supervisors in this chapter.

THE SUPERVISION PROCESS

As you examine the process of supervision, you can see how each of the managerial functions is carried out. Office supervisors *plan* and *organize* their work experiences to meet their firms' needs for effective and efficient operations and their employees' needs for job satisfaction. To meet both kinds of needs, an organization must be created in which employees make major contributions to the organization's goals and at the same time attain their own personal objectives.

Supervision also involves **leading**, which is concerned with motivating the workers so that the objectives of the organization will be attained. In exercising the leadership function, supervisors place special emphasis on the human resources, for it is only through people that things happen. Office supervisors find that optimum productivity is obtained when they plan and organize their information activities around the needs and talents of their workers. Supervisors find, too, that productivity is improved when the workers are led, not pushed, into doing their best. To attain the goals that have been jointly established by the office supervisor and the workers, the supervisor must create an environment in which the workers can grow both personally and professionally.

Finally, supervision involves *control*—obtaining *actual* performance that matches as closely as possible the *desired* performance. The practical aspects of supervising involve the performance of a certain job by the *best method* and by the *best person* in order to obtain the *best results*. A well-trained office supervisor is therefore needed to assure the accomplishment of these three aspects of carrying out a job.

The Responsibilities of Office Supervision

In the small office, we usually find that an office manager directs all the information-processing activities. As the office work and the staff expand, a centralized department for word processing may be developed under a trained supervisor. Further expansion may require the appointment of supervisors for centralized departments such as records management, computer operations, mailing services, and reprographics. Whatever the organization or the number of supervisors, the jobs of office supervision are essentially the same. The jobs require working with human beings—superiors, peers, and subordinates—to develop and carry out the plans of office work, to establish systems and procedures that include the measurement of the work, and to improve the work systems wherever possible.

All supervisory positions involve responsibility, which flows in several directions—*upward* to higher management, *horizontally* to peers (supervisors of equal rank), and *downward* to subordinates. Other responsibilities include *coordinating* the office work to be done and *self-development* as the supervisor prepares for growth and promotion in the business organization. An outline of each of the office supervisor's key responsibilities and its direction is provided in Figure 7-1.

To carry out each of these responsibilities effectively, office supervisors must first be able to manage their own time. Many office supervisors spend the bulk of their time on projects that produce few benefits. In order to get the most benefit out of their working hours, these supervisors must realize that they probably cause most of their own time problems. Thus, the need emerges for office supervisors to undertake a program of **time management**, as described in a later chapter. In such a program, all resources, including time, are efficiently used so the supervisors may achieve their important professional and personal goals.

Figure 7-1

The Office Supervisor's Responsibilities (page 1)

SUPERVISOR'S RESPONSIBILITIES TO OTHERS IN THE BUSINESS ORGANIZATION

Upward responsibilities to higher management:

1. Ascertaining and carrying out what management wants done.
2. Keeping superiors informed of what is being done in the department and passing along ideas for improvement.
3. Accepting full responsibility and accountability for the work in the department without "passing the buck."
4. Referring matters requiring superior's attention promptly without bothering superiors unnecessarily.
5. Interpreting the employees' needs to management, and vice versa.

Horizontal responsibilities to peers (supervisors of equal rank):

1. Cooperating with peers in the same manner that subordinates are expected to cooperate with each other.
2. Helping coordinate the work of the department with that of other supervisors for the good of the firm.
3. Permitting interchange and promotion of good workers among departments.

Downward responsibilities to subordinates:

1. Aiding in selecting, orienting, and training new workers.
2. Motivating subordinates to assume greater responsibilities.
3. Assisting employees to know what to do and how to do it and checking the results.
4. Evaluating employees periodically and recommending promotions, salary adjustments, transfers, and dismissals.
5. Delegating authority and responsibility in order to develop understudies.
6. Developing harmony, cooperation, and teamwork.
7. Building and maintaining employee morale and handling grievances promptly and fairly.
8. Maintaining discipline and controlling absenteeism and tardiness.
9. Taking a personal interest in subordinates without showing partiality.
10. Using courtesy, tact, and consideration in treating subordinates as human beings.

Figure 7-1
The Office
Supervisor's
Responsi-
bilities
(page 2)

Responsibilities for **coordinating** the office work:
1. Planning the systems, procedures, and methods.
2. Distributing the work load fairly.
3. Coordinating the work of different units if this is necessary.
4. Seeing that the work is done correctly and on time.
5. Anticipating difficulties and peak loads in the work.
6. Maintaining the quality of the work to be done by setting standards.
7. Studying, developing, and using new methods and equipment to reduce and control costs.
8. Training understudies so that absences, overload, and other interferences with the amount and the flow of work may be handled efficiently.

Responsibilities for **self-development**:
1. Constantly analyzing and attempting to improve personality traits, such as self-control, analytical ability, personal appearance, ability to instill confidence within subordinates and others, initiative, punctuality, courtesy, leadership, and fair play.
2. Studying the organization and personnel of the entire firm to develop the maximum departmental cooperation, train understudies, and study the requirements for the next supervisory job in the line of promotion.
3. Assuming membership and actively participating in professional organizations.
4. Studying up-to-date literature that will aid in improving the work in present and future positions.
5. Continuing formal education in the areas that will aid in work performance.
6. Developing an effective time-management program in which all resources, including time, are efficiently used to achieve important professional and personal goals.

The Human Approach in Office Supervision

We do not become supervisors merely because we meet the test of being the best workers and because we know intimately the operations of our departments. Although these requisites are important, as supervisors we must use the *human approach*, which means that we must be specialists in dealing with human resources. In working with people, supervisors are continually being appraised as to their genuine value as leaders. Determining the work to be done and how to do it is the easiest task of supervision because it deals with the *objective*, or *tangible*, phase of the position. Most important, and more difficult, however, is the *subjective*, or *human*, phase of supervision. Herein lies the secret of motivating and leading employees.

Office supervisors must possess certain personal qualities to command the respect and loyalty from workers and to ensure maximum efficiency. Foremost among these attributes listed in Figure 7–2 is the ability to treat subordinates as human beings.

Discipline

The words **discipline** and *disciple* can be traced to the same root, meaning "to teach so as to mold." Many people, however, think of disciplining as reprimanding or punishing rather than teaching or molding. To be effective, however, true discipline should *teach* at the same time it *corrects*. Discipline should be constructive and consistent and should enable employees to learn so their behavior and performance in the future will be changed. Consider the following comments made by two supervisors as they talk to a worker returning from lunch 25 minutes late:

Supervisor A: *(rushing from her desk to confront the tardy employee as he enters the work area)* Tim, you're 25

minutes late! So, you can just make it up after quitting time today.

Supervisor B: *(calling the tardy employee, Tim, into her office)* Tim, what happened today that caused you to be late in returning from lunch? Helen has been waiting for you to get back so you two could process the orders you were pricing. You know, Tim, each of us is needed at our workstation on time each day in order to meet our quotas and earn that bonus! Will you and Helen be able to pick up the slack in the next hour to make up for your tardiness?

It's obvious that Supervisor B is the one who looks upon Tim as a human being and is able to discipline effectively.

Need for Discipline. The need for discipline is closely related to such problems as absenteeism, tardiness, low productivity, and poor quality of output. Behavioral scientists believe that such problems are associated with employees' boredom and disinterest, which result from their abilities not being fully used. These specialists look upon human talent as a valuable resource like any other capital resource such as the building housing the workers. They suggest that when human resources are under-utilized, the end result is costly and inefficient operations. Some behavioral scientists feel that we dedicate ourselves to our work in relation to how well the work meets our needs for satisfaction and self-worth. Thus, if work and the work environment do not support our needs, we hold back on our energies; thus, our lack of action severely reduces the organization's cost effectiveness.

Figure 7-2
A Checklist
of Qualities
That Make
for
Excellence in
Office
Supervision

A Profile of Successful Office Supervisors

Regardless of their age or sex, or the size, location, and structure of their organizations, successful office supervisors possess the following qualities:

1. *Ability to treat subordinates as human beings.* Supervisors strive to be "one of the employees" without sacrificing any dignity of the position. Supervisors cannot be too intimate because with intimacy often comes leniency, and with leniency comes loss of respect and confidence. Similarly, supervisors cannot be cold, aloof, or arrogant. The goal of office supervisors is to be sensitive to the needs of others by achieving a workable blending of human relations skills.

2. *Attitude of leader rather than of boss.* Office supervisors win the utmost cooperation by being willing to coach subordinates and work constructively with them to develop desirable performance levels. Innovation and new ideas are encouraged.

3. *Fairness and open-mindedness.* In all dealings with workers, supervisors are candid, honest, and direct. Supervisors are willing to see both sides of problems and to solve them fairly and reasonably so that no resentment remains in those against whom a decision goes.

4. *Willingness to be available for advice.* Supervisors are available for counseling and are patient and understanding when dealing with workers and their personal problems. Effective supervisors display a high level of integrity and trust that is respected by subordinates.

5. *Dependability in keeping promises and providing support.* Supervisors keep all promises made to workers and support them when dealing with other departments and top management. Supervisors follow up on important issues and provide feedback to subordinates on how they are doing.

6. *Objectivity.* Supervisors are fair and unbiased in their relationships with subordinates. Supervisors avoid playing favorites among employees and also avoid giving the appearance of doing so.

7. *Ability to delegate responsibility and authority effectively.* Supervisors involve subordinates in the establishment of mutually agreed upon goals. Clear direction is provided by stating goals and standards clearly and by delegating responsibility and authority.

Developing a Disciplinary System. Not all violations of office rules and conduct deserve the same treatment. For example, in one company, the office supervisor may orally warn a worker who has been tardy twice during the workweek. However, this same supervisor may recommend the immediate discharge of a worker who is caught trying to sell cocaine to a co-worker.

Therefore, a system of progressive disciplinary actions should be designed so that employees are informed of each kind of misconduct and its penalty. Often the disciplinary actions progress from (1) oral reprimands or warnings to (2) written reprimands to (3) time off without pay to (4) discharge. Since the objective of such actions is to correct behavior and performance, employees should be given a clear statement of their required behavior and the consequences of continued misconduct.

Counseling

In the office, our personal problems often affect our efficiency. Therefore, a supervisor should be available to talk with workers as the need arises or to refer troubled workers to the appropriate person either within or outside the company. Some firms that are unable to support a staff counselor or psychologist maintain contact with an outside professional counselor whose services are called upon as needed. Small firms often pool their resources so they can share the services and the cost of such a consultant.

Many medium-size and large organizations have developed employee assistance programs that specialize in providing aid and counseling. An **employee assistance program (EAP)** provides specially trained persons who diagnose and offer help in solving personal problems that affect employees' job performance and attendance. Employees are aided in solving problems such as alcoholism, family or marital distress, financial troubles,

Employee counseling helps solve employee problems that contribute to poor productivity.

nervous or emotional disorders, poor physical health, drug abuse, and legal matters.[1] In firms having an EAP, supervisors can refer their troubled workers directly to the EAP. Thus, the supervisors are freed from becoming involved in the personal lives of their employees, whose personal problems in turn are handled with the utmost confidentiality and competency by professionally trained counselors.

Office supervisors should note any emotional disturbances among workers in their departments and know how to react. The supervisor should watch for symptoms of emotional difficulties, such as a marked change in a worker's behavior pattern, as when a punctual worker suddenly develops a high tardiness record. A worker who persistently complains of headaches and nausea may be showing signs of psychosomatic illness (physical symptoms with an emotional base). A worker who has a series of minor accidents is probably troubled; for such accidents may often be the result of inattention, and inattention is a sign of preoccupation. A bigger problem then any of these, however, is alcoholism, which may indicate a deeply rooted emotional problem that workers are unable to handle alone. In these cases, the office supervisor is responsible for helping workers recognize their problems and for urging them to seek proper professional help before they are dismissed from the company.[2]

How far supervisors should go in talking with employees about their personal problems or personal relations with co-workers depends upon the perception, sympathy, judgment, training, and counseling experience of the supervisors themselves. In counseling, supervisors should listen sympathetically; only through such listening can

---

[1]For additional information about employee assistance programs, see James T. Wrich, *Guidelines for Developing an Employee Assistance Program* (New York: American Management Association, 1982).

[2]The topic of alcoholism is discussed in further detail in Chapter 12.

they come to understand their workers' problems and learn why these problems are affecting productivity. The supervisor can sometimes help a disturbed worker by granting a leave of absence or suggesting where assistance may be found. But the supervisor should avoid assuming the role of psychologist or human relations counselor in problems unrelated to the job.

When employees seek help, however, on how to improve performance or how to prepare for career advancement, supervisors should freely pass along their opinions and recommendations. Supervisors have a responsibility to provide their workers with guidance not only on how to prepare themselves to meet performance standards but also on how to acquire the skills and knowledge to advance their careers.

Career Goal Planning

Office workers may look to their supervisors for help in formulating clear, practical career goals. Many office workers ask questions about promotional opportunities in the firm, such as, "What are the prospects of my being promoted to department head or supervisor?" "What steps should I now be taking to prepare for the new position?" Although most workers cannot be guaranteed a specific organizational slot in the future, the supervisor, fully supported by top management, can aid workers in planning their career goals. In **career goal planning**, the supervisor works with the employees to assess their personal strengths, weaknesses, preferences, and values; to select and formulate career goals; to develop action plans so the workers can carry out their goals; and to put their action plans to work.

Performance Appraisal

Much of the office supervisor's counseling and career goal planning is concerned with **performance appraisal**, in which the employee's work is evaluated and constructively criticized. In appraising the performance of subordinates, supervisors must measure (1) how well the employees have done the work assigned, (2) how well they can do work that may be more demanding, and (3) to what extent they can be depended upon to carry out directions if no one is available to provide close supervision. Such constructive appraisal of employee performance is a valuable tool that can be used by office supervisors to strengthen the supervisor-subordinate relationship. Employee appraisal is discussed in detail in the following chapter.

MOTIVATING THE OFFICE WORKER

One of the major downward responsibilities of office supervisors is to **motivate**—to create the kind of environment in which workers are enthusiastic and have a desire to work. This is best accomplished by treating workers as human beings, not as machines that can be turned on and off automatically. In addition to possessing desirable personal qualities, supervisors must see that the necessary psychological conditions, as well as material satisfactions, exist in their departments. In this section, we will discuss some of the factors that aid in creating an environment of worker enthusiasm and desire to work. Interwoven throughout the discussion are several theories of motivation that were briefly mentioned in Chapter 1. We shall also examine another theory of motivation, expectancy theory, which, along with the others, guides the office supervisor to an understanding of what motivates human behavior.

Building and Maintaining Morale

Morale refers to our mental and emotional attitudes toward the tasks expected of us by our group and our loyalty to that group. A high level of morale, or *esprit de corps*, exists when we perform our work with a feeling of satisfaction and enjoyment. Such an attitude creates a feeling of enthusiasm and happiness during and after working hours. The desires, interests, and feelings of most human beings are somewhat alike; and when supervisors help to satisfy them for us, our morale is improved. Improved morale results in our doing more and better work and enjoying life at the same time.

Unless a proper level of morale is built up and maintained, growing distrust and dissatisfaction may develop among employees. The company and its interest in its workers must be "sold" to the workers by a sincere and continuous effort that takes into consideration their needs, as illustrated in Figure 7–3. This **hierarchy of needs**, as identified by the psychologist Abraham Maslow, shows that human beings have two sets of needs—primary and secondary.

Primary Needs

Primary needs consist of basic *physiological needs* (food, water, clothing, shelter, rest, air, etc.) and *safety needs* (security, protection against physical and mental dangers and

future deprivation). One thread of continuity tying together both kinds of needs is security, of which job security and personal security are fundamental.

Job Security. As employees, we want to know that our jobs are necessary and permanent and that we will be provided a basic salary with pay increases based on performance, promotional opportunities, and seniority. There should be a degree of permanence in the fundamental company plans with which the employees should be familiar. No changes in these plans should be made without giving the employees advance information and an explanation, especially if the plans may affect their jobs.

One effective means of improving morale and meeting the workers' need for job security is to make the company's intentions clear to the employees and to keep them informed of conditions that affect their firm and their positions in the firm. Small group meetings, bulletin board announcements, manuals, and house organs or company

Figure 7–3
Maslow's
Hierarchy of
Needs

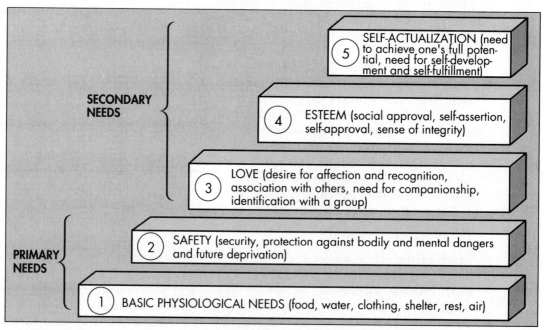

newsletters are effective aids in such a program of communication.

Of prime importance to morale is the existence of fair and uniform wage and salary rates. Workers are interested in their own rates of pay. However, they are also interested in what wages are being received by workers doing similar work in other offices and by employees doing the same kind of work for about the same length of time in their own departments. As discussed later in the text, the pay rates for each job classification should be put into written or printed form so employees know how far they can rise within any given classification. Workers should be told how standards were developed; nothing is so demoralizing to the workers in a department as a belief that pay rates are determined arbitrarily, that employees doing similar work are being paid widely divergent salaries, and that the pay rates are not commensurate with the earnings of the company.

Personal Security. Certain contingencies in life exist for which almost all of us try to prepare. Among these contingencies are our health, employment, retirement, and death. Business firms, either by choice or through the stimulation of union efforts and contracts, try to recognize these contingencies and do what they can to improve their employees' situations. Many firms attempt to meet the safety needs of their workers through employee benefits, such as hospitalization insurance for employees and their families, medical service, life and health insurance, pension plans, unemployment compensation, and guidance and counseling.

Maslow theorized that once the *primary* needs have been well satisfied, they no longer motivate. It is then that the secondary needs stimulate the worker.

Secondary Needs

As you see in Figure 7–3, secondary needs consist of *love* (desire for affection, association with others, need for com-

panionship, identification with a group), *esteem* (social approval, self-assertion, self-approval, and sense of integrity), and *self-actualization* (need to achieve one's full potential and need for self-development and self-fulfillment).

According to Maslow's theory of motivation, one *secondary* need does not have to be completely satisfied before the next need emerges. The needs pattern differs from one office worker to the next, and thus supervisors cannot assume that only one approach can be used to motivate all of their subordinates toward attainment of the firm's objectives.

Love. Here, when we speak of the love and affection need, we are referring to the unselfish loyalty and warm attachment that one person has for another. When our need to feel important and do something worthwhile is recognized and fulfilled, a high level of morale is established. Employees should know and feel the importance of their jobs and their work to the firm. Explaining the "why of the job" and showing employees how their efforts contribute to attainment of the company goals are also helpful in creating a feeling of importance. Recognition should be constantly stressed and, if possible, should be emphasized by developing group projects and teamwork.

Poor supervision can cause us, as employees, to lose our identity and give us a feeling of unimportance. We feel our lack of importance if we are unable to express ourselves in connection with our work. Poor supervision becomes evident when our supervisor criticizes us in front of our co-workers, plays favorites, becomes unfriendly, and shows a lack of understanding of basic human relationships.

Supervisors must recognize their workers' exceptional work and length of service if the love and affection need is to be met. As far as exceptional work is concerned, some companies prefer to pay bonuses established on one of several bases, such as units produced or time saved. Other firms use merit ratings, whereby outstanding performance is rewarded either by a pay increase within a given job classification or by promotion to a higher classification. Other companies favor incentive wage systems, of which there are many basic types and numerous variations, such as piece rates, and base wages plus piece rates.

Length of service is usually recognized by an annual increase in salary, by an annual bonus tied in with the length of employment, or by a combination of the two. Some businesses reward long and faithful service by distributing company stock or by giving employees a share in the profits.

Esteem. This need, which includes both self-esteem and esteem by others, is shown in our desire for achievement and freedom of thought and in our search for status, prestige, and reputation in the eyes of others. Some behavioral scientists feel that management's failure to create jobs that utilize fully the talents and skills of workers often makes work a less satisfying experience than it could otherwise be. As a result, for many persons work becomes a boring time in their lives.

Self-Actualization. The opportunity for self-actualization—the achievement of our full potential—is not only part of our feeling important on the job and in the firm but also part of our personal self-development. In the management theories contributed by behavioral scientists, workers are viewed as having great potential and constantly searching for significant ways to develop themselves. Office workers bring this aspect of themselves to their jobs, and they therefore desire work and work-related experiences that will contribute to meeting this self-actualization need.

Motivation-Maintenance Theory

Money is the oldest motivator, and most companies still rely heavily on salaries and employee benefits as a motivating force. However, some behaviorists compare the giving of more and more money with heroin—it takes more and more to produce less and less effect.

According to the **motivation-maintenance theory** developed by Frederick Herzberg, environmental conditions such as heating, lighting, and ventilation; quality of supervision; and pay are examples of *hygienic (maintenance) factors*. We know that pay is related to productivity, but it is peripheral to the job itself;[3] that is, pay is not an intrinsic part of the job but, instead, is an element that lies outside the work and the workplace. When a hygienic factor, such as pay, is felt by workers to be inadequate, it functions as a *dissatisfier*, which means that it has only the potential to affect performance negatively. When the pay factor is adequate, however, it does not motivate the workers to greater productivity but instead makes it possible for the other set of factors, the *motivators*, to function. Included in the set of motivators are opportunities for workers to say how their jobs are to be done, recognition of the workers and their accomplishments, and a feeling that the workers are using their talents and developing as individuals.

The positive feelings that may be aroused as a result of hygienic work conditions, such as a word of encouragement from the office supervisor or a pay increase, last only a short time. When employees are highly motivated and find their jobs interesting and challenging, they are able to tolerate considerable dissatisfaction with the hygienic factors. Although the hygienic factors cannot be ignored or slighted, a full measure of all of them does not make jobs interesting nor bring about the attainment of the firm's goals. The task of the supervisor is to increase the use of such motivator factors as achievement,

---

[3]See Chapter 1, page 21.

recognition, the work itself, responsibility, and advancement. Thus, we find at the core of Herzberg's theory the concept that the factors which cause employee dissatisfaction are different from those which cause employee satisfaction. Supervisors must therefore work on both sets of factors to avoid discontent and to provide the best conditions for employee motivation.

Job Enrichment

Motivation theory includes the assumption that we want to do a good job, but we need to be challenged. Herzberg believed that if employees are to be motivated, meaningful changes must be made in their jobs. The workers must be given challenging and interesting work through which they can assume responsibility. By means of **job enrichment**, a job is redesigned by building into that job higher-level responsibilities and authorities and more challenging content. This provides the qualified and cooperative individual the opportunity for achievement, recognition, and growth that makes the job a satisfying and a meaningful experience at which the worker is motivated to perform well. The individual's accountability for his or her own work is increased as a complete, natural unit of work is assigned to the employee. The worker is then granted additional authority as new and more difficult tasks are introduced to the job.

For example, let us say that 75 employees are working in the accounting-policyholder services section of an insurance company. In the past, these workers operated in groups to perform three phases of information processing: (1) coding the changes to be made in policy contents, (2) recording the receipt of premium payments, and (3) reviewing the accounts to check upon the accuracy of the recorded information. Each of the three functions was performed in sequence (serially) by different groups of workers. As a result of redesigning the jobs,

the three separate functions were combined into a single job called an "account analyst." Thus, today, instead of performing only one part of the service for a large number of accounts, each analyst is responsible for the entire procedure for a smaller number of accounts. With such a change in procedure, the firm anticipates increased productivity since the delays that occurred as the information-processing work flowed from one workstation to another will be eliminated.

As a result of having altered the work design in order to enrich jobs, companies expect to improve quality, increase productivity, raise levels of job satisfaction, reduce absenteeism and turnover, and possibly reduce the size of the work force. However, opposite results may occur. For example, when more responsibilities are added to a job, the worker may immediately ask for more money. The redesign of several tasks into a new, more complex job may lead to increased requirements for floor space and the duplication of office furniture and equipment. Outside consultants may have to be hired to design and execute the work-related changes. Also, considerable time and money may have to be spent to train the work force to perform the new work satisfactorily. Therefore, firms should weigh the possible benefits to be gained from a job enrichment program against the potential increased costs of (1) wages and salaries, (2) required changes in facilities, (3) implementing the new work design, and (4) training employees to perform the newly expanded jobs.

Delegating

As we saw earlier, **delegating** is the process of entrusting work to others who are qualified to accept responsibility for doing the work. Implied in the process of delegating is the granting of sufficient authority to get the work done and an understanding by all concerned of the results to be accomplished.

Office supervisors have a responsibility to themselves and to their subordinates to delegate effectively the authority and responsibility for the work to be done.

As effective leaders, supervisors plan for more efficient operation of their departments by strengthening the confidence of their subordinates and developing their initiative and capability. Supervisors have a responsibility to their company to inspire their workers to assume new responsibilities and to explore new methods on their own. Supervisors must realize that to a great extent the future of their company lies in the hands of those who report to them. By effectively delegating work, supervisors can help their subordinates prepare for advancement to higher level positions in the firm.

Unfortunately, however, many supervisors are unable to delegate because they do not fully understand their role; or they mistrust their subordinates' abilities to do the job and feel that the work will not be done properly unless they do it themselves. Some supervisors enjoy doing a task so much they are reluctant to let someone else handle it. Supervisors also fail to delegate because of psychological reasons—the fear of competition, the fear of losing credit and recognition, and the fear that their own shortcomings and weaknesses will be exposed. Many times these fears cause poor work, low productivity, and a serious breakdown in morale among the workers in a department.

Similar psychological feelings of insecurity and lack of motivation may account for a subordinate's resistance to accepting more responsibility, as evidenced in Douglas McGregor's views of worker behavior.

Authoritarian vs. Participative Organizations

After studying traditional managers, McGregor concluded that their approaches to managing workers and their work were based on the assumptions labeled Theory X in Figure 7–4. McGregor presented an opposite set of assumptions, labeled Theory Y, as a more realistic assessment of managing workers and their work.

According to the traditional view of supervising workers and of working, **Theory X**, the subordinate is characterized as irresponsible, selfish, and apathetic. Thus, managers and supervisors who evaluate worker behavior from this point of view conclude that restrictive controls are necessary. An example of such restriction is the supervisor who exercises "tight" control over all aspects of employee performance. Those who adhere to Theory X believe in a work-centered organization that relies on the traditional concept of authority—the right to command. Because such organizations are so dependent upon authority, they are often called **authoritarian organizations**.

Theory Y, on the other hand, outlines some critical features of managing workers and human motivation that spring from controlled experiments by highly trained researchers. In essence, this theory points to the fact that we have wants or needs that are never completely fulfilled. The assumptions of Theory Y represent the behaviorist's faith in the capacity and potential of workers. This in turn leads supervisors to create conditions under which all workers have the opportunity to achieve their full potential. Those who adhere to Theory Y emphasize democratic relations in their organizations, which are often called **participative organizations**.

Supervisors must be willing to share their knowledge and experience with their subordinates so that they may more actively participate. In fact, qualified subordinates should be trained to step into their supervisors' jobs as a result of their supervisors having delegated the work. As supervisors free themselves of work through delegation, they become available to assume new, higher-level responsibilities, which may lead to new job opportunities for them.

Figure 7-4
McGregor's
Traditional
and Current
Views of
Worker
Behavior

Theory X The Traditional View of Worker Behavior	Theory Y The Current View of Worker Behavior
1. The average person dislikes work inherently.	1. The average person does not inherently dislike work but, depending on conditions, may find work to be satisfying or punishing.
2. The average person will avoid work if he or she can.	2. People will exercise self-direction and self-control to achieve organizational objectives under certain conditions.
3. Most people must be coerced, controlled, or threatened with punishment to get them to work toward the achievement of organizational goals.	3. People will seek to attain their firm's objectives if there are sufficient rewards provided.
4. The average person prefers to be directed, to avoid responsibility.	4. Under proper conditions, the average individual will seek responsibility.
5. The average individual has relatively little ambition and wants security above all.	5. The capacity to use imagination and originality is widely found in the population.
	6. In our modern society most people do not utilize all their mental potential.

Source: Douglas McGregor, *The Human Side of Enterprise*, reprinted with permission from McGraw-Hill Book Company.

Participative Management

Subordinates who accept responsibilities for the work delegated to them gain practical experience in **participative management**. When this management technique is used, workers are given a voice in determining what they are to do, how they are to do it, and how they are to be appraised. A great motivating force comes into play for those put in charge of a portion of the department's work, given the authority to make decisions that spell success or failure, and then rewarded for what is accomplished. In this way, when subordinates become involved in identifying and solving office problems, more of their personal needs—especially status, recognition, and self-actualization—are being met. Participative management,

therefore, increases employee motivation because workers identify more closely with the company, develop greater team spirit, and, most important, work harder to achieve the goals they have helped to establish. To reflect this spirit of participation, some companies no longer refer to their work force as "employees"; instead, in these firms, we find "partners," "associates," "stakeholders," and "team members."[4]

In their search for ways to improve productivity, companies use a variety of motivational techniques designed to involve their employees. Various formal programs of employee participation are found—from the

[4]Jolie Solomon, "When Are Employees Not Employees? When They're Associates, Stakeholders . . . ," *The Wall Street Journal* (November 9, 1988), p. B1.

task forces, suggestion systems, and problem-solving committees described earlier to management by objectives and employee attitude surveys presented in this chapter. (In a later chapter, we shall examine a popular participation program—the quality circle.)

Even with the availability of employee participation programs, we may question to what extent companies make use of motivation techniques at their disposal. For example, in a Harris/Steelcase survey of office workers and top-level executives, 61 percent of the office employees said that participative management is very important to them; however, only 28 percent stated that their work environments have such a management style. Agreeing with the workers, the executives said that only 25 percent of their firms have participative management programs. In contrast to the employees' responses, however, only 44 percent of the executives thought that participative management was very important to the employees.[5]

Although participation programs hold promise as a means of motivating employees, such programs are sure to fail when supervisors resist their establishment. Many supervisors, concerned solely with their own self-interest, see no benefit for themselves in the programs. They worry about their jobs and resent any loss of power and control when worker involvement increases. In one way or another, these supervisors fall into a pattern of passive resistance.

The most common reason for resistance to employee participation programs is that supervisors refuse to sacrifice their power, control, or authority.[6] To overcome this prob-

lem, supervisory training programs should stress that supervisors will find their roles enhanced as more time becomes available for planning and organizing as well as for innovative activities. Thus, the need exists to increase the involvement of supervisors in upper-level planning sessions so they may more actively participate in decision making and thus improve their own managerial skills. Such participation aids supervisors in better understanding their roles in changing corporate culture and in learning how to define their goals and to manage people more effectively.

Theory Z Organizations

In Chapter 1, the term *Theory Z Management* was introduced to explain the nature of a management style formulated by William Ouchi. In his study of companies in Japan and a comparative analysis of those in the United States, Ouchi identified firms that have a Theory Z organization.

The **Theory Z organization**, which closely resembles the Japanese style of management, relies greatly upon long-range planning; strong, mutual worker-employer loyalty and trust; and those elements listed in Figure 7–5. Ouchi stresses that the special abilities of the individual worker are more important than the contents of the job description. According to Theory Z, workers should be hired for their talents. Further, jobs should be designed around the workers' talents rather than trying to fit workers into preset job descriptions. In firms that have experimented with the theory by adopting flexible work schedules, for example, workers are given a great deal of freedom to make their own decisions about work. Rather than relying upon technological change in itself to bring about increased productivity, Theory Z calls for managers and supervisors to redirect their attention to human relations.

In contrasting the organizations of the United States and Japan, Ouchi notes that Japan's homogeneous structure, a fairly

---

[5]"Office Talk," *Personnel* (October, 1988), p. 12. The survey of 1,031 office workers and 150 top-level executives from around the country was conducted in December, 1987, and January, 1988, by Louis Harris and Associates and sponsored by Steelcase, Inc., an office furniture manufacturer in Grand Rapids, Michigan.

[6]Michael H. Schuster and Christopher S. Miller, "Employee Involvement: Making Supervisors Believers," *Personnel* (February, 1985), p. 25.

Figure 7–5
Charac-
teristics of
the Theory Z
Organization

> ### The Theory Z Organization Provides:
>
> - *Stable, long-term employment* where employees expect to stay on the job for their lifetime, under no assumption they will be laid off.
>
> - *Moderately specialized careers* and rotation of workers through different kinds of jobs.
>
> - *Slow evaluation and promotion* to ensure that no one is advanced into a position of responsibility until complete job commitment occurs.
>
> - *Decision making by consensus*, a natural result of workers having become completely socialized in the culture of their organization.
>
> - *Individual responsibility*, which results from collective decision making and a commonly shared culture.
>
> - *Strong emotional well-being* among workers who believe in collective responsibility and action.
>
> - *Concern for each subordinate* as a functioning whole person, with emphasis placed upon the working relationships among people.

uniform culture, encourages mutual trust and cooperation. This, in turn, allows collective enterprises like large corporations to grow and prosper since a strong paternalistic bond exists between workers and their firms. However, not all Japanese management practices can be transplanted into American life. For example, Americans place a high value on their mobility and have cultural values that do not agree with the practice of lifelong employment. Americans often feel it is good for them and for the company if they change jobs. However, Ouchi found that some firms in the United States have characteristics of the Theory Z organization and have used some of the Theory Z practices such as problem solving by collective project teams, reducing working hours for all employees during a recession, and permitting semi-autonomous work groups to govern their own jobs to improve productivity.

AOMs and office supervisors, in their search for increased office productivity, can profit by examining the ways in which American and Japanese managers look for means to enhance the quantity and quality of their firms' output. Supervisors cannot view their human resources merely as the means to a financial end. Instead, supervisors should implement the concept that workers who are involved with their jobs and their companies are the key to increased productivity.

Management by Objectives and Goal Setting

In his book, *The Practice of Management*, Peter F. Drucker first introduced the widely accepted concept of management by objectives, a technique that has long been associated with George S. Odiorne.[7] In **management by objectives (MBO)**, objectives are set forth for every area where performance and results directly and vitally affect the survival and prosperity of the

---

[7]For the development and presentation of the concept of management by objectives, see Peter F. Drucker, *The Practice of Management* (New York: Harper and Brothers, 1954). Also see George S. Odiorne, "How to Succeed in MBO Goal Setting," *Personnel Journal* (August, 1978), pp. 427–429, 451. Also, George S. Odiorne, "MBO: A Backward Glance," *Business Horizons* (October, 1978), pp. 14–24.

In MBO workers become involved in increasing their productivity.

organization. The technique of MBO may be used to appraise performance, reward performance, train to improve performance levels, and motivate workers to do better.

In using MBO as a motivational technique, subordinates and their supervisors meet face to face to agree mutually upon practical goals to be achieved. The individual goals to be set may be either operational or developmental. **Operational goals**, such as redesigning an outmoded information-collection system, define job expectancies and relate to performance improvement. **Developmental goals**, such as improving one's attendance on the job, recognize identifiable gaps in the personal qualifications of a worker for the present position and for future placement. To be realistic, the goals must be attainable and challenging enough to require effort for their accomplishment. The goals should also motivate the workers to use their talents and skills to the fullest to improve personal performance.

Under guidelines set by the supervisor, the workers set specific targets for their own objectives (such as arriving five minutes early each morning), commit themselves to the attainment of these targets, and evaluate themselves with respect to their performance in meeting the objectives. Thus, individual workers are encouraged to assume greater responsibility for planning as well as for appraising and measuring their contributions in meeting organizational objectives. This in turn aids in meeting the ego and self-development needs of the workers that might otherwise have been ignored.

Feedback must be provided so the employees' progress toward each of their goals may be monitored by the supervisor. For example, each goal mutually agreed upon is evaluated by the supervisor during a periodic performance review. At that time, subordinates are given the opportunity to discuss any problems they might be having. At the time of the performance review, new goals may mutually be set for the next time period. Thus, the performance review emphasizes concrete, measurable goals, such as a 75 percent reduction in the cost of wasted supplies, rather than the traditional, intangible, and unmeasurable personality traits, such as "attitude."

Expectancy Theory of Motivation

The expectancy theory of motivation was developed by psychologists who see workers as thinking persons who have beliefs and anticipations about future events in their lives and thus raise questions similar to those given above. According to **expectancy theory**, our motivational force to perform depends upon the expectancy that we have concerning future outcomes and the value that we place on these outcomes. Victor H. Vroom defines an expectancy as a "momentary belief concerning the likelihood that a particular act will be followed by a particular outcome."[8] Thus, your belief that "working

---

[8]Victor H. Vroom, *Work and Motivation* (New York: John Wiley and Sons, 1964), p. 170.

overtime will improve your image in the boss's mind" is an expectancy. For you, such an expectancy serves as a guideline by which you can plan to fulfill your personal needs. The theory suggests that you have managed your personal motivation depending upon what you expect in terms of the three-way relationship among (1) effort, (2) performance, and (3) rewards for performance. If you had seen little relationship among the three factors and were faced with a backup of work at the end of the day, you may have decided, "Why bother? Forget it!"

For the office supervisor, the expectancy theory provides yet another basis for trying to explain the direction of employee behavior and to evaluate those environmental factors that affect behavior. Thus, this theory, along with all the others described in this chapter, aids the supervisor in learning what motivates employees and in understanding the relationships among effort, performance, and reward.

ETHICS AND VALUE SYSTEMS

As individuals differ, so do their ethical concepts and value systems. Personal guidelines or policies for everyday ethical conduct are needed in the office. Like all policies, a code of ethics must be capable of being enforced. Many problems facing today's office supervisors—problems that suggest clashing or poorly understood value systems—come about in an attempt to apply traditional supervisory methods to employees who have a different work ethic. To manage effectively, office supervisors must adapt their means for achieving organizational goals to the value systems of the people who do the work.

Ethics

In the Harris/Steelcase survey cited earlier, the office workers were asked what they considered the most important charac-

teristics of their office environments. Of the workers interviewed, 89 percent said that "management that is honest, upright, and ethical in its dealings with employees and the community" is very important; however, only 41 percent said that this description characterizes their current employers.[9] What do we mean by "ethical conduct"? Let's take a few minutes to examine this word *ethics*.

Ethics is a systematic study of the part of science and philosophy that deals with moral conduct, duty, and judgment. Your concept of what is and is not ethically and morally right stems from your religious convictions, personal philosophy, and motives. Look at the list of office practices shown in Figure 7-6 and decide which of them are or are not ethically and morally right.

The inspiration for ethical behavior must originate at the top level of management, filter down through middle management, and permeate the business organization. The best guarantee of high standards of morality in business is that subordinates work under the direction of men and women who themselves have high standards. For at least one-third of each working day, supervisors enter into social relationships with their subordinates. During the remaining two-thirds of each day, the attitudes, ideals, and beliefs that the employees have formed while at work in the office are being carried back and relayed to society—the families and friends of the employees. Thus, supervisors have a social responsibility to set a good example for their employees. The ethical and moral conduct of supervisors, as leaders, must rise above their own personal and individual motives and needs.

In communicating with their superiors, supervisors should strive to report all the facts honestly, accurately, and objectively. Supervisors must train themselves and their workers to avoid distorting the facts in order

---

[9]"Office Talk," p. 10.

Figure 7-6
Determining
an Office
Ethics Quo-
tient (OEQ)

WHAT IS YOUR OFFICE ETHICS QUOTIENT (OEQ)?

As you examine each of the office practices described below, indicate with a check (✔) on the scale at the right how you judge the ethics and morality of the practice. After you have evaluated all 12 practices, add your points to obtain your OEQ. An interpretation of your OEQ is given at the bottom of the form.

OFFICE PRACTICE	ETHICS SCALE		
	(A) Unethical or Immoral	(B) Possibly Unethical or Immoral	(C) Ethical and Moral
1. Employee A, knowing he will be arriving late, asks B to punch in for him at the time clock.			
2. C leaves her work station (a nonsmoking area) about ten times each day to smoke a quick cigarette in the company lounge.			
3. D occasionally leaves his office in the morning and the afternoon to go to the company lounge, where he sips a little vodka from the flask in his locker.			
4. E puts a few ballpoint pens and a box of paper clips in her purse before leaving the office.			
5. During the lunch hour, F sits in his car in the company parking lot and smokes pot.			
6. G places weekly long-distance calls to her grandmother and reports them as business calls to the switchboard operator.			
7. H, who does not want to be bothered with incoming calls or visitors, tells his secretary, I, to inform all callers that he is not in.			
8. Each time J passes the desk of K, K whistles at her.			
9. To obtain her job with the company, L exaggerated her educational background on the application blank to show she had a two-year associate degree.			
10. M, working in accounts receivable, "borrows" some of the incoming receipts in the form of cash, with the intention of repaying the "borrowed" amount next payday.			
11. N, a terminal operator in the medical department, supplies the psychological file of a worker to a manager who wants to see if the worker might crack under stress.			
12. O, a payroll clerk, leaks information about present salaries earned by company personnel and the increases planned for these workers.			

Determine your OEQ and its interpretation by assigning the following value to each check mark: Column A, 5 points; Column B, 2 points; Column C, 1 point. Add the point values of all check marks to obtain your OEQ.

OEQ	Interpretation
42 to 60 points	You adhere to an exceptionally high level of morality and ethics in the office. Your supervisor looks upon you as a morally and ethically straight person.
24 to 41 points	You often hedge on issues and feel fairly secure and safe by being inconsistent. Your supervisor sizes you up as a fence straddler, one from whom it is difficult to obtain a clear-cut yes-or-no answer.
fewer than 24 points	Your low level of ethical and moral conduct in the office differs significantly from the norm. Your supervisor is obligated to impose strict controls upon your job performance and work habits.

to fill a psychological need; all too often communication lines become warped by the biases of the sender. In reaching decisions, the goal of supervisors should be to discipline their thinking into a logical, orderly process, rather than to jump to conclusions impulsively. In working with subordinates, supervisors may find it easy to abuse their authority, with the result that employees feel "let down" and unsupported in their actions. To gain employees who will work with him or her, a supervisor must work with them; be kind, fair, and just; and sincerely praise the satisfactory performance of the workers.

Basic to ethical and moral conduct is loyalty. Without this fundamental quality, no supervisor, no office, and no business firm can perform at the peak of potential capability. When supervisors are unable to give allegiance to the authority of their firms, they find themselves in a position of conflict, which in turn hinders them from being loyal to either themselves or their companies. The only workable solution to the problem of office supervisors who cannot abide by the policies and principles set forth by their firm is for them to find jobs in other companies where they can be loyal.

Value Systems

A **value system** is the sum of our moral and social perceptions of those things that are intrinsically desirable or valuable. As a result of our experiences and education and the customs and traditions of the culture of which we are members, we develop and cultivate values that will satisfy our personal needs. If office workers can look upon their working lives as a real contribution not only to their co-workers and the firm but also to society, they may find opportunities to satisfy their love, esteem, and self-actualization needs. If, on the other hand, office workers view themselves as being saddled with boring, unchallenging work, the opportunities to find satisfaction and

happiness and meet their needs are practically nil.

The 1987 INC./Hay Employee Survey found that employees of small and midsize private companies (firms with 10 to 500 workers) were more satisfied with their jobs and had more respect for their companies than employees in large organizations. The study also showed that employees in small firms bring enthusiasm to new jobs, no matter what size the company, and that employee motivation is a major force behind the extraordinary growth of the firms. The president of the Hay Group's Research for Management stated that the companies are also successful because they have managed their people in ways that keep their involvement and sense of partnership high.[10]

In another study dealing with changes in employee attitudes, the Opinion Research Corporation found that in the mid-1980s (a time of general economic recovery and declining unemployment) employees had a more favorable view of their companies and their management than they did several years earlier. The findings showed that employee involvement programs, quality circles, and excellence programs have increased. On the other hand, we find that downsizing (reducing the size of the work force) is becoming a common practice, layers of management are being removed, and support staff is being decreased. Thus, the resulting goals of higher production and profitability are being placed on smaller staffs.[11]

The findings above are in contrast to earlier research studies which found that significant numbers of Americans were dissatisfied with the quality of their working lives. Discontent was found at all occupational levels—blue collar, white collar, and

---

[10]Curtis Hartman and Steven Pearlstein, "The Joy of Working," The 1987 INC./Hay Employee Survey, *INC.* (November, 1987), pp. 61–71.

[11]Brian S. Morgan and William A. Schiemann, "Employee Attitudes: Then and Now," *Personnel Journal* (October, 1986), pp. 100–106.

middle management—where dull, repetitive, seemingly meaningless tasks offer little challenge or autonomy. Some office workers compared their work environment with a factory—work that is segmented and authoritarian directed. Some felt that their tasks of operating direct-entry terminals and of transcribing in word processing centers have much in common with the robot-like activities on the automobile assembly line. Others noted, with the growth in size of their company, that they had become separated, isolated, or divorced from the mainstream of daily work life. Their contributions, when acknowledged by the supervisor, were only impersonally noted. Some felt that they, as office workers, were looked upon by their supervisors as part of the hardware they were operating. They were acknowledged as human beings apart from the hardware only when errors were made or rules were not followed.

Much of the dissatisfaction expressed by office personnel with job content and supervisory styles is caused by a mismatching of values—a conflict between the work ethic of today's worker and the supervisory styles of the past. This situation has come about mostly because work systems have not changed fast enough to keep up with the rapid and wide-scale changes in the value systems, attitudes, and aspirations of workers. Many workers, as a result of their increased educational and economic status, find that having an interesting job is as important as the economic benefits derived from the job. Pay and employee benefits are still important, but they must support an adequate standard of living and be perceived as equitable. However, high pay and a broad employee benefits program alone do not lead to job (or life) satisfaction. As Peter F. Drucker so aptly observed, "To make a living is no longer enough. Work also has to make a life."[12]

Today's office supervisors are working with many persons who have become more inner directed about all aspects of their work. These employees are looking for a more meaningful work experience from the organization. They want to be shown that their work adds value and satisfaction to their lives. They want to see that the quality of their well-being is improved as a result of their job performance. They want to be recognized and wanted for the talents and skills they possess and to feel that their abilities are being used to their full potential. As the younger, more educated employees demand more satisfying jobs, they seek greater participation in those decisions that affect their work. Some managers and supervisors rely solely upon their own value systems to determine the goals of the firm and the means for achieving these goals. However, managers must try to understand other people's value systems and involve them in designing the systems and procedures to be followed.[13] One approach that may be used to learn more about the workers' value systems, their attitudes, and their work frustrations is to conduct attitude surveys and climate surveys, as discussed below.

Attitude Surveys

An **attitude survey** is a periodic polling of workers to determine the moods and feelings of workers toward supervisory treatment, salaries and employee benefits, their jobs, and the firm. For example, a company may ask its workers to rank on a scale of 1 to 5 ("very poor" to "outstanding") how they view elements such as the following:

Your company:
1. As a place to work.
2. Provisions for job security.
3. Wages and salaries paid.
4. Employee benefits offered.

---

[12]Peter F. Drucker, *Management: Tasks, Responsibilities, Practices* (New York: Harper & Row, Publishers, Inc., 1974), p. 179.

[13]Vincent F. Flowers et al., "Managerial Values for Working: an AMA Survey Report" (New York: American Management Association, 1975), p. 44.

Your management:
1. Ability of top management.
2. Ability of immediate supervisor.
3. Cooperation among departments.

Your job:
1. Opportunity to take part in decision making.
2. Challenges provided by the work.
3. Level of interest in the work.
4. Amount of pay received.
5. Relationship between job performance and salary increases.

By surveying employees at regular intervals, such as once each year, and by comparing employee responses to the questions raised, the supervisor can spot changes in employee opinions and gain insight into the workers' wants and needs. With little investment in time and money, the company, and especially its supervisors, can obtain very significant results that can go a long way toward improving employee motivation.

Climate Surveys

In a similar vein, companies may conduct a **climate survey** to determine "weather conditions" by identifying among the workers any prevailing winds of discontent, impending storms, temperatures reaching the boiling point, and so on. The climate survey is a "no-holds barred," two-way feedback process—an interpersonal exchange between supervisors and subordinates in which unwarranted employee gripes can be explained and legitimate ones discussed. Thus, in feedback sessions, supervisors are obligated to face up to and correct any unpleasant situations. Of course, the success of such feedback sessions hinges on the willingness of supervisors and managers to open themselves to close scrutiny by their subordinates.

Attitude surveys and climate surveys aid supervisors in learning what employees expect since the surveys raise basic questions that most workers usually ask themselves about their work situations. Most employees want answers to questions such as, "What's in it for me?" "How important to me are the rewards for working at this job?" "If I try harder, will it really make a difference in my performance?" "Am I really rewarded for what I produce?" "If I improve my performance level, will I receive an increase in rewards?" "If I don't improve, what will be the consequences?"

SUMMARY
1. In exercising the functions of planning, organizing, leading, and controlling, office supervisors assume specific responsibilities in their business organizations: to those in higher management, to their peers (supervisors of equal rank), to their subordinates, to their firms for coordinating the office work, and to themselves for self-development. To assume each of these responsibilities effectively and efficiently, office supervisors must be able to manage their own time more productively.
2. In using the human approach in supervision, office supervisors need to understand the theories of motivation such as the hierarchy of needs; motivation-maintenance; job enrichment; Theories X, Y, and Z; participative management; management by objectives and goal setting; and expectancy.
3. To create the kind of office atmosphere that positively affects worker performance and enables effective leadership, supervisors must acknowledge the ethics and value systems of today's office workers and understand that dissatisfaction may occur when there is a mismatching of the ethics and values of today's office workers and the super-

visory styles of the past. Above all, the office supervisor, by example, must set

the standard for moral and ethical conduct and loyalty.

GLOSSARY **Attitude survey**—a study of the moods and feelings of workers toward supervisory treatment, salaries and employee benefits, their jobs, and the firm.

Authoritarian organization—an organization that subscribes to the traditional view of supervising workers—Theory X—and thus is very dependent upon authority.

Career goal planning—the process of working with employees to assess their personal strengths and weaknesses, selecting and formulating career goals, and developing action plans that workers can put to work to carry out their goals.

Climate survey—a two-way feedback process in which superiors and subordinates, working in small units or individual departments, provide for interpersonal exchange of opinions.

Delegating—the process of entrusting work to others who are qualified to accept the responsibility for doing the work, granting of sufficient authority to get the work done, and mutually understanding the results to be accomplished.

Developmental goals—the objectives that recognize identifiable gaps in the personal qualifications of a worker for the present position and for future placement.

Discipline—the teaching or molding of employees in a constructive and consistent manner so that they may learn to change their behavior and performance in the future.

Employee assistance program (EAP)—a plan that provides specially trained persons who diagnose and offer help in solving personal problems that affect employees' performance and attendance.

Ethics—the systematic study of that part of science and philosophy dealing with moral conduct, duty, and judgment.

Expectancy theory—the view that a person's motivational force to perform depends upon the individual's expectations concerning future outcomes and the value he or she places on these outcomes.

Hierarchy of needs—the view that human beings have two sets of needs, primary and secondary.

Job enrichment—the view that to motivate employees, jobs should be redesigned by building into those jobs higher-order responsibilities and authorities and more challenging content.

Leading—the management function of motivating workers so that the objectives of the organization will be attained.

Management by objectives (MBO)—the view that objectives may be set forth for every area where performance and results directly and vitally affect the survival and prosperity of the organization.

Morale—the mental and emotional attitudes of persons toward the tasks expected of them by their group and their loyalty to that group.

Motivate—to create the kind of environment in which workers are enthusiastic and have a desire to work.

Motivation-maintenance theory—the view that hygienic (maintenance) factors are related to productivity, but peripheral to the job itself. When hygienic factors are present, they do not motivate people to greater productivity but instead make it possible for the other factors, the motivators, to function.

Operational goals—the objectives that define job expectancies and relate to performance improvement.

Participative management—a management technique in which workers are given a voice in determining what they are to do, how they are to do it, and how they are to be appraised.

Participative organization—an organization that adheres to the democratic relations found in Theory Y, where all workers have the opportunity to achieve their fullest potential.

Performance appraisal—the evaluation and constructive criticism of an employee's work.

Theory X—the view of worker behavior in which workers are characterized as irresponsible, selfish, and apathetic.

Theory Y—the view of worker behavior in which, depending upon conditions, the average person may find work to be satisfying, will seek responsibility, and will strive to attain the firm's objectives.

Theory Z organization—an organization, modeled after the Japanese form of management, that relies greatly upon such factors as long-range planning; strong, mutual worker-employer loyalty and trust; stable, long-term employment; slow evaluation and promotion; and decision making by consensus.

Time management—a program in which all resources, including time, are efficiently used to achieve one's important professional and personal goals.

Value system—the sum of one's moral and social perception of those things that are intrinsically desirable or valuable.

FOR YOUR REVIEW

1. Describe the five types of supervisory responsibilities. In what directions do these responsibilities flow?

2. "Supervisors must use the human approach." Carefully explain the meaning of this statement and indicate its relevance for the office supervisor.

3. Is it possible for supervisors to teach at the same time they are disciplining workers? Why or why not?

4. How are employees and their supervisors aided by the company's employee assistance program?

5. In counseling employees, to what extent should a supervisor delve into the employees' off-the-job personal problems?

6. What is morale? How is morale related to the needs of workers?

7. Describe the different kinds of primary and secondary needs that are found in Maslow's hierarchy of needs.

8. How may a company provide job security and personal security as it tries to meet the primary needs of its workers?

9. In their working lives, what do employees search for in an attempt to satisfy their need for recognition?

10. Explain the relevance of Herzberg's motivation-maintenance theory to the concept that the major motivator of workers is the size of their paychecks.

11. How are motivator factors and hygienic factors related to Herzberg's motivation theory?

12. How can job enrichment serve as a means of motivation?

13. What is delegating? What are the underlying reasons why many supervisors do not delegate or delegate ineffectively?

14. Contrast the underlying assumptions of McGregor's Theories X and Y of worker behavior.

15. Explain how participative management may serve as a motivating force.

16. For what reasons do office supervisors sometimes resist the establishment of employee participation programs?

17. Describe the main features of the Theory Z organization that distinguish it from the traditional type of organization found in the United States.

18. Explain how management by objectives may be used as a motivational technique.

19. How does the expectancy theory of motivation aid the office supervisor to explain employee behavior?

20. What is the best guarantee of high standards of morality in the business world?

21. What role do value systems play in employees' attitudes toward their working lives?

22. Explain how attitude surveys and climate surveys may be used by an organization to learn more about its employees' value systems.

FOR YOUR DISCUSSION

1. Martin Rhodes, supervisor of the mailing center at Hennessey, Inc., asked Peter Gibbs, a mail clerk, to step into his office. Rhodes began to discuss Gibbs' poor attendance record. While his time reports for the past month were being reviewed, Gibbs began to cry. How would you, as Rhodes, handle Gibbs' crying?

2. Todd Hunter, a former marine captain, was recently employed to head a department in which morale had slipped considerably in recent months. Hunter's supervisor was aware of the morale problem and informed Hunter accordingly. At the first meeting with his boss, Hunter indicated that the strength and the success of any departmental operation depends 25 percent on the number of employees and 75 percent upon its morale. Furthermore, Hunter stated that the essentials of morale in a business firm are the same as those in the Marine Corps: (1) respect for the officers or supervisors, (2) discipline, and (3) training.

   Do you agree with the statements made by Hunter? On the basis of these facts, discuss the various methods by which a desirable level of morale may be developed and maintained in the department.

3. Dee Terry, assistant manager of accounts payable in a large accounting department, was helping Helen Roth, a data-entry operator, with some month-end reports. Terry uncovered

a mathematical error made by Roth and called it to Roth's attention. Being confronted with her mistake, Roth yelled at Terry: "You're embarrassing me in front of all my co-workers. How can you do this?" As Terry, how would you respond to the screaming Roth?

4. Carlos Rojas, an office supervisor, is so eager to do a good job that he always comes to the office manager before making a decision affecting office procedures in his department. In the past two months, Rojas has called upon the office manager no less than ten times for advice. In nine of these instances, the office manager recommended what Rojas would have done himself. What would you do in this instance if you were the office manager, assuming that Rojas is otherwise doing a good job?

5. You are taking a new job and you have the choice of whether you will report to a male or a female supervisor. Would it matter to you if your boss were male or female? If you have a preference, how do you explain it?

6. As the instructor continues with his lecture on motivational techniques, a neighboring student turns to you and remarks, "I think a lot of this motivation stuff is for the birds. We all know that motivation comes from within—you either have it or you don't." What is your reaction to this student's statements?

7. While attending a three-day seminar on "Improving Office Productivity," Randy Barkan calls his office four times each day, punctually at 10:00 A.M., 12:30 P.M., 2:00 P.M., and 3:30 P.M. As the supervisor in charge of communications, Barkan feels obligated to check in with his workers at least four times each day to see if things are running smoothly in his absence. What do you see as the most pressing problem facing Barkan in his supervisory relations with his subordinates? What solution can you offer to solve this problem?

8. Rose Emilio is office manager and head accountant for a small company in southern California. Emilio has read much about employee motivation and wants to apply some of the suggested techniques. However, she is aware that not enough money is available to grant salary increases and bonuses and that the budget will not permit the purchase of new equipment to ease the work load of her staff. Faced with such severe monetary constraints, Emilio asks you what steps she can take to motivate her workers. What advice can you offer her?

9. You have been asked to design a disciplinary system which recognizes that not all infractions deserve the same treatment and that each penalty should fit the violation. Of the following list of employee infractions, which do you consider serious enough to justify either suspension or discharge with the first offense? Be prepared to defend your answers.
   a. Taking an unexcused absence.
   b. Stealing.
   c. Gambling on company premises.
   d. Falsifying the petty cash records.
   e. Smoking in a smoking-prohibited area.
   f. Working while under the influence of drugs.
   g. Achieving less than satisfactory job performance.
   h. Sleeping on the job.

SOLVING CASE PROBLEMS

Case 7–1 Solving a Problem of Employee Morale

Zachary Allen has worked in the accounts receivable department of a dress manufacturing firm for eight years. In spite of a company rule against bringing coffee to work areas, Allen, like other workers, has always brought coffee to his workstation and at times would bring coffee to his co-workers. Last week when Andre Merrin was promoted to supervisor of the department, he told the workers that a number of changes would be made in the department, including enforcement of the rule against bringing coffee into the work area.

Several workers complained about Merrin's announcement, but all stopped bringing coffee to their workstations, except Allen. Merrin ignored Allen's violation of the newly resurrected rule for two days. On the third day, Merrin called Allen into his office and gave him a one-day suspension. By the end of that week, Merrin was shocked when he saw an all-time low in his department's productivity. Even several workers who never drank coffee were complaining bitterly.

How do you recommend Merrin solve his major morale problem?

Case 7–2 Improving the Status of Office Supervisors Who Are Misfits

One afternoon as Mary Beeman, an administrative manager, was returning from the company lounge to her office, she happened to overhear one of her supervisors, Claude Ferguson, talking with a department head, Bill Hunt. Although the voices were muffled, Beeman heard the essence of their conversation, which was something like this:

Ferguson: . . . I would go back to my old job of auditing freight bills any day if I wouldn't lose out on the bucks and my status. . . .

Hunt: I'm just as unhappy in my supervisory job as you. I just don't feel fit for my job. You'll never know how many days I wish I were back operating that terminal!

Back in her office Beeman wonders about other supervisors and department heads who may feel they are misfits. She questions to what extent such dissatisfaction may account for the increased loss of productivity in the office operations. She sits back and begins to think about what she, as administrative manager, can do to solve the problem of supervisors who are unhappy on the job and who feel they are misfits.

Assume the role of Beeman and prepare a remedial program for top management to consider in which your objective is to improve the quality of supervision by selecting supervisory personnel who will fit the jobs and be happier with the quality of their daily work.

8

Training, Appraising, and Promoting Office Personnel

GOALS FOR THIS CHAPTER

After completing this chapter, you should be able to:

1. Identify the principles of office training and describe how they are applied in an effective training program.
2. Describe the essential psychological factors that must be provided in the development of an office training program.
3. List the outcomes to be realized by a firm that conducts an effective office training program.
4. Describe the methods and techniques that are commonly used in conducting an entry-level training program for office personnel.
5. Identify the methods and techniques of instruction that may be used in supervisory training and development programs.
6. List the purposes for which employee performance appraisal is undertaken and describe the commonly used methods of conducting such appraisals.
7. Describe the essential characteristics of a successful promotion plan and list the factors that should be considered in promotion decisions.
8. Identify the factors to be considered in developing a termination procedure.

In today's Information Age, entry-level workers present challenging training problems. In addition to learning specific tasks, entry-level workers sometimes need basic education and retraining of their skills in order to become productive on the job. For example, in a report dealing with the development of a quality work force, two-thirds of the employers consulted stated that the supply of entry-level applicants was insufficiently prepared in the basic skills of reading, writing, mathematics, and communication. Further, it was noted that the basic skills gap between what business needs and the qualifications of the entry-level workers available to business is widening.[1] Part-timers and workers with years of job seniority also often present training problems because of their long-established work habits that may need to be improved or modified.

All three types of workers—entry-level, part-time, and older—need to know how to do their jobs better and often need to learn new jobs. Supervisors and managers also need to keep up-to-date regarding modern management practices and technological changes occurring in their fields.

We find that the larger the organization, the greater the tendency for an impersonal relationship to develop among office workers and their supervisors. When such a relationship exists, employees feel unimportant and experience feelings of insecurity and lack of recognition for their efforts and achievements. Many offices try to solve such human relations problems by developing effective procedures for appraising their employees' performance.

Office workers must be provided with opportunities for continuing growth and development so they can acquire the needed skills, knowledge, and attitudes in order to prepare themselves for more advanced

---

[1]*Building a Quality Workforce*, a joint initiative of the U. S. Departments of Labor, Education, and Commerce (Washington: Superintendent of Documents, July, 1988), p. 13.

203

positions in the firm. Training and development programs must also meet the needs of the workers' present activities and responsibilities. Thus, such programs should lessen the need for training after promotion and provide for smoother transition upward.

In this chapter we shall examine the nature of several different kinds of training programs, along with employee appraisal and promotion. Also, we shall see the need for AOMs and office supervisors to follow a well-planned termination procedure when discontinuing the employment of workers.

TRAINING

Training is the process of providing individuals with an organized series of experiences and materials that comprise opportunities to learn. What takes place within the individuals—that is, what changes occur in their behavioral patterns and attitudes—is known as **learning**. The money that a company spends for training pays dividends as a result of fewer errors, greater productivity, and less turnover. Like any business activity, training has no value unless it aids in achieving the goals of the organization by contributing to better performance. Training should help a firm attain goals *directly* by increasing productivity, improving the quality of work, and reducing costs; and *indirectly* by improving the skills, attitudes, and work habits of employees and by increasing their knowledge and experiences.

Objectives of Office Training Programs

Before any training program can be undertaken, we must answer the question, "What are the goals of the training to be offered?" As shown in the model illustrated in Figure 8–1, we must clearly identify the objectives of the training program, its courses, and its instructional content in order to show their relation to the objectives of

the firm. Included among the broad goals of office training programs are:

1. To provide **entry-level**, or *initial*, **training** by which employees qualify for entry-job assignments.
2. To provide **upgrading training** for present employees to improve their knowledge and skills in their occupations.
3. To provide **retraining** of workers whose job assignments change.
4. To provide **supervisory training and development** to qualify workers for the added responsibilities and challenges of higher positions.

The objectives of training are developed from the knowledge and skills actually required for job performance, and these objectives must be clearly defined, understood, and communicated to trainees. Each unit of instruction should be based on the knowledge and skills possessed by the trainees before the training program gets under way. Further, the new learning materials must be within the reasonable achievement level of the trainees.

Principles of Office Training

We may look upon the office training program as a subsystem of the major business system, human resources, as discussed earlier in the text. Along with the other subsystems of human resources—hiring, orienting, appraising, and terminating—the effectiveness of office training depends upon the extent to which management is committed to support the program, the proper assignment of responsibility to line managers, and the care and skill with which the training program is planned, implemented, and evaluated.

In Chapter 2, you read about several principles that underlie efficient management and healthy organization. How effectively these principles are applied, like the principles of office training described below, is measured by the performance of

Figure 8-1
Model for an
Office Train-
ing Program

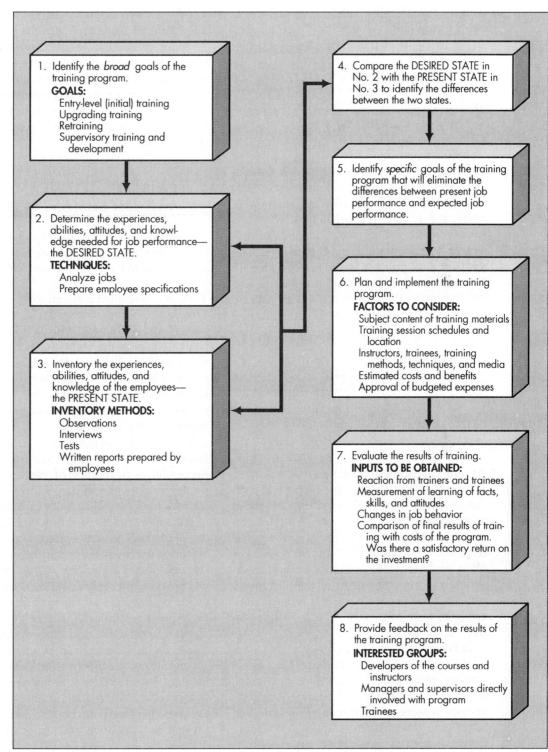

1. Identify the *broad* goals of the training program.
   GOALS:
   Entry-level (initial) training
   Upgrading training
   Retraining
   Supervisory training and development

2. Determine the experiences, abilities, attitudes, and knowledge needed for job performance—the DESIRED STATE.
   TECHNIQUES:
   Analyze jobs
   Prepare employee specifications

3. Inventory the experiences, abilities, attitudes, and knowledge of the employees—the PRESENT STATE.
   INVENTORY METHODS:
   Observations
   Interviews
   Tests
   Written reports prepared by employees

4. Compare the DESIRED STATE in No. 2 with the PRESENT STATE in No. 3 to identify the differences between the two states.

5. Identify *specific* goals of the training program that will eliminate the differences between present job performance and expected job performance.

6. Plan and implement the training program.
   FACTORS TO CONSIDER:
   Subject content of training materials
   Training session schedules and location
   Instructors, trainees, training methods, techniques, and media
   Estimated costs and benefits
   Approval of budgeted expenses

7. Evaluate the results of training.
   INPUTS TO BE OBTAINED:
   Reaction from trainers and trainees
   Measurement of learning of facts, skills, and attitudes
   Changes in job behavior
   Comparison of final results of training with costs of the program. Was there a satisfactory return on the investment?

8. Provide feedback on the results of the training program.
   INTERESTED GROUPS:
   Developers of the courses and instructors
   Managers and supervisors directly involved with program
   Trainees

people in achieving results. As you study these principles, see how they are applied in the model shown in Figure 8–1.

PRINCIPLE OF COMMITMENT

Management must be committed to providing an organizational climate that stimulates continued learning and growth.

Without the support of top management, office training efforts are likely to have little lasting impact. The quality of the training program is greatly influenced by top management, which sets the policies designed to support the training effort. The goal of such policies is to create a climate that will lead to the healthy personal and professional development of all office workers who participate in the training program.

PRINCIPLE OF RESPONSIBILITY

Line managers must be assigned responsibility for organizing and administering the office training program in their own departments.

As line managers, office managers must accept as one of their prime responsibilities the training and development of their subordinates. Also, they must be willing to be evaluated on how well they carry out this responsibility. Although OMs may aid in planning, organizing, conducting, and evaluating the training activity, their greatest contribution lies in helping their subordinates apply to their jobs what they have learned from training.

In large firms, the OM is usually provided staff assistance to help administer the office training program. Staff training personnel may aid in planning and coordinating the various aspects of the training program and in training the instructors and the trainees. In smaller firms, an office supervisor is usually personally responsible for training subordinates in acquiring the skills and knowledge needed to perform their jobs. Often the supervisor does not have the assistance of a training specialist. If help is needed, the supervisor may call upon another supervisor, a representative from the human resources department, or a specialist outside the company.

PRINCIPLE OF PLANNING AND IMPLEMENTATION

The organization must accurately identify its training needs and specify clearly how the objectives of training are to be implemented.

With its investment in an office training program, a company expects that the funds budgeted for training will be spent on the right people in the right positions and that the resources will be used to achieve the goals of the firm. Thus, effective planning and implementation require that adequate emphasis upon training be properly placed within the organization.

The specific experiences, abilities, attitudes, and knowledge needed for the successful performance of each job should be determined and clearly stated by undertaking a program of job analysis, as explained in the following chapter. Next, an inventory of the workers' present experiences, abilities, attitudes, and knowledge may be determined through observations, interviews, tests, and written reports prepared by the workers. The needs of the jobs are then compared with the present inventory of worker experiences, abilities, attitudes, and knowledge. As a result, the differences can be identified and specific training objectives, oriented toward meeting the needs of the trainees, can be stated. Thus, the training objectives express the gap that needs to be bridged between present performance and expected performance.

The person responsible for developing the office training program should prepare a plan that considers each of the factors listed in Step 6 of the model in Figure 8–1. In estimating the costs of planning and implementing the training program, the following factors should be included:

1. *Time costs*—time lost when employees and in-house instructors are off the job.
2. *Instructional costs*—salaries of instructors as well as development, publication, and use of training materials by the instructors.
3. *Transportation costs*—bringing personnel together for training.
4. *Facilities costs*—rental, food, and lodging.

PRINCIPLE OF EVALUATION

A sound office training program should provide for periodic evaluation and measurement of its effectiveness.

The results of any office training program—entry level, upgrading, retraining, or supervisory training and development—must be evaluated in order to determine the extent to which the objectives of the training function were achieved. For certain office tasks, such as data entry, billing, and filing, the volume and accuracy of work produced serve as measures of the skill level attained. Or production figures may be used that are based on the percentage of workers who meet job standards or accomplish the task within the time required to do the job. Performance standards, discussed in a later chapter, are created through a work measurement program and serve as one means by which the effectiveness of new office employees and their rates of learning may be measured. By means of standards, it is possible to determine at what point in the training process trainees should be able to handle a normal work load on a full-time basis.

Indirect measures of the effectiveness of training include the savings realized as a result of error reduction, less absenteeism, and decreased employee turnover. However, difficulty arises when evaluating the effectiveness of training in human relations or social skills. The outcomes of desirable attitude development and modification of behavioral patterns are not easily identified, let alone reviewed and measured.

To measure and evaluate the effectiveness of an office training program, the person in charge of the program should follow the steps listed in Figure 8–2.

PRINCIPLE OF FEEDBACK

The results of the training program should be effectively communicated to all groups needing feedback.

Those who designed the training program and the instructors need feedback in order to make improvements that will assure better results in the future. The managers and supervisors directly involved with the program are often charged with making decisions about future training programs. Therefore, they need to know the results of the training program in order to decide how much money should be allocated to future programs. Finally, the trainees need to learn how well they did in the program and how their performance compared with that of their co-workers.

Psychological Factors in the Learning Situation

To develop an effective office training program, attention must be given to several essential psychological factors in the learning situation. Often a well-planned training program suffers simply because one or more of these factors has been overlooked or was not adequately provided.

As we saw earlier in this chapter, learning is any change that occurs in the previous behavioral patterns and attitudes of the

Figure 8–2
Steps in
Measuring
and Evaluat-
ing the
Effective-
ness of an
Office Train-
ing Program

1. Establish standards of learning time against which the progress of trainees may be checked.

2. Test trainees on the abilities, skills, attitudes, and knowledge acquired.

3. Provide for the instructor to rate each trainee at the beginning, during, and at the end of the training program.

4. Keep records on the progress of each trainee.

5. Develop data on trainee performance before, during, and after training.

6. Obtain feedback from the trainees about what they liked in the training program, what they disliked, and what suggestions they have for improvement. Such information may be obtained by having the trainees fill out questionnaires at the end of the course or program. Another approach makes use of group evaluation where, in small teams, each trainee is stimulated to think about what has been learned. Thus, the trainees are given a chance to check their reactions with others in the group.

7. Check the results of the training program against its objectives.

8. Follow up on the trainees by periodically observing the long-range effects of their training.

trainees. The product of such learning is called a **habit**. The psychological factors discussed in this section surround the learning situation, which leads to the development of desirable work habits. Therefore, these factors should be reviewed by OMs and supervisors not only to refresh their own knowledge but also to help others in their group who may be providing training.

Motivation

Office workers are motivated by certain needs, but workers differ from one another in the relative importance of these needs at any given time. Among those needs that can be satisfied through training activities are the needs for safety, recognition, esteem, and self-actualization. Thus, those responsible for training must recognize the workers' needs and use them as a basis for motivating the employees.

In motivating office workers, the trainer must set performance standards that are realistic and attainable during the training sessions. For example, in the word processing center of a company, an average, fully quali-

fied word processing operator can keyboard original text at a rate of 5.25 pages each hour. However, during a program of upgrading the word processing employees, the trainer incorrectly adopted a standard of 6.5 pages each hour. By trying to meet such an unrealistic performance standard, the trainees became frustrated, anxious, and confused, all of which caused stress and hindered learning.

Knowledge of Results

A knowledge of results is a strong incentive at all stages of the learning process, but such feedback is especially needed after the initial enthusiasm of the learning situation has diminished. The person in charge of training should inform the new learners that their rates of improvement during the practice sessions on a complex task are not expected to be steady. At first, improvement is rapid, with a considerable portion of the total task being mastered in the first few trial sessions. However, each of the following trial sessions contributes decreasingly to the learning process.

The trainees should also anticipate those occasions in many learning situations, especially in the development of skills, when progress does not occur. On these occasions, the trainees are said to have reached a **plateau**—a period of time or a level of learning where no observable improvement occurs or where the rate of increase in learning levels off. Trainees should understand the nature and function of a plateau so that while it lasts, their discouragement and anxiety will be reduced. Reaching a plateau may result from ineffective work methods, or it may come about because of reduced motivation. With proper guidance by the trainer, the real cause of the plateau may be found.

Reinforcement

A **reinforcer** is a condition following a response that results in an increase in the strength of that response. Examples of possible reinforcers are:

1. Approval and recognition from the trainer.
2. The trainee's personal feeling of accomplishment that follows good performance.
3. Self-satisfaction in arriving at a correct answer to a problem.
4. Information about one's progress and achievement on the job.
5. Additional assistance or support provided by the trainer to the trainee.
6. Monetary rewards for attaining and exceeding quantity and quality standards.

Once the desired behavior occurs, it should be reinforced so that the chances of its recurring will be increased. Reinforcement of learning is generally most effective if it occurs immediately after a correct response has been made, such as the proper performance of a task. As pointed out on several occasions in this textbook, especially in Chapter 7, managers and supervisors too often rely upon money as the sole reinforcer. However, less tangible factors such as those listed above may prove more important in meeting employees' needs.

Practice

Few, if any, office trainees would hope to learn how to keyboard by merely reading a book on the subject. Most know that the development of keyboarding skill depends upon practice. Office trainees should be given frequent opportunity to practice their job tasks with relevant learning materials and in the same manner that they will finally be expected to perform their work. For example, the payroll clerk who is being taught to operate a computer should have ample opportunity to practice keyboarding while using payroll problem exercises. The practice exercises may be instructor-directed or computer-aided experiences, and the materials should indicate possible pitfalls that the trainee should guard against.

Massed Training Versus Spaced Training

In planning the courses of instruction for an office training program, instructors must decide whether the training sessions will be massed or spaced. An example of a *massed* training session is two highly concentrated three-hour periods. A *spaced* (or distributed) training session might be six one-hour periods. Usually practice sessions that are spaced out over several time periods, with rest or other activities intervening, result in more rapid learning and more permanent retention than if the same amount of practice is concentrated in a single period.

Whole Versus Part Learning

To determine whether learning by parts or by the whole is the most efficient approach to learning a task, the nature of the task must be studied. If the task can be broken down successfully into component parts, it probably should be broken down to facilitate learning. Otherwise, the task probably should be taught as a unit.

Often a trainer is an experienced worker who may think of the task in larger units than the trainee can readily grasp. A good trainer knows how to break down the units of information into sizes appropriate for the learner. The trainer must then arrange the units of information into their proper, logical sequence. In a small office, the supervisor-trainer may present some phase of his or her job in the order in which the supervisor performs that job. However, an entry-level worker does not learn in that same order and thus may become frustrated and confused. A good supervisor-trainer knows how to organize the information into a logical learning sequence by proceeding from the known to the unknown and from the simple to the complex. This means that the training should begin where the trainee is at present and not where the trainer has determined the trainee should be.

Individual Differences

The extent of individual differences among trainees affects the type and amount of instruction as well as the training methods and techniques by which the learning materials are presented. To provide for individual differences in the training program, the trainees are sometimes grouped according to their capacity to learn as determined by scores on their preemployment tests, such as aptitude tests. The test scores provide a basis for offering a different or an extended type of instruction to meet the varying needs of the groups. For example, the trainer may find that in teaching one group of workers how to master a complex skill, the language level must be kept relatively simple, the skill broken down into easy learning segments, or the training spread out over a relatively long period of time.

Outcomes of Effective Office Training

The principles of office training and the factors at work in the learning situation are directly related to the major objective of the training program—to develop office personnel who have learned to improve performance and are using the new learning on the job. With the attainment of this goal, the following outcomes will become evident.

An Improved Competitive Position for the Firm

Office workers who have participated in training and development programs aid in maximizing the company's profits and improving its competitive position. The training experience helps the workers satisfy their own needs to do a good job and reach a high level of productivity. Thus, production is increased and costly errors are reduced. As a result of the improved performance of its employees, a firm realizes additional economies in the production of its goods or services. Closely allied to this outcome are the cost-reducing factors of standardization and uniformity of output, both of which characterize the end results of effective training.

Better Preparation of Employees for Promotion

Supervisory training and development programs that utilize the best available methods and techniques prepare office personnel to take advantage of promotional opportunities in their firms. Thus, when there is a change in business conditions, such as expansion, qualified workers are available to fill the newly created positions. Also, if employees are well trained, the illness, death, reassignment, or resignation of other workers will have little effect upon the smooth operation of the business.

More Self-Confident Office Employees

Well-trained, confident office workers lessen the need for close supervision. Training increases the self-confidence of workers, which means that well-trained employees will ask fewer questions and will cooperate more readily with their co-workers. As a result, the burden of the supervisor is reduced and the morale of all workers is improved.

More Effective Employee Performance Appraisal

Training that is relevant to the real world and geared to the individual needs of office workers enables superiors to appraise employees' capabilities more effectively. As pointed out later in this chapter, employee performance appraisal, in turn, helps to ensure proper placement of employees in the organization. Therefore, turnover caused by unsatisfactory adjustment to the job should be reduced. Also, employee interest in the job should be increased because of a more thorough understanding of the work and its relation to that of other employees.

ENTRY-LEVEL TRAINING

As we saw earlier, entry-level training is designed to qualify employees for their initial job assignments. The following discussion pertaining to the instructional staff and the methods and techniques of entry-level training applies equally to upgrading training and retraining.

Instructional Staff

Instructors assigned responsibility for the entry-level training program should possess *human relations ability, leadership ability,* and *technical ability.* Those in charge of training, whether a first-line supervisor or a training director, must know enough about human nature, behavioral patterns, and attitudes to realize that trainees should be accepted as they are. In trying to adapt new employees to work situations, even the most skilled trainer cannot completely remold personalities or greatly alter the behavioral patterns of the employees. The trainer can, however, create the kind of environment in which employees accept the need to change their attitudes.

The trainer should have had experience in exercising the managerial functions of planning, organizing, leading, and controlling in order to develop the skills, attitudes, and work habits of the trainees. The trainer must be technically competent in order to command the respect of trainees and to impart to them the knowledge and skills required to qualify them to produce a quality product or service.

In companies large enough to provide formal in-house training, special instruction programs or "training for trainers" are often provided. In some firms, special instruction training consists of attendance at seminars, lectures, and vendor-sponsored workshops. In other companies, the human resources department may train the trainers and evaluate their presentations.

Conducting the Training Program

In-house training programs are conducted by a variety of persons. In large firms with formal training programs, instructors or specialists on the company staff are frequently used to conduct the training. Sometimes outside specialists, such as college or university professors and consultants in training, are called upon to provide the entry-level training. Qualified line managers and first-line supervisors are also often assigned the training responsibility.

In many small firms, the responsibility for training rests with the first-line supervisor, who is the most important part of the entry-level training program. The manner in which this person handles the responsibility is very important. The supervisor's subordinates must be permitted to apply their knowledge and skills and to be independent and professional. Otherwise, the supervisor becomes an obstacle to their effectiveness as well as to his or her own. In firms having a training department, that department may provide assistance to the supervisor, who, often conducts the training. The responsibility of the supervisor goes beyond conducting courses, however. It is the supervisor's job to be alert to the training needs of workers and to opportunities for meeting these needs. The supervisor's job is to see that training which cannot be provided personally is obtained from some other source and to follow up on the training when it has been completed.

Training Methods and Techniques

Of major concern in the selection of any entry-level training method or technique is the kind of change the training is intended to bring about. The purpose of the training, whether to increase knowledge, to improve skills, or to influence attitudes and change behavior, strongly influences the method or technique to be selected. Other factors that must be considered when selecting a particular training method or technique include the number of trainees and their location; their similarities and differences in education, experience, abilities, functions, and occupational levels; the abilities of the trainers; the instructional space, equipment, and media available for the training program; and the cost of the method selected in relation to the results expected.

The training methods described in this section are as follows: on the job, lecture, company courses of study, job rotation, and vestibule training. In conjunction with these training methods, entry-level training, upgrading, and retraining programs make use of programmed instruction materials, computer-assisted instruction, and television. Each of these techniques is briefly described below.

On-the-Job Training (OJT)

The most common method of training entry-level office employees is on-the-job training. **On-the-job training (OJT)** provides the office trainee with the knowledge and skills needed to perform a job while using the

A good trainer provides information and skills that will enable a new employee to master a new job quickly.

actual equipment and materials required by the job. By means of OJT, a new office worker learns about his or her job by working at the job on a one-to-one basis under the direction of a co-worker, a first-line supervisor, or a department head. Along with teaching the needed knowledge and skills, the trainer often discusses problem areas peculiar to the department and may delegate certain responsibilities to the trainee. This trainer-trainee relationship also provides an opportunity for close and continuous shaping of behavior within the work environment. However, the value to be gained from OJT depends upon the teaching or coaching ability of the trainer to whom the new worker is assigned.

On-the-job training is well suited for teaching many office operations, such as opening and sorting incoming mail, billing customers, posting to customers' and vendors' accounts, and operating the switchboard.

Lecture

A **lecture** is a nonparticipative, one-way communication technique in which an instructor imparts much factual information to a group in a relatively short period of time. The lecture method may be supplemented with demonstrations, either in person or on film, transparencies, or videotape. For example, the lecture and demonstration may be used to explain how to take a physical inventory of office supplies, how to reconcile the monthly bank statement with the bank account balance, and how to process an incoming sales order.

Of all training methods, the lecture method is probably the least expensive, easiest to use, and most universally used and understood. However, the lecture, whether presented in person, on film, or by television, is limited in its ability to influence attitudes and shape behavior since the method cannot discriminate among the needs of trainees. Further, trainees receive little motivation because they are unable to participate actively in practicing what they are taught.

Company Courses of Study

Company courses of study may be provided by the firm either during or outside work hours. Many large firms, such as American Telephone and Telegraph Company, General Electric Company, General Motors Corporation, International Business Machines Corporation, Johnson & Johnson, and Xerox Corporation, have set up their own educational facilities for entry-level training. Such in-house training, in spite of its expense, may be the best solution for firms that require large numbers of office workers. In other companies, entry-level training may be provided in conjunction with public institutions, such as high schools, trade and vocational schools, junior and community colleges, and four-year colleges and universities; and in cooperation with private institutions, such as business colleges. For example, a firm may enter into a partnership with local high schools and provide work-study courses in computer operations. The students are paid while training at the company and are given competency certificates from their employers along with their diplomas from their high schools when they graduate.

Job Rotation

In the **job rotation** method, trainees learn a number of functions in a relatively short period of time as they rotate through the various departments of the company or sections of a department. Trainees may be assigned to jobs solely as observers. Or they may be assigned specific job responsibilities so they become personally involved in the operations and learn a set of skills as they move from one job to the next. For example, when recruiting general office and secretarial workers, one company does not hire employees for a specific job but instead assigns them to a training center. The new employees are assigned to various temporary jobs from one department to another. However, they always return to the center for further training until positions for which they are qualified become available.

Vestibule Training

Vestibule training, used primarily for skills development, takes place in an area away from the site where the job is usually performed. In this area, the trainee's future workstation, including a duplicate of any equipment to be used, is simulated. Vestibule training is often used in those situations where the trainees have little knowledge of the jobs to be performed such as the information processing activities handled by a retail sales associate; or where there are strict demands on the accuracy and quality of work such as that performed by a bank teller.

Programmed Instruction (PI)

Programmed instruction (PI) is a self-instruction method in which the learning materials are presented as small units of information. The information is structured so that the learner proceeds in a step-by-step sequence from the basic elements of a skill or concept to more difficult material. Programmed instruction materials are effectively used when teaching specific skills and knowledge, such as how to fill in sales report forms properly and uniformly or how to understand the technical processes of photocopying equipment.

Computer-Assisted Instruction (CAI)

By means of **computer-assisted instruction, (CAI)** or *computer-augmented instruction*, trainees have simultaneous access to a computer, usually through terminal input-output units. The lessons, based on programmed instruction concepts, consist of explanations or lectures with questions and quizzes programmed on the computer with an immediate response or reinforcement furnished by the computer. Some CAI systems use sound and pictures (on slides, film, or videodisk) in addition to computer screens to present information.

CAI can be used to teach a variety of skills.

CAI may be used, for example, to teach us how to compute wages and salaries and to prepare a payroll. The computer informs us if our answers are accurate, tells us where and how to proceed next, and informs us of how well we are doing. Further, in most CAI systems, we can easily go back and repeat a section until we have mastered it. Defense Department studies have shown that students learn about 30 percent faster using computers than in traditional classrooms, a figure that has been adopted as a rule of thumb in industry as well.[2]

Television and Films

Television and films offer many advantages in the development of entry-level training, retraining, and upgrading training programs. Videocassettes and recorders can be easily used and transported to various locations for use. Videotapes may be reedited and updated to meet changing training requirements and erased and used again. Videotape and films bring into the learning situation scenes and other audiovisual materials not possible in the usual lecture approach. Also, the training sessions can be repeated at various times during the day or evening. Several companies may share the cost of producing a training program that meets their common needs and therefore be able to obtain outstanding instructors who otherwise would be unable to come to the individual firms to participate in training sessions. However, before deciding to use television and films as supplemental training aids, all cost factors—equipment, trained personnel, and installation—should be carefully evaluated and compared with the benefits expected.

The effectiveness of training by television and films depends upon how closely the program content is related to the specific

---

[2]Nancy Madlin, "Computer-Assisted Training," *Management Review* (June, 1987), p. 56.

learning objectives established. Further, the program content must be directly related to the viewer reactions or behaviors that are expected or desired by the instructor planning the audiovisual program.

Teleconferencing

By means of **teleconferencing**, as we shall see in a later chapter, three or more people at two or more separate locations are tied together by telephone. As the cost of travel skyrockets, some companies have found *audio* (sound) teleconferencing to be a cost-effective means of presenting their training courses. Besides traditional lecture-type training sessions, management seminars may be held over telephone lines. Consultants, faced with high travel costs, use the telephone as an economical way to deliver their training seminars. *Video* (sound and visual) teleconferencing, a much more expensive medium of training, has been used mostly by large organizations able to justify

Audio teleconferencing enables companies to avoid the expense of transporting all seminar participants to one location.

the costs of using this technique for training or for other communications.

SUPERVISORY TRAINING AND DEVELOPMENT

Earlier in this chapter we saw that the goal of *supervisory training and development* is to qualify workers for the added responsibilities and challenges of higher positions within the firm. Having a definite plan for promoting qualified office workers to supervisory positions improves the morale in all departments. Nothing is more discouraging to conscientious employees who have worked many years for a company than to learn that persons outside the organization were given preferred consideration when promotions were made.

Many companies provide in-house training for their first-level supervisors and middle managers. In most of these firms, the training programs are scheduled on a regular basis, such as four hours a week for six weeks or one day a month for six months. In some instances, the programs are scheduled as needed, while in the largest companies management training programs may be presented on a continuing basis.

A major part of any supervisory and management training and development program is the training conducted by organizations outside the company. Participation in outside programs is more common for middle managers than for first-level supervisors. Training outside the company includes attendance at professional or trade association meetings, career seminars, and university development programs.

Instructional Staff

In companies having in-house training programs for first-level supervisors and middle managers, the person usually responsible for the program is a training/

development manager or a human resources officer. In other firms, line managers, assisted by staff personnel, are in charge of the training program. The training program should be carefully planned and organized so that potential supervisors and middle managers obtain full knowledge of the work to be done and its place in the total organization. A knowledge of what work is to be done and how it is to be done can be obtained by work experience in the departments, by a study of the operations manuals that many firms have developed, or by working on studies with a systems and procedures department in the firm. Information relating to company policies, promotion paths, authority, and responsibility may be obtained from company manuals, organization charts, and personal consultations with senior executives.

Training Methods and Techniques

Supervisory training and development may be provided by many kinds of formal education. As indicated above, supervisory training may be carried out entirely in-house by the company. Or the company may cooperate with nearby educational institutions in providing evening classes in areas such as financial management, business communications, ethics, and basic computer concepts. Supervisors may take advantage of home-study courses and executive development programs offered by the American Management Association, which sponsors courses for managers, and the Administrative Management Society, which offers a series of advanced management training courses. Some firms engage management consultants to conduct such intensive courses.

The one-to-one training methods and techniques used in entry-level training programs, described on pages 211 to 215, are also found in supervisory and development training programs. However, other methods and techniques of instruction have been designed to deal with the more complex topics and concepts found in training prospective office supervisors and middle managers. Several of these methods and techniques are described below.

In-House Seminars and Workshops

At in-house seminars and workshops, a discussion leader may instruct the trainees, or the leader may guide the trainees to reach a decision partially or entirely by themselves. Seminars and workshops are effectively used in training prospective supervisors and managers in human relations and in changing group attitudes and behaviors by using case histories. This training may be followed by on-the-job coaching from a leader skilled in human relations.

Mentoring

Mentoring is a training arrangement whereby senior managers (*mentors*) impart their expertise to younger managers and supervisors (*protégés*) in the company. Experienced mentors pass along their knowledge of the values, culture, and management styles of the organization; help new managers and supervisors to get along with people; and teach specific job skills. Successful mentoring depends upon the interaction skills of both the mentor and the protégé. Therefore, it is crucial that the mentor be carefully matched to the protégé. For this reason, the protégés may be asked to interview several mentors before choosing one to serve as a coach.

Some firms allow several years for their formal mentoring programs, while other companies limit the formal activities to about six months. After this time, the participants are encouraged to continue their relationships informally; often lasting friendships are formed. The mentors are responsible for assigning challenging projects to the younger managers so that they are exposed to meaningful, real-life learning experiences. Mentors benefit by receiving *psychic*

Dialog on the Firing Line

SHERRY CRONE
President
Dimension 11 Ltd.
Management and Customer Service Consulting
Regina, Saskatchewan, Canada

BA, University of Manitoba
Public Relations Certificate, University of Regina
Teaching Certificate, Brandon College

As President of Dimension 11 Limited, Sherry Crone is a public relations, customer service, and human resources consultant assisting companies to maximize the effectiveness of their people. A member of the National Speakers Association and The Speakers Bureau International, Ms. Crone is a dynamic speaker and seminar leader who has made presentations to such diverse groups as Saskatchewan Government Insurance, Federal Express, Manitoba Health Organization, Mary Kay Cosmetics, and the Institute of Canadian Banks. She has worked for and with the media as well as for one of the largest insurance companies in Canada.

QUESTION: As a tool of career development for the female office manager, how do you rank attendance at seminars that stress leadership skills for women? What benefits do women gain from participating in seminars and workshops?

RESPONSE: All seminars are valuable in expanding one's knowledge and expertise in becoming a better leader. Those that stress leadership skills for women often have an added edge for young women wishing to advance. They indicate the pitfalls that one may encounter and help them recognize their strengths and areas needing development. These seminars also assist leaders in looking at others positively, a major benefit when one has a staff. It is helpful to be *aware* of the challenges one might encounter. With this knowledge, it is easier to plan a successful career path that accepts the challenges and still accomplishes one's goals.

income—the personal satisfaction and peer recognition gained from passing on their experiences and knowledge in developing the talents of protégés.

Role Playing

Role playing, a training technique also known as *play acting* and *psychodrama*, calls upon potential supervisors and other trainees to act out their own parts or those of others under simulated conditions. The supervisor may assume the role of a high-level executive and "act out" a solution to problems that would face the executive on that level. Other trainees act as observers, and afterward their immediate superior or training specialist evaluates the performance.

Decision Simulation

Decision simulation, commonly known as *business games*, is based on a model that simulates the actual business or one of its functions. The objectives of the method are to furnish insights into organizational behavior, to promote teamwork among participants, and to teach at the behavioral level.

In playing a game, competing groups of supervisors or middle managers assume certain roles in the management of a company. They are given a description of the mythical business firm and asked to perform tasks and make organizational decisions, often with the aid of a computer. The decisions to be made may be related to improving the company's position by taking such actions as cutting costs, improving production, and increasing sales.

In-Basket Training

In the decision simulation technique referred to as **in-basket training**, the prospective office supervisor is given a brief description of a higher-ranking position. Next, the trainee is "promoted" to that job and given a representative sample of the problems—usually memos and correspondence—as they might arrive in the mail. Within a specified period of time, the trainee must make all decisions and solve all problems, ranging from taking action on reports and letters to settling conflicts among co-workers.

Case Study

When the **case study** is used, each supervisor-trainee is given a written history of a problem or situation that exists or has existed in the business firm. After the background information available for decision making has been studied, each trainee presents a solution to the problem in class. The trainees then evaluate the decisions reached by each other and learn to relate the solutions to the enterprise as a whole and to perceive the interrelationships of people and events. After having evaluated their own decisions, the trainees may be told what actually took place in the business firm. As you have seen when solving the case problems in this textbook, there is rarely a single solution to a case problem; however, like you, trainees gradually develop insights into management behavior as a result of having analyzed and discussed several possible solutions.

Incident Process

In the **incident process**, a group of potential supervisors is given a series of incidents that occur in a mythical company. However, only a minimum of related information is supplied. The supervisors themselves must obtain all additional data needed and then make the decisions. The objective of this training technique is to teach the supervisor-trainee how to examine all facets of the incident and to engage in research by gathering data from many sources.

Assessment Centers

Assessment centers use simulation exercises similar to the kind of work situations employees will find on higher-level jobs. The centers are also used to identify managerial talent among workers and sometimes as part of the appraisal process when promotions are being considered. A series of exercises is used to test the qualities most organizations consider important in management: organizational planning, problem analysis, judgment, ethical and moral conduct, decisiveness, leadership, interpersonal sensitivity, and initiative. Typical exercises include in-basket decision making, leaderless group discussion, simulated interviews, analysis problems, and fact-finding problems. The simulated exercises are observed by specially trained persons who work together as a team to pool their observations and arrive at a consensus evaluation of each participant. Some firms train their own managers to act as assessors, while other companies rely upon outside psychologists and consultants.

APPRAISING THE OFFICE WORKER'S PERFORMANCE

In **employee performance appraisal** or *performance evaluation*, the relative value of an employee's traits, personal qualifications, attitudes, and behavior is appraised. You will want to remember that in performance appraisal, the evaluator studies and analyzes the performance of the *employee*, not the job held by that employee. The evaluator may use the information obtained from performance appraisal for the following purposes:

1. To determine salary increases and to make decisions regarding promotion, transfer, and demotion.
2. To enhance the worker's morale, to contribute directly and indirectly to self-improvement, and to stimulate confidence in management's fairness.
3. To stimulate employees to improve their work.
4. To discover workers' needs for retraining and promotional training programs.
5. To uncover exceptional skills among employees.
6. To furnish a tangible basis for the termination of unqualified or unfit employees.
7. To help assign work in accordance with the worker's ability by furnishing infor-

mation for the proper placement, career counseling, and guidance of the worker.
8. To aid in validating the selection process, especially in the areas of interviewing and testing.
9. To help settle disputes in arbitration cases.

From this list, we can conclude that performance appraisal should provide a fair treatment of all employees, an objective rating, and a feeling by employees that they are not ignored or overlooked.

Methods of Appraising Employee Performance

Several commonly used methods of performance appraisal are briefly described in Figure 8–3. Some companies use two or more of these methods, or a modification of each method, to design their appraisal programs. Companies that have installed a program of work measurement and work standards, as discussed later in the text, may use their work standards in conjunction with most appraisal methods. Since work standards are aimed at improving productivity, their use makes possible a more objective and accurate appraisal of the office worker's performance.

An Illustrative Performance Appraisal Form

The two-page appraisal form shown in Figure 8–4 is designed for use in evaluating white-collar workers. Note that space is provided to record the employee's attendance over a six-month period. This form is well designed, with five degrees contained in the range of each of the seven factors to be evaluated. The rater is further aided by a brief but clear definition of each of the degrees. On the second page, space is provided for the rater to record comments about the employee's potential leadership ability and to record any other information that may aid in appraising the employee's performance. The form also provides space for the rater to indicate an overall opinion

Figure 8-3
Methods of
Appraising
Employee
Performance

1. **Rating scales,** in which factors dealing with *quantity* and *quality* of work are listed and rated. A numeric value may be assigned each factor and an effort made to weight the factors in the order of their relative importance. The rating scale is a widely used method of evaluating performance because it is economical to develop and easily understood by the worker and the evaluator. A major weakness is that each evaluator is apt to interpret differently the factors (such as Knowledge of Work) and the degrees describing that factor that are marked off along the scale (such as Excellent, Good, Fair, Poor).

2. **Narrative** or **essay,** a commonly used technique in which the evaluator provides a written paragraph or more covering such topics as an employee's strengths, weaknesses, and potential. The narrative method is often used in evaluating office workers although there is a disadvantage in the varying length and content of the narratives. Since the narratives touch on different aspects of performance and personal characteristics, they are difficult to combine for comparison purposes.

3. **Management by objectives (MBO)** or **goal setting,** in which a number of short-range goals or objectives that appear to be within the capabilities of the worker are established. The goals, agreed upon mutually by the employee and the supervisor, become the job performance standards by which the employee is evaluated for the period of time for which the goals are established.

   The method rests on the premise that the only real measure of how we perform is whether we achieve specific results. Thus, management by objectives, as discussed in Chapter 7, is *results oriented* rather than *trait oriented.* Although not practical for use at all levels and for all kinds of office work, the method provides for systematic goal setting and performance reviews that concentrate upon the work accomplished rather than upon problems related to personality traits and characteristics.

4. **Simple ranking** or **grading,** in which all employees are classified by rank as best, second best, third best, and so on throughout the entire employee group. Employees are evaluated on their overall usefulness and value to the firm and no attempt is made to describe and evaluate their performances, traits, qualifications, or characteristics. The simple ranking method is useful only in very small companies with fewer than 25 employees where a suitable criterion has been established as the basis for the rating.

5. **Rank order** or **order of merit,** in which the evaluator ranks all employees in order from the best to the poorest on the merits of performance and specific factors such as quantity and quality of work. This method, which takes considerable time and is very subjective, is successful to the extent that employees accept the criteria used for the rankings and respect their rater's honesty.

6. **Forced distribution,** in which employees are rated on only two characteristics: *job performance* and *promotability.* A five-point job performance scale is used, and the supervisor is asked to allocate 10 percent of the workers to the best rating, 20 percent to the next best, 40 percent to the middle group, 20 percent to the group next to the lowest, and 10 percent to the lowest group.

   The method forces the rater not to rank too many workers on the highest or the middle scale. Also, the rater will not appraise the poorest workers as medium or fair since they must be placed among the lowest 10 percent.

7. **Paired comparison,** in which each employee is paired with every other employee in the group. For example, by comparing each pair of workers in the order processing and billing department, the rater decides which of the two workers is more valuable. When making each comparison, the supervisor underlines the name of the preferred worker on a specially prepared form. The employee's score is obtained by counting the number of times his or her name is underlined. After all workers in the group have been thus compared, a list is prepared to show the rank of each employee in order of merit, according to the number of times his or her name was underlined.

   The paired comparison method is workable only in very small groups of 10 to 12 employees; in larger groups, the job of rating becomes overly burdensome and time consuming.

8. **Factor comparison,** in which numerous phrases or questions referring to specific factors are listed, such as those in Figure 8-4. The rater checks the statement or answers the question "yes" or "no" to describe the appropriate characteristic of the worker being appraised. A numeric value is provided for each statement or question, and the complete rating is obtained by totaling all statement values. Using this method, the rater thinks critically about the employee's performance in terms of each important factor and is able to make a study of the worker's specific strengths and weaknesses.

Figure 8-4
Appraisal
Form
Designed for
Evaluating
White-Collar
Workers
(page 1)

EMPLOYEE APPRAISAL

EMPLOYEE'S POSITION	DATE	EMPLOYEE'S NAME	PERIODIC APPRAISAL
Designate concisely, such as senior clerk, unit teller, stenographer, etc.			Return to personnel dept. not later than
unit teller	*11/6/91*	*Jana Markham*	*Nov. 8, 1991*

Briefly describe nature of specific duties:

Receives funds for deposit, disburses funds, proof of cash daily, completes fill-in for savings bonds purchased.

ATTENDANCE RECORD

MO.	LATE	ABSENT
May	1	1
Jun	3	0
Jul	2	3
Aug	2	2
Sep	4	1
Oct	0	3
TOTAL	12	10

QUANTITY OF WORK
Consider volume of work produced consistently

Unsatisfactory output	Limited. Does just enough to get by	Average output	Above average producer	Exceptional output
☐	☐	☒	☐	☐

QUALITY OF WORK
Consider accuracy and neatness

Very poor	Not entirely acceptable	Acceptable accuracy and neatness	Very neat and accurate	Exceptionally neat and accurate
☐	☐	☐	☒	☐

COOPERATION
Consider cooperation with associates and supervisors

Entirely uncooperative	Reluctant to cooperate	Adequately cooperative	Very cooperative	Unusually cooperative
☐	☒	☐	☐	☐

DEPENDABILITY
Consider amount of supervision required and application to work

Unreliable and inattentive	Needs frequent supervision	Generally reliable and attentive to work. Follows instructions carefully	Very reliable and conscientious, needs little supervision	Extremely reliable and industrious
☐	☐	☒	☐	☐

ABILITY TO LEARN
Consider ability to understand and retain

Very limited	Requires repeated instructions	Learns reasonably well	Readily understands and retains	Unusual capacity
☐	☒	☐	☐	☐

INITIATIVE
Consider originality and resourcefulness

Lacking	Routine worker	Occasionally shows initiative	Better than average	Outstanding
☐	☒	☐	☐	☐

JUDGMENT
Consider ability to evaluate situations and make sound decisions

Poor	Not always reliable	Good in most matters	Reliable	Decisions most logical and well founded
☐	☐	☒	☐	☐

Recommended Increase: *$75.00* biweekly

By *Toshi Akeo*
Supervising Officer

Approved by Personnel Committee effective: _____

Next Review *May, 1992*

OK to FILE

OVER

Figure 8–4
Appraisal
Form
Designed for
Evaluating
White-Collar
Workers
(page 2)

LEADERSHIP
Consider ability to gain
cooperation, inspire
confidence and direct
people

(Does employee presently do supervisory work? Yes_____ No _X_)
Indicate your opinion of employee's ability:

Markham needs to "open up" and try to help her co-workers more. She seems to shut herself off from everyone except the customers at the window.

REMARKS: Furnish any additional information which you believe may be helpful in more fully evaluating this employee

None

WHAT IS YOUR OVER-ALL OPINION OF THIS EMPLOYEE:

Unsatisfactory	☐
Poor	☐
Fair	☐
Good	☒
Very good	☐
Outstanding	☐

SINCE EMPLOYEE'S LAST APPRAISAL EMPLOYEE HAS

Improved	☒
Made little or no change	☐
Has slipped back	☐

This employee has been informed regarding any unfavorable factors reflected in this report by *Toshi Akeo*

Date *11/6/91*

Employee's reactions: *She agrees with evaluation of her being "up tight" around co-workers. Blames her "coldness" on bad situation at last place of employment.*

Your Comments: *Will purposefully try to "cultivate" more during next few months. Will add duties that bring her more directly in contact with co-workers.*

_____*Toshi Akeo*_____
DEPARTMENT HEAD OR SUPERVISOR

_____*Charles O. Rollins*_____
OFFICER

FOR PERSONNEL DEPARTMENT USE ONLY _____

of the employee and to record what improvement, if any, has taken place since the last appraisal. Any unfavorable factors discovered during the appraisal are discussed with the employee, and his or her reactions are noted along with the rater's comments.

Weaknesses of Performance Appraisal Forms

When using any appraisal instrument, the rater should be concerned that the form provides information that aids in meeting the purposes listed on page 219. However, an examination of employee performance appraisal forms indicates that some contain certain weaknesses, such as the following, which should be avoided:

1. *Too many questions or characteristics to answer, check, or rate.* Only enough factors and degrees should be given to provide a fair and reasonable picture of the work being done and of the employee who is doing it. Too many questions take too much time and may cause careless or routine and superficial ratings. Probably six or eight factors, each with five or six degrees, are sufficient in most instances.
2. *Poor phrasing of the questions.* Using detailed and descriptive phrases motivates the rater to use more careful judgment than if he or she has only to check general terms. Instead of using such words as "very good," "good," "fair," or "poor" to describe a factor, phrases such as the following should be used: (a) Shows a high level of intelligence in doing work; (b) Shows some intelligence and initiative in performing work; (c) Understands simple routines and follows instructions; and (d) Little comprehension of work, needs constant instruction.
3. *A pattern in the arrangement of the descriptive phrases for each factor.* To provide for a less biased evaluation by the rater, the form should be arranged so that for some factors the highest rating

degree appears first, and for others the highest rating degree appears last. Alternating or otherwise differentiating the order of the degrees requires the evaluator to make an individual appraisal of each factor.

Frequency of Performance Appraisal

The performance of office workers is being *informally* appraised in a never-ending process by their supervisors who observe, evaluate, and coach them on a day-to-day basis. This kind of appraisal is one of the supervisor's downward responsibilities to aid workers in improving their performance, to heighten their motivation, and to solve job-performance and human-relations problems on the spot by "striking while the iron is hot." However, this continuing type of appraisal is not an adequate substitute for *formal* employee appraisal, which is discussed in this section.

In most companies, the performance of office workers is evaluated once each year; however, more frequent reviews can be arranged in the event of promotional openings, poor performance, or outstanding performance. Often during an entry-level worker's probationary period or during the first year on a new job, appraisals are made more frequently. Thus, a firm with a probationary period of six months may evaluate the new office workers at the end of one month, three months, and six months; thereafter, the employee is placed on permanent status and reviews are scheduled annually on the anniversary of the employee's hiring date. Anniversary-date reviews are very important to employees; therefore, supervisors should not postpone the review of employee performance even if the reviews contain a great deal of negative criticism.

Who Should Appraise Employees?

In answering the question of who should appraise employees, it seems logical that the evaluation should be made by those who come in direct supervisory contact with the workers. In many large companies, you will find that the appraisal is made by the employee's immediate supervisor and is reviewed by both the next higher-level manager and the human resources department.

Generally the appraisal is discussed with the employee, who in many companies must sign the appraisal form to indicate that it has been discussed with him or her. The appraisal then becomes part of the employee's permanent personnel record. Sometimes the office worker may be given a copy of the appraisal. In many instances, the office workers have the right to appeal or to protest the performance appraisal. State laws may provide for employees to place counterstatements in their personnel records. If the employees are represented by a union, the appeal may be made through the regular grievance procedure. In nonunion offices, the appeal procedure is informal. It may consist of the employees' noting their disagreement with the appraisal, either in discussion with the supervisor or a representative from the human resources department or in writing on the appraisal form.

PROMOTING

Successful promotion plans are definite, systematic, fair, and followed uniformly. The basis of promotion is the organization chart, developed after a systematic job analysis as described in the following chapter. Each employee should understand the responsibilities of his or her position, the line of promotion, the requirements for the next higher job, and the salary to be expected, which should not be less than the minimum salary for the higher classification or rank.

A promotion plan must have the confidence of the employees. To provide for promotions based upon objective data and not solely upon personal opinion and assessment, the human resources department should maintain a current personal data bank on all employees. These files should include information on all employees, such as age, education, experience, special abilities, physical condition, absences from work, tardiness, suggestions offered by the employee to the firm, any disciplinary action taken, and most important, the periodic appraisals of worker performance.

Commonly we find that promotions are granted as rewards for successful work done in a previous position. The firm senses that status and compensation can be increased only by moving a person up the organizational ladder. However, these firms must develop a greater awareness that each position requires different skills and attitudes and that success in one area does not, in itself, qualify a person for promotion to a higher position. Thus, promotions should be related to the specific requirements of the new position. As a result, individuals will not be promoted solely because of their success in previously held jobs, longevity, or their personal loyalty to the firm or to their superiors. Although these factors are important indicators of a person's overall contribution to the firm, they should be used only as part of the promotion criteria. Other criteria that are more indicative of success on the future job include a complete knowledge and understanding of the duties, responsibilities, and requirements of the new position; interviews and tests that have been checked for their validity and reliability; promotion trials, which, as explained later, give the prospective candidate an insight into some of the new duties, followed by an evaluation of performance; and participation in assessment centers, where the potential of the candidate for promotion is judged by a team of trained observers.

Publicizing Job Vacancies

Companies use several methods to inform office employees of job vacancies for which they may apply. The most common method of publicizing job vacancies is to post notices on bulletin boards. Job posting is a procedure highly recommended by the Equal Employment Opportunity Commission and other agencies charged with enforcing equal employment opportunity laws and regulations. Generally there is a limit on the length of time the notice must remain posted and the time during which employees may bid for the job. However, in many companies, employees may bid at any time until the job is filled.

Memos may also be sent by the human resources department to supervisors, who announce the job openings to their subordinates. For example, one firm issues to all its supervisors a weekly report that lists all current openings. Other approaches to publicizing job vacancies include listing the openings in employee publications and announcing any openings at supervisory meetings. Also, some firms operate a job preference system that gives employees an opportunity to indicate interest in certain types of jobs should openings occur.

Identifying Employees' Promotion Potential

Companies may use a skills inventory or human resources information system to provide names of employees who are eligible for promotion when vacancies occur. More frequently, however, companies make use of their performance appraisal system, which includes an evaluation of their employees' promotion potential.

Some firms seek outside professional help to evaluate their employees' potential for promotion. Management consulting firms may be called upon to test employees and to conduct interviews in an attempt to determine which employees possess the abilities and characteristics for promotion. For example, one management consulting firm gives personality tests to obtain a better understanding of the employees' attitudes

and opinions and to help determine the employees' future benefit to the company.

In large companies, psychological testing is sometimes used to observe and to evaluate workers in order to locate future managerial ability. Also, we saw earlier that companies may use assessment centers to identify employees who are suited for higher positions.

Factors Considered in Promotion Decisions

Many companies take seniority, or length of service, into account when making promotion decisions concerning office jobs. However, seniority is rarely the *only* factor examined. When making promotion decisions for office jobs, the following factors are commonly given more consideration than seniority:

1. Ability to perform the work.
2. Previous work record.
3. Previous experience or education.
4. Recommendation of supervisor or department head.
5. Interview ratings.

Other firms, especially governmental offices and companies that are unionized, place more emphasis upon seniority when promoting office personnel. These firms feel that people who have served loyally for a long period merit recognition. The philosophy of basing promotions upon seniority tends to stabilize employment and to reduce turnover. Seniority should not be adhered to rigidly, however, since it may become an arbitrary check on younger workers. Also, promotion based solely upon seniority may result in a somewhat stagnant staff. New ideas and ability to perform the work must be given recognition, even at the expense of seniority. Otherwise the younger and perhaps more creative, aggressive employees will seek work with a competitor or maybe start in business themselves, with either action possibly being detrimental to the firm.

Probationary Periods

Many firms provide a probationary period for newly promoted employees to prove themselves on the new job. Most probationary periods last three months or 90 days. Some firms provide **promotion trials** for positions that have been vacated. Under this approach, promotion in position or change in responsibilities is made with the consent of the person being transferred. The promoted employees are given the option of returning to their previous jobs if they are unsuccessful or unhappy on the new job. The time limit for exercising such an option may range from one week to six months, with three months being a very common time limit. Often there is a stipulation that returning to the old job is not guaranteed unless it is still vacant or another suitable vacancy exists.

Horizontal Promotion

Employees may reach a level in their departments at which the future is not very promising because there is little turnover and the departments are not expanding. Therefore, consideration should be given to transferring such capable workers to other departments where promotional opportunities are greater. This type of transfer is really a form of promotion—a **horizontal promotion**—though there may be no increase in salary or rank. It is a promotion because in the new position there will be an earlier chance for advancement.

Transfers

Transfers and promotions are related, although not all transfers are promotions. For instance, a transfer may be necessary because an employee has been improperly matched to the job. As a result of the transfer, the employee is moved to a position for which he or she is better qualified and where the worker's capabilities will be challenged. Of

course, such a transfer can be made only where the firm has a staff sufficiently large enough to absorb the transferee.

The fundamental purpose of transferring employees is to stimulate them out of the monotony, and perhaps inefficiency, in which their long service may have placed them. Some firms believe in the practice of developing understudies and therefore have a regular schedule of transfers so resignations, promotions, reassignments, deaths, and illnesses of employees do not seriously affect the office work. There is always someone who can step in and do the work. This policy also stimulates the worker since few workers will feel that their services are indispensable or that "the firm cannot get along without them."

Other firms have rush and slack periods either during the month or during certain periods of the year. By having a series of employee transfers, workers obtain experience in a variety of positions, thus enabling the office manager to shift workers during the busy seasons.

The closing section of this chapter deals with another objective of employee appraisal—to furnish a tangible basis for the termination of unqualified or unsatisfactory employees.

TERMINATING THE OFFICE WORKER'S SERVICES

In small and medium-size companies that have no human resources department, office supervisors are responsible for terminating the services of unqualified or unsatisfactory office workers. In larger firms, the responsibility for firing office workers is usually handled by the human resources department according to a standard procedure. Regardless of the size of the firm, few things in life are as traumatic for office workers as losing their jobs. Although firing may not be a pleasant task for the office supervisor, if it is done humanely, the supervisor can aid in creating a better organization in the long run.

Developing a Termination Procedure

Basic to the firing of any worker is the existence of a well-planned termination procedure that satisfies the union agreement, if any, and government regulations, such as those described in Chapter 6. Personnel records must be objectively and consistently maintained to reflect up-to-date, accurate data so that the cause for termination is well documented. Above all, the termination procedure should be planned to ensure a fair hearing for the worker as well as legal protection for the employer.

Firing should not come as a surprise to an office worker, although there may be an occasion when for justifiable cause a worker is fired on the spot. For example, most companies have a policy that if an office employee reports for work intoxicated, the worker is subject to immediate discharge. Prior to most terminations, however, the worker will have been forewarned by means of warnings and reprimands, performance appraisals, or in counseling sessions and meetings with the supervisor. Thus, as a result of actions taken earlier, the worker should know that he or she has not met the company's expectations.

The *exit interview* should be carefully planned and held in privacy. The interview may be scheduled near the end of the workday so that the terminated worker does not have to confront any peers in the office following the meeting. During the exit interview, the worker's unsatisfactory performance as compared with expectations should be objectively reviewed. The continued failure of the worker to meet goals should be indicated. The worker's strengths and weaknesses can be spelled out by the supervisor; and if possible, the worker may be aided by indicating where his or her strengths may be better utilized. The decision

to fire the worker must be clearly stated along with the date upon which the worker's duties are to cease. The worker should be informed of the procedure to follow in obtaining his or her last paycheck. If the company plans to respond to reference checks about the fired worker, the worker should be so notified and both parties should agree on what will be cited as the reason for termination.

The person conducting the exit interview must avoid becoming emotionally involved with the worker, personally insulting him or her, or being highly critical of any personal qualities outside the worker's control. The interviewer should listen carefully for any feedback from the dismissed worker that will aid in improving future job performance in the department.

Employment and Termination at Will

Under the **employment-at-will** doctrine, the employee and the employer have the right to enter freely into the employment relationship and to sever this relationship at *any* time for *any* reason. Under this rule, the employer's power to discharge workers went unchallenged for many years, during which time many companies had little regard for their human resources. Today, however, this absolute right to discharge is disappearing. Employees have filed suits against their employers, arguing that they have been unjustly discharged. As we shall see, many companies, in turn, are taking steps to avoid such claims.

Over the past 50 years the employment-at-will doctrine has been gradually eroded. For example, unionized employees may be fired only for "cause" or "just cause." The *just-cause standard* requires that a job-related, valid reason must exist for the discharge. Further, Civil Service rules protect from arbitrary dismissal the majority of employees working for the federal, state, or local government. Employees are also protected by a variety of state and federal statutes that prohibit discharge based on the employee's religion, national origin, race, sex, age, physical or mental disability, or union activity. Even with this extensive protection provided by law, it is estimated that private industry discharges about 1 million employees each year without granting a fair hearing and that thousands of employees are unfairly terminated each year.[3]

Today the courts are becoming more sensitive to the personal rights of workers and the growing awareness of the social need for job protection. Of course, employers have the right to fire employees who have poor safety records, refuse work orders, produce poor-quality work, are absent without excuse, or are unqualified to perform the work. However, the power of employers to terminate arbitrarily is being curbed more and more. Since 1980, the courts in 46 states have said that job-security promises may constitute legally binding contracts.[4] States have ruled that employers

cannot fire employees (union or nonunion) if the terminations are unfair. Therefore, in order to avoid costly lawsuits, companies have revised their employee handbooks, application forms, and advertising materials to make sure that there are no statements implying permanent employment or job security. Some companies have set up internal *dispute-resolution systems*, such as arbitration, in an attempt to avoid possible lawsuits. More attention is being paid to the issuance of performance appraisals that show candid evaluations of employee performance. Disciplinary or critical discussions with employees are being carefully and completely documented and retained for a reasonable period of time, such as five years.

As a result of court rulings and the prospect of further state legislation that will affect employment at will, many companies have taken a closer look at their employee relations programs. Companies are also paying much closer attention to selecting, orienting, training, appraising, promoting, and terminating their employees. Office managers have become increasingly concerned with the adoption of an attitude of fairness in their dealings with the company's most valuable asset—its human resources.

---

[3]George E. Stevens, "The Fading of Firing-at-Will," *Management World* (March, 1985), p. 9.
[4]Aaron Bernstein, "More Dismissed Workers Are Telling It to the Judge," *Business Week* (October 17, 1988), p. 68.

SUMMARY

1. The office training program must be built upon sound principles of learning if office personnel, with their diverse needs, are to function efficiently. The program must provide for effective application of those psychological factors that create a meaningful learning situation.

2. In designing its entry-level training program and its supervisory training and development program, the firm must carefully evaluate the wide array of training methods and techniques available. From these, the firm should select those that best meet the needs of the

persons who plan the training programs and of those who implement the training.

3. Office supervisors must know how to undertake performance appraisals so that all employees are fairly treated and objectively evaluated. In light of the eroding employment-at-will rule, supervisors must be familiar with the methods or techniques of conducting such appraisals to make sure that candid evaluations of employee performance are obtained and documented. Proper employee performance appraisal aids the firm in developing and retaining employees

who are more self-confident, properly matched with the requirements of their present jobs, and prepared to meet the requirements of those jobs that lie ahead on the promotional ladder.

4. Since office employees may be found to be unqualified for their positions or per-forming unsatisfactorily, a well-planned termination procedure is needed to make sure that the workers to be discharged are given a fair hearing in which the rights of both the workers and the employer are protected.

GLOSSARY

Assessment center—a training center that uses simulation management exercises to provide the same kind of work situation trainees will find on higher-level jobs.

Case study—a written case history that trainees study for problem solving and class evaluation.

Computer-assisted instruction (CAI)—a training method in which trainees operate terminal input-output units to learn materials that have been programmed on the computer; sometimes called *computer-augmented instruction*.

Decision simulation—a training method based on a model of an actual business or one of its functions, in which competing groups of trainees assume managerial roles, perform tasks, and make decisions for the mythical business firm; also known as *business games*.

Employee performance appraisal—the study of an employee's traits, personal qualifications, attitudes, and behavior; also called *performance evaluation*.

Employment at will—the doctrine which states that the employee and the employer have the right to freely enter into the employment relationship and to sever this relationship at *any* time for *any* reason.

Entry-level training—the training designed to qualify employees for entry-job assignments; also called *initial training*.

Habit—the product of learning in which changes occur in previous behavioral patterns and attitudes.

Horizontal promotion—the transfer of an employee to another department where promotional opportunities are greater than in the present department.

In-basket training—a training technique in which trainees assume higher-level positions and solve a representative sample of problems under the pressure of time.

Incident process—a training method in which, after trainees are given a series of incidents occurring in a mythical company and only a minimum of related information, they must obtain all additional data and make decisions.

Job rotation—a training method that exposes trainees to a number of functions in a relatively short period of time by rotating them through the various departments of the company or sections of a department.

Learning—the changes that occur in trainees' behavioral patterns and attitudes as a result of training.

Lecture—a nonparticipative, one-way communication technique in which an instructor imparts factual information to a group in a relatively short period of time.

Mentoring—a training arrangement whereby senior managers (*mentors*) impart their expertise to younger managers and supervisors (*protégés*) in the company.

On-the-job training (OJT)—a type of training in which the trainees are provided the knowledge and skills needed to perform their jobs while using the actual equipment and materials required on the jobs.

Plateau—a period of time or a level of learning where no observable improvement occurs or where the rate of increase in learning levels off.

Programmed instruction (PI)—a self-instruction method in which learning materials are presented as small units of information, with learning proceeding from basic to more difficult materials.

Promotion trials—the promotions made with the consent of the persons being transferred and with the promoted employees given the option of returning to their previous jobs if they are unsuccessful or unhappy on their new jobs.

Reinforcer—a condition following a response that results in an increase in the strength of that response.

Retraining—the training provided for workers whose job assignments have changed.

Role playing—a training technique in which trainees act out their own roles or those of others under simulated conditions; also called *play acting* and *psychodrama*.

Supervisory training and development—the training designed to qualify workers for the added responsibilities and challenges of higher positions.

Teleconferencing—a telephone service (both audio and video forms) that ties together three or more people at two or more separate locations.

Training—the process of providing individuals with an organized series of experiences and materials that comprise opportunities to learn.

Upgrading training—the training designed to improve an employee's knowledge and skills in the job presently held.

Vestibule training—the training that takes place in an area away from the site where the job is usually performed, with the workstation simulated and the necessary equipment provided.

FOR YOUR REVIEW

1. Distinguish between the concepts of *training* and *learning*.

2. Describe the several broad goals that may be included in the office training program.

3. Contrast the role of the office manager in a large firm to that of the office supervisor in a small company in organizing and administering the office training program.

4. How should the administrative office manager proceed in evaluating the effectiveness of the firm's office training program?

5. Identify the groups that need feedback on the results of the training program. For what reasons do these groups need feedback?

6. What kinds of learning reinforcers may be used by a trainer to strengthen the desired responses in the behavior of the learners?

7. Which kind of practice—massed or spaced—usually results in more rapid learning and more permanent retention of the learning materials? Explain.

8. Describe the outcomes of effective office training.

9. What are the three abilities that should be possessed by the person in charge of initial training?

10. Define the role of the first-line supervisor in conducting the office training program in a small firm.

11. Contrast on-the-job training to job rotation as an effective method of training entry-level office employees.

12. What advantages can be cited for on-the-job training as contrasted to vestibule training?

13. Describe how mentors are used in a supervisory training and development program.

14. For what purposes may the information obtained from employee performance appraisal be used?

15. Describe how the narrative method is used in appraising employee performance. What are the disadvantages of using this method of appraisal?

16. Briefly describe the procedure followed in using the management by objectives (goal-setting) method to appraise employees.

17. What are the characteristics of a successful promotion plan?

18. What steps can a company take to prevent its workers from being promoted solely because of their success in previously held jobs?

19. What factors are usually considered when decisions about promotions are being made?

20. To what extent should seniority be considered in the promotion of office personnel?

21. A horizontal transfer may, in effect, be a promotion. Explain.

22. What points should be kept in mind by the office supervisor who is developing a termination procedure?

23. With the erosion of the employment-at-will rule, what steps have companies taken to protect themselves from lawsuits involving the possible unfair termination of workers?

FOR YOUR DISCUSSION

1. Toward the end of 1988, *Time* magazine reported: "As much as a quarter of the American labor force—anywhere from 20 million to 27 million adults—lacks the basic reading, writing, and math skills necessary to perform in today's increasingly complex job market. One out of every 4 teenagers drops out of high school, and of those who graduate, 1 out of every 4 has the equivalent of an eighth-grade education."[5] What steps can companies, regardless of their size, take to bridge this so-called literacy gap?

2. In some offices, the responsibility for entry-level training is assigned to one of the older office workers. What are the advantages of using an older worker as a trainer? What kinds of problems may emerge when a company follows this approach?

3. What benefits may a company realize by having its entry-level training program for word processing personnel conducted at a nearby community college? Under what

---

[5]Christine Gorman, "The Literacy Gap," *Time* (December 29, 1988), p. 56.

conditions do you think that such a cooperative training program between a business firm and a community college is not beneficial?

4. Many company managers and executives believe that the movement from supervisor to manager is just the beginning of a natural progression toward successively higher levels of status and pay in the organization. How, then, do you explain that sometimes the best way to destroy good supervisors is to promote them?

5. You have just learned from your boss that one of your subordinates and your very best friend, Maryanne Houston, must be laid off as part of your firm's cutback, which resulted from a recent takeover by a Japanese holding company. Houston has been with your firm for more than 20 years and during this time she has become like a "sister" to you. Is there a kind way to terminate the services of your best friend?

6. Last Friday when Debra Stevenson left work at the Collins Company, she was an executive secretary. When she reports in for work on Monday morning, she will be assuming a new position, supervisor of general office services. What kind of "people" problems may face Stevenson as she undertakes her new post? As her superior, what steps should you have taken prior to her promotion in order to alleviate any potential "people" problems for Stevenson?

7. Several common weaknesses of performance appraisal forms are listed on page 223. Using this list, evaluate the employee appraisal form in Figure 8–4 on pages 221 and 222.

8. Jeanne Tibaud is the office manager at the Ontario Company, which has been faced with a decline in demand for its long-play records. As a result, the officers of the firm, which is nonunion, have decided to reduce the office staff by 75 jobs. What guidelines can you offer Tibaud, now faced with making the decision of who stays and who goes?

9. When Tim Reynolds applied for a job at the Proudfoot Company, he was told by an interviewer that he would be with Proudfoot as long as he did his job. Three months later, Reynolds was fired after a bitter disagreement with his supervisor. What are the implications of this happening in view of the increased attacks upon the employment-at-will doctrine? What precautions might Proudfoot take in order to avoid any possible lawsuits in which terminated employees claim they were unfairly discharged?

SOLVING CASE PROBLEMS

Case 8–1 Planning a Training Program for Personnel in the Payroll Department

Anita Fumero has just graduated from high school and has accepted the job of payroll clerk in the home office of the Cohen Oil Company. The job consists of auditing weekly time cards and entering variable payroll information (regular hours worked, overtime hours worked, updated wage and salary rates, etc.) onto a disk for processing by the computer. This is Fumero's first job, and she has no business background other than one semester's cooperative work experience (clerk-typist) as part of her course requirements.

It is your plan, as supervisor of the payroll department, to have each new worker, such as Fumero, properly trained before actual employment begins. Your budget allows you to pay all new workers an hourly wage of $8 during the initial training period. After having successfully completed the entry-level training program, the new workers will be placed on an annual salary of $17,500 to $18,750 during the three-months' probationary period. The payroll department, with its 20 office workers, has had an annual turnover of 25 percent.

Outline a complete plan for training the entry-level office workers in your department.

Case 8-2 Handling the Termination Interview

Dennis Parrott, supervisor of records management at the Madison Steel Company, has just called Jon Sofranko, a clerk-typist, into his office on Friday morning.

Parrott: Jon, we no longer need your services. The company based this decision on some performance problems you have. I don't have any details about your severance pay, but I am sure Maria in Human Resources can answer all your questions.

Sofranko: (shocked and deeply hurt) I don't understand. Just three months ago you gave me a raise.

Evaluate Parrott's approach in terminating the services of Sofranko. How do you recommend that this interview should have been handled?

9

Office Job Analysis

GOALS FOR THIS CHAPTER

After completing this chapter, you should be able to:

1. Identify how the information obtained from a program of job analysis is used in the office.
2. Describe and evaluate the methods of gathering and analyzing job information.
3. Point out the characteristics of well-written job descriptions and job specifications.
4. Compare and contrast the several methods of job evaluation by identifying the major features of each method.

We analyze an office job to learn how the work may be done in the one best way by the best qualified person and at the fairest salary that will produce the largest volume of satisfactory work. Thus, office job analysis is a major problem-solving activity, where workable solutions lead to improved office productivity.

As you see in Figure 9–1, the activities involved in analyzing office jobs are:

1. **Job analysis**—the process of gathering information about a specific job and determining the principal elements involved in performing it. As you shall see later, the major means of gathering job information are questionnaires, interviews, and observations. Usually job analysis is performed as the first step prior to job evaluation.
   (a) **Job description**—an outline of the information obtained from the job analysis, which describes the content and essential requirements of a specific job or position.
   (b) **Job specification**—a detailed record of the minimum job requirements explained in relation to the job factors (skill, effort, responsibility, and working conditions) so the job can be easily rated during the job evaluation process.
2. **Job evaluation**—the process of appraising the value of each job in relation to other jobs in order to set a monetary value for each specific job.
3. **Work measurement and setting work standards**—the procedure for determining the time required to complete each job or task and for setting up criteria by which the degree of work performance may be measured.

The first two phases of job analysis are explained in this chapter. We shall examine the third phase, work measurement and setting work standards, in a later chapter.

Figure 9–1
The Activities Involved in Analyzing Jobs

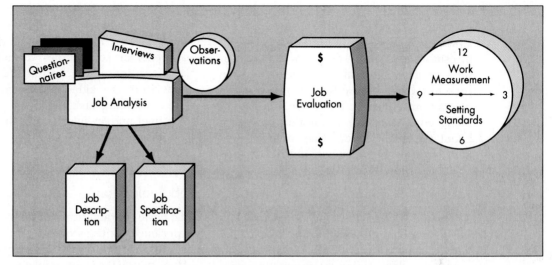

USES OF OFFICE JOB ANALYSIS

In this section you will learn about a number of activities in the office that depend upon the information gathered through job analysis.

Recruiting and Retaining Office Employees

Job analysis is fundamental to the preparation of job descriptions and job specifications, which are used in recruiting, selecting, orienting, training, and promoting office personnel. When properly undertaken, job analysis places a firm's office personnel practices on a nondiscriminatory basis by meeting the requirements of federal legislation such as the Equal Pay Act, the Civil Rights Act, and the Age Discrimination in Employment Act. As you saw in Chapter 6, these acts require all job applicants and employees to be accorded equal treatment, regardless of their race, color, religion, sex, national origin, and age.

The Uniform Guidelines on Employee Selection Procedure, also discussed in Chapter 6, require employers to devote special attention to job analysis when justifying any selection procedure that has an impact on a certain race, sex, or ethnic group. When firms undertake a validity study of their employment practices, they find that an ongoing job analysis program is vital, especially when employment practices, such as transfer, demotion, or promotion, are challenged in court.

Office supervisors who orient and train employees find job descriptions and specifications a great help in spelling out the job routines that must be emphasized in teaching correct work procedures and desirable performance levels. Job descriptions and specifications are also needed by those charged with preparing or selecting aptitude and proficiency tests to make sure that the tests are a valid measure of job content and requirements.

Distributing realistic job descriptions and specifications to employees enables them to understand better the specific duties of their jobs. Thus, any misunderstandings concerning performance expectations will be reduced. Also, employees will be more likely to accept explanations as to how work grievances are handled.

Well-developed job descriptions clarify the relationships between jobs, job functions, and departments and aid in establishing harmony and balance within the organization structure. A department promotion plan can be established through the use of job descriptions to show the real differences between present jobs and those that lie above in the promotion sequence. Therefore, employees being considered for promotion can learn about the qualifications they must possess in order to perform the new duties.

Job Simplification

As a result of studying jobs, the analyst can facilitate the employees' jobs by identifying and eliminating wasted motions. For example, when filling in insurance claim forms, a secretary was found leaning far to the left and stretching 28 inches to grasp a blank form and insert it into the typewriter. In studying just this one phase of the task, the analyst found that by relocating the stack of blank forms, the secretary eliminated stretching and reduced the reach to 12 inches. Job analysis, therefore, brings about simplification and improvement of jobs, which allows workers to perform more efficiently and more economically. As a result, office employees spend a smaller amount of effort in order to accomplish greater results.

Job Standardization

Job analysis leads to standardization of job content as revealed by the job title. For all employees holding the same title, the office supervisor has an accurate picture of what the employees do on the job; how and why they perform the work; the skills involved in work performance; and the physical demands, such as lifting and carrying, that are made upon employees.

Job standardization improves the supervisor's ability to control operations; for once the job contents have been standardized, it is easier to measure the output of employees holding the same positions. The

supervisor can measure the work produced on each job and set production standards, which in turn may be tied in with bonus payments or some other forms of incentives for increased output. Also, office supervisors are aided in assigning certain time-consuming tasks to lower paid office personnel and in planning equitable workload assignments to make sure all essential work is accomplished.

Job Evaluation

The basic characteristics of jobs—education, experience, skills, working conditions, and health and safety requirements—directly affect the differences in jobs and their relative worth. These characteristics are identified through job analysis and then used in evaluating and pricing the jobs. Job evaluation, which is fully described later in this chapter, is undertaken to justify the payment of wages and salaries in relation to the relative worth of the jobs.

GATHERING AND ANALYZING JOB INFORMATION

The analysis of office jobs rests firmly upon obtaining reliable job information. The office manager, or the person charged with analyzing jobs, must decide which method of gathering job information will be most effective at minimal cost. The principal methods of obtaining job information are described below.

Questionnaire Method

A variety of questionnaires is used for obtaining job information. Questionnaires may be designed by the firm's OM or job analyst to meet the special needs of the organization. Or consultants, who design their own questionnaires or purchase them from various psychological services, may be employed to gather and analyze the job information. Some questionnaires consist of as few as four or five questions; others may be three or four pages long. Whatever the form of questionnaire, its results must be analyzed and interpreted in the form of job descriptions and specifications that provide management with a knowledge of the job requirements.

Designing the Questionnaire

Relatively simple questionnaires may be designed for use in small firms. On such questionnaires, two groups of questions are often found. In the first group of general questions, the employee is asked to give information such as the following:

Description of duties.
Special knowledge required for the job.
Experience required to qualify for the job.
How long a period of time must be spent on the job before the employee feels capable of working without supervision.

In the second group of questions about job routines and tasks, the employee is asked to indicate:

Daily routine tasks performed.
Tasks performed weekly.
Tasks performed monthly.
Special tasks performed.
Other job-related information.

To obtain data on the frequency or time spent on different tasks, employees may be asked to keep *work logs* or *diaries*. Work logs, often called *time logs*, are also used in connection with work measurement and the setting of standards, as we shall see in a later chapter.

If the office force is made up of a large number of employees, you will find a much more structured questionnaire used. A **structured questionnaire** requests information on whether a specific task is part of the jobholder's job and tries to learn the importance the jobholder attaches to it. A

structured questionnaire, such as the job information sheet illustrated in Figure 9–2, is given to employees so they may describe their jobs in accordance with the instructions on the form. Each employee's write-up is edited by the employee's immediate superior and submitted to a job analyst. The analyst follows up with the employees and their supervisors to obtain any additional information needed to complete the job analysis.

Techniques of Using Structured Questionnaires

Many job analysis techniques that rely heavily upon the use of structured questionnaires have been designed to provide special types of job information.[1] Brief descriptions of two basic questionnaire techniques are given below.

Position Analysis Questionnaire (PAQ). Using the PAQ, we analyze and document only those activities performed by the worker. A few questions pertain to the employee's description of the job and the compensation received; the remaining questions examine the kind of worker behaviors required and the type of environmental factors surrounding the job. The questionnaires may be completed by an analyst during an interview with the jobholders or their supervisors or while observing the work as it is being performed. The questionnaire form is designed so that the results may be optically scanned and then analyzed on a computer.

Task Inventory/Comprehensive Occupational Data Analysis Programs (TI/CODAP). This collection of computer software products is designed to analyze and report job information that has been collected through questionnaires called task

---

[1]For detailed information about these techniques and others that may be used in analyzing office jobs, see *Handbook of Wage & Salary Administration* (New York: McGraw-Hill Book Company, 1984), Chapter 7.

Figure 9–2
Job Informa-
tion Sheet
(page 1)

JOB INFORMATION SHEET

Instructions

Present Job Title —Enter the name by which the job is now called.

Department — Enter the general office department in which the job is located.

Description of Duties — This portion of the job description is to be a series of numbered statements, each of which describes a task or major step of your job.

1. Introduce each task or major step with an action verb and follow it by a concise statement that tells what you are doing, and where appropriate, include an account of how the task or major step is done.

   If additional space is needed for the completion of your Job Description, please attach another sheet.

2. Tasks or major steps are to be written in descending order of frequency of performance: i.e., the task on which the most time is spent is listed first, and the task on which the least time is spent is last.

3. Minor steps or tasks are to be combined and written in one catch-all paragraph at the end of the Job Description.

Questions 1 through 14 — Complete each of these questions as it relates to your job.

After completing the Job Information Sheet, give it to your supervisor.

Your Name____ BERNARD AMATI _____ Date Issued __4/16/--__
Present Job Title__ PAYROLL CLERK __ Date Due __4/23/--__
Name of Your Supervisor__ JANICE BRADLEY __ Dept. _PAYROLL ACCOUNTING_
Description of Duties: _VERIFY TIME SHEETS; KEYBOARD WEEKLY PAYROLL DATA INTO COMPUTER SYSTEM; PREPARE BANK DEPOSITS; RECONCILE BANK STATEMENT AND PAYROLL ACCOUNT; DISTRIBUTE PAYCHECKS_

1. **EDUCATION REQUIRED.** Indicate the minimum schooling required for your job by check mark. ✓
   No schooling required_____ 2 yrs. high school_____ 4 yrs. high school___✓___
   Technical high school_____ Special schooling_____ College_____
   Do you make any reports? No _✓_ Yes___ If yes, what are they? _____

2. **EXPERIENCE.** The minimum experience required for your job.
   Months: 1_✓_ 2__ 3__ 4__ 5__ 6__ 7__ 8__ 9__ 10__ 11__ 12__
   Years: 1__ 2__ 3__ 4__ 5__ 6__ 7__ 8__

3. **TRAINING.** The minimum training required for your job.
   Months: 1_✓_2_3_4_5_6_7_8_9_10_11_12_
   Does your job require many skills? No_ Yes_✓_If yes, enumerate and describe briefly. _____
   KEYBOARDING ON COMPUTER TERMINAL; USING 10-KEY PRINTING CALCULATOR

   How often does your job repeat itself? Per Hour ___ Per Day___ Per Week _/_ Per Month _4-5_

4. **PHYSICAL DEMANDS.** What kind of equipment do you use? _TERMINALS CALCULATOR_
   What is the maximum weight of your work in pounds? Lifting __3-5 lbs.__
   Pulling_____ Pushing_____ The heaviest work is done__percent of working time. Your work position is
   Sitting_✓_ Standing__ Walking _✓_ Holding steadily__ Lifting overhead__ Bending__

Figure 9–2
Job Informa-
tion Sheet
(page 2)

5. MENTAL OR VISUAL DEMANDS. What accuracy is required on the job? _____*100%*_____
Are the hands and eyes constantly coordinated? _____*YES*_____
Are operations automatic? No____ Partly ✓ Yes____

6. RESPONSIBILITY FOR EQUIPMENT. Are you responsible for any equipment? No____ Yes ✓ If yes, describe the
equipment_____*TERMINAL AND CALCULATOR*_____

What is the cost of possible damage to equipment? No damage____ Minimum $*25* Maximum $*1500* Do you repair
equipment? No ✓ Yes____ If yes, what kind?_____

7. RESPONSIBILITY FOR MATERIAL OR PRODUCT. Are you responsible for any materials? No ✓ Yes____ If yes,
what are they?_____
How much spoilage may occur? Loss in dollars $____ What is required to avoid spoilage?_____

Can the spoiled work be repaired? No____ Partly____ Completely _____
Enumerate and briefly describe various materials you have to recognize.
_____
_____
_____
_____

8. RESPONSIBILITY FOR SAFETY OF OTHERS. How many people may be injured if carelessness would occur? *1*
Are there hazards that may cause injury? No ✓ Yes ____ If yes, what are they?_____
_____
_____
_____

9. RESPONSIBILITY FOR WORK OF OTHERS. Are you responsible for work of others? No ✓ Yes____ How Many?____
For new employees only?____ How Many?____

10. WORKING CONDITIONS. Are the working conditions Agreeable?____ Disagreeable? ✓ Which disagreeable
conditions affect your job? Noise ✓ Fumes____ Cold____ Hot____ Changes in temperature____ Dirt____
Dust____ Oil____ Steam____ Too wet____ Glare ✓ Somewhat dark____ Drafty____ Other_____

11. UNAVOIDABLE HAZARDS. Which accidents may occur? Burns____ Shock____ Cuts____ Crushed Fingers____
Injury to ____Feet____ Eyes____ Ears____ Lungs____ Is your health affected? No ✓ Yes____ If yes, in what
way?_____

12. SUPERVISION. Received from_____*JANICE BRADLEY*_____
Weekly ✓ Daily____ Hourly____ Do you supervise? No ✓ Yes____ If yes, how many workers?____ Weekly____
Daily____ Hourly____ Do you make your own decisions? No____ Yes ✓ Do you inspect someone else's job? No ✓
Yes____

13. Would you prefer to be transferred to another job? No ✓ Yes____ If yes, which job could you perform?_____

14. REMARKS. Give additional information which has not been covered and which may assist in a better description of
your job._____
_____
_____
_____
_____
_____

inventories. The *task inventory* is designed to obtain information about the jobholder's education and training; major items of equipment, tools, and materials used on the job; and the jobholder's assessment of the skills and abilities needed to perform the job. The rating of the task items is created by the job analyst, jobholder, supervisor or manager, and, where appropriate, a union representative. The task ratings are analyzed by computer to provide a variety of reports that give information in areas such as job classification, recruitment and selection, career planning, performance evaluation, and training.

Advantages and Disadvantages of Using the Questionnaire Method

Among the advantages of using the questionnaire method are:

1. Information is obtained rapidly, especially when compared with the time-consuming activity of personally interviewing each worker.
2. Computer programs are available so that the job information obtained by questionnaires may be quickly organized and analyzed, with printouts providing data to be used in a variety of applications. Programs are also available for checking statistically the validity of questionnaire results.

Several disadvantages characterize the questionnaire method of gathering job information:

1. It may be difficult to design or obtain a questionnaire that is sufficiently thorough to secure all the data required by the job analyst. Unless the questions are precisely and clearly worded, it may be difficult for jobholders to communicate the information requested and for the analyst to interpret the information supplied.
2. So many questions may be asked that the questionnaire becomes overly complex

and confusing. As a result, the jobholders may give misleading or incomplete responses because they do not take time to complete the form correctly.
3. Some employees are not skilled in properly analyzing their jobs and thus may exaggerate the importance of their jobs. Or, they may underemphasize those phases of their jobs that require a fairly large percentage of their total work time.
4. The personal touch is lacking since the jobholders are called upon merely to fill out a questionnaire rather than discuss their job content with an interviewer.
5. In order to obtain reliable and valid results, the completed questionnaires require careful analysis and editing, all of which are a costly means of obtaining job information.

However, the questionnaire method does serve as a starting point in the job analysis program. Despite the disadvantages just given, you will find the questionnaire commonly used, often in conjunction with the interview or observation methods, which are discussed in the next sections.

Interview Method

The **interview method** requires the job analyst to spend time in meeting with the employee and the employee's supervisor in order to gather information about the job. Thus, this method is often costlier than the questionnaire method. However, for some types of job analyses, the interview may be conducted at the employee's workstation so the job may be observed at the same time. Of all methods of obtaining job information, interviews or conferences with the supervisor and the jobholder are most commonly used.

The effectiveness of the interview method depends greatly upon the skill of the analyst, who must be trained to deal with people in order to receive their full cooperation. At the beginning of interviews, rapport with the jobholders must be established so they are at ease and will not be hesitant in replying to the questions asked. When collecting information, the analyst must be objective so that personal bias does not influence the data being recorded. All information recorded should be read to the employees to confirm its correctness. Following the interview, the employee's supervisor should be consulted to verify the accuracy of the information obtained.

Observation Method

In addition to gathering job information by the questionnaire and the interview methods, the analyst may observe workers while they are performing their tasks. The **observation method** permits the analyst to obtain job information firsthand and to become acquainted with the working conditions, the equipment used, and the requirements for special skills, such as finger dexterity. For jobs that are relatively simple and repetitive, such as statistical typing, the observation method may be effectively used. For other types of jobs, the analyst may select one of the other methods or a combination of methods. In using the observation method, the analyst must establish rapport with each jobholder in order to put the worker at ease.

In some large companies, you will find that the analyst obtains data about job-performance times from the industrial engineering department. The time-study engineer in such a department is concerned with observing and studying all aspects of the job, including skill requirements, physical and mental effort required, job environment needs, and information flows, which may not be precisely stated in job descriptions. These factors are necessary, however, for preparing performance standards, as explained in a later chapter.

Combination of Methods

The questionnaire, interview, and observation methods may be combined when undertaking a job analysis. Here are brief summaries of three techniques that involve a combination of the methods.

Critical Incident Technique (CIT)

Rather than provide a complete description of the job, this technique defines a job in terms of the specific *behaviors* necessary to perform the job successfully. By means of structured questionnaires, interviews, and observations, incidents are gathered from supervisors, jobholders, and analysts. These incidents describe behaviors that are observed to be critical to job performance and that reflect particularly outstanding or poor performance. The descriptions of the behaviors are then reviewed, edited, and grouped into categories of general behavior dimensions, such as "the ability to work in an environment that requires a moderate degree of trust" or "the ability to work in an environment that requires an exceptionally high degree of accuracy, tact, and diplomacy and a high degree of confidentiality."

A job analyst may interview and observe an employee at his or her workstation.

Functional Job Analysis (FJA)

Using this approach to analyzing jobs, you would examine the *interactions among the work, the workers, and the organization*. The FJA technique centers upon:

1. Identifying the purposes and objectives of the organization.
2. Identifying and describing the tasks performed by workers.
3. Analyzing the workers' tasks.
4. Developing performance standards that describe the amount of time spent by workers on tasks at each functional level.
5. Developing training content related to the skills needed to perform the tasks.

To obtain all this information, analysts review background information on the present jobs, interview workers and supervisors, and directly observe the work as it is performed.

Job Element Method (JEM)

When using the JEM, you are concerned with identifying the *elements* that workers use in performing their jobs. Examples of job elements include knowledge, skills, abilities, and personal traits. Workers and supervisors meet in brainstorming sessions to identify and rate the elements used in performing jobs. The elements are rated as to whether they represent minimum, satisfactory, or outstanding levels of job performance. Next, the ratings are further defined and described in the form of task statements, which are analyzed to determine those requirements needed to perform the job. The task statements form the basis for preparing job descriptions, which are explained in the following section.

JOB DESCRIPTIONS

The results of the job analysis are expressed in the job description or the *position description*, as it is often called. From the job description, you may develop job specifications separately or combine them with the job description. The analysis of jobs and the preparation of job descriptions may entail a period of one year or more before you have refined the descriptions to the point where they become a valuable tool to be used by managers and supervisors in all departments.

As a result of changes in factors such as methods and procedures for processing information, personnel needs, budgetary control techniques, and equipment obsolescence, you should review and revise the job descriptions each year, if possible. You will want to provide office workers with easy access to the file of job descriptions so they can improve their performance, be fully aware of the dimensions of their jobs, know who in the firm can aid them in their work, see how their performance will be evaluated, and become aware of their opportunities for advancement.

Writing the Job Description

The job description must be clearly written, with all statements expressed as simply as possible. The terms used should be widely accepted or carefully defined since the descriptions will be used by several persons for different purposes, including wage and salary surveys. There is no prescribed amount of information that should be included in a job description. However, it should contain enough information to ensure that the job can be accurately evaluated. *The job—not the person holding the job—is to be described as it is; no modifications should be made in the description for what the job ought to be or may become in the future.*

The job titles and descriptions should compare as closely as possible with the standardized descriptions listed in the *Dictionary of Occupational Titles (DOT).*

Other valuable sources of job information are the *Occupational Outlook Handbook*[2] and the three salary surveys—office, data processing, and management—undertaken each year by the Administrative Management Society. The position titles and descriptions of office personnel used by the Administrative Management Society in its survey of office salaries are shown in Figure 9-3. Other organizations that conduct periodic wage and salary surveys include the American Payroll Association, American Management Association, Association of Information Systems Professionals, Data Entry Management Association, Dartnell Institute, Temp Force, Bureau of National Affairs, and Bureau of Labor Statistics.

Typical Job Descriptions

Figure 9-4 shows a job description for a *nonexempt* (entitled to overtime pay for hours worked over 40 during the workweek) office position, computer operator. Note that the latter part of the job description presents the employment standards (employee specifications) and job specifications. Sometimes positions are grouped and described concisely, as shown in Figure 9-5, which presents an accounting-finance grouping of six position titles and descriptions for managers.

---

[2]Both the *Dictionary of Occupational Titles* and the *Occupational Outlook Handbook* are available from the U.S. Department of Labor (Washington, DC 20402: U.S. Government Printing Office).

The *Handbook*, which is revised every two years, groups occupations according to the *Standard Occupational Classification Manual*. The *Handbook* is a useful resource that supplies valuable assistance to all persons seeking employment. For each occupation, the *Handbook* gives information about job duties, working conditions, level and places of employment, education and training requirements, advancement possibilities, job outlook, earnings, and other occupations that require similar aptitudes, interests, or training. Also available from the Department of Labor is the *Occupational Outlook Quarterly*, which is designed to keep employment planners and counselors informed of current job developments between the biennial editions of the *Handbook*.

JOB SPECIFICATIONS

A job specification describes the minimum requirements of the job, such as the educational, experience, and personal qualifications that you see listed in Figure 9-6. The job specification is used primarily as the basis for rating the job in the process of job evaluation. Job specifications are the natural outcome of job analyses and, as we saw previously, may be combined with job or position descriptions. For example, in Figure 9-4 on pages 245 and 246 the specifications for the job of computer operator are combined with the position description.

Job specifications are often used in recruiting, training, and counseling workers because the education and experience specifications imply what qualifications a person should possess in order to be hired. However, we can make more effective use of the **employee specification** (such as the employment standards in Figure 9-4), which states the minimum qualifications a prospective employee must possess in order to be considered for employment. When the job specification and the employee specification are brought together, the interviewer has accurate data for matching the job applicant to the job opening.

JOB EVALUATION

Job analysis and its components—the job description and job specification—are needed before you can determine the relative value of each job. The aim of job evaluation is to develop an equitable payroll policy based on the estimated or measured worth of each job in relation to other jobs. When jobs are properly evaluated, employees doing similar work under similar working conditions are paid about the same salary. However, worker experience and level of skill, the cost of living, the supply and demand of office workers, government regula-

Figure 9-3
Position
Titles and
Descriptions
for Office
Personnel

POSITION TITLES AND DESCRIPTIONS

A WORD PROCESSING OPERATOR—Uses word processing equipment to input and edit typed documents with established quality and time standards. Proofreads and edits own work. Equipment includes the use of standalone or shared-logic word processing system utilizing a CRT terminal.

B SENIOR WORD PROCESSING OPERATOR—Uses advanced word processing equipment and/or functions to produce and revise complicated documents, such as lengthy technical and statistical reports from complex source information, including the retrieval of text and data. May provide training and assistance to new or less experienced operators. May also schedule workload.

C ACCOUNTING CLERK—Checks, verifies, and posts journal vouchers, accounts payable vouchers, payroll, or other simple accounting data of a recurring or standard nature.

D SENIOR ACCOUNTING CLERK—Maintains a complete set of accounting records in a small office, or handles one phase of accounting in a larger unit which requires the accounting training needed to determine proper accounting entries; reconciles entries; prepares accounting reports; analyzes accounting records to determine causes of results shown, etc. May direct work of other clerks.

E PAYROLL CLERK—Prepares input for each payroll including salary adjustments, special payments, tax allocations, and deductions. Codes and maintains time sheets. Prepares payroll bank deposits, and audits and balances payrolls. Assists in preparation and payment of payroll taxes. Prepares appropriate journal entries for expensing of salaries.

F CREDIT AND COLLECTION CLERK—Performs clerical tasks related to credit and collection activities. Includes performing routine credit checks; obtaining supplementary information; investigating overdue accounts; and following up by mail and/or phone to customers on delinquent payments.

G CLERK TYPIST—Produces drafts and/or finished copies of documents from a variety of originators. Form and content usually follow standard guidelines. May perform other clerical duties of minimum difficulty.

H GENERAL CLERK—Performs basic office or clerical duties on short assignments and tasks which are highly structured in accordance with established procedures. This is a higher-level position than a file clerk, involving a variety of routine and semiroutine duties.

I SENIOR GENERAL CLERK—Performs diverse clerical tasks requiring some analysis, judgment, and a detailed knowledge of departments and/or company policies and procedures dealing with the incumbent's area of responsibility, such as claims operations, etc. May direct and check work of other clerks.

J FILE CLERK—Performs general alphabetical and numeric filing, sorting, and cross-determining. Locates and removes material upon request and keeps records of its disposition. Maintains and updates files according to an established system. May deliver files, copy material from files, and purge outdated material.

K MAIL CLERK—Sorts and opens incoming mail for distribution. Sorts, stamps, and dispatches outgoing mail. May distribute and collect mail.

L SHIPPING/RECEIVING CLERK—Performs manual and clerical duties related to the receipt and shipment of goods. Maintains records and processes paperwork for goods received and shipped according to established procedures.

M PURCHASING CLERK—Draws up purchase orders. Verifies specifications of purchase requests. Obtains prices and specifications. Compiles records, such as items purchased or transferred between departments, prices, deliveries, and inventories. Confers with suppliers concerning deliveries. May verify bills from suppliers with bids and purchase orders.

N SECRETARY—Performs a standard range of secretarial duties in a smaller company or for a supervisor in a larger firm. Duties may include taking dictation; transcribing from notes and/or dictation equipment; screening calls; making appointments; handling travel arrangements; answering routine correspondence; and maintaining filing systems.

O SENIOR SECRETARY—Performs standard and advanced secretarial duties for a smaller company or for middle management personnel in a larger company. Composes and/or takes and transcribes correspondence of a complex and confidential nature. Position requires a knowledge of company policy.

P EXECUTIVE SECRETARY/ADMINISTRATIVE ASSISTANT—Performs a full range of secretarial and administrative duties for member of executive staff. Handles project-oriented duties and may be held accountable for the timely completion of these tasks. Relieves executive of routine administrative detail. Position requires an in-depth knowledge of company practice, structure, and a high degree of secretarial/administrative skills.

Q LEGAL SECRETARY/ASSISTANT—Performs secretarial and/or administrative support services for a legal department or firm. Position requires some knowledge of legal terminology. May perform legal-related research activities.

R PERSONNEL CLERK—Performs clerical tasks relating to personnel activities. Includes checking employment applications for completed information; administering preemployment tests; maintaining personnel records; following up with new employees regarding insurance and benefit information; maintaining attendance records; assisting with projects.

S SWITCHBOARD OPERATOR/RECEPTIONIST—Receives and directs incoming calls; greets visitors; performs basic clerical tasks.

T CUSTOMER SERVICE REPRESENTATIVE—Provides guidance and assistance to customers regarding problems with accounts or merchandise. Duties include searching records; investigating problems/complaints; policy interpretation; response preparation and adjustment; and correction of records.

Source: *1989 Office Salaries Report*, Administrative Management Society.

Figure 9–4
Job
Description
for a
Computer
Operator
(page 1)

EXHIBIT 6: JOB DESCRIPTION OF A NONEXEMPT POSITION

Computer Operator   Nonexempt 213.382
Job Title   **Status   Job Code**

July 1, 1987   Olympia, Inc. — Main Office
Date   **Plant/Division**

Arthur Allen   Data Processing — Information Systems
Written by   **Department/Section**

Juanita Montgomery   7   406
Approved by   **Grade/Level   Points**

Senior Computer Operator $16,900 — $19,660 — $22,540
Title of Immediate Supervisor   **Pay Range**

SUMMARY

Operates digital computer and peripheral equipment under general supervision. Performs other assignments as required.

JOB DUTIES

1. Follows specific technical and scheduling directives.
   .1 Follows technical directives and assigned schedules under spot-check supervision.
   .2 Processes data according to defined procedures and schedules.
2. Operates digital computer and associated peripheral equipment.
   .1 Monitors equipment; maximizes operating time; minimizes program errors.
   .2 Analyzes error messages; identifies possible causes.
   .3 Notifies proper authorities of machine malfunctions and program errors.
   .4 Corrects errors within specified areas of authority and responsibility.
   .5 Stores outputs and completed inputs in proper location.
   .6 Performs preventive maintenance as specified.
3. Reviews and analyzes data inputs.
   .1 Recommends changes in scheduling and application to maximize efficient use of equipment.
   .2 Assists in testing new applications.
4. Maintains logs and records.
   .1 Details individual running time of each program.
   .2 Records all equipment malfunctions and program errors.
5. Receives, stores, and maintains D.P.C. inventory.
   .1 Unloads delivery truck.
   .2 Maintains stockroom in orderly manner.
   .3 Maintains stock records.
   .4 Notifies appropriate authorities of inventory requirements.

Source: Adapted, by permission of the publisher, from "Job Descriptions—Critical Documents, Versatile Tools, Part 4: Getting it on Paper," by Richard I. Henderson, SUPERVISORY MANAGEMENT, February 1976, pp. 14-15, © 1976 by AMACOM, a division of American Management Associations, New York. All rights reserved.

**Figure 9–4
Job
Description
for a
Computer
Operator
(page 2)**

EMPLOYMENT STANDARDS

1. Knowledge and ability:
   .1 Must know basic principles of operating a digital computer and associated peripheral equipment.
   .2 Must be able to read and understand technical computer operation manuals.
   .3 Must be able to follow prescribed standards and procedures.
   .4 Must be able to follow computer scheduling instructions.
2. Physical requirements:
   .1 Must be able to lift and store 60-lb. boxes.
   .2 Must be able to load and off-load 20-lb. disk packages.
   .3 Must be able to stand for ten hours a day.
3. Emotional demands:
   Must be able to withstand relative high pitches and levels of noise.

ACCOUNTABILITIES

Timely completion of assigned schedules.
Prompt recognition of machine malfunctions.

JOB SPECIFICATION

Factor	Subfactor	Degree	Substantiating Data	Points
Knowledge	Education	4	Requires completion of vocational-technical program or equivalent on-the-job training.	64
Knowledge	Experience	4	Equivalent on-the-job training may be up to one year.	64
Knowledge	Skill	5	Requires ability to operate medium-size computer and peripheral equipment.	63
Problem Solving	Interpretation	4−	Analyzes error messages and takes corrective action in accord with procedures manuals and operating practices.	38
Problem Solving	Compliance	4−	Requires ability to read and understand technical computer operations manual.	37
Problem Solving	Communication	4	Must maintain records of operation and communicate results.	53
Decision Making	Interpersonal	2+	Notifies authorities of machine malfunctions and program errors.	28
Decision Making	Managerial	3−	Follows technical direction and assigned schedules under spot check supervision. Has no supervisory responsibilites.	35
Decision Making	Assets	2+	Has some opportunity for influencing the planning and control of work assignments.	24
			Total Points:	406

Figure 9–5
Accounting-Finance Grouping of Six Management Positions

MANAGERS IN ACCOUNTING AND FINANCE

A   ACCOUNTING MANAGER—Responsible for the general accounting records and operation of the accounting systems, including gathering and reporting of correct financial information to management. Establishes internal control of procedures and is responsible for developing, adapting, or revising the accounting systems. Projects accounting data to show effects of proposed plans on capital investment, income cash position, and overall financial condition. Assures standard accounting procedures are adhered to.

B   AUDITING MANAGER—Responsible for audits of financial records and practices to appraise and verify the accounting accuracy of records, financial statements, and reports. Determines that accepted accounting principles and policies are followed and evaluates the adequacy of the accounting systems and controls. Develops recommendations for improvements of records, procedures, and internal controls. Prepares audit reports and trains auditors at entering professional levels.

C   COST ACCOUNTING MANAGER—Devises cost-accounting systems and processes and supervises the compilations of information to determine and record costs by department, division, cost centers, product, and other groupings. Devises classifications for labor, material, expenses, and other items for computing costs of new products or services. Prepares reports, including manufacturing budgets, plant financial statements, operating control reports, and variations from standard costs. Develops methods of calculating and controlling costs.

D   CREDIT & COLLECTION MANAGER—Responsible for credit and collection activities. Establishes procedures for investigating, granting and controlling credit, and collecting accounts due. Determines credit limits. Supervises mailing of collection letters and attempts to collect delinquent accounts. Investigates new customers' credit ratings and arranges term of payment. Prepares reports showing status and amounts of credit and collections, and delinquent accounts.

E   PAYROLL MANAGER—Supervises payroll functions, including the computation of deductions; preparation and verification of payrolls; maintenance of payroll records and reports; preparation of reports for federal, state, and local government agencies; and processing of payments to employees. Determines that proper controls are followed to assure wages, salaries, and deductions are being paid in accordance with established policy and labor agreements.

F   ACCOUNTS PAYABLE SUPERVISOR—Supervises the processing of accounts payable, including maintaining records of amounts owed, verifying invoices, computing discounts, and preparing vouchers for payment. Also responsible for the preparation of accounts and other reports as needed.

Source: *1989 Management Salaries Report*, Administrative Management Society.

tions, collective bargaining agreements, and competitive conditions also influence the salaries paid of fice workers.

In this part of the chapter, we shall examine two methods of job evaluation—nonquantitative and quantitative. In the following chapter, you will read about the pricing of jobs and the determination of pay ranges.

Nonquantitative Methods

In the *nonquantitative methods* of job evaluation, jobs are evaluated according to

Dialog on the Firing Line

MICHAEL F. EMIG
Principal Consultant
The Wyatt Company
Washington, DC

BA in Psychology, Lafayette College
MA in Organizational Behavior, Southwest University
Michael Emig is in charge of Compensation Consulting
services of The Wyatt Company's Washington, DC office.
Prior to joining The Wyatt Company, Mr. Emig served
as the Chief Human Resources Executive at Timex and
The Penn Central Corporation and has been responsible
for the compensation and benefits functions at Chase
Manhattan Bank, Bendix, and the American Express
Company. He gained consulting experience as President
of Praxes Management Concepts, a firm he founded. He
has been frequently quoted in national publications and
is a guest lecturer on salary management at George Mason
University and Marymont College. Mr. Emig is a member
of the American Compensation Association and past
President of the New York Association of Compensation
Administrators.

QUESTION: In the management of today's offices, we
hear much about the need for the firm to form a
partnership with its workers, to look upon employees
as shareholders in a team effort, etc. With all this emphasis
on participative management, what has happened to the
role of job evaluation? Is it alive and well, or is it on
the way out?

RESPONSE: Organizations face a choice—pay
everyone the same, or pay them differently. As soon
as that decision is made, a very challenging problem
must be solved: On what basis should employees'
pay be differentiated? Job Evaluation is a foundation for sound salary management practices.

Job evaluation *is necessary* because it is

- *Demanded* by employees.
- *Needed* by managers as a tool.
- *Better understood* owing to media attention,
  legislation, etc.
- *Technically advanced* by computerized predic-
  tive models.

The criteria against which the effectiveness of
job evaluation methods should be judged include:

- Does the organization realize an efficient and
  profitable "return on the compensation investment" it makes in its employees?
- Do managers understand the method and have
  the administrative tools to apply it effectively?
- Do employees understand, accept, and have
  confidence in the method so as *not* to view it
  as a barrier to productive behaviors?

Employee participation in policy level discussion
is increasing. Input from the people who know
best—the person in the job—is being solicited and
used. Through focus groups and structured
questionnaires that test for content and definition,
job definition can be clarified and validated.
Interactive PC systems that enable an employee to
do self-assessment, plan training/development
paths, etc., formalize and facilitate employee
involvement in these very important processes.

The strong emphasis on *paying for performance*
has put additional stress on evaluation methods.
Organizations have found that "merit pay" not only
doesn't work well but actually exacerbates
employee relations sensitivities, if the evaluation
foundation isn't constructed soundly.

One must first define what the employee is to
do, and determine the relative value of that before
the issue of *how well it is done* can be addressed,
measured, and rewarded.

Employee involvement in these processes yields
more valid, workable, and productive results for
all interested parties.

Figure 9-6
Job Specification for Position of General Clerk A

> **JOB SPECIFICATION**
>
> **Job Title:** General Clerk A
>
> **Qualifications: Educational**—High school graduate.
>
> **Experience**—Two or more years with company as General Clerk B. Experience in office systems and procedures.
>
> **Personal**—Speed and efficiency in handling volume of detail. Ability to instruct others in clerical jobs. Ability to supervise work of others.
>
> **Duties:** 1. Handle mail and dictate correspondence.
> 2. Check, index, and file important records and correspondence.
> 3. Handle all payroll records and reports.
> 4. Summarize and tabulate cost information and records.
> 5. Receive, take care of, and account for petty cash and office funds.
> 6. Supervise work of general clerks in routine jobs.
>
> **Promotional Opportunities:** Advancement to accounting clerk after two years.
>
> **Salary Range:** $1,095–$1,575 a month.

their relative or estimated difficulty. The two methods that we shall examine are (1) ranking and (2) job classification.

Ranking Method

The **ranking method**, also known as the *rank order system*, is the simplest and oldest method of determining the economic value of a job. Using the ranking method, we analyze and rank the individual jobs according to the difficulty and the overall responsibility of each job. Jobs are ranked according to job titles *from the most important to the least important* (or vice versa) in relation to their contribution to the business. We assume that the salary increases as the job becomes more difficult. This is not always true, however, because sometimes a salary is determined by the working conditions, level and amount of responsibility, or experience involved. A simple ranking of office jobs is given in Table 9-1.

Often an evaluation committee consisting of supervisors and department heads ranks the jobs. They may do the ranking in terms of job titles alone or by combining titles, job content, and compensation rates. The number of ranks assigned will vary with the number of jobs or positions and the type of business organization. In Table 9-1, for example, the 20 jobs making up one activity field—office and clerical jobs—are arranged in rank order from 1 through 16.

Two types of job-ranking methods sometimes used are the *card-ranking method* and the *paired-comparison method*. In both methods, the supervisors are asked to rank the jobs in the order of their importance from highest to lowest, or vice versa.

Card-Ranking Method. When using the card-ranking method, we place each job title on a 3″ × 5″ index card. Next, we arrange the cards in order of the relative importance

Table 9-1
Simple
Ranking of
Office and
Clerical Jobs

Rank Order	Job Title	Median Monthly Salary (Midpoint of Salary Range)
1	Administrative Office Manager	$2,820
2	Systems Analyst	2,690
3	Programmer/Analyst	2,235
4	Programmer	1,910
5	Executive Secretary/Administrative Assistant	1,665
6	Computer Operator A	1,565
7	Secretary A	1,505
8	Lead Word Processing Operator	1,460
9	Computer Operator B	1,415
9	Accounting Clerk A	1,415
10	Secretary B	1,330
10	Word Processing Operator	1,330
11	General Clerk A	1,290
12	Accounting Clerk B	1,245
13	Data Entry Operator A	1,240
14	Switchboard Operator/Receptionist	1,200
14	Clerk-Typist	1,200
15	General Clerk B	1,160
15	Data Entry Operator B	1,160
16	File Clerk	1,070

Note: Titles and median salaries are illustrative and for comparison purposes only.

of the jobs to the company, ignoring the present salary of the jobs, the historic position or status of the job in the company, and the performance of any particular employee holding that job. This approach to job evaluation provides an effective analysis of jobs without the influence of established, historical precedents and appears more like an independent survey based upon sound operations. If there are too many jobs to be thus ranked, it may be necessary to rank them first by groups of jobs and then to rank the jobs within each group.

Paired-Comparison Method. In the paired-comparison method, we rank each job against another job of comparable ranking on the basis of the total difficulty of the job. The greater number of times a job is ranked as more difficult, the more important the job becomes. One type of form used in the paired-comparison method is shown in Figure 9–7.

Advantages and Disadvantages of the Ranking Method. You may use the ranking method satisfactorily in very small offices where comparatively few jobs (fewer than 25) are to be evaluated and where the employees respect the employer's integrity in ranking jobs. One advantage of the method is its simplicity; it is easily understood. However, the rating is extremely subjective and is often incorrectly based on the employee who is performing the job rather than on the job itself. Also, the relative ranking of jobs depends greatly on current salary and wage rates, which fluctuate with economic conditions.

The ranking method may be installed without much expense. However, some grievances and loss of time may occur when the rater is unable to explain why one job is slotted above or below another because there are no objective studies to back up the established salary or wage rates. Then, too, the evaluation process often becomes unwieldy when there is a large number of jobs. Finally, it is unlikely that there is any one person who knows all the jobs and is thus qualified to evaluate them.

Job Classification Method

The **job classification method** is an outgrowth of the ranking method. This method has long been used by civil service authorities in evaluating office and clerical workers and in granting periodic salary increases. Before the jobs are classified, the analyst selects a number of predetermined classes or family groupings on the basis of common features, such as levels of responsibilities, abilities or skills, knowledge, and duties. The jobs are then analyzed and grouped into those specific classes in order of importance according to the job and the work performed. Thus, it is assumed that each job involves duties and responsibilities that fit into the respective graded classification.

One method of grouping jobs in a classification chart is shown in Table 9–2. The nature of the work is combined with the salary range to show that there is a direct relationship between the rating of the importance of the job and the salary paid. In this table, the four family groupings are clerical, secretarial, accounting, and data

Figure 9–7
Form Used in Paired-Comparison Method

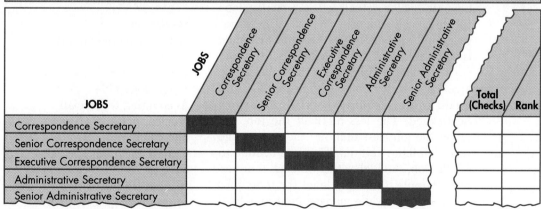

Directions: Compare the first job in the first column with each job in the slant columns. If the job in the first column is considered to have greater value to the firm than the job in the slant column, place a check mark (✓) in the box below the job in the slant column. Repeat process until all jobs have been compared. Tally check marks to find rank of jobs.

Table 9-2
Breakdown of Job Classifications by Job Levels and Weekly Salary Ranges

Job Level	Weekly Salary Range	Midpoint	Family Groupings			
			Clerical	Secretarial	Accounting	Data Processing
1	$225–$275	$250	File Clerk	. . . .	. . . .	. . . .
2	$240–$300	270	General Clerk B	. . . .	Order Clerk	. . . .
3	$250–$310	280	Clerk-Typist	. . . .	Accounting Clerk B	Data Entry Operator B
4	$280–$340	310	General Clerk A	Secretary B	Accounting Clerk A	Data Entry Operator A
5	$300–$360	330	. . . .	Word Processing Operator	Payroll Clerk	Computer Operator B
6	$310–$390	350	. . . .	Secretary A	. . . .	Computer Operator A
7	$355–$475	415	. . . .	Executive Secretary	. . . .	. . . .
8	$375–$485	430	. . . .	. . . .	Junior Accountant	. . . .
9	$400–$500	450	. . . .	. . . .	. . . .	Programmer
10	$440–$580	510	. . . .	. . . .	Chief Accountant	Programmer/Analyst

Note: Titles and median salaries are illustrative and for comparison purposes only.

processing. Under each of these family groupings, the jobs are ranked according to their importance, which in turn is influenced by the salary range.

The General Schedule. The most common example of the job classification method is the **General Schedule** used by the federal government for virtually all of its civilian jobs (professional, scientific, clerical, administrative, and custodial). The General Schedule is composed of 18 job classes (GS-1 through GS-18) with the job classes differing in the levels of job difficulty, responsibilities, and qualification requirements of the work performed. The less difficult the job, the lower the job class number; the greater the responsibilities and qualifications needed to fill the job, the higher the job class number. For example, the entry level for most jobs is GS-3 or 4; middle-management jobs tend

to be in the GS-5 to 10 range; supervisory levels are usually GS-11 to 15. Most workers above GS-15 are in the Senior Executive Service.

Some typical job titles and the levels where you will usually find them are:

Job Title	GS Job Class No.
Messenger	1–3
Office machine operator	1–3
Clerk typist	2–4
Police officer	2–5
Psychology aide	4
Accounting technician	4–9
Nuclear materials courier	5–7
Shorthand reporter	6–9
Communications specialist	5–15
Savings and loan examiner	5–15
Administrative officer	9–15
Program analysis officer	11–15

Advantages and Disadvantages of the Job Classification Method. Like the ranking method, the job classification method is inexpensive to install. Also, like the ranking method, the job classification method may be applied in small business firms or offices; only a small amount of time and few trained personnel are needed to use this method. Since there is usually a hierarchy already present in the office, this method of informally ranking employees may be easily accepted by the workers and serve as a good starting point for the introduction of a quantitative method of evaluating jobs, as discussed in the next section.

The job classification method has the disadvantage of its subjective grading. Also, the rating of jobs by their total content may create distrust among employees. In the same way, the very purpose of this method of job evaluation is defeated if outside influences, such as existing wage rates or qualifications of present jobholders, create a biased effect on the job classification rating.

Quantitative Methods

In the *quantitative methods* of job evaluation, jobs are grouped according to mental, physical, skill, and experience requisites. The two quantitative methods that we shall examine in this section are (1) factor-comparison and (2) point-factor.

Factor-Comparison Method

The **factor-comparison method**, a quantitative evaluation plan, is also known as the *key-job system* and the *job-to-money method*. Using this method, you would rate the jobs in terms of money. Each job is evaluated in terms of the following five critical factors:

1. *Mental requirements* (education, judgment, initiative, ingenuity, versatility).
2. *Skill requirements* (use of equipment and materials, dexterity, precision).

3. *Physical requirements* (strength, endurance).
4. *Responsibility* (for safety of others; for equipment, materials, and processes; cost of error; extent of supervision exercised).
5. *Working conditions* (accident hazard, environment).

Using the Factor-Comparison Method. As the first step in using the factor-comparison method, along with a committee representing workers and management, you select 10 to 20 key jobs that represent a cross section of all the jobs that will be evaluated. A **key job**, or *benchmark job*, is one whose present rate is not subject to controversy and that is considered to be neither underpaid nor overpaid. You can easily identify such key jobs, commonly found in many firms, by using salary surveys. In selecting the key jobs, the committee should select jobs that range from the lowest to the highest paid jobs. The key jobs are next analyzed by each member of the committee. At this time, the committee must also agree on the definition of each of the above five basic factors so each person will be interpreting each factor alike.

The committee next ranks the key jobs according to the five basic factors, one factor at a time, in the order of their relative importance. The ranking should first be arranged numerically, as shown in Table 9–3. Note that in the factor column "Mental Requirements" the highest rank (1) is given to the job of Senior Accounting Clerk while the lowest rank (10) is assigned to the job of Messenger. In the factor column "Physical Requirements," the job of Senior Accounting Clerk is assigned the next to lowest rank (9) while the job of Messenger is assigned the highest rank (1).

Next, the committee establishes the *average* salary for all ranked key jobs, and divides the money value for each job among

Table 9–3
Simple
Ranking of
Key Jobs in
the Factor-
Comparison
Method

Rank	Mental Requirements	Skill Requirements	Physical Requirements	Responsibility	Working Conditions
1	Senior Accounting Clerk	Executive Secretary	Messenger	Senior Accounting Clerk	Data Entry Operator
2	Executive Secretary	Senior Accounting Clerk	File Clerk	Executive Secretary	Messenger
3	Executive Correspondence Secretary	Executive Correspondence Secretary	Executive Secretary	Switchboard Operator/ Receptionist	File Clerk
4	Correspondence Secretary	Correspondence Secretary	Executive Correspondence Secretary	Executive Correspondence Secretary	Switchboard Operator/ Receptionist
5	Senior Typist	Data Entry Operator	Correspondence Secretary	Correspondence Secretary	Senior Typist
6	Switchboard Operator/ Receptionist	Senior Typist	Data Entry Operator	Data Entry Operator	General Clerk
7	Data Entry Operator	Switchboard Operator/ Receptionist	Switchboard Operator/ Receptionist	General Clerk	Correspondence Secretary
8	General Clerk	General Clerk	Senior Typist	Senior Typist	Senior Accounting Clerk
9	File Clerk	File Clerk	Senior Accounting Clerk	Messenger	Executive Correspondence Secretary
10	Messenger	Messenger	General Clerk	File Clerk	Executive Secretary

the five factors according to the importance of the respective factor to the key job. Table 9–4 shows the average weekly salary apportioned to the five basic factors for three of the key jobs ranked in Table 9–3. The assumed weekly salaries are distributed for each factor of the three jobs.

After the weekly salaries have been distributed to the key jobs according to the ranked and evaluated factors, the committee takes the following steps:

1. Pool the rankings in a master reference table such as Table 9–5.

2. List the titles of the key jobs in the first column from the highest to the lowest paid job.

3. Enter the average weekly salaries in the next column.

4. Record the monetary rates, representing the factor rankings for each key job, as well as the rank numbers, under the five major factors.

5. Add horizontally the total distributed money values for each factor to verify the established average weekly salary.

6. Study all jobs that can be compared with the key jobs listed in Table 9–5.

Table 9-4
Average Weekly Salaries Apportioned to Five Factors for Three Key Jobs in the Factor-Comparison Method

Factor	Key Jobs and Graded Salaries		
	Executive Secretary	Data Entry Operator	File Clerk
Mental requirements	$115	$ 45	$ 30
Skill requirements	135	70	30
Physical requirements......	70	60	90
Responsibility	100	60	20
Working conditions	25	90	70
Total weekly salary........	$445	$325	$240

Note: Titles and median salaries are illustrative and for comparison purposes only.

Table 9-5
Job Rankings and Salary Rates in the Factor-Comparison Method

Key Job	Average Weekly Salary	Factor Rankings and Rates									
		Mental Requirements		Skill Requirements		Physical Requirements		Responsibility		Working Conditions	
		Rank	Rate	Rank	Rate	Rank	Rate	Rank	Rate	Rank	Rate
Executive Secretary	$445	2	$115	1	$135	3	$70	2	$100	10	$25
Senior Accounting Clerk............	405	1	115	2	115	9	50	1	100	8	25
Exec. Correspondence Clerk............	370	3	110	3	105	4	65	4	65	9	25
Correspondence Secretary	355	4	100	4	95	5	60	5	65	7	35
Data Entry Operator ...	325	7	45	5	70	6	60	6	60	1	90
Switchboard Operator/ Receptionist	305	6	50	7	70	7	60	3	70	4	55
Senior Typist	300	5	70	6	70	8	60	8	45	5	55
General Clerk........	280	8	45	8	70	10	50	7	60	6	55
File Clerk	240	9	30	9	30	2	90	10	20	3	70
Messenger	225	10	15	10	15	1	90	9	20	2	85

Note: Titles and median salaries are illustrative and for comparison purposes only.

Advantages and Disadvantages of the Factor-Comparison Method. The major advantage of the factor-comparison method in relation to the ranking and the job classification methods is that you have evaluated each job on the basis of five factors basic to the job. Since you have compared each job against a key job, and factor against factor, you are able to obtain a fair degree of accuracy. Also, you can determine not only which job is worth more but also how much more. Thus, the method provides a tailor-made plan of job evaluation that meets a firm's own needs as a result of properly selecting and weighting the factors. Further, once established in a firm, the method can be taught relatively easily to union members and managers.

On the other hand, the factor-comparison method is difficult to explain and communicate to workers. Although the method provides for establishing comparable job factors within the firm, it is inflexible in dealing with salary rates outside the firm. Thus, if a salary level change for a job is brought about by a change in the outside labor market rate, changes must be made throughout the entire salary structure in order to maintain internal equity.

Point-Factor Method

More than 95 percent of the major corporations in the United States use the point-factor method to evaluate their jobs.[3] In the **point-factor method** of job evaluation, each of the basic factors is divided into degrees, and points are assigned to each factor and its degrees. No wage or salary rates are taken into consideration.

----

[3]Edward E. Lawler III, "What's Wrong with Point-Factor Job Evaluation," *Management Review* (November, 1986), pp. 44–48. In this article, Professor Lawler offers strong criticism of the point-factor method. For two rebuttals to his article, see Roger Plachy, "The Case for Effective Point-Factor Job Evaluation, Viewpoint 1," and "Viewpoint 2," presented by Alfred J. Candrilli and Ronald D. Armagast, *Personnel* (April, 1987), pp. 30–36.

Many aspects of office jobs are difficult to evaluate; however, the point-factor method has been found to provide consistent results.

In evaluating most jobs, the four widely accepted factors used in the point-factor method are *skill, effort, responsibility,* and *job conditions.* Since these factors are broad and may be interpreted differently in different situations, each factor is divided into *subfactors* such as the following:

Skill
 1. Education and Job Knowledge
 2. Experience and Training
 3. Initiative and Ingenuity

Effort
 4. Physical Demand
 5. Mental and/or Visual Demand

Responsibility
 6. For Equipment or Tools
 7. For Materials or Product
 8. For Safety of Others
 9. For Work of Others

Job Conditions
 10. Working Conditions
 11. Unavoidable Hazards

Each of the subfactors is divided into a number of *degrees* that serve as a scale for measuring the distinct levels of each factor. The degrees, in turn, are evaluated separately by a number of *points*. For example, the subfactor "Responsibility for Equipment or Tools" may be divided into degrees that are assigned points as shown in Figure 9–8. The sum of all the points for all subfactors represents the total score for the job. In the job specification sheet for a computer operator, shown in Figure 9–4 on pages 245 and 246, the total number of points is 406. Thus, in a firm using the point-factor method, jobs with similar point values would be paid the same salary even though the points are related to different factors.

Advantages of the Point-Factor Method. You will find that the point-factor method is probably less subjective in its approach and provides more consistency of results than any of the other job evaluation methods since each subfactor is clearly defined in terms of degrees. With each subfactor divided into several degrees, you are able to judge quickly and at the same time minimize discriminations and inequities. You are further aided by various computer programs that easily manage the application of the method and the weighting of the different factors and degrees. Since the job is analyzed and rated in its entirety, independently of wage and salary rates, you are not influenced by pressure from unions, workers, or management. The number of points assigned to a job as the result of an equitable rating remains the same until the job is changed. Thus, bargaining for wage and salary rates can be easily accomplished because the job evaluation continues to serve its purpose as a measuring stick.

Disadvantages of the Point-Factor Method. Some critics of the point-factor method feel that it is inflexible or highly rigid because of the limited number of degrees and the fact that the largest number of points depends on, and is assigned to, the highest factor degree. Also, some feel that the point-factor method, with its elements of factors, degrees, and weighting, requires a great deal of time to develop and thus becomes very costly, especially in dynamic companies where job content changes or new jobs are added frequently. Further, use of the method may require the services of outside consultants to install the system and conduct ongoing audits. Then, too, the firm must train and support a large internal staff to administer the plan.

It is claimed that the details and weightings of the point-factor method are difficult to explain to employees. Thus, the staff in charge of administering the plan must educate workers about the nature of the job

Figure 9–8
Subfactor, Responsibility for Equipment or Tools, with Degrees and Points

RESPONSIBILITY FOR EQUIPMENT OR TOOLS		
Degree	**Amount of Responsibility**	**Points**
1	Probability of damage is small. Uses equipment that is difficult to damage. Little or no care required for equipment.	5
2	Some care required to recognize trouble and shut down equipment to prevent or minimize danger. Uses equipment that is subject to damage.	11
3	Moderate care required to prevent damage to power-driven equipment.	18
4	Sustained high degree of care required to control rapidly changing conditions and prevent damage to expensive equipment.	25

evaluation program. In one large firm, the job evaluation supervisor visits each plant at the request of the union or of management and conducts discussion sessions with the employees wherein the evaluation method is fully explained. Thus, a great deal of time and effort are required to implement the method, resulting in substantial costs.

Implementing the Job Evaluation Method

Many trade and professional associations have developed job evaluation plans to meet the needs of their own members, as we saw earlier in this chapter. However, most job evaluation experts recommend that a company not adopt in its entirety the method currently used by another firm. Any plan established and installed by another company or association must be modified to meet the individual needs of the firm involved. For example, the values that are significant to a high-tech computer manufacturer may not be key factors for a low-tech manufacturing firm. Some companies have installed the ranking, job classification, and factor-comparison methods but have discarded them in favor of the point-factor method, especially when the method is used as the basis for compensating rank-and-file

workers. In other companies, two methods of job evaluation may be used concurrently, with each method keyed to different job families. Then, too, modern computer techniques help users to compare the results of various job evaluation methods against each other and thus aid us in deciding which method, or combination of methods, is most appropriate for the company.

Regardless of the method or methods used to evaluate jobs, the firm should discuss with its workers the basis for its job evaluation method. As a result, the workers can see they are being treated equitably. The method or methods used in evaluating office jobs should be clearly set forth in employee handbooks. Also, special programs to explain the information on job evaluation plans should be provided for supervisors and workers. In addition, a formal procedure should be established in which the results of any job evaluation plan may be appealed. For example, in one large manufacturing company, the office supervisor may appeal a job evaluation to the person in charge of salary administration. The evaluation, based upon additional data or interpretation supplied by the supervisor, is then reviewed by the salary administration officer who has the final authority to make any needed changes.

SUMMARY
1. The information gathered in the analysis of office jobs is assembled into job descriptions and job specifications. The descriptions and specifications accurately identify each job and its tasks and spell out the requirements the job makes upon the worker for successful performance.
2. Job information may be obtained by several methods—questionnaire, interview, and observation, or a combination of these methods. The use of computers

greatly aids in organizing and analyzing job data quickly and in statistically validating the job information.
3. Job descriptions and job specifications provide the foundation upon which a company may establish a job evaluation program with the ultimate goal of designing an equitable wage and salary administration plan.
4. In developing an equitable wage and salary administration plan, the value of

each office job in relation to all other jobs must be determined by job evaluation. The person in charge of evaluating the office jobs must determine which of the basic methods—ranking, job classification, factor-comparison, or point-factor— should be used. A company must also decide whether to design its own evaluation plan or turn to outside professional associations or consultants for help in studying and evaluating jobs and implementing the selected method.

GLOSSARY **Employee specification**—a detailed record of the minimum qualifications a prospective employee must possess in order to be considered for employment.

Factor-comparison method—a method of evaluating jobs in which each job is evaluated in terms of money according to five critical factors: mental requirements, skill requirements, physical requirements, responsibility, and working conditions; also called *key-job system* and *job-to-money method*.

General Schedule—a job classification method used by the federal government for evaluating professional, scientific, clerical, administrative, and custodial jobs.

Interview method—a method of obtaining job information in which the job analyst interviews jobholders and their supervisors to determine the job duties performed and the minimum requirements for holding the job.

Job analysis—the process of gathering information and determining the principal elements involved in performing a specific job.

Job classification method—a method of evaluating jobs in which jobs are analyzed, ranked, and grouped into predetermined classes or family groupings based upon certain common denominators, such as levels of responsibility, abilities or skills, knowledge, and duties.

Job description—an outline of the information compiled from the job analysis that describes the content and essential requirements of a specific job; also called *position description*.

Job evaluation—the process of appraising the value of each job in relation to other jobs in order to set a monetary value for each specific job.

Job specification—a detailed record of the minimum job requirements explained in relation to the job factors (skill, effort, responsibility, and working conditions).

Key job—a job whose present rate is not subject to controversy and is considered to be neither underpaid nor overpaid; also called *benchmark job*.

Observation method—a method of obtaining job information in which the analyst observes employees performing their duties and learns about working conditions, equipment used, and skill requirements.

Point-factor method—a method of evaluating jobs in which the factors of skill, effort, responsibility, and job conditions are divided into subfactors, with degrees and points assigned to each subfactor.

Questionnaire method—a method of obtaining job information in which jobholders, often aided by their supervisors and the job analyst, describe their job duties and indicate minimum requirements for holding the job.

Ranking method—a method of evaluating jobs in which jobs are analyzed and ranked according to the difficulty and overall responsibility of each job; also called *rank order system*.

Structured questionnaire—a form that requests information on whether a specific task is part of the jobholder's job and tries to learn the importance the jobholder attaches to it.

Work measurement and setting work standards—the procedure for determining the time required to accomplish each job or task and for setting up criteria by which the degree of performance may be measured.

FOR YOUR REVIEW

1. How is the information obtained from an ongoing program of job analysis used in the office?

2. What are the major advantages and disadvantages of using the questionnaire method of gathering job information?

3. Contrast the interview method and the observation method of gathering job information by examining the advantages and disadvantages of each method.

4. Briefly describe one of the techniques that makes use of all three job analysis methods—questionnaire, interview, and observation.

5. For what reasons should office workers have easy access to their company's file of job descriptions?

6. Distinguish between a job description and a job specification by indicating the purpose of each.

7. Indicate some of the principal uses of job specifications.

8. Explain the procedure to be followed in using the ranking method to evaluate jobs.

9. Why is the job classification method of evaluating jobs looked upon as an outgrowth of the ranking method?

10. Why is the selection of key jobs essential in the use of the factor-comparison method of job evaluation?

11. What are the main advantages in using the point-factor method of job evaluation?

FOR YOUR DISCUSSION

1. Due to a takeover, the Condor Company is downsizing and reducing its workforce by 30 percent. For you, the supervisor of office services, this means that 15 of your people will be laid off. How can the job descriptions of these workers help you and them as you start counseling them about job opportunities in the community?

2. Henri Perrault is the supervisor of information services for Cadeau Communications. Along with the other supervisors and department heads, he feels that the firm is operating very efficiently without any formal job evaluation program. What benefits do you believe the company might obtain by establishing a formal job evaluation program? Do you foresee any potential disadvantages for the company as a result of implementing a job evaluation program? Explain your answers.

3. Elena Pinto, a technical word processing operator, feels that her job should be ranked higher than it is under her company's ranking method. How would you, as Pinto's supervisor, justify to her your ranking of the job she holds?

4. Dwight Hartman, a certified medical assistant, supervises five office workers and two laboratory technicians for Loomis Surgical Services. To assure himself that the salaries being paid are equitable, Hartman has decided to undertake an evaluation of the jobs. Which method of job evaluation do you recommend Hartman implement? Why?

5. Who should have responsibility for determining which jobs in a company are the key jobs? How should the key jobs be determined?

6. Since most office employees have at least a high school education and, in many instances, some college education, they are qualified to write a satisfactory description of their duties. Discuss the relevance of this statement.

7. What qualifications should a job analyst possess? Why?

8. When interviewing Barbara Stein, supervisor of accounts payable, to determine the content of her job, you find that she does not remember many of the things that she does daily, weekly, and monthly. What steps should you take to complete your analysis of Stein's job?

9. By now you have observed your teacher for several weeks and have become fairly well acquainted with the teaching methods used. From your observations, prepare a job description for TEACHER, OFFICE MANAGEMENT. As the job analyst, do you have sufficient information on hand to write a complete description? If not, what additional data do you need to obtain by means of an interview with your instructor?

10. Indicate what method or combination of methods you recommend be used to obtain information about each of the following jobs for use in preparing job descriptions:
    a. Data-entry operator who spends 7½ hours each day keyboarding data from copies of shipping orders.
    b. Receptionist and part-time relief in the mailing center.
    c. Supervisor in the records management department.
    d. Payroll clerk who collects and audits time sheets, calculates gross earnings and withholdings, and distributes paychecks.
    e. Chief editor for a large magazine publisher.

SOLVING CASE PROBLEMS

Case 9–1 Studying the Job Descriptions of Co-workers

In the computer center of DeMille, Ltd., the supervisor of computer operations, Lorna Perrine, has become aware of a serious morale problem among her workers. Perrine believes that much of the problem stems from her workers who are more concerned with their own individual jobs than the overall well-being of the company. For example, this past week she has sensed a conflict among her data-entry operators who appear to be working in isolation as they try to meet each individual operator's goals only; they seem completely unconcerned about the direction in which the firm plans to head. These are the same workers who appear very insensitive to the priorities that have been established by the systems analysts and the programmers.

Perrine believes her people must learn to pull together as a team and become more aware of the firm's perspectives about its future. While she was exploring her concerns with her boss, Daniel Manon, he broke in to say:

> I see where you are coming from, Lorna. What we've got to do is convince these people that they're *partners* in our company. I've got an idea. Let's give each of your people a copy of all the job descriptions for everyone working in the center—the analysts, programmers, computer operators, data-entry operators, and, yes, my job description and yours. Ask them to study all the job descriptions for the next several days and then let's set up a meeting with them. At that meeting here is what I would like us to do. . . .

Prepare a list of the direct questions you would ask your workers to show how their study of the job descriptions can lead to a *team* orientation. What outcomes do you expect the meeting to provide that will enable you to start cultivating a climate in which the workers feel like *partners*?

Case 9–2 Pulling Workers off Their Jobs

At lunch time, Abe Finney was griping to his co-worker, Dee Carmero.

Finney: I'm not supposed to do that work in the mail room. After all, I was hired as a billing clerk.

Carmero: I know what you mean. Terry is on my back, too, to help out with the mail this afternoon. And who's going to be doing my billings while I'm over there in the mail room for four hours?

At the other end of the cafeteria, Finney's supervisor, Marc Terry, was getting an earful from the owner-manager, Tom Struthers.

Struthers: You've got to finish this bulk mailing on time and get those brochures to the post office tonight.

Terry: I know that. But it's not easy with this bunch of prima donnas like Finney and Carmero. They drag their feet when I pull them away from their regular work and put them in the mail room where they can help move the work along.

What do you see to be the main problem as revealed in the conversations? Are the complaints of Finney and Carmero legitimate? Explain. What solution can you offer to Struthers to avoid similar problems in the future?

10

Office Salary Administration

GOALS FOR THIS CHAPTER

After completing this chapter, you should be able to:

1. Identify those persons who may be assigned responsibility for administering the office salary program.
2. List the objectives of the office salary administration program.
3. Describe those factors to be considered when determining office salaries.
4. Enumerate the steps taken in setting a price for office jobs.
5. Identify the different plans for providing salary increases.
6. Describe the types of salary incentive systems that may be used in an office salary administration program.

"I know there's more to life than money, but I can hardly wait to get my hands on that paycheck today!" "Just look at the amount of my take-home pay—somebody in payroll goofed. There's no way my gross salary of $500 could drop to a net of $325!" "I was supposed to get my raise in this check—what happened?"

Do questions such as these about our salaries—a topic so dear to the hearts of us all—ring familiar to you? In this chapter, we shall take a close look at this aspect of our working lives that each of us holds so close—*our salary.*

First, we shall note where responsibility for the office salary program is assigned in the organization. Then, we shall examine the objectives of office salary administration and discuss those factors that are considered when determining office salaries. Next, we shall see how a "price" (salary) is assigned to the value of each office job and how salary increases are awarded. Finally, we shall investigate the nature of individual and group incentive systems.

ADMINISTERING THE OFFICE SALARY PROGRAM

The responsibility for administering the office salary program depends upon the size and structure of the organization. In most companies, regardless of size, the cost of salaries represents a significant part of the total operating expenses; thus, in companies of all sizes we often find the responsibility for salary administration assigned to a top-level officer, such as the treasurer, or one or more key executives in the areas of finance and control.[1]

In small and many medium-size firms, the administrative office manager, aided by a committee of other managers and key executives, may assist in establishing the ob-

---

[1] *1988 Survey of Salaries and the Payroll Profession,* American Payroll Association, p. 2.

264

jectives and policies governing the salary program. Line managers and first-line supervisors, although not part of the formal salary administration committee, are often asked to recommend ways of improving the salary program. These managers and supervisors provide most of the guidance and direction received by office employees; therefore, they must thoroughly understand the program so that they in turn can communicate it to their subordinates.

In the largest companies, the human resources department, with its responsibility for employee relations, sometimes exercises authority over the company-wide salary program. This department, often staffed with a full-time salary administrator, may be responsible for collecting pertinent salary information, recommending policies and procedures, and answering all questions relating to the administration of salaries.

To realize full benefit from the office salary program, those responsible for its administration must communicate to all employees the nature and goals of the program. No matter how technically sound, equitable, and competently administered, the program will be effective only if employees perceive it as such. Employee handbooks, with a section devoted to compensation, are perhaps the most common medium for communicating the objectives of the salary administration program. Other communication media that may be used by the salary administrator are described in Chapter 5.

THE OBJECTIVES OF OFFICE SALARY ADMINISTRATION

Those responsible for any phase of office salary administration must understand its broad objectives. As a rule, you will find that an effective office salary administration program attempts to meet the following objectives:

1. *To attract workers* who will be paid equitable salaries.
2. *To retain workers* by paying them fairly. Employees become dissatisfied and lose confidence in the salary program when they feel that inequities exist. Therefore, the differences in salaries paid workers should be supported by objective employee performance appraisals.
3. *To motivate and reward high-level performance*, determined as objectively as possible by periodic employee appraisal. Periodic appraisal, as we saw in Chapter 8, helps employees learn how well they are performing and ensures communication between office supervisors and their subordinates. Employees thus become aware that their extra efforts and achievements will be recognized and rewarded by means of extra compensation.
4. *To maintain a competitive position* with other companies in the same geographic area. At the same time, the company must be able to control its labor costs in order to realize gains in productivity.

An effective salary administration program helps to attract, retain, motivate, and reward exceptional employees.

To achieve these objectives and to maintain a sound salary program, a company should build its program upon a foundation of job analysis. The importance of job analysis and one of its elements—job evaluation—is indicated in the establishment of *levels* or *grades* for office positions. For each grade or group of jobs, there must be a maximum and a minimum *salary range*, with periodic pay increases based upon the successful performance of work. In order to meet future changes in job content and the reassignment of responsibilities, the office salary administrator must recognize that jobs should be periodically reviewed and analyzed in relation to other jobs within and outside the organization.

In designing its office salary program, the company may consider placing its office workers on an *incentive* basis to reward them for increased production and outstanding work. Before installing an incentive system, the work must be measured and standards set, as explained in a later chapter. In order to set standards, the work must be carefully studied and all unnecessary motions and wasted time must be eliminated.

Finally, an important aspect of the total compensation package for office employees relates to *employee benefits*—the indirect compensation received by workers. When you read the following chapter, you will see that, on the average, employee benefits amount to about 37 cents of every payroll dollar.

In considering the following factors that determine office salaries, firms must recognize the needs of their employees and determine to what extent these needs are being satisfied so that employees are motivated to perform efficiently.

FACTORS TO CONSIDER IN DETERMINING OFFICE SALARIES

Once the office jobs have been evaluated, the next step is to answer the question, "How much should each office worker be paid?" Before we can answer this question, however, we must examine several factors.

Company Philosophy Toward Office Salary Administration

Influenced by the quality of office workers they hope to attract and retain, companies may adopt a policy of paying salaries that are equal to, greater than, or less than the average salaries paid by other firms in the community. Some companies build their salary program around the competition in their area for employees who perform similar types of work. Other companies prefer to relate their salary levels more closely to those of similar firms within the same industry. Firms that provide a wide program of employee benefits may decide to pay a smaller base salary than that paid by other firms not offering such a broad array of benefits.

Some companies have adopted a philosophy toward salary administration that is in keeping with the proposals of behaviorists such as Maslow, McGregor, and Herzberg, whose motivation theories were described in earlier chapters. You will recall that according to Maslow and McGregor, workers are not motivated by their lower-order needs, which money can effectively satisfy, because in today's world these needs are largely met. Therefore, managers turn their attention to the higher-order needs and attempt to provide recognition, status, praise, and opportunities for self-actualization. To meet these higher-order needs, you saw that job enrichment and employee participation have been offered as motivational techniques.

Remember Herzberg's two factors— *motivator* and *hygienic*—that strongly influence workers? Herzberg showed that only the *satisfying* factors are able to improve performance by providing more of what he calls *motivators:* achievement, recognition, advancement, growth, responsibility, and the work itself. Company policies, working conditions, interpersonal relationships, quality of supervision, and pay are *hygienic* or *maintenance* factors. Increasing the hygienic factors will not raise performance, but a decrease in the availability of these factors will lower performance. From his research, Herzberg concluded that money is not a motivator. Managers were thus encouraged to adopt job enrichment rather than money as a means of raising productivity and job satisfaction. Thus, workers would benefit by a greater fulfillment of their higher-order needs.

As we know, the debate still goes on as to what extent money actually motivates. Some critics say that most employees always feel that their lower-order needs are never fully satisfied. Also, many people argue that with increases in the cost of living, as well as changes in life-styles, the amount of money needed to satisfy a person's basic needs has increased greatly. Thus, these critics conclude that not only were the lower-order needs not met in the past, but also they are not being met now; and the amount of money necessary to do so is steadily increasing.

Despite the studies and surveys that have tried to support or deny the role of salaries in motivating employees, supervisors and managers assume today, as they have for years, that money is what most people work for. Money is still viewed as the most important motivator that managers and supervisors have at their disposal. They see dollars as a motivating tool that is tangible, objective, and controllable.

The Firm's Ability to Pay

A basic factor to consider in determining salaries for office workers is that the salaries cannot exceed the firm's ability to pay and still earn a profit. Few companies can afford to keep their employees' paychecks abreast of the inflation rate. Many workers realize that although their income may be more than twice as many dollars as a decade ago, their *buying power* (real earnings after taxes and inflation) is lower. For example, at the beginning of 1989, the average weekly pay, when adjusted for inflation, was no higher than it was in 1973.[2] In 1973, the average 30-year-old homeowner could make the monthly mortgage payment using 21 percent of before-tax monthly pay; in 1984, the payment took 44 percent; since then, that percentage has declined only slightly.[3]

Expectations of Office Employees

Vroom's expectancy theory, which was presented in Chapter 7, describes the conditions that must be met in order to use pay as a motivator. The key elements of this theory may be stated as: (1) EFFORT that results in, (2) PERFORMANCE that results in, (3) REWARDS, as shown in Figure 10–1. By reading the letters **E**, **P**, and **R** from the top to the bottom and horizontally, you see how expectancy theory might work in the case of an office worker.

Like all other employees at every level in the firm, we bring to our jobs our expectations and decisions on how much effort we shall expend to fulfill those expectations. To be reasonably satisfied with our work and motivated to perform, we need a work climate where we can further develop our philosophy of life within which our jobs "make sense." We need a sense of purpose, the will to achieve, and the feeling of being wanted and accepted. As office workers, we expect to get satisfaction from meeting our job challenges successfully and improving our job performance. In turn, we expect our improved performance to result in desired rewards such as equitable salaries, better employee benefits, and improved working conditions.

---

[2]"Are We Becoming a Nation of Burger Flippers?" *Changing Times* (March, 1989), p. 32.
[3]"Homeownership: Who Can Afford It?" *Changing Times* (March, 1989), p. 34.

Figure 10-1
Expectancy
Theory and
the Office
Worker

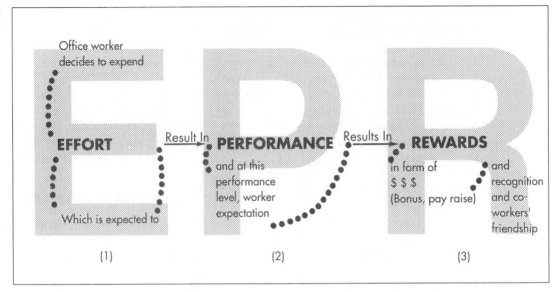

We expect our salaries to provide us with enough money to support ourselves and any dependents and to be able to continue improving our standard of living. We realize that if our salaries do not increase at least as fast as the cost of living, our level of living standards declines. Also, we expect our salaries and pay increases to give us financial security not only during our working careers but also later when we retire.

As office employees, we expect our pay to be fair and reasonable in comparison with that of other workers in the firm. We feel we should make "good" money when we work hard and have the opportunity to earn extra money when we work harder. We want a fair day's pay for a fair day's work; but, in turn, we expect that a fair day's work will be accurately measured. Further, we desire some voice in the determination of our salaries or at least have an avenue of appeal in the event we are dissatisfied with our earnings.

For work well done, we expect recognition at the time of employee appraisal when the company takes note of our quality and quantity of work. In companies that use incentive systems, we want assurance that

additional rewards will be given for an exceptional amount of top-notch work produced. Finally, we expect promotion from within the business firm not on the basis of seniority alone, but also based on merit and our knowledge and understanding of the requirements of the new position.

Office Salaries Paid by Other Companies

In establishing a salary structure for *nonexempt* office personnel (workers who must be paid overtime for all hours worked beyond 40 in a workweek), the most significant factor is the *local going rate*. In many companies, the salary structures for nonexempt office employees are set after serious consideration of the local community rates. To obtain data on office salaries paid for comparable jobs in similar industries within the community or in surrounding areas, the company may use a salary survey.

The Salary Survey

A **salary survey** is a statistical picture of the salaries for certain jobs in a particular geographic area or for a certain industry at a given time. The survey shows only what the responding firms pay their jobholders; the survey does not state nor recommend what administrative office managers must pay comparable jobholders in their organizations.

Although salary surveys are a useful tool in planning and adjusting salaries, we should be cautious when using the surveys for the following reasons:

1. The job descriptions in the survey may not match up with the responsibilities, working conditions, and employee qualifications for the jobs in the company using the survey results. Therefore, we should not use salary survey data as the *sole* basis for relating the pay of one surveyed job to another job in the organization.
2. The survey may be too broad in scope and thus not sample the relevant labor market that consists of all the local companies competing for the same labor supply. For example, national surveys may not give an accurate picture of local labor markets.
3. Salary survey data, especially for high-tech positions, become obsolete very quickly.
4. Human error exists in salary surveys as in any human endeavor; for it is people who complete the survey questionnaires, who enter the data into the computer, and who make mistakes in interpreting the data. Imagine the effect of a keyboarding error that stated the average weekly salary for a Senior General Clerk as $382 instead of the correct amount, $328!

In the *1989 Office Salaries Report*, the Administrative Management Society reported the following statistics for the job title "Legal Secretary/Assistant" found in all types of business in the United States:[4]

[4]*1989 AMS Office Salaries Report* (Trevose, PA: Administrative Management Society), p. 8. See page 244 of this textbook for the job description of Legal Secretary/Assistant.

The **average** weekly salary (the *arithmetic mean*), $415, is obtained by multiplying the number of employees reported for each salary rate by the rate. These results are totaled and then divided by the number of employees whose salaries are reported for the job.

The **quartile** is a measure of position that divides an array, such as the listing of all the salaries paid Legal Secretary/Assistants, into four equal parts. In contrast to averages, quartiles are not affected by the high frequency of salaries at either the high or the low end of a distribution. In Figure 10-2, the **first quartile**, $350, represents the actual weekly salary paid the employee whose salary is more than one-fourth and less than three-fourths of all employees reported for the job.

Figure 10-2
Survey Data for Legal Secretary/Assistant

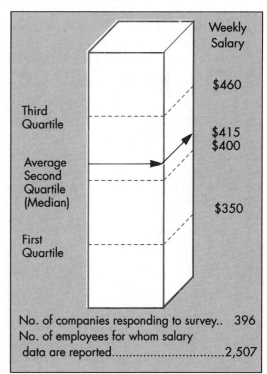

Weekly Salary

Third Quartile

$460

$415
$400

Average Second Quartile (Median)

$350

First Quartile

No. of companies responding to survey.. 396
No. of employees for whom salary
data are reported...............................2,507

Source: 1989 AMS Office Salaries Report.

The **median**, or *second quartile*, $400, is the actual weekly salary of the middle employee in the distribution where half of the employees earn more and the other half earn less. The median is the most representative figure in a survey and, like any quartile measure, is not influenced by extreme highs and lows.

The **third quartile**, $460, is the actual weekly salary paid the employee whose salary is more than three-fourths of all the employees reported for the job. The salaries at the first and third quartiles, $350 and $460, are the limits of the middle 50 percent of the employees reported, as shown in Figure 10–3. Some refer to the spread between these salaries as the **effective salary range** for the job because the salaries at the extremes are disregarded.

Continuing with our preceding example, a newly hired employee, with minimum or no related experience, might commence at the low or minimum weekly salary of $350. (The AMS *Office Salaries Report* shows $345 as the average weekly starting rate for the position.) As the worker becomes more proficient on the job, appropriate pay increases should be provided. If the new employee's caliber of performance is average, the beginning pay rate might be $405, which is the midpoint or the midvalue of the range $350 to $460. ($460 − 350 = $110; $110 ÷ 2 = $55; $350 + 55 = $405.) If the performance is above average, the worker should be paid in the upper half of the pay range, $400 to $460, but in no case more than the maximum, $460.

Obtaining Salary Survey Data

The AOM has available the following means of obtaining salary data:

1. Purchasing the survey.
2. Using a consultant.
3. Conducting one's own survey.

A brief description of each of these sources follows.

Purchasing the Survey. Comparative salary data on 20 benchmark, or key, office positions are found in the annual *Office Salaries Report*, which may be obtained from the Administrative Management Society. These positions are described in Figure 9–3, page 244. Another valuable survey undertaken by AMS is the annual *Data Processing Salaries Report*, which covers 20 key positions, grouped in the job families: General, Systems Analysis, Applications Programming, Systems Analysis and Programming, Computer Operations, and Data Entry. AMS also publishes an annual *Management Salaries Report*, in which salary data are presented for 20 benchmark management positions. Companies participating in any of the salary surveys receive a copy of the report free of charge. For other AMS members, there is a charge for each annual survey.

Figure 10–3

Effective Salary Range Obtained from Survey Data Reported for Legal Secretary/Assistant

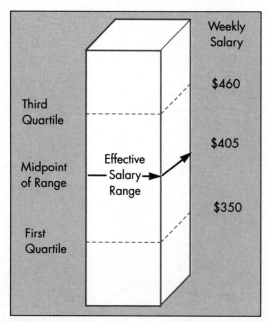

Source: 1989 AMS Office Salaries Report.

Salary data may be obtained free of charge from the Bureau of Labor Statistics, which undertakes the annual *National Survey of Professional, Administrative, Technical, and Clerical Pay* in major cities across the country. In addition to the sources of data on salaries paid office workers listed on page 243, AOMs may receive helpful information from their local employer associations, state and local government agencies, banks, and consulting firms.

Generally the surveys described above are professionally conducted and summarized and are relatively inexpensive. Usually large groups participate in such surveys, and thus statistically sound sample sizes are obtained so that valid estimates of salaries may be made for all office workers. On the other hand, when relating the results of a purchased survey to the job titles and descriptions found within one's own firm, difficulty may be experienced in interpreting the survey data and tailoring the data to meet the requirements of the firm. Further, the company purchasing the survey has not been able to select the benchmark jobs, to choose the questions asked, to select the time the survey is conducted, or to choose the companies being surveyed.

Using a Consultant. Rather than purchase periodic salary surveys or conduct one's own survey, the company may employ the services of a consultant who will professionally conduct, analyze, and interpret the survey. The OM, working with the consultant, is able to help select the benchmark jobs to be surveyed, to choose the questions to be asked and the companies to be surveyed, to select the effective date of the salary data, and to determine the time for conducting the survey. The company employing the consultant benefits from the experience gained by the consultant in working with other companies who have undertaken similar surveys. The major disadvantage of using a consultant is the cost of the service, which may amount to many

hundreds of dollars daily. Therefore, the cost of using an outside consultant must be weighed against the benefits to be realized from this source of salary information.

Conducting One's Own Survey. The greatest advantage realized by the firm that conducts its own survey is that the firm obtains salary data stated in terms of its own compensation program. The individual or committee in charge of preparing the survey questionnaire is able to select the benchmark jobs, specify the questions to be asked, set the effective date of the data and the time for conducting the survey, and choose the companies to survey. The person in charge of conducting the survey must make sure that information is asked about a satisfactory number of stable key jobs. A standard job title should be listed on the survey form for each key job. Since the terminology of job content and the level of responsibility may differ from company to company being surveyed, a description of each job should accompany the questionnaire so that all respondents are provided comparable data about each job.

The disadvantages of undertaking one's own survey include the cost of the time-consuming activity itself and the need for competent, experienced persons to conduct the survey. Often it may be difficult to obtain a random sample or statistically sound sample size since companies may fail to respond to the survey or may supply inaccurate or incomplete information. Thus, follow-up time must be spent in contacting each participant to verify the questionnaire contents before computing, summarizing, and interpreting the data, which adds considerably to the cost of the survey.

Government Regulations

The most important federal statute for the office salary administrator is the **Fair Labor Standards Act (FLSA)**, which is also known as the federal wage and hour law. In addition to this federal law, other federal regulations and state laws must be taken into consideration by the administrative office manager when determining office salaries.

Fair Labor Standards Act of 1938, As Amended

Generally an office occupation is covered by the FLSA if the firm and the jobholder (1) deal with the movement of goods in interstate commerce involving the interstate transmission of documents or (2) require the use of interstate facilities. For example, employees in the home office of an insurance company are covered if the firm operates in more than one state or if the firm's activities involve regular use of the mails or other means of interstate commerce. Bank employees are generally covered by the law because bank activities are essential to interstate commerce. Office employees in a real estate business are covered, too, if they regularly prepare documents that are sent out of state or if they use channels of interstate commerce.

Employees covered under the FLSA must be paid a specified minimum wage, equal pay for equal work, and an overtime premium for all hours worked beyond a certain number. The FLSA also places restrictions upon the employment of children, as discussed below.

Minimum Wages. Unless specifically exempted by the FLSA, all employees must be paid at least the minimum wage, whether they are paid a salary by the hour, by piece work, or by any other method. Under certain conditions, wages lower than the minimum may be paid some employees. For example, full-time students may be employed by retail or service establishments and farms at 85 percent of the minimum wage.[5]

[5]For current minimum wage rates, exemption categories, etc., of the FLSA and other legislation affecting office salaries, see Bernard J. Bieg and B. Lewis Keeling, *Payroll Accounting* (Cincinnati: South-Western Publishing Co., current annual edition), or any payroll tax service.

Equal Pay for Equal Work. The **Equal Pay Act** of 1963 prohibits employers from setting different wages based solely on the *sex* of workers who are doing equal work. Men and women working in the same establishment under similar working conditions must receive the same pay if their jobs require equal skill, equal effort, and equal responsibility. "Equal" in this sense does not mean "identical." However, jobs to be compared under the Equal Pay Act must involve the same primary job function and must require substantially equal skill, effort, and responsibility.

Wage differences between sexes are allowed when the differences are based on a seniority system, a merit system, a payment plan that measures earnings by quantity or quality of production, or any factor other than sex. If there is an unlawful pay differential between men and women, the employer is required to raise the lower rate to equal the higher rate.

What about the salaries paid men and women who are performing jobs not necessarily "equal," but involving "comparable worth"? It has long been held that traditional

The sex of an employee cannot be used as a basis for determining wages.

female jobs (such as clerk typist) are automatically lower paying than traditional male jobs (such as tree trimmer) of comparable worth. Is this as discriminatory as paying a man and a woman different rates for the same job? Unions and women's groups say "yes" and look upon the concept of comparable worth as a way to close the wage gap that has historically existed between "male" jobs and "female" jobs.

Under the concept of *equal pay for comparable worth*, the jobs need not meet any criteria of equality or similarity. Instead, the jobs are compensated according to their intrinsic value to the employer, as determined by one or more of the job evaluation methods described in the previous chapter.

Some states and local governments have adopted comparable-worth policies for their employees in the public sector. If, in the public sector, pay for comparable worth were to become an accepted means of narrowing the gap between wages paid males and females, no doubt private employers would be affected also.

Overtime Hours and Overtime Pay. The FLSA states that overtime, or premium, pay is required for all hours worked in excess of 40 in a workweek. The overtime pay required is one and one-half times the employee's regular pay rate. The law does not require extra pay for Saturday, Sunday, or holiday work; nor does the law require vacation pay, holiday pay, or severance pay. Such types of pay and working conditions may be agreed upon in union contracts, however. Under the FLSA, employers are not required to give rest periods to their employees. If, however, rest periods are given, either voluntarily by the employer or in keeping with the terms of a union contract or a state regulation, the rest periods must be counted as hours worked if they last 20 minutes or less.

Child-Labor Restrictions. The FLSA stipulates that children below certain ages

may not be employed in interstate activities. Thus, a business is prohibited from shipping its goods between states if unlawful child labor was used in manufacturing the goods. Generally the regulations restrict the employment of children under 18 years of age.

Exempt Employees. Certain groups of employees, such as administrators, professionals, and executives, are *fully exempt* from the minimum wage and overtime pay requirements of the FLSA. As an example, let's examine the exempt status of executives.

To be exempted from the FLSA requirements, executives must possess discretionary power (ability to use individual judgment in freely making decisions) and exercise managerial functions. Their primary duty must be to manage the enterprise or at least one of its departments or subdivisions. Generally *primary duty* is defined to mean that executives must spend the major part or over 50 percent of their time in managerial duties. However, employees who spend less than 50 percent of their time in managerial duties may be classified as exempt if (1) they customarily and regularly direct the work of two or more other employees; (2) they can hire or fire employees, or make suggestions and recommendations that are given weight in deciding upon hiring, firing, or promoting; or (3) they customarily and regularly exercise discretionary powers.

Other Federal Regulations

Other federal legislation that may affect the salaries and wages paid and the hours worked by employees are summarized in Figure 10–4.

State Regulations

In most states, minimum wage rates have been established for employees in specific industries. Where both the federal and state regulations cover the same employees, the higher of the two rates prevails. State regulations not only set minimum wages but also contain provisions affecting pay for *call-in*

Figure 10–4
Other Federal Regulations Affecting Salaries and Wages and Hours Worked

Federal Law	Employer Coverage	Provisions for Employees' Wages and Hours
Davis-Bacon Act of 1931	Contractors and subcontractors on federal government contracts of more than $2,000 for constructing, altering, or repairing public buildings	
Walsh-Healey Public Contracts Act of 1936	Those who manufacture or furnish materials, supplies, equipment for agencies of the United States in an amount exceeding $10,000	Workers' minimum wages and overtime compensation are determined by the Secretary of Labor.
McNamara–O'Hara Service Contract Act of 1965	Those who furnish services (such as transportation of mail by railroad, airlines, and ocean vessels) in the United States or District of Columbia in excess of $2,500	

time (compensation guaranteed workers who report for work and find there is insufficient work for them to do), rest and meal periods, absences, meals and lodging, and tips.

Collective Bargaining Agreements

When office employees are represented by a union, the salary administrator must take into consideration the collective bargaining agreement. **Collective bargaining** is a negotiation process between an employer and labor union representatives on work-related issues such as wages, hours of work, and working conditions. Collective bargaining, which was made an instrument of national policy by passage of the National Labor Relations Act of 1935, includes three duties:

1. The duty of both the employer and the employees' representative to sit down at the same table and work to achieve a mutually acceptable labor contract. The **labor contract** is a private agreement entered into by the employer and the

employees for the purpose of regulating certain work-related conditions.
2. The duty of both sides to work sincerely and honestly toward a labor agreement—to bargain in good faith.
3. The duty to limit the bargaining to wages, hours, and other terms and conditions of employment. Over the years, however, the items subject to bargaining have been dramatically expanded and now include issues such as employee benefits, grievance procedures, no-strike clauses, discipline, seniority, and union security.

Thus, we see that the collective bargaining agreement is a policy guide with provisions that the salary administrator must thoroughly understand not only when determining salaries but also when implementing procedures that affect employee earnings and working conditions. We shall examine several of the more important provisions of collective bargaining agreements in the following paragraphs.

1. Of major importance at the bargaining table is the provision for salary increases

during the life of the labor contract. Common in almost all contracts is a **cost-of-living adjustment (COLA) clause**, which is designed to keep the employees' salaries more or less in step with inflation. Such clauses usually provide for salary increases that escalate, or rise, with increases in the cost of living, as measured by an index such as the Consumer Price Index for Urban Wage Earners and Clerical Workers (CPI-W). Thus, we might find that as a result of a 4.5 percent increase in the CPI-W for the year, the union contract provides a COLA increase of 4.2 percent for the year.

2. The provisions of the collective bargaining agreement are binding on both management and labor for a mutually acceptable period of time and are enforceable through mediation and arbitration, or finally through state and federal courts. In **mediation**, an impartial third party tries to bring both sides to a point of common agreement. In **arbitration**, labor and management agree to submit the issue in dispute to an individual arbitrator or a board of arbitration that renders a decision binding upon both parties.

3. The National Labor Relations Board is the agency, created by law, that hears testimony, renders decisions, determines the collective bargaining unit or agency, and prosecutes unfair labor practices.

4. Union shop agreements must be in accordance with prevailing state laws and are void where prohibited by state laws. A **union shop agreement** requires that after workers have been hired, they must join the union or make dues payment within a specified period of time or be fired. (Twenty states have **right-to-work laws**, which ban contracts that make union membership or the payment of fees a condition of employment.)

5. Union dues **check-off** (deducting of union dues from paychecks by the employer and remitting of collections to the union) requires the written consent of the employee.

6. Individual employees can present grievances directly to their supervisors, but the union representative must be informed and given an opportunity to be present.

7. Supervisors may be unionized, but the employer does not have to recognize or bargain with them since they represent management.

8. Employees may *decertify* (eliminate) the union selected to represent them, but only during the 60- to 90-day period at the end of the contract.

9. Workers who hold religious objections to joining or financially supporting a union cannot be required to do so as a condition of employment. However, such employees can be required, under a collective bargaining provision, to contribute to a nonreligious charity a sum equal to union dues and initiation fees.

PRICING THE OFFICE JOBS

Having carefully studied and analyzed those factors that influence the determination of office salaries, the AOM is ready to undertake the important task of *pricing* the individual jobs. In illustrating how pay grades and salary ranges are determined and office jobs are priced, we shall use as our example the point-factor method of job evaluation. As you learned in Chapter 9, this method probably provides more consistency of results than any of the other job evaluation methods. (The techniques of pricing office jobs under the point-factor method may be adapted also to the determination of compensation under the other methods of job evaluation described in Chapter 9.) Figure 10–5 lists the procedure followed when the point-factor method has been used to evaluate office jobs. The steps in pricing the jobs are illustrated in Table 10–1.

Figure 10-5
Procedure
for Pricing
Office Jobs
Evaluated by
the Point-
Factor
Method

1. **Total the points for each job.** You will recall that in the point-factor method, each factor common to a job is divided into subfactors and degrees, which are assigned point values.

2. **List the points for each job,** as shown in Column 1 of Table 10-1. Here, the point values for 19 office jobs, coded A through S, have been arranged from the lowest to the highest. This arrangement makes it possible to add new pay grade numbers if new jobs that exceed the highest point value come into existence or if the high-value jobs are reevaluated and assigned a greater number of points. Also, it appears more logical to have the highest pay represented by the highest pay grade number.

3. **Group the jobs that have about the same number of point values and select logical cutoff points.** See Column 2. The number of job groupings is determined by the number of pay grades to be used and how the jobs naturally group themselves according to pay relationships surveyed in the labor market. After the job groupings have been established, all jobs falling within a particular grouping should have the same basic value. Thus, Jobs F through K, which have point values of 282 through 300, are placed in one pay grade, No. 4.

4. **Establish the pay grades by using a constant progression of points for each grade.** Column 3 shows that seven grades, each with a progression of 40 points, have been set up. There is no acceptable, definite number of pay grades to be used; the number will vary according to the existing number of jobs in the office and the employee job groupings.

5. **Enter the findings from the salary survey** in Column 4. In this illustration, one key job for each of the seven pay grades matched the job description used in the survey; and the average weekly salary for each key job was recorded. Thus, since Jobs A, B, and C are grouped into the same pay grade, No. 1, all three jobs will receive the same pay, an amount to be determined when Job B is priced.

6. **Use the salary survey data to determine the "best fit" for the weekly base salaries,** which are listed in Column 5. In this example, the company's salary administration policy is to set a weekly base salary that approximates the average salary paid by all firms and that is economically feasible in relation to the anticipated sales revenue.

7. **Establish a pay range for each of the base salaries.** Here, it was decided to use the base salary as the midpoint of each range. The company proceeded on the theory that the midpoint represents the "going rate" for each job and decided that any new workers would be hired at a salary between the minimum and the midpoint of the range. This point would not be exceeded unless the job applicant had unusual qualifications.

    A company may set a flat percentage spread around the midpoint of each range, such as the 15 percent spread shown in Table 10-1. Or it may be decided to apply a percentage increase that becomes progressively greater, such as 10 percent for the lowest job level up through 40 to 50 percent for the highest level. If the salary ranges have been accurately developed and kept current, the minimum salary at each level should be sufficient to attract new employees. In setting the salary ranges, as shown in Table 10-1, the maximums should be about 30 to 50 percent above the minimums. Thus, each range has room for rewarding individual differences in experience and job performance. Each salary grade minimum should be about 10 to 14 percent above the minimum of the next lower salary range.

Table 10-1
Steps in
Pricing the
Office Job

(1) Point Values for Each Job Evaluated *Job Points*	(2) Job Groupings	(3) Pay Grades *Grade Points*	(4) Average Weekly Salary of Key Jobs Determined by Survey	(5) Weekly Base Salary	(6) Pay Range
A 180 B 189 C 195	180–195	1 Under 200	B $182	$180	$155–$210
D 225	225	2 201–240	D $195	$200	$170–$230
E 260	260	3 241–280	E $220	$220	$190–$250
F 282 G 282 H 286 I 289 J 293 K 300	282–300	4 281–320	I $246	$250	$210–$290
L 342 M 349 N 358	342–358	5 321–360	M $275	$270	$230–$310
O 365 P 370 Q 384	365–384	6 361–400	O $287	$290	$250–$335
R 410 S 430	410–430	7 401–440	R $332	$320	$275–$370

Source: Adapted and reprinted by permission of the publisher, from COMPENSATION, BENEFITS & REVIEW, © 1974. American Management Association, New York. All rights reserved.

Charting the Salary Rates

A *scatter chart*, such as that shown in Figure 10-6, may be used to show the salary rates and salary distribution at a glance. By examining the chart, we can see any discrepancies in the salaries being paid that need to be adjusted in relation to the pay ranges established. Here, briefly stated, are the steps followed in constructing the scatter chart:

1. *Plot each of the 19 office jobs*, labeled A through S, on the vertical scale in relation to the current salary being paid each jobholder and on the horizontal scale according to the paygrade point values for the jobs.

2. *Plot the midpoint of the lowest and the highest pay ranges to serve as anchor points for establishing the trend line.*

3. *Draw a straight line through the center of both anchor points.* This line is known as the *basic salary curve* or the *salary trend line.*

4. *Draw two more straight lines to determine the upper and lower limits of each pay range.* These lines are drawn at a fixed percentage distance from the salary trend line. In Figure 10-6, two additional anchor points were established on a perpendicular 15 percent above and 15 percent below the midpoint for the lowest pay range. Similarly, two more anchor points

Figure 10-6
Scatter Chart
Showing
Relationship
Between
Weekly Base
Salaries and
Job Evalua-
tion Points

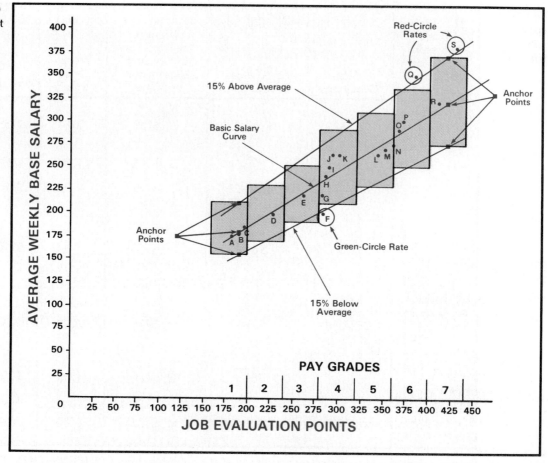

Adjusting the Salary Rates

After we prepare and study a scatter chart, we often find discrepancies in the amounts currently paid employees. Some workers may be receiving more than, while others are earning less than, the recommended averages. We need to adjust such inequities as soon as practical after the pricing of the jobs has been completed.

Rates of fully qualified workers that fall below the minimum line, such as the person holding Job F in Figure 10-6, are known as **green-circle rates**. These rates should be adjusted upward within the pay grade in accordance with the company's salary progression policy. To determine exactly where a worker should fit into the range,

were plotted 15 percent above and 15 percent below the midpoint of the highest pay range. By drawing straight lines through the anchor points above and below the salary trend line, the minimum and maximum salary rates for each pay grade were established.[6]

---

[6]Although the anchor-point method is an accepted practice in establishing salary curves, some authorities claim that the method does not produce a perfect curve. From a purely statistical point of view, the claim may be justified because calculations and plottings established by the method of least squares reflect a somewhat truer curve. For an explanation of the method of least squares, see the accompanying supplementary item, *Practical Experience Assignments for Administrative Office Management*, or any basic statistics textbook.

each worker should be evaluated individually in relation to the salary progression policy and availability of funds.

Sometimes the plotted salary dots appear above the maximum line, as in the case of Jobs Q and S in Figure 10-6. These **red-circle rates** represent overpayments and should be noted for adjustment, such as: (1) training and upgrading the red-circle worker to another job commensurate with the present salary, (2) leaving the employee on the job at the same salary until a promotion opening becomes available, or (3) letting a worker with many years of seniority remain on the job but assign the person additional responsibilities commensurate with the red-circle rate.

Establishing the Salary Progression Schedule

A sound office salary administration program provides employees the opportunity to receive periodic salary increases so they may advance from the minimum to the maximum salary level in their pay grade. The progression system also provides for promotion from one pay grade to another. The spread within a pay grade appears to be an individual company matter that is dependent upon the employees' needs and desires and the firm's financial condition. To motivate employees, the spread of a pay grade should be at least 20 percent. That is, the minimum (or starting) rate is 10 percent below the average salary trend line and the maximum rate is 10 percent above this line. Many companies are likely to have a spread of somewhere between 30 and 40 percent. In Figure 10-6, the spread within each salary range is 30 percent.

Some organizations develop scales of salary grades and ranges similar to that shown in Table 10-2. In this salary scale, each grade consists of a minimum, a midpoint, and a maximum salary. Usually the spread starts at about 30 percent in the lower grades and gradually increases to around 60 percent

A sound salary administration program rewards qualified workers by advancing them to higher levels in their pay grades.

in the higher grades. The scale is designed to show that there is progressively less room open for promotion as employees move up the salary schedule. Thus, the salary ranges for higher levels are wider in order to provide room for recognition of meritorious performance on the same job over a considerable length of time.

Within the individual salary ranges, employees may be provided periodic salary increases under one or more of the following plans, each of which is briefly described:

1. Automatic progression.
2. Cost-of-living adjustment (COLA).
3. Pay for performance.
4. Pay for skills.

Automatic Progression

Some companies grant salary increases according to a predetermined time period. Under the **automatic progression plan**, usually found in union contracts, the salary rate is moved in equal interval steps from the minimum of the range to the maximum,

Table 10-2
Scale of
Salary
Grades and
Ranges

Grade	Range		
	Minimum	Midpoint	Maximum
1	$7,150	$8,200	$9,430
2	7,400	8,500	9,800
3	7,650	8,800	10,120
4	7,900	9,100	10,500
5	8,200	9,430	10,850
6	8,500	9,775	11,250
70	118,300	153,600	188,900
71	124,100	161,300	198,500
72	130,300	169,300	208,300
73	136,800	177,800	218,800
74	143,700	186,700	229,700
75	150,900	196,000	241,100
76	158,500	205,800	253,100

based upon the employee's length of service only. For example, a company might automatically increase an office worker's salary $50 a month for a limited or unlimited number of months. As long as the worker is attaining a standard level of performance, he or she is entitled to receive automatically the set salary increase over a previously determined period of time.

Cost-of-Living Adjustment (COLA)

As you saw earlier, the COLA links a salary increase to a change in the Consumer Price Index. In the following discussion, you will find that other salary increases which reflect improved performance and increased productivity may be given in addition to the COLA.

Pay for Performance

Companies may also grant salary increases on the basis of the employee's job per-

formance. Under a **pay for performance** or *merit increase* plan, the employee's improved job performance is used as the basis for granting salary increases. Where pay ranges have been established, movement from the minimum to the maximum of the ranges is based on the employee's performance as opposed to seniority. Usually a company-wide merit budget is developed each year and divided among the various departments. Individual managers then distribute the monies based on an appraisal of their subordinates' job performance. Merit increases are judgmental and, as such, must be carefully and objectively determined. Care must be exercised that the merit increases reward merit for improvement in the quality of work and not some other factor, such as length of service or loyalty to the firm.

Merit increases should also be kept separate from other kinds of raises, such as COLAs, since merit increases lose their significance when lumped together with other considerations. Office workers must see a definite relationship between their performance and their compensation; or the merit increase becomes forced into a hygienic role, as noted by Herzberg.

The frequency of merit increase reviews varies with the job level. For office workers, the reviews are often conducted every six months during the first year of employment, and yearly thereafter. In some firms, the review is held on the employee's hiring anniversary date or at a time when all employees are being reviewed. In other firms, the time intervals are varied so the merit increases do not become routine and expected. A complete documentation, including all employee appraisals, should be available to support any merit increase decisions.

Pay for Skill

In a **skill-based pay system**, compensation is based upon the knowledge or skills that the person brings to the job, and salary increases are awarded as the employee acquires additional knowledge and skills. Although not widely used, plans for paying workers for their skills appear to be well suited to production workers and possibly to administrative and clerical personnel, and technical and professional persons such as information systems specialists and engineers. Most of the firms that use skill-based pay plans tend to be large organizations such as General Foods, Frito Lay, Sherwin Williams, Shell Oil, Procter & Gamble, TRW, and Westinghouse; and often the plans are installed in new plants that have a small number of workers in a participative management environment.[7]

Those supporting skill-based pay systems claim that the workers become more competent because they are provided a financial incentive for learning *and* performing. When employees have many

skills, they increase a firm's flexibility because they can be rotated among jobs and can fill vacancies when and where they are needed. Further, as the employees acquire more knowledge and skills, they become capable of handling higher-level decision making and problem solving. Thus, an organization can flatten its structure by removing some of the hierarchical layers of middle managers and supervisors. Questioning the potential widespread use of skill-based pay systems, we must consider the huge investment in training that is required and the need for the firm to commit itself to that investment on a continuing basis. Further, not all employees may have the desire to grow and develop on their jobs; instead, they may prefer the stability of a traditional compensation plan where they are paid for one job only and are not required to assume additional responsibilities.

INCENTIVE SYSTEMS

Incentive systems enable workers to increase their earnings by maintaining or exceeding an established standard of work performance. Some AOMs feel that the reward for increased production and outstanding work should be given in the form of promotions when opportunities arise. For many employees, however, the time of promotion is too far away, especially if they lack some of the necessary qualifications. For these workers, an immediate financial reward, such as a salary incentive payment, is a more effective motivator. Some companies recognize improved employee performance and increased output of all their workers—from middle managers to file clerks—by offering *noncash incentives* as a way of rewarding and motivating their personnel. Among gifts offered in lieu of cash we find dinner certificates, TVs and VCRs, video cameras, microwave ovens, personal computers, airline tickets, and days off with pay. Companies find the noncash bonuses

---

[7]Dale Feuer, "Paying for Knowledge," *Training* (May, 1987), p. 58.

Dialog on the Firing Line

RICHARD S. SABO
Assistant to the CEO
The Lincoln Electric Company
Cleveland, Ohio

Undergraduate degree, California University of Pennsylvania
MS, Edinboro University of Pennsylvania
Additional graduate work, Pennsylvania State University and the University of Pittsburgh

Richard Sabo started his business career as a factory worker with Lincoln Electric. In his present position as Assistant to the Chief Executive Officer, he is responsible for a wide variety of activities, including all communications pertaining to the company's world-renowned incentive management program. Mr. Sabo is also Executive Director of the James F. Lincoln Arc Welding Foundation and a member of the American Welding Society, American Institute of Steel Construction, The American Society for Engineering Education, and the Steel Plate Fabricators Association.

QUESTION: Tell us how a typical office worker (nonexempt) is compensated under your company's incentive pay plan.

RESPONSE: Office and clerical staff at The Lincoln Electric Company are compensated with an hourly rate or salary. In either instance, a discretionary year-end bonus is paid when the company is profitable.

Organizations in business for the long term must pay wages and salaries based on local levels whether a particular year has been profitable or not. This necessitates job evaluations to establish base rates. Furthermore, when the company is profitable, the employees have contributed to creating those profits and should share in them. Determining each individual's fair share according to that worker's contribution to profitability is not a simple matter. Job evaluations to establish base rates and piecework pay, as well as strict control of working hours and the size of the workforce, will directly affect profitability. All of these factors require strong management commitment and serious attention on an ongoing basis. Although specific instructions for merit rating exist, the following summary of our merit rating plan highlights the key points.

The process of evaluating each employee's performance must be undertaken and completed twice each year. A merit rating group may consist of a single department, or a combination of individuals from several small departments. Each employee receives a set of four merit rating cards evaluating that person's performance, compared to all others in the rating group, on the basis of four equal categories of indicators. The cards record performance in the areas of dependability, quality, output, and ideas and cooperation.

The merit ratings are a numerical grade determined by the relative position of the individual within the rating group. The guiding principle behind every merit rating decision is that of fairness and honesty. There can be no compromise on these issues, because we are striving to increase individual motivation. Although judgment can and will vary, any suggestion of unfairness or dishonesty will damage motivation for a long time. The primary purpose of merit rating is to determine each individual's relative contribution to the success of the company in that period.

Lincoln freely shares knowledge pertaining to its management system. A telephone call or letter to the corporate headquarters in Cleveland, Ohio, will provide information about this world leader in manufacturing efficiency.

an inexpensive and effective way to increase productivity.

Incentive systems may be used in offices where the work has been measured and standards developed. As noted in a later chapter, the measurement of work and the development of standards are not commonly found in the office. It is estimated, however, that two-thirds to three-fourths of all the work done in offices lends itself to measurement. Thus, the AOM should consider the development of standards, if not for the purpose of installing a salary incentive system, at least for establishing a more effective program of quality control and for increasing productivity. Many firms maintain production records that are used when employee performance is evaluated and recommendations for promotions and transfers are made. Thus, these companies achieve partially the effects of an incentive system.

Salary incentive systems for office workers fall into two major categories: (1) individual incentives, and (2) group incentives.

Individual Incentives

In an **individual incentive plan**, each office worker is paid according to his or her own production or effort. An example of an individual incentive plan is the **piece-rate (piecework) system**. Under the piece-rate system, the employee receives a fixed price or wage for each unit produced. For example, an office employee might be paid for each cassette transcribed, the number of data items entered as input to the computer, or the number of keystrokes entered on a keyboard.

The piece-rate system has the advantage of establishing a direct relationship between what a worker produces and what is earned. Underlying the installation of a piece-rate plan is the measurement of the employee's output. The more routine the work and the fewer the number of different kinds of tasks, the easier the job of measuring the output.

A potential problem that may be found in the use of individual incentives is the social pressure applied by co-workers for an individual to reduce output. Since each person is being paid for individual performance, competition often develops among people doing the same work. Although a certain level of competition is healthy, it becomes unhealthy when the less productive workers put pressure on the more productive workers to reduce their output. This type of pressure—often subtle in nature—may occur over a period of months or even years. Another disadvantage in the use of the individual incentive plan is that it may not reflect the reality of work. With the exception of certain creative positions, such as systems analyst, designer, editor, and research and development professionals, few people can claim sole credit for either the quantity or quality of the product manufactured or the service rendered.

Group Incentives

In a **group incentive plan**, the office worker shares in the achievement of a group of co-workers who are working as a team to produce more than their expected efficiency. Group incentive plans, such as those described below, may cover a small group or an entire department.

Profit-Sharing Plans

Under a **profit-sharing plan**, the payments received by office employees are based on a percentage of the company's profits for the year. Employees can receive cash shares of the profits at regular intervals, or they can defer receiving their shares. In the latter case, their shares are invested by the company and paid to them upon retirement or termination. In the case of death, the value of the employees' shares is paid to their beneficiaries.

To provide a real incentive for workers, the profit-sharing plan must provide a sufficiently large payment to the workers but still permit the company to retain earnings for future growth. The most successful profit-sharing plans provide income to employees that ranges, on the average, from 8 to 15 percent of the employee's annual salary.

In 1989, one of the most extensive and innovative profit-sharing incentive plans was undertaken by the fibers division of du Pont Company. The plan, *mandatory for all nonunion workers but optional for union employees*, is designed to raise efficiency by causing the workers to feel more involved and responsible and to link employee performance to results. Briefly, after a five-year phase-in period, the workers will be earning 6 percent less than their counterparts elsewhere in the company as a result of smaller raises. The employees will receive the 6 percent difference if their group meets its annual profit goal, but nothing if profits fall below 80 percent of the goal. At the 80 percent level, they get a 3 percent bonus; and at 150 percent of the goal, the bonus they receive will put their pay 12 percent above that of their counterparts in other du Pont divisions.[8]

Employee Stock Ownership Plans (ESOP)

Today, millions of office employees own stock in their own companies. An **employee stock ownership plan (ESOP)** is designed to increase the long-term interest of employees in the profitability of their companies. Three types of stock ownership plans are: (1) the *stock option plan*, which at one time was available only to high-level executives; (2) the *restricted stock plan*, traditionally reserved for top executives; and (3) the *stock*

purchase plan, which is offered to all employees.

Stock Option Plan. Although stock option incentives were originally offered only to top management and key personnel, today we find stock options being made available to middle managers and, in some firms, to nonmanagerial personnel. Under a **stock option plan**, eligible employees are given an opportunity to purchase a specific number of shares by a specific date at a given price, which is normally lower than the market price. In some stock option plans, employee eligibility is related to job performance, job function, and length of service.

Restricted Stock Plan. The **restricted stock plan** provides for giving qualified employees actual shares of stock (equity in the company) as an incentive to foster team spirit, to instill loyalty, and, in a firm faced with a hostile takeover, to put more stock in "friendly hands." Generally a company restricts or reserves the offering of shares to its top-level officers; however, today we find some firms offering restricted stock to a wider range of employees. Usually those receiving restricted stock cannot sell the shares until three to five years after receiving them.

Stock Purchase Plan. In a **stock purchase plan**, employees who meet certain length-of-service requirements are given the opportunity to purchase shares of the company's stock at a price usually lower than the current market price. Most firms limit stock purchases to a stipulated percentage, such as 10 percent, of the employee's annual salary. In the more popular stock purchase plans, delivery of the shares of stock is deferred until the employee leaves the plan or retires.

Gain-Sharing Plans

In a **gain-sharing plan**, the savings that are realized from improvements in productivity

---

[8]*The Wall Street Journal* (December 5, 1988), p. B1. Also see "Incentive Pay for Everybody at du Pont," *Training* (December, 1988), p. 12.

are divided among the workers and their employer. Generally gainsharing plans require:

1. A management philosophy that stresses the potential of employees and their need to become involved.
2. A highly structured system of committees in which employees are encouraged to participate in work decisions and contribute ideas on how to improve productivity.
3. A formula that computes and divides the productivity-related savings.

In contrast to most profit-sharing plans that usually pay bonuses once or twice a year, the gain-sharing bonuses are paid more frequently, often monthly.

In one company with 25 plants, everyone from the plant manager to the floor sweeper shares in any savings from productivity increases that lower the base costs. The most productive plants pay bonuses of 22 percent each month.[9] In theory, since all employees working as a team reap the benefits of reduced production costs, they become more cost conscious and thus search for new cost-cutting methods.

Probably the oldest and best-known gain-sharing system is the **Scanlon plan**,[10] which

aims at increasing productivity by stressing the following three elements:

1. *A financial incentive tied to organization-wide productivity.* The incentive or bonus is paid monthly to all workers in the company, from laborer to plant manager, based in most cases on the workers' increased productivity.
2. *A committee system of workers and managers to stimulate increased productivity.* The interlocking system of joint worker-manager committees helps an organization work more efficiently by suggesting ways to increase production.
3. *A philosophy of participative management.* The management philosophy rests upon McGregor's Theory Y assumptions about human motivation, which we examined in earlier chapters. Advocates and successful users of the Scanlon plan believe that all workers are capable of self-directed effort toward organizational goals provided their work gives them the opportunity to take responsibility for their actions and to use their abilities. Further, with workers recognized as a professional resource, the primary task of management is to tap their ideas in order to increase production.

---

[9]*The Wall Street Journal* (May 22, 1984), p. 1.
[10]The plan was developed by Joseph Scanlon, a cost accountant, who in the 1930s led the fight to organize a steel mill into a cohesive body of what is now the United Steelworkers of America.

SUMMARY
1. At the heart of an effective office salary administration program is the firm's ongoing program of job evaluation in which the relative value of each job has been appraised. Only through an intelligently administered program of job evaluation can the firm achieve the objectives of its office salary administration program to attract and retain qualified personnel, to provide fair and internally equitable salaries, to motivate and reward high-level performance, and

to price its goods or services competitively.

2. Among the factors to be analyzed and studied when setting office salaries are the firm's philosophy toward salary administration, the firm's ability to pay those salaries and still realize net earnings, what the office employees expect from their jobs, the salaries paid by other firms in the local labor market, federal and state regulations that specify minimum wages and premium pay for covered employees, and the provisions of a collective bargaining agreement.

3. Because of the significance of the local salary rates paid by other firms, the office salary administrator may find salary surveys useful in pricing office jobs and in adjusting salaries. Salary survey data may be obtained by purchasing the surveys; participating in one or more surveys; using an outside consultant to conduct, analyze, and interpret the surveys; or conducting one's own surveys.

4. After the office jobs have been priced and salary ranges established, a decision must be made on how salary increases will be provided, either by automatic progression, cost-of-living adjustment, pay for performance, or pay for skill. For certain kinds of office work, the AOM should consider the use of an incentive system whereby workers are rewarded for their increased production and outstanding work.

GLOSSARY

Arbitration—the process in which labor and management agree to submit any issue in dispute to an individual arbitrator (or an arbitration board) that renders a decision binding upon both parties.

Automatic progression plan—a type of salary increase in which the salary rate is moved in equal interval steps from the minimum of the range to the maximum, based upon the employee's length of service.

Average—the quotient obtained by dividing the sum of a set of figures by the number of figures in that set; also known as *arithmetic mean.*

Check-off—the process of deducting union dues from paychecks by the employer and remitting the collections to the union.

Collective bargaining—a negotiation process between an employer and labor union representatives on work-related issues such as wages, hours of work, and working conditions.

Cost-of-living adjustment (COLA) clause— a provision in the labor contract that indicates how salaries are to be kept in alignment with inflation, often by linking salary increases to changes in the Consumer Price Index.

Effective salary range—the spread between the salaries found at the first and the third quartiles of a distribution.

Employee stock ownership plan (ESOP)— a group incentive plan designed to increase the long-term interest of employees in the profitability of their company by permitting employees to acquire shares of stock in their own company.

Equal Pay Act—a federal law that prohibits employers from setting different wages based solely on the sex of workers who are doing equal work.

Fair Labor Standards Act (FLSA)—the federal law that sets minimum wages and overtime pay, provides equal pay for equal work, and regulates the employment of children; also known as the *federal wage and hour law.*

First quartile—that position in a distribution of values which is more than one-fourth and less than three-fourths of all the values listed.

Gain-sharing plan—a group incentive plan in which the savings realized from improvements in productivity are divided among workers and their employer.

Green-circle rate—a wage or salary that lies below the minimum of a particular pay range.

Group incentive plan—a compensation plan in which each worker shares in the achievement of a group of co-workers working as a team to produce more than their expected efficiency.

Incentive system—a means of increasing the earnings of workers who maintain or exceed an established standard of work performance.

Individual incentive plan—a compensation plan in which workers are paid according to their individual production or effort.

Labor contract—a private agreement entered into by the employer and the employees for the purpose of regulating certain work-related conditions.

Median—the middle position in a distribution of values; also known as the *second quartile*.

Mediation—the process in which an impartial third party tries to bring labor and management to a point of common agreement.

Pay for performance—a compensation plan in which salary increases are determined by the employee's improved job performance; also called *merit increase*.

Piece-rate system—a compensation plan in which workers receive a fixed price or wage for each unit produced; also known as *piecework system*.

Profit-sharing plan—a group incentive plan in which employees receive payments based on a percentage of the company's profits for the year.

Quartile—a measure of position that divides an array into four equal parts.

Red-circle rate—a wage or salary that lies above the maximum of a particular pay range.

Restricted stock plan—an employee stock ownership plan in which qualified employees are given the actual shares of their company's stock as an incentive to foster team spirit and to instill loyalty.

Right-to-work laws—the state laws that ban contracts which make union membership or the payment of fees a condition of employment.

Salary survey—a statistical picture of the salaries for certain jobs in a particular geographic area or for a particular industry at a given time.

Scanlon plan—the oldest and best-known gain-sharing system, which stresses a financial incentive tied to organization-wide productivity, a committee system of workers and managers to stimulate increased productivity, and a philosophy of participative management.

Skill-based pay system—a compensation plan in which remuneration is based upon the knowledge or skills that the person brings to the job, with salary increases awarded as the employee acquires additional knowledge and skills.

Stock option plan—an employee stock ownership plan in which eligible employees are given options to purchase a specific number of shares of their company's stock by a specific date at a specific price that is often lower than the market price.

Stock purchase plan—an employee stock ownership plan in which qualified employees are given the opportunity to purchase shares of their company's stock at a price usually lower than the market price.

Third quartile—that position in a distribution of values which is more than three-fourths of all the values listed.

Union shop agreement—the requirement that after workers have been hired, they must join the union or make dues payment within a specified time period or be fired.

FOR YOUR REVIEW

1. In a small company, what responsibilities for salary administration might be assigned to the office supervisor?

2. What are the objectives of an office salary administration program?

3. Explain the interrelationship among office salary administration, job analysis, job evaluation, and employee appraisal.

4. In what respect does company philosophy affect the firm's office salary administration program?

5. How do the expectations of office employees exert influence upon the kind of salary program developed?

6. What are some of the limitations of salary surveys when used as a tool in planning and adjusting office salaries?

7. a. In a salary survey, which statistical measure is the most representative figure? Why?
   b. Which measures are looked upon as the effective salary range?

8. What possible drawbacks may be found by the company that purchases its salary survey data?

9. What are the advantages and disadvantages of a firm's undertaking its own salary survey?

10. What are the major provisions of the Fair Labor Standards Act that are of significance to the office salary administrator?

11. Under the Equal Pay Act, when are wage differences between sexes allowed?

12. What are the three duties prescribed by collective bargaining for employers and employees' representatives?

13. How do the procedures of mediation and arbitration differ?

14. What criteria may be applied when evaluating the salary ranges that have been established in a salary administration program?

15. How does the charting of salary rates and salary distributions aid in pricing office jobs?

16. What kinds of adjustments may be made in the case of red-circle rates that emerge when salary rates are plotted on a scatter chart?

17. Contrast the granting of salary increases under the automatic progression and the pay for performance plans.

18. Why are incentive systems sometimes built into an office salary program?

19. What problems may be found by a salary administrator who is considering the use of individual incentives?

20. Explain the operation of a stock purchase plan.

21. Why is participative management a fundamental characteristic of successful gain-sharing plans?

FOR YOUR DISCUSSION

1. In an article dealing with the increasing popularity of skill-based pay systems, the authors opened with this statement: "Pay systems typically pay the job, not the person."[11] How would you proceed to defend this statement? Or do you believe the statement lacks validity?

2. To remedy several inequities in its salary compensation plan, the Dover Company has decided to "promote" several long-term office employees into newly created positions that exist only on paper. What is your reaction to such "phony" promotions? What more effective ways can you offer to deal with the problem of inequitable office salaries?

3. Do you feel that data entry operators should work under an individual incentive plan such as piece-rate? As such an operator, would you be content to work for a firm that uses such a plan? Why?

4. As an office supervisor in the Todd Insurance Company, along with the other exempt supervisors and middle managers, you receive your annual salary increase "up front." That is, the entire amount of the annual salary increase is given to you in a lump sum immediately on your anniversary date instead of in equal payments throughout the year. As an office supervisor, what advantages do you gain under this plan of providing salary increases? What advantages and disadvantages may your company experience as it grants lump-sum salary increases?

5. Sarah Burroughs, one of the three computer operators in your firm's computer center, has just left your office after complaining about her present salary. Burroughs' main gripe is that although she has been with the firm three years, she sees newly hired employees with similar backgrounds being paid as much as she. How can you explain the salary differentials to her?

6. It has been stated that, theoretically, management and workers are always in conflict with each other's interest. Management aims to get as much work as possible accomplished efficiently at the lowest possible unit cost. At the same time, workers strive to obtain as much income and security as possible from their employment. Do you agree that there is such a conflict of interests? If so, why? How can the conflict of interests of management and workers be overcome in part, if not entirely? Explain.

---

[11]Edward E. Lawler III and Gerald E. Ledford, Jr., "Skill-Based Pay, A Concept That's Catching On," *Management Review* (February, 1987), p. 46.

7. Some companies grant COLAs in an attempt to keep their workers' salaries in line with living costs and to avoid having to equate economic increases with merit increases. Other companies prefer to recognize economic fluctuations through the use of merit increases, whereby the COLAs are tied in with the merit increases. What advantages do you see in combining COLAs with merit increases? Do you see any disadvantages in such a practice?

8. Think about a salary increase that you or one of your friends or relatives recently received. Was the salary increase really tied to good performance? Is it realistic to expect that salary increases and good performance should be tied together?

9. The following findings about the comparative salaries received by men and women are taken from studies conducted in recent years:

   a. The majority of working women—75 percent by some estimates—are employed in traditionally female occupational categories, all low-paying. The Bureau of Labor Statistics found, for example, that women account for 99 percent of secretaries, 97 percent of typists, 96 percent of registered nurses, 82 percent of elementary school teachers, and 70 percent of retail salesclerks. The result is "sex-segregated occupations," usually defined as job categories that employ 70 percent of one sex, and what many women's groups call the "feminization of poverty."[12]

   b. In 1986, among full-time year-round workers, women made 64.3 cents for every dollar earned *annually* by men. In 1987, among full-time year-round workers, women made 70.0 cents for every dollar earned *weekly* by men. This reflects a shrinking of the earnings gap between the sexes, reflecting the real gains of the last two decades, during which affirmative action in education and employment led some women to better paying professional and blue-collar jobs. However, the feminization of poverty remains a countertrend. The labor market remains divided by sex and race, while the movement for comparable worth, or equal pay for work of comparable value, remains stalled in controversy.[13]

   What reasons can you advance to explain this "earnings gap" between women and men?

SOLVING CASE PROBLEMS

Case 10–1 Listening to Secretaries Talk about Salaries and Advancement Opportunities

Donald McAdoo, executive secretary with the Phillips Company, recently attended a meeting of the county secretaries' association, where he chaired a roundtable discussion. The discussion focused upon the salaries received by secretaries and their promotion potential. The following comments made by the speakers, with a little of their backgrounds, were recorded by McAdoo:

---

[12]Chris Lee, "Comparable Worth (The Saga Continues)," *Training* (June, 1985), p. 31.
[13]Eileen Boris and Michael Honey, "Gender, Race, and the Policies of the Labor Department," *Monthly Labor Review* (February, 1988), p. 34.

Alma Petersen,
administrative assistant
for 15 years with City
Bank:

I'm sure that my years of service with the bank mean far more in relation to the salary I am paid than my skills and education, or even my title.

Connie Meyers,
secretary for three years
with Industrial Savings
and Loan:

I find that my bachelor's degree means very little insofar as my take-home pay is concerned. Those with only a high school diploma are now being hired as secretaries and their starting salaries are pretty close to mine.

Jerome Tydings,
court reporter for the
county:

I sure can't take my experience to the bank on payday. The county simply won't pay for experience. Last week the county hired a new court reporter and paid her only $500 a year less than I now earn—and I have 12 years of experience!

Harriette Greenfield,
secretary for eight years
with the same supervisor
in Browning-Farmer,
Inc.:

I feel as if I have been with my supervisor for too many years. I could be earning a greater salary if I were assigned to a different department head. Our company's experience shows that a person's salary does not keep up when staying too long with the same supervisor.

1. What appear to be the underlying reasons for the salary inequities presented by the four speakers?

2. Does your experience show that secretaries are getting a fair deal in the market place? Are employers getting a fair deal? Explain.

3. In the role of McAdoo as chairperson, present your closing remarks in which you pass along some recommendations for the speakers as they return to the office the next day. What words of wisdom do you have to offer them?

Case 10-2 Determining the Starting Salary

Tony Guzman, supervisor of information processing for Plumstead Homes, Inc., has been interviewing applicants for two positions of computer operator. (See Figure 9-4, pages 245 and 246, for the job description of this position.) From all the applicants, Guzman has selected two persons who, if the starting salaries are acceptable to all concerned, will commence work next Monday morning.

From the interviews and application forms, Guzman has summarized the following information about the two applicants:

Olivia Harter: 24 years old, single, no dependents; renting an apartment in the suburbs, 25 miles from the Plumstead offices; will be driving to and from work. Was graduated this spring from Nester Community College; cumulative grade point average, 3.7 out of possible 4.0 (B+); area of concentration: business data processing. No prior work experience in field of business nor with computers.

Tom Prinz: 28 years old, married, five dependents; in process of buying home within walking distance of Plumstead offices. Graduated this spring from Nester Community College; cumulative grade point average, 3.8 out of possible 4.0 (B+); area of concentration: business data processing. No prior work experience in field of business nor with computers.

Realizing that Prinz is a "family man" with a mortgage debt hanging over his head, Guzman plans to offer Prinz a starting salary of $25 per week more than the midpoint of the salary range established for the computer operator position. Guzman plans to offer Harter a starting salary of $15 per week less than the midpoint since her financial obligations are fewer and she has no dependents to support.

1. As Guzman's superior, what are your reactions to the starting salaries he has recommended? Do you need any more information about the two applicants before you make a decision to approve or disapprove Guzman's salary offers?

2. In view of the information Guzman has obtained about Harter and Prinz, would the company be proceeding legally if the two starting salaries were accepted and the employees commenced work the following Monday morning? Explain.

11

Employee Benefits for the Office Staff

GOALS FOR THIS CHAPTER

After completing this chapter, you should be able to:

1. Identify the objectives that companies attempt to achieve in providing benefits for their office workers.
2. Describe the legally required payments made by employers to provide benefits for employees and their dependents.
3. Summarize the major features of the payments made by employers to provide medical and medically related benefits.
4. Describe the types of payments made by employers to establish retirement and savings plans.
5. Identify the kinds of life insurance and death benefits usually provided office workers.
6. Give examples of the types of payments received by office workers for time away from their workstations.
7. Identify the major types of benefits that are often provided office personnel as a means of avoiding or reducing their personal expenditures.
8. Explain the role played by the office manager who has been assigned responsibility for the company's employee benefits program—its development, implementation, and cost containment.

Picture this. . . . It's Thursday, March 4, 2010, and you have just entered your office at Futuristics, Inc. Only a few minutes before you had dropped off your five-year-old son and your mother-in-law, age 70, at the FCC (Futuristics Care Center) on the second floor. Seated at your workstation, you call up yesterday's computerized messages on the screen. (You are not working on Wednesday during the month of March this year.) You read a message from FES (Futuristics Educational Services) indicating that your daughter's quarterly tuition for attendance at the local junior college has been received and paid. After scanning the remaining messages, you sit back and dictate into a voice-activated transcriber the remainder of your plan for taking a three-month unpaid leave to work with recovering drug abusers in the city's rehabilitation center. Sound farfetched? Maybe yes; maybe no. Two decades from now it's possible that benefits such as these may be commonplace for office employees. But before we engage in any more crystal-ball gazing, let's see what benefits *today's* office workers are receiving.

Employee benefits (sometimes called *fringe benefits*) include those payments and services that workers receive in addition to their regular wages or salaries. Such benefits may be provided in whole or in part by the employer. Today, employee benefits, which amount to about 37 cents of every payroll dollar, form an indispensable part of the total office salary compensation package. The cost of employee benefits varies widely from company to company and from industry to industry. The amount of benefits paid annually for each employee ranges from less than $3,500 to more than $13,000. In 1988, the average payment was 37.0 percent of payroll, $5.198 per payroll hour, and $10,750 per year for each employee.[1]

---

[1]*Employee Benefits, 1989 Edition*, Survey Data from Benefit Year 1988 (Washington: U.S. Chamber of Commerce), p. 5.

In this chapter we first learn why companies provide such extensive and costly benefits for their office workers. Then, we shall investigate the nature and extent of the major types of employee benefits. Finally, we shall examine the role played by the office administrator in developing, implementing, and controlling the costs of the employee benefits program.

WHY COMPANIES PROVIDE EMPLOYEE BENEFITS

Certain kinds of employee benefits, such as old age, disability, and hospital insurance benefits; unemployment compensation; and workers' compensation, are provided by employers because they are legally required to do so. However, in addition to legislative requirements, companies provide benefits to office employees to meet the following major objectives:

1. *To attract and retain qualified workers.* A company looks upon the cost of employee benefits as an investment in recruiting and maintaining a stable work force. The success of this investment depends to a great extent on whether employees need and desire the benefits and whether they understand and appreciate the value of the benefits provided. As pointed out later in this chapter, employees must be given factual information about the benefits in order to understand fully the efforts made by the company on their behalf in providing such benefits.

2. *To motivate workers to become more productive.* The offering of a benefits package that truly meets the needs of employees aids in creating an environment in which workers will strive to improve their job performance. However, as we saw in the preceding chapter, not all employee benefits are positive motivators. Adding a new benefit to the firm's benefits package does not neces-

sarily bring forth a corresponding increase in productivity. It is doubtful that any increase will be apparent for a prolonged period of time. Further, the offering of a new benefit may adversely affect the attitude and, in turn, the output of some workers.

For example, let's say that a company has expanded its benefits package by offering additional retirement protection for married workers with one or more dependents. Such a benefit usually means little to office workers who are unmarried. Thus, benefits, viewed as hygienic factors by Herzberg, may negatively affect performance. Further, if the workers believe that their benefits are inferior to those enjoyed by workers in other firms, productivity may be affected adversely.

3. *To meet the employees' needs for job security and job satisfaction.* The availability of employee benefits helps a company in partially meeting the office workers' primary and secondary needs, as defined in Maslow's hierarchy of needs. By means of the total benefits package, the company is trying to lessen its employees' concern about loss of salaries because of poor health, layoff, or retirement. In turn, management expects that employees will feel that the company is genuinely interested in their welfare.

4. *To reward employees who improve their performance and increase their productivity.* By means of benefits, the firm can offer incentives, such as profit sharing and stock ownership plans, in return for outstanding performance, improved productivity, less absenteeism, and decreased turnover. Also, benefits such as vacation time and the accumulation of annual credits toward retirement aid in reducing turnover since these benefits are tied in with the length of company service.

5. *To lessen the company's tax burden.* Employers realize tax advantages from their payments for employee benefits

since these amounts represent business operating expenses which are deducted from current income before taxes. Therefore, if a firm spends $200,000 for employee health insurance premiums, the after-tax cost to the firm is only $132,000, assuming a corporate income tax rate of 34 percent.

Also, we find benefits offered to office workers in an attempt to prevent unionization, to fulfill the obligations contained in a collective bargaining agreement, and to meet the competitive pressures brought about by other firms in the community that may offer more comprehensive benefits packages.

NATURE AND EXTENT OF EMPLOYEE BENEFITS

We can analyze the cost of an employee benefits package fairly efficiently if the benefits are first classified into several broad categories, as shown in Figure 11-1. Therefore, in this section, we shall examine employee benefits under six headings: (1) legally required payments, (2) medical and medically related benefit payments, (3) retirement and savings plan payments, (4) life insurance and death benefits, (5) payments for time not worked, and (6) miscellaneous benefit payments. Working with such a classification, the person in charge of the benefits program can evaluate each benefit as to its appropriateness in meeting the workers' needs; and its cost can be compared with similar benefits offered by other firms.

Legally Required Payments

Included under this heading are those legally required, or mandated, payments to federal and state governmental agencies.

OASDHI Benefits

The largest and most rapidly growing phase of the federal government's social insurance program is the **old-age, survivors, disability, and health insurance (OASDHI)** program, commonly called the *social security program*. This program was planned by the federal government to provide economic security for workers and their families. Under the social security program, the *Federal Insurance Contributions Act (FICA)* levies a tax on employers and employees in most industries to be paid to the federal government. Amendments to FICA provide for a two-part health insurance program, commonly known as *Medicare*, for the aged and the disabled. The hospital insurance plan (Part A of Medicare) is financed by a separate tax on both employers and employees. The supplementary medical insurance plan (Part B of Medicare) is voluntary and is financed by those who desire coverage, with a matching payment by the federal government.

Benefits from the OASDHI program are payable monthly to workers and their survivors who qualify under the provisions of the law. Generally as the cost of living rises, so does the cost of the benefits—and so do the FICA taxes for workers and their employers. Social security benefits have been increasing because of the upward drift of wages and prices. However, benefits have not grown so rapidly as prices and thus have declined in terms of real income during periods of inflation, thereby threatening the living standards of the retired.

Unemployment Compensation Benefits

Unemployment compensation insurance is a federal–state program established to provide funds at the state level for compensating unemployed workers in that state during periods of temporary unemployment. Employers are faced with two unemployment taxes: federal and state. Depending upon the

Figure 11-1
Employee
Benefits as a
Percent of
the Payroll
Dollar, 1989

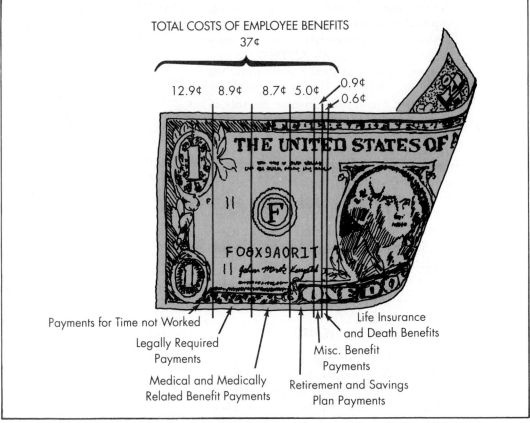

Source of Data: *Employee Benefits, 1989 Edition,* Survey Data from Benefit Year 1988 (Washington: U. S. Chamber of Commerce), 1989.

state law, employees, too, may be required to contribute to the unemployment compensation fund. The state unemployment taxes are used exclusively for the payment of unemployment compensation benefits. The tax paid to the federal government is used mainly for paying state and federal administrative expenses.

Workers' Compensation Benefits

Workers' compensation insurance is a state insurance program designed to protect employees and their dependents against losses due to injury or death incurred during the worker's employment. The cost of workers' compensation insurance is borne by the employer, except in Oregon, where employees also contribute to the state workers'

injured workers, or to their survivors in the event of death, by the state, by the insurance company, or by the employer according to the kind of insurance plan adopted.

State Disability Benefits

Five states (California, Hawaii, New Jersey, New York, and Rhode Island) and Puerto Rico have passed laws to provide **state disability benefits** to be paid workers who are absent from their jobs because of illness, accident, or disease *not arising out of their employment.* Although the five state laws differ with respect to the amount of employer contributions, each state requires employee contributions.

Medical and Medically Related Benefits

In this section, we shall examine several group plans, financed by insurance premiums and fund contributions, that provide future medical and medically related benefits to employees.

Hospital, Surgical, and Medical Insurance

Hospital, surgical, and medical insurance affords office employees protection by covering all or the major part of the hospital, surgical, and medical expenses for employees and their dependents. This type of benefit is very common; and most firms have established group medical insurance plans for their workers, either paying the cost entirely or having the employee contribute part of the cost at a reduced rate.

Employers of 25 or more employees who are subject to the Fair Labor Standards Act and who provide payments for health insurance to their employees are required to offer them the option of membership in a qualified **health maintenance organization (HMO)**. The traditional or "clinical" HMO is an organization of providers (physicians and other health-care workers, and the affiliated hospital, usually housed in a single building) that offers prepaid (by the employer and the employee) medical services to HMO participants. Thus, instead of paying doctors a fee for each service performed, employees who enroll in an HMO pay a fixed premium in advance for all health-care services required during the year.

A newer form of the HMO is the *individual practitioner association (IPA) HMO*. Under this plan, employees are provided a freedom of choice since they may select, from a list of participants, that doctor they wish to see. The worker pays an annual fee for this service, regardless of use.

As an alternative to HMOs, some companies offer their workers the opportunity to participate in a **preferred provider organization (PPO)**. Under a PPO, the employer or insurance carrier develops a list of preferred providers (doctors, hospitals, and other health-care services) that have been selected on the basis of their low cost and high quality. The providers agree to offer their service at a reasonable cost in exchange for a potentially higher volume. Employees may select from the PPO list that physician or hospital they desire rather than be assigned one by the health care provider under a traditional HMO plan.

The Consolidated Omnibus Budget Reconciliation Act of 1985 (COBRA) requires companies with more than 20 employees to offer health insurance to *former* workers and their dependents for at least 18 months. Former employees who opt for the health insurance coverage must pay its full cost plus a surcharge to cover administrative expenses. Even with the surcharge, the group plan rates offered by employers are less expensive than individual coverage. Also, some small companies pay a portion of the continued health-care coverage, even though the law does not require them to do so.

Major Medical Insurance

Many companies have expanded their group hospital, surgical, and medical insurance coverage by providing **major medical insurance**. This insurance plan protects employees and their dependents from huge medical bills resulting from serious accidents or prolonged illness. In many plans, the company pays the full cost of the employee's own medical expense insurance, while the costs for coverage of dependents may be shared by the company and the employee.

Under many major medical insurance policies, coverage ceases after a lifetime maximum per individual has been reached. Other policies set a maximum benefit for each disability period. Most plans require the workers to absorb a certain dollar amount before they are paid benefits, with annual deductibles of $100 or less for each insured person being common. Many major medical plans pay all covered expenses after a specified level of costs has been incurred during the year. For example, a plan might pay 80 percent of expenses until an employee has paid $1,000 in "out-of-pocket" expenses during the year (in addition to the deductible), and then pay 100 percent thereafter.

Some major medical expense plans provide coverage for mental or nervous conditions, with a stated lifetime maximum benefit. Also, alcoholic rehabilitation coverage is often provided to cover the costs of room, board, and services.

Disability Income Insurance

Many office workers receive benefits as a result of their firms' sickness and accident **disability income insurance** plans. The *short-term* plans provide continuing income for workers unable to return to their jobs after they have exhausted their sickness and accident benefits. Generally the short-term disability protection is provided at no cost to employees. Typically, benefits are not payable to employees who are on vacation or on an unpaid leave of absence.

Long-term disability income insurance, an extension of the short-term program, is often made available to office employees at a group rate. Long-term disability insurance, also known as *wage-continuation insurance*, usually provides a benefit equal to 50 or 60 percent of the base salary for the worker who is found by a physician to be totally disabled. The period of payment may range from a few years to a stipulated age, or for life, depending upon the design of the plan. The benefits paid under the plan are usually reduced, up to a maximum monthly amount, by any social security benefits, workers' compensation benefits, or company-provided pension received by the worker.

Dental Care

Dental care has been one of the fastest growing areas of health insurance in recent decades. In its 1988 *Salary and Employment Survey,* Tempforce found that 60 percent of the responding firms provided some type of dental benefit.[2] Nearly all dental plans cover a wide range of services, including preventive care, such as examinations and X rays; restorative procedures, such as fillings, inlays, and crowns; dental surgery; and periodontal care (treatment of tissues and bones supporting the teeth). The plans vary considerably by methods of reimbursement, coinsurance provisions, deductibles, and maximum benefits.

In many dental care plans, the sponsor (employer or union) pays the entire premium for the dental insurance, in which case all members of the group are covered, usually after a brief period of service. In other plans, participation is optional and the participants share the cost with the plan sponsor, usually through payroll deductions. Usually participants may cover their dependents by paying the required premium.

Vision Care

Vision care benefits are normally available to all participants of the covered employee group, usually after a stated eligibility period. Most plans permit the participants to cover their dependents by paying a premium. Vision care coverage provides a variety of services that are not usually covered by regular health insurance plans, such as eye examinations, eyeglasses, contact lenses, and orthoptics (eye muscle exercises). In its *Employee Benefits Survey,* the Bureau of Labor Statistics found that vision care benefits were available to 35 percent of the

---

[2]*The Tempforce 1988 Salary and Employment Survey* (Westbury, NY: Tempforce), p. 19.

full-time employees in medium-size and large firms.[3]

Prescription Drug Plan

Most medical insurance plans cover prescription drugs only when administered as part of hospital care. Therefore, a business may provide a group plan that covers the purchase of prescription drugs. Generally payment for the purchase of prescription drugs is a "co-pay" arrangement, with the employee paying a deductible, such as $1 to $3, and the insurance carrier paying the remainder of the cost.

In a survey of its subscribers, *Personnel Journal* found that 56 percent of all the responding firms have a prescription drug plan. In larger organizations (5,000 employees or more), the number rises to two-thirds; in medium-size (500–4,999 employees) and small (fewer than 500 employees) organizations, the number is at the halfway mark.[4] This finding, along with other results in the survey, supports the conclusion that, generally, larger organizations offer more health coverage options than small and medium-size companies.

Retirement and Savings Plan Benefits

Under this category of employee benefits, we shall examine the major features of retirement and savings plans that provide payments to presently employed, retired, and laid-off workers.

Retirement Income

Generally social security benefits are inadequate for retired employees and their dependents. Thus, most firms modify their retirement plans to supplement the government benefits and thereby attempt to maintain their employees' interest in long-term employment. Although eligibility rules vary among retirement plans, the coverage is about the same for production workers, office employees, and managers. Most of the plans are financed by employer contributions. When employees contribute toward the cost of their retirement benefits, the contributions are usually expressed as a percentage of their annual earnings, such as 2 to 5 percent.

Retirement plans may provide for early retirement, such as between ages 62–65, with a lifetime monthly allowance based on the worker's accrued benefits. For earlier retirement, such as at ages 55–62, the amount of monthly allowance is reduced. If the office worker is forced to retire early because of a disability, a pension benefit is still provided. If an eligible married employee dies before retirement, the spouse receives a payment based on the worker's length of service with the company.

Individual Retirement Accounts (IRA). An **individual retirement account (IRA)**, created by the Internal Revenue Code, is a pension plan that is established and funded by the *individual* employee. Depending upon the existence of a company-funded retirement plan, employees may authorize that either one of two types of contributions—deductible or nondeductible—be withheld by their employer or union. Or employees may place their contributions in individual retirement savings accounts as specified in the law.

The Tax Reform Act of 1986 provides that, under certain conditions, employees may put aside each year the lesser of $2,000 or 100 percent of their compensation *without paying federal income taxes on their contributions*. To be eligible for such *deductible* (tax-free) contributions, the worker must not be a participant in a company-funded retirement plan. Further, the employee must report, for federal income tax purposes, an adjusted gross income less than $25,000 if

[3]*Employer Benefits in Medium and Large Firms, 1988*, Bureau of Labor Statistics (August, 1989), p. 2.
[4]Morton E. Grossman and Margaret Magnus, "The Boom in Benefits," *Personnel Journal* (November, 1988), p. 52.

filing a tax return as a single person, or less than $40,000 if filing a joint return.

An employee who is ineligible to make a deductible IRA contribution is permitted to make *nondeductible* contributions to a separate IRA account. The earnings on the nondeductible contributions are not subject to federal income tax until they are withdrawn. The limit on such nondeductible contributions for a taxable year is the lesser of $2,000 or 100 percent of the employee's compensation.

Simplified Employee Pension (SEP) Plan. By means of a **simplified employee pension (SEP) plan**, employers may make contributions to individual retirement accounts on behalf of their employees. In the operation of an SEP plan, the law sets forth strict requirements, such as these:

1. The amount of the employer's annual contribution to the plan is limited.
2. Employers must contribute for all employees who are 21 years of age or older and who have worked for the employer at least three of the past five years.
3. The SEP plan cannot discriminate in favor of employees who are officers, stockholders, or highly compensated employees.
4. The employer contributions must be fully and immediately "vested."

Vesting. **Vesting** is the process of conveying to employees the right to share in a retirement fund in the event they are terminated before the normal retirement age. The vesting process is linked to the number of years needed for workers to earn an equity in their retirement plans and to become entitled to full or partial benefits at some future date if they leave the company before retirement.

Once vested, a worker has the right to receive a pension at retirement age, based on years of covered service, even though the worker may not be working for the firm at that time. Most retirement plans provide for vesting after the worker has been covered under the plan for a specified number of years. The Tax Reform Act of 1986 provides for full vesting after five years of service, or gradually over seven years (20 percent after three years and 20 percent a year for the next four).

Employee Retirement Income Security Act of 1974 (ERISA). The **Employee Retirement Income Security Act (ERISA)** provides workers with a vested right toward their retirement income benefits and assurance of well-managed retirement plans. It is mandatory that all information concerning the operation of the employer's retirement plan, other benefit plans, and the amount of the worker's accrued benefits be fully disclosed and communicated to the workers.

401(k) Retirement Plan. A retirement plan that has gained popularity is the **401(k) retirement plan**, so called because of its authorization under Section 401(k) of the Internal Revenue Code. Under a 401(k) plan, after employees have at least one year of service, they can shelter a certain portion of their salaries from taxes each year and watch the deferred income grow until time of retirement. The deferred salaries and earnings thereon are not taxed until the employees begin to withdraw the amounts. Most employers contribute matching funds, which, with the employees' contributions, are invested in tax-deferred stock funds, bonds, or short-term investments. Employees are totally vested as soon as they commence deferring part of their salaries, and they receive all earnings from their matched-fund investment if they should leave the company.

Profit-Sharing and Employee Stock Ownership Plans

As we saw in Chapter 10, page 283, profit-sharing plans provide employee benefits that are based on a percentage of the company's profits for the year. Also in Chapter 10, page 284, when you read about group incentives, you learned about another very popular employee benefit, employee stock ownership.

Employees' Savings and Thrift Plans

Under **savings and thrift plans**, the employees' savings are matched, wholly or partially, by the employer and are held in a tax-deferred investment account. Under some plans, managerial employees are permitted to contribute as much as 6 percent of their annual salaries to a matched fund. The company often matches the employees' contributions 50 cents on the dollar; but some companies, such as those in the oil industry, may match dollar for dollar.

Supplemental Unemployment Benefits (SUB)

Many union contracts provide that in addition to state unemployment compensation benefits, private **supplemental unemployment benefits (SUB)** may be paid to employees during periods of layoff. Under a common SUB plan, employers contribute to a general fund a certain number of cents for each hour worked by employees. Employees usually have a right to benefits from the fund only upon layoff and after meeting stated eligibility requirements. In another type of plan, the employer's contributions are paid to a separate trust fund for each employee. Workers are entitled to the fund upon layoff and have a right to the fund when their employment is ended. If a worker dies, the beneficiary is paid the amount of the trust.

Life Insurance and Death Benefits

Group life insurance is a type of protection that covers all employees of a single firm and is designed to provide benefits should a worker die or become totally disabled. For office and plant employees, the life insurance benefit may be an amount equal to one year's earnings; for managerial employees, the benefit may be twice the annual earnings. Group life insurance is *term insurance* that expires when the worker leaves the company unless the employee takes steps to convert it into a private policy. Nearly every large and medium-size firm and many small companies today provide life insurance protection and may pay the entire premium for the office worker's insurance coverage.

The morale-building effect of a group life insurance plan cannot be overestimated, for this benefit relieves employees of much worry and insecurity. In many cases, the group life insurance plan provides for total and permanent disability benefits, accidental death and dismemberment coverage, as well as modest amounts of life insurance for the employee's survivors. Many companies also provide life insurance coverage for their retirees.

Office employees may be covered by their firm's **travel accident insurance** plan when they are traveling on company business. Usually at no cost to employees, this coverage provides benefits in the event of death, disability, and dismemberment.

Payments for Time Not Worked

The benefits discussed in this section represent payments that employees receive for time away from work and for nonproductive periods during the workday.

Vacations

Most office employees receive two weeks' vacation with pay after one year of employment. Many office employees receive three weeks' vacation after 10 years and four weeks' paid leave after 20 years of service. Few employers allow their workers to carry over vacation time from one year to the next. Also, most employers stipulate that the vacation time must be taken away from work; in other words an employee cannot request extra pay instead of time off.

Paid vacations provide employees a needed break from the office routine.

Holidays

In its *1988 Office Benefits Survey Report*, the Administrative Management Society found that 47 percent of all firms surveyed grant between 9 and 11 paid holidays each year. Large companies employing over 500 workers generally offer between 9 and 11 holidays, while in smaller companies, the majority (two-thirds) grant 8 or fewer holidays.[5] Similarly, the *Employee Benefits Survey*, conducted by the Bureau of Labor Statistics in 1986 and 1987, found that in the private sector, employees most commonly received 10 holidays; employees of state and local governments often received 11 or 12 holidays, the result of state and local observances.[6]

Along with the traditional six holidays (New Year's Day, Memorial Day, Independence Day, Labor Day, Thanksgiving, and

Christmas), the following "Monday Holidays" are legal public holidays in most states:

- Martin Luther King Jr.'s Birthday, third Monday in January.
- Presidents' Day, third Monday in February.
- Columbus Day, second Monday in October.

Other days such as Good Friday, Veteran's Day, Christmas Eve, New Year's Eve, and the employee's birthday have become recognized more frequently as paid holidays. Many companies have one or more "floating" holidays, which are designated on different days from year to year. Some firms designate the same "floating" holidays for all employees, while other companies allow employee choice. The holidays most often designated as "floating" are July 3 or 5, the day after Thanksgiving, and the days between Christmas and New Year's.

Sick Leave

Most firms have a company-paid *sick-leave plan* that provides workers with continuing income during short periods of illness. To become eligible for sick-leave coverage, a minimum period of employment is usually specified, with the most common service requirement being three months. Often this requirement is tied in with the end of a probationary period for new employees. The amount of paid sick leave provided office workers may range from 5 to 15 days after one year of service, with the number of days increasing with the employee's length of service.

Maternity Leave

Most firms have adopted formal policies covering *maternity leaves* for office employees. These policies generally have no specific length-of-service requirement for eligibility. Where no maternity leave policy exists, maternity benefits are often provided under a sick-leave policy, as described above. In these firms, the accumulation of sick leave

[5]Jeff Long, "Tracking Trends in Benefits," *Management World* (November/December, 1988), p. 29.
[6]William J. Wiatrowski, "Comparing Employee Benefits in the Public and Private Sectors," *Monthly Labor Review* (December, 1988), p. 6.

days from year to year may be used for maternity reasons. For example, employees with one year of service may receive benefits for two weeks, while five-year employees may be eligible for nine weeks of benefits.

The *Pregnancy Discrimination Act of 1978* bars mandatory leaves for pregnant women that are set at a certain time in their pregnancy, regardless of their ability to work. The amendment requires employers to treat pregnancy and childbirth the same as other causes of disability under employee benefit plans. Also, the reinstatement rights of women on leave for pregnancy-related reasons are protected. Credit for previous service, accrued retirement benefits, and accumulated seniority are provided the woman on maternity leave.

Paternity Leave

Paternity leaves for male employees are increasing in popularity among large companies. Many firms offering paternity leaves permit their employees to use paid vacation or annual leave for such purposes. Some companies provide male employees with time off work under the heading "unpaid paternity leave." The maximum amount of unpaid paternity leave may range from two days to one year for the office staff.

Rest Periods

Rest periods, lunch periods, wash-up time, and other on-the-job time that is paid for— but not worked—cost the employer an average of $674 for each worker employed in 1988.[7] The purpose of providing refreshment breaks and rest periods is to increase the productivity and efficiency of workers, a point that should be communicated to the workers. Most companies provide work breaks, and many firms pay at least part of the cost of snacks. In many

small offices, workers are permitted to take their breaks whenever they have a chance. In larger firms, the break times may be staggered so all workers are not absent from the office at the same time.

Underlying the provision for rest periods is the principle that certain kinds of repetitive work soon become monotonous. This monotony increases fatigue, which in turn slows down production. The work output of employees performing motor-skill tasks, such as data entry, varies at different times throughout the day. Therefore, for this kind of task during an eight-hour workday, it is recommended that work breaks be placed between the second and third hours in the morning and between the sixth and seventh hours in the afternoon.

For office activities that require a high degree of concentration, such as reading information on video display terminals, two work breaks each day may not be sufficient to maintain an acceptable level of performance. Some data entry operators express complaints such as headaches, tension, eyestrain, and neck and shoulder pains, which may be attributed to ergonomic elements such as lighting or the design of the machine, desk, and chair. It has not been conclusively proved that rest periods are the answer to the problems of fatigue and slowdown of production. However, the fact that management provides rest periods shows its concern for the well-being of its employees, which may be the most important aspect of the rest period.

Controlling Work Breaks. The negative attitudes of some administrative office managers toward rest periods may be caused by their inability to control the breaks or because they do not know how to control them. Often the amount of control that the AOM can exercise over the breaks is related to where the employees get their refreshments. It is much more difficult to control the length of the breaks if employees must

---

[7]*Employee Benefits, 1989 Edition*, Survey Data from Benefit Year 1988 (Washington: U.S. Chamber of Commerce), p. 14.

leave the premises at break time. In most offices, employees have access to vending machines and cafeteria services. Some firms control work breaks by permitting employees to eat and drink at their desks because it is felt that if food is consumed while the employees are at their desks, the workers will lose less time.

Although most AOMs feel that rest periods are desirable, they object to the abuse of the privilege. Some AOMs excuse the lack of rest periods by stating that the freedom enjoyed by most office workers makes such breaks unnecessary.

The following guidelines should govern the granting of rest periods:

1. *For some types of work, rest periods are absolutely necessary.* For example, to serve effectively during the entire workday as goodwill ambassadors of their firms through contact with the public, receptionists and switchboard operators should be periodically freed from their sedentary, stressful, and repetitive tasks.
2. *Rest periods should be scheduled when they will be most helpful—not too early in the morning and not too late in the afternoon.* The work breaks should be scheduled so that not all employees are absent from their desks at the same time. Such an approach tends to discourage the overly long "talk" sessions that commonly characterize many breaks. Peer pressure by a co-worker waiting for a worker to return from a rest period may aid in controlling the length of breaks, too.
3. *Definite time limits should be set for the length of the breaks, and these limits should be observed.* Habitual offenders should be reprimanded and, if necessary, discharged. The inability of a few to abide by the rules only sets a poor example for others.
4. *If possible, facilities should be provided for getting refreshments and snacks so*

that the employees do not have to leave the premises.
5. *Supervisors should be held responsible for their workers' abuse of rest period privileges.*

The Cost of Lost Time. Assume that an office employee earns, on the average, $380 each 40-hour week during a 50-week year and spends 20 minutes a day on work breaks. A little over 83 hours—more than 2 workweeks—during the year are spent away from the workstation. The cost of this worker's lost time is about $792. When you add the time employees take for long lunches, leaving work early, being tardy, using sick days when not ill, and extensive socializing, *the costs to business are staggering.*

The cost of lost time becomes clearly evident when the OM makes a few simple calculations, such as those shown in Table 11-1. This table shows for several different hourly rates the cost of *only five minutes lost time* per employee per day. And these costs do not include the costs of employee benefits provided by the employer, which as we saw earlier in this chapter, may be greater than one-third of every payroll dollar!

Other Payments Made for Time Not Worked

Companies may pay their employees for time not worked for other reasons such as the following:

1. *Jury duty.* When office employees are called to jury duty, some may receive full pay from their employers in addition to the payments received from the court. Often, however, if employees are paid jury fees, these amounts are deducted from the pay they receive from the company.
2. *Time off to vote.* Over half of the states have laws allowing employees to take time off from work to vote. Most state laws

Table 11-1
Annual Cost of Lost Time
5 minutes lost time each day during a (5-day work-week in a 50-week year)

Hourly Rate	Number of Employees				
	10	25	50	100	250
$4.25	$ 885	$2,213	$ 4,425	$ 8,850	$22,125
4.50	937	2,344	4,687	9,375	23,437
6.00	1,250	3,125	6,250	12,500	31,250
7.50	1,562	3,906	7,812	15,625	39,062
8.00	1,667	4,167	8,333	16,667	41,667
9.75	2,031	5,078	10,156	20,313	50,781

provide that employees entitled to vote in an election may, upon application to their employers, absent themselves from work for a specified period, without penalty or loss of pay. The state laws that cover time allowed for voting provide for time off that ranges from one to four hours. However, in a growing number of states, time off is granted only if there is insufficient time to vote outside the working hours.

3. *Military training leave.* Employers cannot refuse to grant office employees time off to meet their military training obligations. Many firms treat the required summer training programs as paid leave. Usually in these companies, the employees are paid the difference between their regular pay and what they receive as base pay from the military. In other companies not having a policy regarding military training leave, employees may use their vacation periods for military training and receive accumulated vacation pay in addition to their military pay.

4. *Personal leave.* Paid leave for "personal" reasons or personal floating holidays are being offered more commonly to office personnel. Usually a service requirement, such as three months, is needed before employees become eligible for personal leave, which is often two days each year. Unpaid leaves of absence are often provided office employees for absence due to extended physical health problems, alcohol or drug abuse rehabilitation, mental health problems, educational purposes, extended vacations, and other personal or family problems. Generally there is a minimum service requirement, which may range from one to five years.

5. *Adoption leave.* Some companies provide leave to an employee for the purpose of adopting a child. Often employees are permitted to take time off without pay, usually in the form of unpaid personal leaves.

6. *Funeral leave.* Most companies provide office workers paid funeral leaves, usually of three days' duration, when there is a death in the immediate family.

Miscellaneous Benefits

This final category of benefits includes awards, allowances, other extra payments, and employer-provided programs and services, some of which may represent taxable income to employees. Overtime or premium pay for time worked and incentive bonuses are excluded since they are an earned portion of an employee's regular compensation, as we saw in the previous chapter.

Awards, Allowances, and Other Extra Payments

In this section we shall examine briefly the following three benefits: educational assistance, Christmas bonuses, and relocation expense allowances.

Educational Assistance. Many firms provide educational assistance to their employees, with the result that office workers can continue to grow professionally and to prepare themselves for career pursuits and for promotion to supervisory and middle management positions. Educational assistance may be provided in the form of paid tuition costs or the granting of loans for tuition payments.

Generally under a tuition-aid plan, the company requires that the courses be taken at certain types of educational agencies, such as colleges and universities, community or junior colleges, technical or vocational schools, private business schools, or with professional groups. Another requirement is that the courses be *job-related*; that is, the

An educational assistance plan benefits both the employer and the employee.

courses must maintain or improve skills required in the employee's present work or be required by the employer so that the employee may keep his or her current salary or job. Often the courses may be taken on company time, and sometimes they are conducted on company premises by professors from local colleges or universities.

In some tuition-aid plans, employees are reimbursed the entire cost of tuition for the courses completed satisfactorily no matter what grades are received. In other cases, the amount of reimbursement is tied in with the letter grade received, such as:

100% reimbursement for grade A
 75% reimbursement for grade B
 50% reimbursement for grade C

Some firms also make tuition aid or other educational assistance available to employees approaching retirement age so they can develop new interests or activities.

Depending upon the size and organization of the firm, responsibility for administering the tuition-aid program may be assigned the human resources department, the office manager, or the head of the training and development department. The person with this responsibility should be concerned about the quality of the return being realized from the company's investment in programs of educational assistance. Among the methods available to evaluate the results received by the company are employee performance appraisals, studies of promotion patterns, surveys of the employees' superiors, and interviews with and written reports from employees who have taken courses.

Christmas Bonuses. Many companies give cash Christmas bonuses to their office employees as a gesture of goodwill and to encourage continued employee loyalty and good performance. Other firms base their bonuses on merit, granting them only to workers who have made an extra effort or exceeded predetermined quotas during the year.

Although a bonus is a gift, employees quickly begin to expect it. When business is bad, however, bonuses may decrease or disappear. Giving a worker a cash bonus that is less than the amount received last year tends to cause ill will and can seriously affect morale.

In a union office, the employer may be committing an *unfair labor practice* if a bonus is unilaterally withdrawn. For example, the Christmas bonus may be a gratuity representing a goodwill gesture that has no relationship to the employee's job performance, hours worked, seniority, or position. Thus, the bonus is not a bargainable item. In such cases, the employer can withdraw the bonus for economic reasons without prior notification or bargaining. If, on the other hand, the bonus is part of wages or a condition of employment, good faith bargaining is required preceding the withdrawal of such a benefit.

Relocation Expense Allowances. Many companies offer a relocation expense allowance, often to entice an employee to accept a transfer. The relocation expense package may contain provisions for purchasing the employee's current house, offering a mortgage differential to help in relocating employees who must pay higher interest mortgages, paying legal and closing fees, and paying realtors' commissions.

Programs and Services Provided Employees

Included in this final category of benefits are those programs and privileges provided by employers to enable employees to avoid or to reduce their personal expenditures.

Food Services. In large firms, the operation of cafeterias or "employee restaurants" that supply meals to their employees may become another responsibility of the AOM. In many on-premise food facilities, catering companies have installed vending machines, with employees obtaining food and refreshments at any time during working hours. Company-provided food services are fairly common in large cities where a deluge of several thousand employees from one building seeking meals in a variety of restaurants is not conducive to the best physical and mental well-being of the workers. Also, in the suburbs the office building may be located far away from restaurants. Thus, in-house food service becomes a necessity.

Company Medical Facilities. Very often companies provide first-aid stations and sick rooms. Also, many firms, especially larger organizations, maintain a medical staff that consists of full- or part-time doctors, psychologists, and nurses. Most companies provide preemployment physical examinations, and some firms give periodic examinations to all employees.

Social and Recreational Programs. The social and recreational programs in many firms consist mostly of picnics, employee parties, group tours or trips, and bowling and ball teams. With the additional leisure time resulting from a shorter workweek and flexible work schedules, we find more companies providing additional general-interest programs, sports, and hobbies for the entire family. Some of the types of activities that have become a part of company social and recreational programs are chess or checkers, bridge, concerts, golf, fashion shows, dancing, crafts, glee clubs, fishing, theater parties, and sports car racing clubs. Good recreational planning should provide organized activities for those employees who prefer to spend their leisure time in individual or small-group pursuits.

Most firms feel that the improvement in employee morale is worth whatever it costs to achieve. In some companies, employee associations bear some or all of the expenses of the recreational programs. In other firms, the costs of recreation may be partially defrayed by other sources of revenue, such as income from vending machines located throughout the offices and plant.

Employee Fitness Programs. Committed to the premise that helping employees keep fit improves both their health and job performance, more companies are offering comprehensive fitness programs for their workers. Such "wellness" programs may include aerobics, jogging, and calisthenics. Often the fitness programs focus attention upon high-risk health problems and offer seminars on smoking, alcohol and drug abuse, weight control, proper nutrition, and stress reduction. Some firms provide in-house athletic facilities with custodial services, or they may offer incentives to their workers to participate in programs elsewhere. Companies find the following benefits have been gained from their employee fitness programs: reduced health-care costs and absenteeism, higher morale, and improved productivity.

Career Apparel. Providing wearing apparel for office workers is an important employee benefit in some companies. Over a two- or three-year period, wearing apparel may cost

Employee fitness programs are seen as one means of improving employee health and reducing absenteeism and health-care costs.

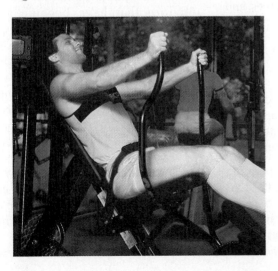

a company several hundred dollars for each worker. In some programs, employees pay for the cost of all their wearing apparel. In other plans, the firm may provide the initial wardrobe, with additional or optional items being paid for by employees. In other instances, the cost of apparel is evenly divided between employee and employer.

Companies that provide career apparel as an employee benefit cite the following advantages: decreased absenteeism and turnover, greater job efficiency and esprit de corps, and a reduction in recruitment costs as a result of more walk-in applicants.

Parking Space. When parking space is provided by the company, employees are saved the cost of renting their own space and are assured of finding a place in which to park. In large metropolitan areas, such benefits represent a significant savings and peace of mind for the workers. Parking lots or garages are provided by many large firms, and in nearly all of these companies there is no charge to the employees.

Counseling and Referral Programs. As you saw in Chapter 7, many companies have established employee assistance programs (EAP) that provide employees with counseling and referral programs for alcoholism, drug abuse, emotional illness, stress, marital problems, and other personal problems.

A company faced with laying off some of its work force may assist and counsel these employees by means of outplacement counseling. An **outplacement counseling** program is designed to assist laid-off workers in applying for unemployment compensation benefits and in obtaining benefits such as medical and life insurance, vacation and holidays, and holdings in the company credit union or stock purchase plan. Outplacement counseling is often undertaken to give the laid-off workers a much-needed morale boost and to help ease them into the world of unemployment. The terminated workers may be counseled in group sessions where they receive advice on interviewing and resumé writing. Some company counselors organize job fairs so the firm's laid-off workers can meet prospective employers.

For those workers approaching retirement age, the company may undertake a program of **preretirement counseling**. In these counseling sessions, matters such as the following are commonly discussed:

Company pensions
Earning money after retirement
Financial planning
Organizations for retirees
Recreation and hobbies
Social security benefits
Wills and inheritances
Health problems of older persons

Financial Services. The most frequently available financial services to office employees are those provided by credit unions. A **credit union** is a financial institution, chartered by the state or federal government, that is organized to assist the employees of a firm in saving money and lending it to one another.

Legal Service Plans. Legal service plans are designed to improve worker satisfaction and performance by handling for the employees such matters as debt difficulties, bankruptcies, and matrimonial disputes. Legal service plans are expected to increase in number as the result of future collective bargaining agreements.

A common type of legal service plan is the *group legal plan*. In this plan, a group of workers with a common affiliation, such as the members of a union or a company credit union, obtain the services of a lawyer or group of lawyers at a discount. Usually the members of a group plan must use the services of a designated lawyer who is affiliated with the plan, although some plans may allow the workers a choice. The fees are paid by the company after the legal services have been performed.

Under the *prepaid legal plan*, an advance payment of fees is made by the company, depending upon the type of services to be provided. For example, the *access plan* provides primarily telephone consultation. However, members are also usually allowed additional services such as brief office consultations and the preparation of a simple legal document each year.

In the *comprehensive prepaid legal plan*, a wider range of legal services is provided the employees. Some plans, designed to meet most of the legal service needs of average middle-income families, cover real estate and housing matters, domestic disputes, traffic accidents, consumer debt problems, adoptions, preparation of wills, and estate planning.

Executive Perquisites. Top-level managers in many firms are often provided **perquisites**, or *perks*, which are defined as privileges, gains, or profits that are incidental to their regular salaries. Some of the most popularly offered perks are use of a personal company car; reserved parking space; periodic free medical examinations; country club memberships; luncheon club memberships; use of company airplane; spouse traveling on company business; stock options; liability insurance for directors and officers; paid memberships in professional, trade, or business associations and civic organizations; financial planning services; and credit cards for business entertainment and travel.

Today executives are receiving fewer perks, which in the past have represented a significant amount of their total compensation. The Internal Revenue Service has imposed tax rules on some financial perks, with the effect that they are treated as earned income for income tax purposes.

Other Programs and Services. Other programs and services that companies may provide their employees include:

1. *Child-care service.* The factors that account for an immense potential demand

for child-care service are shown in Figure 11–2: entrance into the work force by a growing number of women, the increased number of mothers with children under six years of age, and the sharp increase in the number of children under five years of age. However, a relatively small number of companies provide nurseries and day-care services on their premises, as evidenced in the Committee of 500 Survey conducted by the Administrative Management Society.[8] Further, in a nationwide survey of about 10,000 business firms, the Bureau of Labor Statistics found only about 2 percent of the firms were actually sponsoring day-care centers for their workers' children; an additional 3 percent provided financial assistance toward child-care expenses.[9] Indirect benefits, such as work-schedule policies that provide flexible hours of work, voluntary part-time employment, and job sharing, that can aid parents in meeting their child-care responsibilities appear to be far more common than child-care support benefits.

2. *Elder-care service.* This service has not yet become a top priority benefit for most firms. In the *Personnel Journal* survey cited earlier, only 2 percent of the responding firms offer any form of elder care assistance to their employees.[10] Some features of elder-care service include consultation with community agencies on problems of the elderly, referrals to medical services, and home-delivered meals.

3. *Company discounts.* Many firms grant their employees a discount on company

---

[8]Jeffrey E. Long, "Flexible Benefits Move Ahead," *Management World* (March/April, 1988), p. 13.
[9]Howard V. Hayghe, "Employers and Child Care: What Roles Do They Play?" *Monthly Labor Review* (September, 1988), p. 38.
[10]Morton E. Grossman and Margaret Magnus, "The Boom in Benefits," *Personnel Journal* (November, 1988), p. 54.

Figure 11–2
Factors Contributing to Increased Need for Child-Care Service

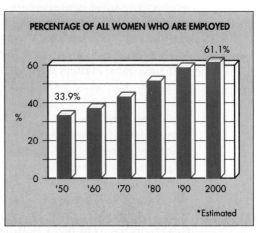

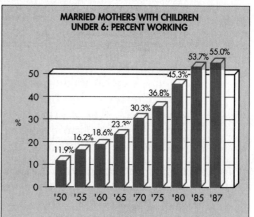

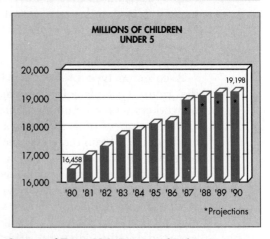

Source of Data: U.S. Bureau of Labor Statistics and U.S. Census Bureau.

products or services, with discounts ranging from 10 to 50 percent or more.

4. *Adoption benefit plans.* Another employee service provided by a growing number of companies is coverage of the expenses incurred by employees adopting children. Under most adoption benefit plans, the amount received by the employee is similar to a pregnant worker's benefits provided under the company's medical insurance plan.

5. *Commuter-assistance transportation programs.* These programs are designed to help employees who usually depend on private automobiles or mass transit when commuting to and from work.

One type of program, *van-pooling*, consists of groups of 8 to 15 employees who ride to and from work together in a van. The vans are either company owned or leased. Or the van-pooling services may be obtained from a third party or a van owner-operator. In the latter case, sometimes the employer agrees to subsidize the fares charged by the van driver.

Carpooling is another popular transportation program that is easy to administer and requires relatively little initial investment by the employer. The main function of the employer is to match up the riders who will commute together in one car. The match-up is usually done by maintaining employee card files containing names of interested workers, addresses, phone numbers, and rider/driver preferences.

DEVELOPING AND IMPLEMENTING A COST-EFFECTIVE EMPLOYEE BENEFITS PROGRAM

Earlier in this chapter you saw that employee benefits are extremely important in attracting and retaining qualified employees and in building positive employee attitudes toward the organization. Thus, with skillful planning and organizing, a company may develop and implement a cost-effective employee benefits package that represents a major factor in the firm's successful operations. All managers, including the OM, and the supervisors must be aware of the different kinds of benefits offered by their company so they can aid in more efficiently managing these benefits and discussing them intelligently with employees.

Often the number of employee benefits grows without a clear purpose or design. Many times a specific benefit is added merely because a competitive firm has recently included the same benefit in its package. Rather than investigate the needs of the firm and its employees, often one person or a committee unilaterally adds benefit after benefit, with a resulting mixture of costly and inappropriate forms of coverage.

The person in charge of the benefits program should avoid overreacting to outside competitive pressures, current fads, and presentations of overly zealous salespersons promoting a new or expanded benefit. Instead, the person developing and implementing the benefits program should turn to the fundamental functions and principles of management in order to manage efficiently an integrated package of employee benefits.

Setting Objectives

You may wish to review on pages 294 and 295 the list of objectives that may be realized by developing a program of employee benefits. A company selects from these objectives those which, when attained, will meet the needs of the workers and the firm. In making the selection of objectives, the company is guided by many factors such as its size, location, extent of unionization, profitability of operations, patterns previously set by the industry, and management's perception of employee needs. Once the objectives have been selected, they must be clearly stated in keeping with the firm's philosophy and policies. Finally, as discussed later, provisions must be made for communicating the objectives to all persons concerned and for making sure by appropriate feedback techniques that the objectives are fully understood.

Assigning Responsibilities

In a small company, we may find that the OM is assigned responsibility and authority for administering the employee benefits program. As indicated in Chapter 1, this person may also be given responsibility for all human resources functions (recruiting, hiring, employee relations, training, employee communications, and wage and salary administration) in addition to information management activities. In fact, in the very small firm, the OM may be assigned all those functions not undertaken by the line departments.

Medium-size companies may employ a specialist to handle the employee benefits plan. Depending upon this person's expertise, he or she may call upon other staff members or outside consultants for help in specialized areas such as law, accounting, and investments. In the large organization, often there is a director or manager of employee benefits who, aided by a benefits committee, is responsible for integrating the management of all benefit plans.

In all sizes of firms, however, first-line supervisors have clear-cut communication and advisory responsibilities. As the linking pin between middle management and the employees, supervisors communicate information about the benefits program, such as length-of-service requirements and changes that have been made in the plan. In meeting their downward responsibilities, supervisors should be available to answer employees' questions about applying for certain benefits and to point out the advantages and disadvantages of particular benefits to the employees. As part of their upward responsibilities, supervisors advise middle management of employee reactions to existing plans and their interests in other benefits not currently offered by the company. To fulfill this upward responsibility, supervisors must first determine the employees' needs, as discussed in the following section.

Determining Employee Needs

A firm should seek its employees' opinions before adopting any new benefit plan or making changes in an existing program. Thus, management can determine how employees feel about existing benefit coverage and whether they have particular preferences or priorities with respect to changes in the benefits program. The company might find that benefits it considers important are not viewed as particularly significant by employees. The reverse also may be true; benefits that have low priority for the company may have high priority among employees. The firm may also find that costly changes in benefits do not necessarily produce the highest level of employee satisfaction. On the other hand, some relatively inexpensive changes may score very high among employees.

To determine employees' needs, the company may use questionnaire surveys and discussion sessions. The questionnaires may be administered at the employees' workstations or sent through the mail to the employees' homes. Interviews (one-on-one, small group, or guided group discussions) with immediate feedback are an effective way to obtain insight into employees' needs in relation to the offering of present and future benefits.

Developing Nondiscriminatory Benefit Plans

The Tax Reform Act of 1986 contained a set of extremely complex rules, known as *Section 89* of the Tax Code, that were designed to discourage discriminatory benefit plans. The Section 89 rules would have made it more difficult and costly for companies to provide generous benefit packages for their higher-paid employees and little or no benefits for others. Originally, the law provided that every company would subject its group life insurance, medical insurance, and similar benefit plans to a complicated testing process to determine whether the benefits were available to most non-highly-compensated employees. If not, the benefits provided to higher-paid employees would be taxed as though those workers had received the benefits in cash. In addition, the company would face tax penalties. However, in late 1989, the Section 89 nondiscrimination rules were repealed.

Because of constant flux in the taxation of employee benefits, new employers who are implementing benefit plans or established employers who wish to amend existing benefit plans should seek legal advice.

Communicating the Benefits Program to Employees

Employers who spend perhaps 30 to 40 percent of their payroll dollars for a benefits program have a right to expect a return on their investment. Thus, the privilege of receiving benefits, those newly emerging as well as those offered in the past, must be communicated to and understood by workers. This means that the benefits must be described in a language and a format employees will remember and understand. Some of the approaches used by companies in communicating their benefits program to employees include:

1. Holding annual meetings of employees and their families where the company's benefits program is clearly explained.
2. Conducting small meetings and counseling sessions led by company managers and supervisors to follow up on questions that employees have asked during the year.
3. Distributing up-to-date handbooks to employees and summary plan descriptions, as required by the Employee Retirement Income Security Act.
4. Mailing a series of letters, over the signature of the chief executive officer, to employees' homes to involve the entire family. For example, letters may be used to announce an updated benefits program to start on a specified date or to outline the revisions to be made in the present benefits program.
5. Presenting a slide film or videotape program to tell employees what their benefits are and how they have been designed to meet their needs.
6. Using the company publications to answer employees' questions of general interest.
7. Preparing posters and distributing payroll envelope stuffers, pocket calendars, and "gadget" benefit calculators that aid in telling the employee benefits story.
8. Using the employee's PC or a computer kiosk, linked to the firm's central data bank, to inquire about the current status of the employee's benefit program, to make changes, and to enroll in new benefits offerings.
9. Using an automated telephone line at any hour to obtain specific, confidential information about benefits coverage.
10. Preparing annual statements that show in detail the employees' earnings and their benefits. The annual statement may take the form of a letter, such as that shown in Figure 11–3, which is distri-

Figure 11-3
Employee
Earnings and
Benefits
Letter

A SAMPLE EMPLOYEE EARNINGS AND BENEFITS LETTER

COMPANY NAME
ADDRESS

DATE

Employee's Name
Address

Dear _____ :

Enclosed are your W-2 forms showing the amount of taxable income that you received from _____ during 19   . Listed below in Section A are your gross wages and a cost breakdown of various fringe benefit programs that you enjoy. In addition to the money you received as wages, the company paid benefits for you which are not included in your W-2 statement. These are fringe benefits that are sometimes overlooked. In an easy-to-read form, here's what _____ paid to you in 19 .

Section A—Paid to You in Your W-2 Earnings

Cost-of-Living Allowance
Shift Premium
Suggestion Award(s)
Service Award(s)
Vacation Pay
Holiday Pay
Funeral Pay
Jury-Duty Pay
Military Pay
Accident & Sickness Benefits
Regular Earnings
Overtime Earnings
Allowances

  GROSS WAGES

Section B—Paid for You and Not Included in Your W-2 Earnings:

Company Contribution to Stock Purchase & Savings Plan
Company Contribution to Pension Plan
Company Cost of Your Hospitalization Payments
Company Cost of Your Life & Accident Death Insurance
Company Cost for Social Security on Your Wages
Company Cost of the Premium for Your Workers Compensation
Company Cost for the Tax on Your Wages for Unemployment Compensation
Company Cost for Tuition Refund
Company Cost for Safety Glasses

  TOTAL COST OF BENEFITS NOT INCLUDED IN W-2 EARNINGS

  TOTAL _____ PAID FOR YOUR SERVICES IN 19-- _____

You have earned the amount on the bottom line, but we want to give your a clearer idea of the total cost of your services to the company, and the protection and benefits that are being purchased for you and your family.

                                                        Sincerely,

                                                        Personnel Manager

---

Source: "The Annual Employee Earnings and Benefits Letter," by Jeffrey C. Claypool and Joseph P. Cangemi. Reprinted with permission of *Personnel Journal*, Costa Mesa, CA, copyright July, 1980; all rights reserved.

buted to every employee in early January.

Controlling the Costs of Employee Benefits

Communications such as those described above aid in making sure that employees are aware of the cost of the benefits provided, especially those for health insurance, which is the employer's most expensive benefit. Figure 11–4 shows the dramatic rise in the costs of family medical coverage over a ten-year period. The estimated average cost to employers for providing health-care insurance for one worker in 1989 was $2,751, which represents a $2,069 increase since 1980, when the same family health policy cost $682.[11] For many businesses, the outlays for employee health insurance outrun their efforts to control the mounting medical costs. Thus, we find companies actively at work trying to *contain*, or reduce within limits, the escalation of their health care costs while at the same time meeting the health needs of employees and their families.

To contain the costs of health care benefits, we find that companies take one or more of the following steps:

1. *Investigate the use of Health Maintenance Organizations (HMOs) and Preferred Provider Organizations (PPOs)*, discussed earlier on page 297. Companies that have been using self-insured, self-funded plans, in which they assume a substantial amount of the risk involved, are now contracting with providers such as HMOs and PPOs to manage their health care programs.
2. *Place more responsibility on employees* to share the costs by raising deductibles, increasing coinsurance, increasing the employees' out-of-pocket limits, and reducing coverage on mental and nervous disorders.

3. *Require review programs* to make sure that medical procedures undertaken by employees are necessary. Thus, some firms are redesigning their health plans to include second surgical opinions, to monitor patient admissions to hospitals, and to offer workers an incentive to have minor surgery in outpatient clincs.
4. *Employ third-party specialists* to aid in establishing information systems, overseeing claims processing procedures, and coordinating second opinions.
5. *Apply case-management techniques*, which include monitoring the course of an employee's illness, supervising and authorizing medical services, and using lower cost outpatient, home, or hospice care instead of hospitalization. Case management is often used in catastrophic illnesses, such as AIDS.
6. *Explore the feasibility of setting up a self-insurance plan*, if the firm is large enough to afford self-insurance. According to the Health Insurance Association, 70 percent of the employees who work for firms with more than 500 people are covered by self-insurance programs.[12] Large companies that provide their own funds to insure employees are exempt from state-mandated benefits and from state taxes on health-insurance premiums. (All states have laws that mandate, or require, employers who offer group health plans to include specific benefits, such as alcoholism treatment, newborn nursery care, orthopedic braces, and breast reconstruction.)

Investigating New Developments in Employee Benefits Programs

The OM, benefits specialist, manager of employee benefits, or whoever may be assigned the responsibility for the firm's

---

[11]Hay/Huggins Benefits Report

[12]David Stipp, "Laws on Health Benefits Raise Firms' Ire," *The Wall Street Journal* (December 28, 1988), p. B1.

Figure 11-4
Rising Costs of Family Medical Coverage

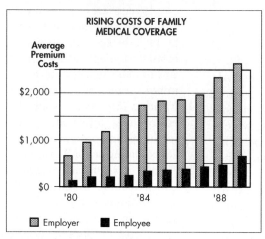

Source of Data: Hay/Huggins Benefits Report.

employee benefits program must keep abreast of new developments in the field of employee benefits. The employee benefits administrator must be informed not only of new kinds of benefits that are being offered but also of innovative ways to provide these benefits to the workers. A relatively new concept in providing employee benefits, the flexible benefits program, is one such development with which the benefits administrator should be familiar. The AMS Foundation's survey of the Committee of 500 shows that flexible benefits plans continue to grow in popularity. In 1988, 24 percent of the companies surveyed had flexible benefits plans as compared with only 20 percent in 1987 and 17 percent in 1986.[13]

A **flexible benefits program**, also called a *cafeteria plan*, is an employer-sponsored benefits package that offers employees a choice between taking cash and certain

qualified benefits, such as accident and health coverage or group term life insurance coverage. The selection is made as the employees determine how many dollars to allocate to each type of optional benefit made available by the employer. Usually each employee receives a specified number of credits to spend on benefits, depending upon the employee's age, salary level, and length of time on the job.

The type of benefits that may be offered under a cafeteria plan is specifically defined by the Internal Revenue Code. Generally only cash and those benefits that are not taxable to employees under the Code are acceptable. These benefits include group term life insurance, group legal services, coverage under accident or health plans, and benefits under a dependent care assistance program. Benefits that are barred from a cafeteria plan include vacation facilities, fitness clubs, summer camps, and vanpools.

Employers can continue to provide tax-free employee benefits, but these must be offered to all employees. Tax-free employee benefits include services that do not cost employers any extra money, such as free stand-by flights given by airlines to their employees, certain employee discounts on goods and services, and routine benefits such as free parking and company-financed eating facilities.

Based on the findings of behavioral scientists, a flexible benefits program assumes that employees are better motivated and more satisfied if they take an active role in developing their own benefits packages. Thus, employees may construct a benefits package that most precisely meets their preferences as dictated by lifestyle, age, family situation, tax bracket, physical condition, and spending needs.

[13]Jeffrey E. Long, "Flexible Benefits Move Ahead," *Management World* (March/April, 1988), p. 12.

Dialog on the Firing Line

DAVID M. MAKSYMOVICH
Senior Field Marketing Representative
Educational Testing Service
Princeton, New Jersey

Educational Testing Service (ETS) provides measurement, research, and related services to educational and business organizations in the United States and abroad. Since joining ETS in 1971, Mr. Maksymovich has managed large operations and clerical staff with an emphasis on customer and client relations. In his present position, Mr. Maksymovich is responsible for maintaining customer relations and promoting national testing programs for licensing and certification in professional and occupational areas.

QUESTION: David, describe the employee benefits program offered by ETS. As you look ahead, what kinds of benefits do you see emerging for your firm's employees?

RESPONSE: ETS was a pioneer in its belief that no one single set of employee benefits can be responsive in a large organization with its wide differences among people in regard to age, family responsibilities, career intentions, and length of service. Therefore, ETS developed a two-part program consisting of:

1. *Basic or core benefits* (life insurance, medical care, disability income replacement, vacation and retirement benefits) that provide a foundation of protection to all staff members. The firm pays the entire cost of this basic coverage.
2. *Flexible benefits* that give staff members choices in most benefit areas to supplement their basic benefits or add new ones. To meet the cost of these benefits, eligible employees are provided with flexible credits—a percentage of their salary based on length of service and position in the company. If the cost of the additional benefits chosen exceeds the workers' flexible credits, the excess cost can be met by salary deductions.

Examples of flexible benefits include: additional term life insurance for employees or dependents, medical care coverage for dependents, dental care for employees and dependents, up to two weeks' additional vacation, and cash to be used for any reason. The program is set up on an annual cycle so employees may change their selection of flexible benefits each year.

Recently the flexible benefits program was modified to provide variable deductibles for medical and dental benefits. Thus, workers use fewer of their flexible credits to purchase the coverage, provided they agree to pay a higher deductible on their claims.

Looking ahead, flexible benefits could certainly include child care, as more mothers join the work force. However, one of the advantages of ETS's flexible benefits package is that if a specific benefit is not included in the overall offering, the employee can set aside flexible credits in the form of cash, to be used for any individual need.

SUMMARY 1. Companies provide benefits to their office workers in order to attain several objectives: (a) to meet legislative requirements, (b) to attract and retain qualified workers, (c) to motivate workers to become more productive, (d) to meet the employees' needs for job security and job satisfaction, (e) to reward employees who improve their performance and increase their productivity, (f) to lessen the company's tax burden, (g) to ward off unionization, (h) to fulfill the obligations contained in a collective bargaining agreement, and (i) to meet the competitive pressures brought about by other firms in the community.

2. In order to evaluate the effectiveness of employee benefits in relation to their cost, benefits may be classified as: (a) legally required payments, (b) medical and medically related benefits, (c) retirement and savings plan benefits, (d) life insurance and death benefits, (e) payments for time not worked, and (f) miscellaneous benefits. The average cost of such benefits amounts to about 37 cents of the employer's payroll dollar.

3. The person charged with developing and implementing an employee benefits program and containing its costs should be guided by the fundamental functions and principles of management in setting the objectives of the program, assigning responsibilities, determining employee needs, developing nondiscriminatory benefit plans, communicating the benefits program to employees, controlling the costs of employee benefits, and investigating new developments in benefits programs.

GLOSSARY **Credit union**—a financial institution, chartered by the state or federal government, that is organized to assist the employees of a firm in saving and borrowing money.

Disability income insurance—an insurance plan that provides continuing income to workers who are ill or have suffered accidents and are unable to return to their jobs.

Employee benefits—the payments and services that workers receive in addition to their regular wages or salaries; also called *fringe benefits.*

Employee Retirement Income Security Act (ERISA)—legislation that provides workers with a vested right toward their retirement income benefits and assurance of well-managed retirement plans.

Flexible benefits program—an employer-sponsored benefits package that offers employees a choice between taking cash and certain qualified benefits; also known as the *cafeteria plan.*

401(k) retirement plan—a plan in which each year employees shelter from federal income taxes a certain portion of their salaries and the earnings thereon until time of withdrawing the funds.

Group life insurance—the protection that provides benefits for all employees in a company in case of death or total disability.

Health maintenance organization (HMO)—an organization of health-care providers that offers prepaid (by the employer and the employee) medical services to HMO participants.

Hospital, surgical, and medical insurance—the protection covering all or the major part of hospital, surgical, and medical expenses for employees and their dependents.

Individual retirement account (IRA)—a pension plan established and funded by an individual employee.

Legal service plan—a program under which employees obtain company-paid legal advice in handling matters such as debt difficulties, bankruptcies, and matrimonial disputes.

Major medical insurance—an insurance plan that protects employees and their dependents from huge medical bills resulting from serious accidents or prolonged illness.

OASDHI benefits—old-age, survivors, disability, and health insurance benefits provided under the Federal Insurance Contributions Act; commonly called the *social security program.*

Outplacement counseling—an employer-sponsored program designed to assist laid-off workers in applying for unemployment compensation benefits and in obtaining company benefits.

Perquisites—the privileges, gains, or profits provided top-level managers in addition to their regular salaries; also called *perks.*

Preferred provider organization (PPO)—an insurance carrier that develops a list of doctors, hospitals, and other services (selected on the basis of low cost and high quality) from which employees select that physician or hospital they desire.

Preretirement counseling—an employer-sponsored program that provides assistance to workers approaching retirement age.

Savings and thrift plans—employer-sponsored plans in which the employees' savings are matched, wholly or partially, by the employer and are held in a tax-deferred investment account.

Preretirement counseling—an employer-

sponsored program that provides assistance to workers approaching retirement age.

Savings and thrift plans—employer-sponsored plans in which the employees' savings are matched, wholly or partially, by the employer and are held in a tax-deferred investment account.

Simplified employee pension (SEP) plan—a plan in which employers make contributions to the individual retirement accounts (IRAs) on behalf of their employees.

State disability benefits—payments from a state insurance plan to workers who are absent from their jobs because of illness, accident, or disease not arising out of their employment.

Supplemental unemployment benefits (SUB)—the benefits provided by an employer's private plan to supplement the state unemployment compensation benefits received by employees during periods of layoff.

Travel accident insurance—a plan of protection that provides benefits to covered employees in the event of their death, disability, or dismemberment while traveling on company business.

Unemployment compensation insurance—a federal-state program established to provide funds at the state level for compensating unemployed workers in that state during periods of temporary unemployment.

Vesting—the process of conveying to employees the right to share in a retirement fund in the event they are terminated before the normal retirement age.

Workers' compensation insurance—a state insurance program designed to protect employees and their dependents against losses due to injury or death incurred during the worker's employment.

FOR YOUR REVIEW

1. What are the objectives that a company tries to achieve by providing benefits for its office workers?

2. Which three categories of employee benefits cost employers the most in 1988?

3. How is the cost of OASDHI benefits financed?

4. What kind of protection do employees gain from (a) unemployment compensation insurance and (b) workers' compensation insurance?

5. What is the major difference between the traditional HMO and a PPO?

6. What protection do employees receive from major medical insurance coverage?

7. Under what conditions may office employees make tax-free contributions to an IRA account?

8. What advantages does an office worker gain by participating in a 401(k) retirement plan?

9. Describe the provisions of a typical group life insurance plan.

10. What is the common practice regarding paid vacations and holidays for office workers?

11. What protection does the Pregnancy Discrimination Act provide for pregnant employees?

12. What is the purpose of providing refreshment breaks and rest periods for office workers?

13. What guidelines should be followed by the office manager in granting rest periods?

14. What is the nature of educational assistance provided office workers in many firms?

15. For what reasons may a company develop an employee fitness program?

16. Explain how a company's outplacement counseling program is of value to laid-off and terminated workers.

17. What kind of help might an office worker expect to receive from the firm's legal service plan?

18. What steps have some companies taken to accommodate working parents who have small children?

19. What are the first-line supervisor's responsibilities in the operation of an employee benefits program?

20. Describe five kinds of communication media that may be used to inform office workers of the benefits provided by their firm.

21. What steps should be considered by a company attempting to contain the costs of its health care benefits program?

22. Explain the operation of a flexible benefits program.

FOR YOUR DISCUSSION

1. As office supervisor in your small company with 150 office employees, you are convinced that something must be done to help solve the problems facing an increasing number of working mothers. However, when you approach your boss with the idea of establishing a child-care center, you are told "Our company is too small. Besides, we're understaffed." However, you don't give up, and now you are considering how your company might operate a child-care program without a huge cash outlay. Help this office supervisor by passing along some suggestions whereby the small firm can economically provide child care.

2. The century-old practice of recognizing retired office workers at the Union Insurance Company has been the holding of a farewell party where the men are presented with gold watches and the women are given gold pendants. As the recently employed office manager of the company, you have been thinking that your firm, as a truly progressive company, has a greater responsibility to those who have served the organization for so many years. You firmly believe that the retirees should be provided with good retirement planning information. Outline the kind of program you would make available to those in your firm who are nearing retirement age.

3. Eight different employee benefits are listed below:
   a. Long-term disability
   b. Pension
   c. Dental
   d. Short-term disability and sick days
   e. Medical
   f. Life insurance
   g. Paid vacation and holidays
   h. After-tax savings/profit-sharing plan

   Assume, first, that you are an office worker in your early twenties, single, with no dependents. Rank these eight benefits to show how important you personally consider them. Next, assume you are an office worker in your late forties, married, with your two children attending college, and with a spouse who is also employed full-time. Now what is your ranking of the eight benefits?

4. Like most employers today, the Troy-Pickering Co. is aware of rising medical costs. Abbie Cruz, director of employee benefits programs, notes that the cost of the firm's medical programs has risen more than twice the inflation rate. Charged with lowering the costs of medical insurance and health care, Cruz has been thinking of ways in which to involve both the employees and management in designing programs that will cut the costs of medical care without decreasing its quality. What suggestions can you offer Cruz to consider as she prepares a program of "cost containment" for medical insurance and health care?

5. At a meeting of the Council on Employee Benefits, one of the speakers stated that any future changes in benefits packages should be directed toward providing a more cohesive package that would benefit both the company and its employees. As you look ahead, which benefits of those presently offered do you expect to become more widespread in their availability to office workers? Now, stretch your imagination and list those kinds of benefits that may emerge by the year 2020.

6. Linda Ferguson, age 55, has just announced to you, her supervisor, that she plans to take advantage of the company's early retirement plan and retire at age 60. Do you

feel that, faced with the prospect of retirement, Ferguson will reduce her productivity during the last five years of her working life? Explain.

7. During his two weeks' vacation, Walter Latham was forced to leave the motel at the seashore and undergo an appendectomy at a nearby hospital. Upon returning to work, Latham indicated to the office manager that, in view of his hospitalization, the company should reschedule his vacation date and treat his former two weeks' vacation as sick leave. As office manager, how would you answer Latham?

SOLVING CASE PROBLEMS

Case 11-1 Improving the Total Benefits Package

The Avery Computer Company, owned by Mr. and Mrs. Harvey T. Avery, has grown during the past ten years from its beginning as a "mom and pop" operation into a corporation with 55 office employees and 280 production workers. From the very beginning, the Averys were never security minded; and thus in the early years they provided their workers only those benefits required by law plus the usual paid vacations, holidays, and group life insurance.

Mrs. Avery has just read an article in *The Wall Street Journal* indicating that some of their competitors in the home-computer field are faced with employee benefits that cost, on the average, $93 each week. The Averys' accountant estimates that the weekly cost of the benefits provided an Avery worker is $77.50. After examining their past operating costs, projecting their future sales volume, and much soul-searching, the Averys realize that they can afford to expand the benefits presently provided their workers. They also feel obligated to do so if they want to retain their workers and avoid unionization. However, neither of the Averys wants to give the employees the impression that the additional benefits are being provided merely to catch up with the competition.

The Averys have come to you, their manager of administrative services, and have asked for your help in modifying the present employee benefits program so an improved package can be presented to the workers at the annual Christmas party in four weeks. In talking with you, the Averys ask the following questions.

1. What would be the most meaningful benefits to offer now?
2. How can we be sure that all the workers need, or even want, the benefits you are recommending?
3. What suggestions do you have for announcing the improved benefits package to the workers at the Christmas party?

Case 11-2 Solving a Problem in Productivity

Jon Kiley, supervisor of the mailroom at McDonegal, Inc., has just analyzed the computer printout showing the production figures for his workers for the first half of this year. Kiley is very discouraged by the department's declining output, which has averaged about 8 percent each month. Kiley has called his workers together to present the "productivity problem" to them and to obtain any suggestions they might have to improve output.

At this meeting, three of Kiley's workers made the following comments:

Brenner: If we had a longer coffee break in the morning, I'd be happier and could do a better job of sorting. (The company has one 15-minute break in the morning and one 15-minute break in the afternoon.)

Pasco: I know I could do a better job if I had longer to enjoy my lunch. I like to drive over to the Double Bar B-Q, and there just isn't enough time to relax after eating. (The company provides a paid lunch period of 45 minutes.)

Wiegand: My sister works at Hannegan's and she tells me they have put in a cafeteria plan for handling all their benefits. Why can't we sweeten up our package and get some more benefits like she has? Then I'm sure all of us could do better.

1. In view of these comments, what do you identify as the major problem in the mailroom?
2. Do you agree with Wiegand that if the benefits were improved, the workers would be more productive on the job?
3. What steps do you recommend Kiley now take in solving the mailroom's "productivity problem"?

12

Personnel Problems and Practices in the Workplace

GOALS FOR THIS CHAPTER

After completing this chapter, you should be able to:

1. Identify the major personnel problems that affect the office workers' physical and mental well-being and describe the practices commonly followed by office managers and supervisors in solving these problems.
2. Describe some of the typical practices followed by firms in solving problems related to job attendance such as tardiness, absenteeism, and turnover.
3. Calculate the rate of absenteeism and turnover for a firm and offer suggestions for an effective program of cost reduction for these two job-attendance problems.
4. Identify the advantages and disadvantages that an organization and its employees may experience when a modified workweek and work schedule are adopted.
5. Describe how a company may minimize the economic effects of a recession by establishing a rotation of layoffs or work-sharing program.
6. List the reasons offered by office workers for joining unions.
7. Describe the role of the office manager in office unionism—before union activity, while attempts are being made to organize, and after the workers become unionized.

Am I fortunate I didn't let Marty drive me home last night after we bowled—she was really high! . . . I just heard that Joe in Purchasing was indicted for possession of crack. . . . Don't breathe a word of this to a soul, but I learned yesterday that John in the office next door has AIDS. . . . Last week I missed work three days, got a lousy evaluation from my boss, and had my car repossessed—I'm getting out of this rat race! . . . Did you hear that our Casanova in Sales finally proposed to Annie? Isn't she still married to Hubby No. 3? . . . Cover for me— just got to sneak out for a few minutes to throw a "nicotine fit." . . . I just got wind that the union organizer will be here tomorrow to ask us to sign authorization cards. . . .

Personal problems and issues such as these often spill over into the workplace and, as a result, affect our job performance and productivity. It is estimated that 18 percent of any work force are affected by personal problems that can influence job performance. Of these affected workers, 12 percent have alcohol- and drug-related problems, and 6 percent have emotional-related problems.[1] When we bring problems such as these into the workplace, our *personal* problems become *personnel* problems for AOMs, who must assume responsibility for assisting us in solving our problems. Knowing how other office managers have solved similar problems strengthens the leadership abilities of managers and supervisors, improves the quality and quantity of their subordinates' work, and aids in creating a better work environment.

In this chapter, we shall examine those work-force issues and problems that are commonly found in offices of all sizes. First, we shall direct our attention to those problems that affect the physical and mental well-being of office employees. Next, we

---

[1]Dale A. Masi and Seymour J. Friedland, "EAP Actions & Options," *Personnel Journal* (June, 1988), p. 62.

shall examine those job-attendance and work-scheduling problems and practices that are concerned mainly with raising the cost consciousness of OMs and their subordinates. Finally, we shall briefly explore the unionization of office workers.

THE WORKERS' PHYSICAL AND MENTAL WELL-BEING

Each day OMs, supervisors, and department heads are faced with a multitude of issues and problems that affect their employees' physical and mental well-being. Each problem requires a fair and equitable hearing and a decision that will be satisfactory to both the company and the worker. The solutions to some of these problems are often found in the employee handbook or the company's policy manual. Other problems require further study and consultation with employees before decisions can be made.

Alcoholism

Alcoholism is a progressive disease characterized by the excessive, repetitive, and uncontrolled consumption of alcohol. The disease cannot be cured, only arrested. Alcoholism is not only a social and physiological problem; it is also considered to be a psychological one. An **alcoholic** is a person who is powerless to stop drinking and whose normal living pattern is seriously altered by drinking. The National Council on Alcoholism estimates that 6 percent of the working population in this country is burdened by serious drinking problems.[2]

Alcoholism has become a serious concern in collective bargaining, and, as a result, union-management committees work together to develop rehabilitation programs for alcoholic workers. Such programs are designed to recognize alcoholism as an

illness, like any other sickness. Today most companies have insurance coverage that pays for detoxification ("drying-out") programs, and many firms provide a paid leave to enable workers "to take the cure."

An employer should develop a straightforward policy regarding alcoholism with the aim of correcting behavior problems in employees before they become unemployable. The company should look upon alcoholism as it would any other disease that affects an employee's output or behavior while at work. In those firms that have instituted some kind of rehabilitation program, the plans usually operate along the lines of the three-step program advocated by the National Council on Alcoholism: (1) education, (2) early detection of the alcoholic by the supervisor, and (3) referral to a treatment center.

Education

The firm must get across to its office workers the fact that alcoholism is a disease and will be treated as such by the firm. Many misunderstandings surround the subject of alcoholism and obstruct the development and operation of treatment programs. The facts on the subject must be given to employees through such media as visual aids, group meetings, and articles in company newsletters and other publications.

Early Detection

The responsibility for detecting alcoholic problems among office workers lies with their immediate superior, usually the supervisor. Supervisors should be aware of the specific signs that denote a case of alcoholism and be alert to the effects of alcohol on employee behavior. The supervisor should closely study and understand the employee's behavioral patterns and visible signs of alcoholism during its several phases, as shown in Figure 12–1. The supervisor must remember, however, that alcoholics strive to hide their problems from others and even

---

[2]Charles E. Shirley, "Alcoholism and Drug Abuse in the Workplace," *Office Administration and Automation* (November, 1984), pp. 24–25.

Figure 12–1
Behavioral
Patterns and
Visible Signs
of Alcoholic
Employees

BEHAVIORAL PATTERNS AND VISIBLE SIGNS OF ALCOHOLIC EMPLOYEES

Behavioral Patterns	Visible Signs of Alcoholism

1. *Early Phase — before employee loses control over drinking*

Drinks to relieve tension.
Alcohol tolerance increases.
Blackouts (memory blanks) occur.
Lies about drinking habits.

Attendance
Arrives late for work (especially after lunch).
Leaves job early.
Absent from office.

General Behavior
Overreacts to real or imagined criticism.
Complains of not feeling well.
Lies.

Job Performance
Unable to meet deadlines.
Makes mistakes through inattention or poor judgment.
Efficiency decreases.

2. *Middle Phase — drinking is less controlled*

Guilt about drinking.
Tremors during hangovers.
Loss of interest in work, co-workers, and current events.
Avoids discussion of alcoholism problem.

Attendance
Frequently takes days off for vague ailments or implausible reasons.

General Behavior
Makes statements that are undependable.
Begins to avoid co-workers who were formerly close associates.
Borrows money from co-workers.
Exaggerates work accomplishments.
Sustains repeated minor injuries on and off the job.
Shows unreasonable resentment.

Job Performance
General deterioration.
Work pace is spasmodic.
Attention wanders, lack of concentration.

3. *Late Phase — loss of control over drinking*

Neglects food.
Prefers to drink alone.
Believes that other activities interfere with drinking.

Attendance
Frequently takes time off, sometimes for several days.
Fails to return from lunch.

General Behavior.
Grandiose, aggressive, or belligerent.
Domestic problems interfere with work.
Money problems, including garnishment of salary.
Hospitalization increases.
Trouble with the law.
Drinking on the job.
Totally undependable.
Visible physical deterioration.

Job Performance
Uneven and generally incompetent.

deny that they themselves have any problems. Thus, the early detection of alcoholics is often the most difficult phase of the rehabilitation program.

Supervisors should not try to make a medical diagnosis of their employees' alcoholic problems nor delve into their employees' private lives. Supervisors should, however, discuss with the employees their declining productivity and carefully document their job performance and behavior. It must be made clear that unless the employees improve their performance or try to solve their problems by treatment, their jobs are in jeopardy. The alcoholic employees should be made to recognize and admit that they have drinking problems and be motivated to accept rehabilitation aid or face the consequences of losing their jobs.

Referral

If the company retains a counselor or a physician on either a full-time or a part-time basis, the supervisor can refer the alcoholic office worker to the counselor or physician. Sometimes we find that the company counselor is a recovered alcoholic who has special empathy for persuading the employee to accept suitable treatment, which may be through a lay group such as Alcoholics Anonymous, a residential alcoholism facility, or a detoxification center. The task of the counselor is to impress upon workers that undergoing and responding to treatment are the only ways to avoid endangering their jobs.

Most small and medium-size companies do not retain a company doctor or counselor on a full-time basis. In these firms, the supervisor can obtain help by consulting the Guide to Human Services in the telephone directory or the yellow pages under a heading such as "Alcoholism Information and Treatment Centers." Information may also be obtained by calling the national Helpline: 1-800-252-6465.

As you saw in Chapter 7, many large companies have established *employee assistance programs (EAPs)* that provide specialized aid and counseling. The office supervisor can refer workers with alcohol problems to the EAP, whose staff will confidentially counsel and refer workers to the appropriate agency.

Drug Abuse

We read that two out of every three people entering the work force today have used illegal drugs and that nearly 40 percent of workplace deaths and about one-half of workplace injuries are directly related to drug or alcohol use.[3] Drug abuse, like alcoholism, threatens the work performance and continued employment of some office workers. A **drug abuser** is one who exhibits strong psychological dependence on drugs, often reinforced by physical dependence when certain drugs are used. Such a person has been taking drugs for some time and presently feels unable to function physically and mentally without them. As a result of the drug addiction, office employees are robbed of their motivation to do their jobs. Further, because their salaries are too small to support their increasing drug needs, they may begin stealing and thus become security risks for the company and the community.

In dealing with drug abuse in the office, the OM should follow a three-step program similar to the one for alcoholism.

Education

Cooperative education efforts with the community and its social agencies represent a major means whereby a company can halt the spread of drug abuse in the office. Many firms have undertaken broad educational programs aimed at initially preventing the use of drugs or narcotics. All of these pro-

---

[3]Patrick R. Tyson and Robert A. Vaughn II, "Drug Testing in the Workplace," *Occupational Health & Safety* (April, 1987), p. 24.

grams support the principle that the only real cure for an *addict*—one who is physically dependent upon drugs—is never to start using drugs. Other companies conduct drug-abuse seminars for their supervisors and set up programs for spotting drug-using personnel. Information about drugs and narcotics may be obtained by consulting the Guide to Human Services in the telephone directory or the yellow pages under a heading such as "Drug Abuse and Addiction—Information and Treatment."

Early Detection

Many organizations use preemployment drug-screening testing of urine and blood, and also test current employees, when reasonable suspicion of impairment or drug use is detected. In a 1988–89 survey, the American Management Association found that, of the companies polled, 48 percent report drug-testing policies; one-third of these companies include a drug test in their preemployment physicals for all newly hired personnel and also test selected current employees when their job performance suggests substance abuse.[4] However, a number of state and federal court decisions may restrict an employer's right to test for drug use and alcohol abuse in the workplace. Some drug and alcohol testing programs have been challenged in that they invade the employee's privacy, do not recognize chemical dependency as a handicap, or are the basis for wrongful termination. Thus, it is often difficult for employers to know when they may test and under what circumstances. For this reason, companies should not initiate a testing program without advice from legal counsel.

In 1989 the Supreme Court ruled that the federal government may require drug testing of some workers in sensitive or safety-related jobs; however, the Court left open any ques-

tions about the constitutionality of broad, random testing. Nevertheless, the Supreme Court decision boosted drug and alcohol testing by government employers in some circumstances, and, as a result, may encourage testing by private employers.

Under the *Drug-Free Workplace Act of 1988*, companies that receive federal contracts valued at $25,000 or more must certify that they are taking specific steps to provide a drug-free workplace. In these companies, all employees must be notified that the manufacture, distribution, possession, or use of illegal drugs is forbidden in the workplace. Each company's antidrug plan must also provide for the counseling of employees and their access to rehabilitation.

To detect an on-the-job user and addict is the major responsibility of the office supervisor, who is closest to the worker. However, it is a much more difficult task to spot the drug abuser than the alcoholic. The addict's symptoms are not always apparent, even to the trained observer. The reaction to a drug usually depends on the user's mood and environment, and the dosage taken.

Cocaine, the "champagne of drugs," is a powerful mind-altering drug whose chronic use can produce chemical dependency, behavior changes, and health risks, including death. Cocaine is used by sniffing it into the nose (snorting), dissolving it in water and injecting it into the blood through a needle (shooting), or smoking it in a free-base form such as "crack" or "rock." It is estimated that there are 4 to 5 million regular users, and every day about 5,000 people try cocaine for the first time.[5] To aid in identifying employees addicted to cocaine, office supervisors should know the signs of abuse and dependency, which are listed in Figure 12–2. When dealing with employees who are heavily involved with cocaine, supervisors

[4]Eric Rolfe Greenberg, "Workplace Testing: Who's Testing Whom?" *Personnel* (May, 1989), pp. 39–45.

[5]Charles E. Shirley, "Alcoholism and Drug Abuse in the Workplace," *Office Administration and Automation* (November, 1984), p. 90.

Figure 12–2
The Warning Signs of Cocaine Abuse and Dependency

WARNING SIGNS—JOB PERFORMANCE

Absenteeism and Tardiness
- A high rate of absenteeism on Mondays, Fridays, and the day after payday.
- Brief disappearances from workstations.
- Frequent tardiness.
- Often on sick leave.

Erratic Performance
- Temporary burst of energy, followed by fatigue and depression.
- Performance swings between extreme highs and lows without reason.

Errors in Judgment
- Arrogant and grandiose.
- Stops listening to others.
- Loss of good judgment.

WARNING SIGNS—SAFETY

Fitness for Work
- May be unfit for work due to irritability, mood swings, nervousness, hyperactivity, and hallucinations.

Frequent Accidents
- More often sustain accidents because of speed and carelessness.
- Easily distracted because of impaired judgment.

Increased Risk to Co-workers
- Ignores safety rules, uses equipment recklessly, and takes unwise risks.
- Bringing cocaine into workplace increases risk that co-workers will begin using the drug.

may obtain confidential information any hour of the day or night by calling the national cocaine hotline: 1-800-COCAINE.

Company officials should be very cautious about accusing employees of drug abuse or addiction or even searching their lockers and personal belongings, for an error in judgment can lead to a costly lawsuit including both the supervisor and the firm. Those in charge of interviewing should be alerted to the telltale signs that may indicate a drug problem. In the case of a suspicious situation, the application form should be carefully checked and searching questions asked about gaps in employment history, frequent job changes, and reasons for leaving former jobs. Previous employers and references should be contacted directly.

Referral

Some companies advise their supervisors not to become involved in a counseling relationship with employees suspected of using drugs. As the law stands, accusing an individual of illegal use of drugs is a cause for libel; and both the supervisor and the employer may be sued. Trying to counsel a drug abuser may cause a supervisor to become involved in the abuser's personal problems and will make it more difficult for the supervisor to reflect accurately the facts in further discussions with the human resources department.

In some companies that have a policy on drug abuse, we find that those who violate the organization code on drugs are immediately dismissed. In other companies, the firm refers to a rehabilitation agency or an employee assistance program those employees who have problems with drugs. These firms do not dismiss the workers unless rehabilitation efforts fail.

Mental and Emotional Illnesses

The absence of job satisfaction appears to be related to a variety of mental and emotional problems, such as psychosomatic illnesses,[6] low self-esteem, anxiety, worry, tension, and impaired interpersonal relations. Factors in the work environment that correlate with these mental health problems are:

1. Low status.
2. Little autonomy.
3. Rapid technological change.
4. Isolation on the job.
5. Responsibility for managing people.
6. Second- and third-shift work.
7. Threats to self-esteem inherent in the appraisal system.

Workers with personality disorders (including alcoholism and drug abuse) may find that their mental health problems stem partially

from stress, job insecurity, unpleasant working conditions, and hazardous work.

Generally most companies have policies for dealing with mental and emotional illnesses among their office workers. Firms rely primarily upon employee magazines, reading rack material, and films that describe the various kinds of mental illnesses and identify the sources of help available to troubled workers. In detecting employees with mental health problems, most firms place great emphasis upon observations made by the first-line supervisors, who focus their attention on the workers' job performance and changes in behavioral patterns, such as their mood swings or increased absenteeism. Because of their pivotal role in identifying workers who may have mental problems, supervisors should be provided with information that will help them recognize mental illness and be able to refer workers to an employee assistance program, a nurse-counselor, psychiatrist, psychologist, family doctor, or medical facility. Generally the office supervisor may find the names of reputable clinics in the yellow pages of the telephone directory under a heading such as "Mental Health Services."

AIDS in the Workplace

AIDS, the acronym for *Acquired Immune Deficiency Syndrome*, is caused by the Human Immunodeficiency Virus (HIV) that attacks primarily the body's immune system. The virus is transmitted by intimate sexual contact; by infected blood entering the bloodstream through the use of contaminated hypodermic needles; or in the case of a newborn baby, either while it is developing in the uterus or during birth when the mother is infected with the virus. As the immune system becomes weaker, the body becomes more vulnerable to infections and cancers. As AIDS progresses, a person becomes overwhelmed by diseases and eventually dies.

---

[6]**Psychomatic illnesses** are ailments evidenced by bodily symptoms or bodily and mental symptoms as a result of a mental conflict. One of the most common psychosomatic illnesses is the stomach ulcer, which can occur in an employee who is unable to cope with prolonged mental stress.

AIDS-based discrimination exists in the workplace, despite all the educational efforts undertaken by governmental agencies, private businesses, the media, and gay and lesbian groups to inform the public that employees with AIDS do *not* pose a risk of transmission of the virus through ordinary workplace contacts. Then, too, the federal and state courts have ruled that AIDS is a handicap and employees with AIDS are entitled to protection against discrimination. This ruling means that the treatment of employees with AIDS should be the same as that for others with any life-threatening, catastrophic, or terminal illness. Thus, an employee with AIDS should be eligible for the same work privileges and medical benefits as a worker suffering from lung cancer.

Most companies have no formal policy for dealing with AIDS. Thus, AOMs, with the support of top management, need to face the issue and develop guidelines for supervisors to ensure that consistent treatment is provided for all employees with AIDS. These guidelines should cover topics such as:

1. The need to respect the confidentiality of infected workers who wish to remain on the job as long as they are able.
2. How to allay the fears and anxieties of employees who believe that the disease can be transmitted by casual social or professional contact.
3. How to prepare employees for working with co-workers who have contracted the HIV virus as well as those with AIDS.
4. The need for an ongoing education program by means of brochures, pamphlets, newsletters, meetings, etc., to convey current information and keep up-to-date on how AIDS is and is not spread.[7]

5. Services provided by the company's employee assistance program (EAP)—professional counseling and support for employees with AIDS, for those being tested for AIDS, and for those groups subject to high risk of HIV infection.
6. Cost-containment measures, such as case management, to deal with AIDS-related medical care. As noted in Chapter 11, case management involves the close monitoring and evaluation of a patient's care to make sure it is as efficient as possible.

Stress

Stress is the physical, chemical, or emotional state we experience at the time of a crisis or when we are subject to irritations and unpleasant situations. Stress brings about bodily or mental tensions and may contribute to serious health problems, such as heart and stomach diseases. Stress has been identified as a major contributor to strokes, cancer, accidents, and suicide. Also, stress aggravates diabetes, multiple sclerosis, and a host of other disorders.

Stress is part of every office worker's life. Some stress may be positive and pleasurable, for it stimulates us to feel more alert, think more clearly and objectively, and function better socially. However, excessive stress becomes *distress*, which robs us of our health and the company of its productivity.

Figure 12–3 lists some of the symptoms of stress identified by office workers and the sources of stress on the job and in the home. Although not all sources of stress can be removed entirely or even reduced, we can learn how to manage stress better.

Some approaches that organizations use to minimize stress include:

1. *Employee fitness or "wellness" programs.* As described in Chapter 11, these programs provide an array of services designed to help employees maintain their mental and physical health and to

---

[7]An excellent directory of organizations, education programs, consultants, and articles focusing on AIDS in the workplace is contained in "The Workplace & AIDS: A Guide to Services and Information," Parts I, II, and January 1989 update, *Personnel Journal* (October, 1987, February, 1988, and January, 1989).

Figure 12-3
Stress—Its
Symptoms
and Sources

SYMPTOMS OF STRESS

Physical symptoms

- Back pains
- Churning stomach
- Exhaustion
- Headaches
- Heavy pounding of the heart
- Hyperactivity
- Inability to sleep
- Nervous tics
- Overeating
- Peptic ulcers
- Skin disorders
- Tight muscles
- Weak or dizzy spells

Behavioral and psychological symptoms

- Accidents on the job
- Alcohol and drug abuse
- Being overly emotional
- Depression
- Excessive smoking
- Feelings of great anxiety
- Inability to concentrate
- Job insecurity
- Loss of control over what appear to be overwhelming problems
- Psychological or physical withdrawal from work environment
- Sexual dysfunction

SOURCES OF STRESS

On the job

- Absence of job description
- Demands of the job
- Emotional needs (caring, love, trust, empathy) not being met
- Fear of, and resistance to, change, especially overnight technological change that may cause displacement
- Having to meet tight deadlines
- Lack of feedback for work well done
- No clear line of command
- Responsibility without authority
- Unpleasant ergonomic conditions such as noise, smoke pollution, crowding, no windows and no natural light
- Worry about forgetting things such as dates, meetings, and names
- Fear of, or distrust of, supervisor and peers

In the home

- Difficulties with children (truancy, drugs, alcohol) and in-laws
- Differences with mate (sex, money)
- Dissatisfaction about role responsibilities

stay well. Some of the services include testing the employee's physical fitness and designing a tailor-made health-management program and providing facilities for jogging, swimming, relaxing in a sauna, and exercising.

2. *Stress-management programs.* Conducted either by in-house personnel or by an outside service, stress-management programs include seminars and clinics where office workers learn relaxation techniques such as meditation and yoga. The programs also offer discussion sessions that focus on physical fitness, hypertension control, healthy dietary habits, and control over alcohol and drug abuse.

3. *Employee assistance programs.* As we have seen earlier, EAPs provide specially trained counselors who work with

employees in alleviating their symptoms of stress and minimizing their frustrations. Employees are aided in planning three-day weekends, vacations, or sabbaticals for rest, rejuvenation, and mental growth and development.

4. *Health incentives.* Some companies offer incentives such as salary increases and "well leave" for employees who do not use their sick leave.

Burnout

Burnout is the total depletion of our physical and mental resources caused by excessive striving to reach unrealistic job-related goals. Burnout affects us at all ages and at all stages of our careers, regardless of our position within the organization. Generally, however, those most affected by burnout are workers with high energy, lofty ideals, and unrealistic expectations.

The symptoms of burnout are similar to those of stress, as listed in Figure 12–3. However, office workers who undergo stress do not necessarily experience burnout. Commonly reported symptoms of burnout include chronic fatigue; emotional exhaustion; job boredom; a negative, cynical attitude toward one's work; unfulfilled need for recognition; moodiness; poor concentration; forgetfulness; and physical ailments such as stomach disorders and backaches. Office employees find that on-the-job stress leads to burnout when they are placed under too many pressures to perform, when they become overly anxious about work problems, or when they seek unattainable goals. Stress in the home, such as family or personal problems, tends to increase the severity of job-related stress and adds fuel to the burnout process.

Figure 12–4 depicts several aspects of office life, each followed by a series of questions, that AOMs should examine with the objective of reducing the risks of burnout among office workers. When AOMs can answer most or all of the questions affirma-

tively, they are assured that their organizations are following an enlightened approach in dealing with burnout. However, even with the best efforts made by organizations to minimize the risks of burnout, the solution to the problem rests with each of us as individual workers. Ultimately, we must (1) remove the cause of the stress, (2) remove ourselves from the stress situation, or (3) manage the situation so that we can take charge of our lives.

Smoking

The problem of employees smoking in the office and its effect upon productivity must receive the attention of the AOM because smoking affects the health, morale, efficiency, and productivity of those being supervised. In addition, sizable costs are associated with smoking in the workplace—excess medical care costs, increased insurance costs, material and labor losses, and reduced productivity and morale. Today many organizations have an official policy regarding smoking in the work area. For example, the 1989 AMS Smoking Policies Survey revealed that of the companies polled, 60 percent have an official policy regarding the rights of smokers and nonsmokers; and, the number of these respondent companies that prohibit smoking in *all* areas of the company rose considerably to 42 percent from the previous year's 25 percent.[8]

Office workers and supervisors who argue against smoking in the office say that smoking is unhealthy and it pollutes the air. Further, it poses an unnecessary health risk to nonsmokers, whose eyes and throats become irritated and whose hearts and lungs may be endangered. Others look upon smoking in the office as an unbusinesslike practice that makes a poor impression on the

---

[8]Jeff Long, "Trend Toward Restricting Smoking Slows," *Management World* (January/February, 1989), p. 42.

Figure 12-4
Checklist for Determining the Extent of Burnout Among Office Employees

---

MEASURING OFFICE EMPLOYEE BURNOUT

Evaluate the steps that have been taken by your organization to minimize the risk of burnout among office employees by answering the following questions. Total the number of your "Yes" answers and see the rating scale below for an interpretation of your score.

	Yes	No
Working Conditions		
1. Can office workers do their jobs without excessive red tape and overly rigid regulations that get in the way?		
2. Is stress limited by avoiding states of emergency in which workers are constantly working under deadlines and always trying to catch up?		
3. Is the ergonomic environment free of negative working conditions such as a high noise level, overcrowding, an uncomfortable temperature, and drab colors?		
4. Are training programs available where office workers have the opportunity to upgrade their skills?		
5. Is there an employee fitness program aimed at encouraging employees to exercise regularly and become more concerned about their health?		
6. Do groups of employees working together have team spirit so that they can offer support and recognition to each other?		
Treatment of Workers		
7. Are outlets provided for workers to express their feelings and voice their complaints, concerns, and frustrations?		
8. Is there an employee assistance program that helps workers at all levels to cope with their lives on the job and at home? If so, are the burnout victims forced to acknowledge that coping strategies must be developed or the burnout is unlikely to subside?		
9. Are employees provided work breaks so that they can refresh themselves or take short walks away from the office?		
10. Can employees sit down to a quiet luncheon?		
11. Are employees obligated to take their earned vacations away from the office?		
Creativity and Rewards		
12. Are employees aware of the significance of their accomplishments and the linkage between their jobs and the company's end product or service?		
13. Are feedback mechanisms and open communication lines available at all levels so that employees know that their ideas and suggestions for improvement will be properly transmitted and acted upon?		
14. Are office workers receiving equitable salaries under the firm's compensation plan?		
15. Beyond dollar rewards, are employees' creative contributions recognized so that their self-image will be improved and their job satisfaction increased?		

RATING SCALE

No. of Yes Answers	Where Does My Company Stand?
12-15	Your company is operating "on all burners" by effectively minimizing the risks of burnout.
8-11	Your company needs to take steps to improve its working conditions and treatment of workers and recognize the employees' creative efforts in order to reduce the risks of further burnout. In other words, your company needs to "stoke the furnace."
1-7	Your company is doing little to minimize the risks of burnout. If no steps are taken to improve the situation, it's going to be a long, cold winter in your office!

public. Also, some believe that office workers who smoke are impairing their own efficiency. Others point out that the non-smokers' right to breathe clean air, free from harmful and irritating tobacco smoke, has become recognized by a number of actions. For example, federal regulatory agencies prohibit smoking on domestic air flights and restrict smoking on trains and buses; and most states and several hundred cities have imposed smoking restrictions in public places and in the workplace.

In view of the reports of the relationship of both active and passive smoking to health hazards, companies attempt to resolve the conflict between the rights of smokers and nonsmokers by:

1. Encouraging employees to stop or reduce their smoking by means of films, posters, literature, and financial incentives (bonuses, pay raises, time off, and gift certificates).
2. Restricting employee smoking to non-work areas, such as lunchrooms and employees' lounges.
3. Permitting a moderate amount of smoking by present employees who feel they cannot quit, but imposing a no-smoking rule for all new employees. In the AMS survey cited above, it was found that 6 percent of the firms polled would not hire smokers.[9]
4. Establishing no-smoking sections in company cafeterias and employee lounges and posting "No Smoking" signs at the office workers' desks.
5. Relocating a nonsmoker from an area where smoking is permitted to a smoke-free environment.
6. Sponsoring a "Kick the Habit" program.
7. Improving the ventilation system and installing electronic air cleaners.

Sexual Harassment

Studies show that at least 50 percent of working women and as many as 15 percent of working men have experienced sexual harassment on the job.[10] Guidelines issued by the Equal Employment Opportunity Commission (EEOC) define **sexual harassment** as "unwelcome sexual advances, requests for sexual favors, and other verbal or physical conduct of a sexual nature," where such conduct affects an individual's prospects for employment or advancement or unreasonably interferes with work performance.

The EEOC guidelines state that harassment on the basis of sex is a violation of Title VII of the Civil Rights Act and that the employer has a duty to prevent and eliminate sexual harassment. A federal appeals court has ruled that a company is liable for the behavior of its *employees* whether or not management is aware that sexual harassment has taken place. The guidelines also have ruled that a company is responsible for the actions of nonemployees on the company's premises, such as when a visiting sales representative harasses the firm's receptionist.

Traditionally the only legal recourse available to a harassed employee was through civil action against the offending employee. Today, however, all complaints are investigated by the EEOC. If sexual harassment is found, the commission can ask that the victim be given a back-pay award, promotion, reinstatement, or other remedies under the Civil Rights Act. If the conciliation process fails, the commission may sue the employer. Therefore, the AOM and all office supervisors must take steps to protect their employees, themselves, and the firm from lawsuits and their costly consequences.

Lawsuits associated with sexual harassment usually involve problems of personal

---

[9]Milo Geyelin, "The Job Is Yours—Unless You Smoke," *The Wall Street Journal* (April 21, 1989), p. B1.

[10]Diane Feldman, "Sexual Harassment: Policies and Prevention," *Personnel* (September, 1987), p. 17.

friction, turnover, disruption, and adverse publicity, all of which affect the firm's productivity. Thus, the firm should establish a clearly written policy that prohibits sexual harassment. A sample policy statement is:

> All employees are to be treated with respect, courtesy, and tact. Conduct that is personally offensive to others will not be tolerated. Abusing the dignity of anyone through ethnic, sexist, or racial slurs or other derogatory or objectionable conduct is cause for disciplinary action. Included in this area of offensive employee behavior are suggestive remarks, physical advances, or intimidations, sexual or otherwise. If you are the object of such conduct, it should be reported to your department supervisor immediately.[11]

The policy must be communicated to all supervisors and employees; and a grievance procedure must be established, or the existing one expanded, to ensure a fair investigation of any complaints.

Office Romances

Romantic relationships sometimes develop in business offices since people are placed in sufficiently close proximity to one another and thus their interactions encourage a relationship. The resulting office romance may pose problems for the AOM and the office supervisor since questions may arise about the interrelationship of the couple during working hours and its effect upon their job performance. In some instances, the couple's actions may result in lower morale and decreased productivity among the office staff; sometimes even jealousy may be exhibited among other workers.

The policies and practices that affect socializing and the development of office romances vary greatly among firms. In some firms, romantic relationships are anticipated and are tolerated until they disrupt work. In other companies, husbands and wives may be barred from working together. Usually, however, there is no policy that prohibits the working together of a couple less formally paired. Other firms discourage socializing by means of explicit rules. In some organizations, there is no objection to the employment of relatives who work together; but there would be adverse reaction to a couple who work closely together, especially when they are in top-management positions.

Nepotism

Nepotism is the showing of favoritism in the employment of relatives. Firms that practice nepotism believe that the employment of relatives, compared with nonrelatives, gives them employees who are more loyal and dependable. At the top-management level, especially in a close, family-held corporation, the employment of a relative may assure continuity of the business and its corporate policies. The relative placed in a junior executive position need not be concerned with "making points with the boss" and can thus concentrate on developing his or her potentialities to the utmost. Some employers feel that relatives working in the same office share a strong sense of responsibility in their work, take more interest in the company operations, and are likely to "fit in" better— all contributing to an improved level of morale.

In other companies, the practice of nepotism brings about problems. Often the hiring of relatives creates jealousy and resentment among the employees. Employees ask themselves, "What's the use of trying?" and as a result the level of morale sinks. The hiring of relatives may also tend to discourage outsiders from seeking employment in a family-held company. Then, too, some firms have found that if relatives are employed and later prove to be unqualified for the job, they

---

[11]*Sexual Harassment, On the Job Sexual Harassment: What the Union Can Do* (Washington: American Federation of State, County and Municipal Employees, 1980), p. 29.

cannot be discharged or demoted as readily as nonrelatives.

Much variation exists in company policy and practice with regard to the employment of married couples. In some offices, the employment of husband and wife makes for a close-knit, harmonious working group; and the recruitment of couples is encouraged. These firms find that they obtain couples with top-level performance because the husband and wife team tend to reinforce each other, share common interests, and understand each other's work problems.

In other offices, the employment of a married couple may bring about marked personality conflicts, especially when both the husband and wife work in the same department or are in a direct supervisory–subordinate relationship. In these firms, the office supervisors cite potential morale problems (jealousy; forced competition; absenteeism; difficulties in scheduling for holidays, vacations, and deaths in the family; and conflicts of interest) in that the couples may not be able to separate their personal and professional lives.

Some companies do not hire married couples. Other companies will employ them but only in separate offices or departments. In still other firms, husbands and wives may remain on the payroll only if they married after meeting on the job. One restriction that appears fairly widespread prohibits one spouse from having supervisory responsibility over another, a rule that often prevents promotion. Then there are some employers who will hire a couple that lives together but will make one of them quit or transfer to another department if the couple marries.

In connection with the employment of relatives and married women, the provisions of the Civil Rights Act must be kept in mind. The EEOC has ruled that it is legal for a company to have a policy against hiring a person whose husband or wife already is on the company's payroll. However, this rule must apply to male and female workers alike.

It is illegal for a company to have a policy against hiring married women unless the same rule is applied to the employment of married men. Also, to discharge women when they get married is illegal unless there is a similar rule for male workers.

Sexual Orientation

Wisconsin, Massachusetts, the District of Columbia, and several cities have enacted statutes, executive orders, and ordinances banning discrimination based on **sexual orientation**—a person's preference in sex or affectional partners. For example, the New York City Human Rights Law defines sexual orientation to mean heterosexuality, homosexuality, or bisexuality. A *heterosexual* is a person who is sexually oriented toward a member of the opposite sex; a *homosexual* is a male or a female who has a sexual desire toward a member of that person's own sex; and a *bisexual* is a person who is sexually oriented toward both sexes.

Millions of homosexuals are employed in public and private business offices, although it is probable that most of their superiors and co-workers are unaware of their sexual preferences. Like heterosexuals, not all homosexuals conduct themselves in a businesslike manner. However, the majority of homosexuals take their work ethics seriously and perform their jobs efficiently. Unlike heterosexuals, however, most homosexuals work daily with the fear of losing their jobs if their sexual orientation is discovered.

Homosexuals increasingly demand a right to work and to live in society without fear, scorn, or humiliation. As a result, a body of case law is developing as homosexuals turn to the courts in an attempt to secure what they consider their constitutional rights.[12] At

---

[12]Phillip J. Decker, "Homosexuality and Employment: A Case Law Review," *Personnel Journal* (September, 1980), p. 756; see also Sabrina M. Wrenn, "Gay Rights and Workplace Discrimination," *Personnel Journal* (October, 1988), pp. 91–100.

the federal government level, homosexuals have gained the right to fair and equal employment in the U.S. Office of Personnel and Management (formerly the Civil Service Commission) as long as their homosexuality does not directly interfere with the jobs assigned them. In the District of Columbia, sexual orientation is one of the several bases upon which it is unlawful for any person to practice discrimination in employment. At the state level, most of the progress made by homosexuals has been through the court system in the area of school system discrimination, where there has been an increased use of the judicial test of establishing a direct link between conduct and job performance.

Although you will find few court cases and little legislation affecting homosexual employment in private industry, in the past the rulings applicable to government employment practices have had long-term impact on the private sector. Therefore, it is important for today's AOM and office supervisor to study the trends of homosexual employment in the public sector; for these trends may be tomorrow's law.

Moonlighting

Moonlighting refers to our holding a second job or working at a second profession after our regular "daylight" job has ended. Generally, like many people, we may hold two jobs in order to maintain a desired standard of living, to pay off debts, or to gain experience for entry into another career field. However, many persons in high-income brackets moonlight not for the dollars involved but because they enjoy the second job, which offers them satisfactions not met by their daylight (regular) job. Some OMs feel that moonlighting decreases the quality of an office employee's work during the day, depletes the worker's energy, and accounts for less attention being paid to detailed work. Other OMs view moonlighting as evidence of a worker's initiative and desire to succeed

and as a safety valve for tensions that have built up during the day on a boring, tedious job.

Moonlighting becomes a problem for the OM when the office workers are frequently tardy or absent, sustain accidents on the job as a result of fatigue, become more argumentative and difficult in their work relationships, or are more easily distracted from their work assignments. Taken together, these costly after-effects of moonlighting exert a major impact on office productivity.

Some companies attempt to deal with moonlighting and its potential problems by banning the practice entirely, which is perhaps as effective as trying to outlaw the grapevine. Such a policy causes the office worker–moonlighter to engage in secretive activities, especially when the firm makes no effort to curtail the moonlighting activities of its supervisors and managers.

Workaholics

Unlike office workers who moonlight usually in order to supplement their earnings, **workaholics** are *emotionally* dependent on their work. Work is their drug; they are addicted to it and cannot stop working. Some moonlighters, struggling to make ends meet, run the risk of becoming workaholics, especially if their added work hours reinforce a work-centered life-style.

There is little agreement about whether workaholism is a disease or merely a useful label for classifying a behavior pattern and life-style. We find research studies that show some workaholics simply prefer labor to leisure. Other psychological reports indicate that workaholics are emotionally disturbed— the product of unresolved conflict, feelings of inadequacy, or defective upbringing. For example, long hours at the office may indicate a family conflict or other crisis.

Office workaholics are easily recognized. They are found working anytime, anywhere, nights, weekends, and holidays. They report in for work long before anyone else and leave the office long after they have become an obstacle to the night cleaning crew. They eat their lunches at their desks between telephone calls and constantly make efforts to "catch up." However, as far as their co-workers can determine, they have never fallen behind.

When there are no tasks to be completed by workaholics, withdrawal symptoms set in. Workaholics tend to become intensely anxious and deeply depressed and may even develop psychosomatic illnesses. Without fully regimented production schedules, the workaholics are out of their natural environment.

In the office, the most frequent problems are not for the workaholics but for those around them. Workaholics tend to create competitive, uncomfortable environments. The perfectionist standards set by workaholics can evoke resentment, which leads to interpersonal conflict or morale problems. For example, the workaholic office supervisor may set unrealistic standards that create more problems than they solve. As often happens, in such situations people find that they cannot work for the supervisor and thus they quit. Workaholics are often stereotyped as loners, desolate, friendless, cranky, and pressured.[13] However, this stereotype does not apply to all workaholics; many may simply be having fun, and for them there is no difference between work and leisure.

The OM should attempt to curb any problems that workaholics may be creating in the office. One approach is to help workaholics recognize their problem by concentrating upon the accomplishment of goals—quantitative and qualitative—during employee appraisals or confidential meetings. The workaholics should be shown how their efforts and styles have created specific problems. For example, the workaholic

office supervisor should be shown that because of his or her ineffectiveness in group situations, many talented subordinates have left the firm. Since the supervisor may respond by commenting about all the hours he or she spends on the job, the OM should concentrate upon the ends to be achieved, not the means.

The key to improving the productivity and performance of office workaholics is to help them gain a balanced perspective on their work and their lives. This requires professional counseling, during which time the workaholics should come to appreciate the benefits of rest and recreation. Office workaholics will probably never change—even if they desire to do so—unless professional guidance is sought. However, most office workers are not addicted to their work; and they probably will never become workaholics even though the risk is there.

Employee Theft

Office employees steal millions of dollars each year by taking advantage of their companies' indifference to the pens, pencils, stationery, staplers, blank diskettes and audio tapes, and typewriter ribbons that find their way into employees' homes and into the classrooms of the employees' children. Control over theft and fraud is a problem in human relations, ethics, and value systems, as discussed in Chapter 7; and the attitude and policies of management contribute to the problem. If managers and supervisors are indifferent toward the rules that have been established and if the atmosphere is one of "Who cares?" the office can become a school for dishonesty.

Some theories advanced by sociologists and psychologists show that how workers perceive their company is related to whether or not they will steal. Thus, if employees believe that their company is exploiting them in their daily relationships, the employees will tend to steal more. Such workers are

---

[13]"When You Love Your Work Too Much," *Changing Times* (November, 1980), p. 68.

searching for an equitable return for the contributions they feel they are making. Sometimes employees who are overlooked or slighted may become frustrated and try to work out a balance between how they behave on the job and what benefits they receive. Often the workers will attempt to remedy the supposed inequity by slowing down their rate of output by not working up to their capacity, wasting time in idle talk, and taking prolonged work breaks—all of which are forms of "stealing."

Some guidelines that the AOM should follow in reducing employee dishonesty follow:

1. *Assign department heads responsibility for developing and enforcing a program of control over the purchase and issuance of supplies.* In such a program of internal control, the person who orders the supplies should not be in charge of their receipt nor issue checks to pay for them. Collusion between dishonest purchasers and suppliers is a frequent cause of large losses. The supplies needed by each department should be estimated and planned for in preparing the budget for each department. Budgeting a dollar estimate, as explained in a later chapter, impresses upon workers the cost of the supplies and creates greater respect for usage. Supplies should be ordered in bulk only a few times during the year in order to reduce the number of orders and the opportunities for employees to "pad" the orders.

2. *Screen all job applicants by investigating their character references and any gaps in their employment history.* Applicants for positions of trust, such as those handling stocks and bonds, and those who are promoted to such positions should be covered by a fidelity bond. A **fidelity bond** is a guarantee by the insurer that the insured firm will be compensated, up to an agreed-upon amount and subject to

agreement on the terms and conditions, for the loss of money or other property resulting from the dishonest acts of the firm's employees.

3. *Require all terminated employees to report to an executive outside the former employee's department.* Thus, the AOM makes sure that the employee's name is removed from the payroll. Otherwise, an unscrupulous person might continue to issue checks in the name of the former employee and cash them with a forged signature.

4. *Set realistic performance standards.* If the standards are not realistic and employees cannot achieve the goals or quotas, they are faced with two alternatives—to fail or to be dishonest. Periodic unannounced spot checks or audits should be taken upon employee performance at all levels in the office. Employees should be informed that such audits are a normal part of internal control. All critical areas of office operations—cash handling, disbursements, and safeguarding of important records—should be inspected and reviewed periodically.

5. *Enforce policies fairly, firmly, and uniformly at all levels.* Double standards of enforcement by the AOM will break down discipline and morale quickly and lessen the employees' respect for the firm, its managers, and its policies and procedures.

JOB ATTENDANCE AND WORK SCHEDULES

In this section, we shall first investigate several problems and practices that pertain to job attendance. Chronic tardiness, absenteeism, and turnover are serious and costly problems for the AOM, particularly during prosperous economic times when many office jobs are available. Next, we shall see how many organizations have modified their work schedules in order to reduce the costs of absenteeism and turnover, raise employee morale, and improve productivity.

Tardiness

The problem of tardiness, which is really a form of absenteeism, is usually handled by a written or an oral reprimand. The reprimand may be followed by payroll deductions, temporary layoff, and termination if the worker is habitually late.

Tardiness in the office is traceable more often to laxness in discipline than to any other cause. Of course, supervisors themselves must set the proper tone by arriving promptly for work. The practice of many companies in not tolerating tardiness except under emergency conditions, such as public transportation delays, car trouble, and driving conditions, proves that it can be controlled. Further, the use of flexible work schedules, discussed later in this section, minimizes the problem of tardiness.

Absenteeism

The absence of employees affects seriously the work of others in most offices unless there are "floating" replacements. In a large company, the human resources department may keep an inventory in its computerized information system of all its employees' capabilities for performing other jobs; thus, employees can readily be transferred to take over the jobs of the absentees. But regardless of the firm's size, the problem is one of management and must be studied carefully. The AOM should analyze the problem of absenteeism by finding out:

1. The extent of absenteeism.
2. The causes of absenteeism.
3. The cost of absenteeism.
4. The action to be taken to control absenteeism.

Extent of Absenteeism

To measure the **absenteeism rate** in an office or a department, the following formula, suggested by the U.S. Department of Labor, may be used:

Absenteeism Rate (%) =

$$\frac{\text{Worker-days lost during period}}{\text{Average number} \atop \text{of workers} \times {\text{Number of work-} \atop \text{days in period}}} \times 100$$

For example, assume that in a bank's computer center an average of 25 workers is employed during a month having 22 workdays. Because of absenteeism, 15 worker-days have been lost. We can calculate the absenteeism rate for that month as follows:

$$\frac{15}{25 \times 22} \times 100 = \frac{15}{550} \times 100 =$$

2.73% rate of absenteeism

After we have calculated the absenteeism rate for each unit, we can compare the extent of absenteeism in the entire firm or among different offices or departments. We can also compare the rate with that of other companies of similar size, in the same industry, and in the same geographic area.[14] The absenteeism rate of 2.73 percent just calculated means that for about every 37 workers in the bank (1.00 ÷ .0273), the firm is carrying one extra employee to take care of the average absence. Assuming an hourly salary rate of $8 and taking employee benefits into consideration, the one extra worker may be costing the bank about $23,000 each year ($8 × 40 hours × 52 weeks = $16,640) + (37 percent × $16,640 = $6,157 for employee benefits).

Data on absenteeism are readily available when the information is stored in a human

---

[14]Comparative data on absenteeism are available in the *Monthly Labor Review*, published by the Bureau of Labor Statistics, and from private sources such as The Bureau of National Affairs, Prentice-Hall, and Commerce Clearing House.

resources database. When workers have been absent from their jobs for a full day or longer, they should be required to report to the OM, their supervisor, or the human relations office before returning to work. Thus, a record can be kept of the workers' absences and the reasons for the lost time. The absenteeism records should become part of the employees' files so the information may be considered at the time of employee appraisal and when opportunities for promotion and salary increases arise.

The individual absenteeism records can be combined and used to calculate an absenteeism rate. Or a report may be prepared for the entire company or for each department that shows the total days' absence during the year, a classification of the reasons for absences, and the frequency of times absent by each employee. Determining the frequency of times absent for each worker aids in locating and controlling chronic absentees, especially those who exhibit a pattern of being ill on Fridays or Mondays.

Causes of Absenteeism

Illness (defined to include alcoholism and drug abuse) and work-related accidents are the most common causes of absenteeism. Some employees seem to avoid working on the slightest pretext of illness; however, others work when they are so ill that they should stay at home.

A company's sick-leave policy may not necessarily invite absenteeism, but it often seems to condone absences. For example, we find that some firms provide full pay for those ill 5 days or less; other companies may provide full pay for an illness lasting 6 to 10 days. If a company encourages absenteeism by neglecting to control it and if employees feel that management is not concerned, they will not make it a priority to show up for work each day. Instead, they may use their sick leave as vacation days to

balance out what they perceive as an unfair working situation. Many employees see the sick days as days "coming to them" for putting up with low pay, poor working conditions, or a disagreeable boss.

Absenteeism rates vary with the ages of the workers. Generally workers under 30 make up a relatively high proportion of chronic absentees. Often their causes for absenteeism are not illnesses, but instead, are low morale and a reluctance to accept the workplace discipline. Among employees in the age range of 30 to 55, the absenteeism rate declines. After age 55, however, the rate tends to increase because of health reasons.

The rate of absenteeism is highest among workers who have relatively monotonous, routine jobs. Office workers who find their jobs unchallenging or oppressive, and who derive most of their satisfaction from outside pursuits, have little incentive to maintain a good attendance record.

Newly hired employees are often found among the most chronic absentees. This points to the need for careful selection of new employees by obtaining information from their former employers about their total *days* absent from the job and the total *incidences* of absence (number of times absent). Generally frequent incidences of absenteeism indicate that leave is being taken for reasons other than illness.

Other causes of absenteeism include family responsibilities, which often account for married women having a greater absenteeism rate than married men since society continues to assign women the traditional responsibility for the home and child care. Another cause of absenteeism is transportation problems, which include commuting a long distance from home to work; reliability of the automobile, van, or bus; and weather conditions.

Cost of Absenteeism

The cost of absenteeism for office employees in a firm can be computed as shown in the following example of a small company having 40 office employees:

```
Total number of sick days paid
    previous 12 months  . . . . . . . . . . . . . 200
    (Based on 40 employees with an
    average of 5 days' absence each.)
Average daily pay multiplied by
    total number of sick days . . . . . . . . ✕ $48
Annual cost of absenteeism to firm . . . . . $9,600
```

The annual cost of absenteeism, $9,600, does not include other costs associated with absenteeism: employee benefits; overtime pay for substitute workers; decrease in employee efficiency; disruption of work flow, leading to missed delivery dates; and costs associated with hiring temporary replacements, all of which could easily double the annual cost.

Controlling Absenteeism

What can we do about the problem of absenteeism? Typically penalties, fines, and incentive bonuses do not produce the desired effects. Penalties and fines, such as payroll deductions for absences the day before or after a holiday, with their demoralizing effects, create hard feelings and job dissatisfaction. Incentive bonuses are usually only temporary in their effect. However, since only a small number of workers are chronic offenders, each of these individual cases should be studied in solving the problem. In the case of chronic absenteeism, many companies enforce the traditional policy of a three-step disciplinary technique: (1) warning, (2) layoff without pay, and finally (3) termination.

Supervisors should be held accountable for the attendance records in their departments. Prior to taking disciplinary action when workers are excessively absent, supervisors should talk over job problems with their workers to discover why the workers are remaining away from their jobs. Such references to the causes of absenteeism may indicate possible solutions to the problem. Every effort should be made to reduce the absences caused by illness and on-the-job accidents. An educational campaign to maintain the health and safety of employees may be undertaken. For example, providing vitamins and free flu shots has been successful in some offices in reducing substantially the absences caused by illness during winter and spring months. Providing satisfactory ergonomic conditions, such as good lighting, comfortable levels of heating and air conditioning, and noise control, may also be effective in reducing absenteeism. Further control over absenteeism may be obtained by modifying the work schedule, as noted later in this section.

Before any policy on absenteeism can be established and chronic absenteeism defined, standards must be set by the firm for the amount of absenteeism that will be tolerated. Recognizing that there are no corporate attendance standards for any employees, The Bureau of National Affairs recommends the following attendance guidelines for any 12-month period:[15]

No. of Absences	Classification
0–2	Excellent
3–4	Good
5–6	Satisfactory
7–8	Poor
9 or more	Unacceptable

Any absenteeism policy should have as its goal the promotion of regular, consistent attendance. The policy should be fair, enforceable, and agreeable to both management and labor. One form of absenteeism policy that meets most of these criteria is called a **no-fault leave policy**, which eliminates the troublesome sick-leave provision and all forms of unlimited leave. Most no-fault leave policies provide a maximum number of days to be absent for any reason,

[15]"Personnel Opinions: How Much Absence Is Acceptable?" *Bulletin to Management* (Washington: The Bureau of National Affairs, Inc., September 21, 1978), p. 1.

such as four to six noncumulative leave days with pay per year. Ordinarily absence due to jury duty, funeral leave, maternity and paternity leave, military leave, educational leave, hospitalization, inclement weather, some kinds of union business, and other company-approved absences are not charged against the no-fault days. Typically most no-fault policies provide for counseling and disciplining those workers who are absent beyond the number of days allowed.

Turnover

Turnover is the amount of movement of employees, voluntarily and involuntarily, in and out of an organization. Most turnover falls in the *controllable* category, which means that the company could have a major influence over whether the employees leave. The remaining turnover is caused by death, accidents, retirement, sickness, military service, or pregnancy. A degree of turnover must be expected and is healthy for the firm. However, it is also costly. For example, when a company loses a computer programmer, the separation costs for the worker and the replacement and training costs for a new employee may be more than $20,000.[16] Since firms may experience turnover rates greater than 20 percent among office workers, excessive turnover exerts a strong influence on the profit picture of the firm.

Turnover Rate

The **turnover rate**, expressed most often in terms of the number of separations from the payroll (quits and dismissals), is computed as follows:

Turnover Rate (%) =

$$\frac{\text{Total number of separations for the time period}}{\text{Average employment for the time period}} \times 100$$

[16]Michael W. Mercer, "Turnover: Reducing the Costs," *Personnel* (December, 1988), p. 38.

Assume that a firm had an average employment throughout the year of 750 and that the number of persons who were terminated totaled 120. We calculate a turnover rate of 16 percent, as shown in the following example.

$$\frac{120}{750} \times 100 = .16 \times 100 = 16\% \text{ turnover rate}$$

In 1988 the annual turnover rate among organizations in the United States and Canada was 15 percent, according to the Administrative Management Society. The turnover rate for companies with under 500 employees averages 18 percent, whereas the average rate for companies employing over 1,000 is 13 percent.[17]

Reasons for Turnover

The reason given most often by office employees for terminating their jobs—46 percent of all terminations—is to take another job. Other reasons for termination are shown in Figure 12–5.

When we analyze the major reason for separation—*to take another job*—we find that the main causes are the desire for better salaries and better jobs, which includes the opportunity for advancement. Thus, in a program of turnover reduction, the AOM must evaluate regularly the salary structure, the employee benefits program, and the promotional opportunities in the firm.

Exit Interviews. At the time of terminating an employee's services, an **exit interview** may be conducted to determine the real reasons for termination. During such interviews, there should be a warm, supportive atmosphere in which the interviewer refrains from criticizing or arguing as the employees give their reasons for leaving. A record of the exit

[17]Jeff Long, "Turnover in the Office Drops," *Management World* (November/December, 1988), pp. 28–29. Each AMS annual *Office Turnover Survey Report* presents average turnover rates, average length of service upon termination, and reasons for termination for exempt and nonexempt employees.

Figure 12–5
Reasons for
Termination

TAKE ANOTHER JOB   46%

LEAVE THE WORK FORCE 14%

DISMISSAL   13%

RELOCATION   12%

RETIREMENT   10%

LAYOFF 5%

Source of Data: AMS 1988 Office Turnover Survey Report, summarized in "Turnover in the Office Drops," *Management World* (November/December, 1988), p. 29.

interview should be made available to interested supervisors and managers so they may be kept informed of the reasons for separation.

Post-Exit Interviews. Some companies make use of **post-exit interviews** in which questionnaires are sent to former employees asking their opinions of the company and their reasons for selecting work elsewhere. The former employees are asked to be frank in their replies; and if they wish, they may omit their signatures on the questionnaires.

Reducing the Cost of Turnover

We can break down the cost of turnover into the following three categories:

1. *Separation costs*—the expenses incurred when an employee leaves the company. Included here are the costs of the exit interview and various administrative and record-keeping activities.

2. *Replacement costs*—the expenses incurred in finding qualified applicants for the job opening. Typical costs are those for advertising the job opening, selection interviews, preemployment testing, and meetings held to determine which applicant to employ.

3. *Training costs*—the expenses incurred to help the new employee learn how to perform the new job. Training costs include the costs for learning materials (booklets, manuals, software, etc.); workshops, seminars, courses; on-the-job training and coaching; and salary and benefits until the new worker can adequately perform the job.

Let us calculate the turnover cost for an individual company. In the following example, we assume a 250-employee firm in which the average turnover cost of each employee is $14,500:

Total number of employees
    separated in past 12 months
    (Based on 250-employee firm
    with 14% turnover rate.)   35

Average cost of employee
    turnover . . . . × $14,500

Annual cost of turnover $507,500

To reduce excessive turnover cost or to control a presently satisfactory turnover rate, the OM should make sure that in the selection process the nature and the responsibilities of the job and the expected results are carefully explained to each job applicant. Job applicants should be presented a realistic picture of the job at the time of the interview. That is, the job should not be "oversold," nor should it be "undersold." Thus, any reservations the applicants may have about the work to be done can be investigated prior to employment. Employees must be carefully matched to the job openings, and opportunities must be provided the workers to achieve what they expected when they were hired. Employee creativity and self-improvement should be encouraged, jobs should be kept as challenging as possible, and opportunities for advancement should be pointed out.

Modified Workweeks and Work Schedules

To aid in reducing the costs of absenteeism and turnover, many organizations have established workweeks of less than the standard 40 hours and with different kinds of work schedules that resemble only slightly the traditional 9-to-5 workday. In many instances, companies find that by adopting a modified workweek and one of the alternative work schedules, they are able to raise the office workers' morale, with a resulting improvement in productivity. Then, too, by modifying their work schedules, companies show they are responsive to the needs of workers who want more time away from the job. Alternative work schedules permit jobs to be shared by two employees, work to be completed in the home, and work to be done by employees on a permanent part-time basis. Each of these different kinds of workweeks and work schedules is described in this section.

Compressed Workweek

A **compressed workweek** is a work schedule in which the usual number of full-time hours are worked in fewer than five days (the regular workweek). For example, the *4/40 workweek* is a fixed workweek schedule that consists of four workdays, each of which is ten hours in duration. When it was introduced, the 4/40 workweek represented a radical departure from previous trends since historically labor unions and other groups have tried to reduce both the number of days worked each week and the number of hours worked each day.

The compressed workweek was first introduced mainly in small and medium-size nonunion firms as a means of improving employee morale by providing more flexible leisure time and enabling workers to schedule such things as dentist appointments outside of work time. It appears as if, following their rapid beginning in the early 1970s, compressed workweeks have peaked out. A major cause of the decreased rate of growth was the introduction from Europe of a different type of workweek—the flexible work schedule—which is discussed in a later section.

Staggered Work Schedule

Under a **staggered work schedule**, groups of workers arrive at their workplace at different times, according to a master plan. Once set, the hours do not change; and all employees work a predetermined number of hours during the workday. The objective of a staggered work schedule, especially in large metropolitan areas, is to persuade business and government offices to switch from the customary 9-to-5 schedule so a more even distribution of commuting times may be obtained. With staggered work schedules, commuter traffic tie-ups are reduced, waiting times for elevators are reduced, and lobby congestion is lessened in large office buildings. Commuting times may be reduced in length, as a result.

Flexible Work Schedule

The **flexible work schedule**, also known as *flextime* and *gliding time*, replaces the fixed times of worker arrival and departure. Instead, the workday is divided into two different types of time: core time and flexible time. *Core time* is the fixed number of hours during which all employees must be present for work. *Flexible time* is the time employees may choose for their arrival and departure times from the office.

Under a typical plan, shown in Figure 12–6, the span (bandwidth) of the total possible workday, which includes flexible time periods and core time, is 12 hours. Each worker elects to come in at any time from 6 to 9 A.M. and leave at any time from 3 to 6 P.M. The only fixed hours (core time) when all workers must be on the job are the peak work-load hours 9 A.M. to 3 P.M. The two requirements of the plan are that all employees be present during core time and that the required number of working hours be accounted for on a daily basis. Beyond this, working hours can be selected to meet the needs and requirements of each firm. The time at which lunch periods and refreshment breaks are taken may vary.

Since the concept of flexible work scheduling made its appearance, there have been many variations of the plan. For example, in some companies flexibility is provided within the working month. Employees must work the number of hours required during the month, but they may work only during core time for several days and make up the required hours during the remainder of the month.

Flexible work scheduling is found most often in insurance, banking, finance, engineering, government, and other service-type establishments rather than in industrial production or retail stores that have set customer hours. Flexible work scheduling does not work well in operations that are continually interdependent, such as the assembly line. Since the beginning of flextime in West Germany, the concept has been adopted by thousands of firms in the United States. Two surveys show that 25 and 31 percent of the responding companies, respectively, use flexible work scheduling.[18]

Flexible work scheduling, in contrast to the fixed 4/40 workweek and the staggered work schedule, permits employees to have a voice in the conditions and processes affecting their work. Thus, workers actively participate in decision making when they decide to work longer hours if there is more work to be done. Flexible working hours also appeal to workers' needs for more responsibility and more autonomy on the job. The main disadvantages cited by firms having flextime include a lack of supervision during working hours, understaffing of personnel at times, unavailability of key people at certain times, difficulty in scheduling meetings

---

[18]"A Look at Alternative Work Schedules," *Training* (March, 1988), p. 74; survey conducted by the Commerce Clearing House and the American Society for Personnel Administration; *also see* Michael Cregar, "Flextime Continues to Edge Upward," *Management World* (July/August, 1988), p. 14; survey conducted by the Administrative Management Society of its Foundation's Committee of 500.

Figure 12-6
Flexible
Times and
Core Times
in a Typical
Flexible
Work
Schedule

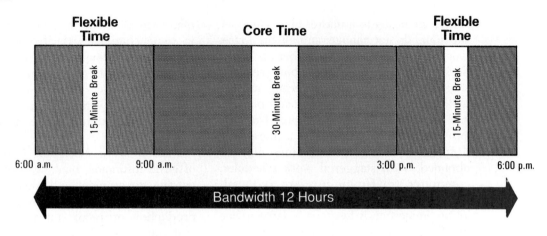

Flexible Time   **Core Time**   **Flexible Time**

15-Minute Break   30-Minute Break   15-Minute Break

6:00 a.m.   9:00 a.m.   3:00 p.m.   6:00 p.m.

Bandwidth 12 Hours

and coordinating projects, and difficulty in planning work schedules and keeping track of hours worked.

Job Sharing

Job sharing is another alternative to the traditional 9-to-5 workday that the AOM may wish to evaluate when scheduling office work and recruiting personnel. In **job sharing**, one permanent, full-time job is shared by two people who generally split their working hours, job responsibilities, and employee benefits. Job sharing appeals especially to working parents with preschool children; to older workers not yet ready to retire; to men and women who want to continue their education; and to full-time employees who want to trade work for more leisure time. Since job sharing involves the whole job with its need for cooperation and commitment, many workers are provided a greater sense of achievement than if they were holding traditional part-time jobs.

Telecommuting

In another application of work scheduling, the AOM schedules work for employees who

work away from the traditional office setting, often in homes where telephone lines link home terminals to a company's central computer. This relatively new application of telecommunications technology to the processing of information at a location other than the office is known as **telecommuting**. One objective of scheduling office work to be completed in the home is to reduce the amount of information processing within the office. Also, in times of chronic shortage of qualified office personnel such as data-entry operators, secretaries, and typists, many qualified workers are available but personal circumstances prevent their working a full schedule in an office away from home.

The advantages to the firm that uses telecommuting include a selection of qualified office personnel from a wide range of applicants, including the physically handicapped; cost savings in reduced office space needed; and the elimination of many employee benefits. Additional cost is incurred, however, for equipment installation, telephone time, and added insurance coverage. Further, the company must ensure data integrity by adopting security measures that permit access to computer files only by authorized telecommuters. For home

Telecommuting provides access to qualified workers who do not wish to hold traditional full-time or part-time jobs.

operators, the major benefit is the freedom of working at their own pace. For example, a home operator may work only part of a day, timing the work to mesh with the firm's rush periods of midmorning and early afternoon.

The major disadvantages for telecommuters are social isolation—the loss of face-to-face contact with co-workers and supervisors, the limitations upon career development and stifling of promotional opportunity, and burnout because of the tendency to overwork at home. Among the problems cited by managers and supervisors are their inability to manage workers from a distance, the difficulties found in interacting with the telecommuters, and the increased supervisory workload due to the additional time required to monitor the telecommuter's work.

Permanent Part-Time Employment

Another alternative work schedule is **permanent part-time employment**, where

regular voluntary employment (not temporary or casual) is carried out during working hours that are shorter than normal. Voluntary part-time employment, which accounts for about 80 percent of all part-time employment, is more common among women than among men; and more young and old workers are found holding part-time jobs than middle-aged workers. The reasons for working less than a full-time schedule include school attendance, family responsibilities, physical handicaps, and a preference for more leisure time.

The occupations in which part-time persons work are mainly routine and low skill, such as service, sales, and clerical workers, and laborers. The higher the job skills and degree of responsibilities, the less likely is a worker to be employed on a part-time basis.

Among the advantages gained by firms using permanent part-time employment are the following: reduced labor costs, with savings in overtime payments and employee benefits; improved job performance and increased productivity; reduced fatigue; and reduced absenteeism. Some of the negative effects that face the AOM when considering the use of permanent part-time workers are increased difficulty in communicating internally, increased difficulty in scheduling work, and increased costs of personnel administration and training.

Alternatives to Layoff

In time of economic recession, a firm may approach the point of laying off indefinitely many of its salaried office employees. One result of such an action is that the laid-off persons will find new, permanent jobs, and thus cripple the firm's plans to expand when the recession has ended. To minimize the economic effects of a recession upon the firm's employees and to preserve the company's work force of qualified employees,

Alternatives to layoffs, such as rotation of layoffs and work sharing, should be investigated by the AOM.

Rotation of Layoffs. Instead of being laid off indefinitely, under a **rotation of layoffs**, office employees may work for four weeks and then be laid off for one week. During the time of layoffs in some states workers can collect unemployment compensation benefits. Rotation of layoffs is not voluntary and offers only a short-term solution to the problems of recession and mounting unemployment. However, the program provides several advantages for employers and employees. Employees are kept on the payroll and thus retain their benefits, which otherwise they might have lost. Unions, generally, cooperate with the firm in its rotation plan since the employed persons continue paying their union dues. For the firm operating under an affirmative action program, the layoff burden is eased since women and minority-group employees do not become the first to lose their jobs. Although the employees take home less than usual pay, most approve of the rotation plan in preference to being laid off permanently.

Most states require a waiting period, such as one week, before laid-off workers may collect their unemployment compensation benefits. As a result, rotation of layoffs becomes less attractive to workers in these states. Therefore, laid-off employees may be aided by their firms, which pay the employees an equivalent compensation during the waiting period and deduct the amount later from their regular paychecks. Another disadvantage lies in a possible increased state unemployment contributions tax for the employer as a result of the increased number of temporary layoffs during the year. Further, problems may be experienced in scheduling the work among those who are rotating their layoffs and in dealing with the

extra paperwork operations in the payroll department.

Work Sharing. Under **work sharing**, a plan of short-time compensation, employees work a shorter week, have their salaries reduced accordingly, and receive partial state unemployment compensation benefits for their lost days' pay. Thus, employees receive partial compensation for their lost wages and retain their jobs and employee benefits. The employers in turn enjoy savings by avoiding the costs of rehiring and retraining.

Ten states have adopted legislation that permits the voluntary use of work sharing as an alternative to layoffs. Available surveys indicate that where these programs have been used, they have generally been well received by both employers and employees. At the same time, the use of short-time compensation has thus far been very limited, especially among larger firms.[19]

UNIONIZATION OF OFFICE WORKERS

As a result of computerized information systems and global company growth, many office workers find that their jobs have become more routine, production-oriented, and depersonalized. In the eyes of many office workers, such jobs have become akin to factory production work. Also, there have been changing patterns of values, attitudes, and expectations among office workers and middle managers, as indicated in Chapter 7. Because of these developments, increased efforts to unionize office workers are predicted, especially among women and minorities.

In this closing section of the chapter, we shall explore the reasons for office personnel

[19]Frank W. Schiff, "Short-Time Compensation: Assessing the Issues," *Monthly Labor Review* (May, 1986), p. 28.

joining unions and the role of the office manager in office unionism.

Why Office Workers Join Unions

Some of the reasons offered by office workers for joining unions are:

1. Dissatisfaction with earnings, promotion opportunities, working conditions, employee benefits, and the relatively weak position of individual workers to influence any changes in these conditions.
2. Job insecurity in that office workers feel there is no guarantee they will not be laid off arbitrarily, especially in periods of recession or when the company is downsizing.
3. Little involvement in implementing new office technology and redesigning job content.
4. Poor handling of grievances by management, which all too often takes a "don't-care" attitude.
5. Importance of employees' work not recognized by the company, which, instead, takes for granted the employees and their work performance.
6. Inadequate channels of communication between employees and management. For example, office employees object to "overnight" conversions to automated office technology without management's informing in advance those persons who will be using the new equipment and procedures.

At the low and middle levels of management, changes in life-styles, value systems, attitudes, and expectations have also produced pro-union sentiment. For many of the same reasons offered above by office workers, some middle managers have expressed their willingness to join a manager's union. Middle managers, too, look for more job security (especially in periods of prolonged recession), higher salaries, and improved employee benefits. Studies have shown that many middle managers favor a change in labor laws that would compel employers to recognize and bargain with manager unions in those organizations where managers have elected to organize.

The Role of the Office Manager in Office Unionism

Many arguments are given both for and against unionism, none of which seems completely unbiased. However, the argument is not a question of being for or against a union for office workers. Rather, as we shall see below, it is a question of what the OM will do about the formation of office workers' unions or attempts to unionize office workers. What the OM does about office unions involves these time-related factors: (1) before union activity starts, (2) while attempts are being made to organize the workers, and (3) after the workers become organized.

Before Union Activity

Long before any union activity might start among a group of office workers, the OM should be listening to employees in order to pinpoint the basic issues that motivate them to seek unionization. For example, by means of attitude surveys, OMs can learn about general areas of employee dissatisfaction and be prepared to answer questions such as the following:

1. Do the working conditions in the office create a desirable level of morale? If not, how can they be improved?
2. How can the work be made more challenging and rewarding by redesigning the jobs?
3. How can the company become more responsive to employee needs for job security in the areas of salaries, promotion opportunities, vacations, suggestion plans,

recreational programs, and other employee benefits?

4. How can the human resources management program and its policies be improved to provide impartial supervision?

Efforts should be made to deal with the office employees' concerns about salaries paid, working conditions, job content, the employee benefits package, and personnel policies in order to compare them with those found in unionized offices. Wherever possible, the salaries paid, working conditions, and employee benefits should be improved so that they equal or surpass those of unionized offices. But these improvements must be properly explained to workers, using the appropriate communication media described in Chapter 5. In one instance, a firm was paying higher salaries than those of unionized companies in the area; but still dissatisfaction with salaries existed among the office employees. This dissatisfaction was due not so much to the company's salary structure as to the employees' lack of reliable information from management about its salary program and exactly how the salaries were determined.

A clear, concise statement of the firm's position regarding unions is needed for the same reasons that other management objectives are stated—to show the firm's commitment to policy and to provide communications to all parties concerned. One such recommended statement of commitment is:

> Our success as a company is founded on the skill and efforts of our employees. Our policy is to deal with employees as effectively as possible, respecting and recognizing each of them as individuals.
>
> In our opinion, unionization would interfere with the individual treatment, respect, and recognition the company offers.
>
> Consequently, we believe a union-free environment is in the employee's best interest, the company's best interest, and the interest of the people served by the corporation.[20]

While Attempts Are Being Made to Organize

If a firm does not provide its office workers with salaries, working conditions, and benefits equal or superior to those offered by unionized offices, it must expect that some dissatisfied workers will seek unionization. Thus, the OM faces the problem of how to deal with a union during an attempt to organize. If the company does not have its own legal staff, the firm should obtain competent legal counsel from outside so the firm will be advised of its statutory rights and obligations and thus avoid possible charges of unfair labor practices. Supplementing such legal help, the OM should be familiar with labor legislation and current labor relations practices.

In many instances when attempts are being made to organize, one or more disgruntled workers contact a union organizer, who is invited to come in to evaluate the situation. Where the opportunity presents itself, the organizer seeks to acquire signed authorization cards from 30 percent of the employees so the union can petition the National Labor Relations Board for an election. The **authorization card** is a formal statement signed by an employee authorizing a named union to represent him or her in collective bargaining. If the union organizer acquires cards from 50 percent plus one of the employees, the union can demand that the employer recognize the union as the bargaining agent and bargain with it. In this case, the National Labor Relations Board certifies the labor organization and the unionization process is complete.

Many employers do not voluntarily accept the signed cards as proof of union interest,

[20]James F. Rand, "Preventive-Maintenance Techniques for Staying Union-Free," *Personnel Journal* (June, 1980), p. 497.

however. Such employers feel they should have an opportunity to tell their side of the story to employees. In this case, the regional office of the National Labor Relations Board sends an investigator to the scene to determine if sufficient interest exists among the workers to form a union. If so, the potential bargaining unit is determined; and an election is called so the employees may vote for or against the union.

Prior to the election, free discussion is encouraged. However, many rules surround an election; and any rule violations constitute unfair labor practices. If over 50 percent of the employees voting choose to join a particular union, the labor organization is certified; and the employer must bargain with the organization in good faith. The employees are next classified by salary and job; and a list of specific proposals covering work-related items such as wages, hours, and benefits is prepared. After the proposals have been approved by the workers, management is presented with the suggested changes. At this stage of the unionization process, a bargaining committee made up of the employee representatives and a business agent from the union meet with management to draw up the contract. After the contract has been approved, union members in each department elect shop stewards to serve as their representatives in dealings with management; and a grievance procedure is established.

Any worker or group can request that another election be held at any time 12 months after the first election. If the employees vote against the labor organization, it is decertified, or eliminated. The employer, however, cannot make such a request or even encourage it.

After the Workers Become Organized

Once the union has been established, management and the employees should work toward achieving the objectives of the firm and those of the union, which will be attained only through harmonious labor relations. New working relationships must be developed between the company and the new union, with a more formal and legal-based system of relationships emerging. As a result, management may find itself much more restricted in future actions and in its decision-making processes.

To create positive union-management relations, management must maintain open lines of communications between all parties involved in the collective bargaining relationship. Also, the company should make sure that the contract is uniformly interpreted and applied by all supervisors and middle managers. Finally, companies should establish rapport and create the best morale-building relationships by working with the union and not against it. At the same time, however, both management and employees must remember that the workers are still employed by the company and that it is the company that hired them, pays them, and expects their support.

SUMMARY 1. Many AOMs and supervisors can easily reach decisions about certain personnel problems and issues that arise in their offices simply by referring to their firm's policy manual or employee handbook.

However, for other kinds of problems that surface (such as those dealing with the sexual and the ethical problems of office employees), or in those firms where policies have not been established nor practices set, the AOM must make a decision that is agreeable to both the office employee and the firm.

2. Today's AOM must learn how to deal head on with many topics that traditionally have been avoided but which are of significance to both sexes at all organizational levels in the firm. This chapter has described a host of office personnel problems, shown how other AOMs have solved such problems, and described the different kinds of policies and practices that may be found in organizations. By acquainting themselves with the information contained in this chapter, AOMs should be able to profit from the successes and mistakes of others.

3. Today's AOMs need to stay abreast of the innovations developing in the modification of traditional time patterns and work schedules and consider alternate work schedules, such as flextime, as a means of meeting the needs of their firms and employees. AOMs—inquisitive, imaginative, and innovative—may wish to consider job sharing, telecommuting, permanent part-time employment, rotation of layoffs, and work sharing as means whereby office employees' fears and insecurities, resulting from recession, downsizing, and unemployment, may be lessened.

4. Faced with a potential increase in unionizing activities among office workers, AOMs must know what part they should play before any union activity surfaces. In the event the workers attempt to organize, AOMs, aided by legal counsel, should have a clear understanding of the fair labor practices in which their firms may engage. If the workers become organized, AOMs must develop new relationships with their company, the workers, and the union and maintain positive, harmonious labor relations in the office.

GLOSSARY **Absenteeism rate**—the extent of unscheduled days absent, calculated as follows:

$$\frac{\text{Worker-days lost during period}}{\text{Average number} \times \text{Number of work-}\atop\text{of workers} \quad \text{days in period}} \times 100$$

Alcoholic—one who is powerless to stop drinking and whose normal living pattern is seriously altered by drinking.

Alcoholism—a progressive disease characterized by excessive, repetitive, and uncontrolled consumption of alcohol.

Authorization card—a formal statement signed by an employee authorizing a named union to represent him or her in collective bargaining.

Burnout—the total depletion of one's physical and mental resources caused by excessive striving to reach unrealistic job-related goals.

Compressed workweek—a work schedule in which the usual number of full-time hours are worked in fewer than five days.

Drug abuser—one who exhibits strong psychological dependence on drugs, often reinforced by physical dependence when certain drugs are used.

Exit interview—an interview conducted at the time of terminating an employee's services to determine the real reasons for termination.

Fidelity bond—the guarantee by an insurer that the insured firm will be compensated, up to an agreed-upon amount and subject to agreement on the terms and conditions, for the loss of money or other property resulting from dishonest acts of the firm's employees.

Flexible work schedule—a work plan under which the workday is divided into *core time* (those hours during which all employees must be at work) and *flexible time* (the time employees may choose for their arrival and departure times); also known as *flextime* and *gliding time*.

Job sharing—a work plan in which one permanent, full-time job is shared by two people who generally split their working hours, job responsibilities, and employee benefits.

Moonlighting—the practice of a person holding a second job or working at a second profession after the regular "daylight" job has ended.

Nepotism—the showing of favoritism in the employment of relatives.

No-fault leave policy—a plan for reducing absenteeism by providing a maximum number of days to be absent for any reason, with provisions for counseling and disciplining workers who are absent beyond the number of days allowed.

Permanent part-time employment—the employment of persons on a regular voluntary basis (not temporary or casual) during working hours shorter than normal.

Post-exit interview—an interview conducted after the terminated employees have left the firm, usually by means of questionnaires sent to the former employees asking their opinions of the company and their reasons for selecting work elsewhere.

Psychosomatic illness—an ailment evidenced by bodily symptoms or bodily and mental symptoms as a result of a mental conflict.

Rotation of layoffs—a program whereby employees may work for four weeks and then be laid off for one week, with the possibility of collecting unemployment compensation benefits.

Sexual harassment—unwelcome sexual advances, requests for sexual favors, and other verbal or physical conduct of a sexual nature, where such conduct affects an individual's prospects for employment or advancement or unreasonably interferes with work performance.

Sexual orientation—a person's preference in sex or affectional partners.

Staggered work schedule—a plan under which groups of workers arrive at their workplace at different times, according to a master plan.

Stress—the physical, chemical, or emotional state experienced by a person at the time of a crisis or when subject to irritations and unpleasant situations.

Telecommuting—the application of telecommunications technology to the processing of information at a location other than the office.

Turnover—the amount of movement of employees, voluntarily and involuntarily, in and out of an organization.

Turnover rate—the extent of movement of employees, voluntarily and involuntarily, in and out of an organization, calculated as follows:

$$\frac{\text{Total number of separations for the time period}}{\text{Average employment for the time period}} \times 100$$

Work sharing—a short-time compensation plan in which employees work a shorter week, have their salaries reduced accordingly, and receive partial state unemployment compensation benefits for their lost days' pay.

Workaholic—one who is emotionally dependent upon work.

FOR YOUR REVIEW

1. Describe the three-step program, advocated by the National Council on Alcoholism, that a company should consider in setting up a rehabilitation program for office alcoholics.

2. Why is it generally more difficult for the office supervisor to develop an effective program in handling the drug abuser than the alcoholic?

3. What practice is usually followed in most firms when working with mentally disturbed office employees?

4. What guidelines should be foremost in the mind of an office supervisor who is confronted by AIDS in the workplace?

5. What approaches may be used by the organization that is trying to minimize stress among its office employees?

6. What aspects of office life are of most concern to administrative office managers when evaluating their companies' programs for reducing burnout among office workers?

7. Describe some of the practices followed by companies in an attempt to respect the rights of smokers and nonsmokers in the office.

8. In a company that has a policy statement dealing with sexual harassment on the job, what responsibilities might typically be assigned the office supervisor?

9. a. What kinds of problems may arise for the office supervisor when an office romance develops between co-workers?
   b. Describe the kinds of policy statements that are often found in companies with regard to office socializing.

10. What arguments can be advanced for and against the practice of nepotism?

11. To what extent are job applicants in private and public employment discriminated against because of their sexual orientation?

12. Under what circumstances does moonlighting become a problem for the office manager?

13. How can the office manager most effectively aid the office supervisor who is a workaholic?

14. List the steps that an administrative office manager should take in setting up a system to control employee dishonesty.

15. What is the usual practice in handling the problem of tardiness?

16. How may the rate of absenteeism, periodically calculated for each department of the firm, be effectively used by the office manager?

17. How may the existence of a formally stated company policy on sick leave condone absenteeism?

18. Describe the operation of a no-fault leave policy. For what reasons might a firm adopt such a policy?

19. What are the major reasons for employee turnover?

20. Describe the operation of a typical flexible work schedule.

21. What is job sharing? To what groups of people does it most appeal?

22. What are the advantages and disadvantages of telecommuting?

23. Contrast work sharing with rotation of layoffs as a means of softening the economic effects of a recession.

24. What reasons are advanced by office workers for joining unions?

25. Compare the role of the office manager in office unionism under each of the following situations: (a) before union activity, (b) while attempts are being made to organize, and (c) after the workers become organized.

FOR YOUR DISCUSSION

1. The average number of office employees on the payroll of the Metro Bank during the past year was 740. Of the 237 workdays that year, the number of worker-days lost was 4,432.
   a. What was the absenteeism rate for the year?
   b. Assuming that each employee was absent the same number of days during the year, how would the number of days' absence per worker be classified according to The Bureau of National Affairs' guidelines (see page 343)?

2. At the beginning of this year, Paula Robard, manager of office services for the Qwik-Trip Company, received from the payroll department the following information about last year's operations:

No. office workers who quit last year	56
No. office workers who were terminated last year	75
No. office workers on payroll at beginning of last year	1,067
No. office workers on payroll at end of last year	1,295

   Robard had earlier estimated $5,550 as the average cost incurred by the company each time an office employee was separated last year.
   a. What was the annual turnover rate last year?
   b. What was the turnover cost to the company for the past year?

3. In the Ludwig Company, the annual turnover rate for female office workers is 23 percent. For male office workers, the rate is 14 percent. The office manager has concluded that male personnel are more stable employees than females. What is your reaction to this statement? What, if any, are the fallacies in the office manager's reasoning?

4. Jeanne Miller has been sitting next to Norman Stewart in the purchasing department of E-Z Bake Flour Company for the past two years. As a result, Miller has become very friendly with Stewart's style of working, his peculiarities, and his strengths and weaknesses. During the past two months, however, Miller has noticed a marked change in Stewart's work patterns and his relationship to her, which in the past has always been warm and comfortable. Now Stewart seems cold toward Miller, who in turn feels "shut

out." From what little conversation there has been recently between the two, Miller has learned enough to feel sure that Stewart is "on drugs," which explains why his work is being affected. Miller is not sure that their supervisor is aware of Stewart's condition and wonders whether she should tell the supervisor. Miller asks you, one of her co-workers, what steps she should take. What would your advice be?

5. Pam Chernov and Michael Rutter have worked side by side for the past seven years in the computer center of Batterby's. Over the years the two have shared very intimate details of their personal lives with each other. This morning Chernov comes to see you, the manager of the center, and says:

> Mike told me this morning he has just seen his doctor, who diagnosed his illness as AIDS. Although we're very close, I can no longer work alongside Mike. I have my husband and children at home—and myself—to think about. You're going to have to do something—maybe move Mike to an office by himself. What's going to happen when the rest of the group finds out about Mike's problem?

You thank Chernov for talking with you and state that after you meet with Rutter, you will follow through. In view of this announcement about AIDS in your company—the first case—what steps should you take at this time?

6. Ever since he was hired as office manager of Kirk's, Craig Donovan has been competitive, ambitious, and aggressive. He impressed top management with his devotion to the work ethic and his expectations of perfection from himself and his co-workers. Donovan thrived on deadlines, relished risks, and lost patience when he did not reach his goals quickly. Then one day the stress of Donovan's job took its toll—a severe heart attack.

   Today Donovan's boss, Garry Minicucci, leans back in his chair, reflects, and asks himself: "Why did this have to happen to a young fireball like Craig? Where did the company go wrong by not having anticipated the stresses of Craig's job? What can we do now?" What answers can you supply to the questions raised by Minicucci?

7. A midwestern newspaper reported that a 22-year-old secretary in charge of a $300 petty cash box secretly withdraws $100 every Friday to bet on horses, ball games, and fights. No guilt for wrongdoing is felt by the secretary, who reasons that all money borrowed from the petty cash fund is eventually returned and no harm is done to the company. Do you agree that the secretary is doing nothing wrong? How can management anticipate and prevent such a practice as this secretary's?

8. Dick Jarvis has been employed as an accountant in the Overell Company for more than 20 years. Over the past few years, Jarvis has developed a drinking problem to the extent that after his "liquid" lunches, he is often unable to do his job well. When the situation gets out of control, Jarvis's supervisor, Inez McGowan, talks frankly with Jarvis about his drinking; and after each meeting, Jarvis seems to work well for about three or four days—but then back to the bottle! Jarvis refuses to join Alcoholics Anonymous, and McGowan is reluctant to recommend discharge in view of his long record of service. What approach do you recommend that McGowan use?

9. Joe Garcia, office supervisor of Benson Oil Heaters, is aware of his company policy that forbids any form of gambling on the company premises. However, each year Garcia

sees (and occasionally participates in) World Series and football pools being organized by the office workers. As Garcia, how would you defend such pools in view of the company's policy against gambling? Is it dishonest or unethical for Garcia, as a supervisor, to participate in any of the pools?

10. Although grievances will never be eliminated, the office supervisor can take steps, especially in nonunion offices, to reduce and prevent large numbers of complaints. Prepare a list of the steps you would include in your program for reducing grievances in the office.

11. Both management and organized labor view flextime as part of a broad picture of changing work conditions. Assuming for a moment that flextime were to become the standard form of workweek in the United States by the year 2000, what changes would you expect to see in working conditions?

12. After reading a news release about the introduction of telecommuting by one of his firm's competitors, Dan Kehoe, supervisor of the word processing center, stated: "The program will never 'fly.' If people work away from the office, how do you know how well they work or if they work at all?" Do you agree or disagree with Kehoe's observations? Explain.

SOLVING CASE PROBLEMS

Case 12-1 Solving Problems of Sexual Attraction and Harassment[21]

When Leon and Beverly first began their relationship, he was one of the top executives in a medium-size company in the Northeast. She was his secretary and recovering from a painful divorce. Leon had experienced frequent extramarital affairs, but this was his first within his own company. As their love affair ended, he found it difficult to continue working with her and began to find fault with her performance on the job. Eventually she was asked to transfer to another department at a reduced salary and status. She felt she understood his motives and, even in later years, did not resent his actions.

As time passed he courted many others within the company, including Susan, the personnel director responsible for EEO compliance. Others in the company suspected that Susan's recent promotion was in part due to Leon's influence.

In the meantime, Leon lost five secretaries in as many years. Eventually, some of them and other women in the firm came to personnel to report what they considered to be annoying behavior and to seek some advice on what to do. Susan suggested that they ignore his advances as "he was harmless and would leave them alone if he understood they were not interested." She even confided to some of them that he had approached her yet had accepted her polite but firm rejection.

---

[21]"Sexual Attraction and Harassment: Management's New Problems," January, 1981, by Jeanne Bosson Driscoll, copyright January, 1981, reprinted with permission of *Personnel Journal*, Costa Mesa, California, all rights reserved.

One of his secretaries, Patricia, let him know she was not personally interested in him. She left the company when Leon began criticizing her job performance. After several months of searching, she began work for another firm in the same city. At that time she wrote his superiors and alleged sexual harassment.

After some careful investigation, the president of the firm confronted Leon and asked for his resignation. Leon resisted, claiming he never forced his attention on anyone and "anyway, most of what I have done and said was just kidding." The president held firm on the grounds that Leon had placed the company in legal jeopardy through his behavior.

Assume that you are the administrative office manager for the company described in this case and that you worked with the president in gathering information about Leon's actions on the job. Discuss the impact of this case on each of the following situations:

1. Your anxiety, as the AOM, when faced with the need to gather information and solve problems relating to sexual attraction and harassment.

2. The increased number of women that have been employed by your firm and the accompanying increase in the number of male/female professional relationships.

3. The kinds of problems that may emerge, which traditionally have caused you and the other managers to look upon feelings of attraction with disfavor.

4. The need for your company to consider its current policies on fraternization.

5. The necessity for your firm to develop a policy dealing with sexual harassment.

Case 12-2 Playing Favorites with Flextime

Shortly after being hired as administrative assistant at DeLullo's, Kathy Rizzo decided she would give up her lunch hours in order to answer the office telephones. In fact, Rizzo made an agreement with Elaine Banes, the office manager, whereby she would be allowed to quit work each day at 3:30 in exchange for giving up her lunch hours. Rizzo saw this move as an excellent way to solve her problem of having someone home with her children when her husband left for night school at 5 P.M. In turn, Banes was pleased to have someone on hand to answer the phones and thus assure customers their calls would be answered during the entire workday.

One afternoon after Rizzo had "flexed out" at 3:30, several of her co-workers came into Banes' office to air their complaints about the favoritism being shown Rizzo. One of the executive secretaries, Andrea Carlos, remarked, "All of us have agreed to give up our lunch hours, too, so we can leave early every day. You know, Elaine, more and more firms are allowing their employees to do this sort of thing—it's called flextime."

Banes patiently listened and then made this statement in support of her feeling that the request was out of the question: "This company can't afford to shut down the office every day at 3:30. We'd be out of business in six months!"

Banes went on to say she was surprised by the employees' request, for she felt they all knew about Rizzo's problems at home—her husband attending school and the need for someone to care for their children. The workers said that they did understand Rizzo's problems and sympathized with her. However, they indicated that they, too, had personal problems—

picking up children at the day care center, avoiding traffic tie-ups during rush hours, being at home when the children got out of school, etc. Carlos wrapped up the discussion by saying, "What's fair for Kathy should be fair for all of us. Think about it, won't you, Elaine? It really isn't fair to play favorites."

Assuming the rule of the office manager, Elaine Banes:

1. How would you answer the complaints made by the employees who met with you?

2. What alternative courses of action are available to you in order to achieve the goals of DeLullo's and still satisfy the needs of your workers?

PART 3

Managing Administrative Services

13

Managing Office Space

GOALS FOR THIS CHAPTER

After completing this chapter, you should be able to:

1. Identify the objectives to be attained by the administrative office manager in the efficient management of space.
2. Describe how the space needs of an organization may be analyzed.
3. Point out the major characteristics of the two principal styles of layout—the conventional plan and the open plan.
4. Identify the advantages and disadvantages that may result from use of the open plan.
5. List the main features of a well-planned "high-tech" office plan.
6. Describe the distinguishing features of the individual workcenter and the group workcenter.
7. List arguments for and against the planning of private offices and open offices.
8. Describe the nature and purpose of the automated workcenter.
9. Apply the space guidelines for efficient work, for personnel, and for furniture and equipment in answering the questions and solving the problems at the end of this chapter.
10. Describe several methods used in the preparation of office layout models.
11. Discuss the factors to be considered by an organization faced with the decision of purchasing or leasing its new office space.
12. Outline the details involved in making an office move and the potential personnel problems that may emerge in such an undertaking.

The systems concept identified in Chapter 1 has important meaning for administrative office managers. When AOMs view their offices as a system, they must consider the following essential elements, which are required to attain the objectives of the office:

1. *Space* in which to work.
2. *People* to perform the work.
3. A *comfortable, satisfying environment* in which to work.
4. *Efficient furniture and equipment* to assist in performing the work.
5. *Facilities* for meeting the internal and external communication needs of the firm.
6. An *appropriate set of records and related information-cycle activities*.
7. *Adequate controls* to ensure that the office system meets its goals.

In the modern office, these seven systems elements are combined into a network of people, machines, and procedures called administrative services. **Administrative services** are support functions that are responsible for meeting all the information needs of the organization.

The graphic model shown in Figure 13–1 outlines the main administrative services needed to produce information in the office and the environment in which these activities are housed, which constitute Part 3 of this textbook. In addition, the model shows the relationship of each service to the other services. The most basic service involves *space* and its direct impact on the office employees who must use it. The management of space and the way in which space contributes to the productivity of office employees are discussed in detail in this chapter.

SPACE IN THE ADMINISTRATIVE OFFICE SYSTEM

Space is an economic resource. As such, we know that space is limited in supply and subject to the changing demands of business. In the central business districts of most large cities in the United States, at certain times the search for more space to house a growing office work force has increased the demand for space and hence its price. At other times, vacancy rates of 30 to 40 percent are reported. So that office space is used effectively, several problems require the attention of the AOM: (1) the year-to-year increasing costs of office space, (2) greater costs of labor for maintenance and building security, and (3) the need to increase productivity and to improve the morale of employees through a better working environment.

From a systems point of view as we see by studying Figure 13-1, machines, office workers, and other systems elements function together to create a product—information—at the lowest possible cost. All of these elements are combined and arranged in the available space, which must be managed in order to be used effectively. Thus, planning, organizing, and controlling activities are required, under the leadership of the AOM.

In the office, information flows in a manner much like the flow of materials in a factory. In each, we find routes or aisles for the movement of people and materials in the shortest possible time. Further, for the sake of efficiency, a strong need exists to keep the number of *workstations* (desks, chairs, and working space) for the loading and unloading of information (or materials) to a minimum without sacrificing the accessibility of the service or the product. Regardless of the type of product (a factory product,

Figure 13-1
Administrative Services Model for the Production of Information

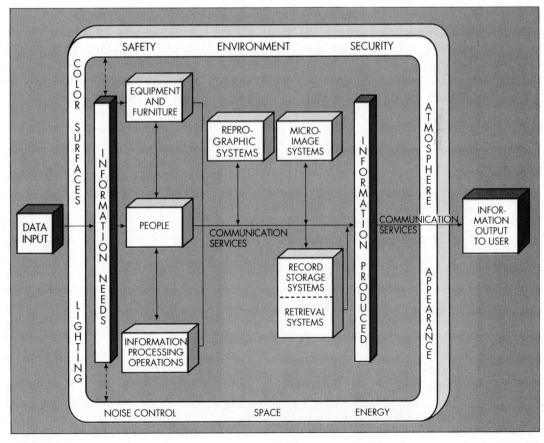

an office paper product, or simply inter-personal communications), how space is planned, organized, and used affects the productivity and morale of workers.

The need to manage space carefully is critical in several situations: when a new office building is being planned, when an old building is being renovated, or whenever a present office is being analyzed with the objective of grouping people, furniture, and equipment more effectively. In such situations, careful planning is required in order to develop and later achieve the objectives of a space management program.

THE SPACE MANAGEMENT PROGRAM

The management of space, like the management of other economic resources, is ongoing and requires periodic attention to ensure that management is getting the most value possible for each "space dollar" spent. For this reason, a formal program for managing space needs to be developed and implemented in the organization. The main features of such a program are discussed in this section.

Planning and Organizing a Space Management Program

When purchasing or leasing a new office site (as discussed later in this chapter) or renovating an existing building, management finds it advisable to consult reliable space planners and interior designers. Such specialists make recommendations based on a complete assessment of economic, efficiency, and esthetic or appearance factors. In addition, these experts place special emphasis on the human needs of the space involved.

Within the large firm, space planning is the responsibility of the firm's facilities engineer. Often a firm uses a project team approach, as found in the matrix organization described in Chapter 2, to help plan and implement the new office design. In such cases, the facilities engineer heads the project team that includes the architect, the designer, systems analysts, industrial engineers, department heads, industrial psychologists, and human resource management personnel. The AOM and key office personnel play a significant role in outlining the work-flow needs of the administrative services in both large and small offices. However, in the small office, technical advice on office design must be provided by outside specialists.

In planning a *new* office building, generally the essential physical features, such as supporting pillars, stairs, elevators, escalators, employee lounges, and cafeterias, can be located where they are most desirable. More frequently, however, a firm moves into an *existing* building where the physical features have been planned by former tenants. Therefore, planning the arrangement of working areas and work flows often is carried on around the present location of fixed factors. This approach also describes the firm that is renovating office space in its present location.

One technique of planning long-range projects, such as a new office layout, uses the Gantt Project Planning Chart. The underlying principle of a **Gantt chart** is that the work planned and the work done are shown side by side in their relation to each other and to time.

Henry L. Gantt, along with Frederick L. Taylor (see Chapter 1, page 15), was a pioneer in the field of scientific management. In 1877, Gantt joined Taylor in his experiments to raise productivity and decrease costs at the Midvale Steel Works in Philadelphia. Gantt's concerns at first centered on the best and fastest method for completing each piece of work.

Dialog on the Firing Line

RICHARD E. KOZITKA
Vice-President, Administrative Services
The Quaker Oats Company
Chicago, Illinois

BA in Journalism, University of Minnesota
Specialized management courses and graduate work,
University of Chicago, University of Michigan

Prior to his position as Vice-President, Administrative
Services for U.S. Grocery Products at The Quaker Oats
Company, Richard Kozitka served as Director, Employee
and Audio-Visual Communications as well as Manager,
Public and Employee Communications at the company.
Current professional affiliations include the General and
Administrative Services Advisory Council of the
American Management Association, the International
Facility Management Association, the Chicago Adminis-
trative Services Roundtable, and the Telecommunications
Forum Advisory Council.

QUESTION: In what ways do you bring below-
management people into the office-planning and layout
process?

RESPONSE: At Quaker we have traditionally
involved nonmanagement people in the office
planning process. Some of our most innovative
concepts have evolved through their participation.

All levels of employees were extensively involved
in planning our new headquarters building that we
occupied in 1987–88. There was a special Relocation
Coordinators Task Force that worked with us in
designing our new facilities, developing new office
procedures to fit the new environment and in executing the move itself. The coordinators, representing the various departments and divisions,
provided substantial "hands-on" insight as we
grappled with the many problems and challenges
involved in moving a workplace and its 2,200 people
from a basically horizontal environment (Chicago's
Merchandise Mart) to one that is vertical (Quaker
Tower). They also offered a great assist during the
move itself as they helped us coordinate the many
details within their respective areas.

In the relocation planning process we used panels
of employees to test various lines of furniture and
equipment before making final decisions. Because
of this involvement in the critical area of seating,
we have had virtually no problems or complaints
about the chairs selected. We likewise involved
nonmanagement employees in decisions regarding
acoustics, mail delivery, telephone coverage, and
design of the new cafeteria and food service facilities, fitness center, and conference rooms.
Employees also helped establish new policies on
a wide range of areas, including smoking.

Very few problems were encountered during and
after our relocation largely because most decisions
and plans were developed with input from
nonmanagement people and reviewed and fine-
tuned with their involvement long before execution.

Later, he became convinced that what really counted were employee morale and motivation.

The Gantt chart is one of the most widely recognized planning methods. In the basic Gantt chart shown in Figure 13–2, project activities are listed along the left margin from top to bottom in sequence of the planned activity. The numbers to the right of the title represent the number of days required to complete the project. Horizontal bars drawn next to each activity and under the appropriate time period make it easy to visualize the planned starting date, duration, and planned completion date. Across from the first activity, the top bar indicates planned performance time; the second bar shows actual performance time. A vertical date line means that the project has been updated. Also, note that some planning phases (such as 3, 4, and 5) may be carried on concurrently, which saves time in completing the layout tasks.

PERT—an acronym for Program Evaluation and Review Technique—is another method for planning long-range projects. PERT is commonly used to determine the time required to complete major projects, such as constructing a large office building, after realistic time estimates have been made of the various activities associated with each project. With the aid of computers, PERT has become an important tool in systems-improvement studies. PERT is discussed in detail in Chapter 21, where an example of a PERT project appears on page 667.

Objectives of a Space Management Program

If our goal is to have a space management program that effectively supports the administrative services function, we must understand the two main elements in the office system. The first element includes the *physical features* of the office. Examples of physical features are the design of the building, which includes window and door locations; stairs, elevators, and escalators; and the plumbing, heating, air conditioning, ventilating, and electrical systems. (Firms that are largely automated require high-tech features that are discussed later in this chapter.) The second main element involves *functional work requirements*. This category includes the information needs of the organization such as department functions and their necessary locations; open and private work areas; special facilities, such as reference (library) services, computer installations, and executive office requirements; the work being performed; the nature and number of employees presently working as well as the number expected for the future; and the equipment and furniture required to complete the work assigned.

By keeping in mind the important space-related factors just mentioned, the AOM develops these specific objectives for an effective space management program:

1. To provide sufficient space that is used to the fullest.
2. To develop work flows that are effective and low in cost.
3. To design workstations that permit the use of good working methods which are in keeping with the work flow.
4. To permit flexibility in layout for possible rearrangement of workstations and for expansion or contraction of space needs.
5. To meet the interpersonal needs of the office staff by providing an environment free of communication barriers.
6. To coordinate the use of space with all related factors in the work environment, such as heat, light, color, and noise control.
7. To assure employees, as well as customers and the general public, of comfort and convenience.
8. To review regularly the long-range space needs of the office and to make improvements as necessary.

Figure 13-2
Gantt Chart
Used for
Planning
New Office
Layout

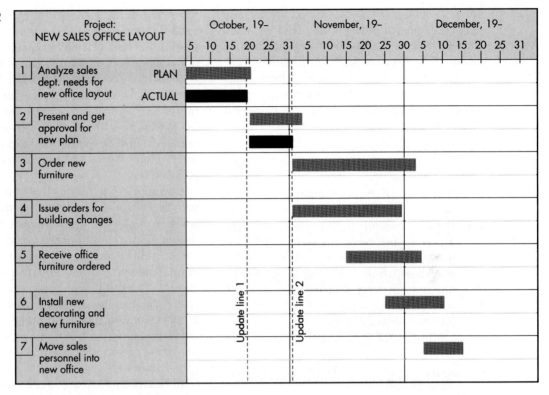

In the remaining sections of this chapter, we shall use these objectives as a frame of reference in discussing the principles of space management that have been developed through the years.

SPACE NEEDS IN THE OFFICE

The organization of a firm directly affects the layout of the office and plant. In many large manufacturing firms, including automotive, electrical appliance, and chemical, the production and office facilities are frequently separated. Many of these firms also have branch or warehouse offices that are decentralized geographically. On the other hand, in service organizations such as banks and insurance companies, paperwork is the main product and hence the office is the main facility provided. Probably the most common type of organization for small and

medium-size offices is a plan in which the main functions of purchasing, marketing, credit, human resources, and administrative services are arranged by departments.

In this section, the office space now occupied and the space needed are examined first. Next, the work flow—of departments or cost centers—and human space needs are analyzed. Finally, the planning of space by functions is considered in relation to the conventional and open plans as well as the type of facility needed for high-tech offices.

Office Space Inventory

Before the many important decisions can be made regarding the best use of office space, much up-to-date, relevant information must be collected. Typical of such information are (1) the organization chart for the office and (2) the operations manual that explains the main functions of the office and the various departments from which the office receives information as well as those departments to which the office transmits information.

To supplement this basic information, AOMs frequently send a space-use questionnaire to each department requesting data on the following basic space needs:

1. Department name.
2. Main functions or responsibilities of the department.
3. Amount and type of contact with the public.
4. Relationship of the department with other departments (that is, which departments are in frequent or regular communication with the department under study and what is the nature of such communication).
5. Number of employees.
6. Functions of personnel in each job category.
7. Type of space each person in the department should occupy.
8. Changes expected in number of personnel and office activities.
9. Equipment presently in use as well as additional equipment expected to be used.
10. Records stored, the volume of records expected in the future, and retention and disposition schedules.
11. Special workcenters, such as private offices, conference rooms, and reception centers, that are needed.

Figure 13–3 shows a form used in surveying the present and expected space needs for an office. The information appearing on the completed form is very useful in analyzing the space needs of the office before the actual design phase of the space management program is begun.

Analyzing Space Needs

From a careful study of the completed form in Figure 13–3, the AOM identifies the

following needs for space in the office: (1) *space for personnel*—working space required by each employee assigned to the department; (2) *support space*—the space required for administrative services, such as mailrooms, word processing centers, reception areas, and conference rooms; and (3) by implication, the *traffic-flow space*—the corridors, aisles, elevators, and lobbies—used by employees, customers, and the general public.

Common sense tells us that it is not difficult to collect information on the present space occupied by a department. However, determining the important work relationships among departments and among employees is complex and requires much consultation and thought before an effective space plan can be created. In this regard we must remember one basic point—*the space plan must follow work flows or work functions rather than space or esthetic preferences of personnel.*

In analyzing space needs at regular intervals, the AOM considers personnel space needs, special workcenters, storage areas, and interpersonal communication needs as reported by the department. (See Figure 13–3.) From the square feet estimated, the AOM must consult space guidelines, such as those presented later in this chapter, to determine how much space should be allocated to each workstation and employee. To these space allocations is added a fixed percentage of aisle space to determine the total square feet needed for the department or cost center. After the head of each department has undertaken annually such an analysis, possibly as part of the budget preparation, a summary of all analyses can be prepared to guide the firm in estimating its total future space needs.

Work Flow Space Needs

Work flow is the movement of information vertically between superiors and subordinates or horizontally among workers on the

Figure 13-3
Form Used
in Surveying
Office Space
Needs

INVENTORY OF OFFICE SPACE NEEDS

Department or Cost Center *ADMINISTRATIVE SERVICES*

Date *DECEMBER 1, 1990*

Office Space:

	Number of Personnel Needed			
	1990	1995	2000	Remarks
Officers, managers, department heads	8	9	9	
Private offices	2	2	2	
Open offices	60	75	90	*1995 – ADD ASST. AOM.*
Administrative/executive secretaries	3	3	3	
Other				*1995 - CONVERT TO DISTRIBUTIVE DATA PROCESSING AND MICROCOMPUTERS.*

General Offices:

	Square Feet Needed			
Officers, managers, department heads	720	810	810	
Private offices	600	600	600	
Open offices	9,000	10,000	10,000	
Administrative/executive secretaries	320	240	240	
Other				

Special Workcenters:

Conference room	250	350	350	*INCREASED NUMBER OF CONFERENCES ON SITE.*
Training room	150	200	200	
Reference services	135	135	135	
Reception center/switchboard	225	225	225	
Computer center	300	200	200	
Reprographics	125	225	225	
Mail room	150	200	200	
Word processing center	350	400	400	*EXPAND WP CENTER.*
Other				

Storage Areas:

Open-shelf filing	—	—	—	*INCREASED USE OF MICROGRAPHICS AND COMPUTER STORAGE.*
5-drawer file cabinets	600	500	350	
Storerooms (supplies, etc.)	120	200	200	
Vault	80	80	80	
Storage (inactive files)	180	250	250	
Other				

same level. The best layout for the work flow is not derived simply from a quick overview of an office operation; rather, it emerges slowly from a feasibility study, as discussed in Chapter 2, or from an intensive analysis of the administrative office system, as explained in Chapter 21. Both studies involve an analysis of the division of labor, the nature

Work-flow space needs must be considered in any space management program.

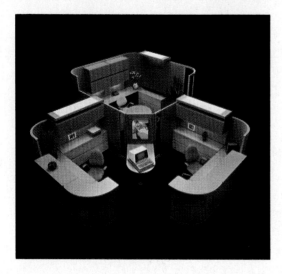

and frequency of information processing documents, and the flow of documents within and, if needed, outside the firm. Also, the frequency and quantity of documents processed, the number of workstations involved, and the time required to complete each work cycle are analyzed.

As we saw earlier, a common method of analyzing information and communication flows is to examine the organization chart. In the chart illustrated in Figure 13–4, the organization is depicted as a matrix. The most frequent communications, shown by the red lines, are often the informal channels. These communication channels are not shown formally on the organization chart but are detected through systems studies of information flow and interpersonal relationships. In space-planning programs, interviews are usually conducted by asking the question, "*Who communicates with whom, about what, under what circumstances, and with what effects or results?*" Answers to the various parts of this question provide useful information for analyzing the flow of communication and work among the office

staff. Figure 13–4 shows a top executive, a second level with four vice-presidents, followed by four equal positions of middle managers and seven positions of first-line supervisors. The flows of information to and from each person are represented on the chart. Both the obvious (open) and the hidden processes of information exchange must be identified before appropriate space allocations can be made to office personnel.

Although Figure 13–4 emphasizes work flows among levels and departments, the same types of communication flows are found within a department. For example, the working relationships that exist between executives and their administrative assistants or between typists and record clerks who file copies of typed correspondence require that the work flow within the office be carefully studied in space management programs.

When office work flow is analyzed for efficiency, it will be found that the *flow is most productive when it is continuous*—that is, when intermittent storage stops or work pauses are eliminated. Therefore, the processing time at each workstation must be identified and verified, transport time between workstations eliminated or reduced, and storage time decreased, if not eliminated. However, much of the success of the space management program depends on how well the AOM understands and meets the special human space needs of the workers.

Human Space Needs

In Chapter 5, we noted that the discussion on nonverbal communication conveys the basic idea that space "communicates" (that is, affects the feelings of people). Research on this topic shows that, because of the unique cultural and personality features of office workers, we should consider certain human needs in providing working space for the office staff.

Each worker needs a certain amount of personal space. **Personal space** refers to an

Figure 13-4
Major Communication Flows in a Company

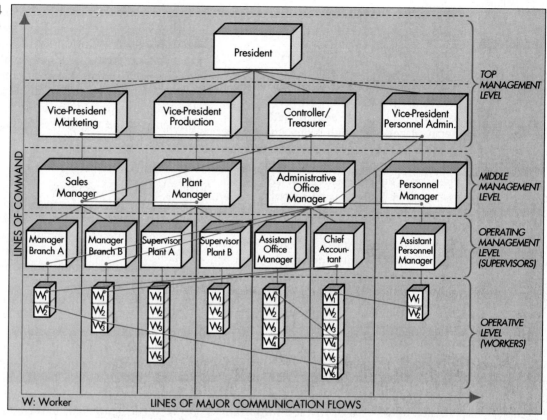

area of privacy surrounding the worker that is important for keeping out other people. This idea is tested, for example, whenever a stranger comes into our homes or into our offices. Under such circumstances, how comfortable do you feel? The amount of personal space required to maintain the psychological comfort of the worker differs between introverts and extroverts. Introverts often prefer to work alone and hence require more privacy than extroverts who like to be with people. Also, the space requirements for people from different cultures vary widely. Anthropology studies show that natives of Middle Eastern countries typically require less personal space than Americans.

Closely related to personal space is the concept of **territoriality**, which refers to the physical area that is under the control of

workers and designed specifically for their use. Hence, no other person can dominate that space. In the office, territoriality is commonly found in the workstation assigned to an office worker. Territoriality is also implied when a secretary is required to knock on the door before entering an executive's private office. Indeed, once within the private office the secretary realizes the feeling of territoriality and higher status held by the executive. With higher status, as communicated by the private office—or, in some cases only a greater amount of office space—power and authority are also communicated.

The AOM must understand the concepts of personal space and territoriality in order to meet the human space needs of the office staff. Personal space—and hence the privacy of the worker—will not be violated if the

AOM observes these three zones in planning space:

1. **Intimate zone**: ranging from skin contact to about 2 feet. This distance is reserved for persons with close emotional attachments, such as very close friends working together on an office assignment.
2. **Personal zone**: ranging from 2 feet to 4 feet. This distance keeps the other person at "arm's length," although reasonably close, as is the case with an office supervisor giving specific directions to a subordinate for reorganizing a report in the office.
3. **Social zone**: ranging from about 4 feet to 12 feet. This distance, especially from 4 feet to 7 feet, is generally maintained in business situations where people work together or salespersons and customers talk. The distance from 7 feet to 12 feet is used for more formal, impersonal situations, such as conferring with one's superior across the desk.

Since much office work requires the interaction of the office staff, it is important that we understand how workplace arrangements affect interpersonal communication. The manner in which the spatial environment acts as an agent to encourage (or, in some cases, to discourage) conversation is commonly observed in cocktail lounges and libraries. The same principles, however, apply in the office.[1]

Another human space need concerns disabled individuals, estimated to represent more than 13 million people in the United States. Of this large group, approximately 18 percent are employed full time.[2] Typical of the space needs of the disabled are handrails; door widths that accommodate wheelchairs; ramps; lowered lavatories and water fountains; and elevator controls with Braille symbols next to floor buttons. Further discussion on providing an effective environment for the disabled is included in the next chapter.

Functional Space Needs

In Chapter 2 we saw that the basic organizational unit of specialized functions is the *department*. This fact continues to be true even though computers and other automated systems have caused many significant changes in organizational patterns.

In planning space needs, the AOM considers the main functions to be performed by each department and the space requirements needed to complete those functions. For example, a sales department with its many external contacts has many different types of operational tasks as compared with an accounting department, which performs tasks of an internal nature and almost exclusively related to automated and paper records.

A functionally sound layout should meet three basic goals: (1) It should provide the best work flow within and between departments and people; (2) it should keep to a minimum the movement and noise that are caused by people as they perform their job tasks; and (3) it should provide as much visual and auditory privacy as the position requires. We will see an expansion of these points in Chapter 14.

OFFICE DESIGN PLANS

To meet the space needs of all department functions, several design plans are available:

---

[1]The earliest studies of the effects of space on people were conducted by anthropologist Edward Hill and reported in two publications: *The Silent Language* (Greenwich, CT: Fawcett Publications, 1959); and *The Hidden Dimension* (Garden City, NY: Doubleday & Co., 1969). Additional references on the relationships of space and human behavior are found in Jean D. Wineman, Ed., *Behavioral Issues in Office Design* (New York: Van Nostrand Reinhold Company, 1986).

[2]*Statistical Abstract of the United States, 1987*, 107th ed. (Washington: United States Department of Commerce, Bureau of the Census, p. 380).

(1) the conventional plan, (2) the open plan, and (3) the "high-tech" office plan. In addition, we find various types of workcenters that may incorporate, as needed, elements of both conventional and open plans. Each of these design plans is described in this section.

The Conventional Plan

The **conventional plan** is a type of office layout characterized by wall barriers that tend to isolate work areas. This design plan, shown in Figure 13–5, provides a specialized work area for a department that promotes productivity. However, critics of this plan believe that it prevents or reduces human interaction and at the same time hinders interdepartmental work flow. Also, the conventional plan makes for an inflexible arrangement and adds greatly to the cost of redesigning the office.[3]

To be used effectively, the conventional plan should be carefully developed. *Departments should be arranged so that the work flow proceeds in an uninterrupted manner and passes through as few hands as possible.* Such planning can be accomplished only after a careful study of administrative systems and procedures, the arrangement of furniture and equipment, and, of course, the needs and preferences of personnel.

Certain design principles should be followed in preparing a sound layout for departments. For example, *departments with much public contact should be located near the entrance to the plant or office; or, if the layout suggests, they may have direct access to hallways in order to minimize traffic flow through open work areas.* Thus, the human resources department and the purchasing department, which have frequent contact with outsiders, should be located near the entrance or reception area. Other departments, such as finance and word processing, should be located near the executive and administrative areas, respectively.

The Open Plan

Sometimes called the *office landscape*, the **open plan** originated in Germany after World War II and has rapidly become a very popular design plan for office layout. This plan brings together the functional, behavioral, and technical factors needed to design individual workstations, work groups, and departments.

Trade associations estimate that 50 percent of white-collar employees work in open-plan offices and that the percentage of open-plan offices will increase to 75 percent in the 1990s.[4]

As we see in Figure 13–6, the open plan features open space, free of permanent walls and corridors. Workstations are arranged by using movable elements such as desks, chairs, freestanding screens, bookshelves, files, and live plants without changing the fixed installations (light fixtures, heating and air-conditioning outlets, partitions, or floor coverings). Each individual grouping of workstations is usually arranged, without regard to windows or other traditional design limitations, in a nonuniform fashion dictated by natural lines of information flow and human communication. Figure 13–7 provides such an example. Starting from the left, the layout includes a middle manager's office followed by a supervisor's work area. More private space for word processing operators is provided at the rear.

In theory, the office landscape is an open-plan model with no private offices. Privacy

---

[3]"How the Open Office Plan Can Save Space and Money," *Office Systems 84* (July/August, 1984), p. 66, as extracted from "A Financial Guide to the Open Plan," Haworth, Inc., One Haworth Center, Holland, MI 49423.

[4]Wilbert O. Galitz, *The Office Environment: Automation's Impact on Tomorrow's Workplace* (Willow Grove, PA: Administrative Management Society Foundation, 1984), p. 94.

Figure 13-5
The Conven-
tional Plan

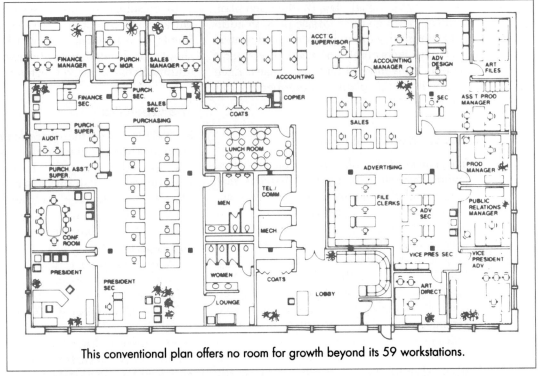

This conventional plan offers no room for growth beyond its 59 workstations.

Source: Adapted with permission from Haworth, Inc., One Haworth Center, Holland, MI 49423.

is provided by using plants and movable, sound-absorbing screens or partitions, usually wired for electricity. The status of workers is determined more by their work assignments than by their locations. High-level executives may have a larger amount of space, a different color desk top, and possibly a different shaped, larger desk; but beyond this, there are few visible signs of rank. In actual practice, however, the open plan is often combined with the conventional plan (called the **American plan**) so that high-level executives can keep their private offices for isolation and confidentiality. Other managers and their staffs are generally located in open work areas close to one another. In the new Quaker Oats Company's corporate offices in downtown Chicago (winner of the 1988 Electronic Office Design competition), all office workers in the 20 floors

share open-plan offices that allow the sun to stream through the floors to every workspace. Executives share this same type of space but their privacy is maintained through the use of full-height panels that can be disassembled and relocated at minimal cost.

Advantages of the Open Plan

Typical of the many advantages of the open plan over the conventional plan are the following:

1. *Lower construction and energy costs.* The open plan permits considerable savings in construction costs, due in large part to the need for building fewer internal walls and hence fewer heating, ventilating, and air-conditioning facilities. In the open plan, a centralized energy system can serve a

Figure 13-6
The Open
Plan

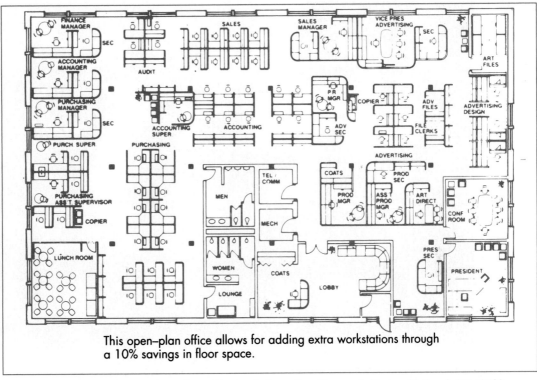

This open–plan office allows for adding extra workstations through a 10% savings in floor space.

Source: Adapted with permission from Haworth, Inc., One Haworth Center, Holland, MI 49423.

large, open space with maximum efficiency. For example, the Eastman Kodak Company constructed 1.5 million square feet of *open office* space at an average cost of about $1 per square foot. The comparable cost of *partitioned dry wall* space would range from $6 to $30 per square foot. Energy costs, too, are lower since about 20 percent fewer light fixtures are needed in a given area because the reduction of walls between offices allows a more efficient placement of the fixtures. Further, the open plan light system can reduce energy consumption by about 40 percent.[5]

2. *More usable floor space available.* In the open plan, the amount of usable space (expressed as a percentage of the total space available) is greater than in the conventional grid plan of row after row of workstations. The open plan shown in Figure 13-6 allows an additional 24 workstations using 10 percent less work area as compared with the conventional design in Figure 13-5. This space economy is achieved by removing the permanent walls and using space-saving arrangements of furniture and equipment.

In landscaped offices, the usable space may run as high as 90 percent. Since the open plan requires less floor space, the square footage required by offices may be reduced by as much as 20 to 30 percent; and, in turn, rental cost per square foot is less than in a traditional fixed-wall office. For example, through the use of workstations that make greater use of

[5]John Pile, *Open Office Space* (New York: Facts on File, Inc., 1984), p. 88.

Figure 13-7
Open Plan
Showing
Work Groups
Arranged
According to
Communica-
tion and
Information-
Flow
Requirements

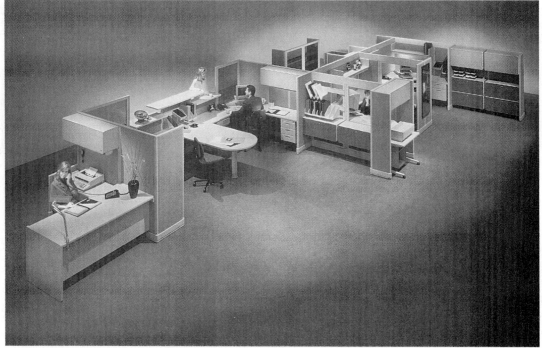

vertical space for storage, often in open-shelf files or in shelves above desks and tables, the open plan reduces the amount of floor space required for each workstation. At the same time it provides a more efficient work area for the individual.

3. *Flexibility of rearrangement.* Office work requirements change periodically, and the open plan provides a flexibility for making changes in layout as work assignments change. Only simple tools are required to rearrange the panels and the component parts that make up each workstation. A rearrangement of facilities within an open-office plan is estimated to cost from 50 cents to $1.50 per square foot compared with $7 to $15 for moves in conventional spaces.[6]

4. *Reduced federal income taxes.* The modular workstations, movable panels, and component parts of the open office can be depreciated over a fewer number of years than the structural elements found in a fixed-wall office building. Thus, the organization is able to lower its federal income taxes as a result of a greater amount of depreciation expense over a smaller number of years.

Most of the tax benefits are available because the panels and components of the open plan are classified as personal property rather than real estate. Since personal property can be depreciated for tax purposes, the firm obtains a lower tax base and lower property taxes. Most dry-wall offices are classed as real estate, which can appreciate (grow in value) and thus result in a higher tax base and greater property taxes.

5. *Fewer communication barriers.* When office walls are torn down, the commu-

[6]Frederick W. Bach, "Tying Up the Loose Ends in the Open-Plan Concept," *Office Systems 85* (March, 1985), p. 59.

nication barriers between managers and employees tend to diminish and psychological barriers tend to be removed also. Employees in a cluster grouping feel freer to ask questions and to come into a manager's work area to discuss problems. Managers, too, have more opportunity to supervise employees since the managers are less isolated in open offices and more in touch with their workers.

Disadvantages of the Open Plan

Surveys taken to determine what conditions office workers prefer are largely based on opinions and thus reflect biases of various types. However, when carefully controlled, such studies can be useful in helping AOMs meet their responsibility for managing space.

Several national studies offer inconclusive results about the use of space. *The Steelcase National Study of Office Environments, No. II*, indicated that 57 percent of 1,002 respondents felt that in an open plan it would be possible to do more work than in the conventional plan or a bull pen type of office.[7] Another study was conducted by the Buffalo Organization for Social and Technological Innovation, Inc. (BOSTI), a nonprofit research and educational organization. BOSTI found that a moderate amount of enclosure is considered very attractive in an office, since enclosure is believed to support communication, increase privacy, and increase satisfaction with floor-space assignments.[8] Two later Steelcase studies, completed in 1987 and 1988, show that office workers in increasing numbers prefer a private office with a door to working in an open plan. However, for reasons cited earlier, both managers and design specialists predict that open-plan spaces, often partitioned to provide some degree of privacy, will be more common than private offices in the future.[9]

As a result of these major studies and other research on worker job satisfaction, many office designers recommend the American design plan, discussed earlier as a mixture of the open plan and the traditional or conventional plan, because of the following disadvantages of the "pure" open plan:

1. *Lack of privacy.* Office workers at all levels complain that the open plan strips them of privacy, especially when conducting personal business. Also, because they no longer have private offices, some managers and supervisors sense a loss of status. Some workers say it is difficult to concentrate with so many people located in one large area. Others report that it is difficult to carry out confidential work. Also, workers feel that they are always under someone's observation. As a result of comments such as these, some firms have replaced the low movable panels and screens with partitions extending from the floor to the ceiling, thus creating movable rooms that are completely enclosed.

2. *Too much noise.* Office workers object to the high noise level that results from the conversations of neighboring workers; the din of machines and equipment, especially the computer printers; and the ringing of telephones. Noise-control techniques to handle such problems are discussed in Chapter 14.

3. *Poorly designed open-plan systems.* When converting from the traditional fixed-wall office to the open plan, some firms have failed to open up their offices. Instead, they have created many very small

---

[7]*The Steelcase National Study of Office Environments, No. II: Comfort and Productivity in the Office of the 80s*, 1980, Steelcase, Inc., Grand Rapids, MI 49501, p. 67.

[8]The six-year research study on the office environment by the BOSTI organization was completed in 1984 and is reviewed in "Using Office Design to Improve Productivity," *Office Administration and Automation* (February, 1985), pp. 26–29, 77–78.

[9]*The Office Environment Index: 1987 Summary Report*, p. 3, and *The Office Environment Index: 1988 Summary Report*, p. 6, both studies completed by Steelcase, Inc., Grand Rapids, MI 49501.

cubicles arranged in mazes that cut off communication and necessary conversation among workers. Other companies have learned that the open plan does not work efficiently for some administrative services, such as legal and accounting, where high levels of confidentiality and concentration are required.

Such poorly designed open-plan systems result from the failure of the space administrator, managers, and designers to (1) plan carefully before, during, and after the installation; (2) consult with office workers who will be affected by the change; (3) educate office personnel about the advantages of the open plan over a conventionally planned office; and (4) control unauthorized rearrangements in which office workers can abuse the open plan by encroaching on their neighbors' space and unnecessarily disturbing others.

Private Versus Open Offices

In the past, the private office has been widely regarded as an important status symbol of executive success. Today, however, the rising costs of office space and the increasing popularity of the open plan cause the AOM to study several factors before deciding whether to design private offices, open offices, or a combination of the two.

Management must weigh the relative advantages and disadvantages of using private offices. The reasons usually given for providing offices are:

1. They create prestige in the eyes of employees and visitors for top management, department heads, and high-level staff people.
2. The confidential nature of the work being done, such as research, planning, and financial report preparation, requires privacy.

3. The work, such as computer programming, requires a high degree of concentration.

On the other hand, the private office makes efficient use of about only 50 percent of the space allocated to it. Thus, the use of private offices is an expensive method of providing utilities, such as heating, lighting, and air conditioning. The private office is relatively inflexible, for its permanent partitions are expensive and difficult to remove; it provides barriers to supervision of employees since the supervisor is separated from the employees; and it sets up arbitrary barriers to oral communications in the office.

The High-Tech Office Plan

Traditionally, office tenants bought space from developers, telephone service and electricity from public utilities, and computers and other equipment from manufacturers. With an increasing use of automated systems, we now find these necessary office services are beginning to be provided by the landlords in the form of "smart" buildings.

A **smart building** is an office building that has a computer for a brain (control device) and a nervous system of cables and electronic sensors that allow the computer to monitor and interact with building conditions. Tenants are able to access the building's computer for telecommunication and automated office services.[10] The landlord of a smart building offers the tenant *building management systems* consisting of fire control and security, energy management, environmental and lighting controls, and

---

[10]J. Thomas Black, Kelley S. Roark, and Lisa S. Schwartz, Eds., *The Changing Office Workplace* (Washington, DC: The Urban Land Institute and Building Owners and Managers Association, 1986), p. 228.

elevator controls. Also the landlord provides *shared tenant services* that include wiring for local and long-distance voice, video, and data transmission, teleconferencing and electronic mail, as well as word processing, copying, and image transmission. (These topics are discussed later in Part 3.) By leasing a smart building, tenants are spared the complex problems of furnishing and maintaining their own automated services. Thus, in the smart building the most up-to-date facilities are constructed in the building for which the tenants pay an additional $2 to $5 a square foot in leasing fees.[11]

SPACE PLANNING IN WORKCENTERS

The office as we know it is a thinking place for information workers. Personnel must be placed at appropriate locations for thinking—that is, for controlling information through each of the stages of the information cycle. In a related sense, the work of the office revolves around communication, the exchange or distribution of information. Each employee, from custodian to chief executive officer, is assigned a location or workcenter, some simple and some highly complex, for performing the work assigned. The concept of the workcenter and special workcenters found in many offices is discussed in the following paragraphs.

Workcenter Concept

The basic unit of office space planning is the **individual workcenter** or *workstation*—sometimes called the *microspace*—where each employee performs the bulk of assigned responsibilities. When all the workcenters are combined, whether departmentally or in some other functional sense, the **group**

workcenter or *total workplace*—sometimes called the *macrospace*—is the result. Consideration of both the individual and the group workcenter concepts is necessary to achieve the most effective use of office space.

Individual Workcenter

In most offices, certain basic furniture and equipment are assigned to each workstation. Such items as a desk or table for a work surface; counters, shelves, and files for storage; machines; and seating facilities are normally required for each worker.

The design of a workcenter should be based on an analysis of the work to be performed, communication requirements (telephone, dictation, interviewing, consulting, etc.), and storage needs. A concern for the environment and related tasks is also required.

Group Workcenter

No one workstation exists by or for itself; rather, it serves as part of a larger group working toward a common goal. All workcenters, therefore, must be space-planned and coordinated to fit into the total work environment.

A department is the typical work setting for groups of workers. For example, personnel specializing in hiring, testing, evaluating, and training workers are housed in a human resources department or division. Each of the many tasks and the workcenters at which these tasks are completed in such a department must be planned so they relate to the spatial needs of the total human resources system of the organization.

The responsibilities of the AOM, as a space administrator, include coordinating all workcenters into an arrangement that facilitates the combined teamwork of the individual members. Three special workcenters must be provided for most modern offices.

---

[11]Ibid., p. 230

Special Workcenters

In many large organizations, special workcenters, such as the reception center, the reference services center (sometimes called the library), and the automated workcenter, are commonly found.[12]

The Reception Center

The reception center serves to promote efficiency in administrative operations and to enhance public relations for the firm. Thus, this area should be well arranged and kept orderly, for visitors get their first impression of the business when they step into its reception center.

The reception center should be located in an area where visitors cannot interrupt the work of employees who may be distracted by the flow of callers. In planning a reception center, at least 10 square feet should be allocated for each visitor; therefore, its size is determined by the maximum number of visitors expected at any one time.

Reading material should be supplied for visitors, who may have to wait until the people they want to see are ready to receive them. As it may be assumed that many of the callers are interested in some product or service of the company, some literature or a display of these subjects should be provided.

The Reference Services Center

To encourage their employees to be well informed on topics relevant to their work, many companies have established libraries or reference services centers. Businesses also

maintain special libraries to further the activities of the organization. As such, the special library is really an information bureau, with a limited number of reference books, technical handbooks, and other publications in the special field of the company.

A firm may obtain assistance in setting up its reference services center by contacting a library consultant (unless the company librarian has sufficient background). The consultant will survey the company's existing facilities and offer recommendations on costs, procedures, space and equipment requirements, and staffing needs.

The Automated Workcenter

To an increasing degree, offices have "gone electronic"; that is, they have adopted computers as necessary information processors. In the 1988 Steelcase study cited earlier, personal computers were used by 71 percent of Canadian workers and 78 percent of U.S. workers for almost four hours each day. For this reason, the AOM must plan workcenters that meet the combined special space needs of both the worker and the computer.

The *automated workcenter* is designed around the **video display terminal (VDT)**, the leading device for entering data into the computer.[13] (Other input hardware is discussed in Chapter 16.) In the design of this modern office workstation, we should consider:

1. *Sufficient space for all types of work.* The VDT is a large device and may crowd

---

[12]For an examination of other special workcenters, such as vaults, interviewing rooms, and conference rooms, see: Susan S. Szenasy, *Private and Executive Offices* (New York: Facts on File, 1984); John Pile, *Open Office Space* (New York: Facts on File, 1984); and Jean D. Wineman, ed., *Behavioral Issues in Office Design* (New York: Van Nostrand Reinhold Company, 1986).

[13]As discussed earlier in this chapter, the workstation is the basic unit of office space planning that includes office furniture and equipment. In the automated workcenter, the most important equipment item is the VDT. Although this is the most common definition of workstation, computer users in the scientific community sometimes restrict the meaning of the term *workstation* to the most powerful desktop computers. See *The Wall Street Journal*, January 15, 1989, p. B1.

Workcenters have been designed to meet the needs of the automated office.

a regular-size desktop. Since the use of paper in manual systems will not be eliminated altogether with the addition of a VDT, thought must be given to alternative locations or larger desktops for performing nonautomated tasks. If not, the result will be an inefficient workplace in which materials are stored off the desk or piled high on top of the VDT. See Figure 14–4, page 414, for suggestions in positioning VDTs in relation to the windows in the workplace.

2. *The technical needs of the VDT user.* Motion economy should be incorporated into the design so that items used most frequently, such as manuals and other references, are within easy reach of the operator. The location and height of the VDT keyboard and display screen should

be positioned to provide the most comfort possible for the operator. Other related environmental factors, such as lighting, noise, air-conditioning requirements, and special furniture needed for the electronic workstation, are discussed in the next two chapters.

3. *The human-social needs of the worker.* As the BOSTI study shows, office workers in the electronic age desire privacy as well as the opportunity to communicate easily with their co-workers. Panels or partitions should be provided to permit worker concentration and to make efficient use of expensive space. The use of five-station clusters shown in Figure 13–8 saves valuable office space and at the same time provides efficient, comfortable, and semiprivate settings for workers using automated workstations. *Executive workstations*, which are automated workcenters for managers, are also appearing in more and more firms, as discussed in Chapter 15.

In some firms, the AOM may be asked to help in planning the computer center. In such cases, we note there are organization-wide implications that call for more extensive knowledge and skills than in planning the individual workstation. Thus, company-wide expertise must be sought along with special consulting services in designing the computer center, as noted in the Yellow Pages of most telephone directories.

PRINCIPLES OF SPACE MANAGEMENT

In this chapter, emphasis is placed upon layout as a major factor in achieving efficiency and worker satisfaction in the office. *Providing sufficient space* and *making the maximum use of that space*, two

Figure 13-8
Open-Plan
Automated
Workstation
with Space
Savings from
Use of Multi-
station
Clusters

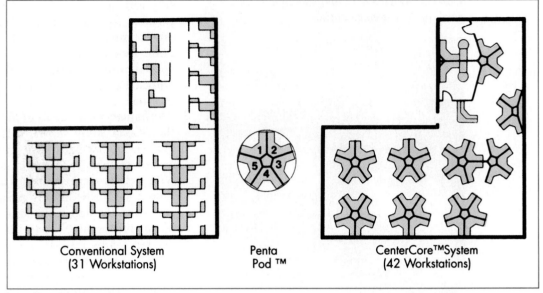

Conventional System
(31 Workstations)

Penta
Pod ™

CenterCore™System
(42 Workstations)

Courtesy of CenterCore

of the key objectives of space management, are vital to administrative office systems, as discussed earlier. This section presents principles, or guidelines, of space management that apply especially to the following components of administrative office systems: efficient work, personnel, and furniture and equipment.

Space Guidelines for Efficient Work

The following space guidelines, which summarize points we noted earlier in the chapter, will aid the AOM in achieving work efficiency:

1. *Use a straight-line flow of information* (such as forms, records, and reports) *rather than a crisscrossing or backtracking of lines* to reduce communication and transportation lines to a minimum.
2. *Provide large, open spaces*, which are better than small room spaces cut out of one area. In such settings, supervision and

control can be more easily maintained; communication with individual employees is more direct; and better lighting, heating, and ventilation arrangements are possible.

3. *Use movable partitions, freestanding screens, and plants as alternatives to private offices with fixed walls.*
4. *Conserve space without cramping individuals in workcenters.* For example, include the space above the surfaces of desks and tables; replace two- and three-drawer file cabinets with more space-efficient models having four, five, and six drawers; provide a common conference area to eliminate the need for private offices; and store all but the working inventory of office supplies in a central storeroom.
5. *Locate offices such as purchasing, sales, and human resources that require contact with outsiders in areas accessible to the public.* However, those offices requiring confidential work or privacy such as

accounting, computer programming, and research and development should be located away from the easy accessibility of the public.

6. *Base space allocation on major work flows,* which function around source documents such as the purchase order, the time card, and the sales invoice. Thus, departments having a great deal of cross-communication with other departments should be located near each other. Examples of this relationship are the human resources and the payroll departments. Also, common destinations (elevators, copiers, restrooms, etc.) should be close together and accessible by direct routes from workstations.

7. *Forecast future work requirements in relation to the projected sales volume.* One guideline to use in such forecasts is the average rate of increase in volume of office work over several typical growth years.

Space Guidelines for Personnel

The number of employees to be housed in a given area both at present and in the future has an effect on the amount of space to be used. Because there are so many variables in allocating space in an office, it becomes difficult to set standards of space requirements, especially the average amount of space required for each employee. The best that can be achieved in setting space standards is to group employees and set minimum and maximum guidelines for each group as follows:

1. *Private offices* vary from 400 to 600 square feet for senior executives to 200 square feet for senior assistants and from 75 to 100 square feet for cubicles or modules in an open plan.

2. In *fixed-wall plans,* general offices have 80 to 100 square feet per workstation in small departments, in units where there

are high-level nonexecutive personnel, or where the visitor traffic is heavy. In large work areas, the space allowance may be reduced to 40 to 80 square feet per workstation.

3. In the *open plan,* the goal is to provide offices with undivided areas of at least 100 feet by 100 feet for 80 to 100 employees.

4. In general, an *automated workstation* requires 10 to 15 percent more space—and in some cases up to 25 percent more when expansion is considered—than the conventional workstation. For example, before automation, the worker needed only a typewriter and writing surface; but after automation, that same worker needs a computer monitor, keyboard, disk drive, disk storage unit, printer, paper storage, and paper.[14] In addition, files should be kept close to those workers who use them.

5. Aisles and corridors will probably require about 10 to 15 percent of the total area of private and general offices.

6. Conference rooms and boardrooms require 25 square feet per person for rooms housing up to 30 persons and 8 square feet per person for areas housing 30 to 200 persons.

7. Central files require about 6 square feet per letter-size (8½ by 11 inches) cabinet and about 7 square feet for the legal-size (8½ by 13 or 14 inches) cabinet. Open-shelf files occupy approximately 50 percent less floor space than file cabinets.

Space Guidelines for Furniture and Equipment

Before furniture and equipment can be effectively located on a new office layout plan, an inventory of all such items (quantity, description, size and use of each item) should

---

[14]Marilyn Joyce and Ulrika Wallersteiner, *Ergonomics: Humanizing the Automated Office* (Cincinnati: South-Western Publishing Co., 1989), p. 108.

be taken. In locating each item on the floor plan, the guidelines in Figure 13-9 may be used. Note that the circled numbers appearing in the figure correspond to the guideline numbers at the left of the figure.

Guidelines for Conducting the Office Space Study

The AOM has two options available for conducting the office space study. The first option is based upon a floor plan drawn by hand to the customary English scale (feet and inches). This method can be quickly converted to the metric scale in case the metric system is used. The second option, still in its early stages of development, uses the computer in the design process.

Preparing Office Layout Models

Several methods of preparing a model of the office layout are described in the following paragraphs:

1. The first method makes use of colored paper cutouts of all types of equipment, such as desks, chairs, file cabinets, and safes. Each piece of furniture and equipment is drawn to the same scale as the floor plan to maintain proper relationships when the cutouts are pasted into position. The scales $1/8'' = 1'$ and $1/4'' = 1'$ are commonly used because of their ease in conversion on a standard ruler. This is the simplest and least expensive method of illustrating a proposed layout.
2. The second method makes use of a plastic template, illustrated in Figure 13-10, which is available from most book and office furniture and equipment stores. The cutout areas indicate the size and shape of the various types of furniture, equipment, columns, partitions, and so on.
3. A third method uses floor space and related items drawn to scale, as shown in Figure 13-11, which are placed upon a floor grid board. The top surface of this

board may be made of cork so the scale models of desks, chairs, tables, screens, plants, and office equipment may be pinned down when set up. After the plan has been laid out, it can be used by managers, supervisors, and workers involved in space planning. Photographs may also be made as a guide for installation.

4. A fourth method—the simulated office space model—relies upon the construction of full-size replicas of selected office areas. In such complete mock-up offices, the office personnel can sit in their actual offices and observe beforehand what their workstations will be like. They can examine and test all the various components, such as the lighting system and storage cabinets. Colors and textures can be evaluated and examined together in the same proportions and arrangements in which they will be ultimately used. This method, possibly the costliest of all, is feasible only when large sums of money are available for space management.

Using the Computer in Office Layout

One of the latest computer applications, **computer-aided design (CAD)**, uses the computer to automate the drafting function. CAD is made possible through programming techniques that assign numeric values to graphic information (such as line drawings and various geometric shapes) for processing and printout or display on the VDT screen. In addition to its use in office layout design, CAD is also used for designing parts, as in the automotive field, for plotting and printing out drawings, and for handling design changes.

Various input methods are available for using CAD. One computer system uses a "mouse," a small plastic device with which the VDT operator can control the movement of the *cursor* (the small position indicator on a VDT screen) for drawing graphics on the

Figure 13-9
Space Guide-
lines for
Office Furni-
ture and
Equipment

1. a. The width of major traffic aisles may vary from 5 to 8 feet.

   b. Less traveled aisles should be 3½ to 5½ feet wide.

2. Aisle space between desks should not be less than 36 inches.

3. In open planning, the plants should grow to between 3½ and 5 feet, unless they are to be used as visual barriers, when 7-foot plants with more fullness and breadth are recommended.

4. a. Desks should generally face the same direction, unless the employees are clustered together in automated work-centers.

   b. Such workcenters should be provided with visual and acoustical privacy, as discussed in Chapter 14.

5. No more than two desks should be placed side by side so that each desk will be on an aisle, thus permitting easy flow of traffic.

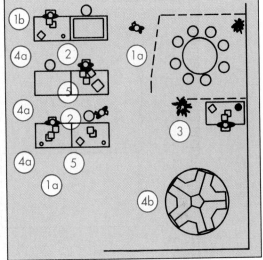

6. Frequently used computer terminals shared by two or more people should be placed as close as possible to the users.

7. Desks should be arranged to give a straight flow of work—that is, so that a person will receive work from the desk beside or in back of him or her.

8. Those whose work requires the most concentration should have the best light. No workers should face the light, and the window light should be at the left of an individual.

9. Space between desks facing in the same direction—that is, the space occupied by chairs—should not be less than 28 inches, preferably 36 inches.

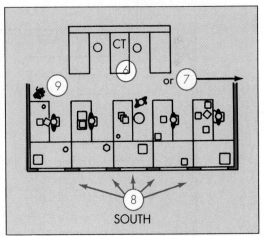

10. If active files open up front to front—that is, to an aisle— the width of the aisle, when the file drawers are open, should not be less than 30 to 40 inches.

11. File cabinets should be placed against walls or railings if possible.

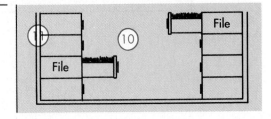

Figure 13–10
Plastic
Template

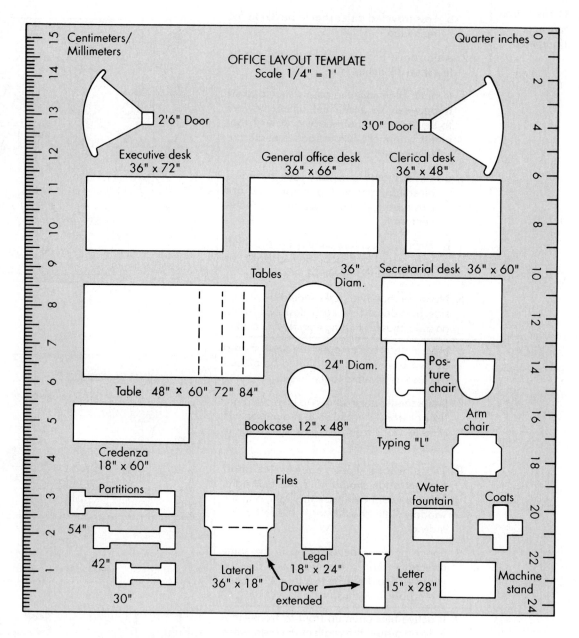

Figure 13–11
Layout
Board with
Scale Models
of Furniture,
Machines,
and
Equipment

VDT screen. When you use the mouse, the movement of your hand is duplicated by the cursor on the screen through electrical pulses sent by the mouse to the computer.[15] Another device, a *light pen*, the size and shape of a pen, is connected to a terminal by wire permitting the operator to draw with the pen on the display screen. This drawing is made possible after the operator calls up a light-pen graphics program stored in the computer. Figure 13–12 shows the mouse and the light pen in use for computerized drawing.

---

[15]Other input devices related to the mouse are the trackball and the joystick. For more information on these devices as well as an increasing number of off-the-shelf packages used in office space analysis and design, consult an up-to-date computer systems/data processing textbook or a reference on office automation, such as David Barcomb, *Office Automation: A Survey of Tools and Technology*, 2d ed. (Bedford, MA: Digital Press, 1989), Chapter 4.

The CAD concept may be used to simulate an office layout. In order to perform this simulation, the operator supplies the computer with information concerning space allocations and workstation dimensions, numbers of personnel to be distributed over the floor space, and space estimates (in square feet) required for performing the functions of the unit. Given all this basic information, the computer can "create" and display the most optimal design on the VDT screen or print out a copy to be used for discussion and decision making. Figure 13–13 shows a computer-aided design projected on a video display terminal for use by the AOM. If desired, this design may be printed out for distribution to other users in the organization.

In another CAD application a layout is projected on one side of the screen along with a listing of the various components to be arranged for use in the layout. Also provided are instructions (add, delete, rotate, and so on). The planner selects an instruction and appropriate component by merely touching a light pen to the corresponding spots on the screen. Finally, the component appears in its updated position on the screen, as preferred by the planner.

RELOCATING THE OFFICE

Even though an effective layout has been designed and put into action, periodically the AOM must review the long-range needs of the space management program (Objective No. 8, page 368). On the basis of such a review, the AOM, representing the space facilities team, may recommend that the office be relocated. Factors contributing to such a recommendation include the rising costs of space (real estate, property taxes, etc.) in the present location; the need to locate nearer the market for the firm's present and future customers; the need for more space to house personnel, furniture, and equipment as a result of the firm's growth; traffic con-

Figure 13-12
Popular
Devices for
Making
Drawings on
the VDT
Screen

A—A Typical Mouse

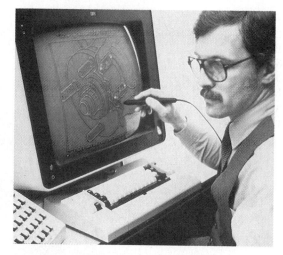

B—A Light Pen

Figure 13-13
Computer-
Aided Office
Layout

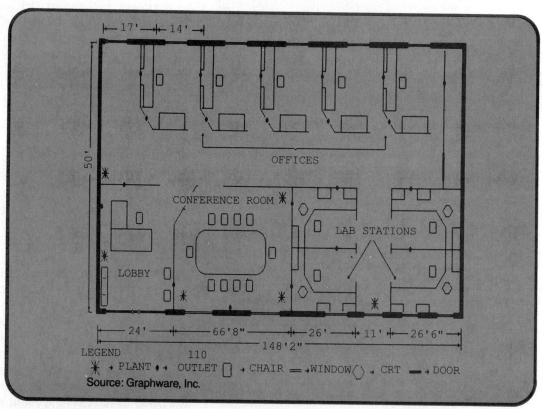

gestion and transportation delays facing workers who commute each day; increased costs of downtown parking; the need to ensure employee safety and reduce security risks; the desire to improve the firm's image by relocating to a more prestigious area; excessive noise from traffic; and inefficient, as well as insufficient, facilities (elevator service, toilets, building management, and electrical capacity for heating, ventilation, computer usage, and air conditioning).

When an organization has decided to relocate, often to an existing building, short- and long-term company goals must be set that include estimates of the personnel needed to attain those goals. The purchase-or-lease decision is briefly examined next, assuming that the firm decided earlier not to construct a new office building. This discussion is followed by some helpful hints on physically moving the office.

The Purchase-or-Lease Decision

The decision to purchase or lease existing office space at a new location should be based upon an analysis of several important factors, as discussed below.

Future Space Requirements

If the space requirements of the organization are going to change rapidly over the next few years, strong consideration should be given to leasing. However, from the viewpoint of reducing income taxes, it may be more economical for the firm to own the space rather than to rent it. For example, the owner of a small company not needing extensive floor space nor a downtown location may reduce the rising costs of office rent and obtain a favorable tax advantage by purchasing a commercial condominium in a suburban location. Income tax deductions may be taken for the mortgage interest and local real estate taxes. Further, the cost of substantial improvements made by the owner may be claimed as reductions in federal income taxes. If the small organization anticipates expanding within the next five to ten years, the firm may consider the purchase of extra space in the condominium, which may be leased until it is needed.

Organizations weighing the decision to purchase or lease office space need to evaluate the net cost of ownership compared with the rental (lease) costs of equivalent space. In calculating the costs of ownership, the following factors should be considered: (1) sales price stated in terms of square feet; (2) interest costs for financing the purchase; (3) maintenance costs (operating and management expenses, association dues, and property taxes); (4) tax bracket of the purchaser; (5) tax benefits from ownership; and (6) the prevailing cost of money (interest rates).

Next, the prospective buyer should compute the rental charges for equivalent space—largely total rent per square foot plus operating expenses—and compare these charges with the cost of ownership in which the owner builds an equity in the business.[16]

Supply of Capital

If the firm is short on capital, it may decide not to tie up its money in the purchase of a building. Rather it may invest the funds elsewhere and obtain a greater return on the investment. Thus, when the supply of capital is tight, we find that leasing may be preferable to purchasing. When leasing is likely, an understanding of the contents of a lease becomes important for the AOM.

---

[16]For making useful comparisons needed in the purchase-or-lease decision, see Kenneth D. Laub, "Tax Act Spurs Development of Condominiums As Offices," *The Office* (March, 1984), pp. 55, 57, 58; Kenneth D. Laub, "Beware Those Hidden Costs When Leasing Office Space," *The Office* (June, 1982), pp. 108, 112, 114; Esther F. Solin, "Erasing the Pains of an Office Relocation," *The Office* (October, 1985), pp. 108–109; and "Getting a Move On," 1988 *Inc. Office Guide*, pp. 14–24.

Contents of the Lease

A **lease** is the agreement between the **lessor** (the landlord) and the **lessee** (the tenant) that transfers possession, *but not ownership*, for a period of time. The lease should set forth clearly the rights of the lessor and those of the lessee in order to avoid any misunderstandings. By means of the lease, the landlord grants to the tenant the privilege of using the property for lawful purposes and without interference providing the terms of the contract are carried out. Although the standard commercial office lease may appear to be a simple business contract, the AOM must understand its contents in order to avoid costly legal problems.

The **work letter** is that portion of a lease which spells out the lessor's and the lessee's obligations for any work to be done to the building and who will pay for it. The work letter should be carefully prepared to consider all possible contingencies so any conflicts about the charges for the completed work may be avoided. The first part of the work letter deals with the plans to be prepared by the lessee and those to be prepared by the lessor. Usually the lessee includes information about the construction and finishing of the office space and the data required (electrical needs, plumbing requirements, weight loads, etc.) for preparing the engineering plans. This section also lists the dates when plans must be submitted by the tenant to the lessor. The second part of the work letter usually deals with the landlord's work and indicates the items to be supplied by the landlord beyond those that are routinely furnished.

The tenant should also consider the effect inflation may have on the type of escalation clause contained in a renewal lease. Although various kinds of formulas are used to determine rent at the time of renewing a lease, often the rent is linked to the Consumer Price Index (CPI) in some way. Thus, as inflation escalates, so does the rental cost to the tenant.

Other important terms of the office lease that should be studied by the AOM include subleasing; options to cancel; options for more space; the hours and seasons for heating, ventilating, and air-conditioning services; and, finally, the rent commencement clause, which states when rent begins. Because a lease is a complex legal document, the AOM should consult the firm's attorney for counsel before completing the lease document.

Resale Value

If the building may be readily resold, its purchase may be a wise move. On the other hand, if there are factors that would limit the resale of the property (such as little or no land for future expansion or for added parking facilities), leasing may be a better choice.

The Office Move

After the decision has been made to purchase and renovate a building or to rent office space, the day arrives when the office must move into the new quarters. Unlike moving a household, the first priority in moving an office is the immediate restoration of production. With intelligent planning over a sufficient period of time and with careful timing of each phase of the move, we can be sure that the job will be done with minimum disruption in the company's normal business.

Checklist for Planning the Move

Basic to the planning for an office move is a detailed checklist of the tasks to be done, with each job arranged in the order in which it should be accomplished. As we plan the move, the tasks shown on the checklist in Figure 13–14 should be completed, or at least considered, by the AOM and others on the project team responsible for moving the office.

Figure 13–14
A Checklist
for Planning
the Office
Move

CHECKLIST FOR MOVING THE OFFICE

Organization	Location	Preferred move date:_____
Person in charge of move	Tel. Number	Actual move date:_____

Instructions: Please check off each subitem as it is completed. When all subitems have been completed, check off the main item as being finally completed.

_1. Determine moving date.
 _a. Consider weekend, not overnight move.
 _b. Make sure new site is ready for the move.
 _c. Verify that the terms of lease permit the move.
 _d. Complete Gantt chart (Fig. 13-2) for detailed moves so all personnel know status of move at all times.

_2. Select mover as early as possible.
 _a. Secure recommendations for reliable moving companies from 2–3 firms who have recently moved.
 _b. Obtain written proposals from each moving company.
 _c. Use proposals to notify project team about details of the move.

_3. Appoint project team and manager to carry out all move responsibilities.
 _a. Select team members, as a minimum: project manager, AOM, and assistant with moving experience.
 _b. Expand project team as needed.
 _c. Orient all personnel about site location, expected move date, and location of workstations in the new quarters.
 _d. Brief personnel at special meetings as needed.

_4. Prepare moving instructions.
 _a. Be complete in every detail.
 _b. Be specific about assignments of staff members and employees assisting in move.
 _c. Include instructions for:
 _(1) Scheduled dates and hours.
 _(2) Details of tagging/marking equipment and furniture.
 _(3) Proper handling of desks, chairs, plants, and other items of equipment.
 _(4) Ordering stationery and forms containing new address and telephone number.

_5. Send moving notices.
 _a. Send new address and telephone number to clients, suppliers, banks, etc.
 _b. Change listing in telephone directory and in the directory of new building.

_6. Prepare layout for each department, area, or cost center.
 _a. Draw all items of furniture and equipment to scale.
 _b. Assign number or color code to each area for ease in putting furniture and equipment in place.

_7. Schedule housecleaning and purge records.
 _a. Conduct "throwaway campaign" 2-3 months before moving date.
 _b. Schedule second housecleaning 1-2 days before the move.
 _c. Consult records retention schedule and destroy unneeded records.

_8. Order cartons for packing.
 _a. Provide sufficient quantity of cartons to each department several days before move so bulky materials can be packed in advance.

_9. Assign code numbers and tag furniture and equipment.
 _a. Stress importance of accurate coding and tagging to each department.
 _b. Assign a different color of tag for each floor (if moving to multistory building).
 _c. Assign a different color of tag to each department if new building is one story.

_10. Set up directional signs at the new site.
 _a. Indicate locations of elevator lobbies, hallways, doorways, offices, private offices, etc.
 _b. Break down large open areas into small sections with each section identified in the directional marking system.
 _c. Post in each elevator lobby a scale plan of the entire floor.

_11. Provide special maintenance crews.
 _a. Inform present and new landlords of need for service personnel (elevator operators, maintenance personnel, security guards, plumbers, carpenters, and electricians).
 _b. Have standby telephone servicepersons instructed to remove all telephone equipment from workstations prior to moving.

_12. Assign guides.
 _a. At old office: provide guides to direct movers on proper sequence of moving items out of the office.
 _b. At new office: provide guides to direct the flow of furniture and equipment as indicated by tags and codes.

_13. Establish an information center.
 _a. Establish at each location—old and new—an area with table and telephone to serve as communication headquarters for employees and movers.

_14. Inspect the site prior to moving in.
 _a. Make final check before the move to reduce delay during the move.
 _b. Check that telephone and electrical services have installed proper equipment and that it is working satisfactorily.

_15. Check the new site immediately after the move.
 _a. Have designer, contractor, landlord, tenant, and manager of project team inspect premises to make sure any damage (marred walls and floors, chipped paint, and dented furniture and equipment) is noted.
 _b. Check to be sure all items to be moved are accounted for.
 _c. Be sure that all liabilities for any move–related damages are determined.

Personnel Problems Related to the Office Move

Whenever we are involved in moving an office, many personnel problems are encountered. Such problems are uncovered when management analyzes its responsibilities to those employees who will be unable to work at the new site and to those who will relocate along with the company.

Employees should be informed of a possible office relocation even before the decision to move is made. After the decision is made, the workers should be told promptly so that those the company will not be able to retain have maximum time to seek other employment. Those in the counseling program or the employee assistance program should make every reasonable attempt to aid these employees in finding new local employment, such as canvassing other employers in the area; granting employees time off for interviews; bringing representatives of public and private employment services into the company to interview employees; assisting in preparing personal resumés; furnishing statements to employees regarding their rights and equities in the various employee benefit plans; and considering the need for severance pay.

Those employees who relocate along with the company to a distant area should be aided in getting settled with a minimum of inconvenience. The chamber of commerce in the new community can help employees by passing along information on such factors as schools, climate, cultural and sports activities, medical facilities, and the location of apartments, hotels, and motels that can furnish temporary housing.

SUMMARY   1. As a space administrator, the OM works toward the goal of creating a well-planned layout that provides a timely, efficient, and economical flow of information to those persons responsible for decision making at various levels in the organization. In designing such a layout, the OM is concerned with meeting space needs and personnel needs so that the layout provides for a continuous work flow. The formal and informal relationships among people in departments or cost centers, the number of employees located in each department, the type and flow of information, and the need for private offices are several important factors that must be studied in order to provide for effective utilization of office space.

2. Three kinds of layout plans—the conventional plan, the open plan, or a blending of the best features of both—plus a new high-tech office plan are used in space management. Each plan has advantages and disadvantages, which must be carefully studied when planning for individual, group, and special workcenters. As an aid in designing layouts, the OM draws upon space guidelines that have been developed for efficient work, for personnel needs, and for furniture and equipment. In developing the layout model, the OM may use either the English or the metric system and one of several layout techniques—colored paper cutouts, plastic templates, cork board grid with scale models of furniture and

equipment, or full-size replicas of office areas. The computer can also be used in designing an office layout.

3. Once the decision has been reached to relocate the office in a new building, the organization is faced with another decision—to purchase or to lease the space. Among the factors to be considered in making such a decision are the future space requirements, the availability of capital, the contents of the lease, and the resale value of the property. Many hours of detailed planning are required to make sure that each phase of the office move occurs on time so there is a minimum disruption in the firm's business. Especially important in the office move is a mutually satisfactory solution to any personnel problems that may arise, such as when some workers decide not to relocate with the company or when employees decide to move along with the company to a new location.

GLOSSARY **Administrative services**—a support function that is responsible for meeting all the information needs of the organization.

American plan—a merger of the open plan and the conventional plan for designing the office layout.

Computer-aided design (CAD)—an application in which the computer automates the drafting function.

Conventional plan—an office layout design characterized by wall barriers that tend to isolate work areas.

Gantt chart—a technique of planning long-range projects in which the work planned and the work done are shown side by side in their relation to each other and to time.

Group workcenter—a combination of all workstations, either departmentally or in some other functional sense; also known as *total workplace* or *macrospace*.

Individual workcenter—a basic unit of office space where each employee performs the bulk of assigned responsibilities; also known as a *workstation* or *microspace*.

Intimate zone—a personal space ranging from skin contact to about 2 feet that is reserved for persons with close emotional attachments.

Lease—an agreement between the landlord and the tenant that transfers possession of property for a period of time.

Lessee—a tenant.

Lessor—a landlord.

Open plan—an office layout design characterized by open space, free of conventional walls and corridors, which brings together all the functional, behavioral, and technical factors to determine the layout of individual workcenters, work groups, and departments; also known as *office landscape*.

Personal space—an area of privacy surrounding the worker that is important for keeping out other people.

Personal zone—a personal space ranging from 2 feet to 4 feet; a distance that keeps the other person at "arm's length."

PERT (Program Evaluation and Review Technique)—a long-range planning technique that is used to determine the time required to complete major projects.

Smart building—an office building that has a computer for a brain and a nervous system of cables and electronic sensors that allow the computer to monitor and interact with building conditions and that tenants can access for telecommunication and for automated services.

Social zone—a personal space ranging from about 4 feet to 12 feet; generally maintained in business situations where people work together.

Territoriality—the physical area that is under the control of a worker and designed specifically for that worker's use.

Video display terminal (VDT)—the leading device for entering data into the computer.

Work flow—the movement of information vertically between superiors and subordinates or horizontally among workers on the same level.

Work letter—a portion of a lease that spells out a lessor's and the lessee's obligations for any work to be done to the building and who will pay for it.

FOR YOUR REVIEW

1. a. What essential elements of the administrative office system are required in order to attain the objectives of the office?
    b. How are these elements related to administrative services in the organization?

2. How does the office compare with the factory as a production unit?

3. What factors are involved in managing space for administrative services?

4. How is the Gantt chart used in planning an office layout?

5. List five objectives of the space management program.

6. What information is sought by the AOM in taking an office space inventory?

7. How does work flow influence the planning of office space?

8. How important to space planning is a study of the company's informal channels of communication?

9. a. Describe the main human needs of office personnel in office space.
    b. What types of distance must be observed in meeting human space needs?

10. What are the main features of the conventional design plan?

11. Define the open-plan concept as it is used in space management.

12. How does the open plan provide for privacy?

13. List the main advantages and disadvantages of the open plan.

14. What special features make up the high-tech office plan?

15. Describe the workcenter concept.

16. List the advantages and disadvantages of providing private offices.

17. a. How important is a reception center to an organization?
    b. How may its space be efficiently planned?

18. a. Describe the automated workcenter.
    b. What special management principles must be applied in designing this type of workcenter?

19. Which offices within a typical manufacturing firm should be located near the public entrance and which should not? Why?

20. What space guidelines are available to aid the office manager in locating desks?

21. Describe the different methods of preparing a model of the office layout.

22. How is the computer used in designing office space?

23. For what reasons may a company decide to relocate its office?

24. In a leasing arrangement a work letter is often used. Describe its value to the lessor and to the lessee.

25. How may a company aid those workers who decide not to relocate with the firm?

FOR YOUR DISCUSSION

1. Joe Creen is presently serving as the president of the local chapter of AMS. Since all chapters have been asked to submit a short, practical article to a forthcoming national AMS publication, Creen asks you, his assistant, to compile a list of typical violations of good office layout that he plans to develop into an article from his chapter. What should your list include?

2. In the law offices of McHugh, Kiernan, and Leedom, there are 32 lawyers, a certified public accountant, 10 legal secretaries, and 14 other employees. The firm is now planning its new quarters, which will be ready late next year. The partners realize they have a lot to learn in their planning. What suggestions can you offer them in the area of initial planning to make sure that a satisfactory space plan is devised for the office?

3. Six typists in the graduation analysis section of your college registrar's office are being retrained as word processing operators using video display terminals (VDTs). Each will be provided with new furniture in a new open-plan design that will replace the present bull-pen setting of the six typists in the general office. As office supervisor, you have been asked by the registrar to recommend a layout that will provide the "right amount" of concentration and privacy for these employees. Prepare a clustered as well as a nonclustered layout for these six automated workstations. Assume that 400 square feet (an area 20 feet square) is presently in use by this group. Defend your choice of the more efficient of the two design plans.

4. Presently six clerks are housed in an open-plan portion of the payroll department that occupies 300 square feet (a space that is 12 feet wide and 25 feet long). Because of expansion, two more clerks must be added to the space presently occupied, as shown in Figure A. Prepare a revised layout that permits eight workstations using the same desk and chair sizes. No additional furniture and equipment, other than a visitor's chair, should be provided for each workstation.

Figure A
Present Pay-
roll Clerk
Workstations

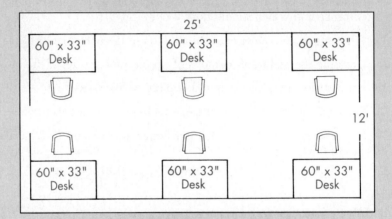

5. Doctors Kim and Lee, specialists in psychiatry, have moved to a new second-floor location in a suburban office building. Two of their last unsolved space problems are the layouts for the reception area and the consultation rooms used by each physician. (The present dimensions of the space are shown in Figure B.) The area is an inner section of the building with no outside window light and with permanent wall construction that must be retained.

Figure B
Layout for
Psychiatric
Office Suite

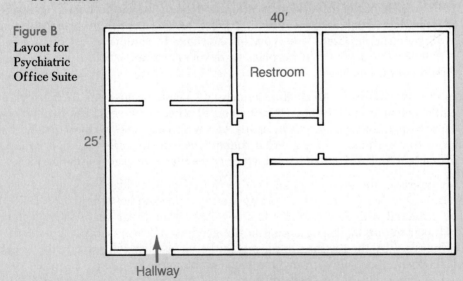

As a 20-year veteran assistant to the two psychiatrists, you are solely responsible for designing the new quarters. Your experience has told you that no more than three chairs are needed in a small waiting room, for the doctors maintain a very orderly one-hour schedule with each patient; hence, there is no waiting line of patients, there are generally no emergencies, and usually the patients come alone.

In each physician's office, there is no need for special equipment. However, several comfortable chairs, a small desk, and a reclining couch for the patients' use should be provided.

Sketch a plan that applies the space management principles in this chapter. Assume that only the two physicians and you as assistant occupy the office and that a small service area for office supplies and other services should be provided.

6. In times of economic stress and reductions in the office budget, you feel that there is no real need for revising your office layout, nor should your office purchase workstation equipment to be used with your new microcomputers. As office supervisor, how can you justify this feeling to your subordinates?

SOLVING CASE PROBLEMS

Case 13–1 Converting to an Open Plan

The Croker Insurance Agency leases a small office space in an expensive downtown location of a midwestern city. Because of the convenient location, the agency hopes to retain this location even though more space may be needed in the next five years.

Recently, the new owners of the building announced plans for a major renovation of the structure, starting with the removal of all nonweight-bearing walls. (In the case of the Croker quarters, only the outside walls are considered weight bearing; thus all inside walls would be removed.) The reason for this decision is to provide opportunities for use of the open plan for modernizing the office with all the advantages this plan offers.

The Croker office layout in Figure C is reduced in size to a scale of $1/10'' = 1'$. In the office, workstations are provided for four agents (salespersons), one secretary-receptionist, an office manager, a vice-president, and president. (The two executives also supervise other business interests of the firm that frequently require small on-site conferences.) Restroom facilities are provided across the hallway from the front entrance to the office suite, which is located on the third floor. Windows occupy the entire west wall (shown vertically at the left on the layout) as well as the short east wall near the secretary-receptionist workstation.

Jo and Jim Croker, executives of the firm, ask you, the office manager, to redesign the office for an open plan that incorporates movable panels to separate the office staff and new workstation furniture and equipment as shown in Figures 13–7 and 13–8.

Prepare a layout of the new office drawn to a scale of $1/4'' = 1'$ that provides the same relative amounts of space for each staff member as found in the present layout. Indicate, in a report, the assumptions (on equipment, work flow, etc.) you made in completing this assignment. Also, provide an estimate of the space savings possible by using the open plan.

Figure C
Conventional
Layout for
Small Insur-
ance Office

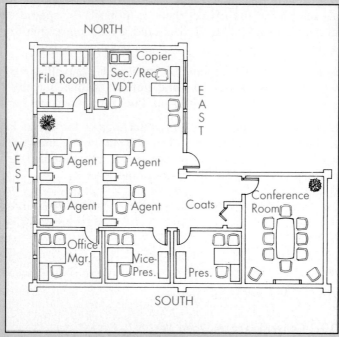

Source: Adapted with permission from Haworth, Inc., One Haworth Center, Holland, MI 49423.

Case 13–2 Maintaining the No. 1 Image in a New Office

Jacob Williams, owner of a management consulting service, is moving his service to a new building in which the office area is 40 feet by 20 feet. There are only two windows in the office, both of which are on one 20-foot wall. The office space will be occupied by:

Jacob Williams, the owner and office manager
Traci Hitchcock, Williams' assistant
Dena Patrick, a secretary
Paul Higgins, a typist, who also serves as receptionist
Irene Kurth, a community college student who works part time

Williams estimates his immediate furniture needs as desks and chairs for all employees, chairs for four visitors, two file cabinets, bookcases, a cabinet and rack for literature, and a coat rack. Williams believes that he would like to have partitions or screens around his office because he does a great deal of dictating and confidential interviewing.

Williams has "roughed out" the tentative location of the employees as shown in Figure D. When he showed his sketch to Hitchcock and Patrick, the following conversation took place:

Williams: Well, here it is—our new home as of three weeks from today. What do you think of it?

Figure D
Williams
Rough
Layout of
New Office
Area

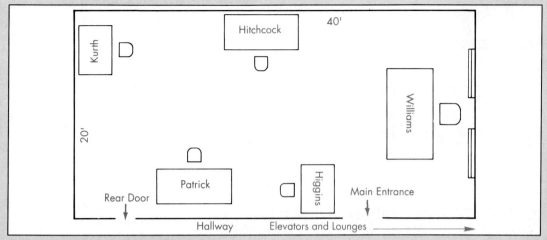

Hitchcock: Sure looks roomy compared with where we are now. But I should have known you would get the windows. Sure must be nice to be No. 1!

Williams: Well, Traci, you know that I have a certain image to maintain, especially when I'm talking with our clients. How do you feel about it, Dena?

Patrick: I see your point about the windows, Mr. Williams. That doesn't bother me too much. I am more concerned about where you have placed my desk. Just look how far I'm going to have to walk every time you call me in for dictation. Why did you put me miles away?

Williams: I put you there so that you can give a helping hand to Paul and Irene. They're still pretty new with us and haven't learned the ropes yet. I need someone to watch over them.

Back in his office, Williams is mulling over the reactions of Hitchcock and Patrick. He begins to think about his "monopolizing" the two windows and his placement of Patrick's desk. He comes to the conclusion that he does not want it to appear that he is appropriating the only two windows in the office. Yet he feels that he deserves the "two-window" status symbol. Also, he believes that close supervision of Higgins and Kurth must be provided.

Prepare a report in which you:

1. Offer suggestions to Williams as he begins to plan the space requirements for his people, the furniture, and the work to be done.

2. React to Williams' feelings that he is entitled to all window space.

3. Include a layout for the new office area, showing the number of square feet you recommend for each employee's workstation.

14

Ergonomics in the Office

GOALS FOR THIS CHAPTER

After you have completed this chapter, you should be able to:

1. Explain the nature of ergonomics as a field of study and describe how ergonomics affects productivity in the office.
2. Identify the key factors in the office surface environment and their effects upon the productivity of office workers.
3. Define these aspects of the seeing environment in an office: the quantity of light, the quality of light, the relative efficiency of daylighting and various artificial lighting systems, and criteria for evaluating lighting systems.
4. Discuss these features of the hearing environment: the measurement of noise, the effects of noise on employee performance, methods of controlling office noise, and the advantages and disadvantages of using music in the office.
5. Identify the basic features of the air environment.
6. Explain the following: how the safe and secure environment affects the level of office productivity, five methods for controlling the physical safety of employees, and five methods for controlling their security and well-being on the job.
7. Discuss the components of an energy management program that includes the conservation of energy in the office.

As the automation of office work increases, we find increasing efforts to make the office staff more productive. Many of these efforts take the form of research studies that generally come to this important conclusion: *The office environment has a strong, direct effect on the quality and quantity of work produced in the office as well as on the morale of all workers.*

Consider for a moment your own experiences with these common environmental problems:

1. Sitting in an unadjustable typist chair—one that had no padding on the seat or back—for four or more hours while typing.
2. Attending a college class during the hottest summer days in which the classroom was not air conditioned, the images shown on a screen from an overhead projector were too small to read, the glare from sunlight invaded your space because of the absence of window shades, and the whispering of students prevented your hearing the instructor's lecture.
3. Operating a video display terminal in a setting in which bright fluorescent ceiling lights as well as the reflections from the outdoor sunlight on your terminal screen caused eyestrain.
4. Undergoing long periods of close-concentration work in a noisy location near the front door of an office which hampered the quality of your work, making you irritable, frustrated, and even considering the prospects of another job.

On the job, such environmental problems lower worker morale and productivity and increase operating costs. To address these serious problems, an environmental field of study known as ergonomics has emerged. Ergonomics comes from two Greek words, "ergon" (work) and "nomos" (laws of). As a field of study, **ergonomics** explains how the performance and morale of workers on the job are dependent on the *physiological* and *psychological factors* in the workers' environment. Ergonomics integrates the use of space, furniture and equipment, and other physiological factors such as light, color, sound, and temperature, to meet the psychological needs of the workers on the job.

When you study all the ergonomic elements that comprise an organization, you are dealing with *macroergonomics*, which integrates such comprehensive topics as organizational structure, company-wide communication programs, and job descriptions of personnel. On the other hand, when you study the individual ergonomic components within a system (for example, people, equipment, and space), you are involved with *microergonomics*. This latter type of study is often performed at the department level; but a truly successful ergonomics program cannot be realized without considering the macroergonomic level throughout the firm.[1]

In this chapter we discover what ergonomics is and analyze its role in the office. Since office automation presents new ergonomic problems to the AOM, methods for ensuring high levels of work in automated workcenters in business and home offices will be discussed. Finally, because most ergonomic factors involve costly economic resources that use energy, the conservation of energy in the office is explored.

ERGONOMIC NEEDS IN THE OFFICE

All office work depends upon the following closely related elements: (1) *human activities* performed in the office, (2) *applications of social psychology* dealing with human behavior on the job, and (3) the *main environmental features* that affect office operations. Thus, it is important for the AOM

to understand thoroughly these elements in order to provide for the ergonomic needs of the worker. Each of these elements is discussed briefly in this section so that a foundation can be laid for understanding the ergonomic processes in the office.

Human Activities in the Office

Research studies completed by major corporations as well as those done in educational institutions classify the activities performed by office workers into four categories: cognitive, social, procedural, and physical, each of which is illustrated in Figure 14-1.[2] **Cognitive activities** are largely mental in nature and revolve around the use of knowledge or judgment. These activities range from simple tasks, such as proofreading, to the complexities included in decision making. **Social activities** involve the interpersonal tasks of two or more persons and also range from simple duties, such as telephoning, to more complex activities, such as conferring. **Procedural activities** refer to the predefined work steps followed by office employees, such as filling out forms, which may be performed simultaneously with other activities, such as reading and writing. Finally, **physical activities** are those tasks that require the use of human energy. Typing and filing or retrieving office records are common examples. Typing, or keyboarding, activities require long hours of continuous strain on the hands and wrist, sometimes resulting in *carpal tunnel syndrome*, a painful medical problem involving progressive numbness, tingling, and pain in the hand and arm. This problem, which is thought to stem from too much pressure on the median nerve in the wrist, may require surgery. The ergonomic design of VDT keyboards may help to reduce the frequency of this common problem.

---

[1]For a highly readable, interesting discussion of the important ergonomic factors in the office considering both macroergonomic and microergonomic levels in the organization, see Marilyn Joyce and Ulrika Wallersteiner, *Ergonomics: Humanizing the Automated Office* (Cincinnati: South-Western Publishing Co., 1989).

[2]Wilbert O. Galitz, *Human Factors in Office Automation* (Atlanta: Life Office Management Association, 1980), p. 40.

Dialog on the Firing Line

MARILYN JOYCE
President
The Joyce Institute
Seattle, Washington

BA, Thomas More College
MEd, Xavier University

Marilyn Joyce founded The Joyce Institute to improve the performance and well-being of people in the workplace. She manages a network of employees and Associates throughout the United States, Canada, and the United Kingdom who provide ergonomics training and consulting services to more than 500 clients, including Ford, AT&T, and the U.S. Library of Congress. She recently coauthored a textbook entitled *Ergonomics: Humanizing the Automated Office* (South-Western Publishing Co., 1989); frequently writes articles concerning ergonomics for trade publications; and presents papers at technical and administrative management conferences. Ms. Joyce is a member of several organizations including the Human Factors Society and the American Management Association.

QUESTION: How much more productive is the employee whose comforts on the job have been assured in the ergonomic office?

RESPONSE: An employee whose comforts have been assured on the job through the application of ergonomics is at least 10 to 15 percent more productive, according to most studies. By "comfort," we mean reduced fatigue, eyestrain, hand/wrist discomfort, back/shoulder pain, and headaches. The BOSTI (Buffalo Organization for Social and Technological Innovation) study says that managers, professional, technical, and clerical workers produce 15 to 17 percent more work when their comfort needs are met by changes in the workstation and environment. A NIOSH (National Institute of Occupational Safety and Health) study indicates a 17.5 percent increase as the result of new seating. The Joyce Institute surveys indicate 10 percent increases in productivity as a result of ergonomics training (health/comfort strategies, work area adjustments, short-term memory training). Most significantly, more than 85 percent of the people who received the ergonomics training reported significant improvement in their health and comfort.

The responsibility for employee comfort is shared by the employer and employees. The employer needs to provide an ergonomically sound workplace and training; the employees need to adjust their workstations to suit themselves and take frequent rest pauses (1–3 minutes) to relax, stretch, and restore circulation. The results are satisfied employees who produce quality work at higher rates of productivity.

Figure 14–1
Classifica-
tion of
Human
Activities in
Performing
Office Work

Social Office Activities
   Telephoning
   Dictating
   Conferring
   Meeting

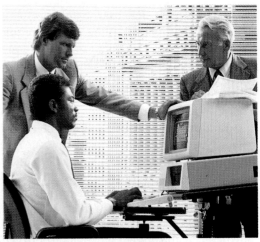

Cognitive Office Activities
   Information development/gathering
   Information storage and retrieval
   Reading/proofreading
   Data analysis/calculating
   Planning/scheduling
   Decision making

Procedural Office Activities
   Completing forms
   Checking documents

Physical Office Activities
   Filing/retrieval
   Writing
   Mail handling
   Copying/reproducing
   Collating/sorting
   Pickup/delivery
   Typing/keying
   Keeping calendars
   Using equipment

Research tells us that there is overlap among the four categories. For example, writing and filing, which require physical energy, also entail the use of some cognitive activities; and telephoning tasks may also involve the completion of message forms. Regardless, the ability of AOMs to create a comfortable and efficient environment depends on identifying the basic tasks in the office and knowing how such tasks can be performed in an efficient manner.

Each of these human activities is performed in both business-office and home-office settings. In the typical business office, we find a greater number of workers and, accordingly, more interpersonal behavior problems than in the home-office setting. In addition, the business office will likely have more rules and greater formality than the home office where typically one worker makes slight modifications in the home setting to provide office space. However, in both locations, ergonomic factors are directly involved in determining how productive and satisfied the workers are.

Human Behavior Problems on the Job

Human behavior problems can cause difficulties for the office manager because these problems are largely intangible and emotional in nature. Many of the problems involve the worker as an individual and deal with status, the need for belonging, and the fulfillment of motivational needs. Problems can also relate to social conditions, such as the degree of satisfaction workers have in working with and for others. Thus, the AOM must take time to study the personalities of workers and attempt to understand their attitudes toward themselves, their work, and their co-workers. All workers—and that includes the AOM—must recognize the need for adjusting to other people's personalities and for solving personal job problems. These subjective aspects of management were discussed in Part 2 of this textbook.

Major Ambient Factors in the Office

The term *ambience* and its derivative *ambient* have gained widespread usage in discussions of our surroundings or environment. Thus, when we speak of **ambient factors** in the office, we refer to those conditions that *surround and affect* the performance of work and the development of worker satisfactions with the work and workplace. Many of these factors are physical since they involve the human senses, such as sight, hearing, and touch. Other factors are psychological in nature (the security that comes from working in a safe place and the feelings that arise from visual comfort and working in an attractive setting) and help to create the communication climate and levels of morale found in the office.

Studies show that today's workers want an office setting that is comfortable and efficient.[3] Thus, offices that cling to traditional, "institutional" layouts having row after row of desks and file cabinets are considered impersonal. A manager's office that seems to be "guarded" by a private secretary, too, seems unfriendly. In contrast, today's office staff wants a workplace that is *flexible, comfortable, safe*, and *understandable* (as far as the use of all resources is concerned); and has *reliable equipment* and *personnel* and *usable, efficient procedures*. In addition, today's office workers seek a personalized ambience that fosters and maintains a friendly atmosphere in which to work.

In order to provide such an environment, employees should be given an opportunity to assist in planning their work areas and to

---

[3]Examples are the Steelcase and BOSTI research studies reported in Chapter 13 as well as the AMS Foundation research studies quoted in this chapter. For a comprehensive view of the most significant ergonomic studies relating to the office, see J. Thomas Black, Kelley S. Roark, and Lisa S. Schwartz, Eds., *The Changing Office Workplace* (Washington, DC: The Urban Land Institute and the Building Owners and Managers Association International, 1986).

bring some of their own personalities into their workstations, such as being permitted to have personal photographs, wall hangings, and plants in their work areas. When employees are given a voice in designing their own workplaces, they develop a greater feeling of belonging and of participation. A higher level of morale and greater productivity result.

Figure 14–2 shows the complex set of ergonomic factors required to achieve an effective office ambience. All of the factors work "side by side" to affect directly the individual worker's job performance as well as the motivation and enthusiasm that a worker brings to the job. Also, as the information in the four corners of the figure shows, important economic resources must be managed by the AOM when implementing the ergonomic system.

Figure 14–2
Influence of Ergonomic Factors on Office Productivity

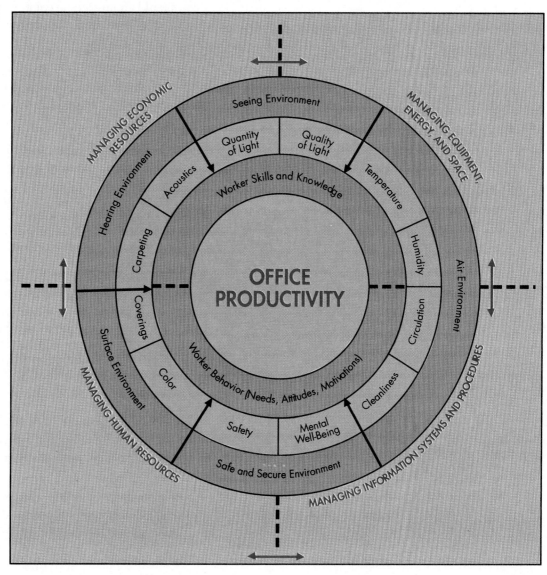

THE SURFACE ENVIRONMENT

The **surface environment** consists of those physical features in the office that are an essential part of the building, its layout, and the work performed. Included in this environment are walls, ceilings, floors, windows, pillars, furniture, and equipment and the coverings placed on them. Another item in this environment is the "plantscaping" integrated within the building. Each of these physical items has a direct effect on the psychological state of the office staff and consequently on productivity and morale.

Effective Use of Color

Color affects our emotions (moods and attitudes) and comfort in the workplace. In addition, color has a direct bearing on the effectiveness of lighting conditions in the office. Therefore, rather than choose colors according to their personal preferences, AOMs should base their color selections upon a serious study of the following factors: (1) the *work functions* that will be performed in the office area, (2) the *physical location* of the office, and (3) the *type of emotion desired* from employees (to stimulate or to relax). With the increased use of the open plan, more attention is required to coordinate the colors used on the office walls with the colors chosen for the individual workstations. Following is a discussion of the emotional effects of color upon the office staff and customers or clients.

Human Reactions to Color

Color sets the mood of an office staff. In this sense, colors can make us feel hot or cold, happy or distressed; and satisfied or dissatisfied with our work space, depending upon the *hue* (the particular shade or tint) of the color, the *lightness* or *darkness* of the color, and the *intensity* (brightness or dullness) of the color. Notice the characteristics of color found in your classroom, library, hallways, cafeteria, and bulletin boards. What is your reaction to these colors?

Table 14–1 lists various color hues and their effects on workers. The *distance effect* tells us how near or far the colored object or area appears to the viewer; the *temperature effect* refers to how warm or cool the color makes the space seem; and the *mood effect* describes how mentally stimulated or relaxed people feel. For example, if you wish to create a cool and calming effect on people, you should choose a blue color of the proper color intensity. Typically people perceive lighter colors such as yellow or yellow-green as bright and cheerful and often respond by keeping their work areas clean and tidy. On the other hand, fast-paced offices may create much worker tension which requires restful colors, such as white or off-white, light gray, and blue.

To create exciting effects, you should choose (but not overuse) orange, red, or yellow colors; on the other hand, remember that dark colors, such as black and brown, often depress workers. For eastern or northern exposures, warm colors such as yellow, peach, brown, and tan are recommended; and for the warmer southern or western exposures, cool colors, such as blue, green, and violet are recommended. Because of its neutrality, white produces no strong reactions although it does increase the perception of light and space. Gray colors are usually not recommended, for they produce a numbing effect. On the other hand, the use of bright, cheerful, nonagitating colors provides contrast and vision-breaks, and results in a restful feeling that is more likely to boost productivity.

More specific ways in which color affects human behavior are:

1. *Brightly colored offices seem cheerful and efficient looking and tend to inspire feelings of trust;* drab, poorly painted offices, on the other hand, convey a feeling of boredom or inefficiency.

Table 14-1
Effects of
Colors on
Workers

Color	Distance Effect	Temperature Effect	Mood Effect
Red	Close	Warm	Very stimulating; increases blood pressure
Yellow	Close	Very warm	Exciting, cheerful; can cause eyestrain if too bright or overused
Blue	Farther away	Cool	Soothing, pleasant, calm; reduces blood pressure and effects of stress; overuse can cause sluggishness
Green (light)	Farther away	Neutral	Unobtrusive, calming; can be gloomy if too dark a shade is used
Orange	Very close	Very warm	Exciting; overuse can cause eyestrain
Violet	Very close	Cool	Aggressive, dignified, stately; can be tiring
Black, brown, or dark gray	Very close Claustrophobic	Neutral	Gloomy; absorbs light; can create fatigue and drowsiness
Gray (light)	Farther away	Neutral	Calming, soothing; can be boring if not highlighted by other colors
White	Farther away	Neutral	Soothing; can be boring if overused; can cause glare on VDT screens

Source: Adapted from Marilyn Joyce and Ulrika Wallersteiner, *Ergonomics: Humanizing the Automated Office* (Cincinnati: South-Western Publishing Co., 1989).

2. *The color of all office surfaces—walls, furniture, equipment, even paper—may cause eyestrain due to improper lighting or reflectance if the colors are not carefully selected.* The result may be eyestrain, headaches, sluggish feelings, and other unhealthy symptoms that cause a staff to perform under par. Under such conditions, worker morale is negatively affected, thinking and concentration powers are diminished, and the accuracy of work is reduced.

3. *The perceptions of people can be changed by the use of color.* For example, office dimensions appear to be changed by the combination of color and light; long, narrow offices seem wider by using darker colors on the narrow end walls and lighter colors on the long side walls.

Square-room monotony in an office can be avoided by painting one wall, preferably the window or opposite wall, a color different from the others. High ceilings seem much lower when painted a color darker than the walls. Also, light colors make a small office space seem larger.

4. *Color helps people to identify key building locations.* Some high-rise buildings use alternating colors for each floor. Thus, when the elevator door opens, the customer looking for the purchasing office immediately recognizes the correct floor when a bright gold color appears (gold being the color code assigned to the purchasing department). A color like red is often used for safety doors because of its attention-getting quality.

Reflection Values of Colors

The colors used in an office reflect light to varying degrees. The **reflection ratio** measures the amount of light reflected from a surface as a percentage of the total amount of light striking that surface. With such a measure, the AOM can restrict the choice of colors to achieve the percentages of reflected light shown in Figure 14–3. Interior designers and representatives of paint manufacturers can provide good advice at little or no cost on the selection of appropriate office colors.

Wall and Ceiling Colors

Since the walls and ceiling constitute the largest surface areas in the office, attractive, psychologically soothing colors should be chosen for these areas. When making such a selection, you should keep this guideline in mind: *Office walls and ceilings should be light enough to reflect light rather than absorb it but not light enough to produce annoying glare*. Table 14–2 lists a wide selection of colors and the percent of light reflected by each color. Generally, a middle

Figure 14–3 Recommended Percentages of Light to Be Reflected from Office Surfaces

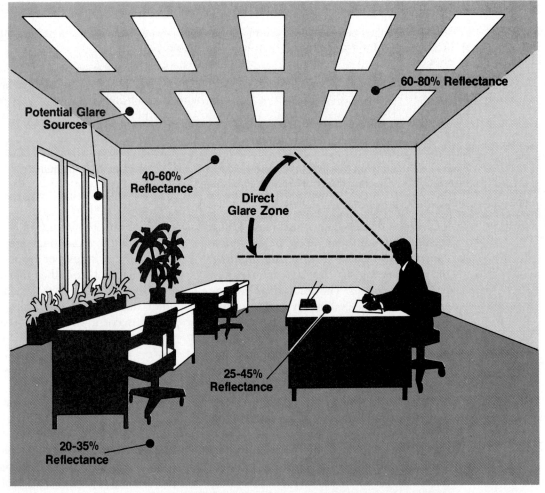

Source: General Electric Company, Lighting Applications Bulletin (LAB) 902-7/5/7R, *Office Lighting* (1989), p. 12.

Table 14–2
Percent of
Light
Reflected by
Various
Colors

Color	Percent of Light Reflected	Color	Percent of Light Reflected
White	82	Golden yellow	51
Gray-white	76	Medium gray	46
Light cream	74	Dark orange.	37
Very light green	70	Copper-yellow	27
Lemon-yellow	67	Medium red	21
Medium pink	60	Cadet blue	15
Very light blue	60	Dark red	12
Light gray	56	Dark green.	10

reflectance range—from 40 to 60 percent—has been found best for office walls. The first four colors in this table are usually recommended for office ceilings and walls because of the high degree of light reflected by these colors. Colors used in an automated workcenter where a computer and documents are being used should have a reflectance value of approximately 50 percent; thus, off-white or white walls should not be used in computerized offices because of the glare that white creates on the VDT screen. Instead, such office walls should be painted medium-light tones like blue or green for offices exposed to sunlight; or beige or rose, which adds warmth to cooler offices.[4] To complement the wall surfaces, artwork has become an important addition to the office. While it is most often used in executive offices, artwork can be used to brighten any dark room, widen a narrow corridor, and tie the decor together.

Since annoying glare may be caused by the application of glossy paint, flat paint should be used for ceilings and side walls.

---

[4]This recommendation was made by the Color Association of the United States, 343 Lexington Avenue, New York, NY 10016, the source of much reliable information on the human response to color in the office.

The use of window shades will also reduce glare in the office.

Furniture and Equipment Colors

The same principles of color selection discussed for walls and ceilings also apply to furniture and equipment selection. In addition, glare must be considered as it is a common hazard caused by the reflection of light from glass tops on desks, other highly polished surfaces, and VDT screens. To prevent this problem, shiny desktops are not recommended; instead, furniture with a non-gloss finish should be chosen. Black or white desktops are too harsh for the eyes. Black contrasts too strongly with the surroundings; white is too reflective. Contrasting changes in light and dark-colored surfaces should also be avoided. The contrast between a white sheet of paper and a dark desktop can cause eyestrain. Therefore, light-colored desktops are recommended. Having a VDT operator look at a dark terminal screen and then quickly glance at white paper unnecessarily strains the operator's eyes. For this reason, manufacturers of VDT equipment select machine surface colors that produce a soft contrast between the light and dark colors in the direct vision of the operators. Also, light characters on a dark background, rather than dark on light, permit easier reading of the characters on the VDT screen.

Floor Coverings

The color of walls and ceilings should be well coordinated with the color and type of floor coverings to ensure a unified, harmonious environment. Of the several types of floor coverings available—carpeting, wood, solid vinyl tile, vinyl asbestos tile, marble, brick, flagstone, and terrazzo, all of which are durable—carpeting seems to be the most popular. However, solid vinyl tile lasts twice as long as carpeting.

High-quality carpeting withstands heavy traffic in areas such as reception centers and hallways. Carpeting also creates a quiet, relaxed atmosphere since its surface absorbs sound. Further, it produces a feeling of luxury, which enhances worker satisfaction and adds to the firm's prestige. Since carpeting is the most comfortable floor covering on which to walk, employee fatigue and accidents—especially falls—are reduced when compared with those reported for slippery tile or concrete. Custodial personnel consider carpeting to be easier to maintain than other types of floor coverings.

Carpeting is available in many colors and designs and is easy to coordinate in various decorating plans. Earth colors (beige, brown, and rust) are especially popular choices due to their ease of maintenance; and tweed or patterned designs are recommended for heavy traffic, high-soil areas.

A careful study should be made of the type of office function (executive or general office, for example) and the traffic volume in each. Once such data are available, carpeting can be assessed regarding (1) *ease of maintenance* depending on fiber, weight, and resistance to soiling; (2) *sound-absorbing qualities*; (3) *control of static electricity*, which is especially important in areas where automated equipment is used; (4) *flam-* *mability*, which is controlled by federal regulations that screen out carpet that is easily ignited; and (5) *resistance to excessive wear.* Reputable carpeting dealers or interior designers can assist AOMs in selecting the best types of carpeting for their offices.[5]

Use of Plants in the Office

To counteract the cold, sterile feeling that automated equipment may bring to the office environment, AOMs make extensive use of plants, or "plantscaping," to personalize work areas. The most popular use of plants on a large scale is in open-office areas where plants are combined with acoustical partitions and modular furniture. In these locations, the plants provide privacy, brighten and warm the area, and add attractive coloring. Plants are easy to place and rearrange when compared with fixed partitions and are simpler and less costly to maintain than partition walls.

Often, office personnel are permitted to choose plants for their work areas even though the company furnishes the funds for their purchase. The presence of the living plants, themselves, has a strong positive effect on morale. The plants in effect become the employees' plants. Studies show that increased productivity and decreased employee turnover result when plants are "recruited" for the office. While small offices may use only a few plants, large firms often require hundreds. In this case, the OM must consider whether the plants should be purchased and maintained by the office staff, purchased and placed under a maintenance contract similar to machines, or leased. The cost of leased plants used for decorative purposes in a business office is fully tax deductible.

---

[5]For other reliable information on carpet selection and care, contact the Carpet and Rug Institute, Box 2048, Dalton, GA 30720.

THE SEEING ENVIRONMENT

The **seeing environment** refers to all the items needed to provide adequate light for performing the work assigned the office. The main goals for the seeing environment are (1) to provide efficient, comfortable lighting and a safe place to work; (2) to help develop a feeling of visual comfort and an esthetically attractive work area, which often includes the effective use of color, as discussed earlier; and (3) to assist in reducing the use of electrical resources, which typically account for approximately 50 percent of the total energy bill. To achieve these goals requires providing the proper quantity and quality of light, factors considered as the most necessary to office comfort by workers taking part in the Steelcase research study cited earlier.

Quantity of Light

To measure the *illuminance* or quantity of light, the footcandle (FC) is used. A **footcandle** is the amount of light produced by a candle at a distance of one foot from the source of light. It can be compared with a *watt* of light, as one watt per square foot produces about 15 footcandles of light. Lighting levels in many modern buildings are in the 90–150 FC range.[6] Such high quantities of light are preferable for paper-based operations because, generally speaking, more light results in easier reading of paper documents, better health and morale, and greater efficiency of employees. Ironically, however, higher quantities of light in the office cause problems for VDT users since it becomes more difficult to read the characters on the screen because of insufficient contrast between the amount of light on the screen and the ambient area in the office.

---

[6]Wilbert O. Galitz, *The Office Environment: Automation's Impact on Tomorrow's Workplace* (Willow Grove, PA: Administrative Management Society Foundation, 1984), p. 71. (AMS and its subsidiary functions have been moved to Trevose, PA.)

Thus, VDT operations should be carried out in areas with lower quantities of light than in the general office. The best "seeing" location for a VDT operator often involves the proper placement of a luminaire (light fixture) and/or the use of outside light as shown in Figure 14–4. As Figure 14–4B implies, there will be no shadows on the workplace with this arrangement, and the amount of light entering the window can be controlled by the use of blinds.

Inadequate amounts of light, on the other hand, induce eyestrain, which in turn may cause such problems as muscular tension, fatigue, and irritability. Inadequate light may also cause poor workmanship, inaccurate work, and lowered production. Most utility companies will measure the amount of light in an office with a light meter and then make recommendations for any changes needed. Little or no cost is involved.

Before making decisions on the quantity of light needed in an office, the OM should understand the visual tasks required of the workers. Some tasks, such as drafting, computer programming, and careful reading of dim photocopies or unclear handwriting, require close detail work and high footcandle levels. Other activities, such as conducting meetings and interviews, involve less concentration and thus require much less light. Table 14–3 shows the minimum levels of light recommended for various types of office work. However, the older office worker will require more footcandles than the minimums indicated in Table 14–3. For people 50 years of age, 50 percent more light is needed than was required when they were young; and for those over 60, 100 percent more light may be needed.[7] To provide such flexible lighting needs as well as to economize on energy used, lighting engineers recommend using a nonuniform system of varying lighting intensity—50 footcandles on work tasks, 30 footcandles in surrounding

---

[7]Ibid.

Figure 14-4
VDT Place-
ment in Rela-
tion to Win-
dow and
Overhead
Lighting

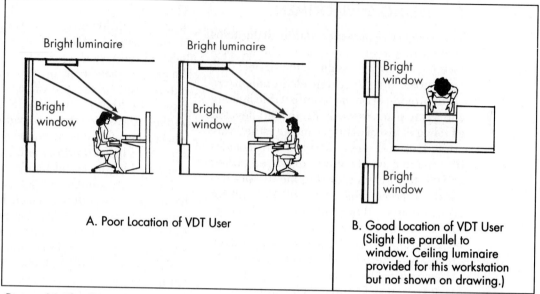

Source: Marilyn Joyce and Ulrika Wallersteiner, *Ergonomics: Humanizing the Automated Office* (Cincinnati: South-Western Publishing Co., 1989), p. 125.

areas, and 10 footcandles in corridors, bathrooms, and core areas (the central part of clustered workstations). This plan reduces the number of fixtures in addition to decreasing lighting and cooling costs.[8]

Quality of Light

The quality of light refers to those features of a lighting system that provide a visually comfortable work area, free of glare or shadows, and which help to create an attractive office climate. The quality of light cannot be measured as easily as the quantity of light, although several yardsticks for measurement are available.

Since the quality of light is directly affected by the brightness of light, that brightness must be kept under control. One useful yardstick for determining the amount of brightness is the footlambert. The **footlambert** is a unit of measure approximating one footcandle of light emitted or reflected. To find the amount of brightness present, the ratio of footlamberts between two surfaces, such as a desktop and the wall area near the desk, must be computed. For example, assume that the brightness of a visual task is 60 footlamberts and the brightness of a dark desktop against which the task is viewed is five footlamberts. A brightness ratio of 12 to 1 is found, which is much too bright and hence will cause visual discomfort. Usually the brightness ratio, which is, in effect, a measure of contrast in two lighted areas, should not exceed 3 to 1.

The **visual comfort probability (VCP)**, another yardstick for measuring the quality of light, is an index of the feelings of the office staff regarding the degree of comfort provided by the lighting system. For example, a VCP of 75 means that at least three-fourths of the people in the worst viewing position in the lighted space find the lighting system comfortable and relatively free from

---

[8]J. Thomas Black, Kelley S. Roark, and Lisa S. Schwartz, Eds., *The Changing Office Workplace* (Washington, DC: The Urban Land Institute and the Building Owners and Managers Association International, 1986), p. 125.

Table 14-3
Recommended
Lighting
Levels in
Footcandles

Type of Office Activity or Area	Range in Footcandles
Visual tasks that are only occasionally performed as in lobbies, reception areas, corridors, washrooms, circulation areas, and on stairs	10–20
Task lighting involving performance of visual tasks of high contrast or large size, as in reading newsprint, typed originals, impact printing with a good ribbon, ball point pen, and felt tip pen as performed in conference rooms, library areas, and in general filing areas	20–50
Task lighting involving performance of visual tasks of medium contrast or small size, as in mail sorting, reading thermal printing, xerography, drafting with high contrast, photographic work, and writing with #3 pencil and softer	50–100
Task lighting involving performance of visual tasks of low contrast or very small size, as in drafting (with low contrast), charting, graphing, reading poor thermal copy	100–200

Source: General Electric Company, Lighting Applications Bulletin (LAB) 205-41507, *Office Lighting* (August, 1985), p. 5.

glare. For paper tasks, a VCP of 70 is recommended; for VDT tasks, however, a VCP of 90 or more is suggested.

Visual discomfort caused by overly bright surfaces (poorly shaded light fixtures and glossy paint finishes on room surfaces and office equipment are common examples) can be easily corrected by proper light fixtures and color choices. Glare, too, causes visual strain and leads to lowered productivity, and muscular and nervous tension. In addition to the problems of glare caused by glossy paint and other shiny surfaces, controlling glare on VDT screens has become a serious problem for the AOM. To reduce glare on such terminals, several control measures are available:

1. Adjust the contrast and brightness knobs on the screen to meet the VCP index of the user.
2. Lower the lighting levels in the areas where VDT equipment is used in order to provide greater contrast and less glare between the surface of the screen and the immediate environment.

3. Tilt the screen, if possible, to the point where viewing is more comfortable.
4. Rearrange the VDT equipment so that office windows are at right angles to the operator (see Figure 14-4). Direct or reflected light will thus be channeled away from the eyes of the operator.
5. Use antireflection filters placed over the screen.

VDT users, especially those using the equipment for long periods of time, report many physical and emotional problems after long hours of operation. Included in the list are eyestrain, blurred vision, backache, and fatigue. However, repeated research studies indicate that nothing inherent in VDT technology causes these problems, and that non-VDT office workers seem to report as many of these problems as VDT users.[9] AOMs are encouraged to make sure that all VDT users take frequent work breaks; have flexible, adjustable equipment that will permit changes in posture; and make consistent use

[9]Ibid.

of glare-reduction methods mentioned earlier. Several years ago a law was passed in Suffolk County, New York, requiring businesses with more than 20 VDTs to give special treatment to those operators who spend more than 26 hours a week at their VDT screens. The law requires that the workers must have 15-minute breaks or a new work assignment after three hours at the machine. Also, the employer must pay 80 percent of the cost of annual eye exams and any eyeglasses that are needed; and all new VDT equipment purchased must be equipped with nonglare screens.[10]

Sources of Light

Two sources of light are available to the office: daylight (natural light) and artificial light.

Daylight

Daylight is a free resource that enters the office through windows or skylights. However, this natural light source must be controlled, especially the direct sunlight that produces glare, visual discomfort, and eye-strain and increases the temperature in the office. However, on cloudy days, no direct sunlight is available; yet people who favor work settings with windows may become depressed if they are assigned to work-stations without access to windows.

Too often daylight is lost by the use of heavy draperies, venetian blinds, or partitions. To use as much daylight as possible, casements, adjustable (louvered) blinds, and window screens that deflect the direct sunlight and reduce glare while still permitting light to enter are recommended. All windows should be regularly cleaned to admit as much natural light as possible since studies show consistently that workers prefer more

daylight rather than more artificial light on the job.

Artificial Light

To supplement natural light, which is not sufficient to meet all the needs of office lighting, three types of artificial lighting systems are used: incandescent light, fluorescent light, and high-intensity discharge lamps.

Incandescent light is produced in filament bulbs such as those commonly used in the home. Such bulbs use much current and give off noticeable heat (only 10 percent of their energy produces light; the balance produces heat). They also produce a steady light that strengthens yellow, orange, and red colors. Incandescent light fixtures and bulbs are less expensive than fluorescent fixtures and bulbs, but they are less efficient because of the difficulty in providing recommended levels of lighting.

Fluorescent light is most commonly produced in long tubelike lamps found in offices and commercial establishments. These lamps do not give off nearly so much heat as incandescent lamps and consume about one-third the wattage for an equal amount of light. A 20-watt fluorescent lamp gives the same light output as a 60-watt incandescent bulb but uses much less energy. The chief advantages of fluorescent lighting are low cost of operation, low heat emission, less glare, resemblance to natural daylight, and an even distribution of light. In addition, the tubes last much longer than incandescent bulbs.

High-intensity discharge (HID) lamps represent a still more efficient form of lighting. These lamps, which have been widely used for street, stadium, and parking lot lighting, are now adapted into office and hallway lighting systems that allow the intensity of light to be controlled. HID lamps use electrical energy two to three times more efficiently than fluorescent systems and as much as six times more efficiently than

[10]Willie Schatz, "Suffolk Law, New Studies Reinvigorate VDT Debate," *Datamation* (August 15, 1988), pp. 39–41.

incandescent bulbs. However, some forms of HID lamps project a yellow light that has produced health problems for office workers—headaches and dizziness are often mentioned. In addition, lamps such as these require the use of an auxiliary device for starting and operating, which produces an irritating humming sound.

The kind of artificial lighting distributed in an office depends on the type of fixture being used. Lighting systems should be designed so the fixtures are spaced (and sometimes ceiling-recessed) according to the needs of the work area and characteristics of the room. *Direct lighting fixtures* furnish light directly to the work surface while *indirect lighting fixtures* project the light to the ceiling to be reflected down to the work surface. Manufacturers of light fixtures publish information on the various fixture options and other data for making wise selections of fixtures and accessories.

Task/Ambient Lighting

Open-space planning requires that satisfactory lighting be available at the workstations. This practice contrasts sharply with the typical lighting plan for the conventional office design that provides recommended footcandle levels uniformly from ceiling fixtures. Traditional ceiling fixtures are not efficient for the open work area, which is broken up by screens, panels, and modular furniture that create shadows on the work surfaces. To remedy this situation, **task lighting** was developed in which the light fixtures are built into the open-plan furniture (desks and cabinets) to light specific work areas. Thus, it is possible to eliminate much overhead lighting and to provide portable lighting that moves with the furniture as it is rearranged.

Ambient lighting uses indirect fixtures or uplights that direct light upward to be reflected off the ceiling onto other surfaces that surround the workstation. Usually ambient lighting is combined with task lighting (hence, the term *task/ambient*) to provide a lighting system offering these advantages: (1) *flexibility*, because of the potential for easy, inexpensive rearrangement of office interiors; (2) *ease of installing and maintaining acoustical panels* in the ceiling because no permanent ceiling fixtures are required for lighting; (3) *reduced glare and reflection* and a greater uniformity in lighting; (4) *lower costs*, as less energy is consumed for lighting the work area, and lighting installation costs are also reduced; (5) *fewer ceiling fixtures and lamps to replace* and easier accessibility to such lamps; and (6) *easier opportunities for office building renovation*, with less wiring for lighting built into the structure.[11] An illustration of task/ambient lighting is shown in Figure 14–5.

Evaluation of Lighting Systems

The ideal lighting system in the office should provide light in the *right amount*, of the *right quality*, in the *right work area*, and at the *lowest possible cost*. Questions to be answered in evaluating office lighting systems are:

1. How much light does the lighting system produce?
2. How much light is actually needed to perform the required tasks? (The age of the workers must be strongly considered in answering this question.)
3. What energy conservation measures are available to keep the wattage used to a

---

[11]Two valuable sources of studies on human reactions to task/ambient and other types of lighting are (1) the federal government study, "Lessons Learned: User Reaction Study—Systems Furniture with Task/Ambient Lighting," which is available from the General Services Administration, Design Action Center, Washington, DC 20405; and (2)Jean D. Wineman, Ed., *Behavioral Issues in Office Design* (New York: Van Nostrand Reinhold Company, 1986), Section III.

Figure 14–5
Task/
Ambient
Lighting in
the Office

minimum? (A list of useful measures is provided in a later section of this chapter.)

4. What appearance does the lighting system create—free from glare, accenting the surface colors appropriately, etc.?

5. How much heat does the light produce?

6. How much light is lost as the bulb "ages"? (Incandescent bulbs, for example, are much less efficient, producing less light as they get older.)

7. Is the system easy and inexpensive to maintain?

8. Is the system safe from fires and shocks? Are fixtures, for example, out of reach of the workers to minimize accidents; or, in the case of task/ambient lighting, can the light fixtures be touched without danger of burns?

9. What is the effect of the lighting system on employees? Rather than emphasizing lighting alone, it is wise to emphasize seeing and the impact that good visibility has on employee mood and efficiency.

Engineers specializing in lighting systems can assist the AOM in developing an adequate seeing environment for the office. In addition, advice can be obtained at minimal cost from the local power and light company.

THE HEARING ENVIRONMENT

The **hearing environment** deals with office sounds, which can be good or bad. When sound, like background music and pleasant conversation, is soothing to workers, it is good and aids office production. However, when sound, like street noises, vibrating office machines, ringing telephones, or squeaky doors, is irritating and distracting, it is bad and hampers production. Unwanted sound is called *noise*, a factor that must be carefully controlled if the office is to be efficient.

To control noise, sound must be measured. The **decibel** (db.) is the unit of measure to determine the relative loudness of sounds, equal approximately to the smallest degree of difference of loudness detectable by the human ear. Thus, the faintest sound that the ear can hear is 1 db.; louder sounds have higher decibel values. Table 14–4 shows common sounds in the work environment, their decibel values, and the relative effect of each sound level (from very faint to extremely loud). In addition, recommended maximum levels of noise for efficient office work are included. Permitting office sounds to extend beyond these levels will result in physical and emotional damage to workers, and in turn, production will suffer.

Sources and Effects of Office Noise

Automobiles, motorcycles, sirens, and trucks account for a majority of the outside noise that is carried into the office. Inside the office, the principal sources of noise are (1) electronic equipment, which is used to an increasing degree; (2) the reduced square footage for each workstation, a trend that places more workers in a given area; (3) more open offices where noise travels more freely between work areas; and (4) the increased use of glass as exterior walls of buildings, which results in more noise being reflected back into the office. Even in the smallest offices, we find several electric typewriters or VDTs with printers, at least one copier, and several telephones, in addition to air-conditioning and heating equipment. Larger offices have more equipment, such as computers and printers and telephones, that link all workstations to each other and to the outside world. Many of these machines are in operation at the same time, thus raising the amount of noise to a very high level. The sound from five typewriters alone has been measured at 80 db., only slightly less than the 90 db. produced by a pneumatic drill in the street. A person has to shout to be heard at 80 db.

Personnel also contribute their share to office noise through conferences, telephone calls, and discussions about work assignments and personal matters. Even the movement of workers from one location to another creates unwanted sound, especially where carpeting is not used as a floor covering.

Uncontrolled noise has many undesirable effects on the workers' health. For example, noise interferes with communication and reduces the workers' ability to concentrate. This in turn makes them irritable, tired, and less productive, which leads to discontent, absenteeism, and eventually to high turnover. Hearing may also become impaired from prolonged noise. Over a period of time, excessive noise can cause loss of sleep from the nervous tension created.

Table 14–4 Common Sounds, Noise Levels, Decibel Ranges, and Recommended Maximum Noise Levels for the Office

Common Sounds	Noise Levels	Decibel Ranges	Recommended Maximum Noise Levels for the Office
Whispers	Very Faint	10–20	
Private office, quiet conversation	Faint	20–40	40 db., for private offices
Average office, typical conversation	Moderate	40–60	60 db., for general offices
Noisy office, average street noise	Loud	60–80	80 db., for data centers
Office machine room, loud street noises	Very Loud	80–100	
Motorcycle and rock band	Extremely Loud	110–130	

Through the years, researchers have studied the effects of noise on office workers. One study, which measured the amount of caloric energy used by typists, found that 19 percent more energy was required in a noisy office. Another study showed that the human nervous system develops stress at 70 db. On the other hand, when noise levels are reduced, beneficial effects, such as decreased typing errors, lowered turnover rate, and general overall increases in efficiency and worker comfort, are found.

Noise problems are intensified by the use of lightweight construction materials in modern office buildings. Also, increasing the size of an office staff may require packing people into insufficient space, which accentuates the problem of noise and calls for strong measures for its control.

Controlling Office Noise

People cannot function well in a "sound vacuum." Rather, a certain level of sound creates a healthy background and helps set a tempo for the work to be accomplished. A properly noise-controlled office keeps sound within comfortable ranges to ensure good hearing and speech privacy.

The Occupational Safety and Health Act (OSHA) restricts noise levels for industrial workers to 90 db. for eight hours; however, this level is questioned by many managers as being too high for industrial workers and far higher than the decibel levels recommended for the office (see Table 14-4). At the state and local levels, organizations such as the National Association of Noise Control Officials are working with the Environmental Protection Agency to limit noise pollution in towns and cities.

An effective noise-control program concentrates on two main areas: (1) eliminating the source of the noise and (2) using sound-absorbing (acoustical) materials to reduce the effects of the noise. For this latter approach, a **noise-reduction coefficient (NRC)** has been developed to measure the amount of noise absorbed or removed from an area. An acoustical screen with an NRC rating of 85, for example, as may be used in an open office plan, absorbs 85 percent of the noise striking it. The highest attainable NRC rating is 95. Figure 14-6 shows a plexiglas cover with a built-in cooling fan for eliminating most of the sound caused by the operation of a computer printer, usually measured at 70-75 db.

All noise-control programs are based on this important fact: *Hard surfaces reflect sounds while soft surfaces absorb them.* A comprehensive noise-control program must apply this idea to each of the noise source problems shown in Figure 14-7. A detailed list of suggestions for curtailing noise relating to layout and location, movement of personnel, inadequate surface coverings, and unprotected equipment is also provided in this figure. One good rule of thumb that you can use for testing the sound levels in any office is this: Can you conduct a normal telephone conversation next to operating machines without shouting? If not, a noise problem exists.

Figure 14-6
Computer Printer with Sound-Absorbent Cover

Figure 14–7
Main Causes
of Office
Noise and
Effective
Principles
and Practices
for Its
Control

Main Causes of Office Noise	General Principles of Office Noise Control	Specific Applications of Noise-Control Principles
1. Poor office layout or location.	1-1. Relocate office to reduce exterior noise. 1-2. Move noisy departments to remote corner locations. 1-3. Locate doors to enhance privacy and stop sound from carrying, especially in open-plan offices.	1-1. Move office from first to, say, tenth or top floor. 1-2. Segregate the printing department from other units requiring work concentration; schedule conferences in private offices. 1-3. Keep doors and windows closed; use acoustical screens for extra privacy; ask that conversations be carried on in low tones.
2. Unnecessary movement of personnel.	2-1. Redesign layout for better work flow and to reduce the amount of walking required of personnel.	2-1. Place workers whose tasks are closely related side by side, thus reducing walking and telephone calls; place machines near the employees who use them.
3. Inadequate surface coverings (where hard walls, floors, and ceilings reflect sounds back and forth).	3-1. Use sound-absorbing coverings on walls, furniture, ceilings, and partitions used in landscaped offices. 3-2. Use "masking" sounds to cover up those sounds that cannot be eliminated but that might be distracting. 3-3. Avoid uncovered floors that reflect rather than absorb sound.	3-1. Use heavy fabrics for draperies, furniture, and inner office partitions. Use carpeting on walls and acoustical tile for ceilings. 3-2. Consider using *background masking sound* (often incorrectly called "white noise"), such as the hum of machines and light fixtures, or music to hide the noise. 3-3. Use sound-absorbing floor coverings such as rubber and asphalt. Carpeting is preferred as the best sound-absorbing floor covering.
4. Unprotected machines and equipment.	4-1. Locate noisy machines in one soundproof location (even though operators' working conditions are not improved). 4-2. Provide acoustical materials at workstations to isolate noise.	4-1. Place word processing and data processing units away from the general office. Hire hearing-impaired persons where noise levels cannot be reduced. 4-2. Use acoustical cabinets (see Figure 14-6) for muffling machine noise and earplugs for reducing noise; mute telephone bells; keep all equipment oiled.

Music in the Office

For most of us, music in the office provides a pleasant background sound that calms the nerves, reduces fatigue due to work strain, and lessens work monotony. Thus, music helps to develop a more efficient climate in which our concentration on work increases, our errors are reduced, and we as employees are better able to enjoy our work setting. However, the benefits received from music in the office depend upon the type of work being performed and the appropriateness of the music for that type of work. The more monotonous or repetitive the work, the greater the soothing effect that music has on relieving mental fatigue.

Common sources that specialize in providing music for the office are vendors, such as Muzak, who have studied what kind of music to use and when to use it; local FM radio stations; and the communication departments of some business firms. Regardless of the source of music, it is important that we keep certain employee needs in mind. For example, studies have shown that music for offices must be more subdued than music for factories; that distracting influences in the music—vocals, loud brasses, or marked changes in tempo—be avoided; and that string and woodwind instruments be emphasized. Also, all types of music should be represented (from classical to popular music).

The music should be confined to the background so as not to become distracting; and it should be turned off for brief periods, possibly totaling 1 to 2½ hours a day. Music should be provided at midmorning and just before lunch and quitting time when fatigue is most likely to be present. While there is a lack of scientific research on the benefits of music for increasing productivity, large firms have reported highly favorable worker reactions to the use of music and also to their being asked for suggestions on the type of music to be played.

THE AIR ENVIRONMENT

The **air environment** refers to the total atmosphere created in the office by the principal air factors—*temperature, humidity, circulation (ventilation),* and *cleanliness.* In this sense, we use the term *air-conditioned office* literally; it is an office where the air has been carefully conditioned for human comfort, including the control of temperature, humidity, circulation, and cleanliness. However, the air environment is very subjective since you may feel too warm and open the window while your co-worker feels too cold and wants to raise the thermostatic settings.

In the Steelcase Study II on office comfort, almost three-fourths of the surveyed workers considered the air environment, especially air circulation and "the right temperature," as very important to their jobs.[12] This is a typical attitude, for a properly maintained air environment improves mental activity and boosts efficiency. Studies conducted on the impact of air conditioning in the office show that when the air was conditioned, productivity increased by almost 10 percent, absenteeism decreased by 2.5 percent, and clerical errors were reduced slightly (by about 1 percent). On the other hand, stale, dry, and dusty air dulls the mind and reduces the output of work, which is especially important since many office activities are largely cognitive. Such air may also lower worker vitality, cause headaches, and produce "four o'clock fatigue."

Temperature

Temperature refers to the relative hotness or coolness of the air measured in degrees Fahrenheit or Celsius. Although there is no

---

[12]*The Steelcase National Study of Office Environments, No. II: Comfort and Productivity in the Office of the 80s,* pp. iii–iv.

temperature level that will please all of us, the American Society of Heating, Air Conditioning, and Refrigeration Engineers suggests that the most comfortable and healthful temperature *for work* is below 70°F. For energy-conservation purposes, thermostatic settings should be limited to 65°F or lower for heating. Such a temperature level is healthful for work if the proper humidity or moisture level is maintained; for we must not forget that the human body constantly generates heat. With normal office activities, such as typing and walking, the production of heat increases rapidly.

The heating or thermal environment is the result of a proper balance in temperature, humidity, and air motion. This environment can be supplemented by outside temperature, solar heat in combination with lighting fixtures that emit heat, and heat generated by large numbers of workers and machines in the office. For example, researchers estimate that the heat produced by the electrical components of one VDT equals the heat generated by one person. Therefore, in an office where each VDT has a full-time operator, the additional heat created is equal to that of doubling the workforce in the room.[13]

Some lighting systems provide enough heat to warm offices without the need for additional heat, depending on the geographical location; and in some cases, the excess heat from the air is stored in tanks for later use when the lights are off. Other systems tie into light fixtures that turn on the lights during the night to help heat the offices. In addition, ceiling height and the materials used in building construction will affect the efficiency of heating.

Important considerations in maintaining proper temperatures in an office are employees' ages, sexes, and body sizes. As a rule, people over 40 require a higher **effective**

temperature (temperature combined with proper humidity) than young people. Women, it has been found, prefer a higher effective temperature than men; and obese people prefer a lower effective temperature than thin people. Thus, we find variation among workers in response to heat for these reasons as well as for the amount of activity involved in one's work.[14]

Humidity

Relative humidity refers to the percent of moisture in the air. Air-conditioning equipment removes moisture from the air (dehumidifies) during the summer months and may add moisture to the air (humidify) during the winter months. A high relative humidity makes us feel colder on a cold day and warmer on a hot day. Generally we feel more comfortable with a temperature of 65 to 70° F if the air is reasonably moist than if the air is dry and the temperature several degrees higher. Automated equipment can tolerate a wide range of relative humidity (from 20 to 80%); but when the humidity level falls below 20%, static electricity builds up. (Static buildup happens when a person walks across a carpeted floor and is "zapped" upon touching a doorknob.) Too little humidity causes magnetic tapes and disks to stick during processing operations and bring about errors. Too much humidity, on the other hand, produces condensation on the electronic parts of the equipment and causes short-circuiting.

The most comfortable range of humidity for most workers is from 30 to 60 percent, which can be maintained by the use of air-conditioning equipment or individual dehumidifiers (in summer) or humidifiers (in winter), depending on geographic location. In addition, static electricity can be partially

---

[13]Galitz, *Human Factors in Office Automation*, p. 99.

[14]For a concise discussion of the human needs to be considered in the air environment, see Joyce and Wallersteiner, *Ergonomics*, Chapter 8.

controlled through the use of antistatic dust covers placed over VDTs during periods of nonuse, floor mats that absorb static carried by visitors or generated by shuffling feet, antistatic sprays for carpeting, or table mats placed under VDTs to "drain" the static on contact.

Circulation

Even though a reasonable room temperature is maintained, the air must be circulated to ensure that we do not become surrounded by air that approaches skin temperature and the saturation point. As a rule of thumb, those of us working in a nonsmoking environment should be provided 12 to 15 cubic meters of outside air per person per hour; and the flow of air should be slow enough so as not to feel drafty. If much smoking is present, 30 to 40 cubic meters of fresh air per person per hour may be required.

This type of circulated air feels cool even though the temperature is high because it speeds up the evaporation of body moisture. Common methods of keeping air in motion are vent fans and blowers. Electric fans are still used to supplement air-conditioning equipment in smaller offices. However, the drafts from fans and ventilators can be annoying to some people.

Cleanliness

The complete air-conditioning system cleans the air of undesirable elements or pollutants. Although there are thousands of possible pollutants in the air, the following three major types are most commonly found in offices:

1. Toxic substances, such as asbestos (a cancer-causing substance found in acoustical tile and air-duct insulation) and carbon monoxide from vehicle exhaust.
2. Sulfur dioxide from heat and electricity production.

3. Undesirable matter, such as soot, dust, chemicals, and metals. In this category is tobacco smoke, which contains nearly 3,000 polluting compounds. In addition, the presence of the smoke produces carbon monoxide, which interferes with the oxygen-carrying ability of the blood. Dust is especially harmful to the operation of VDTs and other items of hardware in the computer system. Also, the building materials and equipment in new offices give off fumes containing formaldehyde; and copiers use chemicals that can pollute the air. Over the course of the day these pollutants are drawn into the ventilation system which may only partially replace the air that is recirculated back into the office.

A cleansed environment is more healthful for workers and at the same time permits complex equipment to function more satisfactorily. A clean, sparkling office suggests a feeling of efficiency and a regard for both customers and employees. To reduce office pollution and to respect the feelings of all personnel, OMs have set up restricted areas in which smoking is not allowed, a practice that is followed in many public and commercial establishments. This, too, ensures cleaner air, as does the use of mechanical air filters that strain foreign particles out of the air. In addition, the air environment will be further upgraded by a regular office maintenance program that includes sweeping, mopping, scrubbing, waxing, and buffing the floors; vacuuming the carpeting; cleaning the draperies and upholstered furniture; and washing and repainting the walls and ceilings as needed.

THE SAFE AND SECURE ENVIRONMENT

Our safety and security are important to our mental well-being both on and off the job. The **safe and secure environment** protects our physical needs as workers; and in so doing, it gives us a sense of well-being that soothes our emotions and improves the total working environment. Thus, the two factors—*safety* and *security*—work together in achieving a comfortable ergonomic level for the office.

Office managers are commonly assigned responsibility for maintaining the firm's safety-security environment, for this is a type of administrative service. Such responsibilities include (1) protecting the firm's assets, especially its physical plant; (2) ensuring that all relevant laws on safety are observed; (3) maintaining the well-being of employees, especially their physical comfort and convenience; and (4) helping to sustain public confidence in the firm, its products, and services, including customer safety while on the company premises.

An office is usually not so hazardous a place in which to work as an industrial plant; nonetheless potential dangers lurk everywhere for which safety measures must be provided. Some of the main safety-security problems in the office and systems for ensuring their control are discussed in this section. Computer security is discussed in Chapter 16, and protecting records is treated in detail in Chapter 18.

Safety Problems

Office personnel are typically not exposed to serious industrial hazards, such as power hand tools, highly poisonous chemicals, and moving machine parts. However, many potential safety problems do exist in the office amid the desks, file cabinets, conveyor belts, and VDTs. In fact, records show that 40,000 office workers sustain disabling injuries and more than 200 safety-related deaths occur each year in the office.[15]

---

[15]Joel Makower, *Office Hazards* (Washington, DC: Tilden Press, 1981), p. 150. Other excellent publications on office safety are available from the National Safety Council, 444 Michigan Avenue, Chicago, IL 60611.

Accidents within the office that frequently occur include:

1. *Trips and falls* caused by thick or loose and torn carpeting; highly waxed floors; tracked-in rain or snow, spilled coffee, and other slippery liquids; dropped pencils, paper clips, rubber bands, and paper; dangling electrical and telephone cords; and broken or loose stairs.
2. *Back problems* caused by improperly fitted chairs (discussed in detail in Chapter 15); leaning back and "flipping" over in a chair with casters; improper lifting; and general poor physical condition.
3. *Electrical problems* caused by improper or lack of grounding of machines, exposed wires, or plugging too many appliances or machines into the same outlet.
4. *Miscellaneous problems*, such as collisions with other persons or with obstructions improperly marked, or unmarked, within the building; falling objects, especially tipping file cabinets; colliding with open file drawers in the aisle; freak accidents with dangling jewelry and neckties near office machines; and horseplay.

As the administrative services manager, the AOM is also responsible for controlling safety problems that occur in areas external to the office. Examples are:

1. Falls and physical assaults that occur in unlighted or poorly lighted exits, aisles, halls, stairways, and parking lots.
2. Fires that occur because of lack of proper control or prevention measures including training programs.
3. Unlawful entrance to the premises caused by unlocked doors or poorly patrolled areas.

Most of these problems can be eliminated or at least reduced in number by the careful application of the control methods presented later in this chapter.

Security Problems

The basic security problem for all office employees is being assured of a job. Beyond this problem, office employees are exposed to many other security risks that relate directly to the work environment. These problems arise in the day-to-day operation of the office and cause stress and general apprehension. Both of these types of mental insecurity can have serious and long-lasting effects upon the person and the job if left unchecked.

Following is a list of typical security problems, some of which are related directly to office safety to be solved by the AOM:

1. *No overall security plan for the firm.* Employees may become anxious about the lack of fire protection when smoke alarms and automatic sprinkler systems are not provided, or if provided, are not checked regularly; employees may not be instructed in the procedures to follow in case of fire; with a lack of effective first-aid training, employees may feel unprepared in case of accident or sudden onset of a medical emergency (heart attack, stroke, or epileptic seizure).

2. *Employee feelings that their basic production and comfort needs are being ignored by their employers.* The Steelcase study, referred to earlier, highlighted employee concerns about the importance of comfortable heating, air conditioning, and ventilation to their productivity. Further, employees expect protection from dangers inherent in the workplace, especially those relating to the use of VDTs. Without such safeguards, insecurities about the job and the employer run high.

3. *Special problems of disabled workers.* Such problems include working in an unstable environment with unannounced changes, such as the rearrangement of furniture; being unable to read colored warning lights in case of fire (for the visually impaired employee); or being unable to hear sirens, signals, or warning alarms (for the hearing-impaired person).

A reduction in security problems can be expected if the control methods discussed next are followed.

Safety and Security Control Methods

Measures to provide a safe and secure environment should be a cooperative venture between management and employees, usually on a company-wide scale. With such participation from all workers in the firm, safety problems ranging from the simplest to the most complex can be understood and adequate measures for their control put into practice. Some of the most common measures for ensuring safety and security are discussed in the following paragraphs.

Safety related to space planning includes providing a well-lighted, dry work space free of debris. Stair treads should be provided, damaged floors repaired, and slip-resistant finishes applied to floors; carpets should be kept in good condition. Desks and cabinets should be arranged so as not to open into walkways, and file cabinets should be bolted together to prevent tipping. Electrical cords and telephone cords should be shortened or taped to the desks. Heavy materials should not be stored on top of cabinets. Equipment should be properly maintained and inspected regularly for health and safety standards. Many OMs conduct a monthly safety check by means of a safety checklist that covers the above items and others, such as policing the general office area, housekeeping, condition of tools and equipment, first-aid supplies, and storage of other materials.

In addition, management must conform to the provisions of two federal acts: OSHA (mentioned earlier) and the Vocational Rehabilitation Act of 1973. Under OSHA, which was enacted in 1970, employers must furnish workplaces free from recognized hazards that are likely to cause death or serious physical harm. Further, employers are required to keep records of work-related deaths, illnesses, injuries, and exposure to potentially toxic materials. Finally, employers must notify any employees who have been exposed to such materials that exceed the set standards. The rights of employees are protected in that they cannot be discharged or discriminated against because they have filed a complaint. OSHA inspectors enforce these standards by visits to the work sites.

The Vocational Rehabilitation Act of 1973 requires all new federal structures and those of organizations assisted by more than $2,500 in annual federal funding to be planned for accessibility by disabled employees. Examples of factors to consider in creating a barrier-free office environment for disabled persons include:

1. Providing appropriate entry doors, preferably of the time-delay type, with the knob 36 inches from the floor. All doors should also be at least 32 inches wide with thresholds as nearly level with the floor as possible. Revolving doors should not be permitted, as they cannot be easily used by people in wheelchairs or on crutches.
2. Allowing enough aisle space (preferably 60 by 60 inches) for wheelchairs to make a 360-degree turn.
3. Keeping desk heights to 28 inches to accommodate wheelchairs. Chairs should have casters for easy mobility and arms to enable disabled persons to lift themselves up more easily.
4. Arranging files so that drawers can be reached from both the front and sides, which eliminates awkward reaches from crutches, canes, or wheelchairs.
5. Providing carts for transporting materials, thus eliminating the need to carry them.
6. Designing the exterior of the building so there is at least one ramp entrance, pref-

erably at least 32 inches wide and at least 30 feet long. This arrangement enables disabled employees and customers to enter and exit the building completely on their own.

The modern, smart office building is designed to meet the safety and security needs of all personnel. Such buildings are commonly equipped with **integrated security systems (ISS)** that bring together under computer control intercommunication systems, burglar systems, and building-wide monitors. Typical features of the ISS in modern high-rise office buildings are closed-circuit television for monitoring the interior and exterior of the building; a burglar alarm control system for protecting exterior doors, vaults, safes and other devices (if entry is attempted to an area outside the permitted times, an alarm is activated); a control system for automated locking and unlocking of exterior and certain interior doors; walkie-talkie and related intercom systems for speedy communication throughout the building; turnkey stations for guards who patrol the building after office hours; fire protection devices that constantly monitor the water supply of the sprinkler system; ionization detectors on each floor that scan the air for traces of combustible gases or smoke; air rescue nets for emergency escapes from high-rise areas; electronically controlled locks on stairwell fire doors to prevent illegal entry into office areas; computer terminals showing the type and location of alarms; and finally, an identification card containing employee photograph, name, number, and other related information encoded for insertion into an access control device to regulate after-hours entrance and exit, and operation of elevators and gates in the parking garage. With such a comprehensive program for protecting employees, such a firm assures the workers peace of mind and protects its investment in facilities.

MANAGING ENERGY IN THE OFFICE

Cutting energy usage and reducing energy costs are ongoing, high-priority problems for all managers. Thus, the AOM shares with other managers the responsibility for studying overall energy needs and for developing energy conservation programs within their firms. Governmental agencies and private industrial and professional associations are assisting in meeting this goal.[16]

The Energy Management Program

Managing energy within a firm requires the same management techniques that are required for managing other functions, such as finance, marketing, and production. Successful approaches to energy management typically include these three steps: (1) Top management appoints an energy manager or coordinator who heads a company-wide energy control committee usually assisted by a representative from each department; (2) an energy audit is conducted to determine

how much energy is presently used in each department and how much is actually needed for efficient operation; and (3) energy conservation goals are set and methods for achieving them are made available. Employees should regularly be made aware of the need to save energy and to reduce energy costs and should know the impact that such savings will have on their jobs.

Energy Conservation Methods

The General Services Administration gives the following energy consumption breakdown for the average office building: lighting, 35 percent; heating, 35 percent; air conditioning, 25 percent; and other energy uses, 5 percent.[17] To reduce these costs, well-operated conservation programs have been developed to cut the use of energy in office buildings by as much as 50 percent. Examples of energy conservation methods available to bring about such savings are outlined in Figure 14–8. Most of these savings can be achieved with little additional cost or training of personnel and the use of a well-constructed, fully insulated office building.

---

[16]Information on energy management is available from the Office of Energy Programs, U. S. Department of Commerce, Washington, DC 20230. Also, local power and light companies will furnish practical suggestions for saving energy in the office.

[17]William Selsky, "Getting a Handle on Energy Control," *Administrative Management* (November, 1978), p. 36.

SUMMARY

1. To be productive, office employees must be housed in a physical setting that is well planned and that possesses the best conditions for meeting their ergonomic needs. Such a setting includes a surface environment made attractive through the effective use of color and plantscaping; a seeing environment that provides adequate amounts of light and high levels of visual comfort; a hearing environment that controls noise yet provides music or other pleasant background sounds to stimulate employees to a high level of work; an air environment with controls maintained through proper air conditioning; and a safe and secure environment that provides for the physical safety and mental well-being of employees on the job.

2. Many aspects of the ergonomic environment can be monitored by computer; but the maintenance of a high level of morale, security, and confidence on the job must be the main, personal responsibility of the OM. Understanding how all these environments contribute to

Figure 14–8
Methods of
Conserving
Light, Cool
Tempera-
tures, and
Heat

Conserving Light

1. Design the light-
   ing system for the
   tasks to be per-
   formed, with less
   lighting in sur-
   rounding nonwork
   areas. The
   task/ambient sys-
   tem reduces energy consumption up to 50
   percent. Individual switches and dimmers for
   each fixture can often be provided to allow
   workers at each station to select desired lighting levels.
2. Provide regular maintenance procedures by
   keeping lighting equipment clean and in good
   working order. Old bulbs should be replaced
   regularly as their output of light is reduced by
   age. Since incandescent lamps are only about
   30 percent as efficient as fluorescent lamps,
   greater use of fluorescent lamps and high-
   intensity discharge lamps should be considered.
3. Turn off lights when not needed for work tasks
   but keep in mind the firm's safety and security
   requirements. In some locations, such as inactive storage areas, lobbies and hallways, every
   other light can be turned off without harm.
4. Use daylight if possible through control of window draperies. Some modern buildings make
   greater use of skylights and atriums to bring in
   additional daylight.
5. Choose light colors on wall surfaces to increase the amount of light available (as much
   as 30 FC, in some cases), which decreases the
   amount of artificial lighting required.

Conserving Cool Temperatures

1. Maintain an efficient
   cooling system.
2. Keep a careful
   watch on thermo-
   static settings.
3. Do not cool un-
   used rooms.
4. Provide shades, draperies, and awnings to keep
   out the heat in the summer months.
5. Wear lightweight clothing. Temperatures
   approaching 80° F and 60 percent relative
   humidity may then be acceptable, with much
   savings in energy, if proper air circulation is
   provided.

Conserving Heat

1. Maintain an effi-
   cient heating
   system. Air filters
   should be
   cleaned or
   changed, and
   vents, flues, and
   burners kept clean.
2. Make effective use of heat generated by the
   human body and VDTs. Through a special
   design, the new headquarters building of the
   American Telephone and Telegraph Company
   is heated solely by body heat generated by
   employees combined with the heat from lights,
   electrical machines, etc. There is also additional heat left over to supply hot water in
   washrooms.
3. Set thermostats lower in winter. Settings
   should be lowered to 65° F during the workday,
   and office personnel should be encouraged to
   wear warm clothing. Generally for each degree
   above 65° F of a thermostatic setting, it will
   cost an additional 3 percent for heating. Overnight and weekend settings should be lowered
   to 60° F.
4. Reduce temperatures in public spaces, corridors, hallways, lobbies, and other nonwork
   areas. In these spaces, people are usually
   moving rather than sitting for hours at a time;
   hence a lower temperature can be tolerated.
   Heat should be turned off in rooms not in use.
5. Program the computer to keep track of ther-
   mostat temperatures in every room and to
   decide whether more or less heat is needed
   and then to activate the necessary equipment.
6. Reduce to a minimum the openings to the
   office. Windows and doors should be checked
   for air leakage; and where constant streams of
   people enter and leave a building, double sets
   of doors should be used.
7. Use solar energy for heating as much as
   possible. With sunlight entering the office, less
   heat is required from the heating plant; but
   shades and draperies should be drawn at night
   to confine the heat.
8. Recycle the heat generated by other sources.
   One firm collects heat through ceiling vents
   and transmits it by fan in order to heat water. In
   turn, the hot water surrenders heat to air from
   the outside as it is mixed with recycled air.

office productivity has become a major concern for all office administrators.

3. All features of the physical environment require the expenditure and conservation of energy. Thus, a well-planned energy management program becomes a necessary function of office management, especially in times of inflation and energy consciousness.

GLOSSARY

Air environment—the total atmosphere in the office created by the principal air factors (temperature, humidity, circulation, and cleanliness).

Ambient factors—those conditions that surround and affect the performance of work and the development of worker satisfactions with the work and the workplace.

Ambient lighting—the use of indirect fixtures or uplights that direct light upward to be reflected off the ceiling onto other surfaces that surround the workstation.

Cognitive activities—those human activities that are largely mental in nature and that revolve around the use of knowledge or judgment.

Decibel—the basic measure of sound, equal approximately to the smallest degree of difference of loudness detectable by the human ear.

Effective temperature—the temperature combined with proper humidity.

Ergonomics—a term that explains how the performance and morale of workers on the job are dependent upon the physiological and psychological factors in the workers' environment.

Footcandle—a measure of the amount of light produced by a candle at a distance of one foot from the source of the light.

Footlambert—a unit of brightness approximating one footcandle of light emitted or reflected.

Hearing environment—that area of the ergonomic environment dealing with noise and its control.

Integrated security systems (ISS)—safety and security control systems that are made up of intercommunication systems, burglar systems, and building-wide monitors under the control of a building's computer system.

Noise-reduction coefficient (NRC)—a measure of the amount of noise absorbed or removed from an area.

Physical activities—those human activities that involve tasks requiring the use of human energy.

Procedural activities—those human activities that refer to predefined work steps followed by office employees.

Reflection ratio—a measure of the amount of light reflected from a surface as a percentage of the total amount of light striking that surface.

Relative humidity—the percent of moisture in the air.

Safe and secure environment—all the factors that protect the physical needs of the workers and give them a sense of well-being that soothes the emotions and improves the total working environment.

Seeing environment—all the items needed to provide adequate light for performing the work assigned the office.

Social activities—those human activities that involve the interpersonal tasks of two or more persons that range from simple duties, such as telephoning, to more complex activities such as conferring.

Surface environment—those physical factors in the office (walls, ceilings, furniture, equipment, and floor coverings) that are an essential part of the building, its layout, and the work performed.

Task lighting—a type of lighting system in which the light fixtures are built into open-plan office furniture to light specific work areas.

Visual comfort probability (VCP)—an index of the feelings of the office staff regarding the degree of comfort provided by the lighting system.

FOR YOUR REVIEW

1. Explain what ergonomics is and how it affects the work produced in the office.

2. How does macroergonomics differ from microergonomics?

3. a. Identify the four categories of human activities performed in the office.
   b. What are some common examples of each human activity?

4. How does the typical business office differ from an office that operates out of the home?

5. What ambience features do today's office workers desire in their workplace?

6. List the main ways that color influences a firm's image and the health, morale, and efficiency of its employees.

7. a. What is the reflection ratio?
   b. How does this ratio relate to the effective use of color?

8. What factors should be considered in selecting floor coverings in the office?

9. What effect has the open-office design had on office ergonomics?

10. a. Define footcandle.
    b. How does the AOM make decisions regarding the number of footcandles required for adequate office lighting?

11. What yardsticks are available for measuring the quality of lighting?

12. How can glare be controlled in the use of the VDT?

13. a. Compare the relative advantages of incandescent, fluorescent, and high-intensity discharge lamps.
    b. Which type of lighting is recommended for general office use?

14. a. How is task/ambient lighting integrated into an office layout?
    b. What are the main strengths of this form of lighting system?

15. What questions should be answered in evaluating an office lighting system?

16. In what ways can sound in the office be measured?

17. a. What physical and emotional effects does noise have upon office employees?
    b. How can these effects be eliminated or reduced in severity?

18. What factors make up the air environment in the office?

19. What measures are available for ensuring a safe and secure environment for office workers?

20. Cite three effective methods for conserving light, cool temperatures, and heat in the office.

FOR YOUR DISCUSSION

1. Since you have recently won a contest that awarded you a personal computer, you are interested in creating a comfortable, productive environment in which to work at home. In addition to your personal work, you have decided to do some part-time computer processing work for others to "help your pocketbook." Discuss the basic requirements of such a work area, classifying your requirements in terms of "essential," "useful," and "nice-to-have" categories.

2. A recent issue of an administrative office management periodical carried this theme: "Plants are a metaphor of life and can have a positive effect on the nature of people." Discuss the meaning and implications of this theme for office productivity.

3. Because of low office salaries in your area, many large offices are staffed with only two types of workers: older workers in their late fifties or early sixties nearing retirement, who complain of feeling cold during much of the winter season; and young workers just out of high school and on their first full-time job, who have the opposite problem— feeling warm much of the time. Can these conflicting reactions to the temperature be resolved? If so, how?

4. The office manager of your firm, Brenda Jefferson, has asked you, her assistant, to evaluate the lighting system in the office. This request stems, in large part, from a company-wide effort to increase productivity and improve the firm's position in the market. Jefferson mentions that the present lighting system (100 percent recessed fluorescent fixtures in the ceiling) is adequate, but she likes the task/ambient lighting concept. However, she feels there may not be enough money available to purchase new equipment to accommodate this new concept; but perhaps the present desk stations can be modified to incorporate the task/ambient idea. Discuss how you would evaluate the present lighting system in an office having 34 workstations. On the basis of this information, decide whether you would accept or reject Jefferson's preference for office lighting.

5. You and the other 20 members of your office staff have become accustomed to the inexpensive energy supplies required to operate your office headquarters. As a result, heating, lighting, and cooling costs have never been questioned. Suddenly, however, you have been given an ultimatum by your office manager to reduce by 15 percent the costs of all forms of energy used in your office. Discuss how you would plan, organize, and implement an energy management program, indicating from whom you would seek advice, and how you would handle the principal human reactions to energy reductions.

6. Anxiety has permeated your 23-person office staff since the recent murder of a veteran night-shift accountant in your firm's parking lot. Also, reports have circulated around the office that personal property has been missing from the workstations and coatrooms. The general manager, Beryl Hunt, has become concerned, for the mental state of the

employees has deteriorated rapidly during the past three weeks, causing a marked decrease in efficiency and accuracy of the work. What was formerly an easygoing group of employees who enjoyed their work and their workplace has changed into a frightened staff. Hunt has discussed her concerns with you, the office supervisor, and has asked that you conduct an audit of present safety-security methods and then recommend whether additional precautions are needed. How will you proceed?

SOLVING CASE PROBLEMS

Case 14-1 Designing an Effective VDT Environment

Over the past three years, the large open-plan office of the Security Insurance Company has installed automated equipment for handling the claims work. Most typewriters have been replaced by word-processor terminals for correspondence personnel, and supervisors and managers as well as claims specialists are provided with VDTs that are linked to the firm's large central computer. However, since obtaining the automated equipment was a top priority, the ergonomic environment within which the equipment is used was put "on hold" until adequate funds were available.

Yesterday, the vice-president of administration, Bill Rogers, called you, the AOM, into his office and made this announcement:

I've got good news. The President tells me to go ahead with planning the necessary equipment, layout, plants—you know what I mean—to make our claims department a model workplace of comfort and convenience in the firm. Within the month I'd like your specific ideas in a report that can be circulated throughout the department and later discussed at a meeting of all employees.

Comply with Rogers' request, by considering the different workstation needs of executives and support personnel, such as administrative assistants, secretaries, word processing staff, and files workers. Assume that the department manager and various supervisors will not be assigned private offices (the open plan does not provide for such office designs) but require privacy. Also, keep in mind that the support personnel need efficient workstations that combine the ergonomic principles discussed in this chapter with the design guidelines illustrated in Chapter 13. Figures 13–7 and 13–8, pages 378 and 384, respectively, should be especially helpful in preparing your report to Rogers.

Case 14-2 Planning the Ideal Office Environment

For the past six months, your company newspaper has featured a column on the qualities of a humanizing, productive office environment. The articles show how other local firms are providing especially fine accommodations for their office workers. On the basis of these articles, workers in many of your firm's departments have "taken stock" of their own environments and find, as they say, "we're coming up short." Since six departments have contacted you, the office manager, about their problems, you schedule a meeting where these widespread environmental problems are uncovered:

a. All departments have an "institutional" atmosphere—row after row of desks and file cabinets; no personal touches, such as plants and photographs allowed; all desks, chairs, and files are identical in all departments; all walls and ceilings are painted a neutral beige color; fluorescent lighting is used throughout.

b. The office building is located at the corner of a busy downtown intersection. Floors are carpeted and ceilings have acoustical tiles installed for control of noise, but still the office seems unusually noisy. Only department executives have private offices.

c. Every workstation (including those of executives) is equipped with a VDT if computerized information handling is relevant to the position. This amounts to approximately 60 percent of all the 210 workstations.

d. Your building "fronts" in all four directions (north, east, south, and west) and occupies four floors served by one elevator.

e. No parking garage or lot is available, but several lots are available within one block of your building.

f. The front door of your building is locked at midnight by the night watchman, a man in his late sixties.

g. Employees feel bored and morale is low since they are not presently allowed to participate in any departmental planning to make changes in their environment.

As you return from the meeting, you chat with your superior, Sara Healey, the Vice-President of Administration, and the two of you come to this conclusion: A full-scale office environmental study is needed. Healey then asks you to prepare an agenda for undertaking such a study as well as a draft of a questionnaire that you might use to request detailed information from each department on "an ideal office environment." Comply with Healey's request.

15

Office Furniture and Equipment

GOALS FOR THIS CHAPTER

After completing this chapter, you should be able to:

1. Enumerate the guidelines to be considered by the administrative office manager in selecting office furniture.
2. Identify the main differences between conventional and modular office furniture.
3. Explain the nature and purpose of the three types of VDT workstations.
4. List the guidelines to be considered by the administrative office manager in selecting office equipment.
5. Describe the four categories of lease agreements that are used in procuring office furniture and equipment.
6. Contrast the advantages of leasing to the disadvantages of purchasing office equipment.
7. Explain how valuation methods such as payback period, break-even analysis, and average rate of return may be applied by the administrative office manager in comparing the relative net cost of purchasing with the net cost of leasing office equipment.
8. Identify the main features of the three principal methods for providing service and maintenance of office equipment.
9. Discuss the need for a well-planned replacement program for office furniture and equipment.
10. List the activities commonly found in the centralized control of office furniture and equipment when this responsibility is assigned the administrative office manager.

To ensure that the ergonomic environment discussed in Chapter 14 is properly maintained, we must give special attention to the selection and use of furniture and equipment, the key physical factors in the office. This is important to remember since the use of suitable tools and the provision for reasonable worker comfort help to create an effective psychological condition in the workers that is essential in achieving high levels of productivity.

Traditionally, office furniture and equipment have been designed and used with the efficiency of space planning and cost consciousness in mind. While these factors are important in "living within the budget," they overlook a more critical consideration—the ergonomic needs of the modern office worker. Thus, in order to manage the furniture and equipment needs of the office, the AOM must understand (1) the nature of the work being performed, (2) the ergonomic needs of the workers as discussed in Chapter 14, and (3) the increasingly complex physical environment of the modern office. For these reasons, the AOM has important responsibilities for selecting, procuring, maintaining, replacing, and centralizing the control of office furniture and equipment. Each of these responsibilities is discussed in this chapter.

SELECTING OFFICE FURNITURE AND EQUIPMENT

As the firm's chief specialist in administrative services, the AOM must be knowledgeable about office furniture and equipment. Thus, we expect the AOM to have on hand, or know where to obtain, up-to-date information about each of the following:

1. Principal types of furniture and equipment and reputable suppliers of each.
2. Reliable data for comparing the effectiveness of competing brands of furniture and equipment.

3. Current prices on all items and, preferably, catalogs representing each major supplier's merchandise.
4. Guidelines for deciding on the need for such furniture and equipment.
5. Knowledge about the impact of the equipment on the information system, particularly the training or retraining needed, the availability of suppliers, and operating costs.
6. Possibilities for standardizing furniture and equipment throughout the firm.
7. Procurement alternatives (such as renting, leasing, or purchasing) and quantity purchasing options.
8. Maintenance, repair, and replacement considerations.

In today's world, we find a seemingly endless number of new furniture and equipment items for the office. For this reason, office managers must take special care to have the best equipped physical environment possible—one that matches the work requirements with the individual needs of each worker. This match can best be ensured with a detailed **workstation analysis** that arranges

Office furniture must be chosen carefully to meet the needs of the office staff and to accomplish the goals of the firm.

in an orderly fashion information about each employee's work and workstation needs. This analysis helps the AOM develop a basic understanding of the principal uses of the various types of office furniture and equipment and assists in making sound decisions regarding the selection of furniture and equipment.

Office Furniture

Generally manufacturers provide furniture that includes filing cabinets, desks, tables, chairs, storage units, panels, and screens as well as other related items for executive, managerial, and employee workstations. The most common types of furniture (with the exception of filing equipment, which is discussed in Chapter 19), will be described in this chapter. Specific guidelines for selecting office furniture are outlined in Figure 15–1.

The cost of office furniture is a significant part of the overall expense incurred to accomplish office work. As a rule, furniture is purchased rather than leased or rented; for it is intended to last for a long period of time. Thus, the OM should give serious attention to the selection and use of office furniture. If properly selected, office furniture can assist the OM to increase productivity, to lower production costs, and to retain satisfied personnel. Both types of general-office furniture—conventional and modular—are discussed briefly in the following paragraphs.

Conventional Furniture

Conventional furniture is a collection of independent furniture components, such as freestanding desks and credenzas, filing cabinets, and bookshelves. The arrangement of conventional furniture in traditional offices typically consists of rows of desks in large, open areas; conventional furniture also is found in private offices and in conference rooms of traditional offices. With the

Figure 15–1
Guidelines
for Selecting
Office
Furniture

Guideline	Aids in Using the Guideline
1. The furniture should contribute to safe and comfortable working conditions.	1. The AOM must understand the nature of the work to be performed and the economy of physical effort as well as the speed of various operations. The edges of furniture should be smooth or rounded to prevent injury to persons or damage to clothing.
2. The furniture should be attractive and harmonize with the office decor.	2. The manner in which productivity is affected by these factors is discussed at length in Chapter 14. This material should be reviewed for a better understanding of esthetic considerations.
3. The furniture should be of good quality, solid construction, and suitable design to facilitate the work to be done.	3. High-quality furniture is usually attractive and economical to maintain. The main alternatives—wood or metal—should be weighed. Metal furniture provides great durability under hard wear and is usually more flexible since it is constructed with interchangeable parts. It is widely used in general office areas. Wood furniture is also long lasting but has the added values of warm tone, rich appearance, and prestige that improves the attitudes of office workers toward their jobs. Wood furniture is usually recommended for executive offices.
4. The quantity of furniture should be sufficient for the number of employees and suitable for the types of tasks performed.	4. Systems studies within each department, along with input from the office staff, will help determine the quantity of furniture needed.
5. The furniture should be adaptable to multipurpose use wherever possible.	5. Office machine stands should be able to serve as VDT tables. Executive desks may be used as conference tables. Tops of counter-high file cabinets can serve as working areas.
6. Specialized furniture should be purchased only if justified by savings in cost, efficiency, and convenience.	6. Furniture such as sorting racks, credenzas, and folding chairs may be desirable, but unnecessary. Existing desks may serve part-time VDT operations.
7. The furniture should meet the preferences of the workers.	7. The workers should assist the AOM in new purchases of furniture. When workers' suggestions cannot be followed, reasons for the decision made should be communicated to them.

exception of chairs, conventional furniture is typically not adjustable. Until the early 1980s, conventional furniture was used almost universally in offices and is still commonly used today; for this reason, conventional furniture remains an important factor for the AOM to understand.

Office Desks. The desk is considered to be the central unit of the workstation. We use it as a working surface for handling information as well as a place to store supplies and collect data. Desks may be broadly classified according to their (1) *physical characteristics* (size and shape or style); and (2) *use* or *function*. Figures 15-2 and 15-3 show examples of desks classified by style and function. These types of desks are available in standard sizes, and as a rule are not adjustable.

Cost is an important factor in the selection of office desks. In most cases, even when a company owns its office building, we make estimates of the space rentals that should be charged against each department and division. For example, we may find that the annual cost of floor space in large-city offices ranges from $20 to $45 a square foot.[1] Then we must consider that a standard-size desk 60 inches by 34 inches occupies a space of over 14 square feet, which, at $30 a square foot, would rent for more than $420 a year. Also, the rental for the chair space, which would approximate 60 inches by 30 inches, or 12½ square feet, would be $375, making a total of $795 for the desk and chair space. However, a desk 48 inches by 30 inches would be satisfactory for many office workers. Such a desk and a smaller chair occupy only 20 square feet of space with a space rental cost of $600 a year, or $195 less than that charged for the larger desk and chair.

---

[1]For a national view of the costs of office space in large cities, see "Office Market Outlook," *National Real Estate Investor* (June, 1988), pp. 58–90.

Tables. Tables serve as desks or desk-substitutes, as a place for sorting when considerable flat work surface is necessary, as a work surface for conferences and meetings, and as a place for storage. For many office jobs, the use of a table is preferred to a desk of any kind and may be more economical. Such a table should contain one or two small drawers, which will be sufficient for most purposes for the person using it.

In many firms where executives and others meet and work together in groups, a large conference table is usually provided. The conference tables found in boardrooms of many large corporations are custom designed to harmonize with the office decor. A wide variety of styles is available—from the traditional rectangular shapes to the more modern boat-shaped, oval, curved, and round styles.

Modular Furniture

Because of the widespread acceptance of automation and the need for office furniture to meet ergonomic requirements as well as the trend toward open-space planning, AOMs recognize the value of using furniture that is adjustable, easy to move, and multipurpose. For these reasons, we see a trend toward the use of modular rather than conventional furniture.

Modular furniture (sometimes called *systems furniture*) is a collection of integrated, interdependent furniture components that can be quickly and easily assembled, disassembled, and rearranged to meet employee and department needs. A **module** is one unit or component of office furniture that has a specific function, such as a desk, an acoustical partition, or a work surface with a pedestal containing several drawers. Each of the separate furniture units is designed according to the modular construction principle. This principle is based upon an approach to building office workstations composed of modules. Functionally designed modular furniture, as illustrated in Figure 15-4, has a panel-dependent

Figure 15-2
Styles of
Desks

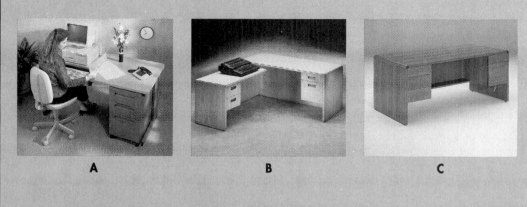

A   B   C

A, B—Single-Pedestal Desks

Single-pedestal, 40" to 60" wide. The term pedestal refers to the unit containing drawers on either side of the desk. To provide additional working space, an extension, known as a return, may be attached to the desk. Returns are available with or without pedestals. Typing-height returns (B) can be attached to desks.

C—Double-Pedestal Desk

Double-pedestal, 50" to 78" wide. Typing platforms, similar to the typing-height return shown above, may be attached. Desks are also available with an overhang at the back and both ends.

workstation with detachable components that can be adjusted to fit a worker's individual needs.

A modular workstation typically occupies less space than that required for conventional layouts. (See Figure 13-8, page 384, especially the reference to the space saved by using Penta Pod over conventional systems.) Vertical panels are used for hanging shelving and storage units in modular layouts while conventional layouts require floor space for shelving and storage cabinets. Modular furniture permits many furniture arrangements, which are subject to both the imagination of the AOM and the limitations of space.

Chairs

Today 75 percent of the work force sits while working. Hence, it is obvious why today's office furniture designers are emphasizing the importance of providing *ergonomic chairs* in the office. We know that physical comfort is closely related to the worker's mental condition upon which performance ultimately rests. In fact, results of the Steelcase survey, referred to earlier in this textbook, show that when 1,004 office workers were asked what makes them comfortable, their two most frequent replies were: "Good lighting" (85 percent) and "Comfortable chair" (73 percent).[2]

It is important that office workers be comfortable to prevent strained posture when sitting for hours while performing their work. The OM can detect signs of fatigue by taking a close look at the workers'

[2]*The Steelcase National Study of Office Environments, No. II*, 1980, Chapter V.

Figure 15-3
Types of
Desks
According to
Functions
Performed

A. Desk for Clerk–Typists and Secretaries

Modular typewriter platforms may be
attached to single– or double–pedestal
desks.

B. Specialized Desk for Word Processing
Personnel

Specialized VDT desks provide built–in
features, such as this model that houses a
compartment for activating the media (tapes
or diskettes) and a storage compartment for
tapes, diskettes, or paper files.

C. Modular Desk System for Data
Processing/Word Processing Personnel

Electronic workstations are engineered to use
modules that provide maximum flexibility for
changing surface heights, depths, and
equipment storage/support facilities.

D. Executive Desk

General–purpose, double–pedestal desks are
commonly used by executives and managers,
either individually or incorporated into a
larger multipurpose executive workstation.

Figure 15–4
A Modular
Workstation

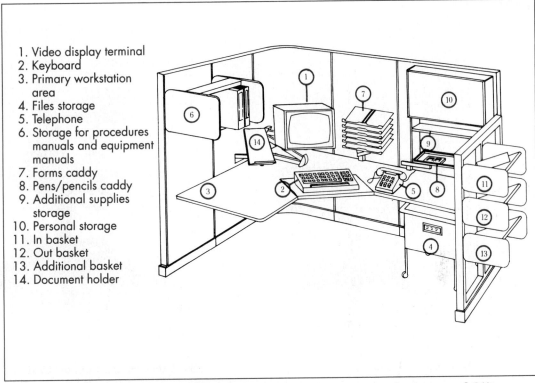

1. Video display terminal
2. Keyboard
3. Primary workstation area
4. Files storage
5. Telephone
6. Storage for procedures manuals and equipment manuals
7. Forms caddy
8. Pens/pencils caddy
9. Additional supplies storage
10. Personal storage
11. In basket
12. Out basket
13. Additional basket
14. Document holder

Source: Marilyn Joyce and Ulrika Wallersteiner, *Ergonomics: Humanizing the Automated Office* (Cincinnati: South-Western Publishing Co., 1989), p. 90.

postures. When workers sit humped over their work with their feet entwined around the chair legs, the chair or the desk or both are not the right height. Such incorrect sitting positions may not be due to careless posture, but rather to defective seating.

As shown in Figure 15–5, the main types of office chairs are classified as:

1. *Executive chairs*, adjustable to the physical characteristics of the person, in swivel and tilt-back styles, and often constructed of wood to match the wooden executive desks.
2. *Administrative support posture chairs*, with or without a swivel base, with or without arms, and adjustable to the physical needs of the person. These chairs are used by secretaries; typists; and word processing, data-entry, and computer operator personnel.

3. *Side chairs*, often straight back with four legs, designed for use by visitors.

All office chairs, other than side or visitor chairs, should be adjustable for height and should swivel. The back support should be vertically and horizontally adjustable. If the back support is provided with a spring tension, the tension should be adjustable. Whenever workers have to bring the work to their eyes, they need armrests on their chairs. If workers have to bring their eyes and arms to the work, they do not need armrests on the chairs. Recent studies of VDT operators have found that proper posture while working in the office not only reduces fatigue and backaches but also improves the health of workers by making them less susceptible to colds and headaches. Healthier employees benefit the firm by reason of less

Figure 15-5
The Main
Types of
Office
Chairs

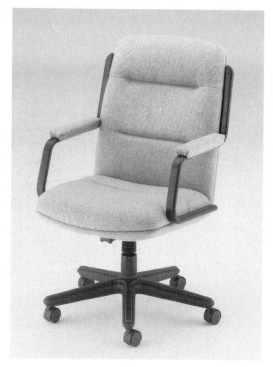

A—Executive Chair

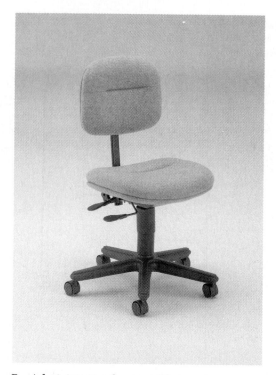

B—Administrative Support Chair

C—Side Chair

absenteeism, fewer errors, a larger volume of production, and, finally, lower costs.

Most office chairs are designed to fit as closely as possible the contours of the body. Saddle seats are one example of the contour designs often used in the construction of office chairs. Correctly contoured seats, especially those covered with foam latex, add to the workers' comfort.

Furniture for Automated Workstations

Furniture for the automated office environment is the fastest-growing segment of the business furniture industry. This growth is due in large part to the rapid influx of VDTs and other computer equipment into every size of office including the home. Many workers are full-time VDT operators, and for this group especially, personal comfort and office productivity depend on the choice of ergonomically sound furniture and equipment.

Three types of VDT workstations are found: (1) the full-time operator's workstation used in computer and word processing systems; (2) the multifunction workstation in which several persons periodically share the use of a VDT; and (3) the executive workstation at which, to an increasing degree, a VDT and related equipment are used by managers. The furniture needed for each type of VDT workstation is briefly discussed in the following paragraphs. The equipment needed to operate workstations such as these is discussed in later chapters.

Furniture for the Full-Time VDT Operator. Working for long hours at a VDT screen "freezes" an operator into one fixed position. The keyboarding and viewing tasks restrict the movement of operators so that much discomfort and many postural problems result. To eliminate such problems, the National Institute of Occupational Safety and Health (NIOSH) recommends that VDT workstations and devices be made as adjustable as possible to allow for the unique physical characteristics of the operator. (See Figure 15–6.) Thus, the workstation for the full-time VDT operator should have the following features:

1. *Detachable keyboards* that permit the adjustment of keyboard height.
2. *Adjustable screen height and tilt* to improve viewing and reduce glare. (Other techniques for reducing glare on VDT screens are discussed in Chapter 14.)
3. *Sufficient leg room* to permit freedom of movement.
4. *Adjustable chair features* (seat height, backrest height, and armrests) as well as the capability of swiveling and movement using casters. Studies show that a seated person changes positions on the average at least once every six minutes.
5. Preferably *an L-shaped workstation arrangement* that enhances the efficiency of motion between the two sections of the workstation. (See Figure 15–3C.)
6. A variety of *hanging components*, as shown in Figure 15–4, to accommodate the normal reach of an operator (22 to 24 inches). Included are storage shelving, task lighting, space for a printer (if needed), and space for performing other nonautomated administrative duties.

Figure 15–7A shows ergonomically designed furniture for a full-time VDT operator. Recent studies by NIOSH and other organizations show that the use of such furniture results in improvements in work produced ranging from 5 to 50 percent. The increased cost can be recovered in fewer than five months through the gains in productivity.[3]

---

[3]M. Franz Schneider, "Why Ergonomics Can No Longer Be Ignored," *Office Administration and Automation* (July, 1985), p. 29. Other excellent treatments of this topic can be found in Wilbert O. Galitz, *The Office Environment: Automation's Impact on Tomorrow's Environment*, Administrative Management Society Foundation (Willow Grove, PA: 1984), Chapter 3; and in Joel Makower, *Office Hazards*, Tilden Press (Washington, DC: 1981), Chapter 4. For good

Figure 15-6
Adjustable
Furniture for
Full-Time
VDT
Operator

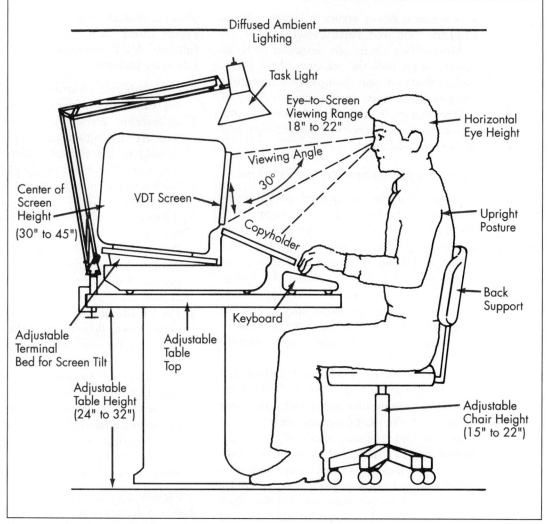

Furniture for the Multifunction Shared Workstation. In many cases, a community workstation is provided in which a group of office workers shares an automated workcenter. Each may use the computer for short periods of time for data processing, word processing, and communication tasks. In such cases, adjustable furniture features

should be provided in the furniture, although this aspect is not so important as it is for the full-time operator's workstation. Many furniture arrangements are available for this type of workstation including the standalone example shown in Figure 15-7B.

Furniture for an Executive Workstation. More and more, automated workstations are being installed in the private offices of executives, to provide them with immediate access to the firm's computerized facilities. In the 1988 Steelcase study, 45 percent of

suggestions on furnishing automated workcenters in the home, see David Gabel, "The Bottom Line on Your Home Office," *Personal Computing* (November, 1984), pp. 64, 67–69, 71–72, 75.

Figure 15-7
Furniture for
Automated
Workstations

A—Furniture for a Full-Time VDT Operator

B—Furniture for a Shared VDT Workstation

C—Furniture for an Executive Workstation

the top executives surveyed reported having a computer in their offices. Of this group, 69 percent reported using the computer on a regular basis.[4] In such workstations, executives can compose letters, make computations, store and retrieve information, and send and receive messages using their VDTs. In the executive workstation, the VDT is used on an irregular basis, as a rule, and thus

occupies a more secondary location in the workstation than is required for full-time operators. Figure 15-7C illustrates an executive workstation that is both functional and comfortable.

Other Furniture and Accessories

The preceding discussion has indicated that desks, tables, and chairs are the key furniture items in any office. While this continues to be true, the forward-looking AOM will mod-

---

[4]*The Office Environment Index: 1987 Summary Report,* p. 18.

ify the working environment as conditions (particularly the layout), the financial resources, and the tastes of management dictate. It has become common to find extra furnishings such as sofas, end tables with harmonizing table lamps, coffee tables, art objects, credenzas, bookcases, planters, privacy screens, office valets or wall and coat racks, and magazine racks in the office. Other accessories commonly found include clocks, safes, bars, office refrigerators, movable carts, and stools. These accessories provide an environment that is more conducive to relaxed work, concentration, and enjoyment of the hours spent on the job.

Office Equipment

In addition to the furniture required for the office, a great array of office equipment is available. The term *office equipment*, as used here, refers primarily to office machines and devices found in the office.[5]

The principal office machines are information machines, such as typewriters, electronic calculators, copiers, telephones, and computers. As such, office equipment is the intermediary between people and their work. It enables employees to accomplish more work in less time with greater accuracy and with better quality. Furthermore, telecommunication equipment helps employees to transmit the results of their work to others over long distances and to receive rapid feedback. The types and brands of equipment and the number of their possible uses continue to grow at an increasingly rapid rate.

The selection of office equipment starts with a feasibility study—introduced in Chap-

ter 4—that seeks to answer two questions: (1) *Is the equipment necessary?* and (2) *If so, which equipment is the best?* To answer these questions, the entire information system is identified and the role of equipment in such a system is clarified. Such a study requires concentrated and extended thought with well-documented answers to the two key questions involved. To assist the AOM in undertaking an office equipment feasibility study, the guidelines for selecting office equipment outlined in Figure 15–8 should prove helpful.

PROCURING OFFICE EQUIPMENT

The procuring of office furniture and equipment is an important and complex responsibility of the OM. Office *furniture*, which is intended to last for a long time, is usually purchased rather than leased or rented. However, the same is not necessarily true of office *equipment*, which is subject to much wear and tear as well as to technological obsolescence.

Purchasing Office Equipment

When a company purchases its office equipment, it owns an asset that it can later sell. Also, the company can reduce its income taxes by claiming as an operating expense the depreciation occurring during the estimated useful life of the equipment.

When buying office equipment, the company may obtain financial aid from the equipment manufacturer. By means of lending programs, some leading manufacturers of office machines and equipment finance a significant portion of their U.S. sales. Customers see such loans as bargains since the interest rate offered by the manufacturer is usually lower than the rates charged by banks. Of course, purchasing office equipment also has disadvantages, which are explained in a later section when the advantages of leasing are explored.

---

[5]For discussions concerning specific types of office equipment, see Chapter 16 (Office Automation), Chapter 17 (Text/Word Processing Systems), Chapter 18 (Information Distribution: Telecommunication and Mailing Systems), Chapter 19 (Records Management), and Chapter 20 (Microimage and Reprographic Systems).

Figure 15–8
Guidelines
for Selecting
Office
Equipment

Guidelines for Selecting Office Equipment	Considerations in Using the Guidelines
1. Equipment should be chosen for any job or task when it helps workers to be more efficient.	1. Where job monotony due to repetitive work tasks is found, a machine should be considered to enrich the job as well as increase production.
2. High-volume (rather than low-frequency or one-time only) applications point to the need for machines.	2. From high-volume applications come better service, more prompt preparation of financial reports, and other good results.
3. Where equipment can provide higher quality of output, it should be used.	3. Compare typewritten with handwritten reports for neatness and legibility.
4. The need for accuracy should be determined; and where internal machine checks and controls can provide such accuracy, a machine should be selected.	4. This guideline relates to numeric data (financial and accounting reports) as well as textual matter. Accuracy of text can be verified through word processing software.
5. Equipment should be installed whenever it will reduce the actual cost of performing office work.	5. The costs of service contracts, of operation and supplies, and of layout alterations required must be considered in calculating the total cost of an equipment installation.
6. To handle urgent work, high-speed requirements, or peak loads in the office work schedule, appropriate equipment should be considered.	6. Some equipment may be shared by several departments if the work schedule permits.
7. Both the capabilities and the limitations of equipment must be carefully considered.	7. Capabilities include ease of use, durability, accuracy, and high operating speeds. Limitations may involve the maximum number of digits that can be handled, size of forms and records to be used, cycling speeds, number of copies required, complexity of mathematic processes, number and capacity of internal storage media, longevity of expected performance, and trade-in value.
8. Both operative and supervisory personnel involved with the equipment should be consulted for their machine preferences.	8. The ease of use and amount of retraining required for proper machine operation should be considered.
9. The availability of ready, reliable maintenance service should receive top priority in equipment selection.	9. The cost of office operations and customer inconvenience increases if equipment is not functioning properly or not at all.

Figure 15–8
Guidelines
for Selecting
Office
Equipment
(continued)

Guidelines for Selecting Office Equipment	Considerations in Using the Guidelines

10. If its usage allows, equipment should be selected that has these features:
   a. Simplicity
   b. Flexibility
   c. Portability
   d. Adaptability
	10. Simplicity is suggested for ease of operation, of learning, and of maintenance; flexibility, for use of the equipment in many situations; portability, for easy movement of machines to be used in several departments; and adaptability, for immediate integration into an existing office system.

11. Before purchase, lease, or rental, equipment should be "test run" in the office situation where it is being considered for installation.	11. For small machines, a one- or two-week trial period is recommended; for the larger, more expensive machines in the computer family, a longer period of time is needed.

12. Standardization of office equipment is desirable, including sizes, styles, and brands.	12. With standardized office equipment it is possible:
	   a. To obtain lower prices through larger purchases.
	   b. To lower the maintenance costs by having fewer brands of machines to service.
	   c. To develop, if necessary, the company's own service department more easily and economically.
	   d. To economize by having one group of employees who can operate any of the machines.
	   e. To train operators more quickly and easily.
	   f. To purchase and use office forms to fit the brands of machines.
	   g. To simplify the computation of depreciation and trade-in value of the equipment.

Leasing Office Equipment

Although office equipment may be purchased outright, it is estimated that about 25 to 30 percent of all newly acquired equipment is leased today.[6] The figure is much higher for firms that have large

investments in material-handling systems, word processing and office equipment, and energy-related equipment, all of which are subject to rapid obsolescence.

An **equipment lease** (similar to the office space lease discussed in Chapter 13) is a contract that enables an equipment user (lessee) to secure use of a tangible asset by making periodic payments to the owner

---

[6]Michael Hofferber, "Leasing: An Alternative to Equipment Purchasing," *The Office* (July, 1988), p. 85.

(lessor) of the asset over a specified time period. Under a lease, which usually extends over a longer period of time than a rental, there is no intent—stated or implied—for the user to obtain equity or to purchase the equipment. *During the life of the lease, the lessor retains ownership of the asset and the claim to any remaining value in the equipment at the end of the lease period.*

Almost all types of office machines and equipment including computers and computer software can be leased. Equipment can be leased from a variety of sources: directly from the manufacturer's distributor; from a local office equipment dealer; from an independent leasing company that leases various brands of office machines and equipment; and from many other organizations that provide some form of equipment-leasing service.

Kinds of Lease Agreements

Since leases can be designed to meet the special needs of the parties involved, we find an almost limitless variety of actual lease contracts. For this discussion, the various kinds of lease agreements will be grouped into four categories: (1) short-term, (2) long-term with renewal option, (3) long-term with purchase option, and (4) sale-leaseback.

The **short-term lease**, which is really a rental contract, is used to obtain extra equipment, such as typewriters and calculators for peak work-load jobs for a relatively short time period. For example, at the time of year-end inventory, a firm may rent several electronic calculators for three or four weeks. The major advantage of this leasing plan is that the needed equipment is made available immediately for a short period of time with the need for little cash outlay. In the computer and computer-driven office equipment field, the short-term lease is referred to as an *operating lease* when client firms want to lease the equipment for a short period of time (two to two-and-one-half years)

because they are unsure as to the type of equipment they will need in the future.

The **long-term lease with renewal option** usually runs between 75 and 80 percent of the useful life of the equipment. On the average, such leases run from three to five years. At the end of the initial lease period, the lease can be renewed. The lease payments during the renewal period should be lower than those in the initial term of the lease since at this point the lessor should be recovering only the residual value (estimated market value) of the leased property.

The **long-term lease with purchase option** is similar to the long-term lease discussed previously except that during the lease period the lessee is building up equity to take ownership of the equipment at the end of the period. The user gains the flexibility of being able to upgrade the equipment, without any penalty, during the lease period. Since the equipment has a tangible value that can be used as a trade-in on new equipment when a new lease is signed, the threat of obsolescence is lessened. Under income tax regulations, this form of lease may be interpreted as a conditional sales contract.

A **conditional sales contract** is a contract in which the user of the equipment, for federal income tax purposes, is treated as the owner of the equipment at the time of signing the lease. Thus, the company may be denied tax deductions for the lease payments. To enable both the lessee and the lessor to arrange terms that result in favorable tax treatment, advice from tax experts, legal counsel, and/or the Internal Revenue Service (IRS) should be sought.

Under the **sale-leaseback** plan, the company purchases its office equipment, sells it to a lessor, and then leases it back under a long-term lease. Thus, the company has use of almost the entire value of its plant assets in the form of usable cash. This plan may prove very economical to the firm in need of working capital for other more productive purposes.

Advantages of Leasing

The advantages of leasing office equipment point up some of the drawbacks of an outright purchase. These advantages include:

1. *Working capital is freed for day-to-day cash flow and thus can be used for more productive ventures.* In some leases, no down payment is required. In other leases, a down payment equal to the first-year's leasing cost may be needed to acquire the equipment. Such minimum stipulations free a firm's capital for other revenue-producing investments or for expansion.

2. *Budgetary control is facilitated and accounting procedures are simplified since the amount of regular lease payments is easily determined.* A hedge against inflation is also provided since the same dollar lease payments are spread over a period of years. Thus, in times of increasing inflation, a constant sum of money paid out five years into the future on a five-year lease will be paid in inflated dollars, which have less purchasing power than the same amount spent in the current year.

3. *Some leases offer the lessee an opportunity to contract out specialized services such as maintenance and recordkeeping which are associated with the use of certain kinds of equipment.* For example, under some leases the lessor services and maintains the equipment for the user, keeps plant asset records, and provides insurance coverage. The lease also relieves the lessee of the necessity of disposing of the equipment when it is no longer needed.

4. *Flexibility, unavailable in other methods of financing, is provided the lessee.* New firms often need equipment immediately but are initially unable to budget substantial funds for lease payments. Under long-term leases, payment schedules can easily be worked out to mesh with the lessee's seasonal pattern of cash flow. For exam-

ple, a deferred-payment lease offers flexibility in payment methods. By deferring its payments, a company is able to generate income before the first lease payment comes due.

5. *Leasing offers the equipment user an additional source of financing.* Lease financing may be available to companies when other sources of financing cannot be obtained on reasonable terms. For example, leasing offers one of the few ways that small companies without access to credit can obtain new equipment.

6. *For companies that use highly specialized equipment, protection may be obtained against the risks of obsolescence.* In many cases the equipment can be replaced during the life of the lease; thus, throughout the lease period, the company can take advantage of the latest advances in technology.

7. *Tax benefits may be realized since the lease payments may be treated as business expenses which are fully deductible for income tax purposes.* As noted earlier, however, under some lease contracts an option to buy during or at the end of the lease period may be looked upon by the Internal Revenue Service as an installment purchase or a conditional sales contract. Thus, the lease payments may not be tax deductible.

   Generally if a lessee anticipates sufficient taxable income, borrowing to purchase equipment offers greater tax benefits and is less expensive than leasing, especially *if methods of accelerating depreciation may be used.* (See the discussion of accelerating depreciation in the section *Replacing Office Equipment.*) Even so, deductible lease payments under short-term leases or leases with variable payment schedules may be attractive to lessees under certain circumstances.

8. *Rapidly expanding companies and those opening branch offices are aided by the package plans of some lessors, under*

which equipment can be added as the needs of the company grow.

9. *Leasing enables the firm to bypass the approval for capital expenditures by top management.* In many firms, the process for obtaining capital appropriations is very complex and time consuming. Thus, by means of leasing, managers can obtain the needed equipment without going through corporate management or obtaining the board of directors' approval.

The Lease-or-Buy Decision

If after we perform a feasibility study, a need for equipment is determined, the relative net cost of purchasing and leasing should be carefully determined before making the decision to lease or to buy. In addition, several other important factors, discussed later in this section, should be considered.

Relative Net Cost of Leasing or Buying

If we wish to use the equipment for more than one shift a day, it may, in terms of direct cost, be more economical for many firms to purchase than to lease the equipment. However, each firm should conduct its own capital budgeting study, as in the case of any other capital investment, by using valuation methods such as payback period, break-even analysis, and the average rate of return on the investment. Each of these methods is briefly described below.

Payback Period. The **payback period** is the period of time over which a capital expenditure, such as the purchase of six computer terminals, will generate cash equal to the cost of the proposal. With this technique, we can estimate how long a company will have to wait in order to recover sufficient cash from the proposed purchase to equal the cash invested in the proposed items to be bought.

When several proposals or projects are under consideration and a payback period is calculated for each one, a selection can be made of the project that is the most

economically feasible. Generally a firm's capital budgeting policy states that any proposal must pay for itself within a specified number of years—the *cut-off point.* A short payback period is usually desired since over a relatively short period of time the company is exposed to less risk of recovering its capital. Further, for the firm that greatly needs cash, a short payback period improves the financial position by creating additional cash inflow.

Cash inflow includes (1) the cash savings that the company anticipates as a result of undertaking the purchase; and (2) depreciation expense, since depreciation is an expense for which no cash is spent by the firm. Thus, the company has available an amount of cash that consists of the net income after taxes plus depreciation.

As an example, let us assume that the cash inflow from a proposed equipment purchase is in equal amounts of $8,000 each year. The cost of the equipment is $24,000, which is divided by the amount of the cash inflow to obtain the payback period, three years. When this three-year period is compared with the firm's cut-off point, the proposal may be rejected, revised before acceptance, or ranked in priority order with other proposals being considered.

Break-Even Analysis. Another method that may be used by the AOM in making the decision to expand operations by purchasing or leasing additional equipment is break-even analysis. In this kind of analysis, the **break-even point** is that level of operations at which the company neither realizes income nor incurs loss. Thus, *it is that point at which revenues and costs (or expenses) are equal.* When the break-even point is charted, as shown in Figure 15-9, the relationship among sales volume, costs, and profits (or income) can be seen graphically. However, before undertaking break-even analysis and charting such a relationship, the AOM needs to understand costs and their behavior as affected by changes in the firm's

Figure 15-9
Break-Even
Chart

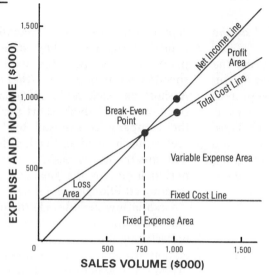

by the straight line parallel to the horizontal sales volume axis. The area below this line is called the *fixed expense area*. At this sales volume, the variable costs are $600,000. The total cost line shows that for a sales volume of $1 million, the total costs are $900,000. The income line, representing the total income to the company, is plotted against the vertical expense and income axis to show that expenses are paid out of income and that the difference remaining is profit. *The break-even point is found at the intersection of the total cost line and the income line.* At this point, a total sales volume of $750,000 equals the total expenses.

Break-even analysis may be used by the AOM in estimating the effects of future actions. For example, if the office lease payments were to increase by $15,000 for each of the next five years, how much must sales increase to cover this growth in fixed costs and still produce a profit of $300,000? If additional part-time office workers were employed, with the variable costs increasing by $45,000, how much must sales expand to cover such an increase? What amount of sales would be needed to break even if variable costs (such as mailing expenses) were reduced by 5 percent but at the same time fixed costs (such as real estate taxes and property insurance) increased by $20,000? Break-even analysis may also be used when evaluating proposed capital expenditures, such as the purchase or lease of new office space. By charting the cost-volume-profit relationship, the effect of the proposed expenditure on the overall financial structure of the firm can be determined.

Average Rate of Return. Another approach the AOM may use to analyze proposed capital expenditures is the **average rate of return**. This method measures the anticipated profitability of a proposed investment by *dividing the average savings to be obtained from the investment by the average amount of the investment.* The rate of return on the

volume of business activity. Also, there is need to be familiar with the fixed and the variable costs involved in the firm's operations.

Fixed costs tend to remain fairly stable (unchanging) over a stated time period even when the volume of business changes. Examples of fixed costs are rent of office space and equipment, real estate taxes, property insurance, and the salaries of administrative and supervisory personnel.

Variable costs change in response to changes in the volume of work activity. Examples of variable office costs are direct labor costs, such as the wages and salaries paid office workers; direct materials, such as stationery and supplies; equipment repair and maintenance expenses; and mailing expenses.

The cost-volume-profit relationships that are inherent in break-even analysis may be shown graphically as in Figure 15-9. In this break-even chart, the sales volume (units produced × unit selling price) is plotted on the horizontal axis, and the expense items (fixed and variable costs) are plotted on the vertical axis. In this example, for a sales volume of $1 million (50,000 units at $20 each), the fixed costs are $300,000 as shown proposed expenditure is then related to certain conditions that have been established by the company. For example, a company may decide that the cost of acquiring the funds that will be tied up in the investment shall be less than, say, 11 percent, which is the amount of interest currently being charged the company by its lenders.

Other Factors to Consider in the Lease-or-Buy Decision

Several other factors that must be carefully studied before a decision is made to lease or to buy office equipment are listed below.

1. *Threat of obsolescence.* Companies that are concerned about their office equipment becoming obsolete as the result of technological advances often decide to lease even though it may be less expensive to buy.
2. *Useful life of the equipment.* Although an analysis of useful life is very difficult to do, a realistic appraisal must be made of how long the equipment will serve the company's needs. For example, in some firms long-range planners are at work designing changes for the future that may radically affect the role of the present computer and word processing installations. To forecast the future, the computer and word processing staffs must analyze the firm's plans and trends for sales, production, and purchases in order to determine the need for new or expanded automated processes.
3. *Amount of base fee.* Often a firm pays a base fee that entitles it to operate the equipment, such as a computer, a certain number of hours each month. Regular overtime usage requires the payment of additional rent, which can be directly determined with the installation of time recorders on the equipment. All terms governing the basic rental period should be spelled out in advance. For example, if the equipment breaks down for a few

hours, is the company charged for these hours or does the vendor assume the loss?
4. *Maintenance services.* The contract to buy or to lease should clearly indicate the type of maintenance services—preventive and repair—that will be provided by the manufacturer or the vendor. The availability of skilled help, when needed, should be determined.
5. *Trade-in value of equipment.* In making cost comparisons between leasing and buying, the trade-in or residual value of equipment at the end of its useful life is often overlooked. With a growing market for used equipment, the firm may realize a substantial trade-in value for equipment that has a systems life shorter than its productive life.
6. *Interest costs.* When comparing the costs of leasing and buying, the firm should consider the rate of interest it pays for borrowed money and the rate it expects to earn on an investment of the funds.

In making a wise decision on whether to lease or buy equipment, the AOM may obtain aid from the firm's own financial specialists and auditors and from independent consultants. Also, many lessors, such as equipment manufacturers, will prepare a detailed analysis of the purchase and lease factors.

MAINTAINING OFFICE EQUIPMENT

As we have seen in the previous discussion, maintenance is an important factor to be considered by the AOM when purchasing or leasing equipment. When any piece of office equipment is purchased, generally there is a warranty period during which time equipment repairs are made by the manufacturer at no cost to the firm. Once the warranty period has passed, however, and unless the equipment is covered by a service contract, any future repairs are charged against the user on a time and materials basis.

Many office machines are operated almost continuously each workday. With automated machines and equipment handling the bulk of information processing, the servicing of these machines becomes a major consideration. When machines and equipment break down, office workers are unable to perform their work until repairs have been made—unless back-up equipment is available.

Depending upon the complexity of the equipment and the number of machines used, the maintenance of office equipment may be provided by internal or external service personnel.

Internal Service

To operate its own service department, a company must be fairly large. Involved in the installation of such a department are the following important costs:

1. The relatively high salaries paid to trained service personnel.
2. The hidden costs of their employee benefits.
3. The cost of retraining the personnel as new machine models appear on the market.
4. The cost of the space and repair equipment allotted to the service department.

External Service

External service may be provided by the manufacturer of the equipment or by an independent service firm under a service contract or on a per-call basis.

Service Contract

A **service contract** (also known as a *maintenance agreement* or *maintenance guarantee*) provides for periodic cleaning and lubrication, inspection, and replacement of worn-out or defective machine parts. Preventive maintenance, which forms a part of the manufacturer's service contract, usually reduces or eliminates the number of breakdowns.

In the servicing of standard office machines and equipment, such as typewriters and copiers, some companies, especially those in small outlying communities, enter into an agreement with a local service firm. For a fixed fee, the service firm inspects, cleans, and repairs each machine in the office at regular intervals.

Per-Call Basis

Some companies find it is more economical to pay for each individual service call as the service is needed. In the case of complex and highly automated equipment, however, repeat service calls are often necessary. When a fixed-fee service contract is used, such calls become the responsibility of the manufacturer or the local service firm.

REPLACING OFFICE EQUIPMENT

With the continuing advances that we see in the information technology field, office equipment becomes obsolete quickly because of newer and better models placed on the market. Therefore, it is necessary for the AOM to select the best machine available at the time of purchase and to use this machine until its efficiency lessens. At such time, the old machine may be replaced with a newer model without too great a loss. This loss can be absorbed by the business if a sound trade-in policy has been established at the time of purchase. Also, at the time of purchasing the office equipment, plans must be made for calculating the depreciation of the property, as described below.

Office equipment may be *depreciated* (written off as an operating expense) over the useful life of the equipment. The Tax Reform Act (TRA) of 1986 established property class lives for various kinds of assets to indicate the length of time over which the cost of different kinds of assets might be recovered. For example, the five-year property class includes assets such as computers and peripheral equipment and office machinery (typewriters, calculators, copiers, etc.). In the seven-year property class we find office furniture and fixtures (desks, files, etc.).

Under one method of calculating depreciation called *straight line*, the cost of the equipment is spread rather evenly over the estimated life (property class life) of the asset. However, since office equipment usually declines in value more rapidly during the first years of its useful life than in the later years, an *accelerated* depreciation method is often more appropriate to use. When using such a method, firms "write off" (or record among the firm's operating expenses) a larger depreciation expense in the earlier years of the asset's life and a smaller depreciation expense during the later years. Thus, the amount recorded as depreciation expense each year more correctly matches the decline in value of the asset during that year.[7]

Whether office machines and equipment are replaced at the end of their estimated useful life or earlier, we still find a need for a well-planned replacement program. Such a program enables a firm to predict accurately each year the exact cost of its equipment. The cut-off point (of operating efficiency and economy) can then be established for each piece of equipment; the number of new items to be purchased can be forecast; and the amount for maintenance during the coming year can be budgeted. A planned replacement program also enables the firm to establish better control over its maintenance costs, especially those that tend to rise during the latter years of machine usage. By closely controlling the replacement

schedule of office machines, the firm can avoid those additional expenses that arise during the period when the equipment is old and requires extensive reconditioning, replacement of parts, and special cleanings. An intangible advantage of prestige and morale is also found in the company that has a planned replacement program. By using such a program, the company presents a businesslike, well-equipped, up-to-date image to its customers, visitors, and employees.

CENTRALIZING THE CONTROL OF OFFICE EQUIPMENT

For purposes of effectively controlling the selection, procurement, maintenance, and replacement of equipment, the office equipment function should be organized on a centralized basis. This is particularly true in large offices where specialized functions are found and where large sums of money are invested in machines and related equipment. Usually the function of centralized control is the responsibility of the AOM and consists of the following activities:

1. Maintaining a current file of information on office equipment and developments in information technology.
2. Setting up a system of centralized control over plant assets that covers the following kinds of information:
   a. Equipment owned, leased, or rented by the firm.
   b. Description of equipment.
   c. Company asset number and manufacturer's model and serial numbers.
   d. Department or cost center assigned responsibility for the equipment.
   e. Date of purchase, lease agreement, or rental contract.
   f. Purchase price plus installation costs or amount of lease or rental payments.
   g. History of maintenance and repair services and costs.

---

[7]For a complete discussion of depreciation accounting, see James B. Bower and Harold Q. Langenderfer, *Income Tax Procedure* (Cincinnati: South-Western Publishing Co., current edition). Also very helpful is the annually updated *Tax Guide for Small Business*, available free from the Internal Revenue Service.

    h. Depreciation expense, accumulated depreciation, and book value (purchase price less accumulated depreciation).

3. Controlling the selection and purchasing or leasing of machines in line with the use to be made of machines.
4. Developing effective procedures for maintenance and replacement of machines.
5. Reviewing periodically all equipment and machine installations to make sure all items remain on company premises.
6. Functioning as a clearinghouse for all equipment needs within the firm and as the contact point for all vendors.

Small offices, too, have need for similar controls over their machines and equipment. Although little specialization of function is found in small offices, the control of such assets should be assigned to one individual.

SUMMARY

1. In selecting office furniture, the AOM must understand that costs and employee satisfaction are affected by the proper choice of desks, chairs, tables, and other accessories. A study of modular furniture layouts will indicate how the rental cost of floor space may be reduced and how employees may work more comfortably and with less physical energy expended. Prior to selecting office equipment, a feasibility study should be undertaken to assure the AOM and others on the project team that the equipment is actually needed and, if so, which equipment will do the job most economically, efficiently, and accurately. Special care should be given to the selection of furniture for automated workstations, keeping in mind the unique features of VDTs and their effect upon operators.

2. When office furniture and equipment are procured, the AOM should carefully study the advantages and disadvantages of purchasing, leasing, and renting. One factor of great importance in making the lease-or-buy decision is the relative net cost of purchasing and of leasing. The payback period, the break-even point, and the rate of return on the investment are commonly determined in calculating the net cost. Other factors to be investigated as part of the lease-or-buy decision include potential technological obsolescence of the equipment, the useful life of the equipment, the cost of the base fee, maintenance service, and the trade-in value of the equipment. Also, a comparison should be made of the interest costs involved in borrowing money to buy the equipment with the rate of return the firm might obtain by investing the funds in some other business transaction.

3. Other important phases of equipping the physical office environment include (1) selecting the most practical approach to maintaining and servicing the equipment, (2) planning a sound program for replacing the office equipment, and (3) providing for effective centralized control over the plant assets whether they are purchased, leased, or rented.

GLOSSARY **Average rate of return**—the average savings to be obtained from an investment divided by the average amount of the investment.

Break-even point—that level of operations at which a company neither realizes income nor incurs loss; that point at which revenues and costs are equal.

Cash inflow—a source of funds provided by savings (net income after taxes) and depreciation expense.

Conditional sales contract—an agreement under which the user of equipment is considered, for federal income tax purposes, to be the owner of the equipment at the time of signing the lease.

Equipment lease—a contract that enables an equipment user (lessee) to secure use of a tangible asset by making periodic payments to the owner (lessor) of the asset over a specified time period.

Fixed costs—those costs tending to remain fairly stable (unchanging) over a stated time period even when the volume of business changes.

Long-term lease with purchase option—a contract in which the lessee has use of equipment for a stated time period, with the choice of purchasing the equipment at the end of the time period.

Long-term lease with renewal option—a contract in which the lessee has use of equipment for a stated time period, with the choice of renewing the lease at the end of the time period.

Modular furniture—a collection of integrated, independent furniture components that can be quickly and easily assembled, disassembled, and rearranged to meet employee and department needs; also known as *systems furniture*.

Module—a unit or component of office furniture that has a specific function.

Payback period—the time period over which a capital expenditure will generate cash equal to the cost of the proposal.

Sale-leaseback—a contract in which a user purchases equipment, sells it to a lessor, and then leases it back under a long-term lease.

Service contract—an agreement between the user of equipment and the manufacturer or other service organization that provides for periodic cleaning and lubrication, inspection, and replacement of worn-out and defective machine parts; also known as *maintenance agreement* or *maintenance guarantee*.

Short-term lease—a rental contract in which a user obtains equipment for peak workload jobs for a relatively short time period.

Variable costs—those costs that change in response to changes in the volume of business activity.

Workstation analysis—a detailed study that arranges in an orderly fashion information about each employee's work and workstation needs.

FOR YOUR REVIEW

1. In order to provide the most service to their firms regarding office furniture and equipment, what types and sources of information should administrative office managers have available?

2. Assume you have been asked to provide a comprehensive set of guidelines for selecting office furniture. What would you include in your set?

3. In the selection of office furniture, how important is the cost of square footage occupied by desks and chairs?

4. a. What is modular furniture?
   b. What are its advantages?

5. Discuss the characteristics of a good office chair. Why is the selection of a chair just as important as the selection of a desk?

6. Identify the main types of office furniture used in automated workstations.

7. Why should a feasibility study be undertaken prior to the selection of office equipment?

8. From the standpoint of equipment usage, what guidelines must be taken into consideration before making the decision to select an office machine?

9. List the advantages of standardizing the sizes, styles, and brands of office equipment.

10. What are the characteristics of an equipment lease?

11. Explain the operation of a long-term lease with purchase option. From the lessee's point of view, what are the advantages and disadvantages of such a lease plan?

12. What possible benefits may a firm realize by leasing rather than buying its office equipment?

13. How may a break-even analysis be of value to the AOM when making the lease-or-buy decision?

14. What factors should be carefully studied before making the decision to lease or buy the needed equipment?

15. What is meant by a service contract for office equipment?

16. Office managers should develop a definite replacement program for their office machines and equipment. Indicate the advantages of such a replacement program.

17. Describe the activities involved in a program of centralized control over the selection, procurement, maintenance, and replacement of equipment.

FOR YOUR DISCUSSION

1. Sources for the purchase of office furniture include manufacturers, dealers, designers, and architects. What advantages and disadvantages might you anticipate as you consider each of these sources of supply?

2. A nationally known office management consultant recently commented at a regional conference that "many office managers make decisions on the procurement of office equipment based on tax savings rather than on the needs of the office." Discuss.

3. The Yusuki Company is considering the purchase of automated information processing equipment with an installed cost of $26,000. However, the firm estimates that this investment will be offset by a savings of $7,000 in its first full year of use. Discuss the kinds of

additional information needed before a decision is made to invest capital in this new equipment.

4. To understand the importance of good seating and related student learning needs, analyze the "workstation" provided for each student in your administrative office management class. As a basis for your discussion, use the furniture selection guidelines provided in this chapter as well as other common-sense principles that might apply.

5. Barry Information Services (BIS) has long had an active program for standardizing office furniture and equipment. Presently, BIS is replacing 300 secretarial and clerical posture chairs at a cost of $38,700. Maryann Ross, office manager of BIS, is finding the selection of office furniture and equipment increasingly difficult. Seven competing firms have offered her chairs that not only look alike and operate the same, and seem to have the same degree of seating comfort, but also cost nearly the same. Ross wants her selection of a supplier to be a wise one. Discuss the procedure you would follow if you were Ross.

6. A leading management consulting firm, with 65 branch offices in the United States, has recently centralized the purchasing of all office equipment through its headquarters office in New York City. Each branch office selects its equipment from a manual published by the company. If, for example, one office wishes to purchase a copier, the branch manager investigates the equipment available in the company's manual and requisitions the purchase of the copier through the central purchasing unit in New York City. What advantages can you cite for this type of centralized procurement of equipment? What disadvantages can be anticipated?

7. For three years your firm has had a service contract on all its office machines but has not taken the time to develop any records to document the service activities on the machines. Recently your supervisor assigned you the responsibility of setting up a record system that would serve as a history of activities on all office machines in the company. What type of information should such a record file include? How should such a set of records be created and maintained?

SOLVING CASE PROBLEMS

Case 15-1 Setting Up an Automated Workstation in the Home

Angie Casper has had seven years' experience with automated processing equipment in the Little Rock area. After the birth of her son two months ago, she decided to resign her previous position and begin a home-based processing service specializing in word processing and customer billing operations. Casper has taken one "giant step" by purchasing a personal computer and the software necessary to commence operations. The remaining tasks of laying out the office and procuring the necessary furniture and equipment for her new service business must still be faced.

Casper has given you the following sketch of the room in her home that will be dedicated to her business:

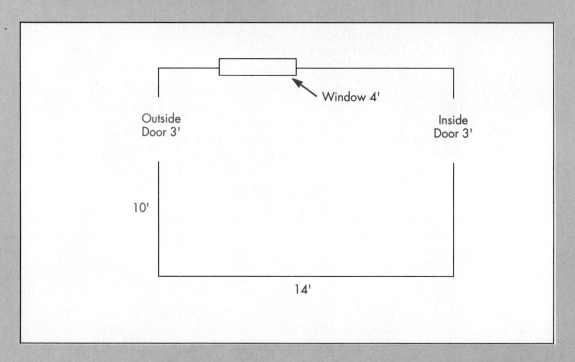

Casper is not aware of what constitutes a sound ergonomic workplace or an efficient use of office space. Accordingly, she asks you, a student of office ergonomics, to make recommendations to her in a very practical way, for she would like to start her business operations within the next month.

Prepare a brief report in which you discuss an ideal office for Casper from the standpoint of (1) ergonomics and (2) furniture and equipment. In addition, develop an easy-to-use checklist of furniture and equipment needed for the room to be operational. Include the physical dimensions and typical costs, which may be found in office furniture and equipment catalogs. No office layout is required, although the furniture and equipment recommended must effectively "fit" the area that Casper has chosen for the office.

Case 15-2 Determining Whether to Lease or Buy Office Equipment

After a slow start in its operations, Rambo Sporting Goods, Ltd. has "turned the corner," financially speaking, and is now experiencing steady growth. As a result, a serious need is felt for additional microcomputers to be used in administration.

To investigate this problem, Lew Kelting, the firm's office manager, completed a feasibility study that showed the need for $40,500 worth of microcomputers, which may be purchased or leased. The results of the feasibility study provided this additional information:

1. At the prices quoted, over a five-year period, the lease payments for the equipment would be $43,750, which includes insurance and all maintenance costs.

2. Annual insurance costs would be $250; the estimated maintenance costs would be $1,500 each year.

3. Kelting has been assured by a reliable broker that the purchase price of the computers could be invested in another endeavor where the interest on the investment would earn $30,875 over a five-year period.

As Kelting's assistant, you are asked (1) to determine the advisability of leasing or buying the equipment; and (2) to furnish any additional information that would be needed before making the lease-buy decision. Comply with this request in memo report form.

16
Office Automation

GOALS FOR THIS CHAPTER

After completing this chapter, you should be able to:

1. Identify the basic characteristics of computers and classify them according to purpose and size.
2. Describe the fundamental phases of computer systems technology and the role of each in the flow of data through the system.
3. Compare the traditional office with the modern office in terms of how the main information functions are integrated.
4. Enumerate the most common applications of information technology in the automated office.
5. Explain the role of feasibility studies in planning and organizing automated office systems.
6. Describe the basic methods used to maintain the security of automated office systems as well as important considerations in evaluating such systems.

Computers are so accessible today that we use them at work, in our homes, and in many other daily activities. No doubt you have also been using a computer to help you with your class assignments. From their earliest years in elementary school, students have become acquainted with computer operations and the many advantages that computers offer. Away from school, computers affect our lives, too. For example, in many homes we find personal computers used to keep business records, to prepare correspondence, and to file address lists, telephone numbers, recipes, and tax records. When you check out at the supermarket, you may find that a scanner, as an input device to the computer, "reads" the price of each item you buy and a printer prepares a slip that itemizes all the items. At any time of day or night when you find you are short of cash, possibly you drive up to an automatic teller machine, which dispenses money from your account. Or perhaps you use your touch-tone telephone at home to complete your school registration each semester. Either directly or indirectly, all of us, in and out of offices, use computer services to process information; in order to use these services effectively, we must become computer literate.

Computer literacy is a broad concept that describes (1) the ability to use or operate a computer, or (2) the ability to understand the capabilities of a computer without being able to operate one.[1] Of these two abilities, the second represents the more basic and more widely acknowledged sign of computer literacy. Four areas in which an understanding of computers should be achieved are illustrated in Figure 16-1. The figure suggests that if we understand what a computer *can do* (its capabilities) and *cannot*

[1]Many research studies reflect the growing interest in defining computer literacy and determining the educational requirements for achieving it. Typical of such studies is *Computer Literacy: The Prejudices, Perceptions and Surprising Realities,* published by Exxon Office Systems Company, 777 Long Ridge Road, Stamford, CT 06902, 1983.

Figure 16-1
The Concept
of Computer
Literacy

Understanding the computer
..what it can do
..what it cannot do
..how it can be used
..the effects of its use on society,
  information systems, and office workers

Computer
Literacy

Using (operating) the computer

do (its limitations); *how it can be used* (its applications); and *the effects of its use* (its implications for information systems and office workers), we are computer literate. This figure does not imply, however, that we must be able to program the computer or handle many of the highly technical aspects of managing a computer system.

The purpose of this chapter is to provide sufficient background on computer fundamentals so that you may develop computer literacy. We place special emphasis on office automation because of the vital role that computers play in the office.

THE NATURE AND PURPOSE OF COMPUTERS

The computer is the central information-processing tool in the modern organization. As an information-systems machine, the computer provides incredible power in the office where information is the principal product. Because of this power, work processes have changed, new work skills and new management challenges have appeared, and tighter systems controls are made available to office managers.

When the computer processes words or numbers, some of its operations are automated. Others, however, are not since the computer operates under the direction of people. *Thus, people are still the dominant force in any computer system.*

A *computer system* typically is composed of the following elements:

1. *Equipment* to convert human-readable data (handwritten or typewritten/key-boarded) into a form that the computer can process. Also equipment is needed for entering and storing data and for later converting the processed data into human language, the output of VDT screens and printers. Usually the equipment in a computer system is called *hardware.*

2. *Programs*, the instructions or *software*, necessary to operate the computer system.
3. *Personnel* who operate, program, and manage the system.

Computer technology is the basis for the automated office systems that move information through the organization. Your ability to use the technology available in today's office begins with an understanding of the basic characteristics of computers.

Basic Characteristics of Computers

In general, all computers receive and process information, retain information as needed in the future, and communicate that information to users. In order to do so, all computers share the following basic characteristics:

1. *Electronic circuitry* (switches) through which the computer routes data to be processed. Present-generation computers use *integrated circuits (ICs)* called **microprocessors** built on very small silicon *chips* (approximately $1/6'' \times 1/8''$). These chips can hold more than one million electronic transistors that perform the many types of electronic switching functions necessary to computing operations. A digital watch, for example, holds about 5,000 ICs and a small computer, about 50,000. The number of ICs can be expanded in many computers which, in turn, increases their processing and storage powers. With such expansion, remarkable increases in operating speeds become possible. For example, many computers operate at the *nanosecond* level (one billionth of a second); and even faster speeds, such as *picoseconds* (trillionths of a second) and *femtoseconds* (quadrillionths of a second), are reported.
2. An *internal memory* that receives and stores the data to be processed and the *program* that contains the detailed instructions necessary to process the data.

The computer's internal memory is divided into many small sections called *storage locations*, each of which has a specific numeric address much like the address given to a residence in a city. When the address is known, we can easily access the data item "residing" in that storage location.

The capacity of a computer is measured by the number of bytes that can be stored in internal memory. A **byte** is a computer term for a basic data character, such as a letter, number, or symbol. One common byte format consists of eight bits plus a ninth bit that checks the accuracy of the data represented. (**Bit** is an abbreviation of the term *binary digit*, the basic value in a numeric system that uses two digits—0 and 1—to represent alphabetic, numeric, and related data within the computer.)

Usually memory is expressed in terms of thousands of bytes. For example, a computer with 640K has approximately 640,000 storage locations, since the letter *K*—an abbreviation of the word *kilo*—represents 1,000. However, in computer circles, K equals 1,024 bytes. A broader measure of computer memory is the *megabyte (MB)*—1,024K or 1,048,576 bytes. For convenience, this measure is frequently rounded to and expressed as one million; thus, a computer with 40MB actually stores 41,943,040 or about 40 million characters.

3. The *ability to perform mathematical operations and machine logic*. For example, the computer can (a) perform arithmetic operations (addition, subtraction, multiplication, and division); (b) determine if a number is positive, negative, or equal to zero; and (c) "decide" whether one of two numbers when compared, is equal to, higher than, or lower than the other. (Alphabetic characters are converted to numeric codes and thus can be compared in the same way as numeric data.) Thus, the computer is

said to have a "logical" ability when it compares numbers and on the basis of such comparisons moves or advances from one set of instructions to another.

4. The *automated control of input, process, and output activities*. The computer is automated in that it self-regulates the flow of program instructions and data to be processed from the various input devices. It can also perform many processing steps and store or print out the processed information as the program directs without the need for human operators. As a result, labor costs are lowered and productivity in the administrative office system is enhanced.

Some computers, called **analog computers**, measure continuously changing conditions, such as temperature and atmospheric pressure, and convert them into quantities. Analog computer applications are commonly found in refineries, chemical plants, and utilities. The computers used in business offices are typically **digital computers**, which count numbers or digits while processing numeric and alphabetic data that have been converted to a numeric code. Since most data processed in business are either numeric or alphabetic, only the digital computer is discussed in this textbook.

Sizes of Computers

The most common way of classifying business computers is by *size*, which refers to their capacity for processing volumes of data. Usually computer size is described in terms of the number of storage locations in internal memory (64K, 128K, 256K, 640K, and so on). The largest computers are called *mainframes*; smaller computers, represented by *minicomputers* and *microcomputers*, have less internal memory, fewer input-output (I/O) units, and more limited storage capacity.

Mainframes

A large computer is referred to as a **mainframe** since it serves as the principal source of power and direction for complex company-wide data processing and telecommunication networks. Large computers provide millions of units of internal memory and can process information at very high speeds with millions—and, as indicated earlier, billions—of operations per second. In addition, we find that mainframes often serve as **host computers**, which direct the input, processing, output, and distribution of information to, from, and among a group of small computers. Mainframes, such as the type shown in Figure 16-2, are typically located in central data processing departments that are managed by specialists in computer science and data processing systems.

Minicomputers

A small computer equipped with integrated circuits and housed in a compact desk-size or desktop cabinet is called a **minicomputer**. (See Figure 16-3.) A minicomputer is a direct "descendant" of the mainframe; and, with

Figure 16-2
A Mainframe System

Figure 16-3
A Minicomputer

the addition of integrated circuits, is able to take over many mainframe responsibilities. Minicomputers are capable of supporting a large number of terminals that perform a variety of operations simultaneously. Typical of these operations are the following: accounts payable, sales systems reporting, interest computations, and word processing. In addition, minicomputers serve as standalone systems in departments and in small firms or as I/O systems attached to mainframes.

Microcomputers

The smallest and least expensive class of computers is the **microcomputer**. Today, as a result of microprocessor technology and availability of peripheral devices for entering, storing, and printing data, microcomputers have become more powerful and fully operational. For these reasons, the lines of distinction separating minicomputers and microcomputers are fuzzy.

A microcomputer is designed for use by one person; hence, we often use the term *personal computer* or *PC*. A typical PC, shown in Figure 16-4A, is placed on a desk and takes up about as much space as a

typewriter and a portable television set. Portable PCs are also available. For example, *transportables* (also called *luggables*) usually weigh 20 to 30 pounds, have a conventional TV-like display screen, and can be moved about easily. Even smaller PCs, called *laptop*, or *briefcase*, computers, weigh from 6 to 20 pounds, have a flat display screen, and can operate up to ten hours on rechargeable batteries. (See Figure 16-4B.) Another model of portable computer is the *box portable*, or *lunchbox machine*, that weighs 14 to 18 pounds and has more features and better displays than the laptop models. Portable computers are used by people whose jobs require them to travel extensively and to make computations, prepare reports, and store records en route. Most portable computers are compatible with the larger machines maintained in the home office. Laptops are also used by students who take notes in class and at the library and then write their reports in their dorm rooms.

The PC has revolutionized the computer industry; and because of its small size, ease of use, and relatively low cost (usually under $5,000), it has been successfully introduced into all types of offices and into millions of homes throughout the world. Over 50 percent of small businesses (those with fewer than 100 employees) use PCs.[2] *Since its use in the office is the primary reason for the tremendous growth of automated office activities, the PC is the main point of emphasis in the discussion of office automation in this chapter.*

Figure 16-5 provides a visual comparison of the PC with the minicomputer discussed earlier. You will note the same types of components found in both systems. Also, observe that the basic PC is limited to one of each component and thus has less processing, storage, and printing power. The

[2]"Small Firms Big on PCs," *The Office* (June, 1989), p. 89.

Figure 16-4
Two Sizes of
Micro-
computers

A—A Typical-Size Microcomputer

B—A Laptop Microcomputer

five components of the PC system illustrated in Figure 16-5 are:

1. A *central processing unit (CPU)*, the heart of the computer system in which computing operations are performed. In the PC, the size of the CPU (measured by the amount of memory provided) ranges from 64K to 512K or more as needed. Microcomputers with 256K hold about 260,000 characters, or about 32,000 words of text.

2. A *keyboard* for entering instructions and data into the system and a *display screen (monitor)* for viewing the data. Some screens are capable of displaying 120 characters across and 256 colors.

3. One or two *disk drive* units in which are placed the media (floppy disks) used to send information to, and store information produced by, the system. One drive unit may hold a hard disk, as described later.

4. A *printer* that produces reports, charts, letters, and memorandums.

We are finding that the desktop PC is becoming more sophisticated and its power

greatly expanded through more powerful microprocessors, networking capabilities, and operating systems designed to handle many tasks. Computer experts refer to these powerful PCs as *workstations*. At one time, these very expensive workstations were reserved for specific applications like engineering and design, which involve much work in graphics. Today, however, computer manufacturers are promoting a broader range of uses for these high-powered machines. As a result, the PC and the computer workstation are becoming more and more similar in their features and capability. (Remember, from our Chapter 13 reference, that in our textbook, we follow the widespread practice in management and use the term *workstation* to describe a unit of office space planning, which includes the furniture and equipment—computer and noncomputer—used by each employee in performing work assignments.)

Personal computers are **user friendly**; that is, they are easy to operate since they require no technical knowledge. Application programs, which include accounting, payroll,

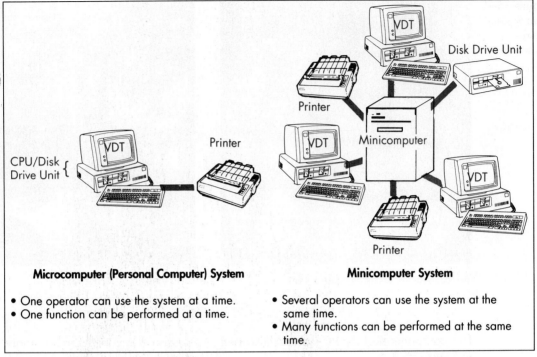

A Comparison of the Microcomputer and the Minicomputer

CPU/Disk Drive Unit

Printer

Microcomputer (Personal Computer) System

- One operator can use the system at a time.
- One function can be performed at a time.

Disk Drive Unit

Printer

Minicomputer

Printer

Minicomputer System

- Several operators can use the system at the same time.
- Many functions can be performed at the same time.

financial planning, graphics, inventory control, production control, and word processing, are readily available. Also, advances in telecommunications technology provide for the connection of PCs to telephone lines for transmitting data among networks of PCs or to minicomputers or mainframes. In addition, the use of PCs in homes and other nonoffice locations has ushered in *telecommuting*, which was discussed in Chapter 12.

COMPUTER SYSTEMS TECHNOLOGY

In administrative office systems, we find that many technologies are combined to provide an automated environment. Even though they perform a variety of functions, these technologies may be classified according to the various phases of the systems model explained in Chapter 4.

Figure 16–6 outlines the basic systems functions and the means by which they are performed in each of the phases of a computer system. To understand the main concepts shown in this figure, let's examine briefly the most common technologies found in automated offices. (More complex systems are explained in detail in advanced references on computer science and data processing systems.)

Input Technology

Technology must be provided to enter into the computer (input) the data to be processed as well as the program that instructs the computer what operations to perform and in what order. Highly skilled technical personnel, known as **programmers**, write computer programs and plan the conversion of unprocessed data onto one or more media. The most common forms of input to the

Figure 16-6
Computer
Systems
Phases and
Related
Functions

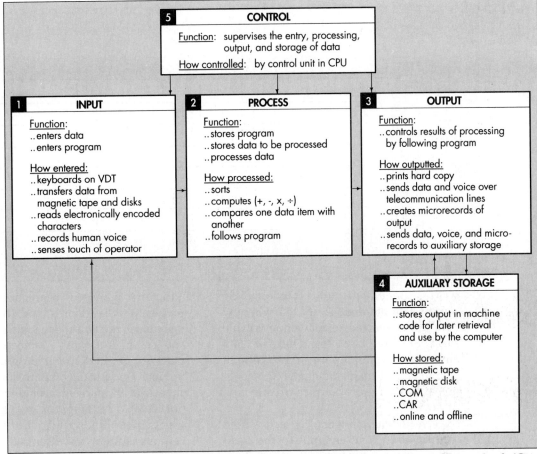

Source: Adapted from Mina M. Johnson and Norman F. Kallaus, *Records Management*, 4th ed. (Cincinnati: South-Western Publishing Co., 1987), p. 335.

computer are achieved by using one or more of the following media:

1. *VDTs (video display terminals)* on which the data and the program are keyboarded.
2. *Magnetic tape*, upon which data are stored as magnetized spots, as shown in Figure 16–7. A typical reel of tape ½ inch by 2,400 feet is mounted on a device called a *tape drive* for use in a large computer system; and from this device the contents of the tape are sent as input to the internal memory of the computer.
3. *Magnetic disks*, which provide storage locations on both sides of the round

magnetic medium. Data are recorded on a disk in the form of magnetized spots arranged in concentric (parallel) tracks on each recording surface. Figure 16–8 shows the storage of one data record on a magnetic disk. In large computer systems, disks are usually arranged in stacks called *disk packs* and placed in a disk drive unit that is used to transfer to the computer's memory the data maintained on the disks. Small computer systems use diskettes, which are discussed in a later section of this chapter.

4. *Scanning devices* that read electronically encoded characters on printed or hand-

Figure 16-7
Magnetic
Tape Code

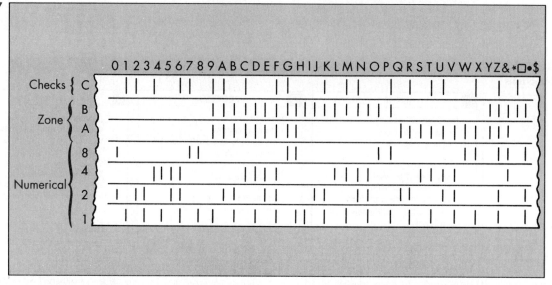

written documents and thus provide **source data automation (SDA)** whereby data are converted to machine-readable form. SDA bypasses the need for data entry by human operators. (Optical-character and magnetic-character recognition readers are examples of this type of device.)

5. *Speech* (the human voice), which is used to a limited extent as input to the computer. Two types of speech-recognition, or voice-recognition, input systems have been developed: (a) isolated speech recognition in which the sender is re-stricted to a limited vocabulary with short pauses between words; and (b) continuous speech recognition in which words are spoken in a natural, connected speech pattern.[3] One computer program, called Sphinx, understands continuous human speech at 94 percent accuracy and does not have to be taught to recognize each user's voice.[4] Voice-recognition and audio-response systems are discussed more fully in Chapter 18.

6. *Graphics and image devices*, such as:
   a. The *mouse*, a device used to move the cursor (the blinking box symbol or blinking underscore) around on the display screen. As the VDT operator moves the mouse, the cursor moves correspondingly, with great precision and speed, on the screen. The mouse, along with the light pen, are illustrated in Figure 13-12, page 390.

Figure 16-8
Data Storage
on a Mag-
netic Disk

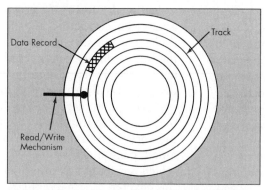

Source: Allen N. Smith, Wilma Jean Alexander, and Donald B. Medley, *Advanced Office Systems* (Cincinnati: South-Western Publishing Co., 1986), p. 221.

---

[3]For an interesting discussion of input technologies including speech-recognition systems, see R. A. Hirschheim, *Office Automation: Concepts, Technologies and Issues* (Reading, MA: Addison-Wesley Publishing Company, 1985), Chapter 4; and Allen N. Smith, Wilma Jean Alexander, and Donald B. Medley, *Advanced Office Systems* (Cincinnati: South-Western Publishing Co., 1986), Chapter 6.
[4]"These Computers Hear You Loud and Clear," *Business Week* (July 4, 1988), p. 112.

b. The *light pen*, an electrical device resembling a pen, that is used for writing or sketching on the display screen to provide input to the computer. As the pen reacts to the light from the screen, the image written or sketched is digitized (converted to a numeric code) by the computer for processing, storing, and printing in the system.

c. Other *touch-sensitive screens* such as the screen upon which the operator enters commands by pressing designated areas with a finger. For example, by touching a file name listed on the screen, the operator can retrieve a desired file from computer storage.

Other input media, such as punched cards and punched paper tape, are generally obsolete and for this reason are not included in this textbook.

Processing Technology

The processing phase in the computer system involves the tasks of receiving input and performing arithmetic, logical, and output operations under program control. The computer unit responsible for this processing is called the **central processing unit (CPU)**, which, as the "brain" of the system, contains the circuits that control and execute the instructions. The equipment and devices that are directly connected to the computer are said to be **online**. This is in contrast with **offline**, which refers to the equipment and devices not directly connected to the computer.

In the CPU, we find three main components as shown in Figure 16-9: (1) the *memory*, (2) the *arithmetic-logic unit*, and (3) the *control unit*, which regulates all processing operations through built-in monitoring capabilities that are beyond the "reach" of the user. The memory unit and the arithmetic-logic unit are explained in this section along with a brief description of the

Figure 16-9
Sequential Flow of Data in the Central Processing Unit of the Computer

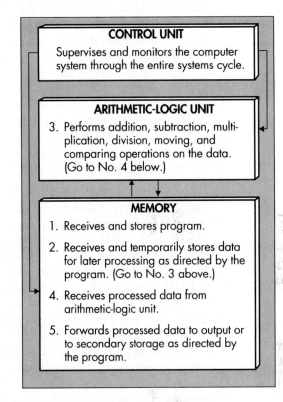

process of programming a computer. The control unit is discussed in a later section.

Memory

Memory or *primary storage* is an area where data and programs are temporarily stored before, during, and after processing. Whenever a program is entered into the computer, it is either stored in memory where it remains until processing is completed or it is retained in memory until needed for further computing operations. In a similar way, data entered from input devices are placed in memory to be available for processing. However, *no actual processing takes place in memory*; this function is reserved for the arithmetic-logic unit. As we shall see below, there are two major types of primary storage.

Random Access Memory (RAM). In the **random access memory (RAM)**, the array of memory locations on one or more microchips is activated when electrical power reaches the unit. At this time, data can be entered into a memory location without regard to any other memory location. *When the power is turned off, all data in RAM are lost.* For this reason, it is important that we store all processed data in the diskette file before turning off the power.

Read Only Memory (ROM). The special type of memory, **read only memory (ROM)**, is permanently programmed with one group of frequently used instructions. No additional data or instructions may be stored in the ROM memory. Thus, the program residing in ROM cannot be changed by the user; only its contents can be read. In contrast to RAM, ROM does not lose its program when the computer's power is turned off.

Both RAM and ROM are *random access*, which means that the computer can go directly (at random) to any set of data without first "reading" each of the sets that have been stored in sequential order.

Arithmetic-Logic Unit

In microcomputers, the **arithmetic-logic unit** is often referred to as a microprocessor, a microchip on which reside the control and arithmetic-logic functions shown in Figure 16–9. In such computers, the data and programs are brought into the microprocessor and executed one step at a time, after which the results are returned to memory. The processing cycle is repeated until all program steps have been completed. This sequence is shown in consecutive-number order in Figure 16–9.

Programming the Computer

No computer can perform its processing tasks unless it is properly programmed. In

order to write an effective program of *instructions*, the programmer must follow the steps in the problem-solving process identified in Chapter 3 and the steps in the systems study cycle discussed in Chapter 4. In particular, these steps are followed:

1. *Analyze the problem and chart the strategy for solving the problem.* Often a *general systems flowchart* using the standardized program charting symbols shown in Figure 16–10 is prepared. In this figure, a general solution to the valuation of an inventory is charted. More specific steps must be created for charting and writing the actual detailed program.

2. *Write and test the program.* In computer systems, the most common programming languages are:
   a. *Business programming languages:*
      (1) *COBOL* (**C**ommon **B**usiness **O**riented **L**anguage)—a high-level language developed for business applications, especially where large volumes of alphanumeric files are handled. (*High-level languages* allow users to write their programs using terms with which they are familiar rather than using the computer's machine code.)
      (2) *RPG* (**R**eport **P**rogram **G**enerator)—a business-oriented language that is highly structured and relatively easy to learn. The language allows users to program many business operations as well as create reports.
   b. *Scientific programming languages:*
      (1) *BASIC* (**B**eginner's **A**ll-Purpose **S**ymbolic **I**nstruction **C**ode)—an easy-to-learn, easy-to-use algebraic language with a small number of commands and simple statement formats. Even though the commands are written in a mathematical-equation format for reasons of simplicity, BASIC is

Figure 16-10 A General Systems Flowchart Using Standardized Program Charting Symbols

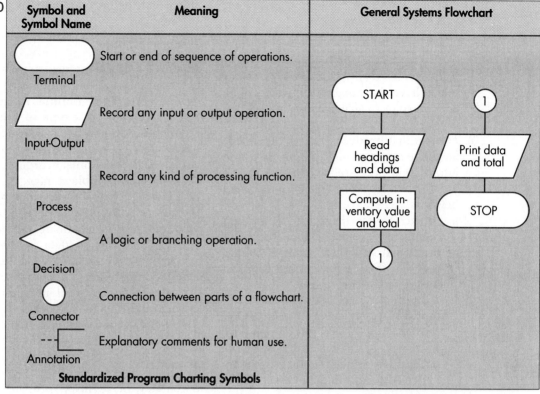

Symbol and Symbol Name	Meaning	General Systems Flowchart
Terminal	Start or end of sequence of operations.	
Input-Output	Record any input or output operation.	
Process	Record any kind of processing function.	
Decision	A logic or branching operation.	
Connector	Connection between parts of a flowchart.	
Annotation	Explanatory comments for human use.	

Standardized Program Charting Symbols

widely used in programming instruction, in personal computing, and in business and industry.

(2) *Pascal*—a high-level language, named for the French mathematician, Blaise Pascal, which is easy to use and is taught widely in schools and colleges.[5]

An *application program*, or application software, refers to a computer program written to perform a specialized computer task. Application programs are available from vendors or software firms for many common applications, such as word processing, payroll, and inventory control. Software purchased from vendors is usually copyrighted

[5]For detailed explanations of the nature and purpose of these programming languages, see James F. Clark and Judith J. Lambrecht, *Information Processing: Concepts, Principles, and Procedures* (Cincinnati: South-Western Publishing Co., 1985), Chapters 13-15.

and thus should not be reproduced without the vendor's permission. Users may also write their own application programs, using the programming languages discussed above.

Output Technology

The output, or the results of the computer processing operations, is prepared according to the program instructions residing in the computer. If the end use of the processed data is a report (text copy) or a completed business document, the results will be printed in planned report form or on a business form, such as a customer invoice or a paycheck. If the output is to be used in later computer processing, as in the case of preparing a payroll or updating inventory data, the output may be placed in secondary storage as discussed later. In this case, the data contained in secondary storage are fed back as input to the system for executing another information-processing cycle.

The most common output devices used in computer systems are:

1. *VDTs (video display terminals),* some of which have the capability for displaying copy in color to enhance the presentation of graphics.
2. *Printers* that produce in plain (decoded) language single or multiple copies of the information processed by the computer. We find two types of printers, as explained below.
   a. *Impact printers* that create the printed output by means of movable print heads that strike the paper through a ribbon, thus transferring the impression onto the paper.
   b. *Nonimpact printers* that have no movable print heads; instead, these printers create characters on paper by means of a process (laser, heat, or chemicals) similar to that used by office copying equipment.
3. *Voice (audio) response units* that create the human voice in two ways: (a) from a prerecorded set of words stored in memory; or (b) from sounds that the computer receives as input and converts to digitized (numeric) form.
4. *Special-purpose output devices,* such as computer output microfilm (COM) and computer-assisted retrieval (CAR) discussed in Chapter 20. Another specialized output device is the *graph plotter,* which is used to make engineering drawings and graphs and charts that are to be reproduced in printed reports.

Storage Technology

Technology provides two types of data storage within the computer system: (1) primary storage in which the data and the program reside temporarily in the CPU's memory unit, and (2) secondary or auxiliary storage in which the processed data are

stored outside the computer on an online or offline basis.

Primary Storage

In addition to the internal storage provided by integrated circuits, another form of primary storage—**bubble memory**—has been developed as a type of miniaturized computer storage. When viewed under a microscope, each unit of storage appears as a small circle, or bubble. In order to represent binary data in bubble storage, the presence of a bubble represents the value of "1," and the absence of a bubble represents a binary value of "O." A 1-inch square bubble package stores 92,000 bits of data in the form of magnetic bubbles that move in thin films of magnetic material. This type of storage provides an economical medium for data storage and, unlike microchip storage, has the advantage of retaining the data in storage when the power is turned off.

Secondary Storage

Secondary, or auxiliary, storage is external storage provided in a computer system because the amount of data that can be stored in internal memory is limited. Secondary storage takes several forms, as explained below.

Magnetic Tape. *Magnetic tape* (Figure 16-7) is commonly used in large computer systems to store serial (or sequential) information, such as the payroll data, by employee number, for all persons in a firm. Magnetic tape must be placed on a tape drive before data can be read onto, or read from, the tape. As is true of most magnetic media, magnetic tape may be erased and reused.

Magnetic Disk. By means of a *magnetic disk* (Figure 16-8), users have direct access to any portion of the tracks on the recording surface. For many operations, this feature is useful as compared with other media, such as magnetic tape, in which unwanted portions of the tape must be sorted through in order to locate the desired data. For example, a disk file provides more efficient storage and retrieval in a college registrar's office since students usually come to the office in random order to get information from their records rather than in alphabetic order.

Floppy Disk. The **floppy disk**, shown in Figure 16-11, is a flexible diskette made of mylar plastic that is encased in a paper or plastic jacket. The floppy disk resembles a small phonograph record. The data, stored in sectors much like storage on magnetic disks, can be retrieved randomly. Used widely with microcomputers and mini-computers, floppy disks provide storage at relatively low cost. A more durable 3½ inch disk is also widely used. It is permanently housed within a plastic casing and can hold more data than a 5¼ inch floppy disk.

Hard Disk. The **hard disk**, made of rigid aluminum, is usually encased within the computer. Since data are stored more closely together on hard disks than on floppy disks, more data can be stored in less space. Because hard disks rotate at a much faster speed than floppy disks, faster retrieval and storage capabilities are possible. Retrieval time is about ten times faster from a hard disk as compared with the floppy disk.

Optical Disk. Another type of secondary storage uses the **optical disk** (sometimes called the *video disk*), which is shown in Figure 20-5, page 620. As we shall see in that chapter, optical disk storage is created when a laser-beam recorder scans a document, film, or slide and then copies it and transfers the image onto a metal disk. Between 50 and 100 times more data can be stored on optical disks than on magnetic disks, and the cost of storing information on optical disks is only a fraction of the cost of storing data on magnetic disks.

Compact Disk-Read Only Memory (CD-ROM). The **CD-ROM** is an optical disk used to store large quantities of data. For example, a 5-inch CD has the storage capacity of about 1,500 floppy disks, or nearly 250,000 typed pages. A 20-volume encyclopedia or the entire parts list for all Honda cars can be stored on a compact disk similar to the CDs you buy at a record store. After you have inserted the CD-ROM into a special peripheral on your PC, you can access the information, read it, save it on a floppy disk, or print it. Many CD-ROM applications are found in systems designed to manage the data for libraries, medical centers, and financial institutions.

Database. A powerful application of secondary storage, such as the CD-ROM, is the *database*. As we learned earlier, a database is a central master file that contains company-wide (or, in the case of a large department, department-wide) information from the major systems of the firm. You may obtain a clear picture of this concept by turning to page 575 and examining Figure 19-4, which graphically shows where the database fits into the data hierarchy in a human resources system. The database concept originated with large computer systems in which data were collected, organized, and stored centrally in a computerized library to be accessed by telecommunication lines throughout the firm. Such an arrange-

Figure 16-11
Inserting a
Floppy Disk
into a Disk
Drive Unit

ment eliminates duplicate files and the related manual storage and retrieval tasks and provides a single information source that furnishes complete, accurate data storage and retrieval. On the other hand, a database has certain weaknesses that include: problems of security (protecting the confidentiality of stored data); expensive technology and file maintenance procedures; the difficulty of sharing department information for integration into a centralized data file; and the company-wide problems that are created when unreliable equipment causes work stoppages and a drop in office productivity.

With the use of software packages called **database management systems (DBMS)**, databases can be distributed, or decentralized, throughout the firm, which allows each user to keep track of an organized collection of files. Thus, any department with a microcomputer can define, create, and process its own set of files on, say, customer records.

On a broader scale, specialized databases are constructed by professional, governmental, and research agencies to provide a huge reservoir of centrally held information for the benefit of subscribers or association members. For example, with a VDT and a communication link, municipal police departments may access state and national databases in search of security and crime-control information.

Control Technology

Two types of control are required to ensure an effective computer system. The first and most important is the set of *human controls* that regulate the performance of managers, supervisors, and workers. (This aspect of control is discussed in a later section, *Evaluating Automated Office Systems*.) The second type of control relates to the *technological controls* that must be functioning properly in the system.

An effectively written and properly tested program is a major type of control, for without it the goal of the computer system cannot be achieved. In addition, control resides in the control unit of the CPU, which operates in the following manner:

1. *The control unit processes the instructions recorded in the program*. It directs the various processing operations spelled out in the program and checks to see that the instructions are properly carried out.
2. *The control unit also "authorizes" the receipt of information from secondary storage units*. It stores the intermediate results of the operations in *buffer storage*, a temporary storage location, until such results are finally stored in auxiliary storage or are printed out.
3. *The control unit then instructs the computer to prepare the results on the appropriate output devices* (printing, plotting, COM, and so on).

The hardware and software discussed in the chapter up to this point apply generally to all computer systems, unless otherwise indicated. However, in the next section, we shall discuss those major applications in information technology that center on the automated office.

THE AUTOMATED OFFICE

Since the office is the organizational function responsible for all phases of the information system, logically the office should be a prime target for automation. However, many offices continue to use traditional systems and procedures despite the availability of computers. In this section of the chapter, we examine the nature of the traditional office and its gradual conversion to automated systems. Also, we shall discuss briefly the benefits of office automation.

The Traditional Office: Separate, Manual Functions

The traditional office relies entirely on manual labor that is supplemented by the use of simple hand-operated equipment, such as typewriters, telephones, copiers, calculators, and filing cabinets. In such a setting, letters are dictated and transcribed; incoming and outgoing telephone calls are handled; reprographic equipment is used for copy making; ten-key calculators prove the accuracy of invoices for customer billing; and copies of the records made in all these operations are filed and later retrieved for use.

Each of these common office tasks exists as a separate, somewhat unrelated operation performed by support personnel. Also, each of these tasks is usually carried out in a separate location—in a private secretary's office, or in a mailroom, typing pool, reprographics center, microfilm reading room, or data processing department. For office operations, this system results in low productivity, high costs, and an inability to provide the best type and level of services to information users inside and outside the firm.

Despite the tremendous inroads made by computers and other information technology, many of the inefficient practices of the traditional office remain. However, as the costs of technology decrease and the demands of office managers for greater productivity increase, gradually more and more phases of the traditional office are being replaced by automated systems, as discussed in the next section.

The Modern Office: Integrated, Automated Functions

Early in this century technology focused on the mechanization of information processing with the development of punched-card data processing systems. In these systems, an integrated family of machine functions was developed for recording, storing, processing, and printing information, which was largely numeric. Later, this type of system evolved into a computer-based operation that further integrated the activities found in the information cycle. As time passed, word processing systems were developed as separate systems for storing, processing, and printing alphabetic information (text). Once it was accepted in business, the word processing system began to use the computer and its peripheral equipment for performing a growing number of functions, including communications. (We shall examine word processing systems in detail in the following chapter.) This *integration* or *merging* of the two principal information subsystems in the office, in turn, sparked a growing trend toward further linkage of information functions. Thus, the term **office automation (OA)** was coined to describe the integration of computer, communication, and related information technologies to support the administrative service responsibilities and to improve the productivity of office personnel.

Ideally, OA seeks to create a *paperless* information system, although from a practical standpoint, creating a *less-paper* office is a more realistic goal. In an OA system, the key steps in the information cycle are handled in the following manner with most, if not all, the steps controlled from one multifunction workstation:

1. *An idea is created and captured* on some type of magnetic medium through the entry of data on a VDT or by using one or more of the input devices described earlier.
2. *The information is processed* in various ways within the integrated system (typically by computer or word processor).
3. *The processed information is reproduced* by an automated microprocessor-based device.

4. *The processed information is retained* in an automated file for use as needed.

5. *The processed information is distributed* electronically to the user. Hard copies can be made available if desired.

Major Information Functions and Systems

In OA, the five operations listed above are integrated into one joint computer-communication system. To understand such a system, let's review the main information functions and the media, equipment, and systems that are discussed throughout this textbook. These factors, identified within five circles in Figure 16–12, are:

Circle 1. Here we see the four main forms in which information appears in the office: data, voice, image, and text (words).

Figure 16–12
Principal Information Functions and Systems in the Automated Office

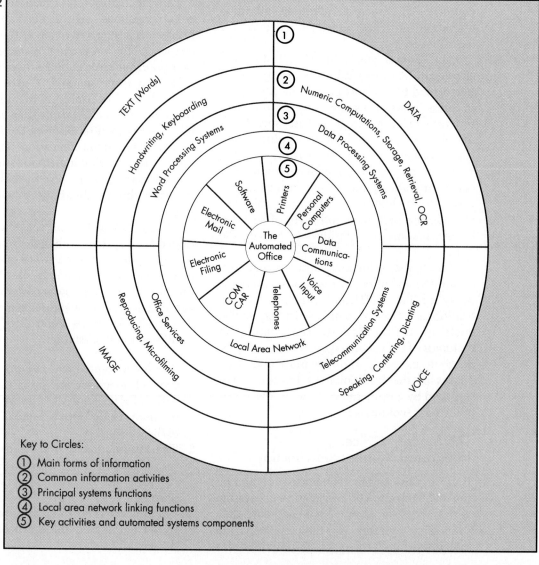

Key to Circles:
1. Main forms of information
2. Common information activities
3. Principal systems functions
4. Local area network linking functions
5. Key activities and automated systems components

Circle 2. This circle shows the basic information-cycle activities that are performed for each of the four forms of information.

Circle 3. In Circle 3 we identify the formal systems that are responsible for carrying out the information-cycle activities.

Circle 4. To link these four systems functions, we find that the organization requires a local area network (LAN), similar to that illustrated in Figure 18-6, page 539. As we shall see in that chapter, a **local area network (LAN)** consists of a telecommunication facility that links together various types of information-processing equipment for transmitting and receiving data.

Circle 5. Finally, Circle 5 shows us the processing power that is available from electronic workstations within the automated office. In such an environment, the computer serves as the major source of automated power and control but is subject to the final decisions of the individuals who have access to the system through terminals.

Automated Workcenters

In the automated office, we find workcenters with VDTs for both the office support (clerical) staff as well as the executives they serve. Let's examine briefly these important facilities of the automated office.

Clerical Workcenters. In the automated office, a *clerical workcenter*, or *clerical workstation*, which includes a VDT, performs many computer-based functions. This workstation links the support personnel (data-entry operators, records clerks, secretaries, and administrative assistants) to the total operating power of the firm's computer system. Through the use of a LAN,

a VDT user in the automated office possesses great information-handling power. Depending on the hardware and software available, some or all of the following clerical-support activities may be carried out at the clerical workstation:

1. *Running data processing programs* for making computations.
2. *Performing word processing tasks*, such as preparing letters and reports.
3. *Storing and retrieving information* from the computer and microrecord files, and transferring documents from one file to another using database management systems.
4. *Printing out information* processed by the computer or information retrieved from the computer files.
5. *Setting up and maintaining electronic calendars* that schedule meetings, appointments, and teleconferences.
6. *Receiving and responding to messages* stored in electronic mailboxes and other electronic mail systems.

In addition, through the use of a switchboard system (discussed in Chapter 18), the VDT operator can use the telephone for interactive voice and computer functions. Thus, each department with clerical workstations has full access to word processing, data processing, and other technologies provided by the firm for use inside and outside the firm.

Executive Workcenters. Early efforts to automate the office included only the clerical support staff. However, experience has shown that managers and other professionals can improve their productivity if they, too, have direct access to automated systems from their offices. Thus, *executive workcenters*, or *executive workstations*, provide managers with immediate electronic access to the firm's database as well as to outside information sources. This type of workstation offers to the executive information-handling capabilities that include:

1. *Preparing text, graphics, and spreadsheets. Spreadsheet* programs display a gridlike formation of rows and columns on the display screen. Each grid box, called a *cell*, is defined by its column and row position. As the data stored in any cell are changed, all data and summary totals linked to that cell's content are automatically updated. Spreadsheet printouts, such as the one shown in Figure 16-13, are often prepared for income statement analysis, budgetary control, forecasting, and other financial analyses.

2. *Receiving and sending electronic mail and voice mail.*

3. *Retrieving data from computer files.*

4. *Checking the electronic calendar* to make sure that all scheduled appointments are met and that no meetings are missed.

5. *Using inside and outside databases.*

Corporate officers, such as controllers, planners, and information managers like the AOM, need "push-button" access to information that an executive workstation provides. Being linked to a LAN allows executives to communicate with one another within the firm as well as with support personnel located at the clerical workstations.

Benefits of Office Automation

The office automation concepts and plans for their implementation described in this section are technologically feasible. They

**Figure 16-13
A Spreadsheet Prepared by a Computer**

```
                    Taylor Computerware, Inc.

          Comparison of Actual vs. Forecasted Monthly Sales

          1st QUARTER

                                              January
                           Inventory   ---------------------------------
          Product Name     Number      Actual    Forecast   Variance
          --------------   ---------   --------   --------   --------

          Dot Matrix Printer  DMP4700  $ 5,600    $ 6,400    ($   800)
          Ink Jet Printer     IJP5300  $ 9,500    $ 8,550    $   950
          VT-100 Terminal     CRT100   $20,400    $16,800    $3,600
                                       -------    -------    -------
               Total                   $35,500    $31,750    $3,750
```

exist, however, in varying degrees of completeness. Where OA is properly planned, organized, and introduced to the workers, productivity can be enhanced in the following ways:

1. *Increased efficiency* (tasks are performed in less time with more output from each worker). Thus, we can make better use of human resources, either by reducing the number of employees or having the same number of employees perform more work.
2. *Greater effectiveness in organizational communication*, including decreased need for meetings because of electronic mail and teleconferencing, which also decreases the need for travel; and a decreased number of telephone calls since internal communication is carried out via the LAN.
3. *Fewer transfers of control* over the work. For example, word processing operators type and edit their own copy rather than have other persons perform the editing.
4. *Better control over the work*: fewer interruptions from telephone calls; a reduced need to depend on workcenters in the firm (data processing and word processing centers especially); higher quality of work because of the ease with which revisions can be made with document-creation hardware; and better, more timely, and more accessible information.

Ideally the benefits of OA may have many positive effects on people. Workers "in tune" with OA experience an improvement in morale, which leads to increased job satisfaction. Faster service leads to increased goodwill and customer satisfaction; and as a result, AOMs and other department managers can better meet the objectives of their individual units.

APPLICATIONS OF AUTOMATED SYSTEMS

Each year we read reports of newly emerging applications of automation. The following discussion briefly examines several applications of automated systems at two levels: (1) mainframe and minicomputer systems and (2) microcomputer systems.

Mainframe and Minicomputer Applications

In addition to the computer applications discussed elsewhere in this textbook, several other examples of successful mainframe and minicomputer operations are described below:

1. *Point-of-sale (POS) terminals*, commonly found in retail stores, use the *universal product code (UPC)* on the label of a product. (See Figure 16–14.) The UPC is

Figure 16-14
Scanning a Bar Code as Input to a Store's Computer

sensed by a laser scanner that is built into the checkout counter terminal. The scanner reads the UPC symbol and transmits this code number to a computer that stores price and other information on all items carried in the store. The computer transmits back to the check-stand the item's price and description, which are instantly displayed and printed on the customer's receipt tape. The POS system speeds checkout operations and allows the collection of complete and accurate information for sales analysis and inventory control.

In some retail stores, we are able to use another computer-based record, the debit card. We give our *debit card* to the check-stand attendant, who inserts it into a device that checks our credit standing. (The retail store has a communication link to our bank's computer where our credit is checked.) If it is approved, the bank charges (debits) our bank account for the amount of the purchase and credits the store's account for the same amount. This paperless transaction eliminates the need for checkwriting.

2. *Automated teller machines (ATM)*, which are terminals found at scattered locations throughout the city that enable us to deposit and withdraw funds, transfer funds from one account to another, and verify account balances. ATMs are part of the *electronic-funds transfer system (EFTS)* used nationally by banks.

3. *Decision-support systems (DSS)* that integrate data from sources inside and outside the firm into the computer files for use in decision making. Managers use DSS to project future operating results based on historical and current data, and by looking at the consequences of a number of alternatives, select a specific course of action.

4. A wide variety of other emerging applications. The technology of *computer-aided software engineering (CASE)* is

being used to automate the job of writing computer programs in the same way that computer-aided design and computer-aided engineering have sped up the work and improved quality in product development.[6]

Computers are widely used to *monitor the work of employees* second-by-second throughout the business day. For example, the computer may be programmed to record the volume of keystrokes per hour, the length of work breaks, the number of errors, and the amount of time airlines agents spend with each caller.[7]

Robots, or automated machines for replacing workers, are programmed to perform an increasing number of tasks in the factory, and plans are in place to extend their use to mechanical-type tasks in the office.

The field of computer science known as *artificial intelligence (AI)* uses the computer to perform functions normally associated with human intelligence, such as reasoning, learning, and self-improvement. AI requires the development of mammoth, highly complicated programs and rules that simulate the logical qualities of the human brain. However, certain human qualities, such as creativity, intuition, and empathy present great problems to the specialists working on the advancement of this highly complex computer application.

Personal Computer Applications

A study published in *Computer & Software News* shows that in medium-size businesses, the percentage of companies that use software for specific PC applications is as follows: word processing, 82 percent; spreadsheets, 80 percent; data management,

[6]"The Software Trap: Automate—or Else," *Business Week* (May 9, 1988), pp. 142–154.
[7]Harley Shaiken, "When the Computer Runs the Office," *The New York Times* (March 22, 1987), p. F3.

58 percent; financial accounting, 51 percent; and desktop publishing (discussed in the next chapter), 22 percent.[8] Further, we expect that companies will realize more savings in these applications through *networking*, as they interconnect their computer systems and terminals. For example, networking enables sales data, entered as part of billing operations, to flow smoothly as the data are fed to the sales department for analysis, to the accounting department for record keeping, to the marketing department for tracking, and to production management for inventory control. The corporate president, when preparing a speech for the stockholders' meeting, can call up from an executive workstation the same sales data for use in the presentation. Thus, networking enhances the efficiency of each application and improves communications within the organization.

The greater availability of easy-to-use PC software extends further the possibilities for using the microcomputer in the office. Such software includes: Lotus 1-2-3®, Quattro®, and Lotus Freelance Plus® for creating spreadsheets, database functions, and graphics; WordPerfect™, Microsoft Word®, and MultiMate Advantage™ for word processing; and dBASE IV® and R:Base™ for database management.

MANAGING AUTOMATED OFFICE SYSTEMS

As an information manager, the OM must know what conditions in the office justify the purchase or lease of a computer system and what services managers and supervisors typically expect of such a system. If planning studies show that a computer system is feasible, other managerial problems, such as or-

ganizing and operating the system, providing security for the systems operation, and evaluating the system, must be resolved. On the other hand, if an in-house computer system is not feasible or if additional computing power is required from time to time, the advantages of using a data services center should be explored. Each of these aspects of managing automated office systems is discussed in this section.

Planning and Organizing Automated Office Systems

Office managers must understand the computer's capabilities in order to make intelligent decisions about which administrative office systems to computerize and which operations to perform using more traditional methods. Such information is usually obtained from a *feasibility study*, which, as we saw in Chapter 4, is conducted to determine whether a system can be improved, and, if so, whether a computer can be economically justified for the system under study.

Conducting Feasibility Studies

A feasibility study group analyzes the information needs of the firm, the proposals of the computer manufacturers for meeting the firm's needs, and the attitudes and opinions of the staff concerning the improvements needed in the administrative office system. Although the study may point to the need for computerizing the system, on occasion the OM finds that the investment in the feasibility study returns a dividend whether or not it is decided to install a computer. For example, such a study often identifies tasks that no longer need to be performed or that can be performed more effectively with the present equipment. In addition, undertaking a feasibility study often increases communications across department boundaries, provides greater insight and understanding of the human and information interrelationships within the

8"Productivity Tool: Mid-Sized Businesses Put Computers to Work," *Personal Computer Special Report*, an advertising supplement to *The New York Times* (November 20, 1988), p. 29.

firm, and improves morale on the part of those who participate in the study. Finally, a feasibility study helps to justify the purchase or lease of a computer and its related equipment.

Generally a computer system is feasible when the following conditions exist in the office information system:

1. *Large volumes of data input, many reusable data files, and frequent references to these files.*
2. *Speedy processing and accurate reporting requirements.*
3. *Regularly scheduled information processing,* such as the weekly payroll or a daily inventory update.
4. *Continuous need for current management information.*
5. *A high probability of reducing the unit costs of processing the data.*
6. *The possibility of providing better service to customers* as a result of more quickly and accurately processing their orders.
7. *The ability to expand the system* if conditions warrant.

Top managers are interested in studying answers to all the questions asked in the feasibility study. The overall costs of installation and operation and the quality and speed of maintenance are also important considerations. Figure 16–15 provides a set of guidelines that will assist the managers of small offices in selecting PCs.

Establishing Automated Office Systems

Various plans for establishing an automated office system are possible, depending on the size of the computer and the goals set for the system. In a small firm, the responsibility for all phases of the minicomputer system might be assigned to the OM and be located in a small computer center. The department in charge of the computer may be organized with a basic staff consisting of a programmer-analyst, a full-time programmer, a computer operator, and a small data-preparation group—all reporting to the computer center manager. A larger computer system requires the same type of organization, which, in turn, would merit a larger and more specialized staff, perhaps reporting to the director of information systems or to a vice-president or director of administrative services.

The widespread adoption of microcomputers in offices of all sizes expands the organizational possibilities for managing computers. In the small office with, say, ten or fewer workers, several PCs may be managed by the OM on a day-to-day basis. A large firm having a mainframe as well as microcomputers may centralize the control of all computers under the person in charge of the computer center even though the machines may be physically located in all departments.

The personnel using the computer systems hardware and software must be carefully chosen, properly trained, and regularly supervised. The Institute for Certification of Computer Professionals (ICCP) maintains two programs for certifying data processing personnel:

1. The *Certificate in Data Processing (CDP),* which is designed for college-trained and experienced data processing professionals. The exam to qualify for this certificate covers data processing equipment, computer programming and software, principles of management, accounting and quantitative methods, and systems analysis and design.
2. The *Certificate in Computer Programming (CCP),* which is designed mainly for senior-level programmers. The CCP exam is more technical than the CDP exam; it covers data and file organization, principles and techniques of programming, interaction with hardware and software, interaction with people, and three areas of specialization.

Figure 16–15
Checklist for
Use in
Micro-
computer
Selection

Selection Factor	Points to Consider
1. Systems capabilities	Word processing and spelling check, database management, financial spreadsheeting, and graphics.
2. Hardware	Computer, a monitor (display), at least one disk drive, and a printer. To display graphics, a graphics monitor and an adapter are needed.
3. Memory capacity	At least 256K, but for a few hundred dollars more, investigate RAM up to 640K; try to get the most memory for the money.
4. Hard disk storage	A minimum of 20MB, unless there are many applications with extensive data files, for which more storage is needed. Check access time, since some hard disks are faster than others. An access time of 80 milliseconds (thousandths of a second) is not exceptional.
5. Expansion slots	By inserting expansion cards into the PC slots, graphics, extra memory, a modem, or a hard disk can be added. A few vacant slots provide flexibility for expansion.
6. Training	Little need to learn to write programs but need to learn how the machine operates and how to run programs.
7. Maintenance and repair	Investigate community and other users to determine sources of reliable service at reasonable rates.
8. Best computer to purchase	Depends on the needs of the user, the tests made on competitive brands, and the reputation of various computers for providing reliable service.
9. Amount of money to spend	Depends on the funds available for purchase or lease and the amount of processing power and software included in the competitive bids.

Individuals hoping to advance in the data processing field are encouraged to become certified in one or both of these programs.

The OM should be acutely aware of the effects on noncomputer personnel when additional hardware is brought into the firm. Fear of layoff, transfer to another job or department, and mandatory early retirement are typical personnel problems that must be given equal attention along with the efficient use of the equipment in the system. By using all available human resource media—company newsletters, bulletin boards, department meetings—to inform the workers of planned changes several months

before the installation date, some of the employees' fears can be averted. But perhaps the best method of allaying fears is for the office workers to spend several hours of hands-on time just "getting to know" the PC. Its simplicity, ease of use, and unusually great operational capabilities alone will "sell" the users on its many advantages.

Maintaining the Security of Automated Office Systems

To maintain the security of automated office systems and to preserve automated records, here are some steps that can be taken:

1. *Protect magnetic media* from improper handling and storage. Just as magnetic tape and floppy disks are sensitive to abuse, hard disks are sensitive to dust and physical shock.
2. *Provide a backup (copy) of magnetic media* for control purposes. Usually two magnetic tapes—the original and a copy—are made. Accuracy of such records is provided in several ways: (a) by internal computer checks, (b) by means of carefully tested computer programs, and (c) by verifying the accuracy and completeness of the data before the data enter the computer system. Also, printouts of the contents of magnetic tapes and disks are used to check the accuracy of stored records.
3. *Establish safeguards that prevent unauthorized entry into the automated system.* The availability of VDTs throughout an organization makes it possible for many employees to access automated files. To guard against the unauthorized entry into an automated system, the OM should consider the use of: (a) *passwords*, which are special words, codes, or symbols that must be presented to the system in order to gain access; (b) *encryption systems*, which scramble data in a predetermined manner at the sending point and decode the data at their destination in order to protect confidential records; and (c) *call-back systems*, which require the computer to verify that the person requesting data is authorized to enter the system, after which the computer calls back such approval to the requesting party.
4. *Use security measures to protect the information in internal memory.* Fluctuations in electrical power, called *power surges*, can alter or even destroy the data within the machine. By installing an inexpensive power surge protector in the electrical outlet, you can eliminate this problem.

Worldwide publicity was given in the late 1980s to another computer systems risk, the *computer "virus,"* which is a contamination of a computer program. The security problem is created when a programmer buries within the software a "virus"—lines of hidden code that cause "out-of-memory" messages, printing problems, and application malfunctions. Running the infected program damages or destroys the software or database files, which results in inaccurate, incomplete, or distorted output, or no output at all! Further, the virus can be passed on to other programs over modems or LANs and thus infect a group of computers that share the same files.

To fight a potential virus invasion, systems analysts recommend: buying a virus detector and/or virus treatment software package to check for the presence of viruses on any existing software; making backup copies of each software package as soon as the package is opened; and from that moment, making copies once a month along with the data entered into the system during that month; reviewing carefully all software before installation; and checking regularly for changes in the size of software programs, for changes in size may indicate human tampering with the program.

Evaluating Automated Office Systems

OMs evaluate automated office systems for the same reason that other systems are evaluated—*to determine how well they are meeting their objectives.* Thus, the computer center or the PC in an individual workstation must maintain a high level of work performance in order to meet user needs. The following objectives of computer systems are useful in the evaluation process:

1. *To provide reasonable assistance in solving the data and word processing*

problems of users. For example, users may be advised to assign preprinted numbers to basic documents, such as bank checks, purchase orders, and invoices, to facilitate accounting for all such records.

2. *To provide effective control over data preparation.* For example, controls should be designed so that there is checking at each step of data preparation (recording and verifying). These steps eliminate the chance of transcription errors and ensure accurate input.

3. *To identify and count all source documents brought to the computer for processing.* This may entail issuing a document receipt that shows document count; first and last document number, if consecutive; and the total number of documents in the batch to be processed.

4. *To use standard procedures for returning documents to the originators for correction before processing.*

5. *To use only properly tested programs to be sure that all output meets the goals of the system.*

6. *To maintain reasonable turnaround time schedules with little variation from one processing period to another.* When such variations occur, major adjustments in user departments are required. These adjustments can cause employee morale problems and delay the completion of work.

7. *To reduce the costs of processing data.* Today, a small business (or a department in a large firm) can purchase a desktop computer system for less than $5,000 and obtain more computational power than provided by the minicomputers of the 1970s and the mainframes of the 1960s.[9]

8. *To maintain tight control over the information stored in computer files.* For individuals, protecting the confidentiality of social security numbers is one prime example of information controls, for this information is widely used by credit bureaus, retail stores, banks, major oil companies, check validation services, utilities, hospitals, motor vehicle departments, employers, and schools and universities.[10]

Occasionally managers turn to a data service center for assistance in processing their firms' data. A **data service center** or *service bureau* is an independent, profit-making organization that specializes in processing data for customer firms. Such centers may be used during peak-load periods when a firm's equipment is not adequate to handle all its needs. Or, small firms without data processing equipment use such a center to meet their major computing needs. OMs find that such an arrangement has many advantages that include: no large investment in computer hardware and software; accurate work; a prearranged turnaround time; savings in the unit cost of processing data because of the service center's skilled personnel, efficient programs, and up-to-date equipment; savings in payroll taxes and employee benefit costs because the user's staff is not increased; and maximum convenience provided the user, such as on-site pickup of data and delivery of processed information. We also find larger organizations making use of *outsourcing*—using external computing centers to handle their internal data processing needs. With outsourcing, a company pays

---

[9]Arnold Rosen, *Office Automation and Information Systems* (Columbus, OH: Merrill Publishing Company, 1987), p. vii.

[10]Maintaining the security of files has become one of the biggest problems in managing computer systems. For a good discussion of such problems, see Arnold Rosen, *Office Automation and Information Systems* (Columbus, OH: Merrill Publishing Company, 1987), Chapter 18, "Information Security."

only for that share of the computer storage and processing time it uses. Those using external computer centers report that outsourcing enables them to reduce overhead, forgo expensive equipment maintenance, and avoid buying bigger

computers each time their data processing demands grow.[11]

[11]Jeffrey Rothfeder, "More Companies Are Chucking Their Computers," *Business Week* (June 19, 1989), p. 72.

SUMMARY

1. This chapter discusses in detail computers and their basic characteristics, which include: electronic circuitry; internal memory; ability to perform mathematical operations and machine logic; and the automated control of input, process, and output activities.

2. Business computers are digital computers and are classified by size. Large computers or mainframes control the data processing needs of entire firms; small computers (minicomputers and microcomputers) operate within departments or in small firms.

3. The growth and expansion in use of microcomputers were spearheaded by the development of the microprocessor on a silicon chip, which extended greatly the storage and processing capability of the personal computer (PC). In addition, it made possible the tremendous growth in office automation, the main emphasis in this chapter.

4. Input technology in computer systems includes the following: VDTs (video display terminals), magnetic tape and magnetic disk drive units; scanning devices; speech; and various graphics and image devices.

5. Processing occurs in the central processing unit (CPU) where the arithmetic and logic operations are performed. Primary storage in the computer system is provided in the integrated circuits and to a lesser

extent in bubble memory. Secondary storage is provided on magnetic tape, magnetic disk (floppy disk and hard disk), and optical disk such as the CD-ROM used in database management systems. All of these operations are regulated by the CPU's control unit.

6. The major kinds of output are the hard copy produced by printers, data displayed on the VDT screen after processing, voice (audio) response units, and special-purpose output devices such as COM, CAR, and graph plotters.

7. In contrast to the traditional office in which the functions were performed as separate operations, the automated office integrates its principal operations into one unified system. Integration is made possible by the use of a communication link (the local area network) capable of transmitting data, voice, image, and text. Two sites for such information transmission are clerical workstations (for support personnel) and executive workstations (for professional and managerial personnel). Ideally each workstation, or workcenter, interacts with other workstations and thereby increases the effectiveness of communications and systems operations.

8. Before a computer system is installed, a feasibility study should be conducted to justify the purchase or lease of a computer and its related equipment. If such a system is justified, it should be set up and

competent personnel selected to keep a watchful eye on operating costs and to maintain security over the information in the files. Whenever a firm's computer facilities are not adequate to handle its needs, a data service center in the community should be consulted.

GLOSSARY

Analog computer—a type of computer that measures continuously changing conditions, such as temperature and atmospheric pressure, and converts them into quantities.

Arithmetic-logic unit—the portion of the central processing unit (CPU) that performs computational and logical operations.

Bit—an abbreviation of the term *binary digit*; that is, one encoded character in the binary coding system.

Bubble memory—a type of computer storage in which large amounts of data are stored in the form of magnetic bubbles that move in thin films of magnetic material.

Byte—a specified number of adjacent bits in binary code that are considered as a unit for making up one position of primary storage.

Central processing unit (CPU)—the main work area or the "brain" of the computer system; its three components are the memory, the arithmetic-logic unit, and the control unit.

Compact disk read-only memory (CD-ROM)—an optical disk used to store large quantities of data.

Computer literacy—a broad concept that describes the ability to use or operate a computer or to understand the computer's capabilities without being able to operate one.

Data service center—an independent, profit-making organization that specializes in the processing of data for customer firms; also known as a *service bureau*.

Database management systems (DBMS)—a computer software package that allows a user to keep track of an organized collection of records.

Digital computer—a type of computer that counts numbers or digits while processing numeric and alphabetic data that have been converted to a numeric code; the most common kind of computer used in business offices.

Floppy disk—a flexible diskette on which the data, stored in sectors, can be retrieved randomly; used widely with microcomputers and minicomputers.

Hard disk—a rigid storage medium, usually encased within the computer, that provides faster retrieval and greater storage capabilities than a floppy disk.

Host computer—a mainframe that directs the input, processing, output, and distribution of information to, from, and among a group of small computers.

Local area network (LAN)—a telecommunication facility that links together various types of information-processing equipment for transmitting and receiving data.

Mainframe—another name for a large computer that serves as the principal source of power and direction for complex company-wide data processing and telecommunication networks.

Memory—the area in the central processing unit (CPU) where data and programs are temporarily stored before, during, and after processing; also known as *primary storage.*

Microcomputer—the smallest and least expensive class of computers; also known as a *personal computer (PC).*

Microprocessor—an integrated circuit built on a very small silicon chip.

Minicomputer—a small computer with integrated circuits that is housed in a compact desk-size or desktop cabinet.

Office automation—the integration of computer, communication, and related information technologies to support the administrative service responsibilities and to improve the productivity of office personnel.

Offline—the equipment and devices that are *not* directly connected to the computer.

Online—the equipment and devices that are directly connected to the computer.

Optical disk—a form of computer storage in which a laser-beam recorder scans a document, a film, or a slide and then copies it and transfers the image onto a metal disk; also known as *video disk.*

Programmer—a highly skilled technician who specializes in writing computer programs and plans the conversion of unprocessed data onto one or more media.

Random access memory (RAM)—the array of memory locations or addresses available on one or more microchips for the storage of data or programs.

Read only memory (ROM)—a special type of memory that is permanently programmed with one group of frequently used instructions.

Source data automation (SDA)—the process of converting data to machine-readable form at the point where the data originate.

User friendly—a computer systems term meaning "easy to operate."

FOR YOUR REVIEW

1. Define the term *computer literacy* and indicate its importance to office personnel.

2. List the basic characteristics that computers have in common.

3. Describe the interrelationships among the three types of computers—mainframe, minicomputer, and microcomputer—in a business firm.

4. Why has the term *personal computer* been given to microcomputers?

5. Describe the various media that are used as input in computer systems.

6. Distinguish between the two major types of primary storage—RAM and ROM.

7. What is the purpose of the arithmetic-logic unit in the computer's central processing unit?

8. Describe the most common forms of output technology used in computer systems.

9. What are the major differences between the primary and the secondary, or auxiliary, storage of data in a computer system?

10. In what way does control, an important management function, operate in a computer system?

11. Compare traditional offices with modern offices in terms of the organization and operation of basic information functions.

12. Define office automation and explain the role of the computer in automating the office.

13. Differentiate between the basic nature and purpose of clerical and executive workstations.

14. Discuss the principal benefits of office automation.

15. List four common applications of mainframe and minicomputer systems.

16. Explain how companies may realize additional savings through the use of networking in their PC applications, such as data management and financial accounting.

17. What is a feasibility study and why is it undertaken?

18. Describe the measures that may be taken to maintain the security of automated records.

19. Identify the principal criteria used by an office manager to evaluate the operation of a computer system.

20. What advantages does an effective data services center hold for a small business firm?

FOR YOUR DISCUSSION

1. An experienced programmer told your class last week that "ATMs operate, in principle, just like the bar code readers in supermarkets." Do you agree with this statement? Discuss.

2. Knowing that you plan a college major in business, your parents have offered to buy you a personal computer for use in many of your classes. But first they need some information and have asked your advice with this statement, "We need to know what type of computer you'd like and·some estimate of its cost." You are happy to comply! Outline for them what type, size, and model of computer and peripheral equipment you prefer and what other equipment and supplies are needed. Also, provide them with an estimate of the costs for this purchase.

3. As you walk around your campus, what additional uses of computers do you find that are not discussed in this chapter? Also, what types of work are being performed manually that you feel should be computerized?

4. Before making a decision to obtain a computer for a firm, the benefits and costs of such a system must be determined. Identify the major costs and benefits of such a system. Which factor—costs or benefits—is more objective and easier to determine? Why?

5. A year ago Peter Massey, your neighbor, purchased a personal computer for use in his rapidly growing stamp business. He has used the computer for inventory and billing applications but is not convinced he is getting enough "mileage," as he calls it, out of his machine. Massey knows of your background in systems and personal computers and asks you to help in evaluating how well he is using his system. Discuss how you would comply with his request.

6. The manager of the accounting department in which you are employed as supervisor of accounts receivable has just told you that all accounting operations will be fully

computerized within three years. The manager justifies the decision to computerize by making statements such as: "Having a PC on each desk will help us reduce staff. The computers will prevent workers from forgetting to enter their transactions. Getting a computer will help eliminate our rapid personnel turnover in the accounting department." Evaluate your manager's reasons for having decided to computerize the accounting operations.

7. Last week you read in your company's newsletter about the plan to give a PC to each of the 14 senior managers. After talking with some of these senior managers, you learn that several have no particular interest in computers. A few tell you that they have no idea how or if they would use them. However, one manager did say that she had some ideas about an information system that she might set up for reference purposes. What is your reaction to the company's decision to order PCs for all of the senior managers? What criteria would you develop to guide you in distributing the PCs?

SOLVING CASE PROBLEMS

Case 16-1 Determining the Feasibility of an Automated Office System

The television station where you work is having more and more difficulty in scheduling and controlling its commercial advertisements. All too often, advertisements purchased by clients are not aired at the appropriate time. The reason for this problem appears to be that the paperwork is not processed in time for the production department to produce the commercials. As a result, the programming department is unable to prepare an accurate schedule of the commercials on the daily programming log.

With advertisements not being aired at the clients' requested times, sales have fallen off and profits have been drastically reduced. As a result, there has been a sense of frustration and hostility among the personnel in the sales, production, and programming departments.

Currently when a commercial advertisement is sold to a client, the salesperson writes an Order Request, which states the content of the ad, the dates and times the ad is to air, the price of the ad, and other billing information. The Order Request is given to the sales department secretary, who types the information from the Order Request on three different forms—(1) a billing form that is sent to the accounting department to initiate the process of billing the client, (2) a production request that is sent to the production department to request production of the ad, and (3) a start order form that it sent to the programming department to authorize the entry of the commercial on the daily programming log.

When the requests are received by the various departments, personnel in those departments must enter the information into their record keeping systems. Currently, only the accounting and the programming departments use computers to keep such records. However, their computer systems are not compatible.

Lauren Langford, the new general manager, has decided that something must be done to curb the loss in revenue. She believes that some type of computerized system is needed to overcome the problems and has asked you to suggest ways to improve the present system of processing information—the sales orders in particular. You know that Langford is interested in automating the process; however, you also realize that she is not "sold" on office automation because of the costs associated with it.

To complete this assignment, provide answers to the following questions:

1. What is the problem that exists at the television station?
2. What approach do you recommend be taken to alleviate the problem?
3. In your opinion, what are some major considerations that will help determine whether it is feasible for the station to computerize its information-processing activities? Discuss.
4. Assuming it is feasible to automate, discuss the type of computer system you recommend be installed.

Case 16–2 Planning a Personal Computer Users' Club

Since your graduation from college one year ago, you have been employed as an administrative assistant to Jacob Williams, the aggressive administrative office manager in a financial services firm that employs 1,450 white-collar workers. The firm has acquired 50 personal computers over the past three years. Typical uses of such machines are financial analysis; management reporting, including spreadsheeting and database management; and preparing internal and external communications by both professional- and clerical-level workers. However, no information has been collected concerning the users' experiences with their PCs.

Williams has a hunch that the results of PC use have been favorable. Also, he believes that the planned increase in the use of PCs justifies collecting information from present users. (The firm has just approved the purchase of an additional 100 PCs over the next 15 months.) For this reason, Williams has obtained the approval of his superior, Monica Perez, to organize a monthly information exchange program called "Let's Get Personal" (LGP) for PC users, those about to become users, and other interested persons. An LGP club could, Williams believes, be a powerful systems communication tool, for he visualizes that there will be a PC on every desk by 2000. Also, you speculate that Williams would like such a club to succeed and serve as a model for other firms, which would be useful to him in his quest for Perez's position. (Perez has announced plans to retire in one or two years.)

Because you have had two years' PC experience (one year on the job and a second year in your college program), Williams has given you this assignment: Develop a "strategy" for organizing and implementing an LGP club in your firm.

In completing this assignment, provide answers to the following questions:

1. What purposes should such a group serve?
2. What management considerations should be identified?
3. How would you recommend that such a program be implemented?
4. What problems can you anticipate in implementing this club?
5. How can such problems be averted or at least minimized?

Prepare your solutions to this assignment in a concise business report in which you apply the report-writing principles discussed in Chapter 5.

17

Text/Word Processing Systems

GOALS FOR THIS CHAPTER

After completing this chapter, you should be able to:

1. Describe the role of text management in the preparation of verbal messages.
2. Describe the written communication process and the role that written communications play in the office.
3. Identify the key written communication media and their purposes.
4. Explain the methods for creating and producing written communications in manual and automated text/word processing systems.
5. Point out the main features of a system for managing text.

In Chapter 5 we highlight the vital role that communication plays in the office and describe the various forms of verbal and nonverbal communication. Although research studies clearly tell us that nonverbal communication, especially that dealing with human gestures, actions, and related behavior patterns, occurs more frequently, verbal communication that deals with *words* (both oral and written) receives more attention. This is true because the most important activities in the office are based on verbal communication. For example, meetings are held (oral communication) to discuss important changes in company products, services, and policies. During such meetings, minutes (notes) are taken and ultimately converted into written documents needed for the operation of the firm. In our research we find that these documents—and the many related records that "flow" from them—receive continued use in the office rather than the oral discussions that take place during conferences and meetings. Further, we see that, on the average, *nine out of every ten pages created by business are strictly alphanumeric*; the remaining one out of ten pages requires some type of illustration, from simple ruled outlines or boxes to statistical graphs to the reproduction of photographs.[1]

To handle this vital function of producing written communications—now popularly known as **text**—organizations apply the latest information technology. Under the "umbrella" term, **text management (TM)**, we find systems that electronically and/or mechanically capture or enter, process, output, and store words and sometimes graphic images. Thus, *TM is to words what a data or computer system is to numbers.* But text means more than words; it means words used to create meaning in messages, usually in sentence form.

---

[1]David Barcomb, *Office Automation: A Survey of Tools and Technology*, 2d Ed. (Bedford, MA: Digital Press, 1989), p. 135.

In this chapter, we discuss written communications and their role in office administration. From this discussion you should understand that (1) the written communication process is a subdivision of the total communication system in the office and (2) we now have many different methods of producing written communications. (In the next chapter we discuss how these messages are sent to their ultimate destinations.) Thus, the contents of this chapter focus on the modern administrative services concept for producing written communications—word processing and a new related tool, desktop publishing.

Shortsighted managers often make the mistake of believing that the production of text is solely a secretarial or an administrative support responsibility and hence give little or no thought to its management. Farsighted managers, on the other hand, realize that *the production of effective written communications is one of their foremost administrative responsibilities* and thus take the necessary steps to ensure that effective TM systems are operating in their firms.

WRITTEN COMMUNICATIONS IN THE OFFICE

For decades, bulletin boards in offices have promoted this conservative message-sending practice:

> # PUT IT IN WRITING!

Such a suggestion clearly implies that written messages offer tangible evidence (that is, a record) of business transactions. Written messages provide security to message senders since such messages can be reviewed whenever necessary; oral messages, on the other hand, are easy to forget.

As we saw in Chapter 5, the preparation, analysis, and transmission of written communications constitute a major portion of the work performed in all offices. Such text messages are usually recommended when the following conditions exist:

1. The message is long (and hence difficult for a listener to recall precisely).
2. The message is complex and detailed, requiring much study.
3. The message must be referred to from time to time.
4. The speed of transmission and feedback is not of primary importance. If these factors are important, oral communications are recommended.

Written communications are recorded messages, such as letters, memorandums, and reports by which we transmit information from senders to receivers. As such, written communications represent an application of the communication process model illustrated in Figure 5–1, page 119. In the case of written communications, the sender is a writer and the receiver a reader, both of whom have responsibilities to ensure the effectiveness of the messages sent. In this section we discuss the responsibilities of senders and receivers and the most common written communication media used in the office.

The Written Communication Process

As background for understanding how the written communication process works, we should be able to answer these questions:

1. Where does the message-creation process start?
2. What role does information technology play in this process?
3. To what extent is the process of creating written messages dependent upon human skills, perceptions, and the motivation to fulfill human needs?

The answers to these questions are rooted in each person—the OM, the office supervisor, and the office employees themselves.

Usually, we create a written communication in the office as a response to a stimulus received. For example, we receive telephone calls or letters from customers that stimulate us to respond. Most office communications are based on this stimulus-response pattern. When the response to a stimulus requires a written communication, a highly complex process is required to prepare, send, receive, and understand written messages using a wide variety of information-processing hardware and software. Figure 17–1 shows this process which, in essence, is a *management process*, for it involves the following management-level responsibilities of the writer:

1. *Planning* the message (Phase 1).
2. *Organizing* the message (Phase 2).
3. *Composing* the message (Phase 3).
4. *Editing* or *controlling* the message (Phase 4).

Figure 17–1
A Model of the Written Communication Process

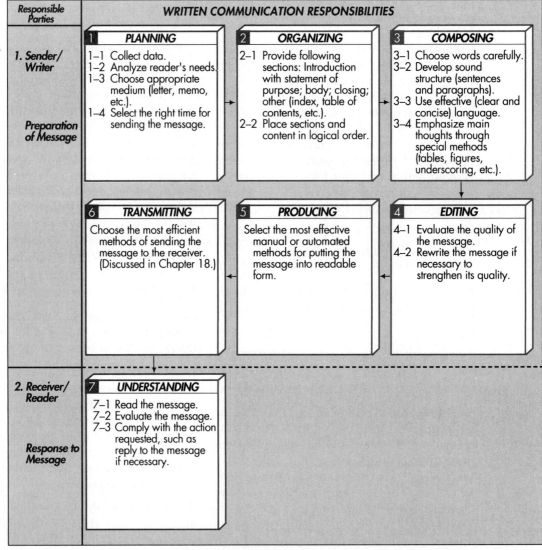

5. *Producing* the message using either manual or automated systems (Phase 5). During this phase, the writer has a basic management responsibility of motivating—getting the receiver to take the desired actions in Phases 3, 4, and 7.

6. *Transmitting* or *sending* the message to the receiver (Phase 6), discussed in the next chapter.

Once we receive a message, we as readers have the important responsibility of *understanding* the message (Phase 7), which is enhanced if the quality of the writing has been maintained at a high level. Frequently we reply to messages received, in which case our roles are reversed. We now become sender/writers and the original senders become receiver/readers. Such a response is known as *feedback*, as shown in Figure 5-1, page 119.

Written Communication Media

In today's computer age, we produce vast numbers of written communications using both manual and automated systems. In this section, we review the most common written communication media produced in manual systems. In a later section, *Automated T/WP Systems*, we discuss automated means of producing written messages.

Internal Written Communications

Internal written communications are created and used solely within the firm. Usually these communications fall into four categories: (1) interoffice or interdepartmental memorandums; (2) reports and related working papers; (3) written procedures, sometimes called standard practice instructions; and (4) manuals.

Interoffice Memorandums. We use *interoffice memorandums* or *memos* within or among departments of a company to record short messages, often in handwritten form, and to speed them to their destinations

with a minimum of time and clerical effort. Interoffice memos are informal, brief, and are produced at very low cost. Usually we destroy memos once their use has been realized. A typical memo is shown in Figure 17-2A.

Reports. As a rule, reports are longer and more formal than memorandums. However, as shown in Figure 3-9, page 84, we often combine reports and memorandums when the need arises. Many large organizations, including federal, state, and local governments, operate reports management programs. The aims of these programs are to eliminate unnecessary reports, reduce the number and cost of report copies, and simplify and standardize (if possible, automate) report formats for ease of reading.[2] The principles of report writing are discussed and illustrated in Chapter 5.

Written Procedures. *Written procedures* are formal instructions that explain step-by-step how to complete a task or solve a problem. Such communications, when properly prepared and understood, ensure uniform, efficient work at a lower cost. Procedures manuals or handbooks are developed in large organizations where considerable detail and many people must be combined in order to accomplish the work. A portion of a written procedure is shown in Figure 17-2B; and a more detailed discussion of procedures is found in Chapter 21.

Office Manuals. *Office manuals* are formal communications of management control developed to acquaint employees with the policies and regulations of the company. In

---

[2]For more information on methods of managing a firm's reports both in computer-generated and in manual systems, see Gail Blount, "Establishing a Reports Management Program," *Records Management Quarterly* (October, 1980), pp. 39–40; and Betty R. Ricks and Kay F. Gow, *Information Resource Management*, 2d Ed. (Cincinnati: South-Western Publishing Co., 1988), Chapter 18.

Figure 17-2
Portions of
Four Key
Internal
Written
Communi-
cations

The G. Alexander Corporation

Interoffice
Memorandum

TO: Managers, All Departments

FROM: Marty Malone, Manager, Facilities Planning *M.M*

DATE: December 8, 19--

SUBJECT: Resurfacing of the Parking Lot

Please remind all members of your department that our parking lot will be resurfaced during the week of December 14-19. During this time, parking spaces will not be available; thus, employees must find parking elsewhere and use the shuttle bus that will be available to bring employees from the main gate to the front entrance of the main office.

If there are questions, please call me at extension 286.

INTEROFFICE MEMORANDUM

A

Glenwood University

Registrars Office
126 Old Main

PROCEDURE: APPLICATION FOR GRADUATION

In order to be included on the graduation list and to receive your degree at the next graduation ceremony, you must follow the steps listed below:

1. Obtain an Application for Degree form at the Registrar's Office, 126 Old Main.
2. Take the form to your advisor's office for approval and signature.
3. Indicate your height (to determine gown size) and hat size.
4. Return the approved form to the Registrar's Office <u>one month</u> prior to graduation.
5. Watch campus bulletin boards for reminders.

Jolene D. Scarputo, Registrar

WRITTEN PROCEDURE

B

ARRANGING PARTS OF THE REPORT

The report may consist of all the thirteen parts enumerated below. These, in turn, may be divided into three main divisions: preliminaries (1-7), text (8-10), reference matter (11-13). (Parts 8-10 are the main divisions of the report, such as chapters, sections, parts, or topics; subdivisions, if desirable; and footnotes.) These should be arranged in the following order, even though in a particular circumstance one or more parts may be omitted:

1. Cover
2. Title page
3. Preface or letter of transmittal, including acknowledgments
4. Table of contents
5. List of tables
6. List of illustrations
7. Summary
8. Introduction
9. Main body or text
10. Conclusions and recommendations
11. Appendix
12. Bibliography
13. Index

Source: Erwin M. Keithley and Philip J. Schreiner, <u>A Manual of Style for the Preparation of Papers & Reports</u> (Cincinnati: South-Western Publishing Co., 1980), p. 22.

CORRESPONDENCE MANUAL

C

RIGHT OF CONSULTATION

It is the desire of the Company management that employees' questions be answered and problems be solved to the satisfaction of all parties. To this end, a problem-solving procedure has been established so that all employees might exercise their right of consultation. The procedure consists of a series of steps as follows:

First, the employee discusses the issue with the immediate supervisor. The supervisor will answer the issue within three working days.

If the employee is not satisfied with the supervisor's answer, the issue may be presented to the Department administration in writing. The administration will answer the issue within five working days.

If the employee is not satisfied with the administration's answer, the issue may be presented to the President in writing. The President will answer the issue within five working days; this decision is final.

An employee who follows this procedure may proceed alone or may select another employee from the Department for assistance. This other employee may attend all meetings to discuss the issue. Assistance is also available from the Personnel Department in following this procedure.

The Company gives its assurance that no retaliation will be made against any employee exercising the right of consultation and that no permanent record will be made of the process.

COMMUNICATION MANUAL

D

addition, manuals are used to assign responsibility for performing certain duties and to establish procedures for performing those duties. With such information readily accessible in printed form, the worker's time is saved and the need for constant repetition of instructions is eliminated.

Manuals should be written in a simple, direct, readable style; prepared as economically as possible; and distributed to all employees requiring the information included. Such manuals should be evaluated and revised regularly to ensure that they are both *usable* and *used*.

Typically we find four types of manuals in large firms: (1) *policy manuals*, for communicating top-level decisions, resolutions, and pronouncements of the board of directors who establish company policies; (2) *organization manuals*, for explaining the organization and the duties and responsibilities of the various departments; (3) *administrative practice manuals*, which contain the standard procedures and methods for performing the company's work; and (4) *departmental practice manuals*, such as the two closely related manuals on communications that are described below.

Correspondence Manual. The correspondence manual is designed to standardize the policies, procedures, and methods of creating correspondence in a company. Typical contents of such a manual include the organization and composition of letters to create goodwill, quality and cost control of company correspondence, word selection, sentence and paragraph construction, mechanical problems of correspondence, and supervision of correspondence. (See Figure 17-2C.)

Communication Manual. The communication manual guides employees in selecting suitable communication and telecommunication services at the least cost to the company.

The advantages and disadvantages of the various media are presented and their relative costs are compared. This information helps the office manager, for example, in deciding when to use the telephone or to send a letter or to arrange a computer conference.

Some companies include in their communication manuals a section that explains to employees those company policies and procedures that directly influence interpersonal relationships. Here, employees are instructed on their responsibilities and rights as well as what steps to take when personal problems, such as grievances, arise. Figure 17-2D shows a portion of a communication manual in which the grievance-handling procedure is outlined.

External Written Communications

In addition to the internal communications produced within business firms, we note a large amount of **external written communications** that are sent to receivers outside the firm. External communications may be sent by telecommunication media, which is explained in the next chapter, and traditional written media (such as business letters, forms, and other papers).

The business letter remains in widespread use because of its value to management. Even though it cannot interrupt an important conference with a loud ring, the business letter continues to be one of the best devices for getting management's attention. Even in the age of automation when telephone and computer communications receive increasing attention, the popularity of the business letter remains. Estimates show that in the United States, several million letters are written every hour of the day, resulting in millions of dollars being spent daily on letter production alone. Communication by mail is a multibillion dollar operation. Note the formats for two modern-looking business letters shown in Figure 17-3.

Figure 17-3
Two Formats for a Modern-Looking Business Letter

WORLD-WIDE TRAVEL SERVICES
1289 Center Street
Lee, MA 01238-3812

October 28, 19—

Mr. Charles E. Sylvestre
91 Leamy Street
Gardner, MA 01440-8687

Dear Mr. Sylvestre

We appreciate your interest in a European trip this coming summer and will be pleased to send you economy tour information as it becomes available. As you requested, we will be on the alert for interesting tours of France, the land of your birth.

Enclosed is a set of suggestions for preparing for such travel, including forms for visa and passport applications. Other brochures will be sent as soon as they are received from the printer.

Thank you for considering World-Wide Travel in preparing your travel plans.

Sincerely

Arthur W. Frawley

Arthur W. Frawley
Manager

dms

Enclosures

A—FULL-BLOCK LETTER

WORLD-WIDE TRAVEL SERVICES
1289 Center Street
Lee, MA 01238-3812

October 28, 19—

Mr. Charles E. Sylvestre
91 Leamy Street
Gardner, MA 01440-8687

PLANNING YOUR EUROPEAN TOUR

Mr. Sylvestre, we appreciate your interest in a European trip this coming summer and will be pleased to send you economy tour information as it becomes available. As you requested, we will be on the alert for interesting tours of France, the land of your birth.

Enclosed is a set of suggestions for preparing for such travel, including forms for visa and passport applications. Other brochures will be sent as soon as they are received from the printer.

Thank you for considering World-Wide Travel in preparing your travel plans.

Arthur W. Frawley

ARTHUR W. FRAWLEY, MANAGER

dms

Enclosures

B—AMS SIMPLIFIED LETTER

TEXT/WORD PROCESSING (T/WP) SYSTEMS

To manage *text*, as mentioned earlier, we must manage *words and related symbols.* Thus, to provide written communications in the right form and at the least possible cost, we must develop an effective text-management system. We now recognize **text/word processing (T/WP) systems** as the most widely used form of text management. Such systems combine *people, equipment, and procedures* for converting words into a final product and forwarding it to the user.

Figure 17–4 outlines the series of general operations we find in all complete T/WP systems (input, processing, output, feedback, control for approving the communications, and for delivery or transmission to the user). The specific mix of people, equipment, and procedures varies from office to office, depending upon needs and available resources.

The T/WP concept has been closely linked to automated systems since it originated in the 1960s with office automation pioneers who developed far more efficient means of recording typewritten text on magnetic tape. This innovation made it possible for typists to erase and rerecord, change, and reproduce text stored on tape, which revolutionized the processing of text. What has emerged since that time, however, is the realization that *all levels of systems for creating and producing text are indeed word processing systems.* For this reason, in this textbook we assume that text management (a new term) and word processing systems are essentially the same. Hence, we will use the letters *T/WP* as an abbreviation of the merged terms, Text/ Word Processing. Also, in this textbook we emphasize the fact that T/WP systems range from simple manual systems to the most automated levels, as discussed in the following sections of this chapter.

Figure 17–4 Basic Steps and Operating Methods in a T/WP System

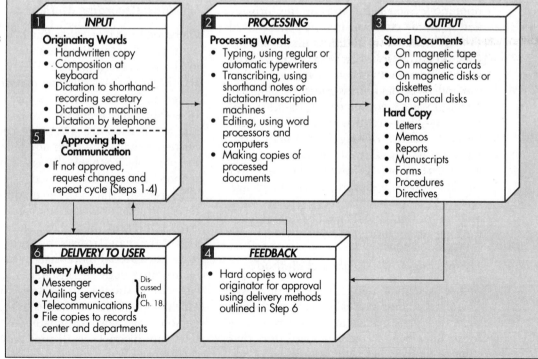

MANUAL T/WP SYSTEMS

In traditional offices, many of which will continue to operate for a long time, research shows us that written communications are created by manual methods. (T/WP specialists call this message-creation process **word origination**.) Next, the words must be converted into a *medium* (letter, report, memorandum, graphic) that is usable and that reflects well upon the originator's employer. This section discusses the most common message-creation and production methods used in manual T/WP systems.

Message-Creation Methods

In manual T/WP systems, we usually create messages in one of several ways. A brief discussion of each method follows.

Handwritten Method

Many business executives favor handwritten messages because they can organize, compose, and edit the messages in one complete operation. Such a method ensures privacy and time for concentration; it can be used in many locations—both inside and outside the office. However, the handwritten method is very slow when compared to other methods. The handwriting may be illegible, which slows the completion of the next step in the message-creation process—the transcription of the message into final form. Despite its significant weaknesses, the handwritten or "yellow-tablet" method continues to be widespread even in an age when office automation seeks to reduce the amount of human effort needed in performing administrative work.

Composing-at-the-Keyboard Method

Some executives and other administrative personnel possess unusual skills of organizing their ideas in their heads and converting these ideas to words at the keyboard and thus bypass handwriting the message on paper.

Similarly, some managers can take a brief outline of a message (words written in the margin of a letter to be answered, for example) and "fill in the gaps" with connected sentences as they compose at the keyboard. This method works well for some workers, since it saves time in handwriting the complete message. However, for most workers with organizing and writing problems, this method is not recommended unless sufficient time is spent, say at the VDT keyboard, to effectively edit each message.

Shorthand-Recording Method

The shorthand-recording method is considerably faster than the handwritten method used to create messages. However, this method requires the presence of both the manager who dictates the message and the secretary who records the message. During this time, both persons are prevented from performing other tasks and are frequently interrupted by telephone calls, office visitors, and other unexpected problems.

Machine-Recording Method

Dictation to a voice-recording machine overcomes most of the disadvantages of the other methods. As input to the T/WP system (Step 1 in Figure 17–4), machine dictation is estimated to be three times as fast as face-to-face shorthand recording and six times as fast as handwriting. Dictation can be performed at any time or in any location since the portable machines discussed in the next section can be easily carried on the executive's person (shirt pocket or purse). From the standpoint of processing (producing) the written message (Step 2 in Figure 17–4), the secretary can transcribe the machine-dictated material more than twice as fast as handwritten copy and faster, too, than poorly recorded shorthand notes. When the machine-dictation method is used, only one person—the word originator—is required; thus, any distractions disrupt only one person's work.

Studies show that, on the average, people can think at very fast rates (about 400–500 words per minute), read about 250–300 words per minute, and compose at the rate of 15 words per minute. With dictation equipment, executives can increase their productivity since their message-creation speeds more nearly approximate their rates of thinking. This saves time and money and allows the word originator to preserve important ideas that often come quickly and, in some cases, fleetingly to mind.[3]

Despite these advantages, machine dictation is not as widely used as might be expected. Many managers refuse to leave the "comfortable habit" of handwriting their messages, where they can easily see and control the results of their work. Others lack the training necessary to dictate in a clear, organized fashion; as a result, they produce garbled, wordy, rambling messages. To overcome these problems, many firms provide training in dictation as discussed later in this chapter. Figure 17–5 summarizes the main characteristics of documents appropriate for each method of word origination.

Recent research tells us that managers equipped with VDT workstations generally use their terminals to key in or create documents whereas those without such hardware are likely to use the longhand/handwritten method (see Table 17–1). Also note in the table that the two most common document creation methods of managers with VDTs were (1) composing at the keyboard and (2) handwriting. Since only 5.2 percent of all managers without VDTs and no managers with VDTs reported using machine dictation, we can see that machine dictation with voice-recording and transcription equipment is still not widely used by the managers in-cluded in this research.[4] However, other studies that do not specifically include the use of VDTs indicate a wider use of machine dictation. How machine dictation works at the manual level is discussed in the next section.

Dictation-Transcription System

As a rule, with a **dictation-transcription system**, messages are recorded on paper or on magnetic media through the process of dictation. These recorded messages must then be converted to final form as needed for use in management information systems. To store the dictated messages, a large number of machine models and brands are available. Each may be used at individual workstations or in centralized locations.

Most manual systems for recording messages use a **discrete** (separate) **recording medium** that is removed from the machine for transcription after the dictation has been completed. Discrete media on which the dictation is recorded in electronic, magnetic form include belts, disks, cassettes, mini-cassettes, and cartridges. The discrete medium can be filed and saved for replaying later or sent through the mail for transcription at the destination.

Dictation equipment using discrete recording media is available in three types: (1) portable, (2) desktop, and (3) central recorder systems. You can see each of these types of recording equipment in Figure 17–6.

Portable Units

Portable units small enough to fit in shirt pockets or purses are available. These units are very popular, due largely to their light weight, low cost, and compatibility with larger transcribing machines. In addition, portable units permit dictation away from

---

[3]For an interesting comparison of the various systems for recording dictation, see "Dictation Systems Are the Ticket to a Faster Thought-Output Track," *Office Systems '85* (October, 1985), pp. 58, 60, 62, 64, 66.

[4]Mary Sumner, "A Workstation Case Study," *Datamation* (February 15, 1986), p. 71.

Figure 17-5
Characteris-
tics of Mes-
sages
Appropriate
for Each
Method of
Message
Creation

If Your Message Has These Characteristics...	Then Use This Method to Create Your Message
1–1 Long messages (more than 250 words). 1–2 Special formats that are easier to write than talk about, such as tables, charts, and graphics. 1–3 Other documents(confidential, classified, etc.) that are not appropriate for the other methods of message creation.	1. Handwritten (longhand) method
2–1 Routine answers to requests for information that can be created by experienced typists/keyboarders. 2–2 Records, such as forms, requiring fill–in.	2. Composing–at–the–keyboard method
3–1 Complex messages needing detailed explanations. 3–2 Longer–than–average messages (200 words and over). 3–4 Multiple messages dictated in 1–2–3 order, each requiring detailed explanations to shorthand recorder. 3–5 Reports of a recurring nature that are familiar to the secretary.	3. Shorthand–recording method
4–1 Short messages, such as letters with fewer than 150 words. 4–2 Well–formatted messages, such as routine sales reports, with standard features ("prompts") that simplify dictation.	4. Machine–dictation method

the office, and thus are valuable time-savers for busy executives and salespersons who are required to make regular reports. The mini-cassettes used in portable machines can easily be mailed to the office, which speeds the preparation of written communications.

Desktop Units

As the name implies, desktop units are larger, heavier, and therefore more stationary than portable units. One type is a dictation-only machine while a second type combines the dictation and transcription functions. Desktop machines are primarily used by decentralized groups of *transcriptionists* (personnel who convert voice-recorded messages into hard copy) with primary responsibilities for preparing written communications. Thus, the desktop system is especially suitable for word originators

Table 17–1
Document
Creation
Practices of
Managers
with and
without
VDTs

DOCUMENT CREATION PRACTICES OF MANAGERS (in percent)					
Method Used	Managers with VDTs				Managers Without VDTs
	Supervisors	Mid-management	Top Management	Average	
Handwriting	35.3	20.5	28.8	28.2	80.0
Composing at the keyboard	59.6	57.0	51.3	56.0	7.8
Shorthand recording	0.0	22.5	2.5	8.3	7.0
Machine dictation	0.0	0.0	0.0	0.0	5.2
Other	5.1	0.0	17.4	7.5	0.0

Source: Mary Sumner, "A Workstation Case Study," *Datamation* (February 15, 1986), p. 71.

who have a secretary and whose work requires considerable correspondence. Such a system is also suitable for those who want to keep communications within their department for security or privacy reasons. With the desktop system, the word originator or secretary has immediate access to the communications.

In small offices, a decentralized dictation-transcription plan is often found, with each department retaining a staff that specializes in T/WP duties. Often one transcriptionist is assigned to serve one or more word originators. In larger firms, greater efficiency is obtained by centralizing this function as discussed in the following section.

Central Recorder Systems

A **central recorder system** is a dictation system where the telephone may be used as a dictation instrument to access a recording device located in the T/WP center. By using the telephone in this manner, we gain wide access to the system which, in turn, permits us to dictate at any hour of the day or night through an outside line that ties into the system. Central systems are most effectively used where there are large numbers of managers who occasionally need to dictate and can share the services of a transcriptionist. This arrangement is more cost effective than placing a desktop unit on

every manager's desk. If a manager travels extensively and has a secretary whose work supports, say, ten people, all of whom create considerable correspondence, a central system with long recording time is necessary.

Typewriters: Message-Producing Machines

A history of the office tells us that, for more than a century, typewriters have served as the principal means of producing communications in a manual T/WP system; further, we know that their widespread use continues. However, some office equipment manufacturers predict the demise of this universally used machine because of the more powerful features possessed by the increasingly less expensive automated T/WP hardware described in the following section.

Even though this prediction seems credible, experienced OMs maintain that the typewriter will remain for many years to come. They cite the many small typing jobs, such as preparing envelopes, labels, file folders, index cards, and the like, that cannot be processed conveniently and quickly with existing T/WP hardware. In addition, there are many small offices in which the present durable typewriter is the only equipment needed to process words.

Figure 17-6
Dictation
Equipment
Used with
Discrete
Recording
Media

A—Portable Unit

B—Desktop Unit

C—Central Recorder System

The two main categories of typewriters are described in the following paragraphs.[5]

---

[5]The manual typewriter is not widely used in the modern office. For this reason, it is not discussed in this textbook.

Standard Electric

The *standard electric typewriter* is intended for large-volume typewriting. This machine is capable of increased output and higher quality copy and requires less human energy than manual machines. On some electric machines, operations such as erasing are mechanized.

Electronic

The **electronic typewriter (ET)** evolved by adding to the standard electric typewriter many automated features made possible by the use of microprocessors. Compared with standard electric typewriters, ETs have fewer moving parts and can perform many additional functions.

With the passage of time, we find more and more optional automated features available on ETs. Illustrations of two categories of ETs are shown in Figure 17–7 along with specific features of each machine. Other intermediate levels are also available.

Many advanced text-editing ETs, called *modular ETs*, incorporate personal computer features into their design, which allow them to perform some nontyping applications, such as spreadsheets. In effect, the operator can flip a switch which transforms the machine from ET to PC mode, giving

the ET limited PC power. Figure 17–7B illustrates an advanced text-editing ET.[6]

ETs have several advantages over electromechanical typewriters and PCs. Secretaries prefer ETs because they are simple to use; they can handle many routine tasks—typing labels, envelopes, and filling in forms—quickly and simply. (Using a PC or a word processor for these tasks can be relatively complicated.) These office workers are comfortable with the technology since it is simple and does not require a long training period. ETs can be built for less money than standard electrics and are much more reliable since they have fewer moving parts. With the many available options, firms can "move up" to ETs when greater capability is desired. Since many office tasks cannot be easily or economically automated,

---

[6]For more detailed information on the evolving relationship of electronic typewriters to PCs, see David Steinbrecher, "Electronic Typewriters Thrive in a World of PCs," *Today's Office* (April, 1987), pp. 18, 19, 23, 24; and Rick Minicucci, "Screen-Based Electronic Typewriters: How Do They Stack Up to PCs?" *Today's Office* (February, 1988), pp. 24–26, 28, 30.

Figure 17–7
Two Models of Electronic Typewriters (ET)

A—A Simple-Correction, Entry-Level Electronic Typewriter

B—An Advanced Text-Editing Electronic Typewriter

an efficient typewriter like the ET serves well the present office market.

A recent survey shows that 85 percent of secretaries who use PCs also use typewriters since PCs are too powerful and too complex for many day-to-day typing tasks.[7] Generally, we should use ETs rather than word processors or PCs if the applications are: (1) one-time interoffice memos, letters, or other documents less than one page long and requiring no revision; (2) labels or envelopes for infrequently used addresses; (3) charts or statistical documents requiring no revision; or (4) filling in infrequently used or single copies of preprinted forms.

AUTOMATED T/WP SYSTEMS

Even with the advent of the electronic typewriter, the copier, and other forms of information technology, the output or productivity of office workers responsible for written communications has remained, at best, constant. At the same time, we observe that the cost of producing written communications continues to increase. To combat this serious problem, automated systems for producing text have been developed to bring the efficiency and economy of computer systems to the office. In this section we discuss in detail the basic T/WP hardware and software used in such systems along with a powerful new application—desktop publishing—that creates many new benefits and challenges for the AOM. In a later section we examine the management of T/WP systems.

T/WP Hardware

In the automation marketplace we find many brands and types of T/WP hardware that offer dozens of features, functions, and

options. However, the role of all brands and types is basically the same: *to create, modify, duplicate, file, retrieve, delete, and store text.* The hardware used in automated T/WP systems shares these basic components, which are shown in Figure 17–8:

1. A *keyboard* (the input unit) on which the layout of the alphanumeric keys is identical to the standard typewriter keyboard. (In some automated systems, the Dvorak keyboard is used, for it represents a more efficient design based on the frequency of alphabetic characters used in the English language.) In addition, there are extra command and function keys.
2. A *video* (or *visual*) *display screen* that enables the operator to see the text. The screen may show a portion or an entire page of text on which revisions to the text (additions, deletions, movement of blocks of copy, correction of spelling errors, and so on) may be made. Additional information about the use of visual display terminals is found in Chapters 16 and 18.
3. A *central processing unit* (CPU) that provides *internal memory* for storing text and the programs to process the text in line with the *logic* of the system that is built into the circuitry of the machine for directing the execution of the programs.
4. *Text-storing media*, such as magnetic tapes, magnetic cards, floppy disks or diskettes, and hard disks, all of which are examples of external storage media.
5. A *printer* that is used to produce hard-copy output of letters, memos, reports, and filled-in forms. Typically, the text that is stored in internal memory is moved to a printer and printed as directed by the program.

The power of automated T/WP equipment lies in its ability to (1) store rough-draft copy, (2) edit the copy so that it reaches the author's high standards of excellence, (3) store the final copy for immediate playback,

[7]Patricia M. Fernberg, "Understanding the Product," *Modern Office Technology* (March, 1989), p. 48.

Figure 17-8
Hardware
Components
in an Auto-
mated T/WP
System

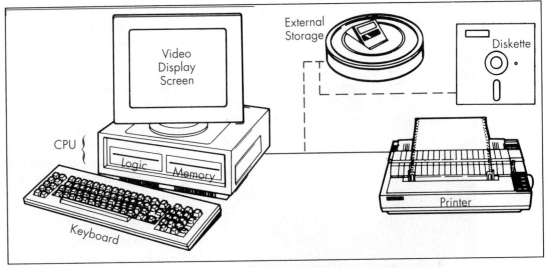

and (4) print out error-free copy. Automated T/WP equipment for preparing and editing text is commonly divided into two classes: (1) standalone word processors and (2) computer-connected word processors. We discuss both of these classes of hardware in nontechnical terms in the following paragraphs.

Standalone Word Processors

A **standalone word processor** is a self-contained system with one terminal. As shown in Figure 17–9, this type of system is composed of a keyboard for the input of the message, a screen for displaying the text, a CPU for editing and processing the text, a printer for producing the hard copy, and a diskette for the external storage of the text or the program for operating the system. (The built-in logic of the system is not illustrated since it is located within the CPU unit of the terminal.)

Some standalone word processors are *dedicated*; that is, their use is restricted to a stated list of T/WP functions built into the hardware. In effect, such dedicated word processors are computers built to perform one type of job only. When multiple standalone systems are interconnected to

share one or more common devices, such as a disk drive or a printer, they are called *shared-resource systems*. Standalone systems are placed on desktops where they can operate independently of other automated equipment. Thus, if one unit fails, the others can still function. However, such units are relatively small and have limitations in processing ability and memory.

Computer-Connected Word Processors

A **computer-connected word processor**, as the name suggests, is a word processing machine that is linked to, and dependent upon, a computer for its operation. In such an arrangement, the computer provides the power for processing the text and for activating the printer to produce hard-copy output. Although we find many different combinations of word processors that edit text, only the two most common arrangements of equipment are discussed in this section.

Shared-Logic Word Processors. In contrast to the standalone system, the **shared-logic word processor** is only one unit in a system of multiple processors and printers that operate simultaneously under the

Figure 17-9
A Standalone T/WP System

direction of a small computer; hence, the term "shared." As shown in Figure 17–10, this type of word processor may also share the services of a printer and diskette files, as well as the larger memory capacity of the host computer.

The shared-logic system is less expensive when many stations are attached to one computer and many word processors can access the same document simultaneously. A major weakness that we see in the shared-logic system is its total reliance on the computer. When the computer is not operating, all shared-logic word processors are "dead."

Microcomputers in T/WP. Because it is low in cost and easy to operate, the microcomputer has been widely adopted for use as a word processor in offices and in homes. By simply loading the personal computer with appropriate T/WP software, an effective system is created for the preparation of written communications. One of the fastest growing computers for creating messages "on the road" is the laptop computer, a lightweight portable device discussed in the previous chapter.

T/WP Software

As we know from our earlier study of computer systems, efficient software must be available to make the hardware perform its "duties." Today we can list dozens of T/WP software packages offering a wide variety of capabilities using natural-language

Figure 17-10
The Shared-Logic Concept in T/WP Systems

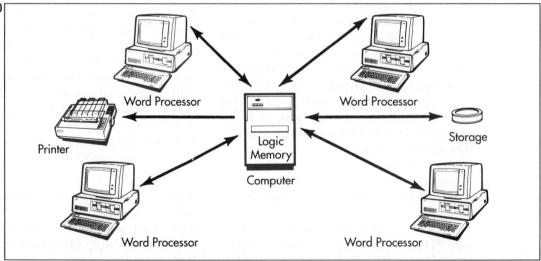

commands. Powerful T/WP software, such as WordPerfect, WordStar, and MultiMate, are periodically updated as new developments in technology occur. What these software packages share in common are the capabilities for performing the basic T/WP functions (editing and indexing documents, creating graphics, and analyzing message composition). Thus, if you want to erase a report file, you can simply key in the word ERASE with the name of the file; or, if you want to move a section of a report, you can define the section and touch the MOVE function key. Such software is simple and quick to learn and generates little fear of learning in the user. The value of these systems can be increased by the use of "*add-ons*," which are software subprograms that offer extra processing power.

Desktop Publishing (DTP)

What began as a software novelty in 1985 has mushroomed into a powerful new application of microcomputers to business. This new application, **desktop publishing (DTP)**, is a T/WP software package that provides for writing, assembling, and designing publications, such as business reports, newsletters, and trade journals, in a business or editorial office.[8] In its simplest form, we find that DTP uses a computer as the basic workstation for preparing and distributing documents, including text, with a variety of typefaces, graphics, and illustrations. Commonly, DTP uses a microcomputer with page layout software and a laser printer to produce a master copy that, to most readers, seems to be very close in quality to that produced by commercial typesetters. This copy is camera-ready since DTP software allows the user to combine at one time T/WP input, graphics input, charts and drawings—everything needed for producing a document. In this system, users function at their microcomputers as writers, editors, and page layout designers; and as a result, users are given control over not only the content of what is written but also over the way it is presented on a page.

Users note considerable savings when they compare the costs of composition and printing of DTP with commercial publishing costs. To publish a 250-page handbook by commercial printers, for example, we might incur a total cost of about $10,000. Using DTP, on the other hand, *two* editions of the handbook can be printed, plus another 750 to 1,000 pages of documentation for $5,000, assuming that well-trained operators are available within the firm.[9]

The hardware needs of DTP systems vary according to the needs of the firm. Typical hardware includes a microcomputer with 640K, an internal hard drive, one floppy disk drive, a mouse, a monitor with graphics capability, and a laser printer. Such a printer is not vital to a DTP system; however, it does ensure more professional-looking copy at one-tenth the noise and much faster speeds (in one case, one page per second) than impact printers. Also, laser printers offer the use of many fonts (a typeface in a specific size and style). Scanners often serve as input devices to bring logos, line art, and photographs onto the screen. Scanners are also used to input and interpret typeset text in various sizes, and optical disks store the completed documents.

The complete DTP process includes these steps:[10]

1. *Designing the document*, which includes developing a "blueprint" as to where to

---

[8]Janice Schoen Henry and Heidi R. Perreault, "Guidelines for Helping Business Education Teachers Choose a Desktop Publishing System: Part I," *Delta Pi Epsilon Tips* (Fall, 1988), p. 1.

[9]William M. Cowan, "Get in the Picture with Desktop Publishing," *Office Systems '89* (March, 1989), p. 52.
[10]Henry and Perreault, "Guidelines for Helping Business Education Teachers Choose a Desktop Publishing System: Part II,"" *Delta Pi Epsilon Tips* (Winter, 1989), pp. 3–4.

place headlines, text, and graphics on the final product.

2. *Creating the text*, which involves using T/WP or DTP software for inputting text and headlines.

3. *Selecting or creating graphics to enhance the document*, in line with the capabilities of the DTP software.

4. *Laying out the page*, which includes making decisions on placement of title, text, and graphics. Other decisions are needed regarding the number of columns, page size, and margin widths, and the setting of "frames" or boxes for holding text and graphics. During document preparation, illustrations can be enlarged or reduced in size, cropped (trimmed electronically), and positioned on a page.

5. *Creating the page*, in which the operator inputs the text and graphics created during the previous steps. To do so requires deciding on typeface size and style, and "sizing" graphics until they fit comfortably in the space allotted. In addition, you must edit and adjust the copy to produce a neat, professional-looking document.

6. *Printing the document*, which starts with a rough draft for proofing; and after getting approval of the proofed copy, producing final hard copy on the laser printer.

Typically firms use DTP for producing catalogs, price lists, sales literature, invitations, business reports, newsletters, notices of employee and corporate activities, and interim and quarterly meeting notices.

Emerging Developments in Automated T/WP Systems

The field of information technology continues to affect all phases of the office, including systems for producing text. Two of the latest developments to emerge are (1) digital dictation and (2) voice-to-print systems.

Digital Dictation

From the earliest days of recorded dictation to the present time, we have recorded the voice in a mechanical, analog form; that is, there has been a one-to-one relationship between the voice and the signal stored on the tape. Stated simply, loud sounds made big "scratches" or impressions and soft sounds created little impressions on the recording medium. In **digital dictation**, vocal sounds are recorded and stored on magnetic media after being automatically converted to digits (the binary numbers, 0 and 1, used in computer systems).[11] When words are stored in numeric form on disks, they can be processed and retrieved in a rapid, random manner in the same way that computers store, process, and retrieve data. Thus, changes in dictated copy (corrections, additions, deletions) can be made quickly since it is a relatively simple matter to locate the digital dictation copy that is stored by a record number. (In contrast, messages in traditional dictation systems are recorded as vocal sounds in sequential order and can be retrieved only by scanning the tape and listening for the desired words.) With digital dictation, messages dictated earlier in the day can easily be reviewed and changed; and instant access can be given to high-priority documents without searching all of the material recorded earlier.

Voice-to-Print Systems

One of the longtime dreams of AOMs has been the development of a "talk-writer," a machine that converts spoken dictation directly to written words and thus eliminates the need for a typewriter. In such a **voice-to-print system**, the word originator speaks directly into a recorder, after which a computer-connected word processing

---

[11]The fundamentals of digital dictation are clearly explained and illustrated in nontechnical terms in "Digital Dictators," *Modern Office Technology* (July, 1984), pp. 126, 128, 132.

terminal converts the spoken words into visual words on the display screen. Areas requiring editing and other text revision can be identified visually, and the dictation is corrected and stored like any other text. One voice-to-print system has a stored vocabulary of 5,000 words, which can be doubled in size through the addition of more software. Some automation specialists predict that voice-to-print systems will be widely used in the early 1990s.[12]

MANAGEMENT OF T/WP SYSTEMS

Historically we could accurately describe the management of T/WP systems for producing written communications as lacking in planning, organizing, operating, and controlling. Written communications were produced using the skills, attitudes, and experiences that the writers brought to the job. A general attitude prevailed that "everyone can write." However, poor writing habits, failure to consider the important impact that written communications have on the firm's future, bottlenecks in work processes, and a host of other problems related to written communications prevented managers from achieving effective administration in the office.

To prevent the recurrence of such problems, we must carefully manage the T/WP system, as we do any other administrative office system. A company-wide communication program must be well planned, carefully organized, and operated by a capable staff. Further, we must place appropriate controls on all phases of the system, as discussed in this section.

Planning T/WP Systems

When an AOM senses the need for greater productivity in written communications,

several planning operations are necessary. As a first step, the AOM conducts a feasibility study to determine the need for, and the practicality of, designing a new or revised system. If the results of such a study indicate the need for a T/WP system, then further planning, including the development of program objectives, must be implemented. We discuss each of these planning steps in the following paragraphs.

Feasibility Study

In the feasibility study, the practicality of developing a T/WP system must be assessed. Usually a special committee is appointed to conduct such a study, with representation from each of the key departments and from various levels of employees. Outside consultants and equipment vendors can provide useful assistance to such a committee. The same general approach is recommended for studying the T/WP needs within a department.

To complete the feasibility study requires collecting information about the present methods and problems of originating and typing/keyboarding information. Questions such as the following should be answered by all departments in the firm:

1. How is secretarial work distributed?
2. What secretarial tasks (typing and nontyping) are performed in each department?
3. How much time is required and taken for each task, and how important is each in relation to the time being consumed?
4. Are secretaries with special skills and abilities called upon to perform duties requiring lesser skills?
5. What word-origination activities occur in each department, in what volume, and requiring what amount of time?
6. What methods are employed by word originators to initiate written communications?

---

[12]For an interesting discussion of voice-to-print systems, see "Dictation: The Super Systems," *Modern Office Technology* (August, 1985), pp. 56, 57, 60, 61, 64.

7. To what extent do word originators revise their communications from time to time and to what extent are standardized communications, such as form letters and paragraphs, in use or desired?
8. What is the estimated turnaround time (the time that elapses from word origination until the finished document is returned for approval)?
9. How much of the work of producing written communications can be adequately measured?
10. How much does the production of written communications cost each department on an annual basis?
11. Should a word processor or a PC with T/WP software be purchased?

The feasibility study often reveals many unrelated, unnecessary, time-consuming tasks; wasted motions; and duplications of work, all resulting in poor work quality and low productivity. Further, when reasonable estimates are computed for the cost of producing written communications, too often such costs are clearly excessive compared with other necessary processes in the firm. These excessive costs point to a need for new efforts in managing the T/WP function.

Objectives of T/WP Systems

The cost-conscious administrator expects top-notch efficiency and high quality in the production and distribution of written communications. This includes a faster turnaround time and an increasingly lower unit cost of producing letters and reports than is normally possible with traditional methods.

Advocates of automated T/WP systems point to the following benefits that should be expected—and hence may be considered as objectives—of such systems:

1. *Increased production of text by executives who use machines for originating communications.* Many word originators are able to increase their dictation speed from a range of 10 to 15 words per minute using the handwritten method to a range of 60 to 80 words per minute using dictating machines. With the growing use of executive workstations, more and more top-level managers create first-draft copy of written communications on their own VDTs.
2. *Higher productivity since the work is performed by expert operators.* The retyping of copy is reduced, and error-free hard copy is obtained as completed paper documents. Much repetitive typing is eliminated. The amount of proofreading required is reduced, and documents may be revised much faster.
3. *Better supervision of the work.* In the T/WP center, operators are supervised by a specialist in the production of written communications rather than by an executive with more general management responsibilities.
4. *More opportunities for measurement of the output,* from simple tallies of documents completed to line counts or keystrokes per day, week, or month. Thus, an incentive system based upon work quantity and quality can be set up.
5. *Better use of equipment and personnel* by providing a system that keeps both the personnel and the equipment busy, thereby reducing the typical peak-and-valley periods in the work.
6. *Closer ties between the company's T/WP center and the data processing system.* In today's administrative office systems, the same hardware can be utilized for both types of systems.
7. *Greater career opportunities in both the T/WP and the administrative-support areas,* with more management positions opening up for the secretarial personnel.

Organizing T/WP Systems

Since T/WP systems are organized according to the special needs of each firm, their organizational plans will vary. This section discusses typical organizational plans for T/WP as well as the personnel needs of this type of system. The selection of equipment, another organizing responsibility of a T/WP manager, is discussed in Chapter 15.

Organizational Plans

Several basic organizational plans exist, ranging from highly centralized to totally decentralized arrangements. As a rule, the more centralized, routinized, and highly specialized the T/WP function becomes to handle large-volume keyboarding operations, the more the personal (human) touch is sacrificed. In the same way, the less centralized and less specialized the word processing function, the more difficult it is to control the work assigned. Typically we find the following basic organizational structures.

Centralized Text Production. A production operation as pictured in Figure 17–11

brings all of the written communication responsibilities together in a central location under a company-wide supervisor. This organizational plan, usually found in large firms, requires large volumes of work, major investments in equipment, considerable training of staff and supervisors, and qualitative and quantitative controls over the work. In effect, it represents automating the production of written communications. Nonkeyboarding duties are directed by an administrative-support supervisor who may report to the T/WP manager. However, even in such a centralized structure, top management usually retains executive secretaries who continue to perform both keyboarding and general administrative duties.

Decentralized Text Production. In decentralized text production systems, small, scaled-down versions of the centralized plan, such as mini- or branch-office centers, are located in major functional areas of the firm. Under this plan, the operators are closer to the word originators and can function more efficiently as a result. Also, more personal contact is possible, and greater job satisfaction is reported.

Other Organizational Plans. Other plans for operating T/WP systems include retaining the traditional secretaries equipped with automated word processors for written communications but using word processing units to handle overflow keyboarding. A modification of this plan has secretaries performing light keyboarding tasks, while extensive keyboarding projects are assigned to a word processing unit equipped with more powerful data-entry capabilities. With this arrangement, the personal contact between the managers and the secretarial staff is maintained while at the same time the several advantages of centralization (especially work measurement, quality control, and data-entry competence) are retained.

Figure 17–11
A T/WP Center

Dialog on the Firing Line

PATTY NELSON
Technical Training Administrator
Intel Corporation
Hillsboro, Oregon

Accounting/Business major,
De Anza Community College

In her position as Technical Training Administrator for Intel Corporation, Patty Nelson's responsibilities include supervising the clerical staff, network administration, systems administration, and administration of the company training course. Ms. Nelson has been employed at the Intel Corporation for nine years holding secretarial positions in die production coordination, marketing, and engineering, and as Administrative Associate. Previous employment experience includes various positions in accounting and administration at Stanford Applied Engineering and as production clerk at the Monsanto Company.

QUESTION: How have enhancements in word processing changed the role of administrative personnel in the last ten years?

RESPONSE: In the last ten years the administrative work force has seen the evolution of both word processing and the administrative support person. Ten years ago word processing was unknown in many offices; administrative personnel used typewriters for all types of documents. With the introduction of word processing, the time needed to type and edit documents has been drastically reduced. With every word processing enhancement the amount of time required to complete projects is reduced further, thus leaving more time to learn other administrative skills. Word processing has given administrative personnel the opportunity to become truly administrative and not just typists. Today, many administrative personnel are learning the necessary skills required for advancement while doing their day-to-day jobs. The ability to do word processing from a personal computer sitting at your desk has opened up unlimited opportunities for all administrative personnel.

When I began working at Intel, I had an electric typewriter at my desk. Using this typewriter I published meeting minutes, handbooks, policies, and procedures, and also filled in forms. When documents required changes, many times they were completely retyped. After about six months I was thrilled to get an IBM typewriter with ten lines of memory. Soon the memory on the typewriter increased to hold one page, then two pages. It was amazing the amount of time I could save by retyping only a few words instead of entire pages. Next I learned to use a Wang word processing workstation. I had to leave my desk to type documents on the word processor, but the memory was unlimited. I was lucky to get one of the first PCs to do word processing in my area. It was just amazing how much time I could save editing and to be able to do it all from my own desk. As I began saving time with the word processing capabilities, I had more time to learn to do spreadsheets and databases. With every software program I learned, I became more valuable and also ready for advancement. When I transferred from a secretarial position to an administrative position, it was the PC experience that was most valuable to me. I began using a PC to do word processing—this made the PC a very useful tool and allowed me to become comfortable with the PC so that learning new software was an adventure, a challenge, but never frightening. Today I use my PC to do spreadsheets, databases, project management, and word processing.

T/WP Personnel

In traditional offices, secretaries, typists, and other types of transcriptionists are responsible for the message-producing tasks. However, firms using more complex, automated systems to produce written communications are interested in obtaining more specialization (and, it is hoped, more productivity) by dividing the office tasks between two types of staff members: (1) correspondence secretaries and (2) administrative secretaries.

Correspondence secretaries (sometimes called *text/word processing operators*) are keyboard specialists capable of far greater keyboarding output per hour than traditional general secretaries, whose keyboarding is continually interrupted by other required tasks. Correspondence secretaries usually perform the heavy-volume keyboarding work in a centralized department under production supervisors, or they may be located in several decentralized areas. In either case, the correspondence secretaries are not assigned tasks such as filing, running errands, and answering the telephone.

In contrast, **administrative secretaries** are freed from large-volume keyboarding responsibilities and thus are better able to handle the remaining office services—answering the telephone, filing correspondence, scheduling travel, arranging meetings, and performing various mailing tasks. Administrative secretaries often work in small administrative-support centers near the executives to whom they report for their daily assignments. *In the small firm, secretaries perform both correspondence and general administrative duties* since separating such specialized functions is not feasible.

To assist T/WP managers in the selection of staff, the Association of Information Systems Professionals has developed standard job titles and descriptions for word processing and related support personnel.[13] The job titles and lines of promotion typically found in a centralized system are charted in Figure 17–12. This chart also serves as a guide in establishing job levels in systems that are not fully centralized.

In a T/WP center, the T/WP manager and the administrative support manager each direct a staff of specialists responsible for written communications and general office services, respectively. The T/WP manager must be familiar with the organization's communication needs and be able to direct the supervisors and the staff in the implementation of the system. Administrative requirements of such a position include managing the budget, developing production controls, and coordinating the services of the center with the administrative support group. In some firms, the position may also be expanded to include responsibilities for photocopying, photocomposition, printing, mailing, and graphic services.

Reporting to the T/WP manager are staff members that include the supervisor who schedules and assigns work; T/WP specialists who, in addition to some keyboarding, may be assigned the tasks of designing complicated documents; proofreaders; and the typists (the T/WP operators and trainees). The staff must possess high levels of language skills. Operators must enjoy production typing; possess at least 60 words per minute as a keyboarding skill; be able to prepare a realistic document on automated keyboard equipment; satisfactorily pass a written English test that measures grammatical usage, spelling, punctuation, and proofread-

---

[13]For detailed information on job requirements for text/word processing personnel, write the Association of Information Systems Professionals, 1015 North York Road, Willow Grove, PA 19090. Additional information can be obtained from the current edition of the *Dictionary of Occupational Titles* available in most public and collegiate libraries.

Figure 17–12
Organization
of Text/
Word Pro-
cessing and
Administra-
tive Support
Personnel in
a Centralized
T/WP
System

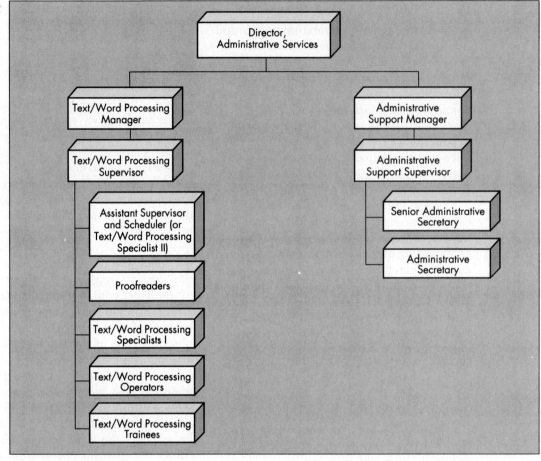

ing skills; and possess good judgment and analytical skills.[14]

Organizing the transcription of written communications in the small and medium-size office starts with the selection of an experienced, well-trained person who can coordinate the work of the word originators and the transcribing personnel. As a full-time supervisor, this person may be responsible for training transcriptionists, setting work standards, measuring the output of each employee, and analyzing the quality of communications produced. In a small office, this person may function as a supervisor on a part-time basis and devote the remaining time to more complex transcribing duties.

Operating T/WP Systems

The operation of a T/WP system requires the development and installation of procedures, standards, and other controls to ensure effective performance. For this task, many T/WP managers initially borrow ideas from other firms and adapt them to their own situations. Professional consultants and word processing associations, too, are excellent sources of information regarding the development of effective operating

[14]Donald A. Nellermoe, "Word Processing Personnel: Entry-Level Expectations," *Business Education Forum* (May, 1989), p. 15.

procedures. However, with more experience, firms develop their own production and time standards based on counts of work produced. Time studies and other work measurement techniques are used as a basis for setting standards, as discussed in Chapter 22. Cost data, such as per-page or per-report costs for keyboarding and proofreading, are prepared for use in analyzing the efficiency of each operator. Further, cost records are maintained for equipment, maintenance, and supplies; and each department is charged for its proportionate share of the communications produced by the T/WP system.

Because most business executives require training in the use of dictating machines, the following procedures for effective dictation are recommended:

1. Collect all relevant information necessary to organize, compose, and dictate the message.
2. Plan and organize the information in a form that facilitates the dictation process.
3. Control the dictation by providing proper sequence of the thoughts to be communicated, by eliminating distracting mannerisms, and by effectively using the voice.
4. Maintain quiet physical surroundings.

The most difficult phase of machine dictation revolves around the mental planning and organizing of the message prior to, and during, the dictation period. Many large firms—especially insurance companies and banks where much correspondence originates—use a step-by-step method to train their correspondents in giving dictation. First, the word originator is asked to write and then read the material to a secretary and then to a machine to avoid dictating too quickly and to ensure clarity of pronunciation and adequate instructions to the transcriptionists. Next, the originator is taught to dictate from an extensive written outline of key thoughts in each paragraph, which is later followed by dictation from a more concise outline. Gradually, as each step is mastered, the word originator becomes able to dictate from a mental outline alone.

Besides this dictation training, such firms periodically review the quality of the letters written through (1) conferences with supervisors, originators, and transcriptionists and (2) the use of a correspondence manual that the firm has developed to guide the originators in improving their work and standardizing their output. Frequently an evaluation report, as shown in Figure 17–13, is used to analyze the work of each word originator. Dictation machine manufacturers also provide instructional materials (films, tapes, and workbooks), and communication consultants are available to assist word originators in learning good dictation techniques and effective letter-writing skills.

Controlling T/WP Systems

Like other administrative office systems, T/WP systems must be carefully controlled if the system is to meet its goals. As Figure 17–1 on page 496 suggests, effective writing is a very complex process that requires considerable planning and organizing as well as the use of important human skills. Particularly important to the management of the written communication process is the control of the quality of the messages produced and the costs of preparing and transmitting the messages.

Quality Controls

The quality of written communications involves the originator's writing skills and concern for the needs of the receivers (clients, customers, and so on). The following problems should receive top priority in controlling the quality of written communications:

1. *Poor writing quality.* While most people can write well enough to be understood,

Figure 17-13
A Transcriptionist's Report Evaluating the Quality of Dictation

Evaluation of Dictation

| Name of Word Originator *M. Thomas* | Department *Customer Service* | Date *4/14/--* |

As a help to you in planning and organizing your future dictation, I am sending you the following list of difficulties that I encountered recently while transcribing your dictation:

✓ Dictation was started before the recording medium (tape, disks, or belts) was in motion.
_____ Dictation continued beyond the end of the recording medium.
Dictation was, as a rule,
_____ too fast _____ too slow ✓ too loud _____ too faint
_____ Enunciation was not clear.
_____ Proper names or unusual words were not spelled out. Examples are:
_____
_____

✓ The location of corrections in dictated material was not given.
✓ Length of letter or memo was not given.
_____ No indication was given that paragraphs or tabulations were to be inserted.
_____ No instructions were given on how to set up the transcript.
_____ No instructions were given at the beginning on the need for extra copies.
_____ The extra number of copies needed appeared in the middle of the memo or letter, or at the end of the dictation, instead of at the beginning.
_____ No indication was given as to beginning or end of quotation, indentation, or tabulation.
_____ No mention was made of the number of the recording medium when dictation was continued on two or more tapes, disks, or belts.
Additional comments: _____

If you have any questions or comments on this report, please call the correspondence supervisor at Extension 2847.

S. Presson
Transcriptionist's Name/Number

Distribution: White copy - to word originator with correspondence folder
            Pink Copy - to correspondence supervisor
            Buff copy - to transcriptionist's file

---

one source suggests that "the real art in writing is to be able to write so that one cannot be misunderstood."[15] Writing weaknesses abound, especially those relating to sentence and paragraph structure, organization of the message, and a knowledge of sound writing psychology. However, these problems can be overcome through intensive self-study and the use of communication clinics. Some useful guidelines for creating effective written communications are outlined in Figure 17-14.

[15]*Correspondence Management* (Washington: General Services Administration, National Archives and Records Service, Office of Records Management, 1973), p. 1.

2. *Use of gobbledygook.* Excessive use of technical terms or gobbledygook often causes the reader to misunderstand the message the sender meant to convey. It is preferable for management to emphasize sending clear, straightforward messages, omitting all gobbledygook.
3. *Excessively long response time.* Responses to written communications received in the office should be prompt, for delays can lose customers and slow down operating effectiveness. By utilizing faster production methods—such as machine dictation of letters and standardized, preprinted (form) letters—most messages can be answered within hours rather than days or weeks. The use of

Figure 17–14
Guidelines
for Creating
Effective
Written
Communi-
cations

1. Write for your reader, keeping in mind the purpose of the message and the background of the reader.

2. Organize facts in a logical order.

3. Use simple, familiar words.

4. Use action verbs.

5. Keep sentences as brief as possible but vary length to maintain interest.

6. Maintain good transition and flow within paragraphs.

7. Create a friendly, positive, sincere tone.

8. Give careful attention to appearance (neatness, placement, and appropriate form).

9. Proofread carefully to avoid mechanical errors (spelling, punctuation, capitalization, and incomplete sentences).

10. Read carefully before signing. Remember that the message represents you and your organization or company.

automated T/WP equipment also speeds up the production and distribution of letters.

4. *Lack of sound communication controls.* Without controls over the communication function, the problems outlined in this section occur repeatedly. However, with a realistic management program that includes setting policies and standards for all communication media, the company can effectively meet its objectives of conveying information between the firm and its customers or, internally, between management and employees or departments. To achieve these goals means identifying and maintaining the quality of written communications, improving the systems for producing documents, and reducing correspondence costs.

Cost Controls

While the actual costs of business correspondence vary from office to office depending upon local circumstances, all offices share a common set of factors that must be controlled if costs are to be held in line. Unfortunately, too many executives either do not understand what these factors are or do not consider the cost of correspondence to be significant enough for concern. Such persons fail to recognize the tremendous

volume of such correspondence and the time required to produce it, which quickly accumulate to a very high office cost.

The basic time-related factors that must be considered when analyzing correspondence costs are:

1. *Preparing and giving dictation,* which cover the time required for jotting down notes, consulting records, conferring with others, and actually giving dictation. For the average-length letter of 175–185 words, it is estimated that 10 minutes are required for preparation, and from 5 to 10 minutes for actual dictation.

2. *Transcribing,* which covers the work of the secretary or the transcriptionist. For the average-length letter, the actual keyboarding takes 15 to 20 minutes.

3. *Reviewing and signing the average-length letter* take 2 more minutes of originator time. (See Table 17-2.)

In addition to these basic costs, we find costs of stationery, supplies, mailing, filing, and general office overhead (such as depreciation and utilities expenses).

The Dartnell Corporation estimates the costs of dictating, typing, mailing, and filing an average business letter in the United States to be $10.26, which represents an increase of more than 84% in ten years. This letter

Table 17–2
Time Factors
in Creating a
Typical 175-
Word
Average-
Length
Letter

Message-Creation Action	Time Estimates (in Minutes) Required by Using		
	Dictation to a Shorthand-Recording Secretary	Dictation to a Machine	Form Letters
Planning what to say	10	10	0
Dictating	10	5	0
Looking up a letter	0	0	1
Transcribing—keyboarding . . .	20	15	1.5
Reviewing—signing	2	2	.5
Total minutes	42	32	3

cost is based upon face-to-face dictation involving an executive word originator, with a weekly salary of $868, and a secretary/transcriptionist, with a weekly salary of $376. These two salaries represent the largest cost factors ($2.89 for the 8 minutes of dictation time and $2.81 for the estimated 18 minutes of secretarial transcription time). Thus, labor cost is the factor where the greatest savings can be made.[16] Note, for example, in Table 17-2 the savings in time that are realized as the method of originating words moves from dictation to a shorthand-recording secretary to the use of form letters where no executive dictation time is involved. For an executive earning $50,000 a year (or about 40 cents a minute), such dictation costs alone would range from $2 to $4 for each average-length letter.

The major objective of a program to control correspondence costs is to reduce the critical labor time necessary to produce each letter or memorandum without impairing its effectiveness. To achieve this objective, consider carefully the following suggestions:

1. *Learn to write short letters and interoffice memorandums.* They are more effective and save time not only for the dictator and the transcriber but also for the reader.

2. *Teach word originators how to prepare for efficient dictation.* All dictation should be done at one time, as early in the day as possible. All necessary information should be on hand so uninterrupted dictation may be completed. Also, letter writing should be scheduled in accordance with its urgency and importance. A good rule to follow is to answer all mail the same day it is received, if possible. However, this should not be done if it results in unnecessary overtime costs.

3. *Eliminate unnecessary dictation* by training transcriptionists to compose replies to routine correspondence.

4. *Use form letters and automated keyboarding equipment where applicable.* Form letters play an important part in reducing the cost of correspondence if they are carefully prepared and intelligently used. (See Table 17-2.) For example, preprinted postal cards or form letters may be used to acknowledge incoming letters when no special answer is required.

5. *Conduct correspondence-improvement clinics.* Having a communication consultant in the organization examine all copies of letters and make suggestions for reducing their length and improving their quality will help to improve the corre-

---

[16]"1989 Business Letter Cost Pushes Over $10," *Dartnell Target Survey* (Chicago: The Dartnell Corporation, 1989), pp. 1–4.

spondence function. The application of the guidelines shown in Figure 17–14 will also assist in preparing more effective written communications.

6. *Use simplified letter styles to reduce keyboarding time.* One such letter style developed by the Administrative Management Society is characterized by (a) use of block form (all letter parts begin at the left margin), (b) omission of salutation and complimentary close, (c) subject line typed in uppercase letters, and (d) three or more blank lines left for the originator's signature. (See Figure 17–3B, page 500.) Advocates of this letter style have found

that about 10 percent of typing time can be saved on a 96-word letter.

7. *Answer letters by telephone whenever possible*, especially when no written record of the reply need be kept.

8. *Record handwritten answers to incoming queries in the side or bottom margins of the incoming documents and make copies of these documents to send out as answers.* The originals can then be filed, which requires less space and thus less cost.

9. *Limit the number of copies of correspondence prepared* since many copies are later thrown away. Filing time as well as supplies costs are thus saved.

SUMMARY

1. Many methods are available for communicating information within and outside the firm. Where a record of these messages is needed, written communications, which include internal communications (memorandums, reports, procedures, and manuals) and external messages (principally letters) are used.

2. Written communications are produced in manual and automated T/WP systems. In manual systems, dictation-transcription systems are used for originating the messages, and both standard electric and electronic typewriters are used for transcribing the messages. In automated systems, messages are transcribed, stored, and, in some cases, transmitted on electronic machines with keyboards, display

screens, and logic components. Later, the messages can be printed or stored on magnetic media.

3. In the modern T/WP system, we use hardware (standalone word processors, computer-connected processors, and microcomputers); software for editing and indexing documents, creating graphics, analyzing composition, and desktop publishing; and personnel with appropriate training and experience.

4. T/WP systems must be properly managed. To do so requires planning and organizing, developing a highly trained staff, procuring efficient equipment, and preparing appropriate control procedures.

GLOSSARY

Administrative secretary—an office worker who is freed from large-volume keyboarding responsibilities in order to handle the remaining office services in a T/WP center.

Central recorder system—a dictation system where the telephone is used as a dictation instrument to access a recording device located in the T/WP center.

Computer-connected word processor—a word processing machine that is linked to, and dependent upon, a computer for its operations.

Correspondence secretary—a keyboard specialist who is employed to convert words into a finished communication in a word processing center; also called a *text/word processing operator.*

Desktop publishing (DTP)—a T/WP software package that provides for writing, assembling, and designing publications, such as business reports, newsletters, and trade journals, in a business or editorial office by the use of computers, especially microcomputers.

Dictation-transcription system—the equipment and procedures used to record messages on paper or on magnetic media through the process of dictation.

Digital dictation—vocal sounds that are recorded and stored on magnetic media after being automatically converted to binary digits.

Discrete recording medium—a separate magnetic record for storing dictation that can be removed from the dictation machine for transcription after the dictation has been completed.

Electronic typewriter (ET)—an electric typewriter to which automatic functions have been added by the use of microprocessors.

External written communications—messages that are sent to receivers outside the firm.

Shared-logic word processor—one unit in a system of multiple processors and printers that can operate simultaneously under the direction of a small computer.

Standalone word processor—a self-contained T/WP system with one terminal.

Text—the written communications composed in the office.

Text management (TM)—a system that electronically and/or mechanically captures or enters, processes, outputs, and stores words and sometimes graphic images.

Text/word processing (T/WP) system—a combination of people, equipment, and procedures for converting words into a final product and forwarding it to the user.

Voice-to-print system—the process in which a word originator speaks directly into a recorder, after which a computer-connected word processing terminal converts the spoken words into visual words on the display screen.

Word origination—the process of creating messages.

Written communications—the recorded messages, such as letters, memorandums, and reports, by which information is transmitted from senders to receivers.

FOR YOUR REVIEW

1. Of the two types of communication in the office (verbal and nonverbal), which receives more attention and why?

2. What is text management, and what systems phases are required in this process to produce words?

3. Under what conditions are written communications, rather than oral communications, recommended for use in the office?

4. What steps occur in the written communication process?

5. What types of written communication media are often used in internal and external office communications?

6. Of what value are office manuals as tools of managerial control over the communication function?

7. Describe the composition of a text/word processing system.

8. What methods are commonly used in creating messages in a manual T/WP system? Which method is fastest and why?

9. What advantages does a discrete recording medium offer in the transcription process?

10. Compare the principal uses of standard electric and electronic typewriters.

11. What are the main components of automated T/WP equipment?

12. How do standalone word processors and computer-connected word processors compare?

13. List four powerful software functions commonly performed in an automated T/WP system.

14. Explain what desktop publishing (DTP) is and how text is created using DTP software.

15. Cite two important developments that are emerging in automated T/WP systems.

16. What steps should be taken to determine whether a firm can justify establishing a T/WP center?

17. Identify several key reasons for the existence of problems in written communications. What effective controls may be applied to eliminate these problems?

18. Why is the time factor stressed as the most important component of correspondence costs to be reduced?

19. Outline the various organizational plans for operating a T/WP system.

20. Differentiate between the typical responsibilities assigned to correspondence secretaries and administrative secretaries.

21. What measures are available for reducing correspondence costs?

FOR YOUR DISCUSSION

1. "Write like you talk" has long been a suggestion of specialists in business communication. Yet, many business letters and reports sound formal and anything but conversational. How do you explain this continuing gap between theory and practice?

2. Early in this chapter, "text" was defined as "words"; yet you know from your study of computer systems in Chapter 16 that such systems also process words. Is this definition of "text" contradictory or in error? Discuss what you believe the authors mean by their definition; also, improve on it if possible.

3. After a recent promotion to assistant office manager, you have interviewed and hired a new secretary who will commence work in two weeks. During the interview, the job candidate asked one question (What is your concept of mailability?) that continues to bother you since you had no good response. What answer should you be prepared to give—and defend—when the question is asked again—as it will?

4. Last week a new four-part supplies requisition form was distributed to all 30 departments in the Jansen Company. Attached to each package of forms was this note, "This new form must be filled out completely before any requisitions for office supplies will be approved. Call Extension 4827 if there are questions." Discuss the communication effectiveness of such a procedure that must be followed by 400 office employees in the firm. What improvements in communications would you suggest?

5. On your computer network, Kevin Kelly, your new supervisor, sent you the following draft of a short letter—in very rough form, he said. Your VDT screen shows this message:

> Dear Ms. Avery I am very pleased an excited to be able to inform you that are latest T/WP sofware updates are off and runing. I know you will be as happy to learn of this hapning as I am to write you about it? So, why not let me explian all it's advantages to you! I just hapen to be in your city Teus all day and can stop into your office at your convience. A discription of what I have to show you is inclosed for your information to accomodate your needs. Yours truly,

Edit this message—on a VDT if available—so that it is grammatically and mechanically correct, reads well, and gets the desired response—an appointment to explain your firm's new T/WP software packages to an *unhappy* client. The return of her goodwill is very important to your firm.

6. Because of your enrollment in an administrative office management class, you have been asked to help organize a communication manual by a friend who manages a 20-person office staff. Discuss the skills and nonskills content needed in such a manual.

7. As administrative office manager for Nardi Engineering Consultants, you sense that the cost of the keyboarding and transcription work in your firm is excessively high—perhaps as much as 30 to 40 percent above the costs of doing similar work in nearby firms. From your analysis of keyboarding/typing work patterns and costs during the past six months, you have concluded that most of the problems can be attributed to (a) improper employee selection due to the shortage of qualified clerical help; (b) the absence of any valid preemployment tests for measuring the skills, aptitudes, and interests of job applicants; (c) the fact that beginning keyboarders/typists are poorly trained and have little knowledge of business systems, work costs, English fundamentals, and spelling; (d) inadequate supervision, including a certain amount of laxness in discipline; and (e) no records of the production rates of the clerical staff. How can each of the problems cited above be resolved, given your goals of improving the quality and quantity of the work and at the same time reducing the work costs?

SOLVING CASE PROBLEMS

Case 17-1 Identifying Basic T/WP Skills for Keyboard Composition

One week after taking your first position following graduation, your supervisor, Donna Brown, announces that all word originators will receive new word processors and are expected to create their own drafts of messages at their keyboards. Each word originator will then forward his or her drafts on the computer network to T/WP operators who will produce final copy. In addition, Brown mentions she would like your input regarding what information you need in order to comply with this policy.

You, like most of the other nonclerical employees, know how to type using the touch system, but know little else about any aspect of message composition at the machine. Using an available VDT or electric typewriter, do the following:

1. Create a sample message and during the process list from beginning to end what skills and other information you need to ensure that your message drafts are produced satisfactorily.

2. Organize your ideas into a usable outline of key points that can be taken to class during which time discussion will be provided for refining the draft.

3. After class, edit the draft so that it has a professional-looking appearance. Hand the final copy to your instructor as directed.

Case 17-2 Designing a Collegiate T/WP System for Students

As you complete your study of T/WP systems, your instructor writes on the chalkboard: *"The proof of the pudding is in the eating."* The instructor elaborates by saying that you can demonstrate your overall understanding of T/WP systems by designing a prototype system for the preparation of written assignments in your class as well as in every other class in your school. The assignment, as discussed, has these two main objectives: (1) designing a basic system that combines the main concepts found in all T/WP systems (manual or automated); and (2) offering practical suggestions for other students who must regularly apply the concepts in the preparation of reports and other written communications required for their classes.

Several sources of T/WP equipment were identified in the discussion about this case: (1) equipment available at a student's place of employment; (2) word processors, personal computers, or standard electric typewriters at home; or (3) equipment available at the college for student use in preparing written assignments.

Based upon this discussion, prepare a report in which you:

1. Provide a drawing of the basic T/WP functions required to produce written assignments for students in your college. A review of the elements making up the model of the written communication process will assist you in completing this first task. (See Figure 17-1, page 496.)

2. Develop a list of practical suggestions for using the T/WP facilities available to you personally. In your list include (a) "do's and don'ts" in composing, producing, and sending written messages and (b) ideas to ensure the effective use of the T/WP facilities available to you. A review of this chapter as well as Chapter 5, especially the sections, *Barriers to Effective Communication*, page 128, and *Report-Writing Principles*, page 136, will be helpful in solving the second part of this case problem.

18

Information Distribution: Telecommunication and Mailing Systems

GOALS FOR THIS CHAPTER

After completing this chapter, you should be able to:

1. Identify the basic components of telecommunication systems and their purposes.
2. Discuss the various tools of telecommunication systems that relate to the transmission of voice, data, text, and image messages.
3. List the telecommunication services that are most important to the administrative office manager, giving reasons for the important role each plays in administration.
4. Describe the key phases in managing a telecommunication system, giving special attention to the problem of reducing telecommunication costs.
5. Indicate how the basic principles of management can be applied to the mailing function.
6. Contrast the techniques for handling external mail with those available for handling internal mail in the modern firm.
7. List five practices used to control mailing costs in the office.

As a phase in the information cycle shown in Figure 1–4, page 7, **information distribution** transmits or moves information from the place in which it is processed to the point where it will be used. In the office, much information continues to be transmitted by telephone, a term that comes from two Greek words—*tele*, far, and *phon*, sound—which explains the basic purpose of this universal "information-movement" device. The telephone instantly transmits sounds over distances too far for the human voice to carry. The ease of use and general availability of the telephone have made it a necessary tool in the modern office.

During the past few decades, the basic functions of the telephone have expanded; and a broader term—*telecommunications*—has been coined to reflect more accurately the expanded services. **Telecommunications** *involves all communication processes designed for sending and receiving voice (sounds), data, text, and image messages by wire and wireless methods.* In our increasingly complex and competitive world, telecommunications involves the linkage of the telephone and the computer, and a host of new customer services is now provided by communication utility firms (*common carriers*).

Telecommunication systems, as a basic tool of administrative office management, are discussed in this chapter. In addition, we shall examine effective mailing systems as a vital method for transmitting messages over long distances. Special emphasis is given to ensuring the proper use and control of operating costs in both of these information-distribution systems.

TELECOMMUNICATION SYSTEMS

To maintain a competitive edge, both small and large firms recognize the need for effective communications. Successful large businesses expand from local to national and multinational concerns because we as consumers accept their products and services and because of the firms' abilities to compete. Much of this growth depends upon communication facilities that enable firms to respond quickly to the demands of markets and suppliers of raw materials wherever they are located.

Smaller companies use voice communications to an increasing degree for speeding up the flow of information. With such simple devices as the telephone and some of its services described later in this chapter, orders can be received and processed, raw materials and supplies purchased, personnel recruited, and financial transactions processed. With the advent of microcomputers that are within the price range of the small office, the telephone is commonly linked to the computer, which opens up many new opportunities for improving communications.

In this section you will see that all telecommunication systems revolve around the same basic concepts found in the communication model shown in Figure 5–1, page 119—a sender-receiver relationship built around a message. However, in the case of telecommunications, the media may differ in certain cases. Elements in a telecommunication system may be classified as (1) *voice communication*; (2) *data communication*; (3) *text communication*; and (4) *image*, or *graphic communication*. Messages sent in telecommunication systems require a certain **bandwidth**—the amount of space needed to transmit messages on telecommunication channels similar to the number of lanes on a freeway system. Voice systems require a narrower—hence, less expensive—bandwidth than nonvoice systems.

Both wire and wireless methods of telecommunication are used in and between organizations, as shown in Figure 18–1.[1] Also, both methods are used in *local area, metropolitan area*, and *wide area* (long-distance) *networks*, which are discussed later in this chapter.

Figure 18–1 outlines the principal types of messages sent through telecommunication channels and the networks available for sending these messages. Each type of message—voice and nonvoice—is discussed in detail in this chapter. Other related uses of telecommunication systems in the office (word processing, reprographics, and microimages) are also shown in this figure. A discussion of these uses can be found in the textbook chapters shown in parentheses.

THE TOOLS OF TELECOMMUNICATION SYSTEMS

Specialists in telecommunications classify the tools or technology used in their systems according to the basic nature of the message transmitted. The technological "tools" used in each of these message-sending systems are discussed in this section.

Voice Communication Tools

In a **voice communication system**, messages are originated by speakers and sent by wire or wireless methods to listeners who receive and respond to the messages. Generally we should use voice communications rather than written messages when the following conditions exist:

1. The message to be sent is short and simple.
2. The speed of transmission is important.
3. There is no need for lengthy study or for later reference to the message. However, by using recording equipment, voice messages can be retained for later reference.

---

[1]Wire communications have greatly expanded because of the introduction of fiber optics as replacements for copper wires. **Fiber optics** are fiberglass threads along which units of information are translated into light waves by a laser beam and then "pumped" through the glass fiber. With fiber optics, message transmission is much faster and less expensive since more messages can be sent over networks in a given period of time and in a more reliable fashion. This is true since fiberglass threads are not so subject to atmospheric conditions as copper wires.

Figure 18-1
The Princi-
pal Elements
in a Tele-
communica-
tion System

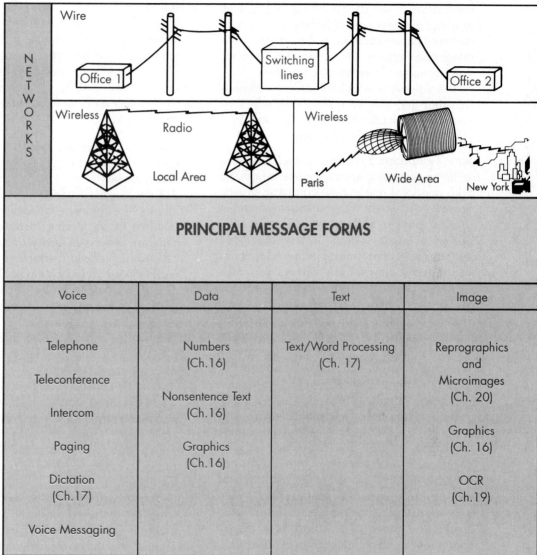

Voice	Data	Text	Image
Telephone	Numbers (Ch.16)	Text/Word Processing (Ch. 17)	Reprographics and Microimages (Ch. 20)
Teleconference			
Intercom	Nonsentence Text (Ch.16)		
			Graphics (Ch. 16)
Paging	Graphics (Ch.16)		
Dictation (Ch.17)			OCR (Ch.19)
Voice Messaging			

4. The personal touch found in face-to-face communication is needed.

Other circumstances may suggest the need for voice communications, such as when the channels we use for sending written messages are overloaded. A telephone call, for example, gets more immediate attention from an executive than a special-delivery letter on the executive's desk. In some cases, a voice message is more easily received, as in a dim or dark hallway or when workers have to move around frequently in their work environment.

Each of these criteria should be evaluated carefully by the AOM in considering the communication needs of the office. When most of these conditions are present, a voice communication system should be considered.

Telephone Systems

As we see in Figure 18-1, the basic telephone has been incorporated into telecommunication systems that handle images or graphics and text as well as voice. However, the basic nature and common purpose of the telephone remain the same—to transmit voice messages between two persons.

The volume of telephone calls determines the kind and size of system needed. Two basic types of telephone systems—key and switching—are discussed below.

Key Telephone Systems. A small business, at the outset, may have only one telephone with one local line. As the company grows, however, it needs more telephones and a greater number of lines which require the use of a larger system. A **key telephone system (KTS)** has two or more telephones connected to several telephone lines, each of which can be reached by each telephone set. For typically fewer than 50 to 60 users, the KTS is the main form of telecommunication in the small office.[2] A typical example is the KTS with a six-button set shown in Figure 18–2A. With this equipment controlled by efficient switchboard operators, each telephone provides access to all central office lines for both incoming and outgoing calls. One of the buttons permits placing a call "on hold"; another may be assigned to an intercom system. In today's modern office, an increasing number of telephones transmit more than voice messages, as we shall see later in this chapter. When the number of telephones in use becomes too large (more than 50 as a rule), a switching system must be installed.

Switching Systems. A **switching system** receives and distributes internal and external calls without the need for a switchboard operator. The earliest switching system—the **PBX,** or **private branch exchange,** was operated manually by a switchboard operator where the number of extension telephones was not great and the volume of calls was not heavy. Gradually electronic functions were built into the PBX and the **private automatic branch exchange (PABX)** was created. When operating under computer control, PABX switching systems perform many time-saving calling tasks, such as the following:

1. *Executive override,* which enables an operator to cut in on another extension that is in use.
2. *Automatic call distribution (ACD),* which allows the sharing of calls among a number of answering locations so that calls are served in order of arrival; and *call-waiting display,* which provides the worker with an indication of the number of calls waiting to be answered. Another feature, called *camp-on,* extends an additional call to a busy station.
3. *Conference calls* in which three or more persons are connected for local or long-distance conversation.
4. *Automatic call back,* which alerts a user when a desired number is no longer busy and then redials the desired number.
5. *Automatic least-cost route selection,* which completes outgoing calls automatically over the least-expensive route available.
6. *Call forwarding,* which automatically transfers calls to another internal or external telephone number. A related feature, *hunting,* routes calls automatically to an alternate station when the called station is busy.
7. *Automatic dialing* of frequently called numbers. A device similar to that shown in Figure 18–2B can store up to 60 numbers in its memory for local and long-distance calling and "remember" the last number dialed manually. Programming to add new numbers or to change numbers already stored takes only a few seconds. Another dialing aid is *speed dialing,* which allows calls to be completed internally and

[2]G. Gordon Long, "Technology Is Enhancing Telephone and Fax Systems," *Office Systems '89* (January, 1989), p. 16.

Figure 18-2
Modern
Equipment
in a Key
Telephone
System

A—Key Telephone

B—Telephone with Automatic Dialing Features

externally by dialing an abbreviated number. Many of the most automated telephones are equipped with boards or screens on the telephone console for displaying the number called or other pertinent information.

8. *Hands-free operation*, which allows two-way communication without lifting the telephone handset.

9. *Night service*, which routes calls normally directed to one station to an alternate destination. This is a useful service during lunch breaks and after normal business hours.

The number of telephone features continues to grow, and, if properly applied, will help to improve productivity in the offices of the future.

Intercommunication Systems. For many employees making internal calls, an outside line is not necessary. When many internal calls are made, an **intercommunication** (or **intercom**) **system** should be considered. This system is a privately owned, small-scale

telephone system that ties together all departments. Typically, two types of intercommunication systems are found: telephone-based systems and dedicated systems. Both types of systems transmit information rapidly and enable personnel to remain at their desks. Thus, productivity is enhanced.

In *telephone-based systems* the intercom functions are built into the telephone unit as an added capability of the PBX or PABX systems. Such an intercom system requires low installation charges and offers privacy as well as excellent sound quality. Its main drawback is the potential danger that internal calls may block incoming or outgoing telephone calls.

A *dedicated system* uses a unit that is separate from the telephone. In such case, the problems of blocking telephone calls and tying up a switchboard are eliminated. However, a dedicated system must be leased or purchased, which adds to overhead costs.

Manufacturers of intercom equipment provide many options including the following:

1. *Hands-free operation*, which lets users talk into a speaker without the need for a handset. Thus, users are free to work with their hands, search through files, or move about.
2. *Handset systems that give privacy to workers*. These units can be installed on desks (Figure 18–3A), walls, or in drawers to avoid distractions or being overheard by a caller from another workstation. A "silent," dedicated intercom system is shown in Figure 18–3B. In this system a quiet audio "beep" announces incoming messages on the display dial. Each work-station is assigned its own one- or two-digit number to use in identifying the sender. Messages up to 64 characters in length are repeated automatically on the dial until a response is received.
3. *Priority features* that allow a designated station to cancel or interrupt ongoing conversations in order to transmit urgent messages.
4. *One- or two-conversation arrangements* between managers and their staffs, or simultaneous conference calls to a number of stations.
5. *Tie-in between the intercom system and centralized support centers*, such as the text/word processing center, enabling all word originators to dial a number on the intercom set, dictate their correspond-ence, and have it keyboarded without leaving their desks.

Since intercommunication machines con-nect two or more departments within a firm, an interdepartmental systems study must be conducted to determine the most effective equipment installation required. For exam-ple, after one large insurance firm installed a new central filing system, it became clear that new communication services would be required since telephone requests for files were being delayed due to other uses of the telephone system. As a result, a private inter-com system was installed, making it possible to request files without disturbing regular telephone conversations.

Voice-Recognition and Audio-Response Systems

A **voice-recognition system**—sometimes called *speech recognition*—is a computer-based system in which the computer "understands" and records the human voice as input and performs operations based on this input. In order to recognize a voice, the computer system stores patterns of words that must be matched to words that we speak; and only when the spoken word is in the computer "library" does recognition occur. Small systems provide 500- or fewer word vocabularies and the largest systems, from 10,000- to 20,000-word vocabularies.

Voice-recognition applications include data entry, instructions for controlling various systems, dictation, and a wide range of specialized functions. Such systems bypass the need to convert the message to written form. Thus, we no longer must learn to operate a terminal but only to speak in a manner that a computer can understand. With this system, data-entry errors, such as the transposing of digits or the misspelling of words, almost disappear; and processing responses by the computer to the messages are immediate.

A typical example of a voice-recognition system involves an incoming telephone call from a customer. The call is transmitted to the voice-recognition device of the person called, at which point the voice message is translated into the digital (numeric) code required for computer processing. Because of certain peculiarities of human speech (dialects, slurring of words, speaking too fast or too slowly, and speaking indistinctly), we notice limitations to this type of system; but these restrictions can be overcome. Currently customer ordering, internal ordering of parts from stockrooms, and hotel and airline res-ervation systems accept voice entry rather

Figure 18–3
Intercom
Systems

A—Voice Intercom System

B—Visual Intercom System

than requiring speaking in person to an order clerk.

In an **audio-response system**, a computer-activated voice answers questions using a vocabulary stored in the system. Such systems have been in widespread use for years in the time-of-day and temperature-reporting systems arranged through local telephone companies. Also, in account-inquiry systems in banks, customers can simply request their current account balance and a mechanical voice responds. A larger system is illustrated in the freight-carrying industry where shipment status reports must be furnished 24 hours a day. In one such system, with an 800-word vocabulary, a customer dials a toll-free number to receive quick, concise shipment status reports (route data, trailer numbers, times of arrival and departure, etc.) delivered by a computer-generated voice. Responses by voice alert people more rapidly than visual messages, and labor costs are reduced by eliminating the need for human operators.

Wireless (Radio) Communication Systems

As distances increase between senders and receivers of messages and as the channels of communication by wire become over-loaded, managers turn to *wireless* (or *radio*) *communication systems* for transmitting messages of all kinds. With wireless methods, significant savings are realized since the expense of installing wires is not required. Traditional wireless systems, such as paging, as well as modern systems (cellular telephones and microwave and satellite systems) are discussed briefly in this section.

Paging Systems. We use **paging systems** to locate persons—often executives, doctors, and emergency personnel—who are away from their desks or workstations. Typically, paging systems are available as one-way radio receivers (pocket-size equipment such as "beepers") that receive short-duration messages in the form of voice, a digital readout, or a "beep" up to several miles from a paging transmission center. After you, the paged party, receive a message, you may access the caller over regular telephone lines. Currently, doctors, sales representatives, and others who must maintain close contact with their firms represent the largest users.

Some paging systems are telephone-based. In such a system, each executive is given a number that must be dialed for paging. When the number is dialed, a signal corresponding to that number will sound. As soon as the executive hears the sound, he or she goes to the nearest telephone, calls the switchboard, and receives the message. Two-way contact is thereby provided.

Cellular Telephone Systems. The **cellular telephone**, or *mobile telephone*, is a radio-based wireless communication system for receiving and transmitting voice messages within a limited geographic area, such as a large city or an overall area of approximately 25–30 miles. The cellular telephone system uses individual phone units that pick up signals being transmitted from multiple radio towers provided in each of the areas covered. The system is tied together by a computer system that switches signals from one "cell" or geographic area to another as the user moves, usually in an automobile. Typical local users—sales and field service representatives of firms operating within a few miles of the main office, real estate agents, and doctors and medical technicians who need to maintain contact with their offices or with hospitals—spend a significant part of their working day in their automobiles. Advances in communication technology permit cellular phones to be used nationwide. While the cellular telephone permits such persons to keep in touch with their "bases" of operation, it has several disadvantages. Such disadvantages include high costs of equipment and relatively high costs for service. Figure 18–4A shows the cellular telephone concept and Figure 18–4B, a

typical cordless telephone used in its operation.[3]

Microwave and Satellite Communication Systems. Microwave and satellite communication systems represent further extensions of the cellular telephone concept. In a **microwave communication system**, a radio-relay system sends signals between towers located many miles apart. (See Figure 18–5A.) The signals are amplified and retransmitted until the message reaches its destination.

A **communication satellite (Comsat)** consists of two or more ground transmitter-receiver stations and a satellite "parked" in space above the earth. Information is beamed from the transmitter on earth to the satellite, where the message is directed to a receiving point at another earth location. (See Figure 18–5B.) As an example of the use of Comsat, *Time* magazine in New York City prepares the copy for its latest weekly edition and transmits the copy (text and color) in under one minute by Comsat to its remote printing facilities all over the United States near the points of distribution. Thus, the magazine is ready for local distribution; and the typical problems of length of time, distance, and cost are greatly reduced.

Data Communication Tools

As information systems become more complex, management relies on high-speed interstate communications systems that send and receive information of all kinds at high rates of speed in several forms—voice and, to an increasing extent, nonvoice (data, text, and image) form. The limitations of voice communication systems, discussed earlier,

---

[3]Thomas J. Housel and William E. Darden III, *Introduction to Telecommunications: The Business Perspective* (Cincinnati: South-Western Publishing Co., 1988), p. 174. This publication offers, in nontechnical language, a comprehensive discussion of telecommunications from a managerial point of view.

Figure 18-4
A Cellular
Telephone
System

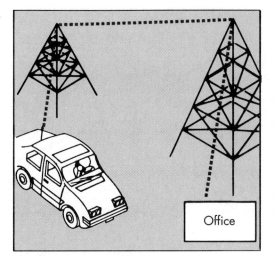

A—Cellular Telephone Concept

B—A Typical Cordless Telephone in Operation

are widely acknowledged. Consequently, we find that much of the data transmitted over long distances use data communication systems.

In a **data communication system**, the computer or other electronic systems are combined with the telephone system to send prerecorded data over long distances at electronic speeds to be received by a related device at the destination. In this setting, the *data* represent, to a large degree, (1) numeric records and words in *nonsentence form* essential to the operation of business functions, such as accounting, finance, banking, order-entry statistics, and remote data processing; and (2) symbols, such as @, #, $, %, &, and the Greek letter symbols commonly used in business statistics.[4]

Basic Data Communication Concepts

Data communication has rapidly evolved into a highly complex profession that

---

[4]Early data communication systems were limited to the transmission of nonvoice information. With the passage of time and the integration of many communication forms, modern data communication systems have been developed for sending and receiving both voice and nonvoice information. However, their main thrust remains the same—to transmit nonvoice information to remote locations.

includes computers, engineering communications such as the telephone system, and electronics. To understand it thoroughly, we must have a technical background beyond that necessary for managing the modern office. However, if you are holding a position as an AOM, you will be responsible for office communications; hence, you must understand the following basic nontechnical concepts that underlie the data communication process:

1. *Data communication systems specialize in the movement of information through networks of interconnected machines.* In telecommunications, a *network* is simply a series of points connected by one or more communication channels.

   In the automated office discussed in Chapter 16, you are likely to find local area networks. A *local area network (LAN)* is a telecommunication facility that links together various types of information-processing equipment (most commonly by coaxial cable) for transmitting and receiving data. A LAN permits departments to: (a) share resources, such as all PC operators using one departmental printer; (b) exchange interoffice mail

Figure 18–5
Common
Wireless
Communica-
tion Media

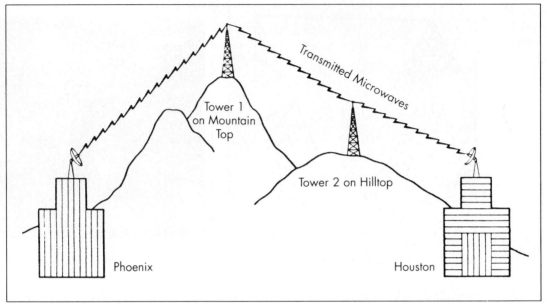

A—A Microwave System

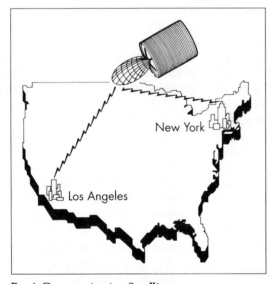

B—A Communication Satellite

with other computer users in the office building; (c) keep track of how often software is used, by whom, and for how long; and (d) provide an efficient method of handling interoffice communications. Figure 18–6 shows a typical LAN.

A **wide area**, or *long-distance*, **network (WAN)**, discussed later in this chapter, covers a large geographic area and is composed of dedicated and private or public channels for transmitting and receiving messages.

Recently an intermediate-distance network, the **metropolitan area network (MAN)**, has been developed. MANs are networks covering a geographic area of up to 30 miles (50 kilometers), that are capable of transmitting voice, data, text, and image signals at the same time. We expect MANs to be used to connect common carrier long-distance service to local lines as well as to serve companies needing a local network of great capacity.

2. *The simplest form of data communications involves data transmission only.* This process requires the use of sending and receiving equipment linked to a communication medium, such as a telephone line or a microwave system.

3. *The computer-based communication process is more complex than a transmission-only system.* The computer-based process involves *capturing* or *entering* data, frequently using the VDT, processing such data by computer or

Figure 18-6
A Local Area
Network
(LAN)

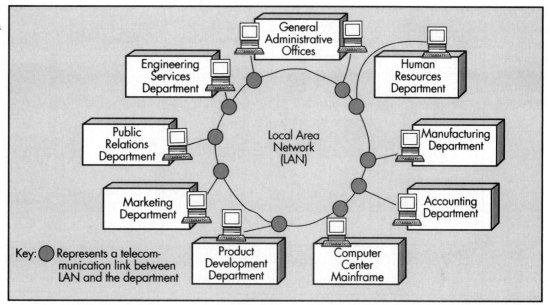

related word processor, and transmitting the data over one or more communication facilities.

The computer-based data communication system in its most simplified form is shown in Figure 18–7. Note that the data must first be entered into the system, typically through one or many VDT keyboards. Within the terminal, the data are encoded automatically in digital (numeric) form as a series of discrete binary electrical impulses (1s and 0s) for processing in the local computer or for transmission in unprocessed form to a destination computer. Next, the electronic digital codes representing the computer output must be converted to an *analog code*—that is, a continuous electronic signal "analogous" to the sound being transmitted—by a device called a *modem* in order to be acceptable to the telephone system.[5]

---

[5]**Modem** is an abbreviation for *modulator-demodulator*. This device converts the digital code of the computer into an analog code used by the telephone system. Modems are also used to convert an analog code back to digital code for use within the computer-based data communication system, as shown in Figure 18–8.

With this code conversion accomplished, the data are transmitted by telephone line to a modem at the destination. This time the coded signals are converted back to digital code form so that the computer—a digital machine—can process, store, or route the data. The controls for handling the automated phases of this system reside in a *front-end processor*, which takes some of the burden off the computer. The results of computer processing can be returned to any terminal located in any part of the world.

Organizations with complex information-processing requirements and with widely dispersed office locations make great use of data communication systems. For example, a multinational firm with a main office in Chicago receives and transmits information to its Paris branch office with the same efficiency as to its Louisville branch office. (See Figure 18–7.) With these capabilities, management can expect such administrative improvements as:

Figure 18-7
Basic Components of a Computer-Based Data Communication System

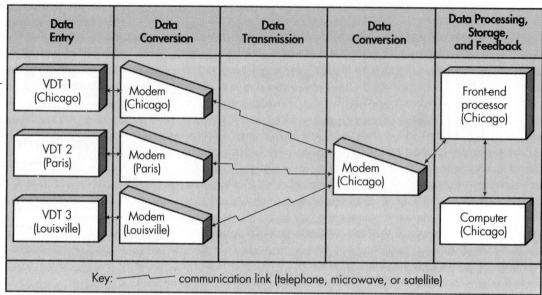

Reduced time in preparing payrolls and delivery of orders.

- Added operating efficiencies because all distant branches are tied together and more current information is available to all.
- Reduced costs from more efficient order handling, inventory control, and data processing.
- Improved customer service stemming from better stock availability, better work scheduling, and prompt delivery of orders.

Data Communication Equipment

Two types of equipment are basic to the operation of a data communication system: (1) *telephone* or *related wireless equipment,* and (2) *computer systems equipment and software.* The first category is highly technical in nature and is typically outside the direct responsibility of the AOM. The second category, on the other hand, is an AOM's responsibility. As explained in Chapter 16, the computer systems equipment includes computers, principally mainframes and microcomputers, and terminals (VDTs). Each of these equipment items, as com-

ponents of a telecommunication system, is briefly discussed below.

As we saw earlier, a *mainframe* is a large computer that processes large amounts of data at very fast speeds; and a *microcomputer,* or personal computer, is a small computer that can be adapted with software packages to operate in a data communication system. We may think of these two types of computers as terminal equipment when they are connected to an internal (LAN) or external (WAN) network. Modems are required for conversion of the computer data, which is in digital form, to the analog form required by the telephone system. Both mainframes and microcomputers can be equipped with built-in jacks for a telephone plug in order to link the computer hardware to the telephone system for transmitting electronic messages.

The most common application of data communications is a host mainframe with a network of computer terminals connected to it.[6] Typically, we find three categories of

[6]Housel and Darden, *Introduction to Telecommunications,* p. 73.

terminals, which are described below in increasing degrees of automation:

1. A **dumb terminal** is a data-entry terminal with an alphanumeric keyboard and printer (the teletypewriter) or a video display terminal (VDT), which is connected to a mainframe via a communication link. A dumb terminal has no capability for processing data on its own (that is, of being programmed); rather it can only receive, display, and send information through its communication link to the mainframe. Specialized applications of dumb terminals include banking terminals that accept coded identification cards and/or keyed input to permit banking transactions to be carried out automatically; point-of-sale terminals for automating retail sales transactions; and industrial data collection terminals operated by factory workers to collect production control, inventory, and timekeeping information.

2. A **smart terminal** is a dumb terminal to which have been added more powerful features capable of processing operations independent of the mainframe. It may have a limited amount of memory with a built-in program, which cannot be altered by the user. Typical uses of smart terminals involve composing electronic mail, editing messages, and controlling attached printers and other input devices. By performing these operations, a smart terminal reduces connect time to the mainframe and thus, overall telecommunication costs.

3. An **intelligent terminal** is programmable by a user and can operate independently of the computer system to which it is attached. Since an intelligent terminal can store internally its own operating instructions, it can operate as a computer as well as a terminal. For example, the operator of an intelligent terminal can direct the device not only to display a business in-

voice on the screen but also to compute the extensions and totals on the displayed document. As such, this top-of-the-line terminal removes many of the routine storage and processing tasks from the mainframe, which then has added time for more important jobs.

Text Communication Tools

The preparation of text, commonly called word processing, is treated in detail in Chapter 17 along with the hardware, software, and systems needed to manage the *text-producing* function. In this section, we shall examine the tools for *transmitting* text messages.

Electronic Mail

As the name implies, **electronic mail** is the process of delivering mail electronically. However, it is more a concept than a technology, for the "umbrella" term "electronic mail" includes a broad range of devices that substitute the transmission of electronic codes over wire or wireless for the physical delivery of paper documents through the mails.

Electronic mail transmits information in many forms from terminals within organizations or via public service networks, such as MCI Mail, Western Union's Easy-Link, or Tymnet's On Tyme. Its most common use has been in firms with three or more locations, 50 or more employees, and a large volume of communications that must be delivered under the pressure of time. The basic process of sending and receiving electronic mail, as well as the major types of equipment for doing so, are charted in Figure 18–8. Each type is covered in this section.

Facsimile. The facsimile, or *fax*, **process** permits exact copies of written, printed, or graphic information to be sent and received over regular telephone lines as well as by

Figure 18-8
Electronic
Mail
Methods

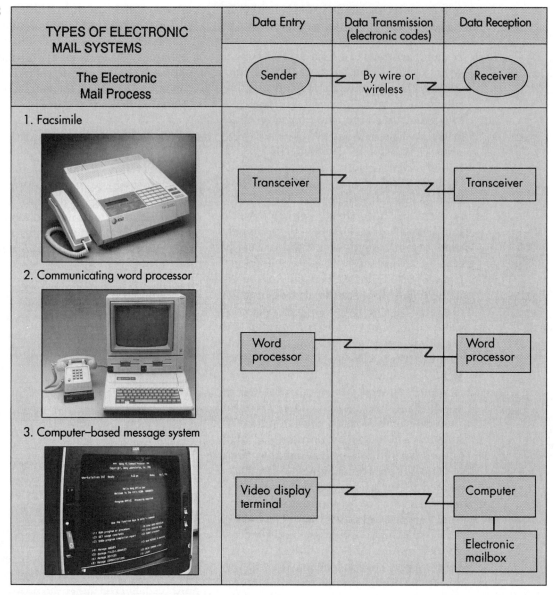

TYPES OF ELECTRONIC MAIL SYSTEMS	Data Entry	Data Transmission (electronic codes)	Data Reception
The Electronic Mail Process	Sender	By wire or wireless	Receiver
1. Facsimile	Transceiver		Transceiver
2. Communicating word processor	Word processor		Word processor
3. Computer-based message system	Video display terminal		Computer / Electronic mailbox

satellite. Thus, handwritten notes, signatures, forms, drawings, and other graphics may be sent over long distances in a kind of "remote photocopy" process. In addition, with software provided by communication carriers, such as Western Union, we can send fax messages directly from computer terminals or our PC. At the sending end, a *transceiver* (equipment that both *trans*mits and re*ceives*) scans or "reads" a document and converts the data to electronic signals to be sent by wire or wireless. At the receiving end, a second transceiver accepts the message and decodes it to produce an exact error-free copy (a facsimile) of the original document. (Only black, white, and gray characters can be transmitted.) In a few seconds, the receiver has an exact copy of an original document at less than a dollar per page. Any offices that are linked by telephone can be connected by facsimile equipment, as shown on Figure 18–8.

Over the last few years, facsimile has achieved major acceptance in business firms. Users are now "faxing" documents as common practice. Even company letterheads and business cards display an alternate fax number beneath the company telephone number. Fax users can make quick copies of documents, let callers leave voice messages on the fax machine, or use the telephone built into the machine to make calls.

Fax is especially valuable for international communications since, in effect, it eliminates time differences because the message can be stored until the receiver is able to retrieve it. At the same time, fax has destroyed an important period of communications "float." While writing a letter takes time to compose, type, seal in an envelope, stamp and post, fax does not give an executive time for second thoughts. (A recent study shows that the average manager is interrupted by telephone calls and fax messages every *four minutes*.)[7] By sending fax messages, we give the receiver a suggestion of urgency when in fact the message may be routine. In addition, since many fax machines are installed in the mail room or some other central location, information-security problems arise. To prevent this type of problem, the most advanced machines store communications that receivers may retrieve only by punching in a code or using a passkey.

Communicating Word Processor. Some of the advanced word processors discussed

in Chapter 17 have communicating capabilities. Thus, on a **communicating word processor**, after a document is keyboarded, edited, and recorded, the entire message is transmitted over telephone lines at the push of a button. At the destination, the message can be displayed on the word processor screen or printed out. As a result, at the receiving end, rekeyboarding is eliminated as is the need to proofread and make corrections a second time. Most major word processing systems have these capabilities.

Computer-Based Message System. A sophisticated type of electronic mail is the computer-based message system, sometimes called an *electronic message system (EMS)*. In a **computer-based message system**, specialized instructions or programs are added to an existing computer system in order to send and receive written messages electronically almost anywhere in the world. Each system user is assigned a computer storage area called an **electronic mailbox**, which is identified by a location code or a special user-name code. At the sending site, a user keyboards a message on the VDT keyboard and directs the message to the receiver's electronic mailbox at the destination. Here the message is filed until the receiver makes an inquiry of the system. At a convenient time, the receiver sits down at a similar VDT and keys in his or her name and authorization code. On command, the system instantly prints a list of senders and their incoming messages (by subject only). The reader then decides which messages to view on the terminal screen and has them printed out if desired. Other messages are left in the computerized file for later reading. In this system, the sender and the receiver are not required to be in simultaneous communication, which eliminates the expensive time "game" called *telephone tag* in which an office worker keeps calling back until the called party is available to talk. Studies show that about 75 percent of all

---

[7]Jon Ferry, "Fax Copiers Hurt Productivity, Management Consultant Says," *Philadelphia Inquirer*, September 6, 1989, p. 5-C.

telephone calls do not reach the intended receiver on the first try, which costs, at the vice-presidential level, an average of $10 per completed call.[8]

This computer-based system enables office personnel to handle from 25 to 30 mail items an hour, which is comparable in time to placing 5 or 6 telephone calls. Problems can be handled in their order of importance, and multiple copies of messages can be sent to persons on a distribution list. Not counting the cost of the terminals, such messages can be sent for less than $1 each.

A slight variation of the electronic mailbox is a computer-based system called **voice mail** or *voice store and forward system*. In this system, the telephone, the computer, and a special recording device are used for immediate or later delivery of one-way voice messages. The person placing the call enters the code number (in effect, the voice-mail address) of the person being called and dictates the message into the telephone. This message is automatically converted into digital or numeric form for immediate delivery. If the person called is not in the office, the message is stored in the computer's mailbox. Later, when the recipient dials the code number of his or her mailbox to obtain messages, the computer reconverts the messages of the callers into their own voices. Such voice mail can be stored indefinitely and transported to many persons.

Videotext

Videotext is a telecommunication process in which textual data—and sometimes graphics—are transmitted to specially adapted television sets. Videotext allows users to interact with each other and various databases through computer systems. One example of videotext is the Viewdata system that uses a telephone network or cable tele-

vision network. Information is provided through a special editing terminal that permits the user to construct pages for sending copy to the Viewdata computer for storage in a central computer file. To retrieve information, the user must have a Viewdata television set or a special adaptor to a regular television set. Access to the computer system is gained by dialing the computer's telephone number. If the call is answered, the user must supply an approved password or passnumber after which a link is established and communication can begin. A related process, **videofax**, enables users of video equipment to send still images, such as photographs, over public or dedicated telephone lines in the same manner that documents are sent via conventional fax devices. Photographs in color may be printed on the color unit at the destination.

Image Communication Tools

Image communication involves communication symbols that are mainly transmitted in nonword, nonvoice, and nonnumber form. Three categories of image communication are available: facsimile, video, and graphics. However, with the many advances made in information technology, including the integration of functions originally performed by one-function machines, we find that the distinctions among the methods of transmitting messages become more blurred with the passage of time. For example, *fax* was originally designed for transmitting drawings, signatures, and charts that earlier methods of sending messages could not handle; now, however, fax machines transmit all forms of nonvoice communication, as we noted earlier.

Video, or television, *transmission* provides audiovisual communication on an interactive basis. *Graphics*, as output from the computer, are most frequently used by engineers in the design of cars, airplanes, bridges, water systems, electronic equipment, and houses

---

[8]David Barcomb, *Office Automation, A Survey of Tools and Technology*, 2d Ed. (Bedford, MA: Digital Press, 1989), p. 174.

because it is much less expensive to build a computer system to create models than to build and test the physical models themselves. The transmission of video and graphics communication requires broad bandwidths (1,000 times the bandwidth of voice transmission) and hence considerable cost.[9]

TELECOMMUNICATION SERVICES

With the onward march of telecommunication technology, the entire world becomes accessible through the standard office telephone. Business firms grow larger as they merge with national and international companies; and their offices, scattered around the globe, develop an enormous "thirst" for useful information. Thus, many complex business operations require "by-the-hour" global communication services to compete in the international world of commerce. The need for maintaining worldwide military security and facilitating global financial services has also increased the demand for greater telecommunication efficiency. To meet these needs, the telecommunication industry has responded with an impressive array of services that continues to expand with the passage of time. In this section, we shall discuss briefly the services most widely used in office administration. They are (1) leased lines; (2) voice communication services, (3) data communication services, and (4) integrated telecommunication services.

Leased Lines

A **leased line** is a telegraph or telephone line between specific points that is made available to subscribers on a full-time basis. Such a line is useful for large-volume, point-to-point transmission of voice, data, text, and

image messages for a flat rate. Leased line rates, which are based on the message-sending capacity of the communication line and distance spanned as well as terminal charges, are substantially lower than those for an equivalent number of single telephone channels.

Other leasing arrangements are available to business subscribers. From common carriers, such as U.S. West Southern Pacific Communications, users may lease private lines that provide dial-up lines in which users can call, or be called by, any interconnected telephone in a distant area.

Voice Communication Services

We noted earlier that voice messages have several advantages over other message forms; and for this reason, voice communication services remain a very popular means of transmitting messages. This situation is expected to continue, using the services we discuss in this section.

Centrex

Centrex, or *central exchange*, provides direct inward dialing in which all local and long-distance calls go directly to the number dialed. Thus, a call into a company is made without first having to go through an operator. In turn, employees make all internal and outgoing calls by dialing direct. (Usually the caller dials a "9" to get a local telephone line.) Centrex is considered worthwhile when at least 90 percent of all users desire to reach an individual extension rather than a department. However, a central operator is not available in the typical Centrex system so that the called telephone often goes unanswered when left unattended (except when the telephones are programmed with the call-forward feature). Also, nearby workers are often committed to answering extension telephones that continue to ring when unattended, which interrupts their concentration. Answering devices are

---

[9]Housel and Darden, *Introduction to Telecommunications*, p. 45.

effective remedies for this problem as well as for recording calls after regular hours when the office is not open for business. An alternative is to have incoming calls channeled to a central answering center after a predetermined number of rings using call-forward.

WATS, 800-, and 900-Number Services

Wide Area Telecommunications Service (WATS) is a long-distance telephone service for sending voice, data, text, and image messages at discounted rates. WATS charges are based on two components: (1) a fixed-access charge for each subscriber and (2) a usage charge that varies with the length and number of calls made.

Two forms of long-distance service are available: outward and inward. *Outward WATS* is designed for only outgoing calls in which the user dials a number in the same way as an ordinary long-distance call. Inward dialing is available under an *800 number*, a service created and still maintained by AT&T for placing toll-free calls. With the *900 number* service, callers pay a small fee (typically 50 cents) for voice information, such as voting in public opinion polls and receiving financial information.

WATS has become an efficient communication tool in many organizations. It facilitates placing sales calls to customers and suppliers and enhances fund-raising and maintaining good investor relations. The 800 service is widely used in media advertising and sales literature. Allowing customers to communicate toll free helps to increase sales and gives greater customer satisfaction. When properly used, these long-distance services can reduce toll costs by as much as 70 percent, depending on the volume and length of conversations.

Users can obtain assistance in the proper use of long-distance services from their local long-distance carriers. The computers of some firms also provide assistance by monitoring long-distance calls, which is

helpful in detecting improper telephone usage.

With the deregulation of the telecommunication industry (discussed later), alternatives to the Bell System's WATS service are now offered by other common carriers, such as US Sprint and MCI Communications Corporation. AOMs in large organizations with many distant customers should compare the costs of these highly competitive services before deciding which WATS service to acquire.

Foreign Exchange (FX)

Foreign exchange (FX) is a long-distance service that permits a telephone in a distant location (within or outside the United States) to be connected to a local telephone. For example, by using FX, a customer in Des Moines may be immediately connected to the London or New York office of the ABC Corporation by dialing a local number instead of ABC's long-distance number. For businesses making frequent calls between distant locations, FX is more economical than regular long-distance calls. The ABC Corporation, in this case, would subscribe to this service between the two cities.

Data Communication Services

In addition to the voice communication services discussed earlier, we typically find three data communication services: (1) Telex and Teletex, (2) electronic banking services, and (3) database access.

Telex and Teletex

With **Telex**, an international telegraph network operated by Western Union, small and medium-size firms lease existing public utility lines and rent teletype equipment to transmit long-distance messages. A main drawback of Telex compared with facsimile is the need for an operator to type all outgoing messages in order for them to be sent. This results in the possibilities of data-entry errors and slower processing speeds. Also, there is no provision for transmitting graphics. To overcome these problems, a new service called Teletex was created.

Teletex is a high-speed, desk-to-desk message service that allows users to type, edit, and transmit nonvoice messages over telephone lines to their destinations. In addition, Teletex permits the automatic sending and receiving of calls with facilities for storing incoming and outgoing messages. The speed of Teletex is estimated to be 30 times faster than Telex. For this reason as well as the greater number of other capabilities provided, Teletex is expected to cause the phaseout of Telex systems.

Electronic Banking Services

Electronic banking services allow bank transactions to be carried on without making direct personal contacts with tellers. In addition to the use of automatic teller machines (ATMs) discussed in Chapter 16, another electronic banking service allows customers with personal computers and modems to perform most of their banking functions from home. Often this home service is offered to customers at a low cost or free (for a short time or trial period). Not only does this service provide added convenience for customers, but it also helps the bank to automate most of its labor-intensive functions, particularly the work of tellers.

Database Access Service

Database access is an information-retrieval service in which the user, usually through the use of a modem, calls up a database and secures the information needed. Such dial-up services are available for most professional fields and for general users. For example, physicians access medical databases provided by organizations, such as the National Institutes of Health, to help diagnose patients' conditions. Business executives may subscribe to databases, such

as CompuServe or Dialcom, that carry a variety of information, allow computer conferencing, and provide electronic mail functions. Users subscribe to these services for a monthly fee. Students in a growing number of colleges and universities have free access to databases, such as OASIS and ERIC, that are maintained by their central libraries. Thus, students can be linked to computer-catalogued library references from their dormitory or apartment telephones; or they can access various commercial databases from their college libraries.

Teleconferencing

A study by Cross Communications, Inc., found that 80 percent of all meetings in the United States last under 30 minutes, 35 percent are held only to exchange information, and telephone conversations can be substituted for 60 percent of the face-to-face conferences.[10] One useful alternative to the business conference is the **teleconference** in which telephone lines or satellites tie together three or more people at two or more separate locations. Teleconferences have proven very successful, especially since several forms of teleconferences have been made available.

Audio Teleconference. An **audio teleconference** is the simplest, least expensive, and most commonly scheduled kind of teleconference since it requires no more than a telephone or speakerphone and operator assistance to be connected to the other participants. Audio teleconferences are designed to replace regularly scheduled "fly-in," on-site meetings of key people who already know one another and can conduct business using this medium. The audio teleconference, however, is not a replace-

---

[10]Tom Jenkins, "Take Audio Teleconferencing and Meet Without Traveling," *Office Systems '85* (April, 1985), pp. 100, 102, 104. For a comprehensive discussion of audio, video, and computer conferencing, see David Barcomb, *Office Automation*, Chapter 8.

ment for the once-a-year gatherings that are held for the purpose of meeting new people, sharing a key event (unveiling a new computer system, for example), or attending a meeting at which face-to-face negotiation is needed.

Experience has shown that audio teleconferences are more democratic and objective than other forms, far shorter in length, and hence less expensive. Audio teleconferences work best for exchanging information, giving directives, brainstorming and other forms of creative thinking, resolving minor conflicts, presenting proposals, conducting cooperative problem solving, and making decisions.

Video Teleconference. The **video teleconference**, or *videoconference*, which is more personalized and costlier than its audio counterpart, combines the audio dimension of voice with color television. The use of a video teleconference helps to humanize a telecommunication event in the same way that any face-to-face communication helps to develop personal rapport. However, research has shown that this type of teleconference is suitable for only 8 percent of the face-to-face meetings for which an audio teleconference alone is inappropriate and suitable, too, for only 4 percent of *all* meetings.[11] Figure 18–9 illustrates equipment that may be used in a video teleconference.

A related video teleconference system— the **electronic blackboard**—permits handwriting or graphics on a chalkboard to be photographed and sent over telephone lines to widely scattered locations. At the receiving end, the message is displayed on television screens. At the same time, telephone connections carry two-way voice messages to discuss the visual messages with the audience. Frequently we find the electronic blackboard used in centrally located classes taught by an instructor some distance away.

---

[11]Barcomb, *Office Automation*, p. 213.

Computer Conference. The use of electronic mail, voice mail, and other types of telecommunication has changed the ways in which office workers communicate. Because of our overwhelming acceptance of the VDT, it is natural that we find conferences being conducted using such computer facilities.

A **computer conference** allows people who are geographically separated to exchange information in a convenient fashion through the use of computers. Today's business executives conduct computer conferences on PCs or portable display terminals while traveling or at home. Instead of meeting face-to-face in one place at the same time, the participants "meet" via their VDTs, which are arranged in an interconnected network.

In a computer conference, users dial up (check into) their computer communication files to determine all the messages waiting for them to be displayed on the screen. In turn, the user composes, edits, and sends messages to the other participants in the conference and thus may take part in many different conferences that are being recorded in the computer conference network. Usually the messages range from one to five lines, and often only short phrases are used. Since these messages are short, they require little file storage. The user may read the messages on the VDT screen or print them out as hard copy similar to electronic mail. However, electronic mail is usually sent from one person to another; in contrast, a computer conference involves a "many-to-many" type of communication where groups of individuals "converse" with one another when each feels inclined.

Integrated Telecommunication Services

Traditionally all machines used in the office performed single functions. Telephones and radio networks carried only sound, and fax carried only visual messages. With each

Figure 18-9
Video Tele-
conference
Equipment

successful breakthrough in information technology, more and more functions were combined, or integrated, into one multi-function service. Several of the most important services that have been integrated in telecommunications are as follows:

1. *Integrating voice and data communications.* In the Displayphone Plus, two telephone line inputs provide concurrent voice and data communication. Also, this device provides hands-free options, a tickler file with audible alarm signaling, and small computer capabilities including memory, processing, and data storage. Figure 18-10A shows the integration of telephone, input keyboard, and display screen with a menu for the selection of subjects to be processed.

2. *Integrating voice and video communications.* Figure 18-10B shows a Photophone

that sends and receives still pictures over regular, dial-up telephone lines in as little as seven seconds. Using standard telephone jacks, this device transmits pictures of people, objects, text, or drawings without the need for technical knowledge or special telephone charges. Incoming pictures are automatically displayed, with the previous picture stored and available for recall.

3. *Integrated Services Digital Network.* Most telephone service is based on analog codes for transmission in which separate lines are required for transmitting voice, computer data, video, and images. With an entirely new transmission technology, known as the **Integrated Services Digital Network (ISDN)**, data are carried in telephone channels using *digital* (0 and 1) signals. Thus, all four forms of communication mentioned above can be trans-

Figure 18-10
Integration
of Voice,
Data, and
Video
Communi-
cations

A—The Displayphone: Integrating Voice and
Data Communication

B—The Photophone: Pictures and Sound by
Telephone

mitted along the same line simultaneously. ISDN enables otherwise incompatible computer systems to communicate with one another; and greater amounts of information can be transmitted much more rapidly through ISDN than with analog equipment.[12]

Before decisions are made on telecommunication services, the AOM should carefully study the information needs of the firm, as discussed in the next section.

MANAGING TELECOMMUNICATION SYSTEMS

The modern organization could not exist without telecommunications, for this administrative service has become essential to large-firm and interfirm operations alike. However, even though they are widely used, telecommunication systems are often badly abused. As we discussed earlier, communication systems must be carefully planned and organized; and controls must be established over their costly operations. We must exercise

the same care in the operation of telecommunication systems, as we see in the following paragraphs.

Planning and Organizing Telecommunication Systems

"Planning First—Hardware Last" is a slogan long advocated by systems consultants. Since modern telecommunication systems normally involve all departments, we find that a total-systems approach is necessary in order to study the communication needs of the entire firm. One effective way to plan such a study is to appoint an ongoing committee of personnel who represent all departments and who know firsthand the communication needs of their units. Most manufacturers of communication equipment will provide, without obligation, consultants to survey the needs of the company. In fact, the willingness of a sales representative-analyst to perform this service may be used as a guide to the dependability and reliability of the company represented.

A telecommunication system must be organized using the objective approach to problem solving discussed in Chapter 3. This

<hr>

[12]Janice Castro, *Time* (March 30, 1987), pp. 50–51.

approach requires following certain logical steps, such as:

1. *Define the information problems facing the business.* Typical problems include late arrival of information, obsolete and inaccurate data, and mutilation of records.
2. *Gather and analyze the facts relating to the problem.* Special attention should be given to these features of information systems:

   - Type of information distribution (one source to one receiver or one source to many receivers).
   - Information volume, such as the average daily volume of messages currently in the system, the average number of characters in each message, and the average daily total transmission time.
   - Form of the information (hard copy, magnetic tape, or visual display).
   - Accuracy of the information. For example, greater accuracy is required of numeric information when sending a communication satellite into space than is required of alphabetic information when sending a business letter.

   Typically the most common human errors are made in data entry and in telephone dialing.

3. *Consider the urgency of the information.* Considerable ranges in urgency exist in firms. For instance, there is less urgency in sending out accounting statements than that required for making air reservations for an imminent flight.
4. *Determine the cost of the system.* Cost should not be evaluated in terms of dollars alone but rather in light of the benefits accruing to the organization for the dollars invested. Also, improved customer service and the effect of good communications on competition should be considered.

Some firms recruit telecommunication personnel from their computer departments as well as from the common carriers, such as AT&T, MCI Communications Corporation, and Allnet. Usually, we find that a firm's employees are familiar with the organization, its communication needs, and the existing hardware. Smaller firms obtain the services of consultants from professional associations such as the Data Processing Management Association, the Society for Technical Communication, and the Society for Management Information Systems. In addition, vendors of communication equipment are valuable sources of personnel and training. Other sources of personnel are discussed in Chapter 6.

Because of the technical nature of telecommunications, the AOM is not likely to be in charge of staffing such a function, nor will the AOM be responsible for procuring the equipment. Rather, he or she may serve on a committee for planning and organizing such a function, for office communications constitute a major portion of the total communications workload. However, all members of such a committee should understand the history of telecommunication equipment.

Prior to 1969, telecommunication equipment and services were purchased or leased from common carriers. However, with the landmark Carterfone decision of 1968, it became legal for other firms to provide equipment to telecommunication users. These firms—called **interconnect companies**—offer a variety of voice, data, text, and image communication equipment that can be connected to the lines of the common carriers. In 1980 the Federal Communications Commission ruled that data processing and telecommunication firms may freely compete in the telecommunication equipment market. Further, in January 1984, under court mandate, the Bell System divested itself of its operating companies, making them independent firms competing in the telecommunication market. The result of these decisions has allowed equipment production and prices to be ruled by competition rather than by monopoly. The market has, to use a common term, become "deregulated."

Business executives now face a complex array of options in the procurement of telecommunication equipment. In long-distance calling, there are dozens of carriers, such as AT&T, Microwave Communications, Inc. (MCI), and Allnet; and telephones and telephone equipment of varying prices and models may be obtained from local retail outlets as well as from carriers. Also, there is wide variation in the availability and quality of service. For these reasons, the office manager should take special pains to study carefully the needs and message traffic patterns of the firm, as discussed earlier.

Establishing Telecommunication Controls

Basically, control involves defining the information requirements of each department— *who sends what type(s) and number(s) of message(s) to what destination(s) under what circumstances?*

An appropriate means of consolidating information on the use and control of all telecommunication media is the communication manual, discussed in Chapter 17. Such a manual provides company guidelines on all phases of telecommunication equipment and services within the firm and helps employees to make wise choices in the use of alternate telecommunication methods. Thus, the manual serves as a yardstick by which the effectiveness of the telecommunication system can be measured. A firm may simplify the collection of such information regarding its telephone requirements by using a form, such as that shown in Figure 18–11, for both inside and outside calls. By compiling data from each of the extension telephones, the analyst is able to determine which features of the telephone

system are needed and which are largely provided for personal convenience.

Some companies periodically monitor their telecommunication usage by the hour to determine which departments send the most outside messages. As a result of such studies, the communication patterns of departments can be determined and the type of equipment needed to serve such departments can be justified. More economical use of the telecommunication equipment results. Many times equipment vendors as well as the local telephone company will conduct a free traffic study, showing both the amount and type of messages sent, for guidance in determining how much equipment and how many operators are required at each hour of the day. Further, they can offer assistance in using the telecommunication system and in selecting and training personnel.

Reducing Telecommunication Costs

Telecommunication costs continue to spiral to the point where they rank third on the list of corporate expenditures, exceeded only by labor and rental costs. And when we examine the total telephone expenses, we find that from 70 percent to 90 percent of all such expenses relate to local and long-distance calls.[13] To control these costs, large firms use telephone management systems that often are linked to an automatic switching system. One such system, called the *station message detail recording*, makes records of all outgoing calls. As we see in Figure 18–12, typical information that is collected and reported by this system is the station number or extension making the call, the number dialed, and the duration and cost of the call. With such information, an AOM can determine the type of usage of each station and the source of unauthorized calls.

---

[13]Janet A. Tufford, "Planning and Controlling Telephone Costs," *Office Systems '89* (February, 1989), p. 34.

Figure 18-11
A Telephone
Usage
Report Form

TELEPHONE USAGE	Department *Human Resources*	Ext. No. *806*
Employee Name *Jane Marner*	Position Title *Administrative Assistant*	

INSTRUCTIONS
In the space below (1) record the number of calls placed and received during the day and (2) record the average call length (in minutes using the code provided). Reasonable estimates of calling information are satisfactory.

No. of Calls/Day
Small (S)   = 1–3
Average(A) = 4–7
High (H)   = 8+

Calls Placed: CP
Calls Received: CR

Call Length (in Min.)
Average (A)   = 1–3
Above Aver. (AAv) = 4–7
Long   = 8+

Number of Calls /Day						Comments	Length of Call (in minutes)		
Internal		Local		Long Dist.			A	AAv	Long
CP	CR	CP	CR	CP	CR				
A	H					I CALL THE BOSS' OFFICE EVERY HOUR WITH ROUTINE MESSAGES TO THE DEPT. SECY.	✓		
		S	S			OCCASIONALLY I TALK WITH THE EMPLOYMENT SERVICE AGENCIES TO FIND NEW EMPLOYEES.		✓	
				A	S	TALKS TO HR OFFICES IN BRANCH PLANTS ABOUT RECRUITING AND TRAINING PROBLEMS.			✓

Thus, a system of this type gives some measure of the effectiveness of telephone usage.

Whether a telephone management system is available or not, both small and large firms should consider these cost-reduction suggestions regarding the use of their telephones:

1. *Compare the costs of mail, telephone, and other communication media*; and provide instructions in their proper use.

2. *Request from the telephone company an itemized list of its service and equipment charges.* Also, request the telephone company to conduct a survey to determine how intensively the equipment is being used. With such information, alternatives to the telephone company, such as interconnect companies and other common carriers, can be considered and

the most economical equipment and services chosen.

3. *Keep records of all toll calls.* Department managers should stress that each user keep a daily log of all toll calls made, including the purpose of the call. If calls are placed by switchboard operators, a similar log should be kept by the operators so all toll calls may be charged back to the calling departments. These records may be compared against the monthly invoices to ensure accuracy of the call record. (Only authorized personnel should be permitted to place toll calls using telephone credit cards.) If many toll calls are being made to one area—the rule of thumb is 300— the installation of a WATS line or an equivalent long-distance service may be justified. Whenever there is heavy telephone traffic between two widely

Figure 18–12
A Telephone
Extension
Detail
Report

TELEPHONE EXTENSION REPORT					Ext. No. 806
Date of Call	Time of Call	Called Number	Call Length	Cost of Call	Account Charged
03/01	09:25	515-287-7821	00:10	04.85	0604-2000
03/01	15:30	214-346-0091	00:05	03.75	0604-2000
03/02	08:45	319-338-5782	00:25	12.90	0604-2000
03/31	14:40	405-123-8543	00:12	05.75	0604-2000
Total			02:15	42.25	

separated cities, foreign exchange service should be considered.

4. *Provide monthly summaries to each department concerning the equipment cost, the volume of toll calls, and other communication charges or credits assigned to that department.* With this information, department managers can better meet their responsibilities for staying within their operating budgets.

5. *Publicize economical calling practices.* For example, unusually long calls should be discouraged, even though rates for time beyond the first minute are given a discount. Thus, the shorter the call, the lower the cost. Savings of as much as one third can be realized by direct dialing as well as by calling after 5 P.M., which is reasonable for calls to West Coast offices from the eastern half of the United States. Greater discounts (up to 60 percent) are available for night and weekend calls. While credit-card calls provide a record of calls made, such calls triple the cost of many toll calls.

6. *Periodically remind employees to keep personal calls at an absolute minimum.* A survey of personnel directors in *Fortune* 1000 companies found that the average employee makes and receives 3.14 personal phone calls daily and spends almost 5 minutes on each call. On a yearly basis this employee spends 62 hours—over one and one-half weeks—in personal on-the-job phone calls![14] Some firms use their computers to check on this type of expensive problem.

7. *Provide experienced, well-trained telephone operators who can give undivided attention to placing and receiving special calls.* All personnel should be instructed to answer and place their routine telephone calls rather than through third parties—usually secretaries—which saves time. The proper use of company and city directories also expedites incoming and outgoing calls.

MANAGING MAILING SYSTEMS

Even in the age of telecommunications, the mails continue to be the lifeline of business. Each year more than 150 billion pieces of mail are handled by the U. S. Postal Service (USPS), a number that continues to climb by 5 percent a year.[15] And hundreds of thousands of parcels are processed by alternate mail services, such as the United

[14]"Personal Phone Calls," *Small Business Report* (February, 1985), p. 16.
[15]Richard Lipkin, "Postal Service Ponders Its 21st Century Prospects," *Insight* (August 22, 1988), p. 13.

Parcel Service (UPS). Many large firms receive more than 100,000 pieces of mail daily and frequently send an equal number of items. The rise in the cost of energy, including transportation costs, and the continuing increase in postage rates create the need for effective management of a firm's mailing system.

Business mail may be classified as *internal mail* (interdepartmental or intradepartmental mail which is distributed by messengers, conveyors, and delivery vehicles); and *external mail* (incoming and outgoing). Since mailing services exist for all departments of a business, the mailing center is a key part of the company's communication system. Good mailing service ensures the quickest, most economical, and most direct flow of mail from the sender to the receiver, reduces delays in completing work, and creates a positive image with customers. The mailing center therefore enhances all business relationships.

Historically, we find that the mail room has been one of the most neglected departments in the company. It has been characterized by low pay for its staff, high operating costs due in part to wasted postage, lack of work standards, poorly utilized space or too little space provided, and lack of supervision. Many of the related functions, such as copying, folding, stuffing, and bulk-mail sorting have been performed in a haphazard fashion outside the mailing center. Too often the result has been, at best, a "get-by" operation. To overcome these problems, the mailing system should be organized and operated according to sound management principles.

Planning and Organizing Mailing Systems

Before setting up a new or revised service function, management typically considers whether to centralize or to decentralize the function. While there are strengths and weaknesses in each of these organizational patterns, the general trend continues to be a centralized organizational plan for mailing services. Such a plan may take two forms. In some offices, both internal and external mail are handled through a centralized mailing department. In other offices, incoming mail is handled centrally by one person or department; and outgoing mail is processed by the department in which it originates. In a small office, one person may handle both incoming and outgoing mail.

Proper planning and organizing are needed to bring about savings in time and costs, not only in the mailing center but in other departments as well. Such economy is achieved when higher paid office workers are released from the time-consuming necessity of interrupting their regular duties to attend to matters that can be handled more efficiently by the mailing department. The mailing center personnel can also bring increased specialization to their work, a fact that becomes increasingly essential as more and more mailing services become mechanized. With the centralization of mailing services, operations for handling both incoming and outgoing mail are more easily systematized and supervised; and labor-saving devices can be applied where feasible. The fact that the mailing service is centralized makes it more accessible—and usually more valuable—to the departments it serves. Overall improvements in control then tend to follow.

Key steps in planning and organizing a mail system include (1) providing a trained staff; (2) developing an effective internal mailing system; (3) designing an efficient mailing center, as shown in Figure 18-13; (4) procuring efficient mailing equipment; (5) developing efficient operating procedures; and (6) using automated mailing equipment when feasible. Each of these steps is discussed briefly in this section.

Figure 18-13
Main Components and
Work Flows
in a Modern
Mailing
System

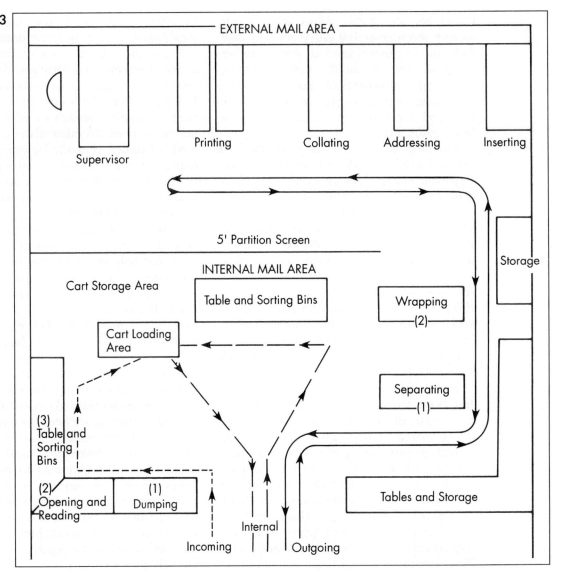

Providing a Trained Staff

In the small organization, a part-time office employee may combine the duties of mail clerk with those of messenger, file clerk, or another related job. On the other hand, the large organization appoints one person as full-time mailing center supervisor and

provides this person with sufficient workers to handle the operation satisfactorily.

The supervision of the mailing function requires an experienced person who understands the company organization, the mailing routines, the regulations of the USPS, and alternate methods of sending mail. Such a person must also be able to recruit, train, and command the respect of the staff, which usually includes one or more clerks in addition to delivery personnel. The following duties are usually assigned to the mailing center supervisor and staff:

1. Designing an efficient mailing center. See Figure 18–13.
2. Handling incoming and outgoing mail.
3. Developing schedules for pickup and delivery of mail.
4. Providing internal messenger and mailing services to all departments.
5. Selecting and training personnel for the mailing center.
6. Procuring the necessary equipment.
7. Performing related nonmailing duties, especially those pertaining to copying and collating tasks that are sometimes assigned to the mailing center staff.

Developing an Effective Internal Mailing System

In the small office, internal mail is carried manually from one desk to another. Larger firms, with higher volumes of mail and more specialization, typically use one or more of the following mailing systems:

1. *Personal messengers*, which save the time of executives and other high-pay personnel in transporting interoffice communications. The retention of such service depends upon the number of delivery locations and the distances between them, the time provided for delivery, the bulk and weight of the papers to be delivered, and finally the cost of the service.
2. *Office conveyor systems*, which are recommended for systems in which large amounts of paper are circulated on a continuing basis and such paperwork can be distributed to fixed locations. Such systems minimize the movement of office workers and hence increase worker productivity by decreasing wasted hours

spent away from the workstation. *Horizontal conveyors* transport papers between workstations in an upright position between two stationary guides that are moved by a motor-driven belt beneath them. Such conveyors, as shown in Figure 18–14A, are fast (several hundred feet a minute), quiet, clean, and safe, but they cannot climb vertically from one floor to another.

For sending internal mail from one floor to another, *vertical conveyors* are used. This equipment consists of a series of trays spaced along a vertical chain for moving documents. (See Figure 18–14B.) The chain moves in one direction only and is motor driven in a space resembling a small elevator shaft, thereby linking all floors. Incoming mail is thus brought in consecutive order to each floor.

An alternative system for handling both horizontal and vertical mail is the *self-propelled delivery vehicle*, as pictured in Figure 18–14C. This vehicle is battery driven and follows an invisible, horizontal guidepath—a fluorescent chemical line painted on the office floor—that is coded to stop the vehicle for pick-up and delivery of papers to departments. After a preset stop-time interval, the vehicle automatically resumes its travel route in order to maintain its published schedule. Several vehicles can be operated under computer control and used to summon, enter, direct, and exit an elevator for providing mail service to all floors of a building. Its use eliminates the need for costly vertical distribution systems.

Designing an Efficient Mailing Center

Adequate space is required for handling all incoming, outgoing, and internal mail procedures. As shown in Figure 18–13, all three of these routines are arranged in a straight-line sequence that reduces backtracking and delays in processing. Additional

Figure 18-14
Office Con-
veyor
Systems

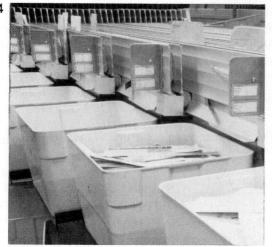

A—Horizontal Conveyor

B—Vertical Conveyor

C—Self-Propelled Delivery Vehicle

space is provided for the supervisor's workstation away from the main mail routine traffic. Nearby space has been allocated for related mail-preparation activities. From this adjacent room the mail items are returned to the outgoing mail area for final processing, which includes sealing and affixing postage.

Modular furniture is recommended for the mailing center; for it permits many arrangements of tables, sorting units, and shelving.

Furniture that is selected should be durable to withstand the heavy usage common to this function. Making such decisions is facilitated by an analysis of the volume of mail and how it must be distributed.

Procuring Efficient Mailing Equipment

When considering which equipment to use in the mailing center, a systems point of view is needed; that is, the center must be viewed as a smoothly running, unified combination of various mailing functions upon which the entire organization must depend. Thus, the equipment must be selected in relation to its contribution to overall efficiency of the operation and to the time it saves employees. *A good measure of the need for, or worth of, a machine is whether the value of the employee's time saved is greater than the depreciation and cost of the machine used.* If so, the purchase of the machine is worthwhile.

Today, we find a wide variety of furniture and machines for handling *incoming and outgoing mail.* The most common types of furniture and equipment used in the mailing center include:

1. *Sorting bins and tables.* As we see in Figure 18–15, sorting bins attached to tables speed up the sorting and disposition of the mails. A wide variety of types of bins is available to provide the greatest number of bins per square foot of floor space.

2. *Postage meters.* Postage meters are leased from the manufacturer and licensed for use by the USPS. The meter prints the amount of postage and accounts for government revenue under official "lock and key." The postage is paid in advance just as when buying ordinary postage stamps. Or through a toll-free number, a postage-by-phone system may be used to reset the meter in 90 seconds.

    Postage meter equipment offers several advantages: speed in sealing, stamping, and stacking the mail; elimination of waste and misuse of postage; and better control over postage costs. Also, by means of the postage meter, the firm's trademark, slogan, or advertising message can be imprinted on the mailing piece at the same time the postage impression is made.

3. *Addressing machines.* These machines range from hand-operated portable models to large, automated models which imprint a complete name and address on a label or envelope faster than a typist can keyboard a single line. Some models imprint account numbers, district or territory codes, and sales representatives' code numbers. Automated versions of addressing machines are described later. In selecting addressing machines, the size of the mailing list, the frequency of mailing, and the size and variety of labels used should be considered.

4. *Folding and inserting machines.* For volume mailings, such as promotional mail, routine billings, or bulletins, folding and inserting machines are necessary. Some of these machines fold, insert, and seal units of three or more mail items at one time at a rate of more than 5,000 units per hour.

5. *Mailing scale.* Probably the simplest but most essential item of equipment is the mailing scale. Studies have shown widespread problems with overpayment of postage because of an inaccurate scale or the underestimating or overestimating of postage required when no scale is available. The accurate weighing of mail eliminates these problems as well as the delays of mail returned because of insufficient postage. Electronic scales described below are especially valuable in the precise computation of postage for all types of mailed items.

Developing Efficient Operating Procedures

The mailing center staff is responsible for developing effective operating procedures that cover all phases of the mailing function. Whenever feasible, these procedures should substitute machines for manual operations in the center in order to reduce the high costs of labor.

Particularly important are the following procedures that help to assure sound operations:

Figure 18-15
Typical Mail Room Furniture and Equipment

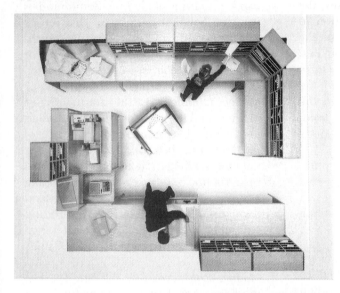

For incoming mail:

1. *Ensure early delivery of mail from the post office* by the use of company or private delivery service vehicles that pick up the mail at the post office.
2. *Sort personal and company mail, and then time-stamp the first-class mail for prompt delivery to addressees.* A register or log should be used for recording the receipt of important mail.
3. *Establish and maintain efficient schedules for the delivery of mail to all departments.* If possible, mail should be processed and delivered within one hour after it is received or one hour after the beginning of the workday.

For outgoing mail:

1. *Understand and apply the postal regulations* and observe carefully the dispatch time schedule of the post office, airlines, UPS, and other private carriers.
2. *Maintain a prompt, regularly scheduled pickup service so mail received in the mailing center during working hours is dispatched the same day.*
3. *Develop an efficient routine for processing the outgoing mail.* In some firms, the outgoing mail is handled departmentally, in which case each department seals, stamps, and mails its own correspondence. Firms having a centralized mailing unit may deliver mail to the mailing center with the letters folded and inserted in envelopes, leaving only the sealing and stamping to be done by the center personnel; others deliver the addressed envelopes with enclosures, giving the mailing center the additional duties of folding and inserting.

For general mailing center operations:

1. *In small offices, combine the activities of the mailing unit* with other services, such as filing and copying. Some employees in the filing and reprographics units may in turn be assigned to the mailing unit during rush periods.
2. *Periodically check the postal scales* against USPS scales to ensure accuracy and dependability.
3. *Ensure proper conformance to the center's standard operating procedures by*

periodic evaluation of the center's operations. Standards for routine mail-handling tasks, such as folding, inserting, addressing, and opening mail should be developed.

4. *Discourage the handling of personal mail except under unusual conditions.*

Using Automated Mailing Systems

New equipment frequently emerges to automate further the mailing function. For example, *electronic scales* have digital panels powered by a solid-state circuit to compute and display the most economical rate for letters or parcels. When rates change, a new programmable memory unit is inserted. One unit computes two mailing fees, with one meter used to determine USPS fees and another meter for computing fees for UPS parcels. In this system, a printer records (on invoices or other documents) the date, dollar amount, and parcel identification number.

More advanced systems integrate the feeding, sealing, postage imprinting and postmarking, and stacking of envelopes. An even more advanced system that includes a computer processes billings, statements, and letters; and word processing software has automated the printing of addresses on labels that can be affixed to envelopes by machine.

Controlling Mailing Costs

Improvement of office productivity demands that AOMs find more effective methods of controlling mailing costs.[16] Basic to the achievement of such controls are a thorough knowledge of the postal regulations and a company-wide education program that stresses the impact of needless communications on mailing costs. Some cost-cutting practices used by the mailing center in a large firm are outlined in Figure 18–16.

---

[16]Useful publications for office managers interested in reducing costs are Robert L. Foster, *The Business Mailer's Handbook* (Englewood Cliffs: Prentice-Hall, Inc., 1978), and *Everything You Need to Know about Mail* (Dallas: The Drawing Board, Inc., 1978).

SUMMARY

1. To handle the growing number of messages that must be transmitted over long distances, a wide range of telecommunication services has been placed at the disposal of management. Voice communications that incorporate expanded telephone, intercommunication, voice recognition, and audio-response systems are being increasingly used by office administrators.

2. Wireless communication is achieving greater acceptance by business firms. In this category are microwave and satellite communication systems. In addition, firms use paging systems for in-plant and local-area messages and cellular telephones for communication from moving vehicles.

3. Many messages require more than the transmission of the voice. For this reason, large firms, particularly those with many widely scattered branches, develop data communication systems that frequently merge the computer and the telecommunication network to send all forms of communication, such as electronic mail, and to transmit nonsentence words, numbers, and graphic information. Used in this electronic delivery method are facsimile, communicating word processors, and computer-based message systems.

4. In telecommunication systems, many services are required, depending on system size and the volume of messages sent. Some firms place special importance

Figure 18–16
Practices for
Controlling
Mailing
Costs in a
Large Busi-
ness Firm

Help Us Cut Mail Costs

Let's follow these cost-cutting practices	Then the result will be . . .
1. Update your mailing lists at least once a year.	1. A decrease in the materials and handling costs (of material being mailed).
2. Combine mailings whenever possible. Enclose all branch mail in one envelope at the close of the day.	2. Sending two letters in one envelope--cuts first-class mail costs in half.
3. Reduce the weight of mailed items. Condense letter length; reduce enclosures; use both sides of letter paper except official letterhead; reduce weight and size of stationery.	3. Places mailing in lower weight class.
4. Use first-class postage (not air mail) for all letters within the continental United States (except bulk mailings).	4. Delivery as speedy as with air mail except for overseas mail where airmail postage is recommended.
5. For rush items, consider overnight delivery service, such as Express Mail, for delivery of domestic letters and parcels. Other alternatives: See below.	5. Speedy delivery at reduced costs.
6. Use special delivery service only if necessary.	6. Prompter delivery to the addressee.
7. Insure mail items accurately.	7. Insures items according to their actual, not their declared, value.
8. Use registered mail only when the item has insurable value. Otherwise, use the less expensive certified mail.	8. Provides a receipt for the sender. Certified mail does not insure the value of the mailed item.
9. Use: a. Bulk mail when there are 200 or more items to be mailed at one time. b. Business-reply envelopes instead of enclosing stamped return envelopes.	9. a. Large decrease in mailing costs; actual costs of items mailed available. b. Our post office collects the regular postage plus a small fee for the reply privilege.
10. Print in advance the envelopes for branch mail. Computer-printed labels should be used if possible.	10. Saves cost of typing addresses each day.
11. Use window envelopes to eliminate the typing of the recipient's name and address.	11. Eliminates typing name and address on the envelopes and the problem of matching the addressed envelope with the appropriate letter.
12. Substitute postal cards for first-class letters in sending short messages (making announcements to customers, for changes in addresses, etc.).	12. Reduces first-class mail costs by 40 percent.
13. Use presorted mail privileges available upon application to the post office. Check with the mailing center supervisor (Ext. 124). Use ZIP + 4 code for identifying more specific address locations.	13. Saves several cents per item by presorting by ZIP codes and delivering bundles to the post office. ZIP + 4 code provides further discount.

OTHER MESSAGE-DELIVERY METHODS FOR CUTTING COSTS

A. The Telephone: Use for two-way communication unless a hard copy is needed. B. The Mailgram: Use for delivery by USPS and Western Union to any U.S. address the next business day.	C. Private Delivery Service: Use for fast delivery of all mail (other than first-class). Compare costs of UPS, Federal Express; see the yellow pages. D. Electronic Delivery Methods: Call the Computer Center, Ext. 214.

on these services: leased lines, Centrex, long-distance calling using WATS lines, 800- and 900-number lines, foreign exchange, and teleconferencing; and a growing list of other telecommunication services.

5. Within the firm, messages are sent via personal messengers, conveyor systems, and self-propelled vehicles. To send and receive mail at the lowest cost and in the shortest time, a centralized mail center is usually set up with appropriate staff, equipment (including an increased number of automated machines), and procedures. The center manager is committed to the most efficient use of mailing services and must be aware of alternate methods of delivery.

GLOSSARY **Audio-response system**—a system in which a computer-activated voice answers questions using a vocabulary stored in the system.

Audio teleconference—the simplest, least expensive, and most commonly scheduled teleconference requiring only a telephone or speakerphone and operator assistance to be connected to the other participants.

Bandwidth—the amount of space needed to transmit messages in telecommunication channels.

Cellular telephone—a radio-based wireless communication system for receiving and transmitting voice messages within a limited geographic area.

Centrex—a central telephone exchange that provides direct inward dialing in which all local and long-distance calls go directly to the number dialed; also known as *central exchange*.

Communicating word processor—a word processing machine that has the capability of transmitting and receiving messages over telephone lines.

Communication satellite (Comsat)—a communication system that consists of two or more ground transmitter-receiver stations and a satellite "parked" in space above the earth.

Computer-based message system—a form of electronic mail in which a computer directs the received messages to be filed in electronic mailboxes later to be accessed by persons as their needs require; also known as *electronic message system (EMS)*.

Computer conference—a form of teleconferencing in which geographically separate persons communicate with each other through the use of computers and appropriate software packages and communication links.

Data communication system—a powerful information-transmitting system that merges the computer, the telephone, and other electronic systems to send prerecorded data over long distances.

Database access—an information-retrieval service in which the user calls up a database and secures the information needed.

Dumb terminal—a data-entry device with an alphanumeric keyboard and printer (the teletypewriter), or a video display terminal that is connected to a mainframe via a communication link.

Electronic blackboard—a telecommunication service in which a chalkboard message is photographed and transmitted over telephone lines to distant television receivers.

Electronic mail—the process of delivering mail by electronic signals over telecommunication lines, thus eliminating the need for the physical delivery of paper documents.

Electronic mailbox—a computer storage area identified by a location code or a special user-name code for the storage of an individual's electronic mail.

Facsimile—a form of electronic mail that permits exact copies of written, printed, or graphic information to be sent and received over regular telephone lines as well as by satellite; also known as *fax*.

Fiber optics—fiberglass threads along which units of information are translated into light waves by a laser beam and then "pumped" through the glass fiber for transmitting information in a telecommunication system.

Foreign exchange (FX)—a long-distance telephone service that permits a telephone in a distant location (within or outside the United States) to be connected to a local telephone.

Image communication—messages that involve communication symbols transmitted in nonword, nonvoice, and non-number form.

Information distribution—that phase of the information cycle in which information is transmitted or moved from the place of processing to the point where it will be used.

Integrated Services Digital Network (ISDN)—an information-transmission technology in which messages are carried in telephone channels using digital (0 and 1) signals.

Intelligent terminal—a device that is programmable by a user and which can be operated independently of the computer system to which it is attached.

Intercommunication (intercom) system—a privately owned, small-scale telephone system used to tie together all departments within a firm.

Interconnect companies—those firms that offer a variety of voice, data, text, and image communication equipment that can be connected to the lines of common carriers.

Key telephone system (KTS)—a voice communication system having two or more telephones connected to several telephone lines, each of which can be reached by each telephone set.

Leased line—a telegraph or telephone line between specific points made available to subscribers on a full-time basis.

Metropolitan area network (MAN)—an intermediate telecommunication network, covering a geographic area of up to 30 miles, that is capable of transmitting voice, data, text, and image signals at the same time.

Microwave communication system—a radio-relay system that sends signals between towers for ultimate delivery of messages to distant locations.

Modem—an abbreviation for the term *modulator-demodulator*. This device converts the digital code of the computer into analog code used by the telephone system and also converts the analog code back to digital code for use within the computer.

Paging system—a system used to locate persons who are away from their workstations.

Private automatic branch exchange (PABX)—a privately owned telephone switching system that performs many time-saving calling tasks under computer control.

Private branch exchange (PBX)—a privately owned switching system for manually handling telephone calls where the number of extension telephones is not great and the volume of calls is not heavy.

Smart terminal—a dumb terminal to which have been added more powerful features capable of processing operations independent of the mainframe.

Switching system—an exchange for receiving and distributing internal and external telephone calls without the need for a switchboard operator.

Telecommunications—all the communication processes for sending and receiving voice (sounds), data, text, and image messages by wire and wireless methods.

Teleconference—a telephone service that ties together three or more people at two or more separate locations.

Teletex—a high-speed, desk-to-desk message service that allows users to type, edit, and transmit nonvoice messages over telephone lines to their destinations.

Telex—an international telegraph network operated by Western Union.

Video teleconference—a type of teleconference that combines the audio dimension of voice with color television; also known as *videoconference*.

Videofax—a telecommunication process that enables users of video equipment to send a still image, such as a photograph, over public or dedicated telephone lines in the same manner that documents are sent via conventional fax devices.

Videotext—a telecommunication process in which textual data—and sometimes graphics—are transmitted to specially adapted television sets.

Voice communication system—a telecommunication system in which messages originated by speakers are sent by wire or wireless methods to listeners who receive and respond to the messages.

Voice mail—a system in which messages are stored in digital form in the computer and later delivered in the caller's voice when the called person requests such messages from the computer's mailbox; also known as *voice store and forward system*.

Voice-recognition system—a computer-based system in which the computer "understands" and records the human voice as input and performs operations based on these inputs.

Wide area network (WAN)—a telecommunication facility that covers a large geographic area and provides public and private channels for transmitting and receiving messages; also called a *long-distance network*.

Wide Area Telecommunications Service (WATS)—a long-distance telephone service for sending voice, data, text, and image messages at discounted rates.

FOR YOUR REVIEW

1. What are some of the expanded services offered in telecommunication systems for the modern organization?

2. Identify the conditions that should be considered before designing a voice communication system.

3. What improvements in basic telephone equipment have expanded the use of this medium in the office? How do these improvements aid in expediting office work?

4. Cite several of the automatic functions that have been added to the telephone. What are the main advantages of such functions?

5. What features of intercommunication systems enable the office manager to communicate more effectively?

6. Define audio-response and voice-recognition as used in telecommunication systems. What are the purposes of each?

7. List some common wireless communication systems. What significant savings can be realized by using wireless rather than wire communication systems?

8. Explain how a cellular telephone operates.

9. Do cellular telephones and microwave and satellite communication systems operate in a similar fashion? Explain.

10. What is meant by the term *data communication system*? Explain the basic concepts underlying the data communication process.

11. List the main types of equipment used in a data communication system.

12. What is a terminal? Briefly describe the most common types of terminals.

13. What types of equipment and processes make up the collective term *electronic mail*? Identify the comparative advantages of each type of equipment.

14. What are the principal advantages of using facsimile?

15. Identify the principal services offered in voice communication systems.

16. Define *database access* and explain through an example how this service works.

17. Identify three types of teleconferences and the typical uses of each.

18. In what ways are telecommunication services integrated in the modern organization?

19. Prior to developing a telecommunication system, what factors should be analyzed and studied?

20. Cite five specific ways in which telephone costs may be reduced and controlled.

21. In the age of automation, what circumstances justify the use of personal messengers in offices? What alternate means are available for transporting materials within the office?

22. In what ways can mailing operations be automated?

23. What are some of the principal methods available for reducing the costs of mailing services?

FOR YOUR DISCUSSION

1. As an office manager, you have overheard several of your employees use curt, and sometimes offensive, language in telephone conversations with your customers. How would you *approach* the solution of this problem and still retain the good will of your workers?

2. Intuition tells you that many of the employees in your office are tying up the telephone lines with unauthorized personal calls for many hours each week. How can you obtain information on this problem without undue prying? Once you have reliable information, how can the problem be resolved?

3. On Monday morning, you checked into your electronic mailbox and found the interoffice memos listed below. Each memo should be answered, in memo form as shown in Chapter 3, and sent to the electronic mailboxes of your correspondents (or use an equivalent method to be determined by your instructor). Indicate at the beginning of each message whether the message should be classified as urgent, regular (routine), or confidential.

   a. From Barbara Mingo, Accounting Department

      Message: I'm still planning on having lunch with you on Tuesday. Is 12:15 still OK with you?

   b. From Max Kolanski, Stockroom Supervisor

      Message: The inventory supply of your department letterhead stationery is quite low. Have you any changes to make in the present design? If not, should I reorder the usual quantity—10 reams—for delivery in four weeks?

   c. From Leslie Van Dorn, Director of Human Resources

      Message: Effective this date, office employees are required to report their absences from department meetings to their supervisors unless specific permission for missing a meeting is given by the supervisor. Notify all employees in writing. Let me hear from you at the end of this month regarding the effectiveness of this policy.

4. During the past six months you have surveyed all your office personnel and uncovered these communication "situations" that may become potential problems in your office:

   a. Workers are writing many memos because the memo seems to be the only way they can reach groups of people.

   b. Workers are frequently busy on the phone, away from their offices, or tied up in meetings.

   c. Your customers have difficulty contacting specific personnel in your office.

   d. Many people on your staff handle the thankless chores of call coverage or message taking.

   e. Your customers have a continuing need to communicate after local business hours.

   f. Branch offices in your firm are scattered across all four time zones in the continental United States.

   g. Your executives, who are frequently away on business, have difficulty calling for their messages.

   Explore the nature of each "situation" and how it could result in a communication problem for your firm. What recommendations do you have for improving or preventing such problems?

5. Your instructor issues this challenge to you: "Class, a mailing operation is nothing more than a vital system in a firm. Prove it by constructing a systems chart, similar to Figure 4–5, page 97, for an overall mailing system. Include both incoming and outgoing mail." Comply with your instructor's request.

6. The following statements represent your employees' attitudes toward the usage of their telephones:

a. *Clerical worker*: I have the right to use my desk phone as much as I want so long as the boss doesn't say anything.
b. *Staff member*: Without that phone on my desk, I'm nobody in this company.
c. *Middle manager*: What I use the phone for is *my* business.
d. *Top management*: I'd give anything to get the blasted thing disconnected so I can get some work done.

What are the implications of these attitudes for you, the person responsible for getting the most value from your telephone system? Discuss.

SOLVING CASE PROBLEMS

Case 18–1 Analyzing Small-Business Telecommunication Problems

Berta's Country Crafts (BCC) handles consignments of quilt and other sewing patterns, and do-it-yourself kits of small country furniture and accessories for a national market. After a meteoric rise in sales with only five years' business experience, Berta Kallsen, the owner-manager, has organized a nationwide mail-order business built around a country theme depicting her base of operation in rural Iowa. Her office and sales staff is small, consisting of:

1. One office supervisor, Clare Kallsen, who handles all correspondence.

2. One sales order clerk, Anne Gay, who is responsible for processing all sales orders.

3. Two stock clerks, Meg Thompson and Kim Zerbe, who receive shipments of merchandise to be sold from contact persons. (There is a contact person in each of seven midwestern states who "scouts" the territory in search of items to be offered on consignment through the BCC catalog.) The stock clerks also fill orders.

4. Two part-time workers who are hired during busy holiday seasons.

As business increases, so do the telecommunication problems. The contact persons call "collect" into Kallsen's office three or four times a day. Typically, they place long-distance calls, which are growing more expensive. Often, too, they are forced to play "telephone tag," hoping to find Kallsen, who makes all management decisions, in her office. With a growing number of mail orders also come collect calls from customers who register complaints about the merchandise received. In the rush to fill orders, no one has given serious thought to the importance of a well-organized telecommunication system.

Kallsen turns to you, a new part-time worker with much office experience, to help resolve the problems identified. Specifically, she asks you to find out (1) what problems exist, (2) what can be done about them, and (3) how to prevent such problems from recurring.

How would you proceed with such an assignment? On whom would you rely for assistance? What types of forms are needed to report communications problems? Consolidate your suggestions in a brief written report to Kallsen.

Case 18-2 Planning a Mailing Center

While you complete your degree program, you are employed part-time as an administrative assistant to the director of a national professional society located on your campus. Your office is directly in charge of all society operations on more than 500 campuses throughout the United States. The mailing operations are growing by leaps and bounds, with correspondence going to each chapter office at least twice a week.

Recently you moved into a new office, but unfortunately no prior planning was performed regarding the mailing function. As usual, in your opinion, the mails "come last." Because of their importance, however, your supervisor asks you to draw up a "blueprint," in concise report form, that will help the office to set up, maintain, and control all mailing operations. For the time being, no telecommunication equipment is planned, although such equipment may be needed.

Draw up a "blueprint" that will serve as a master guide to the organization for developing, operating, and periodically evaluating their mailing system.

19

Records Management

GOALS FOR THIS CHAPTER

After completing this chapter, you should be able to:

1. Describe the records management function in the modern organization and the objectives of records management programs.
2. List the various levels in the data hierarchy and the importance of this concept to records managers.
3. Discuss the principles of forms management and the role that each plays in a records management program.
4. Identify each of the key phases or steps in a records management program, and explain the importance of each phase in records control.
5. Compare manual and automated systems for storing and retrieving records.
6. Explain the basic methods of organizing and operating records management programs.
7. Discuss the most common methods used to evaluate the effectiveness of a records management program.

To begin our study of records management, let's "set the 'record' straight," to use an old political cliché. As you study our economy and the ups and downs of business activity, don't you often hear about the global use of computers with their "invisible" records on tape and disk? Or, the wonders of fax and other forms of electronic mail that send records around the world? At the same time, however, don't you many times hear office workers ask for "a hard copy," or a computer printout of important records? Or, these same people who ask their subordinates to "make me a copy," or repeat many times daily, "xerox it, please." The answer to these questions and requests is, of course, "yes," because of a simple and very basic point: *In an increasingly automated world, people need, demand, and use paper records or automated records converted to paper form in order to perform their responsibilities.* Thus, paper records continue to serve as the most basic medium for storing information.

To verify this point, look about you. As you visit the offices of your physician, your dentist, your attorney, your banker, or your academic advisor, in what form do you find most of the records? And in what form do you receive monthly statements for paying your utility bills, your cable television charges, your annual automobile license and insurance premiums as well as your college course grades and tuition bills? The answer *has been, is, and will be, for the foreseeable future, paper records.*

Organized human activity relies completely on information that is "captured" on records. Government regulations and the complex information needs of businesses require that millions of additional records be prepared each year, which further increase the mountains of records processed by an office. The huge size of the paperwork load staggers the imagination of the most experienced office manager. One systems authority estimates its size in this way:

1. Over 2.1 million pages created *per minute*. (Included in this category are computer printouts, photocopies, letters, and other documents.)
2. One billion pages created *per working day*, which, laid end to end in paper cartons, would create an unbroken wall seven feet high stretching from Maine to California.
3. File cabinets which store 24 trillion pages, or about one carton of paper for every man, woman, and child on earth.
4. A doubling of the amount of stored information every four years, at the present rate of records production.[1]

With the growth of records comes a host of problems that seriously affect office operations and administrative costs. Typical problems include creating too many unneeded records, overloaded file drawers and folders, too many misfiles and duplicate records, a lack of understanding of the role of records and their overall costs, and a serious lack of training in the management of records. To prevent or solve such problems, records management programs have been developed as a vital responsibility of administrative office management. All such programs are organized around the life cycle of records—from their creation through their destruction or permanent storage. In this chapter we examine (1) the basic principles of records management including the management of forms, (2) the records life cycle in manual and automated systems, and (3) programs for managing records.

THE RECORDS MANAGEMENT FUNCTION IN THE ORGANIZATION

A **record** is written or oral evidence that information has been collected and kept for use in making decisions. The most common

records (such as forms, correspondence, reports, and books) are written and appear on paper. Oral records capture the human voice on tape which is stored in cassettes or on other magnetic media. Less obvious to the human eye are records that appear on film, such as movies, photographs, and microfilm. Even less obvious are the "invisible" records produced by computers in an intangible, magnetized form on tapes, disks, and other storage media.

Each of the major business functions—finance, production, marketing, and human resources—creates and uses its own set of records. External records are sent to customers, creditors, and others outside the organization. Such records include purchase orders, sales invoices, billing statements, checks, and form letters. Also, departments create internal records for use solely by employees within the firm. Examples of internal records are memorandums, requisitions, time cards and time sheets, journals and ledgers, and reports used in presenting data gathered from other records. Without proper management, the number of records (especially the internal ones) becomes excessively costly and, finally, goes out of control.

About two-thirds of all records involve correspondence, reports, and operating papers used in administration. The remaining one-third are forms, which are used to store information of a recurring nature that may be used inside or outside the firm.[2] In service firms or service departments, the ratio of forms to total records may be much higher. For example, in an insurance company or in a typical purchasing department, two out of three paper records may be forms.

A **form** is a specially designed record upon which *constant* information is preprinted, with space provided for the entry of variable

---

[1]David Barcomb, *Office Automation*, 2d ed. (Bedford, MA: Digital Press, 1989), p. 5.

[2]Lura K. Romei, "Electronic Forms: Winning Against High Costs and Obsolescence," *Modern Office Technology* (April, 1989), p. 42.

information. For example, on a bank check, the words *Pay to the order of* (the *constant* information) are preprinted on the form. The name of the payee entered on the blank line represents *variable* information. Forms are used in administrative systems to simplify and standardize the recording and use of information in order to facilitate decision making. In addition, *filled-in forms become records that assist in the accumulation and transmission of information for historical or reference purposes.*

The Relationship of Records Management and Forms Management

Traditionally, the management of office forms has been considered to be an area of responsibility separate from the management and control of records. As we noted earlier, however, records and forms are closely related administrative tools. In many service industries, such as insurance and banking, forms often comprise as much as 75 percent of the total number of records in use. Thus, *completed (filled-in) forms represent a common illustration of business records.* For this reason, a study of records management must involve a study of forms as well as other business records (see Figure 19–1). Therefore, in this textbook *we include forms management in a discussion of the overall records management program.*

The Records Management Program

When we demand more and more information in the firm, we are, in effect, demanding that more and more records be created. At the same time, the capabilities for handling such a demand grow at an even faster pace as technology provides more efficient automated systems. To help AOMs in the proper control of records, the federal government—and later state and municipal governments and private industry—

developed programs in records management. **Records management *is an organization-wide administrative service responsible for creating and maintaining systematic procedures and controls over all phases of the records life cycle.*** (Figure 19–2 shows these phases as responsibilities of the records manager.) As such, records management is an important function upon which all departments of the organization depend. By means of both manual and automated procedures, the modern records function has developed into a vital administrative service. In turn, this service has added new responsibilities to the AOM or an equivalent position, the director of administrative services, as shown in Figure 19–1. This field also offers many new opportunities to qualified persons desiring challenging positions in management.[3]

Objectives of Records Management

Like any other administrative function, records management should be goal oriented and service minded. By this we mean that objectives, or goals, for the program must be set up as standards against which the performance of the program can be measured. In addition, the program must provide useful services to all departments. In order to do so, the program objectives must include:

1. *Providing accurate, timely information* as economically as possible whenever and wherever it is needed in the firm.
2. *Developing and maintaining an efficient system for the records life cycle*—creating, storing, retrieving, maintaining,

[3]The leading professional organization specializing in the management of business records is the Association of Records Managers and Administrators (ARMA), Inc., 4200 Somerset Drive, Suite 215, Prairie Village, KS 66208. In addition to publishing an excellent magazine, the *Records Management Quarterly,* and other practical references, ARMA sponsors a professional certification program for records managers, the Certified Records Manager (CRM) program, as well as local, regional, and national conferences.

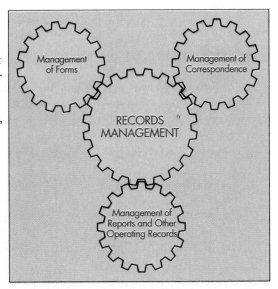

Figure 19-1
Relationship of Records Management and the Management of Forms, Correspondence, and Other Operating Records

and disposing of the firm's records. Figure 19-3 outlines each of the specific phases in the records life cycle and the most important objectives of each phase. Each of these phases is discussed at length in a later section of this chapter.

3. *Designing and using effective standards and evaluation methods* relating to the management of the records, equipment, and procedures.

4. *Assisting in educating personnel* in the most effective methods of controlling and processing the company's records.[4]

The Data Hierarchy

To an increasing extent, the computer directly affects the records function in the firm. As a result of using the computer on an organization-wide basis, AOMs and records managers have developed a much broader view of the organization and how its parts work together. (This point of view represents the central focus of the systems school of management discussed in Chapter 1.) From their need to consider the entire firm as one production unit, administrators look at records on a company-wide basis, studying their common purposes and features and noting particularly how these features are interrelated.

---

[4]The General Services Administration (GSA) of the federal government has developed a continuing education program in records management that emphasizes the management of correspondence, reports, forms, directives, and mail as well as records maintenance, disposition, and program evaluation. Handbooks on each of these topics are available from the Superintendent of Documents, U. S. Government Printing Office, Washington, DC 20408.

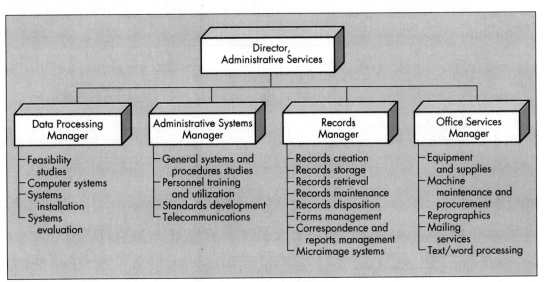

Figure 19-2
Placement and Responsibilities of Records Management in the Administrative Services Organization

Figure 19-3
Objectives of
a Records
Management
Program

RECORDS CREATION Objectives	RECORDS STORAGE Objectives	RECORDS RETRIEVAL Objectives	RECORDS MAINTENANCE Objectives	RECORDS DISPOSITION Objectives
1. Eliminating needless records from present files.	1. Providing classification and coding systems for records storage.	1. Providing immediate access to the information requested.	1. Developing a classification system for retaining records.	1. Setting up an inactive records center (or storing records in a commercial center).
2. Controlling the creation of records.	2. Selecting proper storage equipment and supplies.	2. Developing efficient procedures for charging out records.	2. Surveying departments to determine type and amount of records kept.	2. Reducing records to microform wherever possible.
3. Designing records for efficient use.	3. Developing and maintaining well-controlled file storage and protection procedures.	3. Controlling the return of records to the files.	3. Setting up a retention schedule.	3. Transferring outdated records from active to inactive storage.
4. Applying cost standards and controls to records creation.	4. Selecting and training files personnel.		4. Protecting and preserving active and inactive records.	4. Developing control procedures for inactive storage and for destruction of records.

Figure 19-4 shows how a portion of a common human resources record—the employment application—fits into the overall structure of information in the firm. The **data hierarchy**, sometimes called the *file structure* or *file organization*, is a five-level organization structure of information that ranges from the most basic level—the *character*—to the broadest level—the *database* or *library*. As you move from lower to higher levels, observe how each successive level represents a *group of related data units*

found at a lower level. Thus, a *data field* (level 2) represents a *group* of related characters (level 1); a *record* (level 3) a *group* of related data fields (level 2); a *file* (level 4) a *group* of related records (level 3); and a *database* or *library* (level 5) a *group* of related files (level 4).

Note the strong emphasis on the *group concept* and how this concept helps us to understand the data relationships in the files. In your college, all students taking principles of accounting can be treated as a group for

Figure 19-4
Data Hierarchy in a Human Resources System

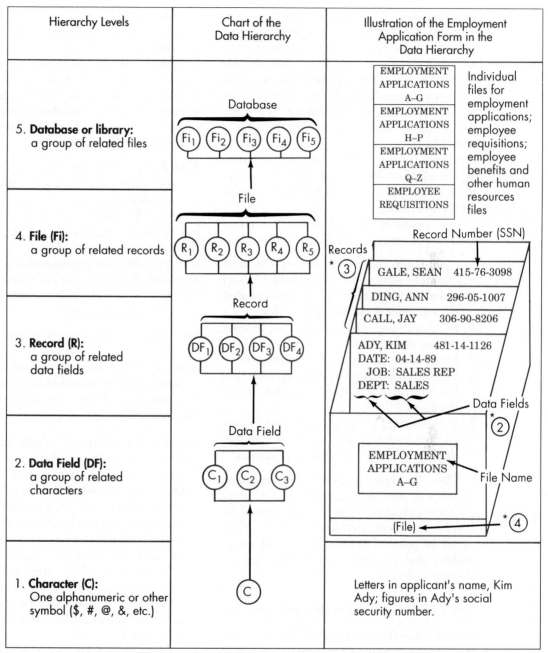

Hierarchy Levels	Chart of the Data Hierarchy	Illustration of the Employment Application Form in the Data Hierarchy
5. **Database or library:** a group of related files	Database Fi₁ Fi₂ Fi₃ Fi₄ Fi₅	EMPLOYMENT APPLICATIONS A–G / EMPLOYMENT APPLICATIONS H–P / EMPLOYMENT APPLICATIONS Q–Z / EMPLOYEE REQUISITIONS — Individual files for employment applications; employee requisitions; employee benefits and other human resources files
4. **File (Fi):** a group of related records	File R₁ R₂ R₃ R₄ R₅	Record Number (SSN) Records *③ GALE, SEAN 415-76-3098 DING, ANN 296-05-1007 CALL, JAY 306-90-8206
3. **Record (R):** a group of related data fields	Record DF₁ DF₂ DF₃ DF₄	ADY, KIM 481-14-1126 DATE: 04-14-89 JOB: SALES REP DEPT: SALES Data Fields *②
2. **Data Field (DF):** a group of related characters	Data Field C₁ C₂ C₃	EMPLOYMENT APPLICATIONS A–G — File Name (File) ← *④
1. **Character (C):** One alphanumeric or other symbol ($, #, @, &, etc.)	C	Letters in applicant's name, Kim Ady; figures in Ady's social security number.

* Circled numbers refer to the corresponding hierarchy levels in the left column of this figure.

examination and grading purposes. For scheduling examinations, only the time and place for a specific course examination need be posted. In the examination example, this posting or grouping has the same effect as posting a notice that lists the name of *each person enrolled in the course*. Through grouping, the basic concept underlying a data hierarchy, the entire set of data can be accessed (retrieved for use) at one time, which eliminates the need for an item-by-item reference to each individual element (student name).

Understanding the data hierarchy assists the records manager in many ways, such as:

1. In designing forms and files since the data hierarchy shows how many characters and spaces are required to provide the needed data in manual and computer files.
2. In classifying, coding, and sequencing related information.
3. In detecting duplicate data on records.
4. In building a logical, operational structure for all related records in the firm's database.
5. In converting paper records to automated records in which precise record size and other operating data must be provided.

Thus, the data hierarchy provides many benefits to records managers since it gives a comprehensive "view" of the firm's information system and the interrelationships of all its parts. The effectiveness of information storage and retrieval operations is thereby enhanced.

Types of Forms Used in Records Systems

In addition to the "geographic" classification of records—external or internal—discussed earlier, AOMs also classify records according to the number of copies made. Thus, we find (1) *single-copy,* or single-ply, *records* commonly used within a department solely for its own needs, and (2) *multiple-copy records* made up of an original and one or more

copies. Multiple-copy records are used to transmit information outside the "creating" department or to provide additional information for other departments or for persons outside the firm. Both types of records are used in manual and automated systems. The forms needed in each type of records system are discussed briefly in the following sections.

Flat Forms. The *flat form*—a single sheet of paper often used as a single-copy record—is the most common type of record in manual systems. Examples are sales tickets and billing forms. Because of its simplicity, the flat form is the easiest of all forms to design and reproduce on reprographic equipment. Flat forms that cannot be produced internally may be purchased from a stationery dealer or a forms manufacturer.

Specialty Forms. A much broader category of forms in manual systems is the **specialty form,** so called because special equipment is required for its manufacture or use. Figure 19–5 shows common specialty forms that have the following features:

1. **Carbonless forms** in which impressions from one copy to another are made without the use of carbon paper. This type of form is sometimes called NCR ("no carbon required"). On a carbonless form, an image is made when the special coating on the back of one sheet is brought against the face of the following sheet under pressure. Up to eight copies can be made on a typewriter; up to four copies, with a ballpoint pen; and with an impact printer in the computer system, the maximum is five copies.

   Carbonless forms eliminate smudging of copies and the soiling of hands or clothing as well as the time wasted with insertion or removal of carbons. Also, there is no need to dispose of used carbon sheets, which eliminates security problems in government offices and the need

Figure 19-5
Specialty
Forms

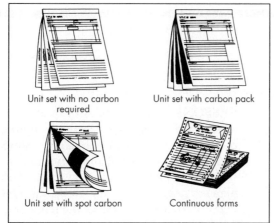

Unit set with no carbon
required

Unit set with carbon pack

Unit set with spot carbon

Continuous forms

for burning or shredding carbon paper. However, carbonless forms are more expensive—from 20 to 30 percent—than comparable carbon forms.

2. **Unit-set forms** that are preassembled with inexpensive one-time-use carbon paper interleaved between the perforated sheets. This type of construction permits easy removal of the nonperforated carbons. Unit sets are also constructed using carbonless papers. Although such forms are expensive to print, their use is justified by the great savings realized in the typist's or keyboarder's time. For example, with a six-part form requiring five lines of typing, 64 percent of the operator's time can be saved using unit-set forms.

3. **Spot-carbon forms** in which only certain areas of each copy have carbon coating. Thus, confidential or unneeded information will not be readable on each subsequent copy of the form. Such a design withholds or conveys information to users as the needs of the information system dictate.

4. **Continuous forms**, or *fanfold forms*, that consist of a series of connected forms folded in a prearranged manner and perforated for easy separation of each form. Printed forms, such as invoices and special accounting forms, are designed in

continuous single- or multiple-copy sets with preassembled carbonless or carbon sheets arranged in proper numeric order. Often such sheets are perforated with holes on each side, which permits fastening the forms to an aligning device on the writing machine. The result is an accurate registration across and down each form and the elimination of the need for aligning each form in the machine. Continuous forms save employees' time by reducing the manual operations of collecting, inserting, removing, and separating the sheets as compared with the use of automatic bursting machines for the separation of sheets of continuous forms.

Automated Records Systems

With the steady progress made by computer technology, many automated systems use machine-readable printing on specialty forms, as shown in the examples in Figure 19-6. **Magnetic Ink Character Recognition (MICR)** is a system used by banks to interpret and process numeric data that have been recorded in special magnetic ink characters on checks and other business papers. Automatic equipment is used to read, sort, and transmit to a computer the data printed on the business forms for further processing, such as the preparation of customer bank statements. Examples of such MICR characters in Figure 19-6 are the bank's Federal Reserve routing number and the customer's account number recorded in machine-readable form.

Optical Character Recognition (OCR) is a scanning system for reading numeric and alphabetic data that have been printed in a distinctive type style on business forms and records. As each character on the business document is read by an optical character reader, it is translated into electrical impulses that are transmitted to the computer for processing. On the OCR form in Figure 19-6,

Dialog on the Firing Line

ALICE KARSJEN
Administrator, Group Records Management
The Principal Financial Group®
Des Moines, Iowa

FLMI (Fellow in the Life Office Management Institute)
As Administrator, Group Records Management, for The
Principal Financial Group®, Alice Karsjen provides
technical expertise and assistance for maintaining record
systems in paper, microfiche, microfilm, and electronic
form. Her responsibilities include audit and analysis of
current systems to develop the most efficient and cost-
effective storage and retrieval methods. She works with
Group departments to educate staff about records management procedures, designs formal plans, develops
quality control methods, and maintains an operations
manual. Ms. Karsjen teaches a records management
course at a local community college and is active in ARMA
International.

QUESTION: What effects have computers had on the
quantity of records produced as well as on your efforts
to control records in your organization?

RESPONSE: In an industry that is information
intensive, instant access to the computer database
provides a way to give quality customer service
and to achieve control and efficiency in document
storage. Using computers as part of the records
management plan in our group insurance department dramatically reduces the number of times we
need to access a document file to obtain information. However, there is an increased volume of
records produced.

One example of how records storage has become
more efficient is in our production of the office
copy of routine monthly customer communications.
The paper copies formerly required a large amount
of space and maintenance. Now, storing them on
computer output microfiche (COM) minimizes
those problems.

Using computers also helps maintain our paper
files and microfiche by providing computer-
assisted retrieval, a quick way to request document
files and lists to identify records that can be
transferred to inactive storage.

One major challenge created by using computers
resulted from the large amount of paper output.
At first we printed output on 11″ × 17″ paper, which
was inconvenient to store. We remedied the
situation by producing the output in small print on
8½″ × 11″ paper, reducing retention periods and
storing any output needed for longer time periods
on COM.

Computer usage continues to grow and will
provide more solutions and challenges for future
records and information managers.

Figure 19-6
Forms for
Automated
Records
Systems

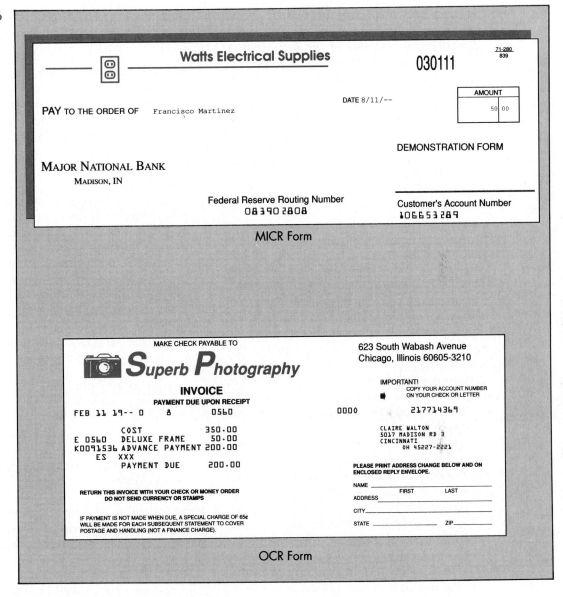

the customer's name, address, and invoice amount are printed in OCR type. Other electronic records appear on magnetic media, such as tape, disk, and diskette (discussed in Chapter 16) and on microfilm, which is covered in the next chapter. In addition, forms that are programmed to

appear on the VDT screen are also used. These "intangible" nonpaper forms are discussed in the section, *Designing Efficient Forms in the Records System.*

These forms and a host of management reports are generated in an *automated records system*, which integrates the equipment, software, procedures, and operating data to support the day-to-day management activities of the organization. A leading type of software in such a system is the *database management system*, which is designed to store, change or update, sort, and retrieve related information about entities, such as documents, customers, accounts, and employees. The database as an office automation concept is covered in an earlier chapter.

PRINCIPLES OF FORMS MANAGEMENT

In Part 1 of this textbook, basic principles needed to manage the office were specified: principles of management, principles of organization, principles of problem solving, and principles of communication. All effective AOMs must be principles conscious, for such an attitude toward work responsibilities enables managers to understand the office dynamics required to ensure a high level of productivity in the office.

The records manager, to be an effective administrator, must also apply certain basic principles. With the wide variety of information needs and the equally wide variety and complexity of forms and records, certain guidelines must be followed to ensure proper management of records. Thus, a sound records management program is built upon four basic principles that pertain to forms: (1) the principle of use; (2) the principle of standardization; (3) the principle of effective forms design; and (4) the principle of centralized control. Each of these principles is discussed in the following section.

▌*PRINCIPLE OF USE*

Forms should be approved and made available only when their use is justified.

This principle is basic. A form should be created for use only when these conditions are met:

1. When certain information, such as orders, requests, and instructions, must be collected for use in the administrative system.
2. When the same type of information must be recorded repeatedly. With the constant information preprinted on each copy of the form, time is saved in information processing.
3. When it is necessary to have all information recorded in the same place on each copy of the form, as in the case of duplicate copies. This arrangement serves as a check on the completeness of the record and ensures identical information on all copies.
4. When it is desirable to fix responsibility for work done by providing spaces for signatures of those responsible for the work.

▌*PRINCIPLE OF STANDARDIZATION*

The physical characteristics of the paper and printing styles used in all forms should be standardized to improve operating efficiency and reduce costs.

Standardization of forms affects primarily their physical characteristics—size, quality of paper stock, color, and printing styles.

Size of Forms

The number of approved form sizes should be kept to a minimum. Forms are printed on standard-size sheets of paper stock, such as 17″ by 22″. Odd-size forms, which cannot be cut from standard-size sheets without waste, increase printing costs. Odd-size forms also contribute to increased office costs by making the filing and handling tasks more difficult, often requiring the purchase of odd-size envelopes or containers for transmittal through the mail. Before the size of any form is selected, a study should be made of the envelopes, file cabinets, and mechanical equipment to be used with each form. Table 19–1 shows the size of common forms that can be cut without waste from standard-size sheets of paper stock.

Quality of Paper Stock

A second factor affecting the standardization of office forms is the *quality of paper stock*. The durability and ease of handling the forms, as well as the length of time that the forms may be kept, are determined by the quality of stock. Paper stock is sold by the ream (usually 500 sheets) and in multiple packages of reams by the carton. The weight is figured by the ream in 17″ by 22″ size. For example, a ream of 17″ by 22″ paper that weighs approximately 20 pounds is called *substance 20, or 20 lb. stock.*

For multiple-copy forms, weight is particularly important because it determines the number of copies that can be made in one writing. The weight of the stock used also affects mailing costs.

The physical handling that a form receives must also be considered in deciding upon

the quality of stock to be used. Normal treatment, such as that given an invoice form, can be provided for by using a relatively inexpensive sulfite (wood-pulp) paper. On the other hand, company stationery, such as letterhead sheets and matching envelopes, are usually printed on more expensive cotton-content bond paper, which is a hallmark of quality and prestige for the firm. Extremely hard treatment received by some factory orders requires a tough sheet with great tensile strength so that the paper will not crack after many foldings. Some forms, such as shipping tags, are printed on cloth. Sometimes we find it advisable to use a celluloid facing to protect such forms.

The manner in which the form is filled in determines the finish of the paper to be used. Forms completed in ink must be printed on nonabsorbent paper that withstands erasures and that prevents the ink from "bleeding." Forms created on some types of duplicating equipment must be sufficiently absorbent so the inks will dry quickly and not offset on each succeeding sheet being duplicated. Continuous multiple-copy forms are usually printed on a lighter weight of paper with a medium finish to

Table 19–1
Standard
Form Sizes

(1) Size of Form (in Inches*)	(2) Standard Sheet That Permits Form in Column 1 to Be Cut Without Waste (in Inches)	(3) Number of Forms Obtained from Single Standard Sheet	(4) Number of Single Forms Obtained from One Ream of Paper
2¾ × 4¼	8½ × 11	8	4,000
2¾ × 8½	17 × 22	16	8,000
5½ × 8½	8½ × 11	2	1,000
5½ × 8½	17 × 22	8	4,000
8½ × 11	17 × 22	4	2,000
8½ × 14	17 × 28	4	2,000
11 × 17	17 × 22	2	1,000

*The equivalent metric sizes are available from the American Paper Institute and from forms manufacturers.

ensure copying legibility. If the finish is too hard, however, the paper fibers will be so flattened that they will not readily receive the carbon image. If the finish is too soft, the surface of the paper will be rough, which results in poor copying qualities with part of the copy being clear and other parts unreadable.

Most business forms are printed on the **commercial writing class** of papers, a group of writing papers commonly used in ordinary business transactions and for advertising purposes. The types of paper falling under this heading are bond, copy or onionskin, ledger, index, and recycled, each of which is described in Figure 19–7.

Color

Colors used on office forms should be standardized. The use of carefully selected colors expedites the routing, sorting, and filing of forms. Forms may be color coded to indicate departments, branches, or other divisions to which copies are to be sent or in which they are to be used.

Printing Styles

Printing styles should be standardized since a uniform typography improves the appearance and readability of forms, thus reducing the possibility of error.

PRINCIPLE OF EFFECTIVE FORMS DESIGN

Sound forms design should be based upon the use of the form in the system and should ensure the effective recording and flow of information in the firm.

The designer of forms must know what information is needed, by whom, and in what order as well as the physical requirements of each form. Such physical factors as the form's size, quality, and color must be combined with the functional needs of the form. Guidelines for designing forms are presented later in this chapter.

PRINCIPLE OF CENTRALIZED CONTROL

The entire life cycle of the form, including its approval, design, use, distribution, and replacement should be centrally controlled.

Too many offices create new forms and perpetuate all the old forms without seriously questioning their need. This problem can be avoided by providing a program of records management under the direction of an office administrator, such as the records manager in a large firm or a files supervisor in a small firm. Various aspects of a centralized records management program are discussed later in this chapter.

THE RECORDS LIFE CYCLE

A record, like the information system of which it is a part, follows a set of steps during the time it is used in the office. These steps, or sequential phases in the life of the record, are called the **records life cycle** and are outlined in Figure 19–3, page 574. They include creation, storage, retrieval, maintenance, and disposition. Each phase of the records life cycle is discussed in this section.

Records Creation

Everyone in the firm, from a file clerk to the corporate president, creates and uses records. Managers write letters, support staff fill in forms and compose and circulate memorandums, and computers print out multicopy reports. Thus, all personnel should understand the need for justifying the creation of their records and the need for records control. (Frequently, a telephone call or a face-to-face conversation can substitute for a memo or a letter.) Without control measures, records continue to multiply and

Figure 19-7
Types of
Paper and
Recom-
mended Uses
in Records
Systems

Type of Paper	Characteristics of Each Type of Paper	Recommended Uses
1. Bond	Fine appearance and durability; good erasing quality and uniformity of finish and color; more expensive than other commonly used papers.	Use sulfite (wood-based) bonds for standard office papers. For legal forms, insurance policies, and letterhead stationery, use cotton fiber bonds.
2. Copy	Lightweight paper, such as onionskin.	Use 9–11 lb. stock for carbon copies and for permanent records where little bulk is desired. If the number of copies needed exceeds 5, use 7 lb. stock.
3. Ledger	Heavier card-like stock with a good writing surface that withstands abuse (erasing and creasing).	Use 20–40 lb. ledger paper for accounting and other systems records. Also use for looseleaf records.
4. Index	Heaviest paper stock with smooth finish that withstands more rugged wear than ledger paper. Common weights are 43, 53, 67, and 82 lbs.	Use for machine-posted records, punched cards, and index and library files.
5. Recycled	Paper stock produced by adding new fibers to waste paper. Cost is lower than paper manufactured entirely from original wood pulp. Appearance is not as refined as bond paper.	Use for most internal records but avoid using for external records.

soon clog the firm's communication channels. For this reason, the records management program begins with records creation.

Records creation is a preventive maintenance program that seeks (1) to determine who creates records and why; and (2) to ensure that only supervisors can authorize the creation of records in their departments. Also, reasonable procedures should be developed for obtaining supervisory approval to revise old forms or design new ones, subject to the design guidelines discussed in the following section.

Approving Requests for New/Revised Forms

A procedure for approving requests for new or revised forms should include (1) a formal written request with documentation regarding the need for the form, (2) a central control log showing the date and nature of the request and the decision made regarding the request, and (3) preparation of the approved design of the form.

Designing Efficient Forms in the Records System

The forms designer must have access to information compiled in systems studies in order to find answers to the *who, what, when, how, where,* and *why* questions concerning a form's use. Thus, a designer must understand the needs of (1) the person preparing the form, (2) the printer or reprographic department producing the form, and (3) the personnel and equipment involved in mailing and filing the form.

A well-designed form is easy to fill in and easy to read and use. Moreover, it clearly defines what information is needed in its preparation and simplifies the task of data handling. In turn, such a form creates a better attitude on the part of the users, which results in increased efficiency and decreased costs.

Guidelines for Efficient Forms Design. Figure 19–8 outlines efficient guidelines for designing forms. By following these "rules," you will avoid poor design problems and at the same time ensure the creation of an efficient, usable form. To analyze the design of a form, note that Figure 19–9A shows a poorly designed form in which the guidelines are not observed. Figure 19–9B, on the other hand, demonstrates the use of most of the effective design guidelines. The circled numbers in this figure correspond to the five design guidelines outlined in Figure 19–8.

By carefully studying the forms shown in Figure 19–9, you will understand how efficient forms design can be achieved. Note, however, that the form in Figure 19–9B is printed on standard-size paper (8½″ by 5½″), which you cannot see since the figure has been reduced in size to fit the textbook page.

Computer-Designed Forms. With the increased popularity of microcomputers, we find the creation of more forms called "soft-copy" forms (in contrast to "hard-copy" forms that appear on paper). A **soft-copy form**, created by using a computer program on forms design, appears on the VDT screen for the entry of data into the computer system. In some systems, a "mouse" or "joystick" is used as an input device for creating horizontal and vertical lines for completing the design of the form.[5]

Once designed, the blank form is stored in a computer file for later use. To use the form, a data-entry operator or secretary "calls" the blank form from the file for display on the VDT screen. At that time, the operator fills in the form by entering data from the *source document* (the hard-copy record from which information is obtained) into the blank form displayed on the screen. The operator may then store this information in the computer file for later use or for printing a hard copy of the filled-in form for use in the information system. Figure 19–10 on page 588 shows a partially filled-in VDT form.

An even more automated method for designing forms makes use of a smart form. A **smart form** is an automated form that is created with a special set of forms design and fill-in instructions stored in a file in a host computer. With this software, the computer is able to combine two separate automated files—a file of data to be filled in on a blank form, and a separate blank forms file. When the blank form is called to the screen, it looks like the ones commonly used in offices. But when an operator enters data into the form, the form "helps" fill itself out under the direction of the software. To tell the smart form what to do with the data entered in each blank, you create a "form map" of software instructions. When you create such a "map" for an invoice form, you must tell *each blank* (1) what to do with the data to be filled in (such as perform an automatic calculation); (2) in what other locations these data should go on the form and on other forms; (3) what other forms to include (in the case of collecting a set of related forms); and (4) what criteria to use for validating data (that is, for determining whether the data should be letters, numbers,

---

[5] A new and promising input device is called the *sensor frame*, which looks like a deep picture frame fitted over the VDT screen. When the operator reaches into the frame with the hand, the frame's sensor detects the hand movement and reproduces it on the screen, which offers great potential in creating new systems designs. For an explanation of this device, see "Computers You Control with a Wave of Your Hand," *Business Week* (February 20, 1989), p. 142.

dollars, how many digits, how many decimal places, and so on). For example, by accessing an existing database "by itself," a smart form can compute and add the sales tax to an invoice form as well as fill in the address, telephone and customer account numbers, and billing instructions on an order form. With this highly automated form, you can fill in, approve, revise, and file forms as well as distribute copies on a VDT network *without paperwork*!

Records Storage

With all the attention given to computers and magnetic storage media, it might be natural for us to feel that the era of the file cabinet has ended. This, however, is not the case. In small and large offices alike, manual filing systems continue to furnish the majority of storage service.

Experience shows clearly that an office filing system cannot manage itself, regardless of how well it is organized. On the contrary, AOMs must carefully consider many important administrative factors such as the following: (1) setting up effective filing systems, (2) organizing the files, and (3) procuring filing equipment and supplies. Subsequently, the effectiveness of the filing equipment must be evaluated, as discussed later in this chapter.

Filing Systems

Quick access to all types of stored records—whether they are on paper, film, or magnetic tape—is assured with an effective filing system. The term **filing system** refers to the procedures and methods used to classify, sort, and store records for fast retrieval. We use two systems, *alphabetic* and *numeric*, which we subdivide in this manner:

1. Alphabetic Systems
   a. Correspondence filing (by name)
   b. Geographic filing
   c. Subject filing

2. Numeric Systems
   a. Numeric filing
   b. Chronologic filing

Most firms use both of these systems. For example, a credit office may maintain accounts receivable files in alphabetic order by customer name; a purchasing department, its purchase orders in numeric order; a human resources department, its personnel requisitions in files by type of position (subject); or a traffic department, the incoming receipt of goods in files by delivery dates or by a time-of-day scheduling chart (chronologic).

Organization of the Files

The requirements for records systems differ from office to office, depending on the size of the office staff, the nature of business operations, and such factors as competition and government regulation and control. Two plans of files organization are commonly found in offices: **decentralized filing** and **centralized filing**. A variation of the centralized filing plan, called *network filing*, may also be found. The advantages and disadvantages of each form of files organization are given in Figure 19-11 on page 589. The AOM must weigh carefully the strengths and weaknesses of each plan and arrive at a suitable compromise. Frequently both decentralized and centralized filing plans are used by large organizations, as their needs dictate.

Filing Equipment and Supplies

In the selection of filing equipment, the AOM should first consider the intended use of the equipment and then the savings possible through standardization of equipment and supplies. Other factors the AOM should study before an investment is made in filing equipment are (1) the types and sizes of records; (2) managerial preferences for requesting information; (3) the appearance, design, space-saving features, and durability of the equipment; (4) its capability for saving

Figure 19-8
Guidelines for Designing Efficient Forms

GUIDELINES FOR DESIGNING FORMS

1. *Identify and sequence the data to be entered on the form.*
   a. Make a list of all data items needed by the forms user.
   b. Arrange the items in the order of fill-in or the order in which they are extracted from the form. For example, if a purchase order is prepared from the information on a purchase requisition, the sequence of data on the two forms should be identical. For automated systems, efficient keyboarding of input data requires the same sequence for the computer system form as that appearing on the source document.
   c. Keep related information together. Place personal data (name, address, sex, date of birth) in the same section of the form.
2. *Provide a simple, efficient design.*
   a. Eliminate unnecessary information. For example, do not request age on a form that requests date of birth.
   b. Eliminate any request for information that is discriminatory. A request for data on religious or ethnic background may be discriminatory and should be avoided.
   c. Avoid using horizontal ruled lines for typewritten fill-in. Use horizontal and vertical ruled lines to subdivide the form into sections, each of which is composed of related data items. An employment application form typically has a personal data section, a work experience section, and a references section. Rule or "box-in" each section to enhance fill-in and readability.
   d. If possible, use a box design that requires a check mark rather than writing for fill-in and that uses upper left captions (box names) to identify each box. (See Figure 19-9B.)

   e. Specify sizes and weights of paper stock needed on the form in line with requirements of the machines, such as typewriters, and equipment, especially file cabinets. Use standard-size paper stock, standard typefaces, and standard (familiar) terms on the form.
   f. Adapt spacing on the form to the method of fill in (machine or handwriting). For handwriting, ¼" vertical space is adequate; for typewriting, double spacing (½" vertical space) is satisfactory.
3. *Provide proper identification for the form.*
   a. Assign a form name (located at the top of the form) that reflects its function and a number (usually placed at the bottom of the form) that indicates its age. The form number also serves as a cross check in referring to the form in a requisition for forms or in a written procedure in which the form is used.
   b. Label each copy of a multicopy form at the bottom with the name of the main user (Sales Copy, Customer Copy, Human Resources Department Copy).
4. *Include clear instructions for using the form.*
   a. Locate short fill-in instructions (such as "Prepare in triplicate") at the top of the form.
   b. Place lengthy instructions (such as legal requirements accompanying many purchase orders) on the reverse side of the form.
5. *Choose the best available source for printing the forms.*
   a. External sources: printing firms with capabilities for producing complex, multicopy forms.
   b. Internal source: the firm's printing, reprographics, or word processing departments including desktop publishing equipment.

Figure 19-9
An Internal
Form Show-
ing Poor and
Efficient
Design

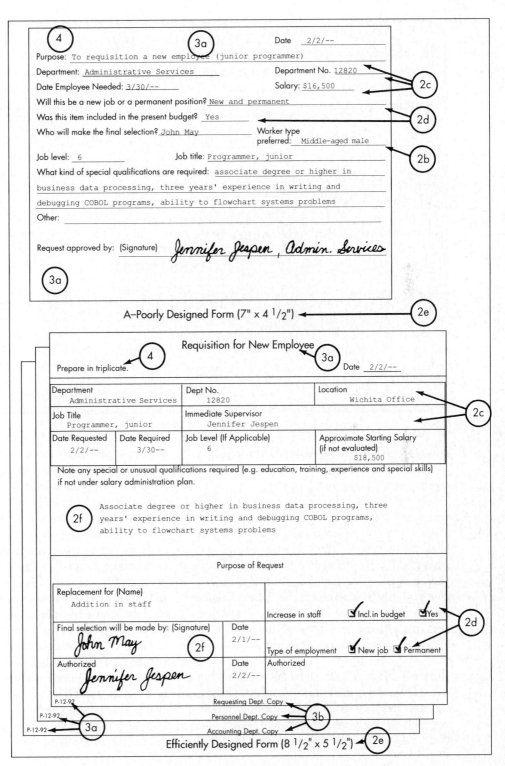

A—Poorly Designed Form (7" x 4 1/2")

Efficiently Designed Form (8 1/2" x 5 1/2")

Figure 19-10
A Computer-
Designed
Form

RECORDS INVENTORY

DEPT	INVENTORY TAKEN BY	DATE
Human Resources	Mary Taylor	6/12/91

SUPERVISOR OF FILES	PHYSICAL TYPE OF RECORDS	_X_ ACTIVE
S. Smith	printed material	___ INACTIVE

RECORDS SERIES TITLE	___ NONRECORD
Retirement Program Regulations	_X_ RECORD

DESCRIPTION OF SERIES (FUNCTION AND PURPOSE)

ERISA regulations on retirement program; useful in maintaining the firm's benefits package.

Figure 19-10 A Computer-Designed Form

worker time; (5) the type of security required for the records; and (6) the cost of the equipment.

Records vary widely in size from small cards to large drawings and blueprints. As a result, many different kinds and sizes of files are required. Filing equipment may be classified as (1) vertical, (2) horizontal, (3) visible card, (4) rotary, (5) mobile, and (6) files for special-purpose records (see Figure 19–12). The storage of computer-generated and microform records is discussed in Chapters 16 and 20, respectively.

Vertical Files. The **vertical file** with one to six drawers is the most common filing cabinet. In it, we store cards as well as larger documents, such as letters and reports, *on their edge* for easy accessibility. The file

drawers pull out from the front of the cabinet. In standard letter-size (8½″ by 11″) cabinets, the file width measures 15″; for legal size (8½″ by 14″), 18″. The file depth for both ranges from 24″ to 28½″. These dimensions involve important space considerations, with approximately 6 square feet as a general space requirement for each vertical file cabinet. Figure 19–13 on page 592 illustrates how we can achieve better use of floor space by increasing the number of file drawers and at the same time decreasing the amount of floor space needed for a given number of files. Also, less stooping and walking are required of files personnel; and as a result, the filing work is accomplished more quickly and easily.

A **lateral** (or *side*) **file** is a vertical file in which the long side of the cabinet opens out.

Figure 19-11
Advantages
and Dis-
advantages
of Three
Files Organ-
ization Plans

Type of Files Organization	Advantages of the Plan	Disadvantages of the Plan
Decentralized filing—each office maintains its own filing system; the work is performed by employees who have other work to do.	Privacy of confidential records is maintained; delays in obtaining records from the centralized department are avoided; and records filed are not required by other departments.	This plan results in needless duplication of equipment; less efficient personnel to do the filing work as they have other tasks to perform; and sometimes a confusing filing system since one department's filing methods may be different from others.
Centralized filing—records of general value throughout the firm are stored in one location.	Control over creation, retention, and disposition of all records is more easily achieved; more personnel efficiency is possible since the files are placed in the hands of specialists; needless duplication of equipment, supplies, and records is avoided; related records are kept together; and more uniform filing methods are followed, which results in greater accuracy and quicker retrieval.	Workers have access to confidential information; delays occur in obtaining records—forms to be filled in, charge-out procedures, messenger delivery problems; much stored information is never requested by other departments.
Network filing—department files are located within each department, but centralized control resides in a central records management department. A *locator index* is maintained centrally for records that are filed in each department for quickly tracing the location of all records.	In general, this plan has the advantages of the centralized and decentralized plans.	In general, this plan has the disadvantages of the centralized and decentralized plans.

(See Figure 19–12A.) Since this arrangement does not entail pulling out a drawer as in the case of the filing cabinet, it requires less depth and results in savings in floor space. Also, because we can view the entire contents of the drawer when it is opened, we gain quicker access to the records.

To eliminate dust and fire hazards, manufacturers provide models with doors or retractable roll-out shelves that can be opened to provide additional working space. Lateral files are also available without doors (the open-shelf concept), which allows an unlimited view of the folders. Open-shelf

Figure 19–12
Common Types of Equipment for Filing Records

A—Lateral (Side) File

B—Open-Shelf Vertical File

C—Visible Card File

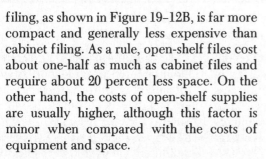

D—Motorized Rotary File

filing, as shown in Figure 19–12B, is far more compact and generally less expensive than cabinet filing. As a rule, open-shelf files cost about one-half as much as cabinet files and require about 20 percent less space. On the other hand, the costs of open-shelf supplies are usually higher, although this factor is minor when compared with the costs of equipment and space.

Horizontal Files. A **horizontal file** is used for storing papers or records, such as maps

and drawings, in a flat position. Often horizontal filing equipment of counter-high design is purchased so that, at no extra expense, the files may also serve as a counter-high working area.

Visible Card Files. The **visible card file** shown in Figure 19–12C permits complete visibility of the key reference data (names, account numbers, and telephone numbers, for example) recorded on the edge of each card. The speed with which the cards can

Figure 19-12
Common
Types of
Equipment
for Filing
Records
(continued)

E—Mobile File (Movable Shelves)

F—Motorized (Power-Driven) File

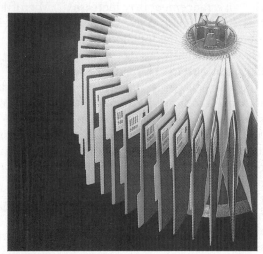

G—Floppy Disk File

be located and entries made justifies the use and cost of this type of equipment. Visible card files are available in the form of trays that lie flat horizontally in a cabinet, on revolving racks, or in loose-leaf book binders.

Rotary Files. In a **rotary file** the records rotate in a circular fashion around a common hub; and documents may be removed or added by rotating the file to the desired location for access. (See Figure 19–12D.) Larger rotary files are motorized, permitting

an operator to have push-button control over a cabinet of record trays to bring the desired work to desk or counter height.

Mobile Files. As shown in Figure 19–12E, a **mobile file** uses sliding shelves placed on tracks in order that the shelves can be moved together when not in use. Such shelves can also be moved apart as needed to create double-access aisles or moved to other locations on the track as needed. Mobile files permit a file clerk to work on both sides of

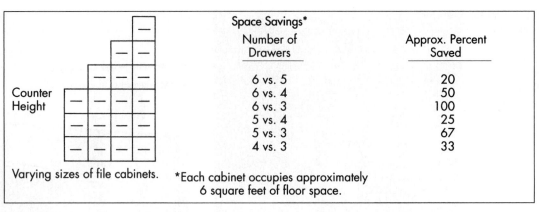

Figure 19–13
Space
Savings
Achieved by
Using Verti-
cal Filing
Equipment

Space Savings*	
Number of Drawers	Approx. Percent Saved
6 vs. 5	20
6 vs. 4	50
6 vs. 3	100
5 vs. 4	25
5 vs. 3	67
4 vs. 3	33

Varying sizes of file cabinets.   *Each cabinet occupies approximately
6 square feet of floor space.

a shelf and reduce by up to 50 percent the amount of floor space required for the files. However, such an arrangement may increase the amount of time needed to access most files since it eliminates the possibility of several clerks concurrently using various shelves in the same system. This is because when one shelf is accessible, the shelves behind it are not. Another type of mobile file, *motorized* or *power-driven equipment*, provides trays on movable shelves for the storage of records. Such shelves are powered by an electric motor and mounted on a frame inside the cabinet using a revolving motion similar to the operation of a Ferris wheel. Any shelf can be brought to the front of the machine (and to the operator) by pressing one of a series of buttons mounted on a control panel. (See Figure 19–12F.)

Automated Files. Filing equipment is also needed to store special-purpose, nonpaper records. For example, floppy disks used in word processing and computer systems are stored in protective envelopes in desk-top files (see Figure 19–12G), in ring binders, or in folders with special pockets for accommodating the pliable disks. The folders may in turn be stored in file cabinets. Minidisks and magnetic cards also used in word processing systems are stored in a similar fashion. Magnetic tapes that record the results of computer operations are stored on reels in round metal boxes that in turn are filed on open shelves for easy retrieval. Microfilm files, including optical disk files, are covered in the next chapter.

Records Retrieval

A records storage system is ineffective unless it can provide information immediately upon request. Thus, **records retrieval**, the process of locating stored information, is a critically important phase of records management.

Manual Retrieval Method

Under the manual retrieval method, a worker goes to the file and extracts the record desired. Such a system is simple in theory but is often difficult to put into practice. For example, when an AOM asks a secretary to "Get that report on our plans for reducing labor costs for next year from the files," the search may be unsuccessful. The files may not divulge any report with the key words "reducing labor costs for next year." More than anything else, the difficulty in this case involves a problem in communication. The secretary must search for the record using the words given by the requester; if unsuccessful, the secretary must find synonyms (cutting, worker pay, etc., for the key words listed above) and use them in the search until the record is found.

Frequently, an index of manual files is set up to help locate filed information when users ask for a record on a basis different from that by which the record is filed. In a human resources department, for example, records might be filed under the employees' social security account numbers. When employees' records are requested by name, however, there is need for an index file of employees' names cross-referenced to their social security numbers.

The specific procedures for retrieving information vary to a great extent from office to office depending on whether a small-office manual system (largely worker controlled) is involved or whether an automated storage and retrieval system is used.

Automated Retrieval Method

To understand the automated retrieval of information, we must first remember that such systems store information in various locations (within the computer or on tapes or disks outside the computer). Such information is stored in invisible, coded form and must be accessed by the computer for use by the office staff. To do so, this procedure is usually followed:

1. A record is requested by entering the file label information into a VDT.
2. The computer compares the label information in Step 1 with the label information in its files.
3. When located, information is printed out by the computer or displayed on the VDT screen, as instructed.
4. No controls are required other than those built into the hardware and the program. The original records remain on tape or disk after being printed or displayed. Thus, there is no need to return the retrieved record to the file, as is required in the manual storage system.

In other cases, paper documents are coded, for identification purposes, and the coded list of documents (an index) is then stored in the computer. The paper document is then filed manually. To locate a document, an operator must access the computer index to find the location of the stored document in the file.

Specialists in the information sciences, especially computer and library, have spearheaded efforts to increase the number of records retrieval operations by computers. Several of the most successful automated retrieval systems—those dealing with information retrieval in an office automation network and microfilm records—are discussed in Chapters 16 and 20, respectively.

Records Maintenance

Records maintenance refers to the set of service activities needed to operate the storage and retrieval systems. These activities include classifying records; developing efficient procedures for operating the records system; updating, purging, and retaining records; and preserving or protecting the records. Only the retention and protection activities are discussed in this section, for these are management-level responsibilities as opposed to the other records maintenance tasks that are usually delegated to clerical support personnel.

Records Retention

Deciding how long each record should be kept in the files is a decision based upon a survey of all existing records (mentioned earlier as a key factor in all records management programs). From such a survey of the records needs and uses of all departments—typically done using the questionnaire method of data collection—a **records retention schedule** is prepared. This is a document describing how long each key record is to be kept in the files.

The records retention schedule is based upon policies of the firm that relate to (1) microfilming papers, (2) transferring materials to inactive storage, (3) protecting the records, and (4) destroying the records. Such internal policies must also observe provisions of federal and state laws and regulations, including the statutes of limitations in the various states, regarding the retention of records.[6] Based on these recordkeeping requirements and the specific needs of the firm, most companies classify their records in four ways: *vital, important, useful,* or *unnecessary.* Records considered vital or important are retained indefinitely; those considered useful may be retained for several years; and unnecessary records are destroyed. Special care should be given to the retention of tax-related records that continue to play a highly important role in the administration of most offices. Figure 19–14 outlines the retention periods for common office records, as extracted from one firm's records retention schedule.

Protection of Vital Records

Historically, vital records were stored in steel file cabinets for protection from fire, theft, or some natural hazard. For additional protection, more expensive facilities, such as vaults and safes, were provided. With the increase in government regulations, as discussed in Chapter 6, we find it essential for a firm to provide additional types of protection to ensure the confidentiality of employee records. Records retention schedules also place additional responsibilities on the AOM or the records manager for protecting records.

When accurate operating information about a firm's customers, creditors, inventory, and employees is lost through theft or

some disaster, the business may be forced to close. To protect against such an occurrence, business executives insure their property, including business records, against risk of loss. However, information is a unique asset and difficult, if not impossible, to replace; and no insurance protection is available for the loss of information contained in records. Therefore, the following special measures are frequently provided to protect all vital records:

1. *Special fire-resistive housing* includes files, vaults, and safes both on and off the premises. Magnetic tape is highly flammable, requiring safes that keep interior temperatures below 150°F.
2. *Dispersion* entails transporting vital records to locations away from the business site. Small firms may combine their resources with those of other firms and establish cooperative storage centers or use commercial centers. Large firms can exchange records among their branch offices to ensure adequate protection.
3. *Duplication* pertains to reproducing vital documents so copies may be stored in locations away from the original records. Microforms and magnetic tape records are especially easy to reproduce.
4. *Standard fire discipline* permits no smoking around computer installations, keeps combustible materials cleared from storage areas, and ensures that vault doors are closed when not in use. In addition, adequate smoke alarms, proper sprinkler systems, and fire extinguishers should be installed.
5. *Restricting access to the files,* which includes maintaining close controls over keys that unlock file cabinets, using photographic identification cards or magnetically encoded cards or buttons (mounted on a panel near the door knob) that permit access through designated doors at stated times, providing internal alarm systems and motion detectors that spot movement in the files area during

---

[6]For the provisions of federal laws and regulations relating to the retention of records, see *Guide to Records Retention Requirements* (Washington: U. S. Government Printing Office, published annually) as well as records retention references prepared by the American Institute of Certified Public Accountants. State statutes on tax and payroll records vary widely. Thus, you should check with your local accountant or your state tax commissioner for specific details.

Figure 19-14
Portion of a
Records Re-
tention
Schedule

Record	Retain (Years)	Record	Retain (Years)
Accounts Payable Invoices	7	Production Records	1
Attendance Records	7	Purchase Orders	3 AE
Bank Statements	3	Sales Commission Reports	3
Check Registers	P	Sales Correspondence	7
Checks, Canceled	7	Stock Certificates, Canceled	7
Correspondence, General	2	Time Cards	7
Depreciation Schedules	P	Work Orders: Cost $1,000 or Less	3
Employee Withholding Statements	4	Work Orders: Cost More Than $1,000	6
Expense Reports (Employee)	7		
General Journal	P		
Income Statements	P		
Inventories	7	**Legend**	
Job Descriptions	3 or SUP		
Licenses (federal, state, etc.)	UT	AE: After Expiration	
Mailing Lists	SUP	OBS: Until Obsolete	
Office Equipment Records	6	P: Permanently	
Payroll Records	7	SUP: Until Superseded	
Price Lists	OBS	UT: Until Termination	

certain time periods, and employing around-the-clock guard service.

In addition, we must take certain steps to preserve automated records commonly used in the office:

1. Diskettes used in word processing and computer systems must be protected from improper handling and filing, especially from the danger of fingerprints, dust, and scratches.
2. Usually two magnetic tapes—the original and a copy—are required for control purposes. Both are filed manually by a control name or number. Accuracy of such records is provided in several ways: (a) by internal computer checks, (b) by means of carefully tested computer programs, and (c) by verifying the accuracy and completeness of the data before such data enter the computer system. Also, printouts of the contents of magnetic tapes or disks are used to check the accuracy of the stored records.
3. The availability of VDTs in each department makes it possible to access automated files, which presents a problem over which the records manager has little centralized control. Safeguards to protect automated records against unauthorized use include (a) **passwords** that employees must use to retrieve data; (b) **encryption systems** that scramble data in a predetermined manner at the sending point in order to protect confidential records (the data are decoded at the destination); and (c) **call-back systems**, which require that the computer verify that the person requesting data is authorized to use the system, after which the computer calls back such approval to the requesting party.

The major threat to the security of information in manual and automated systems is people. The computer virus, discussed in Chapter 16, is but one of many security problems caused primarily by people in the office system.

Records Disposition

The last phase in the records life cycle, **records disposition**, or *disposal*, involves two types of records: inactive records that may not be destroyed and are transferred to lower cost storage; and other records that are no longer needed and that must be destroyed. Procedures for the systematic transfer and destruction of records are discussed in this section.

Transferring Inactive Records

The decision to transfer records to inactive storage should involve records center personnel and the members of each department responsible for the records. Several transfer practices are available, depending upon the nature of the records operation.

Periodic Method. One transfer practice, called the *periodic method*, requires filed materials to be examined at fixed intervals of six months or one year. All materials considered inactive are placed in inexpensive record boxes and sent to inactive storage. However, periodic inspection is a laborious job and may interfere with more pressing work; for this reason, inspection may receive a low priority.

Duplicate Equipment Method. In the *duplicate equipment method*, last year's materials are kept in inactive file cabinets located next to the present active files. At the end of the year, the contents of last year's files are sent to inactive storage; and the present year's file becomes the "back" file. Although this method is fairly expensive in terms of equipment needed, it is very efficient.

Continuous Method. Under the *continuous* or *perpetual method*, records are transferred to inactive files as they reach a certain age or when it seems likely they will no longer be used. Such a method works well with client files in law offices, customer files in real estate offices, or job files in construction firm offices where the termination of a job usually means very infrequent, if any, reference to the files. For other types of offices, the continuous method may be considered rather inefficient.

Storing Inactive Records

In the small firm, transferred materials should be kept in that part of the general office area that is least used. (Examples are storerooms or unattractive, inaccessible portions of a main office.) Housing for inactive files should be of inexpensive but durable construction, usually fiberboard, and kept in an orderly manner so desired information may be located without too much delay.

In larger offices, a *records center* or *archives* is often set up for storing the inactive records of all departments. With these facilities available, records personnel periodically transfer the contents of the file cabinets to cardboard storage cases on steel racks that extend to the ceiling of the records center. With less-expensive storage containers arranged compactly, the costs are about one-fourth the price of active storage; and annual savings can be sizable.

Rather than set up their own archives, some firms prefer to use commercial records centers, which offer a wide range of services at a low per-record storage cost. In addition to providing centralized storage, commercial records centers offer specialized services such as regular records destruction, inventory control, reference activity reports, file purges, copying and microfilm services, and access to records by telephone. Experience shows that over 95 percent of all references to records in commercial centers are handled over the telephone.

Destroying Obsolete Records

Each year stored records that are no longer required should be destroyed. To avoid the destruction of useful records, department managers should be notified when materials are to be destroyed. An authorization form signed by the department manager should be used and retained in the records center (or in the files of the small office) as evidence of the final disposition of the records. Within the office, *paper shredders* are often used to destroy records containing confidential information. Documents may also be sent to local paper companies to be recycled if the information on the records is not confidential in nature.

ADMINISTRATION OF THE RECORDS MANAGEMENT PROGRAM

To achieve the objectives of a full-scale records management program as outlined in Figure 19-3, page 574, the required management functions must be planned and put into action. These functions are explained in this section.

Organization of the Records Management Program

Because records management is one of several information service functions in administration, we place records management on the organization chart alongside other related services. Figure 19-2, page 573, shows a typical setting for records management in the large organization. In such a setting, the director of administrative services, often a vice-president position, is responsible for such major information functions as data processing, administrative systems, records management, and office services. In such cases, the records manager is responsible for meeting the records management program objectives specified earlier as well as administering other technical services, such as microfilming, which is discussed in the next chapter. Also, such

a manager may coordinate forms management activities and word processing systems with the appropriate department managers.

In the small firm, this degree of specialization will not be found; but the same general administrative functions remain. For example, a human resources manager may be able to handle administrative services, such as systems analysis and data processing. In another firm, the office services manager may handle personnel selection, placement, training, and general office management functions including records and forms control, while the systems and data processing services may be the responsibility of another person. Most important is that related work be grouped together and assigned to those individuals who by aptitude, interest, and training are most highly qualified for such assignments.

An important part of the process of organizing a records management program is to provide competent personnel to staff the department. In turn, these personnel are responsible for achieving the objectives outlined in Figure 19-3.

Records Management Personnel

Because the records management program involves the entire organization, an executive familiar with the information needs of the total firm, its objectives, and its structure should be chosen as records manager. This position requires a generalist who can manage people and promote and coordinate the program among all units of the firm. Such a person should also be familiar with accounting, finance, and other business administration areas as well as be a specialist in information storage, retrieval, and files management. Although records managers need not be computer experts, they should understand the concepts and applications of computer, word processing, and telecommunication equipment, particularly as these machines involve the creation and distribution of records.

Two levels of records specialists typically report to the records manager, as we see in Figure 19-15. At the *supervisory level*, the records supervisor selects, trains, and evaluates the staff and advises departments on records policies and procedures. At the same level, microfilm and forms supervisors design and install new systems. At the *operating level*, records clerks assist in sorting, storing, retrieving, and performing other operating duties. Larger firms also employ clerks with special assignments in the microfilming of records; forms and records analysts also assist in the design of new records. In more highly automated systems, such positions as documentation clerk, tape librarian, and program record clerk may be found.

Records Space and Equipment

Today's records operations require far more than smooth-gliding file drawers and neat-appearing file rooms. First of all, the great expense of office space requires that special space-conservation measures be taken to get the most productivity at the least cost. Both people and equipment must be spatially arranged in a manner that promotes an efficient work flow and an attractively designed work area using the principles discussed in Chapter 13. This means providing well-lighted, air-conditioned areas that are convenient to users and which save filing and retrieving time. Confidential materials should be kept away from the general public, and access should be denied to unauthorized personnel. A discussion of the equipment responsibilities of the records manager is found in an earlier section of this chapter.

Operation of the Records Management Program

As we have seen, a variety of operating responsibilities is found in the records management program. Two of these responsibilities are considered basic: (1) the responsibility for developing efficient procedures for performing the work, and (2) the responsibility for identifying and controlling costs. Each is discussed briefly in this section.

Developing Efficient Procedures

In cooperation with supervisory personnel, the records manager must develop efficient procedures for operating the program. To do so requires making decisions on:

1. The specific responsibilities of the program.
2. The assignment of duties to each member of the records management staff.
3. The necessary priorities that must be established for the completion of the work.
4. Instructions on how to accomplish the assigned work.
5. Deadlines for the completion of the work.
6. Methods for evaluating the work and the personnel in the program.

For example, operating procedures must be developed for indexing, storing, and filing correspondence; for retrieving and controlling outgoing records; for designing and purchasing forms, equipment, and supplies; and for hiring, training, and appraising employees. In the development of these procedures, both operating efficiency and

Figure 19-15
Position
Levels and
Titles in
Records
Management

Position Level	Position Title
Managerial	Records Manager or Records Administrator
Supervisory	Records Supervisor Micrographics Supervisor Forms Supervisor
Operating	Records Clerk Micrographics Clerk Forms Analyst Records Analyst Documentation Clerk

cost consciousness must be given major consideration.

Controlling Records Costs

In manufacturing operations, cost accounting has long been used to determine the cost of each work unit produced. In the office, on the other hand, little attempt has been made to identify and control paperwork costs. However, with costs continually rising and with administrative work taking more and more of the profit dollar, AOMs are stepping up their efforts to isolate and control records costs. Figure 19–16 identifies the specific records costs in administrative work that must be controlled.

Calculating precisely the cost of records management becomes a complicated task because of the variety of factors, such as salaries and office rent, that affect cost. However, certain basic cost elements can be determined. For example, records management studies show that, on the average, each file clerk is responsible for 12 four-drawer file cabinets; and for every ten file clerks there is one supervisor. A file clerk is paid

$13,500 a year, on the average, and a supervisor, $17,000. The purchase price of each four-drawer file cabinet is $360. Using these figures and other costs obtained from records system studies, the approximate annual cost of maintaining one four-drawer file cabinet may be estimated as follows:[7]

File clerk's salary	$1,125
Employee benefits (37%)	416
Overhead (Supervisor's salary)	142
Cost of cabinet, recovered over ten-year period (ignoring trade-in value)	36
Floor space, 6+ square feet, @ $30 per square foot	180
Supplies (per cabinet and transfer supplies)	176
Total yearly cost of maintaining one four-drawer file cabinet	$2,075

---

[7]The basis for this computation is the article by Joseph E. Casurella, "CAR Versus Paper Files: Hard Facts about Software Driven Systems," *IMC Journal* (January/February, 1988), p. 14, which was amended and updated by other paperwork management cost studies.

Figure 19–16
Records Costs in Administrative Operations

Cost Factors	Specific Records Costs	Percent of Total Records Cost
1. Personnel	Clerical and supervisory salaries Employee benefits	70–80
2. Supplies	Forms and stationery Folders, cartons, and labels Printing Postage	10–15
3. Space for active and inactive records	Owned space Rented or leased space Taxes Utility expenses (telephone, light and heat) Janitor service	5–10
4. Furniture and equipment	Cost recovery of assets Rental and lease charges Maintenance expenses	3–7

Personnel Costs. While each of the other cost factors offers good opportunities for saving paperwork dollars, the records manager must give primary attention to reducing the costs of personnel, which typically represent from 70 to 80 percent of total records costs. Salaries, for example, may be controlled through better selection and training of workers and through improved work methods and performance standards for the processing, storage, and retrieval of records. In addition, the records manager must regularly stress the important effect that better use of staff time, equipment, and supplies has on profit.

The Cost of Supplies. The principal records supplies needed in the office are stationery, forms, filing materials, printing, and postage; among these supplies, forms usually generate the greatest costs. While the axiom, "Paper is cheap," may be relatively true, the functional costs of filling in, using, distributing, and filing forms are extremely expensive since they require the use of human effort. Many systems experts estimate that functional costs range from 25 to 50 times higher than the physical costs of the paper and print used for the form. For this reason, records management programs set up functional files in which all forms having identical or similar functions (recording, listing, ordering, and requesting) are grouped together. With such forms groupings, it becomes easier to spot duplicate forms and opportunities to eliminate, consolidate, or standardize forms.

The following suggestions for reducing the cost of supplies should be considered:

1. *Provide close supervision of department copiers* to reduce the number of unauthorized forms.
2. *Establish standard procedures for all phases of the forms management program* so clear guidelines about the physical costs of paper and ink used in printing the form

and the more important functional costs involved with the form's use are brought under control.

3. *Take advantage of the savings resulting from large-quantity purchases of forms.* Usually such quantities can be developed through grouping forms by categories, such as unit-set forms and continuous forms.
4. *Print all flat forms internally on a firm's own duplicating and word processing equipment.* For runs of less than 10,000, internal printing is more economical than using the services of an outside printer.
5. *Use white paper wherever possible rather than the more expensive colored paper.* The destination of each copy of the form can be printed at the bottom of the form to facilitate its distribution.
6. *Reduce in number the different paper items (forms, letterhead sheets, and envelope sizes and types) to the minimum actually required.* This practice in turn simplifies quantity buying, warehousing problems, and inventory control.
7. *Design forms so printing costs can be controlled.* For example, by avoiding the use of a department name, employee name, or similar information, the form does not become obsolete so quickly nor is its use restricted to a specific department or office. The number of copies of a form should be reduced to the minimum required, as extra copies add to the cost of printing, stocking, filing, and distribution.
8. *Consider postage costs when specifying the weight of forms and stationery.* Through the course of a year, the use of 20 lb. rather than 36 lb. paper stock will result in considerably lower postage costs.
9. *Reuse as many of the stationery and forms supplies as possible,* and wherever possible use the less expensive recycled paper for internal forms. If possible, use the reverse side of an incoming letter for the reply, which saves the cost of second

sheets and reduces the number of items to be filed.

Suggestions for reducing many of the other administrative costs in the records management program are discussed in the next section.

Other Costs of Administering the Records Management Program. In addition to the cost-reduction suggestions already discussed, the following suggestions should help the AOM increase efficiency and reduce costs in administering the records management program:

1. *Centralize those files used by all departments.* In the data processing departments of many firms, a data bank under the control of the computer serves this centralized file function.
2. *Provide an efficient layout for the records center that will speed up the flow of records to and from the files.*
3. *Purchase durable equipment and supplies that speed up the completion of the work.* It is estimated that the typical file drawer is opened and closed 100,000 times during its useful life. Thus, cheap cabinets would be wasteful under such heavy usage. Poor-quality supplies, too, interfere with efficient filing because they must be replaced constantly. Special equipment, such as map files and blueprint files, should be procured for records that do not fit into regular letter-size or legal-size file drawers.
4. *Develop efficient operating procedures,* such as regular schedules for the collection and distribution of materials to be filed or to be delivered from the files. Also, efficient methods for transferring inactive records to the archives should be used.
5. *Consider the microfilming of records* in lieu of storing records in transfer cases, as discussed in Chapter 20.
6. *Carefully check the volume and quality of work that should be done in the records*

center. During rush periods, workers from the mail department may be added to the regular records center staff.

7. *Obtain the expert services of specialists in records management.* Representatives of filing equipment and supplies manufacturers can help in the selection and installation of equipment and often in the analysis of files. Records analysts working as independent consultants are also available for this purpose.
8. *Develop a records management manual that contains all program policies and operating procedures.* Such a manual helps to fix responsibilities for carrying out all phases of the program and assists in the training of employees and in the systematizing of records control practices throughout the company. The small office may incorporate these control techniques in an operations notebook for use by the files personnel and the AOM.

Evaluation of the Records Management Program

How well is the program meeting its objectives? is the question we should ask the administrator of any business function, including the records manager. Although the question is simple, the evaluation of records management programs is complex because of the company-wide scope of such programs. Evaluation involves assessing the performance of personnel (which was included in an earlier discussion) and, as explained in this section, the efficiency of the files, filing procedures, and filing equipment to be sure each is functioning properly in the system.

One rule of thumb recommends that an evaluation or audit be conducted at least every two years to answer the types of questions shown in Figure 19–17. As soon as weaknesses in the records management program have been identified by the audit,

Figure 19-17
A Records
Audit
Checklist

Audit Factor	Specific Questions
1. Scope of the records management program	a. How is the program organized? b. How many files are in use?
2. Type of filing system and retrieval methods	a. What filing systems are used? b. What types of controls are used (charge-outs, cross-references, etc.)? c. How are records retrieved and what is the average wait-time for retrieval?
3. Records personnel	a. Who does the filing and finding? b. How are records clerks supervised? c. What kind of performance standards are in effect?
4. Records users	a. Who uses the files? b. What access do users have to the files?
5. Records control procedures	a. Are filing policies and procedures set up? b. Is a records manual available and in use? c. Are records retention and disposition programs in effect? d. How are private, confidential, and department files protected? e. What special provisions are in effect for protecting automated records?

corrective measures, such as improved records controls, can be instituted.

Using Efficiency Ratios

Through the years, records managers have created guidelines for evaluating the efficiency of the records program. Expressed as **efficiency ratios**, the most useful of these guidelines are:

1. The **files activity ratio**:

$$\frac{\text{number of files requested}}{\text{number of records filed}}$$

To illustrate, a records management audit shows 600 documents requested out of a total file of 12,000. The files activity ratio is .05, or 5 percent. A reference ratio of 5 percent or less is normally considered low and points to the need for transferring records from active storage to archives or possibly even destroying them. On the other hand, if the ratio is 20 percent or greater, the files are considered active and should be retained.

2. The **files accuracy ratio**:

$$\frac{\text{number of records found}}{\text{number of records requested}}$$

For example, 9,250 records out of a possible 9,500 requested are located. This means that there is 97.37 percent accuracy for the filing system and that the files are in excellent operating condition. If this ratio falls below 97 percent, the files should be studied carefully, especially for these problems: (1) too many private files (as in executives' desks), (2) improper indexing and coding, (3) poor charge-out procedures, and (4) insufficient cross-indexing and cross-referencing.

3. The **retrieval efficiency ratio:**

$$\frac{\text{time (in seconds) to locate records}}{\text{number of records requested}}$$

The retrieval efficiency ratio measures the speed with which records are found and verifies how files personnel spend their time. A ratio of .75 (retrieving 80 records in 60 seconds) suggests an efficient records system and a productive files operator. Files efficiency standards are typically developed in a firm's work measurement program, as discussed later in the textbook, and should be included in the records manual.

With these common measures of efficiency as evaluation tools, we can obtain objective data on the operating effectiveness of the records program. Such data can then be used for further improvement of the total records management program.

Evaluating Filing Equipment

Because records personnel depend heavily upon tools and equipment in the performance of their work, an objective appraisal of such equipment should be made as one measure of the efficiency of the filing system. In such a study, all of the following components of the filing system that interact with the equipment should be included:

1. *The time required to use the equipment,* including the relative merits of using such equipment as open-shelf versus drawer file cabinets.
2. *The methods used by the workers,* such as whether the use of certain equipment decreases the transportation time of records.
3. *The flexibility of the equipment to meet changing needs.*
4. *The reliability of the equipment to function* and *the availability of service* to ensure minimal machine downtime.
5. *The costs of purchasing and operating the equipment.*
6. *The materials,* such as guides and folders, *required in using the equipment.*
7. *Miscellaneous factors,* such as the training required of personnel to use the equipment, and the space required to use it.

SUMMARY
1. To control the growing number of records, many of which are office forms, companies have developed records management programs. In large firms, these programs are a part of the administrative services functions; in small firms, records management is an added responsibility of the AOM.
2. Records management programs cover the life cycle of a record: (a) the creation phase, which seeks to prevent the origination of unneeded records but which requires the effective design of all forms initiated; (b) the storage phase, which includes the supervision of all filing procedures, equipment, and supplies; (c) the retrieval phase, which aims for speedy access to paper as well as to automated records; (d) the maintenance phase, which covers a survey of all records, the development of a schedule for retaining such records, and provision for adequate

protection of the records; and (e) the disposition phase, which is concerned with transferring and storing inactive records and destroying unneeded records.

3. Records management programs must be properly organized and operated. During such operations, evaluation of the program is carried out using special techniques, such as the records audit, efficiency ratios, and appraisals of the effectiveness of personnel and the filing equipment.

GLOSSARY

Bond paper—a type of paper used for letterheads, office forms, and certificates where fine appearance and durability are essential.

Call-back system—a records protection measure in which the computer verifies that the party requesting a record is authorized to use it.

Carbonless form—a form in which impressions from one copy to another are made without the use of carbon paper; also called *NCR paper.*

Centralized filing—an organizational plan in which records of general value throughout the firm are stored in one location and controlled by one centralized records department.

Commercial writing class—a group of writing papers commonly used in ordinary business transactions and for advertising purposes.

Continuous forms—a series of connected forms folded in a prearranged manner and perforated for easy separation of each form; also known as *fanfold forms.*

Copy paper—a lightweight writing paper used for making carbon copies; an example is onionskin.

Data hierarchy—a five-level organization structure of information that ranges from the most basic level—the character—to the broadest level—the database or library; also known as the *file structure* or *file organization.*

Decentralized filing—an organizational plan in which each office division maintains its own filing system.

Efficiency ratios—the guidelines used by records managers to evaluate the effectiveness of their records programs.

Encryption system—a computer system safeguard that scrambles data in a predetermined manner at the sending point in order to protect confidential records.

Files accuracy ratio—a measure used to evaluate a records system in which the number of records found is compared with the number of records requested.

Files activity ratio—a measure used to evaluate a records system in which the number of records requested is compared with the number of records filed.

Filing system—the procedures and methods used to classify, sort, and store records for fast retrieval.

Flat form—a single sheet of paper often used as a single-copy record.

Form—a specially designed record having constant information preprinted on it with space provided for the entry of variable information.

Horizontal file—equipment for storing papers or records, such as maps and drawings, in a flat position.

Index paper—a heavy, durable paper used for machine posting of manual records, punched cards, index files, and library files.

Lateral file—a vertical file in which the long side of the cabinet opens out; also called *side file*.

Ledger paper—a type of paper that has a good writing surface for use with pencil or ink and that will withstand heavy use because of its card-like strength.

Magnetic Ink Character Recognition (MICR)—a system used by banks to interpret and process numeric data recorded in special magnetic ink characters on business forms.

Mobile file—equipment in which files move on a track in order that the shelves can be moved together when not in use, or on motorized Ferris-wheel type arrangements in which the records are brought directly to an operator seated at a console.

Network filing—an organizational plan in which records are retained in each department but controlled centrally.

Optical Character Recognition (OCR)—a scanning system used for reading numeric and alphabetic data that have been printed in a distinctive type style on business forms.

Password—a code used to protect records and retrieve data in an automated records system.

Record—written or oral evidence that information has been collected and kept for use in making decisions.

Records disposition—a phase of a records management program that is responsible for transferring and storing inactive records and for destroying unneeded records.

Records life cycle—the steps or sequential phases in the life of records that include creation, storage, retrieval, maintenance, and disposition.

Records maintenance—a set of service activities in a records management program needed to operate the storage and retrieval systems.

Records management—an organization-wide administrative service responsible for creating and maintaining systematic procedures and controls over all phases of the records life cycle.

Records retention schedule—a document describing how long each key record is to be kept in the files.

Records retrieval—the process of locating stored information.

Recycled paper—the waste paper that is reduced to a pulp state by paper manufacturers before new fibers are added for the production of economical second-use papers.

Retrieval efficiency ratio—a measure used to evaluate a records system in which the time (in seconds) to locate a record is compared with the number of records requested.

Rotary file—equipment for storing records in which the records rotate in a circular fashion around a common hub.

Smart form—an automated form that is created with a special set of forms design and fill-in instructions stored in a file in a host computer.

Soft-copy form—a VDT-designed form that appears on the terminal screen for the entry of data into the computer system.

Specialty form—a form that requires special equipment for its manufacture or use. Types of specialty forms include carbon-less forms, continuous forms, unit-set forms, and a wide variety of miscellaneous forms requiring special printing processes.

Spot-carbon form—a form on which a carbon coating has been applied only to certain areas in order to convey or withhold information from employees as the needs of the information system dictate.

Unit-set form—a preassembled form with carbonless paper or one-time carbon paper interleaved between the perforated sheets.

Vertical file—a filing cabinet that contains one to six drawers in which records are stored on edge.

Visible card file—equipment for storing records that permits complete visibility of key reference data.

FOR YOUR REVIEW

1. a. What reasons may be given for the constantly increasing number of records that are produced in the office?
   b. In what form would you expect to find most of the records in the offices in your community?

2. Define *record* and *form* and show how the two terms are related.

3. a. What is the data hierarchy?
   b. Of what value to the records manager is an understanding of this concept?

4. List the most common types of forms used in manual systems and in automated systems.

5. Identify the four principles of forms management with which the records manager should be familiar.

6. What is meant by *standardization* as it is used in forms management?

7. Describe briefly the main types of paper that make up the commercial writing class.

8. What characteristics should be present in order to label a form "well designed"?

9. Explain how the design of forms may be automated.

10. a. Identify the most common types of filing systems.
    b. When is each most likely to be used?

11. Compare the advantages and disadvantages of decentralized filing, centralized filing, and network filing.

12. What advantages do open-shelf files offer over vertical file cabinets?

13. a. What types of files make up the mobile files category?
    b. Explain how each type of mobile file functions.

14. How does the manual retrieval of records differ from the automated retrieval of records?

15. What is the purpose of a records retention schedule?

16. Besides storing records in fire-resistive files, what other methods are available for protecting records?

17. Distinguish between the periodic and the continuous methods of records transfer.

18. a. Describe the organizational setting for records management in a large firm.
    b. How does this setting differ in a small firm?

19. a. Define the various levels and types of positions typically found in a records management program.
    b. What competencies are usually required of the records manager?

20. List the main records costs in administrative operations, from the highest to the lowest percent of total records cost.

21. In what ways is the cost-effective records manager able to cut the costs of operating the records management program?

22. What evaluation measures are used to assess the efficiency of records management programs?

FOR YOUR DISCUSSION

1. At a recent conference you heard the keynote speaker discuss the "hidden" costs of operating an office. As a result of these comments, you have considered the "above-board" and the hidden costs involved in the use of forms. List examples of both types of costs, and discuss ways of eliminating or controlling such costs.

2. The records manager asks you, an administrative assistant, to prepare a "model" of an efficiently designed form. Discuss what features such a model should possess.

3. As the office manager of Campus Copiers, a copy-making service located across the street from your school's campus, you must frequently hire part-time workers to handle copying, assembling, binding, and other related tasks. Usually such workers are students. To collect job-application information, you need a simple form that will be used in making hiring decisions. The form will be filled in either on the office typewriter or by hand. Your assistant suggests the following information arranged in a 6" × 4" format. Evaluate the proposed design.

Figure A
Proposed
Applicant
Information
Form

6"

4"

Name _____   Days available _____

Address_____   Hours available _____

Telephone number _____   Hours desired _____

Additional information:

4. The three efficiency ratios (file activity, file accuracy, and retrieval efficiency) appeal to you as simple, useful techniques for evaluating your filing system. What organizing and operating procedures must be set up in order to use these ratios in your records center?

5. To most department managers in your firm, records management sounds like a fancy name for filing. Yet you know from your experience as an office supervisor that this area of work is much more comprehensive in scope. What steps could you take to change this stereotype of records management in order that a management orientation to the subject might be developed in your firm?

6. In a large hospital, Harry Wong, the hospital administrator, is searching for better methods of handling the expanding volume of records. Reporting to the hospital administrator is the director of the medical records department, who supervises 40 word processing personnel, file clerks, and general office workers. The director has compiled the following list of urgent problems and discussed the priorities for solving these problems with Wong:
   a. On the average, 600 X rays are developed and processed daily (none of which is destroyed).
   b. Records for 300 outpatients and 2,500 inpatients must be handled daily, with Medicare forms adding to the problem by 15 percent each year.
   c. Approximately 15,400 health insurance forms were processed during the past 6 months.
   d. No central depository of records is available.
   e. Physicians are growing more impatient with the slow retrieval of medical records from the files but are resisting the use of microfilmed records.

   Assuming the accuracy of these facts and the existence of other equally pressing problems, you, as assistant to the director, are asked to recommend to Wong a comprehensive plan for improving the records management practices of the hospital, including records retention and protection programs. The plan must first be discussed with the director before it is forwarded to the office of the hospital administrator.

7. You have been assigned responsibility for helping to design an invoice form from the draft shown in Figure B on page 609. This draft was prepared in handwritten form by the user department, Accounts Receivable, in Integrated Paper Products, located in your city. The actual size of the form is 7½" by 9". Evaluate the design of this form using the principles of forms design presented in this chapter.

SOLVING CASE PROBLEMS

Case 19-1 Building an Understanding of Systems Thinking in Records Personnel

Early in your administrative office management class, your instructor emphasized the importance of systems thinking. At the same time your class was assigned the responsibility of visiting, in small groups, records centers in medium-size and large offices in your city. Each of the eight groups was to visit one office, observe the procedures in use, and report their findings to the class.

When the groups reported to the class, these general conclusions were drawn:

Figure B
Draft of
Invoice
Form

7½″

INTEGRATED PAPER PRODUCTS   PAGE #_____

                                             DATE_____

SHIP TO _____   REMIT TO _____
        _____   _____
        _____   _____

9″

CUSTOMER NAME _____   INVOICE #_____
SALES PERSON'S NAME _____   CUSTOMER #_____
SALESPERSON NUMBER _____   SHIP VIA _____
TERMS_____

| STOCK# | QTY. | DESCRIPTION | PRICE | AMOUNT |

TYPICAL ORDERS   AVERAGE 5 ITEMS SOLD

SAMPLE ENTRY:
| 0024615 | 0060 | WHITE 20# SULPHITE BOND | 5.75 | 345.50 |

                                     AMT. DUE _____
                                     AMT. REMITTED _____
                                     BALANCE DUE _____

1. All the records personnel were friendly and answered all questions asked. In all cases reported, such persons seemed to be most concerned about the neatness of their files and their work areas and having all their filing work "caught up."

2. These personnel seemed to work in their "own little worlds," in that filers only placed records into, and took records out of the files; coding clerks only coded records; and supervisors seemed to oversee their workers from a "safe" distance.

3. Generally each records supervisor appointed a liaison person in each department to coordinate their records work with the records center. As a rule, little personal communication existed with these liaison persons; they seemed "to do their own thing" within their departments.

4. Computers were used throughout the firms, but only paper records—including hard copies of computer records—were responsibilities of the records supervisors. Several supervisors

mentioned that "one of these days we'll have to think about automated records systems." The average tenure on the jobs was 17 years.

On the basis of class discussion, your instructor assigns a report in which you are to do the following:

1. Develop a systems chart for a records center using as your references Figures 4–2, 4–3, and 4–5, pages 93, 95, and 97, respectively, in the textbook.

2. Recommend ways of building an understanding of systems concepts in the records personnel, specifically addressing the conclusions noted above.

3. Discuss what objections records personnel would likely have to your recommendations, and suggest how these objections could be overcome.

Case 19–2 Designing a Soft-Copy Form for a VDT

To meet increasing competition, Osaka Hardware, Ltd., has created a bold new policy: it will accept all orders from customers for one-day delivery by overnight courier. Orders will be taken over the telephone or by facsimile by a staff of VDT operators, who will then key the information into the VDT. The computer will then assist in filling the orders and automatically create an invoice for each customer.

First, however, a soft-copy order-taking form must be designed for use on the VDT. As an office intern for Osaka, you are asked to draft a design for such a form—one that can be approved and given to the programming staff for final design and execution.

To complete your assignment, you are given the following specific directions:

1. Consider the items on the invoice form in Figure B, page 609, as typical information needed for the soft-copy form to be designed. Assume you are limited to 60 horizontal spaces on any one line for filling in the form. Some abbreviations may be required in the entry of data.

2. Provide reasonable-size data fields of information for this form in line with a study of the records system, which shows:
   a. The maximum size of the customer name field is 40 spaces.
   b. Total address (street, city, state, and ZIP Code) can be accommodated on three 60-space lines.
   c. Customer numbers are made up of 7 digits.
   d. The maximum size of Osaka invoice numbers is 7 digits; unit (style) numbers, 7 digits; quantities ordered, 3 digits; description, 34 characters; and unit prices, 4 whole-number digits plus 2 decimal digits.
   e. No order in the past has involved more than 10 items.
   f. All sales are based on catalog information; thus, there is no salesperson information to be recorded.

Using the systems information cited above, prepare a design for a soft-copy form that can be used on the VDT for taking orders. The examples in Figures 19-9B and 19-10 should assist in completing this assignment.

20

Microimage and Reprographic Systems

GOALS FOR THIS CHAPTER

After completing this chapter, you should be able to:

1. Identify the various types of microrecords and the principal uses of each.
2. List the criteria for deciding when to use microrecords.
3. Discuss the various stages involved in managing microimage systems.
4. Explain the role of the computer in automating microimage systems and the increasing use of optical disks as an alternative to microfilmed records.
5. Point out the differences between duplicating and copying processes, and explain the principal benefits to be gained from using the copying process.
6. Discuss the main components of a program for managing reprographic systems.

In all the offices we've worked in or visited from time to time, records have been *the* common method for storing and using information. While most of these records are paper documents, we expect nonpaper records to increase dramatically in the future. With the aid of an expanding information technology, we find more and more paper records being microfilmed; and huge numbers of records are being copied or reproduced in other ways. Both of these technological systems—records stored as very small (micro) images on film, and reprographics, which relates to the reproduction of records—are discussed in this chapter.

MICROIMAGE TECHNOLOGY

Business records have been photographed and reduced in size on microfilm for more than half a century. During this time, the microimages of records have generally been called *microfilm* and the process for converting paper records to reduced size, *microfilming*. Thus, the process of microfilming results in the creation of a **microrecord**, the name for a paper document that has been converted to microfilm. (*Note, however, that it is still a common business practice to consider microfilm as the generic classification for all types of microrecords stored on film.*)

Later, to reflect the expansion of services available in the microfilm field as well as the integration of microfilm with other technologies, the term *micrographics* was created. Most recently, to reflect a growing emphasis on the form and size of the record, the total system for creating, using, and storing microrecords has been called a **microimage system**, an important subsystem in the total information system. Along with this changing emphasis, a leading professional association in this field—the National Micrographics Association—changed its name to the Association for Information and Image Management (AIIM).[1] Figure 20–1 outlines in greater detail the full set of procedural steps involved in creating, using, and storing a microrecord.

This chapter presents for you, the student of administrative office management, as well as for AOMs and their staffs, a nontechnical discussion of the technology involved in the highly technical microimage field. As such, the discussion emphasizes in layperson language two key, basic aspects of a microimage system: (1) the storage, retrieval, and use of the most common types of microrecords (steps 6–9 in Figure 20–1), and (2) the management of microrecords in manual and automated systems. The remaining aspects of microimage systems (steps 1–5 in Figure 20–1) are more highly specialized and require the attention of personnel with technical training in the field.

Types of Microforms

Although all microrecords are photographed onto film, many different types of microforms are available. Usually microrecords are divided into two broad classes: unitized and nonunitized. The **unitized microform** is prepared as one complete set or unit of data, such as a payroll file, and does not include any unrelated material. The **nonunitized microform**, on the other hand, frequently contains random or unrelated items of information from many departments of a firm on the same continuous length of film. This type of microform is illustrated by microfiche, aperture cards, and filmstrip in jackets. The largest users of microrecords are the federal, state, and local governments in the public sector and utilities, insurance firms, and financial institutions in the private sector.

---

[1]This leading professional association fosters more effective use of microimage technology through a comprehensive educational program that includes seminars, conferences, and practical publications. AIIM is located at 1100 Wayne Avenue, Silver Spring, MD 20910.

Because of its simplicity and widespread usage, roll film—the principal nonunitized microform—is discussed first. The microforms commonly included in the unitized category (microfiche, aperture cards, and microfilm strips inserted into plastic jackets) are described later in this section.

Roll Film

Roll film is a continuous length of microfilm 16mm, 35mm, or 105mm in width and 100 feet in length on which original documents are photographed and reduced in size for storage. Note the drawings of the three sizes of roll film inserted in this paragraph.

16mm Roll Film

35mm Roll Film

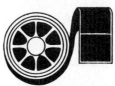
105mm Roll Film

It is the most frequently used—and usually is considered the most economical type of microrecord. The width of film selected depends on the size of the original material to be photographed, the desired reduction ratio for the microimage, and the intended use of the microrecords. The **reduction ratio** expresses the number of times the size of a record is reduced photographically. For example, a page from this book measures 7¾″ × 9½″. If a typical reduction is used, the book is reduced at the ratio of 24 to 1 (expressed as 24×). This means that the microimage is 1/24th the width of the original page, or about .32 inches wide and would look similar to this drawing:

Figure 20-1
Procedural
Steps in
Operating a
Microimage
System

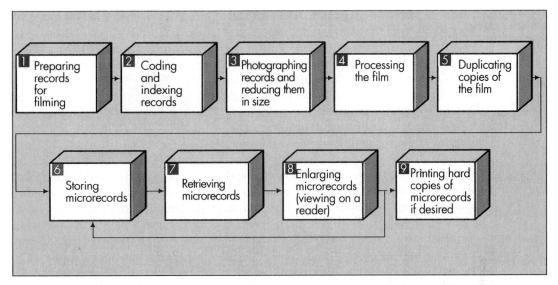

Thus, a 16mm roll of film that is 100 feet in length would hold more than 4,000 textbook pages.

Administrative office managers use roll film for filing large volumes of records stored in sequence, such as employee time sheets, correspondence, checks, and sales records in a very small space at a very low cost. Generally 16mm film is used for storing alphabetic and numeric data, such as correspondence, checks, and invoices. The wider 35mm film (and less frequently, 105mm film) is used for storing microimages of larger documents, such as X rays, newspapers, and maps. Microrecords produced by the computer output microfilm process discussed later are stored on 105mm film.

When the film is in negative form, we can use it to reproduce a positive film roll. The negative may then be sent out to an off-site facility for vital records protection. Unlike other types of microforms, roll film makes browsing and updating difficult. To add related documents requires splicing, which is a slow and costly process.

Storage of Roll Film. Roll film is easily stored on reels, similar to the storage of movie films or the magnetic tapes used in computer systems. Other methods of packaging roll film are cartridges and cassettes, which ease the handling of microfilm rolls. In these containers, the film is protected from fingerprint smudges and other possible damage. The use of a cassette also eliminates the need for rewinding since each cassette provides both "advance" and "reverse" features. Similarly, cartridges are self-threading.

Retrieval of Roll Film. Microrecords are indexed and coded so that they may be quickly retrieved. Before being photographed, the paper records are sorted in the same order as for paper-based files. Later as the sorted records are photographed, code marks are recorded on the film adjacent to each microimage or frame. One common coding system uses a type of identifier or "flash" (similar to a flash card) between regular sections of the filmed material (usually every 20 feet of film) to assist the user in determining the section of the film being scanned. Sequential numbers may also be placed on the film to identify each frame.

Once the documents have been coded and photographed, an index of the coded frames is created manually to assist in their retrieval. This index contains information about the microrecord file, such as the subject or invoice number of each stored document, the roll film number, and the code number of each frame. The original documents may then be retained or discarded.

To retrieve a record from a roll film file, the user consults the index to determine the appropriate reel of tape, cassette, or cartridge. This container is then located and placed in a **reader**, a device that enlarges or magnifies the microrecord to its original legible size and projects the image onto a viewing screen. (See Figure 20-2.) Generally microrecords are stored sequentially along the length of the film, like magnetic tape recordings, so that the user can advance a film or move it backward as the retrieval needs require. With motorized units, the user obtains the index location of the desired microrecord from a separate index. This information is then entered into the keyboard of the unit, which searches for and locates the desired record.

Microfiche

Microfiche (pronounced "mĭcrofēsh") means small index card and refers to a microform that appears in a grid pattern on a transparent sheet of film. (See the drawing shown below.) The most common

size of microfiche is 6″ × 4″ (or 108mm by 105mm). Because of their light weight, eight 6″ × 4″ microfiche can be sent by first-class mail at the one-ounce rate.

A special type of microfiche, **ultrafiche**, permits very high (ultra) reduction ratios, commonly from 150 to 400×, and sometimes as great as 2400×. (In one notable example of an ultrafiche record, the entire contents of the King James Bible—approximately 800,000 words stored on almost 800 pages— were microfilmed onto a fiche measuring less than two inches square.) Banks use ultrafiche to record customer transactions. Other large organizations, such as General Motors Corporation and Sears, Roebuck and Company, use ultrafiche for storing catalog and parts data. Copies of fiche records may be duplicated easily and inexpensively for mailing throughout the world. Updating is accomplished in two ways: (1) by replacing an obsolete fiche with a current one, or (2) by using **updatable microfiche** in which a

Figure 20-2
Microrecord
Readers

A—Desk-Top Reader

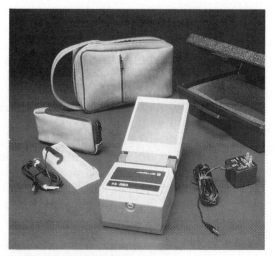

B—Hand-Held Reader

special camera erases an obsolete record and places a new image over the erased record. Another version of updatable microfiche affixes the word "Void" or "Superseded" over an obsolete microrecord and adds a current or updated record to the same microfiche.

Storage of Microfiche. A microfiche record is as easy to store as any other 6″ × 4″ card and hence makes use of standard vertical card filing equipment. As the microfiche drawing shows, the format of the microfiche permits the placement of an eye-readable index along the top margin of the record. Since microfiche has become increasingly popular for storing active records, we find that such records are stored in a convenient location near their point of use. A typical means of housing small numbers of microfiche is a desktop tray (shown in Figure 20–3A) or a looseleaf ring binder. Larger numbers of microfiche are stored in cabinets, shown in Figure 20–3B.

Retrieval of Microfiche. Microfiche records that are stored in small quantities at or near the workstation are retrieved like regular file cards. The user manually scans

the top margin of each fiche, which bears the indexed information by which the record is stored. As soon as we locate the desired fiche, we can physically remove it from the file and place it in a reader in order to locate the appropriate frame for viewing.

When large files of microfiche are maintained, automated storage and retrieval systems are used. One microfiche storage and retrieval system uses up to 100 positions of code along the top edge of the fiche for storage in standard or electromechanical files. When the proper cartridge of fiche is selected after consulting a separate file index, the cartridge is placed in an automatic desk retrieval unit. This unit locates the desired fiche, extracts it from the cartridge, and presents it to the operator for manual insertion in a reader. A more advanced system uses codes in the form of notches that are punched in the top or bottom edges of the fiche. When the operator presses the appropriate buttons or turns the correct dials on the retrieval unit, the unit searches the fiche file for the notch codes that refer to the page and frame numbers of the desired fiche. As soon as the requested frame is located, its image is displayed on the reader screen. The most

Figure 20–3
Equipment
for Storing
Microfiche
Records

A—Microfiche Tray

B—Microfiche Cabinet

automated systems for retrieving microfiche operate under the direction of a computer, a topic that is discussed later in this chapter.

Aperture Cards

The **punched aperture card** shown at the 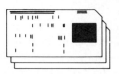 left is a standard-size 80-column punched card with a precut hole over which a portion of 35mm microfilm is mounted. Aperture cards have traditionally used punched-card codes for storage and retrieval. Recently, a **data aperture card** has been introduced with the identical dimensions and weight to the punched aperture cards. The principal difference between the two is that the data aperture card uses one or more lines of computer-readable OCR indexing text at the top of the card for retrieval and display on the VDT screen rather than the human-readable printing and the punched-card codes appearing on the earlier aperture microform.[2] However, the punched aperture card still represents the best, smallest, handiest, and most economic storage medium for blueprints, other technical drawings, and charts. Also, since these records are likely to be used and updated frequently, they are readily accessible as "individual" copies as a unitized record. One card may contain a single microrecord or up to eight images on a single 35mm frame. Besides its space-saving qualities, the punched aperture card has the advantage of permitting the keypunching of information into the card, which aids in the speedy storage and retrieval of the microrecord. Typically, the punched aperture card bears identifying information that is printed in the upper margin as well as punched in the body of the card. It is this information that determines the location of the card in the file.

[2]An interview with Ulrich Welp by Heinz Müller-Saala, as reported in "Advantages of Data Aperture Cards over Punched Aperture Cards," *IMC Journal* (March/April, 1987), pp. 17–19.

Storage of Aperture Cards. Trays and boxes designed for desk-top locations are available to store small quantities of cards. If large quantities of cards are required and retrieval time is critical, motorized bin-type storage systems can be obtained.

Retrieval of Aperture Cards. Like microfiche, aperture cards are separate units (rather than sequential records on roll film) that can be scanned by hand and taken from the file like regular index cards. Or, mechanical sorting equipment can be used to retrieve aperture cards using the identifying information keypunched into the upper margin of the card. These cards can be returned to the files using either the manual or mechanical storage systems.

Microfilm Jackets

Sections of roll film containing blocks of related microrecords may be cut into strips, which are then inserted into plastic jackets 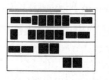 to serve as unitized microrecords. *Microfilm jackets*, as shown in the photograph at the left, are suitable for records that must be retrieved together (such as personnel files), and for convenient distribution of film records through the mails. Filmstrips in jackets may be duplicated directly from the jacket, which eliminates the need for removing the film. In addition, obsolete records may be easily removed from the jacket and new microrecords inserted, which speeds storage operations. The storage and retrieval of filmstrips housed in jackets are similar to the storage and retrieval of microfiche discussed earlier.

Automated Microimage Systems

Thus far, our discussion of microimage technology has been based on two ageless principles of learning: (1) *Proceed from the known to the unknown*, and (2) *Move from the simple to the complex*. The typical microfilm operations described early in this chapter are based on the separate, distinct activities of a manual system similar to those we recognize. One person types a document; another files it. A third person microfilms the record while a fourth person files the microrecord. Such separate activities depend upon the availability and smooth coordination of a group of office personnel in order to have a continuous flow of work from the beginning to the end of the microrecord cycle. When such an efficient work flow is not found, the time used for preparing microrecords is extended unnecessarily; and the cost of such operations is increased. (At this point we move from the simplicity of the manual system to the relative complexity of the computer system.)

As a partial solution to such problems, the computer has been successfully applied to various phases of microimaging. As a result, many of the microfilming functions have been automated, with greater volumes of microrecords stored and more rapidly retrieved and the administrative expenses budget more effectively controlled.

Two of the most significant developments for automating micrographic services are (1) computer output microfilm (COM) and (2) computer-assisted retrieval (CAR). A third automated development, optical disks, has emerged as an alternate medium for storing and retrieving vast amounts of information. Each is discussed briefly below.

Computer Output Microfilm (COM)

One of the first successful efforts to automate microimage systems has produced **computer output microfilm (COM)**. In the COM process, the computer's output (machine-readable, digital data) is automatically photographed and converted to human-readable images on microfilm or microfiche without creating an intervening paper copy. (When the final record is on microfiche, COM refers to "computer output

microfiche.") This process is made possible through the use of a special device called a **recorder** that photographs and reduces the computer output to microimage size on film. As Figure 20–4 shows, two types of COM applications are used: (1) *online*, in which the computer output is sent directly to the recorder similar to the way data are transferred from a computer to a printer; or (2) *offline*, in which the computer output is sent to a magnetic tape drive to be read into the recorder for microfilming independent of the computer. COM recorders produce records, usually on microfiche and sometimes on roll film, for use in the microimage system described earlier.

The COM process eliminates the earlier steps of preparing a hard-copy printout by the computer and then taking the printout to a microfilm camera for filming and reduction to microimage. Great savings may be realized from COM-produced microrecords: (1) savings in the weight of records (40 pounds of computerized paper records can be stored on seven ounces of microfilm), (2) savings in postage from mailing much lighter records, and (3) savings in materials and space for storing the microrecords as compared with storing cartons of computerized paper records. A closely related process— **computer input microfilm (CIM)**—has been developed. Using special equipment, CIM translates uncoded data on microrecords into computer language code for storage on magnetic tape as input to a computer. With COM and CIM available, the computer's role in microimage systems can be expected to grow.

Computer-Assisted Retrieval (CAR)

In addition to its use in COM and CIM, we find the computer has become a powerful tool for retrieving records. **Computer-assisted retrieval (CAR)** is the process of merging the computer (with its fast data storage and data search capabilities) and the microrecording process to access data on microfilm. Storing records on microfilm is

Figure 20-4
The Compu-
ter Output
Microfilm
Process

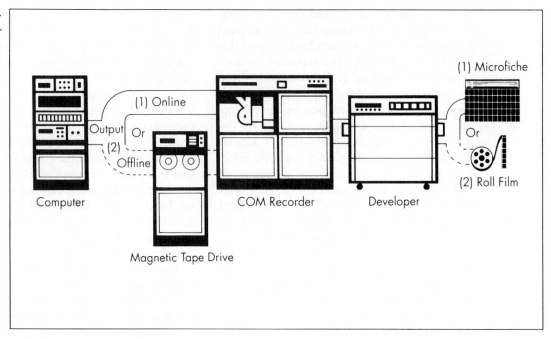

estimated to be 500 times more economical than the storage of data on magnetic tape in a computer system. In CAR, an index of all records in the microimage system is stored in the computer while the records themselves are stored on roll film, microfiche, or aperture cards. The index is created from the codes affixed to each record during the filming process described earlier. Commonly, we find two CAR systems whose main features are discussed in this section.

Basic CAR System. *Basic CAR* is an indirect-access system in which the various types of microrecords are stored manually according to the index code developed at the time of filming. When a microrecord is desired, the operator consults an index register for the identification (ID) code number of the desired record. This number is then entered into the VDT, after which the computer searches its index file for the code number. Once the number is found, the computer displays (or prints out) the location number of the document (the page and frame

numbers of the microfiche, for example, or the frame number and cartridge or roll number of the record on roll film, which is often stored in cassettes). After we locate this microrecord file, we can insert it manually into the reader and scan the file for the desired frame for viewing on the reader screen.

Advanced CAR Systems. In *advanced CAR systems*, the computer performs greater portions of the work required to find and display the desired microrecord. The microrecords used in an advanced retrieval system may be stored in an offline or in an online file. Both file processes require the development of an index of microrecords that is stored in the computer.

In the offline retrieval process, the operator enters the code number of the desired microrecord into the terminal. The computer searches its index file and displays the location number of the desired record on the VDT screen. The user then manually finds the proper microfiche or roll film file and places it in an automatic retrieval device. The desired microimage, with its specially coded ID number, is automatically found in seconds and displayed on the screen once the location/ID number has been key-boarded into the retrieval unit.

The online retrieval process operates in the most automated fashion. As soon as the operator enters the index code number of the desired record in the VDT, the computer searches its index file and then directs the online microimage terminal to locate and display the proper microimage on the terminal screen. The retrieval of microrecords from a COM-generated file may follow this automated retrieval procedure. If a paper copy of the displayed record is desired, the operator simply presses the "print" button on the retrieval device.

One rule of thumb in the microimage industry is that any office that each day files 1,000 or more documents for active use can justify a CAR system. Firms meeting the requirements of this guideline use CAR successfully to reduce labor costs and to improve operating efficiency. However, with increasingly greater numbers of records to store, a new alternate technology using video disks has emerged.

Optical Disks: An Alternative to Microimage Storage

The most powerful alternative to microimage technology is the optical disk (sometimes known as "laser optical disk," "video disk," or "optical digital disk"). The **optical disk** is a mass memory device that stores document images through the use of laser technology. An optical disk, as shown in Figure 20–5A, looks like a phonograph record and is available in many sizes (with diameters of 3″, 5″, 8″, 12″, and 14″). With its extremely high-storage capability, *the cost per unit of optical disk storage is lower than any other disk system*; and the disk will store data for a long time, estimated to be 100

years. Because the images are digitized (converted to numeric code) and stored as data on optical disks, technically these disks are called *optical digital data disks (ODDD)* and abbreviated as OD[3].

We can summarize the principal characteristics of optical disks and the systems in which they operate in this way:

1. *An OD[3] represents the latest extension of the magnetic disk drive introduced in the 1960s.* One commercially available type is **WORM** (Write-Once, Read-Many) **storage**, which limits the user to writing to the disk just once. However, the user is provided many opportunities for "reading out" the contents of the disk.

2. *Data are entered on, and read from, OD[3]s using lasers.* During the data-entry operation, the laser forms a tiny hole—less than one micron in diameter, or 1/100 the width of a human hair—in a thin metal layer inside the disk to represent binary data. (See Figure 20–5B.) Both sides of the disk can be used for data storage. This hole-burning operation gives write-once disks their permanence; at the present time contents of these disks cannot be erased or changed, although a rewritable type of optical disk has been introduced. Read operations use the same laser at a lower intensity to recover the data from the disk. The laser reader reflects back to a sensor if a hole is, or is not, present (the presence or absence of stored information) at an incredible speed—several million bits of data in a second!

3. *Each optical disk can store vast amounts of data.* Disk storage capacities, which are far greater than microfilm, range up to 4 gigabytes (4 billion characters or 2,000,000 pages), equal to the storage capacity of 3,000 standard floppy disks.[3]

---

[3]David Barcomb, *Office Automation: A Survey of Tools and Technology*, 2d ed. (Bedford, MA: Digital Press, 1989), p. 321.

Figure 20-5
Optical Disk Storage

A—Optical Digital Data Disks (ODDD)

B—Holes in Which Binary Data Are Stored on an ODDD

Typically disks are stored online in a "jukebox" containing as many as 100 disks. A user requests a file from a disk in the same way as requested in a CAR system. A copy of the file may be displayed on the VDT screen; or, if needed, a hard copy can be made on a laser printer.

4. *The disk cartridges can be easily removed from the drive*, which allows easy access to the data by other computers. And like other disks, random access is provided to the hundreds of files or large databases stored on a single cartridge.

5. *Operation of the disk drive is identical to that of any other disk drive.* The drive is attached to the computer via simple cables, and its installation typically takes about five minutes.

6. *Records stored on OD³s are subject to the same retention, legality, and control procedures as other records.*

MANAGEMENT OF MICROIMAGE SYSTEMS

In a typical organization, microfilming services were not planned. Rather, they just "grew" as the need to save the space occupied by the volume of common paper records, such as canceled checks and accounts payable files, became critical. When new microforms like microfiche and the aperture card appeared on the market, too often they were added without the necessary coordination among the departments. The result was a set of fragmented, nonstandardized, inefficient, and poorly directed programs. Under such conditions, duplication of equipment occurred and a lack of standardization in storage equipment, indexing, and retrieval prevailed. As a result, operating costs became much higher than necessary.

Before undertaking a carefully developed program to avoid these problems, we must obtain answers to two fundamental questions: (1) When should we microfilm records? and (2) Are microfilm records legal? Answers to these questions as well as considerations for ensuring the effective management of microrecords are included in this section.

When to Use Microrecords

"Why use microfilm?" managers ask. From research studies completed since the 1920s when microfilmed records were first used in business, administrators have recommended converting paper documents to microrecords to meet the following office needs:

1. *The need to conserve space and to reduce the costs of storing records.* Great savings can be achieved by converting paper documents to microrecords, depending on the reduction ratio used. For example, at a 24× reduction, the contents of a four-drawer vertical file cabinet—from 8,000 to 14,000 documents—can be reduced to four or six rolls of 16mm microfilm (assuming that there are 2,000 letter-size documents per 100 feet of roll film). This same four-drawer vertical file cabinet can store 1,000 rolls of 16mm microfilm—the equivalent of 750 to 1,750 drawers of paper documents.[4]

2. *The need for a more efficient records system.* A high number of file searches can be conducted easily, quickly, and inexpensively by an automated retrieval system discussed earlier. Microrecords have uniform dimensions since their sizes are reduced to fit standard microfilm dimensions regardless of their original size or shape. The handling of aperture card microrecords, rather than bulky engineering drawings, also simplifies the records work of the office staff. Also, books, periodicals, catalogs and other library references are often available in microform at a fraction of the paper-copy costs.

3. *The need for maintaining file integrity,* that is, the assurance that none of the documents filmed in sequence is lost or misfiled. The records on microfilm are usually arranged in a fixed sequence, which protects against misfiling, mislaying, alteration, or record loss. Also, AOMs want to be sure that there are no documents charged out so that the file is always complete. Microrecord files ensure such completeness.

4. *The need for periodic duplication of a regularly updated file and for maintaining duplicate records stored in several locations.* An offsite duplicate microfilm file protects against loss of information due to fire or theft. The small size of microrecord packages, the low cost of duplication (one microfiche or jacket holding 50–100 pages can be duplicated for little more than the cost of one paper page on an office copier), and the ease with which such records can be mailed make microrecords a valuable information-storage service in the office.

5. *The need for long-term preservation of records.* Under carefully controlled conditions, microrecords can be preserved for hundreds of years.

With all their advantages, however, microrecords have several limitations. Since they are very small, microrecords require the use of reader equipment to enlarge the photographed records for the user. Such equipment adds to the cost of administrative operations; and since the reader equipment is often bulky, it typically lacks portability. However, recent developments in the manufacture of portable readers have partially overcome this limitation. Usually records that are subject to constant change are not filmed except on microfiche, for the updating of filmed records is a costly process and is more easily carried out on the original paper documents.

---

[4]William Saffady, *Microfilm in Records Management* (Silver Spring, MD: National Micrographics Association, 1982), pp. 10–11.

Other costs attached to microrecords include the costs of filming the original records or similar costs of having records filmed by an outside agency; costs of processors, duplicators, and related supplies; special storing and retrieving equipment; and unique climate controls needed for microrecord files. AOMs must weigh these cost factors against the benefits of satisfying the other needs discussed in this section.

Determining the Legality of Microrecords

If we are to ensure the legality of microrecords in a firm, we must answer two "legality" questions: (1) Is a records retention requirement met by retaining the document image in microform and discarding the paper document? and (2) Are microimages acceptable in courts of law as substitutes for paper documents?

To ascertain the legality of microrecords, AOMs should be familiar with both state and federal legislation on the subject. In 1951, Congress passed the Uniform Photographic Copies of Business Records in Evidence Act. This act established that microfilmed copies of business records (as replacements for the original documents) could be admitted as evidence in courts of law if these conditions were met: (1) the filming occurred in the normal course of business, (2) the original records were accurately photographed in their entirety, and (3) they were legible. Thus, the provisions of this Act, which are still in effect, permit records that meet these conditions to be used as evidence in court.

Most federal and state agencies have their own microfilm regulations concerning the substitution of microfilmed records for hard copies. The Securities and Exchange Commission, for example, allows filming, provided a duplicate of each microrecord is stored separately from the original microrecord. A good guideline to follow is to file a certificate of authenticity as the last document on every roll of film. This certificate is an official record of the firm's routine microfilming policy and provides information about the dates and ranges of the records filmed, the date photographed, and the signature of the photographer. The firm's legal department should prepare this certificate.

Planning Microimage Systems

Even though we assume that a program of microimage services is warranted, we should conduct a feasibility study in order to compile unbiased information on the real need for microrecords. To assist in collecting and organizing the large volume of data needed for such a study, microimage management specialists recommend the use of a systems grid form as shown in Figure 20-6. For the input phase of such a study, answers should be requested for questions such as the following:

1. What are the objectives in a proposed microimage system?
2. What are the characteristics of the files to be microfilmed? (How many items to be filed, how often are additions or modifications made to the records, how frequently is the file consulted, and how long must the file be retained?)
3. What are the characteristics of the documents to be microfilmed? (Are all documents the same size, what are their sizes and condition, are they clear and readable, and are they paper or computerized?)
4. What are the anticipated retrieval needs for the files? (What is the average number of retrievals per day/week, by how many people, in what departments, and in what proximity to each other; and must the entire file be accessed or just single documents within the file?)
5. What kinds of materials and supplies will be needed?

Figure 20–6
A Systems
Grid Form
for Collect-
ing Feasibil-
ity Data for a
Microimage
System

		People	Equipment	Materials	Facilities
I N P U T		1. Document preparation clerks 2. Systems supervisor 3. Delivery and mail service	1. Cameras 2. Worktables 3. Floodlights 4. Meters 5. Duplicators 6. Storage equipment	1. Source documents 2. Unprocessed film 3. Microimage service record forms	1. Preparation area 2. Filming area 3. Temporary storage area
P R O C E S S		1. Supervising work 2. Photographing records 3. Processing film 4. Delivering film to users	1. Tables 2. Cameras and equipment 3. Processing equipment 4. Delivery cart	1. Record forms 2. Film 3. Source documents 4. Processed film	1. Preparation and filming areas 2. Processing area
O U T P U T		Records of worker performance	Same equipment as used for input	1. Microrecords created 2. Records of microrecords created and delivered 3. Source documents retained	Newer storage area in user system

6. What facilities are necessary to start and maintain such a system?

In a similar way, questions must be asked about the volume of paper used; the format of each record; the turnaround time needed to obtain the stored information; how the microrecords will be used; and how the information flows from its origin to its destination. From this wealth of information and a discussion of its implications with departmental managers, the AOM can formulate a plan that shows *anticipated benefits* and *expected costs*. If such benefits exceed costs, a decision should be made to convert to microrecords.

During the process of conversion, the AOM or the records manager should continue to maintain hard-copy files until the records retention committee decides that the original documents are no longer needed. In a manual information system, many active records will still be maintained in their original form. If, on the other hand, the information system is highly automated and the active records can be easily retrieved from the microfile itself, the paper records may be destroyed. However, a duplicate (backup) file of microrecords should be created for security purposes.

Organizing Microimage Systems

Microimage systems should be considered as an important subsystem of the total information system. As such, microimage systems are a complex mix of the equipment, environmental conditions for records storage, personnel, and procedures necessary to provide efficient microrecord operations for the company. In large firms, these responsibilities are assigned to a specialized unit under the supervision of the records manager. In smaller firms, commercial microfilming agencies are used to photograph the records for storage in the firm under the direct supervision of the AOM.

Microimage Equipment

Although highly specialized equipment (cameras to photograph the records, processors to convert the film images into negatives, and duplicators to reproduce copies of microrecords) is necessary in a full-scale micrographic program, only two types of equipment are operated by the office staff. Such equipment, which can be operated with little or no training, includes storage equipment for each of the microrecords discussed earlier, and readers, as defined on page 614. (See Figure 20-2.) There are readers of various sizes and for each type of microrecord. *Reader-printers* combine the reading function and the production of hard-copy printouts of microrecords. To obtain such a printout, the user simply presses a button and a copy of the image appearing on the screen is released from the machine.

Storage Environment

Records on film are highly sensitive to temperature and humidity conditions. Generally the average air-conditioned office is well suited to preserving microrecords. Where controlled atmospheric conditions are not found—as in some company *archives* (inactive records center)—over long periods of time the microrecords may crack, mold, or attract dust or dirt that can scratch the surface of the image. If this occurs, all or a portion of the stored information may be destroyed. Other hazards, such as fire, theft, and unauthorized access to microrecords,

require the same environmental and security controls as given to paper records.

Personnel

A microimage system is typically an administrative service that is delegated to the records manager. Such a program requires certain managerial, technical, and user skills for effective operation. Figure 20-7 outlines these three personnel needs. Due to the simple nature of the reader-printer equipment, most users can be taught the fundamentals of machine operation in a few minutes. The managerial and technical skills, on the other hand, require considerably longer training and extensive administrative experience.

Establishing Operating Procedures

To operate a full-fledged microimage system, a set of effective procedures, as shown in Figure 20-1, must be established. These procedures include instructions for indexing, photographing, and processing records as well as control procedures for ensuring that all records are properly protected. Some of these procedures are entirely manual in nature while others, such as those required for computerizing the microphotography process, operate according to computer program instructions.

The AOM or the records manager should conduct orientation sessions for each department. These sessions should explain in detail the nature and purpose of each of the new procedures, how such procedures are to be carried out, and where assistance can be found if needed.

The principal procedures for operating microimage systems include:

1. *Describing the records to be filmed.* This includes the names and sizes of the records as well as the type and color of paper stock on which they are printed; the volume of records to be filed; whether the records are one- or two-sided; and a

Figure 20-7
Personnel
Needs of the
Microimage
Systems
Program

Managerial Needs	Technical Needs	User Needs
Understanding the microfilming needs of the firm.	Photographing and processing film. Duplicating the film.	Understanding procedures for storing, retrieving, maintaining, preserving, and destroying records.
Designing an effective system of microimage services. Coordinating the use of microrecords throughout the firm.	Procuring, maintaining, and updating equipment.	Using basic equipment (readers, printers, and retrieval or display units) to retrieve information and produce hard copies.
Preserving and controlling all microrecords.	Providing continuous service to users.	Keeping the records manager informed on the effectiveness of the microimage system.

general statement about the condition of the records.

2. *Preparing the records to be filmed.* The person who submits records for filming is responsible for putting the paper records in correct filing sequence, for mending torn pages and crumpled sheets, and for removing staples and other fasteners. If the data on the records are not legible, the records should not be filmed.

3. *Determining the requirements for personnel and equipment.* Information should be obtained regarding (a) the total number of file drawers of records to be filmed, (b) the estimated number of drawers to be filmed per camera per day, (c) the number of cameras required, (d) the total working days required to complete the jobs, (e) the average number of persons regularly assigned, and (f) the number of film readers required after the filming has been completed.

4. *Filming and processing records.* Departments should provide information regarding (a) the desired record size and format, (b) the number and type of duplicate microrecords to be made, (c) the coding system to be used, (d) the desired reduction ratio, and (e) any tests

needed to evaluate the quality of the filmed record.

5. *Packaging and indexing the filmed records.* The nature of the microrecord package, how the processed film is to be indexed, and when and where the records are to be delivered should be determined.

6. *Storing and retrieving the filmed records.* Effective procedures for storing the records should specify (a) the current retention period for each microrecord, (b) how the records are to be filed (alphabetically, numerically, or chronologically), and (c) how to request and retrieve microrecords from the file. Also, logs should be maintained that show how often each of the microrecord files is requested.

7. *Disposing of original records.* The location of the original records for all microrecord files should be noted. In addition, the decisions on disposing of original records (when, how, and by whom) should be recorded.

Evaluating Microimage Systems

Periodically we should evaluate any system to determine how effectively its objectives are being met. The major points in the evaluation of a microimage system include:

1. How well users accept and actively use the microrecord files.
2. The adequacy of the equipment (sufficient number, properly scheduled and allocated among departments, properly maintained and serviced, and easy to use).
3. The quality of environmental controls and protective measures for safeguarding the microrecords.
4. The effectiveness of operating procedures, such as making available to all departments information on microfilm applications; contacts with vendors of equipment and supplies; and effective methods of filming, storing, and retrieving documents.
5. Provision for follow-up studies to improve the service to all users.
6. Careful monitoring and control of operating costs, as discussed in the following paragraphs.

The AOM or the records manager responsible for a microimage system must understand fully the total and the major costs involved in its operation. While the same general costs apply to a microimage system as to other administrative operations as shown in Figure 19-16, page 599, several additional specific factors must be considered. Figure 20-8 outlines the major costs required in the use of space, personnel time, equipment, materials, and supplies associated with microimage systems.

We must consider each of these costs in evaluating the relative economy of microrecords versus maintaining paper records. By obtaining either actual data or reliable estimates for each of these cost factors, the records manager can compute a break-even point to justify or to reject the use of microrecords. Break-even analysis, discussed in Chapter 15, is a useful technique for deciding at what point there is no measurable cost advantage in using microrecords. To make such a determination, the records manager must know, for example, the costs of operating a four-drawer file cabinet for a year as well as the costs of filming, processing, and storing microrecords for the same period of time. In both cases, the cost of space required to store each type of record must also be known. If, for example, the yearly cost of maintaining the four-drawer file of paper records is $500 and the cost of maintaining a microrecord file is $430, we know it is more economical to convert the hard-copy records to microrecords. On the other hand, if the yearly costs for both files are approximately equal, the break-even point is reached. The decision about which type of records system to maintain must then be based on the record manager's assessment of future costs and efficiencies of operation and on an estimate of the size of the records system anticipated for the future.

Figure 20-8
Major Types of Costs in Microimage Systems

Types of Space Costs		Types of Personnel Time Costs	
Storage area		Indexing	Duplicating
Records preparation area		Sorting	Filming
Transportation areas		Filing	Distributing
Related service areas		Retrieving	Supervising
Types of Equipment Costs		**Types of Materials and Supplies Costs**	
Storage cabinets and shelving		Microfilm	
Readers or reader-printers		Storage supplies	
Cameras, processors, and duplicators		Paper and carbon paper	
Maintenance charges and replacement parts		General administrative supplies	

REPROGRAPHICS TECHNOLOGY

Can you imagine any office today as well as in the future that doesn't require making copies of forms and records on a daily, or even an hourly, basis? In fact, one of the most basic systems maintained in the office is copy making. For decades, multiple copies of records were made using carbon paper and three machine duplicating processes. Later, with the application of photographic and telecommunication processes to the task of copy making, a new phase of copying emerged that offers many advantages to the AOM.

Since all these processes share one key function—the *reproduction* of information and records for management—they are called **reprographic systems**. A full knowledge of such topics is essential in order that the AOM be able to provide copy-making information to all areas of the organization.

Reprographic Processes

The earliest form of reproducing copies in an office involved a clerk making a handwritten copy of a record. This slow, painstaking process was later replaced by carbon paper, which continues to offer many economies to the office even in this age of automated copy making. The major use of carbon paper (or carbonless paper, as discussed in Chapter 19) is in the preparation of multiple copies of forms. As a rule, however, other duplicating and copy-making processes have replaced to a great extent the use of carbon paper. Because office copiers have largely replaced duplicating machines and the use of carbon paper, in this section we give major emphasis to copying processes and the growing role of copiers in integrated systems.

Copying Processes

In most duplicating processes, a typist prepares a master copy from an original docu-ment, which is a slow process subject to typing and proofreading errors. In contrast, *when copying processes are used, the information to be reproduced is photographed*, which saves valuable staff time. Because exact reproductions can be made with copiers, the copies are acceptable in courts of law and by government agencies.

Copiers are used in every size and type of office. Such machines are relatively inexpensive and easy to operate as well as very reliable. For these reasons, however, copiers have too frequently been misused for producing many unnecessary copies of records. Thus, it becomes important to manage carefully the reprographics program so that the use of the firm's copiers is restricted to the production of necessary records. Three broad classes of copiers, based on the volume of copies that can be made, are available. Figure 20–9 lists the main features of each copier class.

Advances in electronics and machine design have resulted in a growing number of convenience features in office copiers. The most common features include (1) the ability to reduce the size of documents, such as computer printouts, to smaller-size copy paper, or to enlarge the original document to a more readable size; (2) automatic feeding of documents; (3) collating of copies produced; (4) **duplexing**, or copying on both sizes of a sheet of copy paper in one operation; (5) the use of color toners in throwaway packages for copying documents in a variety of colors; (6) edge erase (eliminating the edge and "gully" (center) in copying from thick, bound volumes; (7) blue erase (ignoring the blue-pencil editing on the original); (8) margin/image shift, which shifts the image to either the right or left for duplexing or binding; and (9) electronic editing (the operator uses an electronic writing instrument to delete or relocate on the copy a portion of the original's image displayed on the screen). This last feature effectively replaces old cut-and-paste methods of

Figure 20-9 Copiers Classified by Volume of Copies Made

Copiers Classified by Volume of Copies Made	Main Features of Each Copier Class
1. Low–volume or convenience copier	Compact units, sometimes portable; produce up to 20 copies per minute; recommended for copy volume levels not exceeding 20,000 copies per month; used as sole copiers in small offices or as satellite units in a decentralized reprographics program.
2. Mid–volume copier	Desk–top units larger than the convenience copier; produce copies at speeds ranging from 21 to 50 copies per minute for firms requiring 20,000 copies per month; or, as floor–console units, for firms requiring up to 100,000 copies per month; used in centralized copy centers.
3. High–volume copier	Floor units that produce copies at speeds ranging from 51 to 90 copies per minute for firms needing 50,000 to more than 200,000 copies per month; includes in this class *copier/duplicators*, which combine the convenience of high–speed copiers with the low per–copy cost of duplicators; used in centralized reprographics departments or in decentralized locations within large firms.

editing copy. Other more automated features of the new reprographics technology are discussed below.

Usually we classify copying processes in two ways: (1) the *wet process*, which uses coated paper and (2) the *dry process*, which may use special paper or plain paper depending on the type of copier used. Plain paper copiers, the most popular copying machines, are used for preparing file copies of correspondence, records to be distributed to other departments, business forms and form letters, transparencies, and drawings. The copies made from such machines can be produced at low per-copy cost and stored and preserved permanently. Wet process copiers using *diffusion transfer* and *stabilization* copying methods have more specialized applications, such as producing copies of photographs and engineering drawings. Information on this type of copier can be found in technical references on reprographics.[5]

[5]Detailed information on office duplicating and copying equipment can be obtained from Buyers Laboratory, Inc., Hackensack, NJ 07601; Datapro Research Corporation, Delran, NJ 08075; and Auerbach Publishers, Inc., Pennsauken, NJ 08109.

Generally office copying processes involve chemical and mechanical operations of a highly complex, technical nature that must be understood by the personnel who sell and service the equipment. However, office personnel can learn quickly the relatively simple methods of machine operation; therefore, technical information is not necessary. For this reason, the discussion of the copying process in this section is limited to a brief description of the xerography process.

Xerography, which is an electrostatic process, exposes a positively charged drum surface to light reflected through lenses from the original document. When light from white areas of the original copy strikes the drum, the charge disappears and a negatively charged black powder (toner) clings only to that portion of the surface still charged—the image area. The image is transferred from the drum to copy paper where it is permanently set by heat. The advantages of xerography include: (1) its ability to copy many colors; (2) no requirement for chemicals other than toner or powder; (3) the use of plain paper; and (4) easy machine operation. Its disadvantages are: (1) the per-copy cost (2 cents and above), which is higher than the costs of duplicating for a large number of copies; and (2) for the low-volume user, expensive equipment that requires special maintenance. Figure 20–9, photo 1, shows a typical small-office copier.

Duplicating Processes

For many years before the advent of office copiers, duplicating processes were the only mechanical means of reproducing copies in the office. Three methods of duplicating were developed: (1) *fluid duplicating* (also called *spirit duplicating* and *ditto*; (2) *stencil duplicating* (also called *mimeographing*; and (3) *offset duplicating*. In each method a master copy of the document to be copied must be prepared and attached to the duplicating machine for copy making. Fluid duplicating requires the use of a special two-sheet set (white paper and duplicator carbon) as the master on which information is hand-written, typed, drawn, or otherwise prepared through the use of a thermal copier. The stencil process master is a porous sheet of tissue coated with a wax-like substance that does not absorb ink. The stencil is prepared by cutting through this coating by writing or drawing with a stylus, or by using a typewriter with the ribbon disengaged. In the offset process, the master copy is prepared in the same manner as the spirit-duplicating master; or it can be photographed directly from the original copy onto a metal master. Offset copy making is frequently used where large-volume, print-quality copies are required.

Copiers have rapidly replaced duplicating machines in most offices because of their ease of operation, fast copy-making rate, relatively inexpensive per-copy cost, and overall availability. However, many small offices—in schools, community organizations, and service agencies—continue to use duplicators. Also, in some offices, duplicating machines serve as backup units in case an office copier is not functioning. To partially automate the reproduction of copies by stencil duplicator, one firm has developed a special plug for hooking up a personal computer to a digital mimeograph machine so that documents created on a PC can go directly to a stencil. This machine prints with the same quality as the best laser printer and turns out copies about ten times faster. Its per-copy cost is estimated to be as low as $.01.[6]

Automated Developments in Reprographic Processes

Many of the technical advances in information technology have also included

6"Coming Soon to a School Near You: The Digital Mimeograph," *Business Week* (July 31, 1989), p. 97.

improvements in copying processes. In some cases, we see that these improvements have been brought about by integrating copying equipment with other types of information-processing and communication hardware. Examples of the continuing developments in copying processes include the following:

1. *The copier is integrated with the telephone to transmit facsimile and xerographic copies of information over regular telephone lines.*
2. *Copiers use fiber optics* (discussed in Chapter 18) *to simplify the complex lens-and-mirror systems required in the photographic process.* As a result, copying costs are lowered and the quality of the copies is improved. The printing quality has also been improved through the use of a laser beam, which is a very intense light. Such a beam forms character or type patterns in the copier's printing mechanism under the control of a microcomputer.
3. **Phototypesetters** *are used to create print on a special VDT screen from data obtained from word processing or computer systems or from direct keyboard entry.* The characters on the screen are photographed by an attached photocomposition unit that also directly sets the type for the production of paper records or, commonly, newspapers. The main purpose of phototypesetting is to produce a professional-looking black and white original copy that will be printed on an offset press or photocopied using a compatible copying process.
4. *New computer technologies are making possible the integration of many information functions.* By merging a *microprocessor,* a small computer, with the copying function, an operator can monitor numerous copier functions on the VDT screen as well as messages of the copier's operational status. **Intelligent copier/printers,** which are a cross between a photocopier and a mini- or

microcomputer, combine the capabilities of a copier with those of a computer and phototypesetter. With an intelligent copier/printer, you can create hard-copy images directly from the magnetic files of a computer or word processor. Their "intelligence" or programmability lets you merge logos, signatures, and form-ruling lines into the text as printing occurs. The machine's computer-like capabilities permit receiving, storing, and communicating information in electronic, rather than paper, form from computers or word processing systems; or from other intelligent copier/printers linked by telecommunication lines. This type of copier can store up to one thousand pages of incoming documents in electronic mailboxes until hard copy is needed. Graphics and forms can also be designed using a wide variety of type faces and stored for later use. In fact, the designing of forms and the printing of variable information can be done simultaneously on this equipment. Such a multifunction machine becomes a valuable item of equipment for all text and graphics production in the office. An intelligent copier/printer is shown in Figure 20–10.

MANAGEMENT OF REPROGRAPHIC SYSTEMS

Like other administrative functions, reprographic systems must be managed carefully in order to meet the responsibilities assigned them. These managerial responsibilities include planning and organizing the necessary resources, establishing operating procedures and controls, and controlling costs. Each of these topics is discussed briefly in this section.

Planning Reprographic Systems

Before installing a reprographic services system, the AOM should carefully consider

Figure 20-10
An Intelligent Copier/Printer

the following: (1) the copy requirements of each of the departments in the company; (2) the resources (especially the personnel, equipment, and space) needed to meet the copy requirements; (3) procedures necessary to control the total reprographics operation; (4) ideas from users whose support of the reprographic program is vital to its success; and (5) reliable methods for measuring the effectiveness of the program.[7] This information may in turn help to determine what portion of the reprographic work should be done internally or by an outside firm.

To obtain such information, the manager should ask each department to furnish answers to these questions:

1. How many copies of each form, report, and other documents are required?
2. To whom is each copy sent?
3. How is each copy used and stored?

4. For how long is each copy filed?
5. How frequently are copies reproduced?
6. What size copy is desired for reduction and enlargement purposes?

Much, if not all, of this information may be available from the company-wide survey of records required in the operation of a records management program, as discussed in Chapter 19.

Organizing Reprographic Systems

The size of the firm affects directly the manner in which the reprographic services function is organized. In small firms, for example, one desk-top copier or duplicating machine may be sufficient to handle the copying volume of the entire firm with no special operator required. Large companies, on the other hand, frequently organize centralized reprographic services departments that utilize many machines and highly trained operators. In some cases, copiers and duplicators are placed within individual departments (physical decentralization of machines) even though central control is maintained by reprographic services. Other firms leave both the equipment and its control to the individual departments.

Centralized control of reprographic services is preferred for the following reasons:

1. It makes available specialized personnel who can provide high-quality copy work and take better care of the equipment.
2. It permits a greater variety of equipment and more flexibility in its use.
3. It requires a minimum investment in equipment by reducing the number of duplicate machines.
4. It provides better scheduling of work.
5. Ideally, it increases productivity.

On the other hand, physical decentralization, which is usually self-service, offers each department more flexibility as to what is

[7]For highly useful information on the strength and weaknesses of copiers as well as the copier features that users like and dislike, consult the latest annual copier survey of Datapro Research Corporation, Feature Reports Department, 1805 Underwood Boulevard, Delran, NJ 08075.

copied and also reduces travel and turn-around time. Under a decentralized plan, however, it may be more difficult to maintain company-wide operating standards and controls over the use and maintenance of the equipment. A greater amount of supervision would doubtless be required.

Personnel

The responsibilities for operating the reprographic systems normally fall on the AOM or the supervisor who is in charge of communication services. In a small firm, such a supervisor may be assigned many duties including the responsibilities for the copying function. The day-to-day repro-graphic tasks may, in such a setting, be handled by secretaries and typists. For more complex copy-making needs, the firm may contact commercial printers.

In the large firm, on the other hand, a full-time, specialized supervisor with knowledge of such equipment should be appointed. This type of supervisor has responsibility for selecting and training the staff, for de-veloping sound procedures for scheduling and operating the reprographic equipment, and for establishing the necessary operating controls to conduct a sound program. In addition, the supervisor should plan and conduct a continuing education program among the various departments to ensure that only necessary copies are made. Such a program should cover the legislation on copyrights, which legally recognizes the ownership of original recorded work. In addition to printed materials such as books and periodicals, copyrighted works include recorded lectures, drawings, and photo-graphs that are officially registered with the Registry of Copyright of the United States Library of Congress. Since copying machines are widely used to reproduce materials from copyrighted sources, the AOM or repro-graphics manager should be sure to secure the permission of the copyright holder—

usually the publisher of the material—before permitting such material to be reproduced. If such permission is not obtained, the copyright owner may sue the violator in a civil court. In 1988, the U. S. Congress strengthened copyright laws by ratifying the Berne Convention for the Protection of Literacy and Artistic Works. This treaty, which was ratified by 78 countries, calls for reciprocal protection over the copying of software or films and is designed to eliminate the "softlifting" or illegal copying of copyrighted computer programs.[8]

Reprographics Equipment

With the increasing use of the computer to reproduce and transmit information, most large firms can produce internally the major portion of their copy needs. In fact, with the use of word processors connected to phototypesetters, desktop-publishing soft-ware, and computers, camera-ready copy can be produced error free in a matter of minutes. Even so, such firms as well as a large majority of small firms must select, maintain, and use equipment to meet their copying needs. Figure 20–11 provides a checklist that may be used by AOMs in the selection of duplicating and copying machines. Several models of competing brands of such machines should be evaluated according to the degree of effectiveness of each machine for handling the reprographic tasks required in the office.

Considerable advantage is found in the local purchase of equipment and supplies, especially where service is concerned. Environmental requirements, particularly temperature and humidity, should also be studied for their effects upon machine operation.

Information on equipment selection is readily available from equipment manufac-

---

8"The Battle Raging Over 'Intellectual Property,' " Time (May 22, 1989), pp. 78, 79, 82.

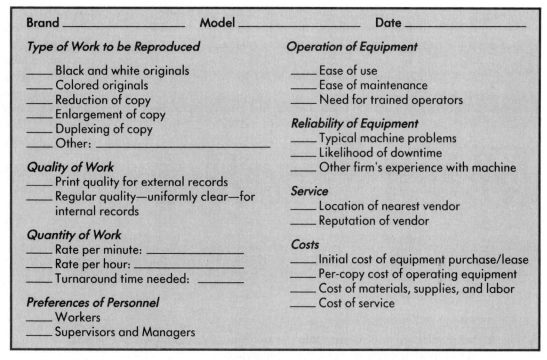

Figure 20-11 Checklist for Selecting Reprographic Equipment

Brand _____ Model _____ Date _____

Type of Work to be Reproduced

_____ Black and white originals
_____ Colored originals
_____ Reduction of copy
_____ Enlargement of copy
_____ Duplexing of copy
_____ Other: _____

Quality of Work

_____ Print quality for external records
_____ Regular quality—uniformly clear—for internal records

Quantity of Work

_____ Rate per minute: _____
_____ Rate per hour: _____
_____ Turnaround time needed: _____

Preferences of Personnel

_____ Workers
_____ Supervisors and Managers

Operation of Equipment

_____ Ease of use
_____ Ease of maintenance
_____ Need for trained operators

Reliability of Equipment

_____ Typical machine problems
_____ Likelihood of downtime
_____ Other firm's experience with machine

Service

_____ Location of nearest vendor
_____ Reputation of vendor

Costs

_____ Initial cost of equipment purchase/lease
_____ Per-copy cost of operating equipment
_____ Cost of materials, supplies, and labor
_____ Cost of service

turers and from professional groups like the Computer and Business Equipment Manufacturers Association and the Administrative Management Society. Managers may also obtain assistance in the careful selection of equipment from such useful periodicals as *Modern Office Technology* and *The Office*, which highlight equipment for information systems.

Space

Along with maintaining standards for good work layout, the reprographic center should provide adequate storage space for the large quantities of copy paper and supplies required. Other needs include a sink for cleaning up after operating the machines, darkroom facilities if photographic equipment is used, and acoustical materials and cabinets to reduce the noise of equipment, which can be annoying to office workers in adjacent areas.

Establishing Operating Procedures and Controls

When we hear the comment that "paper is cheap," we usually suspect a lack of understanding of administrative operations and their costs, which in turn causes the AOM many problems. To prevent these problems from occurring, the AOM should assign the highest priority to setting up efficient operating procedures and appropriate controls for regulating the personnel in the reprographics unit. Since costs are involved in all phases of operations and are of great importance, they are covered later in this chapter.

Personnel Controls

The most effective use of equipment and supplies can be achieved by training one or more individuals in machine operation, machine maintenance, and control of copy quality. This training should emphasize not only the benefits accruing to the entire firm from providing an effective reprographics center, but also the costs of such services and how each employee can help to keep such costs in line.

Reprographics policies should be developed to ensure that only authorized personnel from each department be permitted to use the equipment. Violations of this requirement result in misuse of the equipment, which in turn causes downtime and delays in the completion of work. Also, many unauthorized copies may be made. With such problems, office operating costs increase.

Procedure Controls

Orderly, efficient procedures for operating the reprographic services function must be developed in order to meet the information needs of all departments. The following practices will assist the supervisor of reprographic systems in achieving control over the procedures:

1. *All departments should be informed about the copyright laws and their effect on copying practices in the firm.* Present copying practices must observe the provisions of the copyright law which went into effect January 1, 1978, and which cover what can be copied, how many copies may be made, and the purposes for which authorized copies may be reproduced. Note that "copy" extends beyond hard copy to include other types of media, such as sound (music and lecture), graphics (drawings), and any computer software that is copyrighted. Other materials, such as securities of the United States government (United States bonds, certificates of deposit, and paper money are examples), may not be copied.

2. *A policy should be developed that clearly identifies how each type and quantity of job will be reproduced.* For example, multicolor advertising brochures may require technical design skills as well as special color reproduction available only from commercial printers. Also, the types of copying to be assigned to duplicators, copiers, and other reprographics equipment should be publicized throughout the firm and such regulations consistently enforced.

3. *Some type of record should be created and used to ensure that data on copies made are available to management.* In the small office, the "honor system" may be used by requiring that each user note *how many copies* of *what type of original* were made *on what date* and *by whom* (the user). A form similar to that shown in Figure 20–12 is commonly used in a firm with many departments for each copy request from a department. The form has space for important control information (code number for the type of run, account number of the department to be charged, time received and needed, and proofreading requirements) needed in a university reprographics center. Special instructions may be needed for collating, reducing of copy size, punching, and binding of copies. Unless permission of the publisher of copyrighted materials is obtained, as discussed earlier, some copying requests cannot be approved.

4. *If possible, a trained operator should be provided full time to operate the equipment.* If not, a part-time operator should be available for stated hours, after which the machine should be locked. If no operator is assigned, the machine should be placed near an office supervisor who can monitor the use of the machine.

5. *Shredders should be placed alongside office copiers to destroy unneeded copies of important documents.* Reprographics managers are then able to reduce the risk of corporate information falling into the wrong hands.

Figure 20–12
A Combined Form for Requesting Word Processing and Reprographic Services

Work Received	
Time:	*10:15*
Date:	*4/14*

Typist _____
Document Name _____
Department *Accounting*

Name *Thompson, Meg*
Tel. No. *3-3170*
Date/Time Needed *4/18, 1PM*

☐ Manuscript
☑ Classroom Material
☐ Examination
☐ Corrections
☐ Letter(s)
☐ Other _____
☐ Transparencies/Transofax
☐ Xerox
☐ Exam Service
☐ Copy Center
☐ Communications

No. of pages *2* No. of copies *100* Total *200*
Code # *021*   Account # *Z-247*   C & S _____
To be proofed? *yes*   Backup? _____

Special Instructions:
collate & staple
3-hole punch
_____
_____

6. *Records of equipment usage should be kept.* Some firms keep a log at the machine site and require that entries be made for all copying done. However, this practice lacks accuracy, requires considerable supervision and accounting, and does not provide security over the machine.

   A more effective method of copier control makes use of a plastic access card that must be inserted into the machine before it can be used. Such a card contains information that identifies the department or user number. In addition to activating the machine for making copies, this control device accumulates data regarding the number of copies made so that the appropriate department users may be charged for copies made. (Other stand-alone alternatives to cards are keys, keyboards, or plug-in cartridges that are issued to users who connect the cartridge to the copier, thus "authorizing" the machine to operate and to record and display the number of copies made.)

   Centralized systems use a terminal with a keyboard connected to the copier. Through identification codes, such a system "gives permission" for the machine's use and records operating data, such as user's name and department, copier used, the date and time of access, and the number of copies made. At the end of the accounting period, the computer generates copier usage reports from this information.

7. *To maximize the use of the copier, similar types of copying work should be grouped together to speed the completion of the work.* Job priorities should be established and publicized among the departments—computers can be instructed to monitor and control such priorities—and feedback from department users should be collected regarding the quality of the copying work.

Controlling Reprographic Costs

The number of office copies made annually continues to grow to the point where it staggers the imagination. According to a study by Accountemps, a New York-based temporary office help service, an estimated 350 billion photocopies are made annually, 37 percent of which are unnecessary. A conservative estimate places the cost of these wasted copies at $2.6 billion, about 8 percent of which are reproduced solely for personal use.[9] Thus, the cost of reprographic services represents a large portion of the office budget. Good management of the copying function dictates that a program be set up to identify and control reprographic costs. These topics are discussed briefly in this section.

Identifying Reprographic Costs

If we are to calculate the total costs of providing reprographic services, we must first identify each of the administrative costs. Administrative costs are outlined in Figure 19–16 (page 599), and each must be included in the computation of per-copy costs in a reprographic systems operation.

A large number of *hidden costs* that creep into the reprographic operation are often overlooked because they are not directly a part of the copy-making process but which, on the average, account for 60 to 70 percent of the copier's total cost.[10] These include the costs of:

1. Ordering reprographic supplies and equipment (like getting quotations from suppliers).
2. Storage space and shelving for storing reprographic supplies.
3. Labor involved in keeping stock and handling invoices and other records.
4. Mailing, since a large portion of the output is mailed.
5. Messenger service for work that must be delivered.
6. Overordering and underordering.
7. Charging back all work produced to the user department.
8. Overtime and borrowed help.
9. Furniture and equipment used by supervisory personnel.
10. Supervisor's time.
11. Wasted paper caused by overruns, defective work, and excessive use of paper in preparatory operations.

When these hidden costs—sometimes adding as much as 100 percent to reprographic costs—are brought to light, a much more accurate determination of total reprographic costs is obtained.

Reducing Reprographic Costs

The availability of good controls over reprographic services as well as the constant vigilance of personnel to enforce such controls can help to keep the costs of reproducing documents within reasonable limits. To achieve such controls, we suggest you consider the following points:

1. *Select the most suitable process for the job to be done.* If less than five copies are needed of an original that must be typed, carbon paper is the *least expensive production method*, although you may not agree that it's the most convenient! If 5 to 10 copies of an original are needed, a desk-top copier is more appropriate; and for making more than 10 copies, one of the other duplicating processes should be

---

[9]This 1985 survey was reported in "Costly Copies," *Office Administration and Automation* (July, 1985), p. 16. A later study by Dataquest was reported in Patricia M. Fernberg, "Singing the Copier Blues (and Reds and Yellows)," *Modern Office Technology* (February, 1989), p. 54. In this update, Fernberg projects that by 1992 color copiers will produce more than 2 billion copies in color; and for every color copy, hundreds of black and white copies are made. Thus, the overall number of copies being made continues to increase.
[10]Patricia M. Fernberg, "Copiers: What You Need Is What You'll Get," *Modern Office Technology* (July, 1987), p. 50.

used, if available. Both sides of the paper should be used if possible.

2. *Standardize equipment, methods, and supplies to eliminate an unnecessary variety of machine models from many manufacturers.* Following this guideline permits using uniform supplies bought in large volume from one vendor under quantity purchase discounts. The systems and procedures department, if one exists, should be consulted for advice in increasing the efficiency of reprographic methods, materials, equipment, and personnel. Usually self-service, departmental copiers should be replaced by satellite reprographic centers staffed with full- or part-time operators, messengers, and an office supplies center.

3. *From the current copy-production records, compute per-copy costs and* *make semiannuual surveys of anticipated needs of departments.* Some firms provide usage and cost figures by departments on a monthly cumulative basis compared with the past year's figures. This information helps in planning future equipment needs as well as in developing guidelines for selecting the most cost-effective copying method.

4. *Do not overlook the highly competitive nature of the equipment market and the free services offered by vendors.* Manufacturers' sales representatives can assist AOMs in controlling their reprographic costs and can make suggestions for work improvement. Sales representatives can also provide data on maintenance costs, leasing metered copying equipment, equipment reliability, and free equipment trial plans.

SUMMARY 1. Two types of information systems assist the AOM in providing the information needed in the modern firm. Microimage systems, which use very small records, represent a continually expanding form of compact records storage that started with the photographing of records onto microfilm. Presently there are two types of microrecords (unitized, such as microfiche, aperture cards, and microfilm jackets; and nonunitized, such as roll film) that may be packaged in various ways to facilitate the storage and retrieval of filmed records. To automate these processes, the output of a computer is linked to a device that photographs the records for storage on film. More recently, computer-assisted retrieval, which provides techniques for automating the retrieval of information stored in microform, has been developed; and optical disks have emerged as a highly effective, space-efficient, computerized storage and retrieval medium.

2. A related information systems area is reprographics, a term that refers to the wide range of hardware and procedures for reproducing information. The earliest reprographic process using machines was called duplicating and involved three machine processes—fluid, stencil, and offset duplicating—which have been largely replaced by office copiers.

3. The copying process represents a second method of reproducing information by machines. Xerography, because of its ease

of operation and convenience, has become the most popular copying process. Although all copying processes photograph the records to be reproduced, some copiers are capable of performing multiple functions. Copier-duplicators not only make copies of an original document, but also duplicate the original in large quantities. The intelligent copier/printer is capable of storing data in its memory, making copies of the data in the format prescribed, printing out the requested number of copies, and distributing them by wire to various locations.

4. Most large firms have organized central microrecord and reprographics departments and provide a specialized staff, proper equipment, and adequate space. Small firms, on the other hand, usually purchase microfilming services and some printing services from commercial agencies specializing in these services. All firms, however, should place strong emphasis upon controlling the costs of these operations.

GLOSSARY **Computer-assisted retrieval (CAR)**—the process of merging the computer and the microrecording process to access data on microfilm.

Computer input microfilm (CIM)—the process of translating uncoded data on microrecords into computer language code for storage on magnetic tape as input to a computer.

Computer output microfilm (COM)—the process in which a computer's output is automatically photographed and converted to human-readable images on microfilm without creating intervening paper copy.

Data aperture card—a microform that is identical to the punched aperture card except that it uses one or more lines of computer-readable OCR indexing text at the top of the card for display on the VDT screen.

Duplexing—copying on both sides of a sheet of copy paper in one operation.

Intelligent copier/printer—a machine that is a cross between a photocopier and a computer for providing a wide range of information functions.

Microfiche—a microform that appears in a grid pattern on a transparent sheet of film.

Microimage system—the total system for creating, using, and storing microrecords.

Microrecord—a paper document converted to microfilm.

Nonunitized microform—a microrecord that contains random or unrelated items of information on the same continuous length of film.

Optical disk—a mass memory device that stores document images through the use of laser technology; also known as *optical digital data disk (ODDD*, shortened to OD^3), since the disk stores digitized information.

Phototypesetter—a machine capable of creating print on a special VDT screen from data obtained from word processing or computer systems, or from direct keyboard entry.

Punched aperture card—a standard-size 80-column punched card with a precut hole over which a portion of 35mm microfilm is mounted.

Reader—a device that enlarges or magnifies the microrecord to its original legible size and projects the image onto a viewing screen.

Recorder—a device that photographs and reduces a computer's output into microimage size on film.

Reduction ratio—an expression of the number of times the size of a record is reduced photographically.

Reprographic system—a system related to the reproduction of information and records for management.

Roll film—a continuous length of microfilm, 16mm, 35mm, or 105mm in width, and 100 feet in length, on which records have been photographed and reduced in size for storage.

Ultrafiche—a special type of microfiche that permits very high (ultra) reduction ratios.

Unitized microform—a microrecord that is prepared as one complete set of data, such as a payroll file.

Updatable microfiche—a type of microfiche in which a special camera erases an obsolete record and places a new image over the erased record.

WORM (Write-Once, Read-Many) storage—a type of data storage that limits to one time the writing to disk but that provides many opportunities for reading out the disk contents.

Xerography—an electrostatic process that exposes a positively charged drum surface to light reflected through lenses from the original document.

FOR YOUR REVIEW

1. What procedural steps are involved in the creation and use of microrecords?

2. Identify the various kinds of microforms, and compare the relative advantages of each.

3. How are microrecords retrieved from (a) roll film, (b) microfiche, and (c) aperture cards?

4. What are the nature and purpose of a reader in a microimage system?

5. Define the computer output microfilm (COM) process, and trace the flow of information from the computer to the point of storage.

6. Explain how data are stored and retrieved in computer-assisted retrieval (CAR) systems.

7. Explain what an optical disk is and how it differs from typical media used for microrecord storage.

8. What types of conditions must be present in an office before the use of microrecords can be seriously considered?

9. Under what conditions can microfilmed records be admitted as evidence in courts of law?

10. What are the typical personnel needs to be provided in a microimage systems program?

11. What are the principal procedures needed to operate an effective microimage system?

12. In what ways does an office manager evaluate the microimage program?

13. Differentiate between the terms *duplicating* and *reprographic* processes.

14. What reasons are usually given for the rise in the use of copiers as replacements for most duplicating machines?

15. How are copying processes frequently classified?

16. What is an intelligent copier/printer, and how does it function in the production and transmission of information?

17. What factors should be considered in the process of selecting copiers for an office?

18. What good arguments can be given for the physical decentralization but organizational centralization of reprographic systems?

19. List some of the most common hidden costs that creep into a reprographic systems operation.

20. Outline some of the principal methods for reducing reprographic costs.

FOR YOUR DISCUSSION

1. A long-time friend of yours, Jake Nason, mentions that the number of records maintained in his small insurance office has gotten "out of hand." Nason asks you for suggestions about handling this common problem. What key issues and questions need to be answered before Nason can begin solving his problem?

2. In most of the small offices you have visited, a single copying machine is located in an area that is accessible to everyone. What advantages and disadvantages does such a layout have as far as reprographic cost controls are concerned?

3. "Most office workers consider the costs of copy making to be insignificant compared with other costs in the office." Is this an accurate assessment? If not, how can this common point of view be changed?

4. The department heads in City Hall remain opposed to the idea of converting their inactive records to microfilm for one reason—they believe it would be very inconvenient to go to a reader to use the records. What arguments can you advance to refute their reasoning?

5. Up to the present your employer, a small private business school, has used duplicating machines exclusively for all copy-making purposes in the administrative office. Now, however, the low-cost, simple methods for using convenience copiers have finally been accepted by your office manager, Juanita Mitchell. As a result, Mitchell has announced that a new copier with capabilities of making copies as well as producing transparencies and duplicating masters has been purchased. Mitchell requests that you, her assistant, prepare an outline of "do's and don't's" regarding the effective use of this new machine by the 23 employees and faculty in the school. Mitchell also requests that your outline give top priority to preventing the unauthorized use of the copier so poor copying habits and unnecessary copying costs do not develop. What information would you include in your outline?

6. The offices of Byers Products, Inc., require the documents listed below for the month of February. Indicate which of these items might be reproduced most economically and efficiently (a) on each department's convenience copier, (b) on the large-volume copiers maintained in the firm's reprographics center, or (c) on more highly specialized equipment provided by commercial printers.
   a. 200 copies of time cards for the office employees. The employee's name, clock number, and date are to be inserted on each card.
   b. 20 copies of a 2-page bulletin to be sent to each department head.
   c. 5 copies of the minutes of the directors' meeting held on February 10, to be sent to board members.
   d. 3,000 copies of a 2-page form letter to be sent to prospective customers.
   e. 500 copies of the 8-page newsletter. This company paper, issued monthly to all employees, contains snapshots, illustrations, and reading material.
   f. 250 copies of notices to stockholders announcing the annual meeting on March 15.
   g. 20 copies of a sales analysis report, 8 pages in length, for distribution to each of the 20 district sales managers.
   h. 20 copies of bulletins to typists listing suggestions for improving their work. Similar bulletins are issued weekly to the typists, who keep them in binders for future reference.

7. Representatives of a local microfilm services firm have recently discussed the advantages of converting your paper records system to microrecords. Regardless of the representatives' efforts, the officers of your company remain vehemently opposed to the idea and cite the following objections:
   a. Microrecords are "out of sight" and thus "out of mind."
   b. Microrecords are difficult to retrieve.
   c. Microrecords are more costly to maintain than paper records.
   d. Microrecords are useful only for inactive records.

   What is your reaction to these objections?

8. After studying Chapters 19 and 20, you have become much more conscious of the importance of records. As a result, you make an extra copy of your automobile license, your driver's license, and your automobile certificate of title. Can you legally do so? Discuss.

SOLVING CASE PROBLEMS

Case 20-1 Deciding Whether to Microfilm Paper Records

Barbara Satoko, office manager of Haven Wholesale Plumbers Supply, recently returned from an administrative cost reduction conference. During the conference, Satoko was impressed by the speakers' persuasive appeals for cutting costs by converting paper records to microfilm. As a result, Satoko has given you, the assistant office manager, this challenging assignment: "Find out for me whether our 'small-time' office should consider microfilming our active records (inventory, billing, and correspondence). I think this is 'big-time stuff' for large offices only, but give me your ideas in a short report."

The small office to which Satoko refers has seven full-time employees who spend much of their time creating new files and updating existing paper records related to the more than 4,700 plumbing and heating supplies maintained by the firm. Other common record tasks involve buying from 45 supplies manufacturers and selling to 275 retail hardware stores.

From your study of administrative office management, it seems clear that your assignment requires the study of basic information storage and retrieval systems and procedures in your firm.

1. What steps would you follow in completing this assignment?
2. What types of information—about microfilm as well as your office operations—would be needed? From whom would you obtain such information?
3. What personnel problems should you anticipate? (Note Satoko's "attitude" toward big-office ideas; also, keep in mind that the average tenure of the seven office employees is 17 years.)
4. How would you suggest the findings of your study be presented in order to receive a fair hearing by Satoko?

Case 20-2 Calculating Copying Costs

For several years you've worked as an assistant to Julie Foster, your firm's office manager. In her efforts to control costs, Foster calls you into her office where this conversation takes place:

Foster: Y'know, for too long we've talked about cutting paperwork costs, but no one has done anything about it. Agree?

You: I do.

Foster: Let's do something about it—RIGHT NOW! First, I'd like you to let me know all of the costs involved in making copies on our "repro" equipment; and second, tell me how we can easily and accurately calculate per-copy costs. Give me an example of such a computation so I can better understand this figure and possibly share it with other department heads here in the office.

You: OK, but won't I need some cost and volume figures from you first?

Foster: Sure will. Here is what I think you'll need. Good luck!

Foster hands you a sheet that shows these typical cost figures:

1. Convenience copier with life of 5 years: $6,000
2. Annual maintenance service (10% of copier purchase price) 600
3. 8½″ × 11″ copier paper, cost per ream (500 sheets) 6
4. Chemical additives (toner and developer) for making 15,000 copies 100

   Using this information, calculate per-copy costs for the following copy volumes per month: 1,000, 3,000, and 5,000. Also, point out to Foster how you made your calculations and what costs, either directly or indirectly related to reprographics, are *not* included.

PART 4

Controlling Administrative Services

21

Improving Administrative Office Systems

GOALS FOR THIS CHAPTER

After completing this chapter, you should be able to:

1. Differentiate between an effective system and an efficient system as these terms are used in improving administrative office systems.
2. Identify the prototypes of basic systems improvement and explain their value to personnel responsible for analyzing and designing administrative office systems.
3. List the principal systems communication tools and the typical uses of each.
4. Compare and contrast the work simplification model with the input-output model as guidelines for improving administrative office systems.
5. Describe the major elements that are typically examined in systems improvement studies and the goals that are set for the successful completion of such studies.
6. Discuss the various means that are used to communicate systems improvements, giving reasons for the use of each type of communication.
7. Explain the steps involved in designing, installing, and evaluating administrative office systems.

A *system*, as you recall from your study of Chapter 4, is a *set* of *related elements* that are *linked together* according to a *plan* for achieving a specific *objective*. In the systems study cycle, office workers—the most important systems element—perform six activities in the following order:

1. *Department managers or supervisors send a request to the systems unit for a study of their systems*; or, in a small office, the office manager requests a responsible worker to study one of the office systems.
2. *A survey of the present system is conducted.*
3. *The data collected about the present system are analyzed to determine how well the system is meeting its objectives.*
4. *An improved system is designed and tested.*
5. *The improved systems design is installed (put into operation).*
6. *The system is later evaluated* and its operating flaws corrected.

In this chapter, you will be introduced to methods of improving all types of administrative office systems (AOS). In doing so, we follow these same six steps, confining our discussion to typical manual systems that are basic to all of us. With a review of Chapter 4 and a careful study of this chapter, you should understand not only what AOS are but also how to improve AOS so that the systems goal—high productivity—is achieved.

Examine the world of work about you. In it you'll typically find the following kinds of paperwork systems in operation:

If you want . . .	. . . you must fill out . . .
• To get a job	. . . an application form.
• To get a hotel room	. . . a registration form.
• To go to college	. . . application forms.
• To pay taxes	. . . income-tax forms.
• To buy a car	. . . a loan application form.
• To get married	. . . a marriage license form.

Each of these systems is but *one small portion* of more complex systems at the manual systems level; and, too, each system can be—and often is—a part of a system that is automated in various ways. Generally automated systems involve complex, comprehensive areas of responsibility for controlling vast amounts of information and other resources. The improvement of such systems requires highly technical skills and broad backgrounds, the study of which is beyond the scope of this textbook.

The scope of activities involved in studies of simple manual systems (payroll, inventory control, college registration) is still relatively comprehensive because of the complex nature of most organizations. In such studies, the office manager first identifies all the basic elements in the system—*personnel*; *physical resources, including equipment, machines, and supplies*; *forms and related records required for operating AOS*; *data to be processed*; and *various types of controls*. Next, the office manager determines how these elements interact in the work environment in order to improve the system under study.

In this chapter, the fundamentals of systems improvement are explored first. With this general approach as a backdrop, the major areas of systems studies are highlighted. Once the studies are completed, the newly revised system (or an entirely new system in some cases) must be formally communicated to the user before the system can be installed. Finally, after the revised system has been in operation for an appro-priate period of time, it is evaluated and, if necessary, modified as required.[1]

THE SYSTEMS IMPROVEMENT PROCESS

On the bulletin boards in their departments, many systems managers post this simple, meaningful description of systems improvement studies: *Systems improvement studies help us decide whether we are doing the right thing rather than doing the thing right*. The thinking behind this systems philosophy is based on two important terms used to describe the general requirements for a properly operating system. Such a system should be *effective* and at the same time *efficient*. You may hear people using these terms interchangeably, but in systems circles these words have different but closely related meanings.

A system is **effective** when it is actually *doing the right thing*—that is, producing the desired quantity and quality of goods or services (the output) with the value of its output exceeding the costs involved in the input and transforming/processing steps of the systems cycle. For example, the costs involved in acquiring the labor, space, plant, equipment, and necessary operating data

---

[1]A related type of systems study, the feasibility study, is often associated with automated systems. However, as shown in this textbook, the feasibility study is useful in evaluating the benefits to be realized in adopting many systems changes—in furniture, in machines and equipment, in personnel, and in other systems elements as discussed above.

(the input costs) are added to the costs involved in the processing stage (computing, manufacturing, or related "transforming" operations). If these total costs are lower than the value of the output (a new automobile, an insurance policy, or a typewritten letter), the system is considered to be effective.

On the other hand, a system is **efficient** when it is judged to be operating in an economical manner; or, as mentioned earlier, *doing the thing right*. Usually three factors are considered in evaluating the efficiency of a system:

1. *Time*, which refers to the number of minutes, hours, days, weeks, months, or years needed to complete the output requirements of the system.
2. *Reliability*, an efficiency measure used to determine the accuracy of the system (its freedom from errors).
3. *Cost*, which refers to the dollars spent for all the components required to design and operate the system. (The cost factor usually receives the most attention in systems studies since department managers wage a continuing battle to "live" within their operating budgets. The control of administrative costs is discussed in detail in Chapter 23.)

You will find that analysts and office managers use both effectiveness and efficiency measures in evaluating the productivity of AOS. However, of the two measures, *effectiveness is considered the more basic*, for it directly relates to the attainment of systems objectives, as discussed in the next section.

General Approach to Systems Improvement

We study systems in order to meet one general objective: *to improve the performance of the systems*; that is, to solve present problems and prevent the occurrence of anticipated problems. Analysts find that

problems occur in any of the basic systems phases illustrated in Figure 4-5, page 97, or in any of the systems elements listed earlier in this chapter. However, most problems occur during two phases of a system: (1) *at the input phase*, when problems are reported to the systems personnel from other systems in the organization, and (2) *at the feedback phase*, when the quantitative and qualitative levels of output fail to meet the standards of performance expected. In both situations, the same general administrative problem is recognized: *Personnel performance or the operational levels of the other elements in the system do not meet the system's objectives. The gap between actual performance and expected performance thus represents the extent or severity of the problem.*

A Prototype of Systems Improvement

In order to understand how the systems approach is applied to the improvement of systems, a prototype of the improvement process may be used. The **prototype**, or basic model, shown in Figure 21-1, simplifies our view of the complex relationships found in systems operations and serves as a foundation for most of the work involved in systems studies. Most systems studies emphasize an intensive analysis of the present systems; section A of Figure 21-1 outlines this set of activities. On occasion, however, a department in a firm senses the need for creating an entirely new system. When this condition exists, the prototype is modified slightly, as shown in section B of Figure 21-1. However, in both cases, the same systems study cycle is followed.

The Ideal System

To use the prototype for systems improvement in an effective manner, we must previously have developed a clear idea of an **ideal system**. In such a utopian system, all systems elements function at their most effective and efficient levels at all times. Personnel perform at their peak; machines

Figure 21-1
Prototypes for Improving Administrative Office Systems

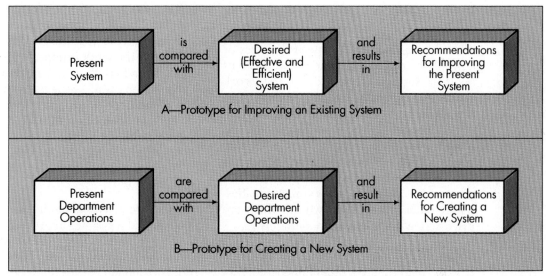

A—Prototype for Improving an Existing System

B—Prototype for Creating a New System

function properly and, with proper maintenance, are not subject to downtime; forms and reports are well designed and function as planned; data are available as needed; controls effectively regulate the system according to the plan; and operating costs are minimized. *Such a perfect system does not—and will never—exist.* However, from a conceptual standpoint, a systems staff benefits by having this idealistic system as a model. Such an ideal "target" provides a sense of direction and motivation to an administrative staff to analyze, design, and install a higher quality system than if such a model did not exist.

The Effective Real-World System

In the real world, we must be practical-minded and recognize that an ideal system cannot be attained. What can be developed, on the other hand, is an effective **real-world system** that provides the best possible service to the departments concerned but subject to certain limitations. As the main element in the system, the human being is prone to fatigue and dissatisfaction on the job. Machines, unlike people, do not become fatigued or dissatisfied; however, machines

are subject to downtime through lack of or careless service. Through human error, inaccuracy, or indifference, forms and reports are often used in an ineffective way. Data may be received late or transmitted to the wrong parties, which results in failure to meet reporting deadlines, thereby delaying business decision making. Controls, even though properly designed, may not be understood or, worse yet, may not be enforced. Thus, standards of worker performance, quotas, budgets, computer programs, and other AOS controls fail to function properly. Under such conditions, operating costs in AOS skyrocket.

Studying all of these elements is complicated by the need for an in-depth study of *each* element if a more reliable, more economical system is to result from the study. Realistically, systems analysts "attack" the study of systems problems in small, manageable portions and often restrict the scope of a study to *one* of the elements mentioned earlier. Specialized systems analysts in large firms use this same approach by identifying the main segments, or parts, of the organization of the system under study, and then studying each segment.

Systems Improvement Models

When the analyst or the AOM wishes to undertake a study of the specific phases of a problem, we find that one of two systems analysis models is used: (1) the work simplification model that has resulted from the application of scientific management to the office and (2) the input-output analysis model, which is an outgrowth of computer systems studies. Whenever complex systems need improvement and highly specialized analysts are available, several mathematics-based models are used, two of which are discussed in the following paragraphs.

The Work Simplification Model

A **work simplification model** describes a set of general guidelines, based upon common sense, for analyzing a system. Behind the work simplification concept is the basic philosophy that all work operations can be improved and that there must always be a better way to perform each task.

A basic model of work simplification may be expressed in question form with the key words capitalized, as shown in Figure 21-2. When a work simplification program is started in the office, this logical sequence of steps is followed in *Phase One* (Data Gathering) in order to facilitate a later analysis of the system:

1. The analyst gathers information about WHAT work is being done.
2. The analyst questions WHERE and WHEN the work is done, WHO does the work, and HOW it is being done.
3. Each step in the sequence is followed by a request for an explicit reason WHY the work is performed in a certain way as well as how it SHOULD be done. These questions are intended to uncover the facts that have the most bearing on the system under study.

This type of verbal model can be applied to all phases of systems improvement studies; for it structures the systems study into identifiable, orderly steps, which make the problem-solving, or systems improvement, tasks easier to complete.

When the data have been gathered in Phase One of the work simplification model, the analyst is prepared to undertake the second phase, Data Analysis. In this phase the analyst probes for answers to questions such as the following:

1. *Can the systems work be ELIMINATED?*
   - Is the system obsolete and of no further value?
   - If the service provided, such as extending credit, results in a loss for the firm, can the service be discontinued?

Figure 21-2
The Work Simplification Model Used in AOS Improvement Studies

Phase One—Data Gathering	Phase Two—Data Analysis
1. WHAT work is being done? WHY? What work SHOULD be done?	1. Can the work be ELIMINATED?
2. WHERE is the work being done? WHY? Where SHOULD the work be done?	2. Can several tasks or forms be COMBINED?
3. WHEN is the work being done? WHY? When SHOULD the work be done?	3. Can the work processes be RESEQUENCED or REARRANGED for more efficient operations?
4. WHO does the work? WHY? Who SHOULD do the work?	4. Can the work be SIMPLIFIED?
5. HOW is the work being done? WHY? How SHOULD the work be done?	

- Can the correspondence operations with branch offices be eliminated by installing electronic mail systems?
- Can the storage of inactive records be assigned to the company archives in order to eliminate the work being performed by the records management department?

2. *Can several tasks or forms be COMBINED?*
    - Can two or more forms be combined into one?
    - Can two related jobs be assigned to one full-time worker rather than to several part-time workers?
    - Can the work of three small decentralized copy centers be combined into one large copy center?

3. *Can the work processes be RESEQUENCED or REARRANGED?*
    - Can invoice checking be assigned to the computer rather than to the office staff?
    - Can reports be edited on a word processor rather than on handwritten copy prior to the automated processing of the reports?
    - Can the items on a form be resequenced in keeping with the order in which the information is used?

4. *Can the systems work be SIMPLIFIED?*
    - Can the number of copies of a form be reduced?
    - Can a mechanical collator be used for the rapid assembly of pages in a report?
    - Can the office layout be changed to provide adjacent workstations for employees working together?

With sufficient time, patience, and attention to detail, the analyst can identify basic questions that require answers if the system is to be improved. Such improvement results in better, faster, more convenient, more simplified, and less costly methods of performing the work. A discussion of the techniques used in work simplification is provided in a later section of this chapter.

The Input-Output (I/O) Model for Systems Improvement

If properly done, input-output analysis generally can be applied to the improvement of all types of systems operations. Thus, an **input-output (I/O) systems improvement model** furnishes a generalized method for analyzing each of the phases in AOS. Such a model is shown in Figure 21–3, which represents a modification of the basic systems model discussed in Chapter 4, pages 97–100.

As you can see in this figure, the topmost priority in studying a system is to determine the objectives of the user department. To illustrate the use of the input-output model for improving systems, assume that in the design of an accounting system, all hourly employees are paid by noon on Friday of each week. In studying the effectiveness of such a system, the analyst must determine the requirements for satisfying the needs of each phase in the system (represented by blocks in Figure 21–3). These requirements include:

1. *User's objectives*: Paychecks available by noon each Friday; all checks and related records accurately prepared; and sufficient security and privacy maintained over the payroll records.

2. *Output requirements*: Same as user's objectives; in addition, copies of payroll records are fed back into the payroll system for use in computing the next cycle of paychecks and the related payroll and tax records.

3. *Input requirements*: Relevant data (hours worked—regular and overtime—rate of pay, deductions, and other payroll information); and appropriate equipment, procedures, and work schedules. Each must be provided early enough in the workweek to complete the required output on time.

4. *Process requirements*: Manual procedures or computer programs that transform the

Figure 21-3
An Input-
Output (I/O)
Model for
Systems
Improvement

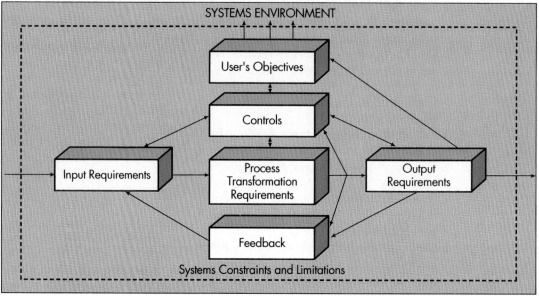

payroll system's data into the output required.

5. *Feedback*: A record of the output—a correctly processed paycheck and related records, such as an earnings statement—as fed back into the system to be used in computing the paychecks for the following pay period.

6. *Controls*: Ensuring that the system operates properly by: (a) checking on the accuracy of the input data, (b) pretesting the computer program or manual procedures, (c) monitoring the arrival time of the payroll data, (d) providing security over the paychecks until delivered to workers, and (e) maintaining a complete set of all records produced in each cycle of the payroll system's operations.

If each of these requirements is met, the output will be accurate and reliable; thus, the user will have faith in a system that has demonstrated its effectiveness and efficiency.

While the input-output model revolves around the various phases in the system, such

an analysis is performed by systems personnel who use whatever techniques are available for problem solving. Thus, analysts ask meaningful questions (illustrated in the work simplification model) in order to gain insight into the operation of each phase of the system (as indicated in the input-output analysis model). In reality, therefore, both models discussed in this section can be used—one as a supplement to the other—in order that the analysis of the system be as thorough as possible.

Other Models

When managers require great precision and predictability as to the likely outcomes of installing a certain type of system, they turn to analysts highly trained in mathematics, logic, and the scientific method of problem solving. For example, sampling models are used to learn the characteristics of a group of people without examining each individual member in the group. In addition, analysts use **operations research (OR)** to determine the best possible solutions to decision-making problems in complex systems. An OR model represents a simplified conceptual picture of the system—usually set up in a mathematical equation—that contains all the factors of primary importance to the problem. Once the model is developed, we can test it to see how well it answers many of the questions asked of a real-world system.

Simulation is a basic OR technique for creating a mathematical model of a real-world system. Simulation involves the identification of alternate courses of action to consider for maximizing profits and minimizing costs after studying the various resources available. Less complex simulation methods use simple logic—or plain common sense—based on good experience to "imitate" on paper or in an oral discussion the same conditions an AOM would find in a real-world problem. Figure 21–4 simulates,

in outline form, a typical set of conditions routinely faced by the manager of a travel agency. By addressing each of these situations, the AOM can begin the problem-solving/systems study cycle using the work simplification model, the I/O model, or both. Another OR technique, **linear programming (LP)**, is used to determine the best mixture of components in a system, such as the best "mix" of operators and equipment to handle an anticipated word processing workload in an office.

Systems Communication Tools

Because of the great amount of detail involved in improving AOS, analysts search for concise, understandable methods of organizing and communicating the detailed operations of the system being studied. One of the most effective methods of commu-

Figure 21–4
Simulating
the Opera-
tions of a
Small Travel
Agency

Typical Operations
1. Customer wants to change reservation to later flight.
2. Telephone customer checks on flight reservations to Hawaii.
3. Airline calls informing travel agency of changed departure times for passengers who made reservations through agency.
4. AMTRAK calls to confirm reservation for waiting customer.
5. Group wants to arrange tour to Washington, DC.
6. Three customers want to be waited on at once.
7. Customer complains about accommodations on his last trip to NYC.
8. Foreigner (with very poor English skills) calls to ask information about one-way ticket to Pakistan.
9. Customer calls for quotation on fare; and upon learning quotation, begins to argue because friend went same route at less cost.
10. Customer calls because she lost her ticket and needs a new one.
11. Equipment (telephone, computer, copier, etc.) breaks down.
12. Personnel problems arise: one clerk 30 minutes late; another, ill on the same day.
Resources Needed to Conduct Operations
1. Personnel
2. Space
3. Furniture, equipment, and supplies
4. Procedures including needed references
5. Operating budget

nicating these operations is the systems chart. Such a chart tells a pictorial, sequential "story" of the system with few or no words required. The proverb, "One picture is worth a thousand words," applies well to the use of charts in systems studies.

A second type of systems communication is the decision table, which emerged in the computer age as a useful device in documenting the makeup of a system. Each of the commonly used systems charts is defined in this section along with a discussion of the use of decision tables. Other systems communication tools, including written procedures and manuals, are explained in a later section of this chapter.

Systems Charts

A **systems chart** is a graphic device used to portray an existing or a proposed system, including the flow of information and the various elements required to operate a system. Charts help the analyst to display information clearly and the user department to understand the problems in the present system as well as the solutions recommended.

Analysts begin systems studies by familiarizing themselves with the entire organization and examining in detail the specific parts of the organization to be studied. If there is no organization chart, the analyst must prepare one that shows the present plan of organization and the role of the departments to be studied.[2]

Many types of systems charts are available, depending on the information needs of the analyst. For example, a **flowchart** is used to show the logical sequence of steps involved in the flow of work, usually in a manual system. A **forms distribution chart** traces the flow of forms and related paperwork through the departments under study. Layout charts, illustrated in Chapter 13, are useful in understanding the problems involved with the management of office space. Information regarding the scheduling of work is often presented on a Gantt chart, also discussed in Chapter 13, or on a PERT chart, which is discussed later. For analyzing work assignments among a department staff, a **work distribution chart**, which identifies and compares the principal tasks of all workers in the system, is a useful tool.

Systems charts are also useful in studying automated systems. However, two charts in particular—the systems flowchart and the program flowchart—are most often identified with computer systems. Both of these charts are discussed in Chapter 16.

Decision Tables

A **decision table** is a tool for presenting the logic and the sequential operations in a system by showing what action must be taken to satisfy each information-related condition. The decision table was originally designed to illustrate the logic found in computer programs; however, we also use it in other systems studies. This type of systems tool is used in situations where the logic and the sequential flow of data cannot be clearly represented on a chart. Decision tables serve as easy-to-follow communication devices for both the systems staff and the nontechnical personnel in the user departments.

A decision table may be very simple and describe only a few conditions, or it may involve dozens or even hundreds of steps. The basic decision table is divided into four sections:

1. The *conditions section* that sets forth in an explicit or implied question form the conditions that may exist in the system.
2. The *action section* that lists the action to be taken for satisfying each condition.
3. The *condition-entry section*, or set of rules, that provides answers ("yes," "no,"

---

[2]The purpose of organization charts is discussed in Chapter 2 along with suggestions for constructing such charts.

or "not applicable") to the questions in the conditions section.

4. The *action-entry section* that indicates by an *X* the appropriate action resulting from the answers entered in the condition-entry section.

Figure 21–5 illustrates a decision table for determining the vacation time and amount of bonus for the workers in a major corporation. Each of the four possible conditions and the actions that may be taken for satisfying each condition can be easily understood by using this simple device.

MAJOR STUDIES IN ADMINISTRATIVE OFFICE SYSTEMS

Analyzing and improving AOS may involve all or only a portion of the elements making up these systems. Depending on the availability of staff and the necessary time and funds, one or more of the following major studies in AOS may be undertaken:

1. Flow of work.
2. Use of space.
3. Forms and related documents.
4. Performance of personnel.
5. Use of equipment.
6. Scheduling of work.
7. Costs of operating AOS.

We discuss each of these areas of study in this section. However, before such studies can be started, it is important that the analyst or the OM has followed the guidelines contained in the systems models discussed earlier and that relevant, accurate, and complete information about the system is on hand.

Work-Flow Studies

In **work-flow analysis**, we study the origination and distribution of documents

Figure 21–5
A Decision Table Showing the Rules for Granting Employee Vacations and Bonuses

	CONDITION ENTRY			
Employee Vacation and Bonus	**Rule 1**	**Rule 2**	**Rule 3**	**Rule 4**
Worker employed for less than 1 year?	Y	N	N	N
Worker employed from 1-2 years?	—	Y	N	N
Worker employed from 2-5 years?	—	—	Y	N
Worker employed 5 or more years?	—	—	—	Y
No vacation	X			
One-week vacation and $50 bonus		X		
Two-week vacation and $100 bonus			X	
Three-week vacation and $500 bonus				X

CONDITIONS
ACTIONS
ACTION ENTRY

Legend: Y = Yes   X = Completion of action statement
N = No   — or blank = Not applicable

and the clerical operations required to process the information. Each of the subsystems in AOS uses a set of key documents around which the work is centered. For example, in a purchasing system, the work involves originating a purchase requisition form, which is sent by the requesting department to the purchasing department for approval. Next, a multicopy purchase order is created and distributed to various departments in the firm, such as accounting and receiving, and to the vendor for filling the order. Both of these internal departments must await the receipt of the item ordered from the vendor before final payment is made.

To document the work flow involved in a typical system, the analyst prepares a flow process chart that records each of the steps in the system. The symbols and definitions used in flow process charting, illustrated in Figure 21–6, are now a part of the "Methods of Charting Paperwork Procedures" developed by the American National Standards Institute. Frequently AOS consultants and representatives of office equipment manufacturers modify these symbols to suit their individual needs.

Figure 21–7 illustrates a flow process chart of the steps involved in typing a purchase order. By studying each of the steps in the flow of work—the operation, transportation, inspection, delay, and storage activities—the analyst is able to compute the time and delay problems detected and from such information develop improvements in the system.[3] Typical problems that can be disclosed by a study of the flow process chart include undue delays in transferring work between workstations; too much duplication of effort at workstations, such as two separate operations for verifying totals on invoices; duplicate forms and work sheets; too much travel or transportation time from one workstation to the next; and unfair work assignments that cause an overworked clerk to delay the processing of information.

---

[3]Note that only the present method of typing purchase orders is shown in Figure 21–7. A similar chart would be prepared for an improved (proposed) method as well as for keyboarding such information on "soft-copy" forms in the VDT. At the top of the chart, numeric data are shown for a proposed method, along with the savings in number of steps and in minutes required to complete the two versions of the system. Thus, the proposed method of operating the system saves five steps and 122.9 minutes, on the average.

Figure 21–6
Standardized Flow Process Chart Symbols

Symbol	Key	Example of Systems Activities
○	Operation	A productive activity (computing, filling in a form, interviewing an employee).
⇨	Transportation	The physical movement of workers, information, or materials.
▢	Inspection	Proofreading, checking, or verifying data.
◗	Delay	A pause (momentary or longer) in the processing or flow of work.
▽	Storage	Temporary or permanent filing of information or materials.

Figure 21-7
Flow Process
Chart of
Present
Method of
Typing Pur-
chase Orders

FLOW PROCESS CHART OF *Typing a purchase order set*

SUMMARY

		Present		Proposed		Savings	
		No.	Time	No.	Time	No.	Time
◯	Operations	6	6.7	4	5.1	2	1.6
⇨	Transportations	3	1.1	2	.8	1	.3
☐	Inspections	2	3.0	1	2.0	1	1.0
D	Delays	2	180.0	1	60.0	1	120.0
▽	Storages	1	—	1	—	0	—
	Totals	14	190.8	9	67.9	5	122.9
	Distance traveled (*ft*)		10		6		4

Department *Purchasing*
☐ Worker ☑ Form / ~~Material~~ *#124*
Chart begins *Step 1*
Chart ends *Step 14*
Chart _____ Page *1* of *2*
Charted by *Jason Carroll*
Date *9/8/--*
Dept. approved *B. J. Falk*
Date *10/17/--*

SYMBOLS

Step No.	Description of Present Method ~~Proposed~~	Operation	Transport	Inspection	Delay	Storage	Quantity	Time in minutes	Distance in feet	Notes
1	Purchase order forms stored in desk drawer	◯	⇨	☐	D	▽	400	—	—	Consider installing
2	Remove 1 purchase order from drawer	◯	⇨	☐	D	▽	1	.1		continuous forms and
3	Move form to typewriter	◯	⇨	☐	D	▽	1	.3	3	form-feeder
4	Insert purchase order form into typewriter	◯	⇨	☐	D	▽	1	.2		mechanism on two typewriters in
5	Type purchase order from purchase requisition	◯	⇨	☐	D	▽	1	4.	—	purchasing dept.
6	Proofread	◯	⇨	☐	D	▽	1	1		
7	Remove form from typewriter	◯	⇨	☐	D	▽	1	.2	—	
8	Place in "P.O. complete" basket	◯	⇨	☐	D	▽	1	.5	3	
9	Wait until 25 purchase orders are typed	◯	⇨	☐	D	▽	—	100	—	Average wait time
10	Pick up batch of completed P.O. forms	◯	⇨	☐	D	▽	25	2.	—	
11	Count number in batch	◯	⇨	☐	D	▽	25	2.	—	
12	Place rubber band around batch	◯	⇨	☐	D	▽	25	2.		
13	Place in Out Basket	◯	⇨	☐	D	▽	25	.3	4	
14	Wait for pickup	◯	⇨	☐	D	▽	—	80	—	daily wait, on the average
	Order typing completed	◯	⇨	☐	D	▽				See page 2 for chart of proposed system.
		◯	⇨	☐	D	▽				

Space-Use Studies

The effective use of space is an important responsibility of the OM and a topic that is closely related to work-flow analysis. In fact, the physical layout of the efficient office is built around the major flows of work, with the workstations arranged to minimize backtracking and wasted motion. Also, the combined ergonomic aspects of the environment must be studied; for these environmental factors directly affect the manner in which the space is used.

In addition to ergonomic studies of office space, we should give attention to **workplace analysis**, which seeks to improve the arrangement of all resources needed to function efficiently at a workstation. (See Figure 21–8A for an example of an inefficiently arranged workstation badly in need of improvement; Figure 21–8B shows how this workplace has been rearranged for more efficient office production.) Also, we should study the flow and frequency of movement of each of the forms and of the workers who transport the records throughout the office. This may be accomplished by studying the office layout, preparing separate before-and-after layout charts for each important system, and drawing lines to indicate the movement of the various papers throughout the organization.

Office layout charts should be prepared for the paperwork transactions that occur most frequently. Studying the direction and distance of movement in the office will point out wasted motion and needless backtracking. Measuring the distance traveled *before* and *after* the changes in the system are made will indicate the distance and time saved in performing the office activities.

Figure 21–9 shows an example of the effective rearranging of office space in order to minimize the movement of workers and the paperwork for which they are responsible. A study of the before-and-after illustrations in this figure shows the waste in steps, time, energy, and money that was eliminated in this space study. The "after" example shows a reduction of approximately 40 percent in distance traveled for the combined flows of mail and other work. In addition, other important savings result from the fact that two VDT operators and their workstation equipment replaced five typists and their workstations in the office under study.

Forms Studies

The systems analyst approaches the study of the forms used by collecting copies of all the key forms in the system. With this

Figure 21–8 A—An Inefficiently Arranged Workstation B—An Efficiently Arranged Workstation

A

B

**Figure 21-9
Before-and-
After Office
Layout
Charts**

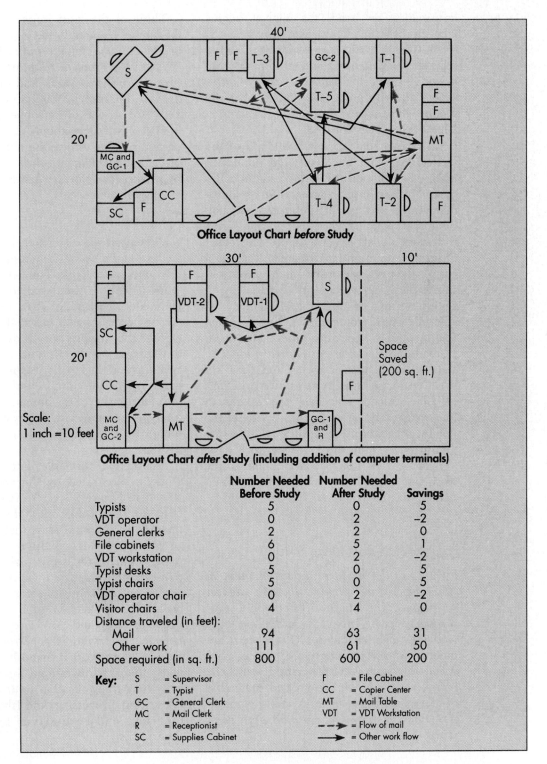

Office Layout Chart *before* Study

Office Layout Chart *after* Study (including addition of computer terminals)

Scale:
1 inch = 10 feet

	Number Needed Before Study	Number Needed After Study	Savings
Typists	5	0	5
VDT operator	0	2	–2
General clerks	2	2	0
File cabinets	6	5	1
VDT workstation	0	2	–2
Typist desks	5	0	5
Typist chairs	5	0	5
VDT operator chair	0	2	–2
Visitor chairs	4	4	0
Distance traveled (in feet):			
Mail	94	63	31
Other work	111	61	50
Space required (in sq. ft.)	800	600	200

Key:

S	= Supervisor	F	= File Cabinet	
T	= Typist	CC	= Copier Center	
GC	= General Clerk	MT	= Mail Table	
MC	= Mail Clerk	VDT	= VDT Workstation	
R	= Receptionist	---→	= Flow of mail	
SC	= Supplies Cabinet	——→	= Other work flow	

information on hand, the analyst begins analyzing the need for each copy of each form. Generally the users of forms in all the related departments are asked to justify the use of all forms. Guidelines for studying this aspect of forms analysis are included in the section, *Principles of Forms Management*, in Chapter 19, pages 580–582.

An analyst may approach a study of the work flow from many vantage points. In addition to the narrow scope (within a department), an organization-wide or multidepartment analysis of such a system may be undertaken, as pictured in the forms distribution chart, Figure 21–10. This chart illustrates the multidepartment routing of a form—the purchase order—and its relationship to the purchase requisition and receiving report forms. In this simplified type of systems chart (sometimes called a *block diagram*), no special symbols are used. Instead, the blocks are provided to identify the various copies of forms and their respective destinations. Scaled-down drawings of file cabinets also help the reader to understand the storage of forms without the need for committing additional charting symbols to memory. Before-and-after versions of this type of chart, similar to the flow process and layout charts discussed earlier, may be prepared.

Personnel Performance Studies

People are the most important element in AOS; hence, we should give the highest priority to the study of personnel performance in the office. Regardless of how well the other elements in the system are planned—machines, furniture, forms, and space—a system will not perform well if the people assigned to do the work are incapable of performing satisfactorily or are undermotivated or simply refuse to do a fair day's work.

Three of the most important aspects of the human element in the system are (1) *the needs and skills of the individual workers*, (2) *the nature and distribution of tasks performed by the workers*, and (3) *the quality of their supervision*. You read about the first and third aspects of personnel performance in Part 2 of this textbook. In the following paragraphs, we discuss the remaining aspect of the human element—the tasks performed by workers and the distribution of such tasks among the office staff.

Task Analysis

Task analysis is a systems technique used by analysts and personnel workers to determine *who does what work*. The necessity of each work activity is then studied and the task eliminated if possible. Task analysis should not be confused with job analysis discussed earlier. Job analysis serves as the basis for developing job descriptions and job specifications and thus spells out the requirements made by the job on the workers. Generally the contribution of the human element to the total performance of the system is determined by the tasks people perform in the system.

A **task** is a definable unit (or piece) of work, as illustrated by the work activities shown in Figure 21–11. We can divide the tasks in most AOS into five *productive* operations: (1) *input tasks* that relate to the receiving and recording of data; (2) *transforming (processing) tasks* in which the data are converted into the form required for the output; (3) *data storage and retrieval tasks*; (4) *control tasks*, such as verifying or proofreading; and (5) *tasks designed to prepare information for transmission to those who must use it*. In addition, there are *nonproductive* operations, such as excessively long transportation routes; time spent in creating, processing, and filing unneeded records; and excessive numbers of supervisors.

Figure 21-10
A Forms Distribution
Chart of a
Purchase
Order
Procedure

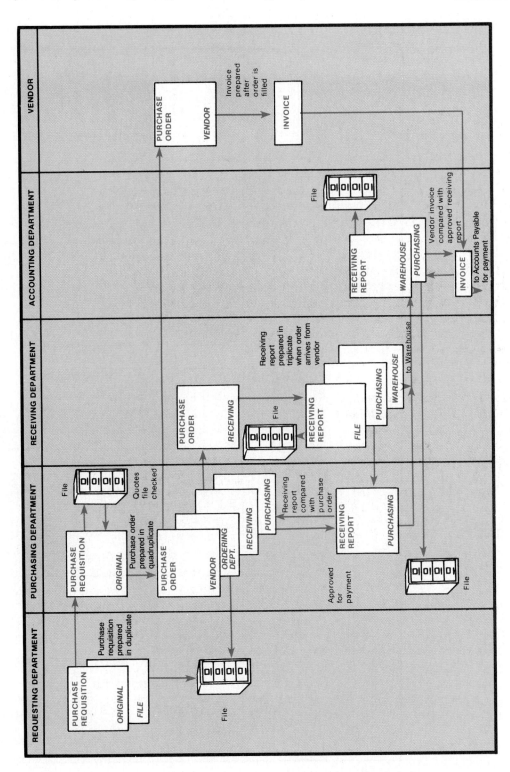

Figure 21-11
Weekly Task Chart for a Purchase-Order Clerk

WEEKLY TASK CHART

Principal Tasks: Completing a purchase order   Employee Name: Carl Snell   Date: 10/17/–

System: Purchase Order Processing   Department: Purchasing   Title: Jr. Clerk

PRODUCTIVE OPERATIONS												NONPRODUCTIVE OPERATIONS	
Receiving Inputs	*Hrs.	Recording	Hrs.	Processing	Hrs.	Storage and Retrieval	Hrs.	Control	Hrs.	Transmitting Outputs	Hrs.	Miscellaneous	Hrs.
Purchase requisition	1.25	Type order data	13.5	Compute totals for each item to be purchased	4.0	Retrieve vendors' catalogs and price lists	.4	Check purchase order data against purchase requisition	1.5	Purchase order (6 copies)	1.25	Carry purchase requisitions from purchase requisition section head to desk	.6
Vendors' catalogs and price lists		Type terms data	2.5	Compute sales tax	.5	File purchase department copies	.6	Confirm major purchases with secretary of purchase agent	1.0	Distribute copies		Carry purchase orders to supervisor	.6
Telephone calls to expedite processing of orders	3.0	Write order information on dept. order schedule	1.0	Compute grand total for each purchase	1.5							Carry file copies to file	.8
		Address envelopes to transmit copies of purchase orders	3.0	Update schedule of outstanding orders	.5							Separate copies of completed purchase orders	1.5
	5.25		20.0		6.5		1.0		2.5		1.25		3.5

*Figures in Hrs. column represent the approximate number of hours required weekly for completing each task.

By completing a task chart listing the duties performed by each worker, an analyst can confirm the *productive* tasks (those adding value to the system) as well as the *nonproductive* tasks (those not contributing value to the system). However, this latter category may include tasks such as supervision, transporting paperwork, and error correction, which are considered necessary in some instances. Although these tasks are necessary in order that the work be processed properly, *the amount of nonproductive tasks as a percentage of the total systems tasks should be held to a minimum.*

Work Distribution

If we complete the task chart in Figure 21–11 for each of the three clerks assigned to a purchasing department, we have laid the groundwork for studying the distribution of the work load among this office staff. We prepare the work distribution chart in order to identify and classify the principal tasks of all the clerks in the office. From the information shown on the work distribution chart in Figure 21–12, the analyst can tell how many work units are produced and how much time is spent on each type of activity for all three clerks. With this type of information, the analyst can obtain answers to such questions as:

1. How much time is *each* clerk (as well as *all* clerks) spending on each type of task?
2. Is the group spending too much time on unimportant tasks or on relatively unproductive work? If so, what are they?
3. Is the distribution of tasks fairly assigned, or are more rewarding tasks needed by certain workers?
4. In what ways can the workers' assignments be rearranged so that the overall performance can be raised and operating costs lowered?
5. How much time is unaccounted for?

Next, the analyst compares the times observed or reported for each clerk performing related work. With this information, the analyst can evaluate the assignments, note the ratio of time used for productive to nonproductive operations, and determine the rates at which the work is performed (as calculated from the work-count figure). For each task reported on the work distribution chart, the analyst can classify the operation as input, transformation (processing), output, or some other systems category by referring back to the appropriate task chart. With this information, the analyst can determine what category of operation is occupying the most time and then concentrate on reducing the time.

Equipment-Use Studies

Because of the continuing increase in the cost of labor, AOMs place much emphasis upon the effective use of labor-saving equipment in the office. An analysis of the use of equipment may be part of a broader systems study, such as total work flow; or the use of equipment may be studied separately.

Most studies of equipment usage start with an identification of the various tasks performed. Once this has been accomplished, the analyst attempts to find out which of the main administrative operations (recording, computing, sorting, filing, retrieving, summarizing, and communicating) are performed by human means and which are performed partially or wholly by machine. The use of machines in performing administrative operations may afford cost savings—usually in labor costs—and thus help to increase profits. In addition, the output produced by machines is usually more legible, neater, and more accurate than that produced by human means. For many applications, such as calculating, machines are much faster than workers; and therefore larger volumes of information can be handled in shorter periods of time. Much of the work in accounting systems is routine

Figure 21-12
A Work Distribution Chart Comparing the Work Performed and Time Spent by Three Clerks in the Purchasing Department

WORK DISTRIBUTION CHART						
Department Purchasing	**System** Purchase Order		**Analyst** Betty Binelli		**Date** 4/14/--	
Productive Operations	Title: Jr. Clerk Name: Carl Snell		Title: Jr. Clerk Name: Sandi Heinz		Title: Jr. Clerk Name: Kim Lee	
	Hrs./ Wk.	Work Count	Hrs./ Wk.	Work Count	Hrs./ Wk.	Work Count
1. Receiving inputs (vendors' lists, purchase requisitions, telephone calls, etc.)	5.25	27	7.0	43	12.0	38
2. Keyboarding order data	13.5	50	15.5	35	20.0	60
3. Keyboarding terms data	2.5	50	2.0	40	1.5	30
4. Writing order information on order schedule	2.4	50	2.0	45	1.0	22
5. Addressing envelopes	1.6	85	1.4	70	1.0	64
6. Computing totals for each item to be purchased	4.0					
Productive time spent	36.5		30.0		36.0	
Nonproductive Operations						
1. Carrying purchase requisitions from purchase requisition section head to desk	.6	50	1.0	50		
2. Carrying purchase orders to supervisor	.6	50				
3. Carrying file copies to file	.8	50				
4. Separating copies of completed purchase orders	1.5	50	2.0	50	2.0	20
Nonproductive time spent	3.5		3.0		2.0	
Summary of Time Spent (In hrs./wk.)						
Productive operations	36.5		30.0		36.0	
Nonproductive operations	3.5		3.0		2.0	
Time not reported	.0		7.0		2.0	
Total time	40.0		40.0		40.0	

and repetitive and lends itself to the use of standardized machine processes. As the power of many machines increases, their sizes decrease; and their operations grow more quiet. Therefore, valuable office space is saved; and the need for installing costly acoustical materials is reduced.

A feasibility study provides criteria for the selection of machines as well as operating information about the system in which the machines are used. Regardless of what type or level of machine is used in the system, the AOM or the systems analyst in charge of studying the use of machines should try to match the benefits of available hardware with the tasks to be performed. If that goal can be accomplished, machines can help to provide an efficient means of performing office work.

Work-Scheduling Studies

One of the most critical elements to control in a system is time; for, as the business axiom maintains, *"Time is money."* All of the labor hours devoted to administrative work are very costly since studies show that labor time is consistently the most expensive factor in producing administrative services. Thus, we must carefully manage the time used in the operation of AOS.

Of special importance to the success of AOS are (1) scheduling techniques that help to reduce the time required for completing work and (2) the concept of time management, which seeks to reduce the amount of time required by individuals in performing their assigned jobs. Time management is discussed in Chapter 22 as one phase of a work measurement and control program; scheduling techniques are discussed briefly in this section.

A major problem in most systems operations is coordinating the flow of materials, energy, and information over a period of time in order to achieve the desired output as soon as possible. The flow of these factors must be orderly, logical, and uninterrupted. One technique developed during World War II to handle such logistics problems is called PERT, mentioned earlier in this chapter. The main function of **PERT**, an acronym for Program Evaluation and Review Technique, is to answer the question, *"How much time is required to complete a project?"* A basic PERT chart for estimating the time required to construct a new office building can be developed manually by following the steps shown in Figure 21-13. A PERT chart for scheduling the time required to construct an office building is illustrated in Figure 21-14. Notice that some events must be sequential (Event B must follow A, and Event H must follow G); on the other hand, other events may occur concurrently (Event C can be completed at the same time as D is being carried out).

Simple PERT charts can be constructed by hand from the mental computations of the systems analyst or the OM when fewer than one hundred activities are involved. When more complicated projects, such as the construction of major highways in an interstate system, are to be charted, mainframes are used to generate such charts, using programs that are written specially for PERT. For smaller projects, we can use PC software for developing Gantt and PERT charts, and the mathematic computations to accompany them.

PERT helps the managers of AOS control the completion of important projects and thereby save money. (Note, however, that an estimated 5 percent of the total cost of a project is often spent for PERT and other scheduling methods; thus, the technique is not cost free.) PERT also is useful with projects that involve many activities stretching out over a period of years. However, the technique calls for realistic estimates of expected completion times. Without such insight, PERT is not useful.

Figure 21-13
Steps to
Follow in
Developing a
PERT Chart

Steps	Comments
1. Determine the activities to be performed, such as digging a basement, writing a computer program, or conducting an employee attitude survey.	An activity takes time to perform and costs money to complete. On a PERT chart, the activity is shown as a line with an arrow pointing in a general direction to the right. Usually a time measure (one week, two months) is indicated on the line.
2. List the events that will occur in the completion of the project.	An **event** is a point in time when an activity starts or when it ends. An event does not consume time or cost money. It is represented by a small circle on a PERT chart. All PERT networks begin and end with an event.
3. Determine the sequence of activities and events from all parties to the transaction or contract. In a building project, for example, the various contractors and suppliers would be able to furnish such information along with estimates of expected arrival times.	Note in Figure 21-14 that some activities can be performed concurrently rather than sequentially, which reduces the time and cost of the project.
4. Assign a reasonable time for completing each of the activities.	A common method is to request three time estimates from knowledgeable persons and to calculate an average figure from these estimates.
5. Construct the PERT network as shown in Figure 21-14. The path through the network requiring the greatest time (134.5 weeks) is called the **critical path.**	If the job is to be speeded up or completed on time, the critical path must be most closely controlled.

Administrative Cost Studies

The importance of controlling costs is well recognized by most OMs. However, at times some managers become so preoccupied with cutting costs (the efficiency goal discussed earlier in this chapter) that they fail to understand the real purpose of AOS (the effectiveness goal). Such systems can meet their broad goal of service to the organization only if they are delivering the required level of service to the users. Thus, a manager should not fall into the trap of achieving lower costs that unfortunately result in substandard service. Rather, *the most basic cost goal should be to reduce costs without impairing service.*

The need to control costs is a continuing theme throughout this textbook. Periodically, this emphasis takes the form of concrete examples showing the OM how administrative costs can be controlled after the various elements of costs have been pointed out. Such cost emphasis is intended to develop a strong cost "conscience" in each worker, which is the basis for all effective cost-control programs. For example, many managers are concerned about "time theft" or lost time (long lunch periods, personal business during work hours, tardiness, and early departure from work), which studies show averages four hours and five minutes weekly. Table 11-1, page 305, shows the tremendous costs

Figure 21–14
A PERT
Chart for
Scheduling
the Time
Required to
Construct an
Office
Building

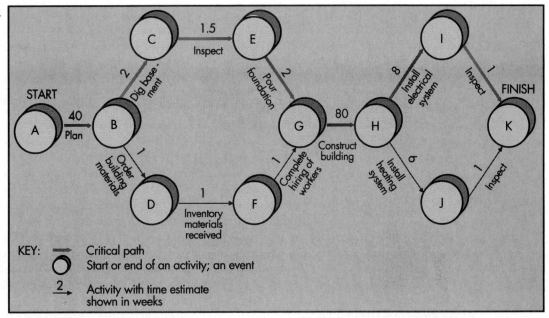

incurred when an office staff loses five minutes of time each day during a five-day workweek in a 50-week year. Time lost has great significance to office productivity as well as to budgetary and cost controls, the main focus of the two final chapters in this textbook, respectively.

Other Studies in Administrative Office Systems

We find several other types of systems improvement studies conducted by analysts depending on the nature of the systems problems and the skills and resources available to the firm. Examples are:

1. *Broad studies of company organization,* which concentrate on the structure of the firm and the comprehensive responsibilities assigned to each division.
2. *Limited-scope studies,* such as motion economy, in which the various motions of the right hand and the left hand are analyzed in order that the fewest and the least fatiguing motions are adopted by workers.

3. *Quality-control programs,* which are installed in some administrative centers that seek to eliminate the following problems: (a) incorrect or inaccurate work; (b) unattractive work; (c) wasted materials and time; and (d) costly reprocessing of work required because of errors. The major thrust in such programs is to provide adequate training of the workers so that errors are prevented and thus do not have to be corrected.
4. *Complex studies to maximize the use of expensive resources.* As mentioned earlier, important simulation problems can be solved on the computer by using appropriate mathematic techniques. For example, suppose a college registrar needs to maximize the performance of all resources (employees and supervisors, space, machines and equipment, computer programs and operating procedures, and time). At the same time, such an administrator is interested in minimizing the costs of the total operation.

To arrive at such an optimum situation, the registrar seeks to determine the best mix of resources for each level of student enrollment anticipated (1,000, 1,200, or some other realistic number), assuming certain levels of productivity for the resources available.

By using simulation or some other appropriate OR technique, an analyst can solve systems problems on paper much more economically than if the real-world system were designed and put into operation before its problems were resolved. The applications of OR continue to expand as administrators increase their knowledge of advanced mathematics, statistics, and other areas of study that relate to the improvement of AOS.[4]

DESIGNING, INSTALLING, AND EVALUATING THE IMPROVED SYSTEM

The goal of systems improvement is a highly productive system—one that is as free of problems as possible. When an analyst has completed a study of the present system, an improved version of that system is designed and presented to the user department for approval. User departments need systems that meet these standards:

1. *Quality standards*: systems that result in a better product or service or require less work than the previous system.
2. *Quantity standards*: systems that have shorter processing or response time; lower costs of production and maintenance; the capability of handling peak work loads and increased levels of productivity; and

fewer errors and a reduced number of breakdowns.
3. *Acceptance by both managers and employees.*

Designing the Improved System

As many of these criteria as possible must be met by the improved systems design. In the design, the OM or the systems analyst plans the proposed system and selects and organizes the elements (people, equipment, furniture, procedures, space, and work flow) in line with realistic objectives set for the system. On occasion there may be situations in which the proposed design must be returned to the systems department for further revision and then resubmitted to the users for final approval.

Before the new system can be formally installed, however, it is put into final form. The main consideration at this stage is good, accurate communication—presenting to the users a system that is clearly defined with understandable, measurable goals and in a form that the user department can implement. For this purpose, two types of systems communications are usually recommended: (1) a documented account of each of the phases of the system, which includes both charted and narrative forms, and (2) a systems manual that integrates the new or improved design into the presently operating system. Both of these types of communications are discussed in this section.

Documenting the Improved System

To illustrate the manner in which a new or improved system is formally presented to a department, we have selected the purchasing system discussed earlier. By referring to Figure 4-2, page 93, we see that the purchasing system is one of the major systems in an organization and that such a system is typically divided into smaller interrelated segments called subsystems, such as ordering, buying, and expediting. How the

---

[4]For more basic information on simulation in manual and computer systems, see John E. Bingham and Garth W. F. Davies, *A Handbook of Systems Analysis* (London: The Macmillan Press, Ltd., 1972), pp. 68–72; and Andrew W. Bailey, Jr., James H. Gerlach, and Andrew B. Whinston, *Office Systems: Technology and Organizations* (Reston, VA: Reston Publishing Company, Inc., 1985), Chapter 5.

Dialog on the Firing Line

J. CLAUDE FERGUSON, JR.
Manager
Andersen Consulting
Philadelphia, Pennsylvania

BS in Chemical Engineering, Ohio State University
MBA, Ohio State University

As Senior Consultant with Andersen Consulting, a unit of Arthur Andersen & Co., J. Claude Ferguson, Jr., is involved in the planning, design, and installation of information systems for clients in a variety of industries. His specific areas of expertise include business and information planning, computer integrated manufacturing, and distribution/logistics systems.

QUESTION: Claude, tell us about the major features of the program used by your organization to orient information systems professional personnel.

RESPONSE: The orientation program for professional personnel at Andersen Consulting, which lasts eight weeks, has three major components. The first component, lasting one week, is a general introduction to the organization. New hires learn about the history and culture of the firm, the office policies and procedures, and how the firm is organized and run. The second component is four weeks of self-study training in the basics of COBOL programming. The orientation culminates in the third component, an intensive three-week programming course, held at our central training facility. The course, which operates on a seven-days-a-week schedule, brings together new hires from around the world. The course simulates the environment of a first client assignment by making each participant directly responsible for a workload of programming, testing, and systems documentation. Although the training facility maintains its own staff, experienced line personnel serve as the primary instructors for the course.

Superimposed over the eight-week orientation structure are informal meetings and discussions among new and experienced personnel. These discussions help new hires to feel as if they are part of the organization, and allow them to begin to understand the nature of their new careers.

Having personally participated in the orientation process both as a new and experienced person, I can say that it is very effective in preparing individuals for their first assignments and introducing them to the culture and methodologies of Andersen Consulting.

details of operating these subsystems are communicated to workers is discussed in the following paragraphs.

Charting the Improved System. Earlier in this chapter we pointed out the variety and purpose of systems charts. From the various charts available, two in particular lend themselves to charting the present system and the proposed improved system. For example, Figure 21–7, page 657, illustrates the processing of information on a purchase order in one department; and Figure 21–10, page 661, shows a broader, multidepartment flow of information on three key forms involved in the purchasing system. Each of these charts can be used to present graphically both the present and proposed systems in their final forms. Through an analysis of the system, the main resources used and the sequence and flow of information through the system can be documented, that is, made a matter of written record on the chart. Also, such charts are invaluable tools to the systems analyst and the OM for educating the user's staff about the improved system.

Writing a Narrative for the Improved System. While charts are useful in documenting an improved system, generally they do not provide the specific, step-by-step details needed to operate the system. For this purpose, a written narrative is required.

One of the most effective forms of narrative is the **playscript procedure**, so named because it follows the format (*who* says *what?*) used by a playwright (see Figure 21–15). This type of systems communication lists, in sequential order, the detailed steps necessary to operate a system and also shows who is responsible for performing each step. Such a simple format is easy to construct and understand; only a few rules must be observed in order to develop this type of narrative. These rules are:

1. *Clearly identify the system* (the purchasing system in Figure 21–15).

2. *Indicate the responsible departments or workers in a separate column.* (See the Responsibility column in the figure.)
3. *List in sequentially numbered order the steps to be followed by the workers to put the system into operation.* (This rule is illustrated in the Procedural Steps column in the figure.)
4. *Start each step or action with a verb* (an action word), thereby shortening and simplifying the language used. This eases the reading load of the user. (See the first word in each of the procedural steps in Figure 21–15.)
5. *Refer to related forms and other paperwork at the earliest reference point.* (Note Steps 1 and 6 in the figure as well as the related chart reference.)

Although only a portion of the system's steps are shown in Figure 21–15, all five of the rules for constructing an effective narrative are illustrated. It is important that the forms distribution chart (Figure 21–10) and the supporting narrative (Figure 21–15) be presented as one communication package when the improved system is explained to all members of the user department. Later changes in the system should be reflected in the charts and the narrative that document the system.

Creating Systems and Procedures Manuals

Many organizations assemble all their systems communications, including the narratives and the charts correlated with the procedures, in various types of manuals. Such communication media can be useful to managers throughout the firm, for they provide a paper "picture" of the main information systems and work flows in the organization. To be useful, these manuals should be distributed to all user departments and regularly updated as changes occur in the systems. For a more complete discussion of manuals, see Chapter 17, pages 497–499.

Figure 21-15
The Play-
script
Procedure

SYSTEM:	Purchasing	DEPARTMENTS INVOLVED:	Ordering (or Requesting)
FORMS:	Purchase Requisition #124		Purchasing
	Purchase Order #507		Receiving
	Receiving Report #632		Accounting
			(and Vendor)
RELATED CHARTS:	Purchase Order Forms Distribution Chart		

RESPONSIBILITY	PROCEDURAL STEPS

Ordering (Requesting) Department	1. Prepares Purchase Requisition #124 in duplicate.
	   a. Sends original to purchasing department.
	   b. Retains file copy in pending file.

Purchasing Department Requisition Section	2. Receives Purchase Requisition #124 from ordering (requesting) department. 3. Verifies approval of #124. (If ordering department head has not approved form, returns for approval.) 4. Verifies prices from quotes file. 5. Forwards batches of approved requisition forms to purchase order section twice daily.
Purchase Order Section	6. Keyboards Purchase Order #507 in quadruplicate. 7. Staples original copy of #124 to purchasing department copy of #507. 8. Files in order pending file by department number.

Installing the Improved System

After the proposed systems design has been approved (usually by the department manager), we are ready to install the improved system. But such an installation process is highly complex, for it means essentially that workers, supervisors, and managers in the department must change their work-habit patterns and their attitudes toward work procedures. A department manager must do a "selling job"—convincing the workers of the values of the improved system, summarizing how users will benefit from the improved system, and communicating this information *before* the system is put into operation.

The systems designer must be on hand to explain the operations of the newly installed system, answer questions from workers, and "guide" its operations until it is working smoothly. Training sessions may be required if new skills or new attitudes toward work must be developed. Thus, a timetable must be developed that schedules all important activities. Workers should not have to be concerned about ordering or checking out machines, writing procedures or designing new forms, changing office layouts, or scheduling training meetings. The person in charge of systems installation should provide all this information, but be flexible enough to make changes in the schedule if conditions warrant. In case the newly installed system needs special "fine tuning," experienced systems analysts recommend *parallel runs*, with the new system operating alongside the old until the new system has been sufficiently tested and can "run" on its own.

Evaluating the Operating System

A system should operate through several complete cycles before it is evaluated. A system whose operations are repeated several times daily can be evaluated after a few days; one that has a monthly cycle will not show reliable results until after several months (that is, several cycles) have elapsed. And systems operating on a once-a-year basis will require two or three years for an accurate evaluation.

To evaluate an operating system, we use many performance measures, with the measure(s) chosen depending on the type of system to be assessed. Some of the most common criteria for judging the performance of systems are:

1. *Time*, which measures the number of clock units (hours, minutes, etc.) required for a particular action to be performed, such as the speed at which data move through a workstation. However, time does *not* measure quality. Two important time measures are (a) *lead time*, or response time, which is the time that elapses before a system responds to a demand placed upon it; and (b) *turnaround time*, which is the length of time required before results are returned. A slow turnaround means a relatively long period of time is required for processing; and a fast turnaround means a short period of time is needed.

2. *Costs*, which are used to measure profit, return on investment, errors in production, and shipping. The principal cost factors encountered in the office are described in detail in Chapter 23. Certainly a cost-effective system requires fewer dollars to operate than a poor system.

3. *Performance of the hardware*, especially its speed, reliability, service, maintenance, power requirements, and operating costs.

4. *Performance of the procedures and software*, which includes computer programs, office procedures, manuals, and other documentation related to operating a system.

5. *Productivity*, which states the relationship of input and processing costs to output level. Thus, to arrive at a productivity measure, we divide the level of output produced by the system by the input and processing costs. High productivity levels are obvious when we find relatively low input costs and high output levels. In this category, the performance of people plays a major part.

6. *Accuracy*, which, as stated earlier in this chapter, is a measure of the freedom from errors obtained by a system. Rates of accuracy, such as the number of misfiled orders or misshipped goods, may be measured by comparing the results of processing from one system to the results from another. Also, the frequency of errors during a time period gives another measure of systems performance.

7. *Systems integrity*, which measures the degree of security and control that can be maintained over the documents and records in the system. High document integrity means that records are safe, confidential, and under systems control at all times.

8. *Morale*, which reflects the satisfaction and acceptance that employees feel toward the system (and their jobs). The higher the morale, the greater the expected work performance level. Although morale is difficult to measure, we can take a fair "reading" of morale by comparing absences and late arrivals that occurred before and after installation of an improved system.

9. *User and customer reactions*, in which responses of persons who use or are affected by the system can be evaluated. Large numbers of complaints from customers concerning errors in monthly statements indicate poor performance at one or more points in the system. Fewer complaints might indicate that the new billing procedure is more adequate than the old one.

SUMMARY

1. All of the phases of the systems study cycle are directed toward systems improvement. During a systems improvement study, all of the elements in a system are identified and, time and resources permitting, studied in their entirety. Realistically, however, smaller scale studies are usually conducted to improve on manageable portions of the system. Two types of systems improvement models are employed in such studies: (a) the work simplification model, which is built upon the same logic that characterizes the problem-solving process, and (b) the input-output model, which furnishes a general approach for examining each of the phases in the system. The available resources and time constraints, as well as the analytical skills of the administrative staff, dictate whether one or both of these approaches are followed. In more complex systems, mathematics-based models are used by operations research specialists.

2. Typically major systems studies focus on the following areas: the study of work flow, which is organized around the origination and distribution of key documents in a system; the use of space; the use and distribution of forms; the performance of personnel; the use of equipment; the scheduling of work; and the control of administrative costs. Often other types of studies are conducted, such as motion economy, quality control, and operations research studies that help the OM predict the outcomes of using various mixes of resources in the office.

3. To design and later install the improved system, various types of communications are used. The most common are: charts that show the sequence, logic, and overall framework of the system; and written narratives that provide the specific details for operating a system. The playscript procedure is one of the most useful formats for narrating such operating steps. After the system has been in operation for a sufficiently long period, it is evaluated to determine how effectively it is performing and to correct any deficiencies found in the system.

GLOSSARY

Critical path—the path or route through a PERT network that requires the greatest time for completion.

Decision table—a tool for presenting the logic and the sequential operations in a system by showing what action must be taken to satisfy each information-related condition.

Effective system—a system that is actually producing the desired quantity and quality of output; at the same time, the value of the system's output exceeds the costs of the input and transforming/processing steps.

Efficient system—a system that is operating in an economical manner, that is, one that is highly reliable and minimizes the time and costs involved in its operation.

Event—a point in time on a PERT chart when an activity starts or ends.

Flowchart—a type of systems chart used to show the logical sequence of steps involved in the flow of work, usually in a manual system.

Forms distribution chart—a systems chart that traces the flow of forms and related paperwork through the departments under study.

Ideal system—a utopian system in which all systems elements function at their most effective and efficient levels at all times.

Input-output (I/O) systems improvement model—a general model for analyzing each of the phases in an administrative office system.

Linear programming (LP)—an operations research technique for determining the best mixture of components in a system.

Operations research (OR)—a method of analysis in which advanced mathematics and scientific techniques are used to obtain the best possible solutions to decision-making problems in complex systems.

PERT (Program Evaluation and Review Technique)—a technique used to record activities, events, and their sequences in a system, with the main purpose of determining the amount of time required to complete a systems cycle.

Playscript procedure—a systems communication that lists, in sequential order, the details necessary to operate a system and who is responsible for performing each step.

Prototype—a basic model.

Real-world system—a system that provides the best possible service to departments, subject to certain limitations.

Simulation—a basic operations research (OR) technique for creating a mathematical model of a real-world system.

Systems chart—a graphic device used to portray an existing or a proposed system, including the flow of information and the various elements required to operate a system.

Task—a definable unit (or piece) of work.

Task analysis—a systems technique used by analysts and personnel workers to determine *who does what work*.

Work distribution chart—a systems chart for identifying and comparing the principal tasks of all workers in the system under study.

Work-flow analysis—a type of systems study that concentrates on the origination and distribution of documents and the clerical operations required to process information in an administrative office system.

Workplace analysis—a systems space study that seeks to improve the arrangement of all resources needed to function efficiently at a workstation.

Work simplification model—a set of general guidelines, based upon logic and common sense, for analyzing a system.

FOR YOUR REVIEW

1. Compare and contrast the terms *effective* and *efficient* as they are used to describe desirable qualities of systems.

2. Explain the nature of a systems improvement prototype and its role in the improvement of administrative office systems.

3. If there can never be a truly ideal system, of what value is the concept of such a system to a systems analyst or office manager?

4. Define what a work simplification model is, and explain how it functions in the systems improvement process.

5. How does the input-output model function?

6. When are mathematics-based models used to improve the operations of systems?

7. List the major types of communication tools used in systems improvement, and state the principal purposes of each.

8. a. What is the main purpose of work-flow analysis?
   b. What type of communication device is commonly used to record the flow of work in a system?

9. Are work-flow analysis and space-use studies closely related? If so, how and why?

10. What types of questions should be answered when office forms are studied?

11. Define *task analysis* and *work distribution*, and indicate the functions of each.

12. What factors should be studied in an analysis of the use of equipment in a system?

13. Describe the nature and purpose of PERT.

14. From the standpoint of administrative costs, how can the attainment of cost reduction result in an efficient but ineffective system?

15. a. What types of documentation are often used to communicate the details of an improved system to the user department?
    b. What are the advantages of each type?

16. Describe the procedures recommended for effectively installing an improved system.

17. List seven of the most common criteria for evaluating the performance of a system.

FOR YOUR DISCUSSION

1. A nationally prominent systems expert once called systems improvement "a war against habit." Why is such a statement made?

2. The business division of your college is headed by a dean on whose staff are two faculty assistants (an associate dean and an assistant dean) and an administrative-level assistant *to* the dean. Also, each of the five departments (accounting, finance, management, marketing, and management sciences) has a chairperson. After drawing a clear chart of this organization structure, use the work simplification model to develop questions that you would need to ask in studying the operations of this organizational system.

3. The office management class in which you are enrolled is the one organization in which all your classmates are "employed." Using the input-output systems improvement model (Figure 21–3), analyze the operations of your class from a systems standpoint. Include as many systems elements in your analysis as possible. Before proceeding with this task, develop a class consensus on the objectives of your exercise.

4. As the office manager for Oat Products, a cereal manufacturer, you are responsible for the work of four general clerks, five accountants, three secretaries, and four typists. In this small office, no one has been assigned the responsibility for maintaining effective systems; for this function is assumed to be an implied duty of the office manager. However, you recognize that you do not have the time to devote to this work. Considering the

size of the office staff, how would you proceed to ensure that the major administrative office systems in the firm are designed and operated in an effective manner?

5. Recently a new set of rules has been proposed to update the system for granting credit in the Jared Jewelry Mart. In an effort to communicate these proposals to all the department managers and to the 20 members of the credit department staff for consideration, Della Hanson, the credit manager, has asked you, her assistant, for help. In particular, Hanson asks that you develop an effective communication that will clearly and logically present the following credit-granting rules that have been suggested:

Application Conditions	To Be Approved By
Applications for credit, $0 to $100	credit supervisor
Applications for credit, $101 to $500	assistant credit manager
Applications for credit, $501 to $1,000	credit manager
Applications for credit, $1,001 to $10,000	credit committee
Applications for credit above $10,000	store president

Using this information, develop a decision table that clearly shows the various possible conditions in the new procedure and what action must be taken to satisfy each condition. Present your table with an attached explanation for its use, as directed by your instructor.

6. Suggest tentative solutions to each of these common work-scheduling problems:
   a. Too many rush jobs.
   b. Little or no information provided about the priority of work assigned.
   c. Advance notice rarely given for long project assignments.
   d. Two supervisors give you equally long and difficult assignments and both tell you that the assignment is "of the highest importance."

7. Typically, the analyst develops a proposal for improving the system and presents it to the department for approval. Unfortunately, too often, a department considers such a proposal to be a personal affront to its competence. Since the user is the boss and the analyst is only an advisor, such an attitude sometimes causes more problems than the systems study eliminates. Discuss the psychological problems created in such a situation. What types of strategies must be put into practice by the analyst in order to guarantee that a proposal will be objectively evaluated by a department manager?

SOLVING CASE PROBLEMS

Case 21-1 Developing Your Systems Analysis "Sea Legs"

"We learn by doing" is a time-honored training principle. To apply this principle to systems improvement and at the same time let you demonstrate your analytical skills in a system that you know best, your instructor makes the following announcement:

Class, I want you to "get your feet wet," so to speak, right here in our class. We have many minisystems in the class that I know are in need of improvement. One deals with attendance; another with seating and layout; still another with grading and returning of term papers and other written exercises. Since the grading and returning of this classwork is a top-priority system of mine, I'd like you to propose to me how this system can be improved. For this assignment, students in the front half of the room will use the work simplification model as their systems improvement model; and the remainder of the students, the input-output model. In two weeks, I'd like to see the results of your thinking. At that time we'll compare the experiences of both groups and combine the "wisdom" of the entire class in developing a general proposal. Don't be afraid of hurting my feelings; just "tell it like it is." I'll be in my office an extra hour—from 3–4 P.M. daily for the next two weeks—to answer questions.

Based upon the specific details provided by your instructor, comply with this assignment.

Case 21-2 Charting a System in a Small Business

In a discussion of systems charting in your office management class, your instructor has emphasized to all the students the ease with which charts can be understood. In addition, the instructor mentions that all systems, even those in the least complicated small businesses, are full of complex and partially hidden details that may be overlooked when data about the systems are collected. To prove this point, the instructor has directed the class to go to restaurants in the local community and, with the approval of the respective managers, to observe the main work flows involved in completing one cycle of a common system in the firm selected.

To complete this assignment, your specific instructions are as follows:

1. Two students are to observe and record the steps involved in ordering, preparing, delivering, and receiving payment for a hamburger in a small restaurant near your school. Each of the two students must observe and chart the system independently so the differences in perception of the events and the relative effectiveness of the recording methods can be discussed in class.

2. For charting the system described in (1) above, use the techniques of flow process charting discussed in this chapter.

3. Prepare a narrative of the charted process using the playscript procedure.

Present this material to your instructor along with a cover letter (sometimes called a letter of transmittal), as directed.

22

Improving Office Productivity

GOALS FOR THIS CHAPTER

After completing this chapter, you should be able to:

1. Cite the benefits to an organization that establishes a program of work standards.
2. Describe in broad terms the kinds of office operations that can be measured in order to prepare work standards.
3. Indicate the preliminary steps involved in preparing for a work measurement program.
4. Evaluate the pros and cons of the different methods for measuring routine office work and for setting standards.
5. Relate briefly how performance standards may be developed for nonroutine office jobs.
6. Describe several techniques used to improve office productivity, paying special attention to the need for developing effective time management programs.

As we look ahead to the year 2000, a major challenge facing administrative office managers will be to improve productivity by involving employees in the integration of technology into the workplace. Equally important in increasing productivity will be our need to improve the morale and job satisfaction of a work force that is becoming more diverse.

Today office productivity is a major factor in the economic struggle to control the mounting costs of administrative operations. In Chapter 3, *productivity* was defined as the relationship between the output of goods or services and the input of basic resources—labor, capital, energy, and materials. Thus, increased productivity depends upon a more effective use of resources, or more output per unit of input. Faced with rising office salaries and increased employee benefits, organizations must closely examine the means available for controlling administrative costs, obtaining more output per employee, and thus improving productivity.

Major improvements in productivity are frequently made through a systems approach to the study of office activities. As we saw in earlier chapters, all systems studies emphasize the role of office personnel, whose skills, knowledges, and attitudes must be used more effectively in order to increase productivity and improve performance. The pressing need for establishing cost-control programs becomes evident when managers in offices that have no formal cost-reduction programs realize that their personnel are being utilized effectively only *one-fourth* to *one-half* of each workday.

Along this line, Val Olson, president of Creative Management Consultants, advanced the *4/8 Theory*, which states that today's white-collar employees produce, on the average, only four hours of effective work out of each eight-hour workday.[1] As

---

[1]Val Olson, *White Collar Waste: Gain the Productivity Edge* (Englewood Cliffs, NJ: Prentice-Hall, Inc., 1983), p. 4.

Employee attitude must be considered when determining how to increase productivity.

defined by Olson's theory, *white-collar productivity does not depend on how fast office employees work but, rather, on how efficiently they use their time.* The theme advanced is that low productivity is a problem of *management* because *management* does not know how to *manage* office time. To solve the problem of how to use the workday effectively, Olson offers a solution that rests upon Leffingwell's principles of effective work—*plan, schedule, execute,* and *measure* the work, and *reward* the worker. These principles, discussed earlier on pages 16–17, can be applied in today's offices to improve productivity, for AOMs have the tools, the know-how, and the human resources. Managers must learn how to release the energies of their human resources, for these workers know where savings and productivity improvements can be made. To apply Leffingwell's principles in productivity-improvement programs, AOMs must make sure that they themselves do not become an obstacle to productivity improvement by accepting the myth that nothing much can be done to reduce administrative costs.

In this chapter we highlight the importance of reducing administrative costs by first investigating the measurement of office

work and the development of work standards. Then, we shall examine several methods used by office workers and their administrators to improve their own productivity.

WORK MEASUREMENT AND WORK STANDARDS

Work measurement is a tool of cost control used to determine how much work is completed and how effectively it is completed. Usually this suggests a measurement of the volume of work and the amount of time required (*quantitative measurements*) as well as the accuracy and appearance of the work (*qualitative measurements*). A **work standard** is a yardstick of performance, or par, which indicates what is expected of workers and how their output can be evaluated. Work standards are tools of managerial control that are best applied to routine and repetitive operations such as keyboarding, transcribing, calculating, filing, billing, and posting. Although we usually exclude nonroutine, semicreative jobs from a formal work measurement program, we can measure some types of nonroutine work to provide useful standards.

By means of work standards, AOMs can determine what quantity and quality of work should be produced. They can then compare this output with the quantity and quality of work actually produced and thus have a basis for managerial control. All work standards are aimed at obtaining *100 percent efficiency,* which is defined as the rate of production at which an average, well-trained employee can work all day without undue fatigue. Or, we can say, simply, 100 percent efficiency means "a fair day's work."

To work at this level of efficiency, we need standards that are reliable, realistic, and attainable under normal, reasonable working conditions. The standards should not be changed too often or confusion will result.

They must be understood both by employees and by management. Also, standards must be flexible in order to meet variations in working conditions. For example, a standard for keyboarding a one-page, 100-word letter of straight copy is not the same as a standard for keyboarding a one-page, 100-word report involving columns of statistical data. Similarly, the standards set for the number of invoices to be filed under an alphabetic filing system and those under a numeric filing system are not the same.

Benefits of a Work Standards Program

By providing data on *quantity* (volume and time) and *quality* (accuracy and appearance), a program of work standards offers the AOM many benefits. Standards aid in:

1. *Determining the cost of the work performed*, an unknown element in many offices. Thus, management is aided in establishing realistic work targets, planning human resources needs, preparing budgets, and measuring the effectiveness of forecasts.
2. *Exercising better control over the scheduling and routing of administrative work*, which results in improved service to customers by reducing the elapsed time for processing the work.
3. *Evaluating employee performance.* Employees know the performance goals expected of them in terms of volume, time, and quality. Further, they know that these are objective figures based upon reasonable working conditions. The superior worker receives recognition for a job well done, and the poorer worker is appraised accordingly.
4. *Installing incentive systems* in which employees' earnings are based upon their productivity.
5. *Evaluating the need for improving administrative office systems and determining*

the feasibility of installing new machines and equipment. The OM knows what volume of production can be maintained and the labor cost of maintaining this volume. Thus, the manager is able to study and to lower the costs of the systems. The OM can realistically compare proposed costs and output with present costs and volume of production and learn whether a gain or a loss will be realized. Thus, the manager is better able to answer questions pertaining to the installation of new equipment and the use of facilities.
6. *Measuring the effectiveness of department operations* by comparing department achievements with the standards. Consistently lower performance by a department or a wide variation in performance levels among several departments indicates that something is wrong. Thus, the supervisor is prompted to study the causes and to correct them.
7. *Enabling the supervisor to measure the effectiveness of a new employee and the rate of learning that has taken place.* At what point should a trainee be able to handle a normal work load? This is the type of question that supervisors must be able to answer so that they may follow up on employees and determine if the necessary training has been provided to ensure a high level of work performance.

In spite of the benefits to be realized from work standards, we see that formal programs of work measurement are not commonly found in many offices, as noted in the following section.

Difficulties in Applying Work Measurement in Offices

In view of the rapid rate of growth in the size and cost of office staffs, we would expect that administrative work would be measured to a much greater extent. However, the measurement concept is not universally accepted. Thus, a top priority of the AOM is to convince both management and subordinates of the need for a work measurement program.

Several reasons explain the low incidence of work measurement in offices. The major reason is that the work is either impossible to measure or that measurement is too difficult and costly to be practicable. People holding this point of view feel that administrative work is so varied and complex that it does not lend itself to measurement. For example, repetitive information-processing operations do not exist in many phases of office work to the same extent as assembly-line operations in manufacturing. Often an office employee processes several kinds of work units—orders, invoices, checks—in a single day. Even though the work may be repetitive, some phases of the job, such as answering and placing telephone calls and looking up information, prove difficult, if not impossible, to measure.

Some people feel that measurement is not needed in those offices where the number of employees is small. In other instances, top management lacks the desire to engage in any work measurement program. It is felt that administrative work is going along well enough, and there is no need to disturb the workers' peace of mind by attempting to measure their productivity. Also, managers and first-line supervisors are often suspicious of and have misconceptions about the nature and intent of work measurement.

Many management consultants contend that most of the reasons offered for the failure to establish a work measurement program in the office are more imaginary than real. They claim, as we shall see below, that most routine and many semiroutine office activities can be effectively measured.

Office Operations That Can Be Measured

Estimates of the amount of administrative work lending itself to measurement range

from two-thirds to three-fourths of all work done in the office. If this major portion of work were measured and work standards prepared, OMs would have a tool of cost control that could improve their office operations and enable them to gain a competitive edge. For measurement and the setting of standards, office tasks should meet three criteria:

1. *Repetitive*—the tasks should repeat themselves, be highly routine, and be done in a consistently uniform manner. Examples: opening the incoming mail, verifying the quantity shipped and the selling prices on sales invoices, posting to customers' and creditors' ledger accounts, preparing customers' statements, and filling in insurance claim forms.
2. *Countable*—the work units can be counted in precise quantitative terms. Examples: 12 cassettes transcribed, 394 forms filled in, or 1,408 letters filed.
3. *Sufficient*—the volume of work must be sufficiently great to justify the cost of its measurement. Examples: filing 600 copies of sales invoices each day, or calculating the regular and overtime hours worked on several thousand time cards each week.

Office tasks that meet these criteria are commonly found in those cost centers or departments that have the largest number of employees performing routine, repetitive tasks. For jobs such as drafting, editing, proofreading, programming, and writing specifications, where the work is semicreative, the task of measurement becomes more difficult, as explained later in this chapter.

PREPARING FOR THE WORK MEASUREMENT PROGRAM

For a work measurement program to be effective, top management must fully support the program and its objectives and actively use the information obtained. The nature of the program and its aims must be communicated to employees so that they fully understand the program. A supervisor must administer the program at each level of office operations. Analysts who have some college training or equivalent work experience and a "feel" for paperwork should be properly selected. Finally, all personnel must realize and accept the fact that the work standards developed are feasible and accurate.

Gaining Top Management's Support

Work measurement must receive complete and unqualified endorsement by those for whom the tool has been designed; otherwise, there is little point in installing the program. Therefore, top management must (1) understand the objectives of the program and how it will work, (2) take an active interest in the program, (3) be willing to make the decisions needed to put the program into operation, and (4) demonstrate in a tangible way that all managers stand behind the program. To do so, top-level managers must impress upon middle managers and supervisors that work measurement is a permanent, ongoing program that must be accepted at all levels in the organization.

Communicating the Program to Employees

Before the work measurement program is installed, the AOM must provide workers with an honest and satisfactory answer to the question: "How is this program going to affect me?" What is important is that the workers understand the work measurement techniques to be used and how the results of the program will apply to them. Thus, employee fears and natural resistance to change will be lessened. Employees must be convinced that they will not lose their jobs as a result of work measurement. They need to understand that the company's usual

amount of turnover will adequately adjust the staff size and absorb the expected increases in productivity.

When informing workers of the program, the timing and the nature of the communication are very important. Rather than have knowledge about the program circulate via the grapevine, we suggest that a letter announcing and fully explaining the program be sent to all employees at the same time and from the same source. Thus, any suspicions and questions on the part of employees may be anticipated before the first phase of the program gets underway.

Administering the Program

The backbone of a work measurement program is the first-line supervisor, for ultimately this person determines the success of the program. If the workers are given adequate supervision and leadership, most of them can meet the performance standards and will do so willingly.

Supervisors must be able and willing to review their operations and to weed out inefficiencies that can cause the failure of their departments to meet the standards. The work of their units must be planned and scheduled and work loads shifted in order to maintain a balance of work among employees. To coordinate the work flow and keep peak loads at tolerable minimums, a supervisor has to plan and consult with other supervisors. Adequate records must be kept to provide a sound basis for performance reports. Importantly, supervisors must evaluate individual productivity and use the results of the program to determine training needs, to prepare people for promotion, and to justify salary increases. Thus, the program takes on meaning in the eyes of the workers; and management is able to identify and to reward outstanding workers.

In training sessions, first-line supervisors are introduced to the program and to the roles they will play. Here, it must be made clear that the results of the program will not dictate how the supervisors' departments are to be operated; nor will their ability to operate the departments be restricted. The program should be introduced to supervisors as a managerial tool that will aid them in doing a better job.

Selection of Analysts

As a means of reducing employee fears about the work measurement program and to prevent any undue resentment, employees from within the firm may be selected and trained as work analysts. Acceptance of the program is better assured when the analysts are known to their fellow employees. An important qualification needed by employees selected from within the firm is the ability to sell their ideas to others. In addition, analysts who have been recruited from within the ranks, such as from the administrative office systems division, are familiar with company routines, methods, and procedures. This knowledge is a valuable contribution when defining methods and setting standards. Although an analyst selected from within the firm must be trained in work measurement, an outside analyst must spend time in getting acquainted with the firm's systems and the individual jobs performed—an orientation that costs the company several hundred dollars each day.

Feasibility and Accuracy of the Standards

Regardless of the office task, some mental and physical effort is required to complete a unit of work; and the amount of productive activity used to accomplish the job can be measured. As noted earlier, there is a natural reluctance by many firms to establish administrative work standards, a fact that must be accepted at the outset when installing a work measurement program. Thus, the OM should be resigned to obtaining something

less than perfection in the program. When the development of a work measurement program is approached from this point of view, the OM will be pleasantly surprised at how much can actually be accomplished through work measurement.

To encourage employee confidence in the standards, the workers must understand how the standards have been developed, what is included in each standard, and how they are to proceed if unforeseen conditions, such as machine breakdowns, occur. Standards must be accurate and consistent, as explained later, for approximate standards do not provide accurate, reliable yardsticks; nor do they gain the confidence of employees.

METHODS OF MEASURING ROUTINE OFFICE WORK AND SETTING STANDARDS

Many of the first attempts to measure office work were clumsy since the techniques used had been designed to measure the output of workers in machine shops and foundries. Because managers applied work measurement techniques that paid little attention to the feelings of the individuals being measured, many of the programs failed. In some cases the discontent among office workers paved the way for unionization activities. Today, however, measurement techniques center around a consideration for human values.

In this section, we first describe several methods used chiefly to measure routine, repetitive office work and to set performance standards. Then, in the following section, we briefly present a few methods for establishing standards for nonrepetitive, semicreative office jobs.

Historical Data

Under the **historical data** or *past performance* method, we study the past production records of various office activities such as transcribing, keyboarding, filing, and billing to measure what was produced in the past. For example, we may measure the output of workers in a text/word processing center by using one or more of the following bases:

1. *By the page, letter, disk, or cassette.* Measurement according to this base is probably the simplest method to use. However, simply counting the number of pages, letters, disks, cassettes, etc., is too inaccurate to be of much value; for letters vary in length, and disks and cassettes hold varying amounts of dictated matter.

2. *By standard lines.* Some companies count the number of standard lines of copy. A *standard line* is usually 60 spaces—15.24 cm (6 inches) for pica type and 12.7 cm (5 inches) for elite type. The number of lines may be counted either by hand or by use of a line counter, which is a cardboard or plastic scale graduated for pica and elite type. Such a base cannot easily be used for tabulated or statistical matter. The standard-line basis is particularly useful, however, where workers are paid on a piece-rate basis.

3. *By weighted lines.* Many word processing centers use the weighted-line count as a means of measuring production. A *line* is defined as 72 characters of typed material on a single-space line, 6 inches long. The supervisor of the center assigns various *weights* to the work according to the difficulty of the material. Some factors considered in determining the weighting include the degree of difficulty in reading, the amount of unusual terminology, and the complexity of format.

4. *By square centimeters (cm²) or square inches.* Some companies use the square-centimeter or square-inch base in place of the standard-line base. In these firms, the production of typists is measured by use of transparent celluloid sheets blocked off in square centimeters or inches. When

a sheet is placed over a letter or a report, the number of square centimeters or inches of typewritten material may be read at a glance. This base is especially satisfactory in the measurement of tabulated material.

5. *By keystrokes.* A commonly used base is the number of keystrokes made at the keyboard. By means of an electronic counter, attached to the equipment, the number of keystrokes can be accurately and automatically recorded by a computer.

The past production of the group of workers, measured by one or more of the bases described above, is used as a means of measuring what employees can do in the future. The *best performance* may be selected as a standard on the theory that "we did it before; we should be able to do it again." Or the average output of the *best* worker and of the *poorest* worker may be used as a standard. The average output may be more reasonable than the best performance; however, the historical data method is little better than having no standards at all. By means of historical data, we learn how long a certain job took *in the past* rather than the amount of time the job should take *at the present* or *in the future*. Built into the performance reporting system are all the inefficiencies present during the period from which the data are drawn. On the other hand, the historical data method can be easily installed at a very low cost; and there is no need for highly trained personnel to administer the method.

Time Log

Another simple method of measuring office work and establishing work standards is the **time log** or *time ladder method*. To use this method, it is first necessary to identify the work activities performed during the day. For each of the various office activities, a simple code number is established. On a time analysis recording sheet, such as the activity log shown in Figure 22-1, employees measure their output by recording the actual time spent and the units of work produced for a period of a week to a month. At the end of the time period, the employees' forms are summarized, reviewed, and edited to isolate any unusual patterns. A time log for the entire department is prepared, upon which each activity is summarized by code number. This report provides the total time spent on each activity in a particular department. Dividing the total hours into the quantity produced converts the data into a rate-per-hour figure and places all the performances on a comparable basis. From these figures, we can establish a standard time for each item being processed.

The major advantage of the time log method is that it can be used with little additional cost. Permanent control over activities can be maintained by continuing to record work assignments on the activity log. The time log method becomes unreliable, however, when, intentionally or not, employees do not accurately record the personal time allowances and absences from their workstations.

Work Sampling

Work sampling is a method of measuring work based on the statistical law of probability. According to this law, observing a smaller number of chance (random) occurrences tends to reveal the same patterns that the observation of a larger number of random occurrences would produce. Thus, by means of work sampling, we take a sufficient number of valid random samples to supply information that would be impractical to obtain by continuous observation because of the time and cost involved.

Using Work Sampling

To learn how the work sampling method is used, let's examine the steps taken by a trained observer to find out how much time a team of office workers spends on the various tasks that make up their work day. In our example, the observer takes the following steps:

1. *Randomly observes the work being performed.* (The time of each observation and the person to be observed were statistically predetermined for the observer.) After each observation, the observer immediately records what the worker was doing when observed, along with a production volume count for each activity. When the sampling is completed, the observer determines what percentage of the total observations is represented by each activity. These results are given on the next page.

Figure 22-1
Time Log
Recording
Sheet

ACTIVITY LOG					
Date: April 15, 19—				Employee:	Renata Corrio
Activity Code	Units Produced	Time			Remarks
		Start	Finish	Elapsed	
43	10	8:20	9:10	50 min.	
38	176	9:15	12:30	3 hrs.	15 min. break
33	52	1:30	2:45	1 hr. 15 min.	
38	91	2:50	4:30	1 hr. 25 min.	15 min. break

Activity	Obser-vations	Ratio	Percent of Total
Filing	100	100/1,000	10
Keyboarding	300	300/1,000	30
Sorting	150	150/1,000	15
Assembling	200	200/1,000	20
Personal	250	250/1,000	25
Total Observations . . .	1,000		100

2. Calculates the total time that employees were available for work during the study:

Name	Minutes	
Lucas	429	
McTavish	429	
Van Horn	324	(part-time employee, 9:30–3:30)
Doerr	Absent	
West	254	(training session 8:45–11:55)
Total Available Minutes . . .	1,436	

3. Multiplies the time, expressed in employee minutes, by each of the observation percentages developed in Step No. 1. The product of each multiplication equals the time spent on each activity observed.

Activity	$\left(\begin{array}{c}\text{Percent} \\ \text{of Total} \\ \text{Obser-} \\ \text{vations}\end{array}\right)$ ×	$\left(\begin{array}{c}\text{Minutes} \\ \text{Available} \\ \text{for Work}\end{array}\right)$ =	$\left(\begin{array}{c}\text{Minutes} \\ \text{Spent} \\ \text{on Each} \\ \text{Activity}\end{array}\right)$
Filing	10	1,436	143.6
Keyboarding . . .	30	1,436	430.8
Sorting	15	1,436	215.4
Assembling	20	1,436	287.2
Personal	25	1,436	359.0
Total	100		1,436.0

4. Divides each activity time by the corresponding volume count (obtained in

Step No. 1) to obtain the unit time, or standard:

Activity	$\left(\begin{array}{c}\text{Minutes} \\ \text{Spent}\end{array}\right)$ ÷	$\left(\begin{array}{c}\text{Work} \\ \text{Counts}\end{array}\right)$ =	$\left(\begin{array}{c}\text{Unit Time} \\ \text{or} \\ \text{Standard}\end{array}\right)$
Filing	143.6	450 cards	0.32 min.
Keyboarding . . .	430.8	110 policies	3.92 min.
Sorting	215.4	600 pieces of mail	0.36 min.
Assembling	287.2	150 applications	1.91 min.
Personal	359.0		
Total	1,436.0		

The unit times calculated above are based on the premise that the percentage distribution of the various activities as they occurred during the random observation period tends to equal the exact percentage distribution that would be found by continuous observation. The accuracy and validity of the study depend upon the care with which the observer performs each step.

Determining Proper Sample Size

The number of observations to be made in any work sampling study depends upon three factors: (1) how much tolerance will be accepted, (2) what portion of time is expected to be consumed by the smallest activity to be measured, and (3) how reliable the results have to be.

Tolerance refers to the degree of accuracy desired. Suppose it is specified that a tolerance of 10 percent will be acceptable. If our study results show that an activity consumed 5 percent of the available time, we are assured that the actual time consumed was within 10 percent of that 5 percent; that is, it was not less than 4.5 percent nor more than 5.5 percent. *The larger the tolerance one is willing to accept, the smaller the number of observations that must be made.*

Besides providing an acceptable tolerance in the sampling study, we must estimate the percentage of time consumed by the least time-consuming activity for which reliable results are required. This is an educated guess made after we have become familiar with the operations of the unit to be studied. The smaller this estimated critical percentage becomes, the larger the sample must be. For this reason, often we set up observation codes so that the smallest activity will account for at least 5 percent of the total number of observations. Whenever possible, we eliminate separate observation codes for those activities that are estimated to consume less than 5 percent of the available time. We can combine these activities with related work codes or group them under a miscellaneous observation code.

As the size of a sample is increased, the reliability of the results also increases. However, nearly every sampling application reaches a point of diminishing returns—the increased reliability achieved does not justify the additional time, effort, and expense required. A sample size that produces a reliability of 80 percent is generally considered to be sufficient for work sampling purposes.

Suppose we are planning a work sampling study with the following requirements:

1. An acceptable tolerance of 10 percent is specified.
2. The critical percentage is estimated to be 5 percent.
3. A reliability of 80 percent has been determined to be adequate.

Given these conditions, the sample sizes shown in Table 22–1 indicate that 3,210 observations must be made.[2]

Further, suppose we decide that greater reliability, say 90 percent, was needed. In that

case, the number of observations for 80 percent reliability shown in Table 22–1 would be multiplied by the appropriate factor given in Table 22–2.

To find the net number of observations (N) required for $P = .05$, $T = .10$, with a reliability of 90 percent, we first identify the correct value for N from Table 22–1:

When $P = .05$ and $T = .10$, $N = 3,210$

Then, using Table 22–2, we find the reliability factor for 90 percent and multiply:

$$N = 3,210 \times 1.601$$

$$N = 5,139$$

Pros and Cons of Work Sampling

If we take enough random samples over a long enough period of time to make the samples representative and valid, the data obtained under work sampling are much more reliable than those we secure from the time analysis method. The major disadvantage of work sampling is the need for trained analysts to set up the study and to perform the required observations. In some cases, the sampling method may prove to be uneconomical if the sample size required to produce valid results is too great. Also, some employees may not fully understand the sampling technique employed and may be skeptical of statistical evidence. Some office employees feel that the analysts are spying on them, while other workers state that they cannot perform naturally while their work is being observed. Some may alter their performance, such as slowing down, so that the sample taken produces a performance standard on the low side.

Using Probability Sampling in Quality Control

Quality control is a regulatory process in which the quality of performance is

---

[2]For those interested in learning how the sample size is derived by statistical formula, consult any textbook in basic statistics.

Table 22-1
Sample Sizes
Computed
for 80 Per-
cent
Reliability

	Net Number of Observations When:			
P is	T is ± 5% (of P)	T is ± 10% (of P)	T is ± 15% (of P)	T is ± 20% (of P)
1%	66,920	16,730	7,440	4,180
2	33,120	8,280	3,680	2,070
3	21,860	5,460	2,430	1,370
4	16,220	4,060	1,800	1,010
5	12,840	3,210	1,430	800
6	10,590	2,650	1,180	660
7	8,980	2,250	1,000	560
8	7,770	1,940	860	490
9	6,840	1,710	760	430
10	6,080	1,520	680	380
15	3,830	960	430	240
20	2,700	680	300	170
25	2,030	510	230	130
30	1,580	390	180	100
35	1,260	315	140	80
40	1,020	260	110	60
45	830	210	90	50
50	680	170	80	40

P = Estimated Critical Percentage
T = Tolerance Factor

Table 22-2
Reliability
Factors

Reliability	Factor	Reliability	Factor
50%	.269	85%	1.227
55	.337	90	1.601
60	.420	95	2.273
65	.517	96	2.496
70	.637	97	2.786
75	.783	98	3.204
80	1.000	99	3.926

*Factors to be applied to sample sizes in Table 22-1 provide indicated degrees of reliability.

measured and compared with standards so that any difference between performance and standards may be acted upon. Under a quality control program, we attempt to recognize and remove the identifiable causes of the defects and the variations from the standards developed for the particular process or operation.

Through the use of probability sampling, we can reduce the costs of some types of quality control. For example, rather than check the output of all billing clerks and record all errors made, we can take a random selected sample of the work produced by each clerk. The sample size required to give valid and reliable findings can be statistically determined so that the costly checking of all records can be avoided. However, many companies continue to use "old-line" methods of quality control, such as 100 percent inspection and reinspection.

Motion Study and Time Study

In most administrative office systems, there is usually one best way in which to perform each operation. By observing and timing workers at their jobs, we can eliminate much wasted motion and effort. However, the purposes of motion study and time study are not synonymous. *Motion* study is used primarily to improve work methods, while *time* study is used to determine time standards. Nevertheless, in relation to measuring work performance and setting standards, motion study and time study are inseparable. To improve an old work method or to introduce a new job, it would be difficult to determine the most desirable procedure without utilizing motion economy. Similarly, the gains realized from the new method could not be measured without time values for comparison.

Motion Study

Detailed motion studies were originated by Frank and Lillian Gilbreth, whose contributions to management thought were discussed in Chapter 1. Motion study is a recognized fundamental of obtaining "the one best way to do work," a phrase used by the Gilbreths, who considered motion study a scientific method of waste elimination. According to their definition, "**Motion study** consists of dividing work into the most fundamental elements possible; studying these elements separately and in relation to one another; and from these studied elements, when timed, building methods of least waste."[3]

In a simple motion study, we visually examine a single operation or a series of operations by means of a stopwatch. However, if management can justify the cost of installing motion study and the time required

for analysis, the precise micromotion study is preferred. The Gilbreths originated the term **micromotion study** when they began to use motion pictures for studying the component parts of an operation. In a micromotion study, we observe and analyze human and mechanical movements in order to reduce a given operation to the fewest component parts in their logical sequence. Instead of relying upon our uncertain eye as an observer, we use a motion picture camera. On each picture frame appears the face of a specially prepared clock called a *microchronometer*, which is divided into 100 sections. Since the clock revolves 20 times each minute, it is possible to obtain 2,000 pictures per minute. The 1/2,000 of the minute time division, shown on each picture frame, is the unit of measurement in a micromotion study.

Micromotion studies are especially useful in studying office work of a repetitive nature and of long-range duration. Although the micromotion technique involves time-consuming methods, expensive motion pictures, and detailed records, the study is worth the expenditure since the entire office operation is being analyzed and recorded simultaneously. As a result, ineffective work motions are eliminated or reduced; and thus overall efficiency is increased.

Following either a motion study or a micromotion study, *standard time data* are determined, which in turn become the basis for determining a fair day's work for a fair day's pay. The standard time data form the basis for determining the most efficient method of doing a particular type of office work. However, as explained below, we must adjust the data to allow for the worker's fatigue and personal needs as well as for delays due to machine difficulties.

Time Study

The main purpose of **time study** in measuring job performance is to establish a *time*

---

[3]Frank B. Gilbreth and Lillian M. Gilbreth, *Applied Motion Study* (New York: Sturgis & Walton Company, now the Macmillan Company, 1917), p. 43.

standard—the time required to perform an operation at an average pace. Another aim of time study is to develop standard time data that can be used for the performance rating of similar operations without making further time studies. (The development of predetermined times is explained later in this chapter.) Time studies are also helpful in comparing relative wage rates as well as aiding in the control of production.

Generally workers accept time standards if they are assured that the time studies have been made under the best standardized conditions. Management in turn expects the operator to perform the job in the established time. Of course, adherence to a time standard requires that all working conditions and job specifications be described in detail.

Unless the time study analyst has gained the confidence of the office personnel, the efforts expended in the study will be ineffective and morale problems will follow. The analyst must be capable of dealing with people honestly, tactfully, and sympathetically. Also, the analyst must build a reputation for making fair and accurate studies by using a systematic and exacting procedure when analyzing operations.

One limitation of the time study method is that a degree of subjectivity is involved in the initial selection of people who will be studied to determine time standards. The employees selected to be observed should be average and fully qualified because such persons are respected by their co-workers. The workers should be chosen for their consistency in using the most efficient movements in working at a normal work pace.

On a time study sheet, the analyst describes each element in the operation according to the sequence in which it occurs. Extreme care must be exercised to see that all operations are included. The analyst must also decide on the number of work cycles to be studied. Generally the more observations made and the more accurate

the basic time, the greater the assurance that unnecessary delays and inconsistencies will be eliminated.

The stopwatch studies cover only the actual time that it takes the observed employees to perform the operational element. Thus, we must adjust the actual time required in order to determine a realistic time standard for all employees. The technique of adjusting individual differences is called **performance rating** or *leveling*. The goal of performance rating is to obtain a theoretical normal time—neither slow nor fast—that average workers require to complete their jobs under standardized conditions.

Since workers cannot produce steadily throughout the day with no interruptions, we must make allowances for the extra time that is not consumed in actual job performance. Therefore, in addition to the normal working time, we determine proper time allowances for delays, fatigue, and personal needs such as walking to the drinking fountain or washing the face and hands. For most office situations, the time allowances are expressed as percentages, which may vary from 10 to 20 percent of the normal work day. Thus, if the elemental times of a particular work cycle add up to a total standard time of 2 minutes, a minimum allowance of 10 percent for delays would increase the standard time to 2 minutes and 12 seconds.

After we have determined all the allowances, our time study is complete. We can then make the necessary entries on a time study observation sheet for a permanent record, and prepare a list of the time standards.

Predetermined Times

The development of **predetermined times** is based on the assumption that if the same motions are used in all work activities and under the same conditions, the time values are constant. Therefore, we can reduce subjective judgment by combining the time values as necessary to synthesize a time standard. In using predetermined times methods, we describe the elements of an operation according to various physical or mental factors. Then, as we analyze a job and divide its elements into basic motions, we assign each motion a time value that is obtained from a table. The total time for all motions involved in performing the element plus the addition of a time allowance for conditions such as delay, fatigue, and personal needs become the time standard for the job. The time values are usually developed from engineered stopwatch studies, micromotion studies, or laboratory studies of work motions. Many of the tables of time values, developed and copyrighted by management consulting firms and professional associations, may be obtained for a fee.

Advantages and Disadvantages of Using Predetermined Times

The advantages of using predetermined times include:

1. *Micromotion or stopwatch time study can be eliminated on many job studies*, thus conserving time in establishing time values and wage rates.
2. *The time standards are more precise, consistent, and objective than those obtained under time study* because the standards do not vary as does the daily efficiency of time study analysts.
3. *Use of predetermined time values may settle labor disputes more effectively.* Predetermined time values are more realistic in settling grievances since the data have been established after much experience and many observations rather than having been based upon a small sample or a possibly faulty time study.
4. *Workers are usually convinced that wage rates based upon the use of time standards are equitable*.

On the other hand, there are several disadvantages in establishing time standards through the use of predetermined times:

1. *There is less personal contact with employees.* Standards set from observation, where the workers who have to live with the standards can actually see the measurement of their work, tend to create greater confidence.
2. *Only those tasks that are highly routine and repetitive lend themselves to measurement by predetermined times.* Thus, the method is unacceptable for studying many office activities.
3. *A higher caliber of staff, requiring fairly high initial training costs, is usually needed* more when synthetic time standards are being determined than under other methods where the staff can be quickly taught the measurement techniques.

Methods for Determining Predetermined Times

There are more than a dozen methods available for determining standard time data, but the basic techniques of each method are essentially the same. Among these methods are Motion Time Analysis (MTA), Universal Maintenance Standards (UMS), Work-Factor (W-F), Methods Time Measurement (MTM), and Master Clerical Data (MCD). We shall describe and illustrate the latter method in the following paragraphs to indicate the basic techniques common to all methods.[4]

Master Clerical Data (MCD)

The *Master Clerical Data (MCD)* method of determining standard time data consists of various categories of elements tailored for

---

[4]The background information on Master Clerical Data (MCD) is reprinted with the permission of H. W. Nance, President, Serge A. Birn Company, 5328 Wooster Road, Cincinnati, OH 45226.

measuring work performed in the office.[5] As a result of the need for more economical methods of measuring office tasks and to provide for new tasks emerging as a result of technological changes in text/word processing, data entry, and photocopying, the basic MCD method was modified. The modified plan, known as MCD-MOD-I, provides for measuring a wide variety of tasks completed on word processing and data-entry equipment.

The basic categories of MCD-MOD-I elements used in measuring office work are shown in Figure 22–2; some of the typical elements are presented in Figure 22–3. Initial use of the method requires training under the guidance of a consultant who has experience in using the basic element categories and the correct techniques for gathering information. Once the person who will be responsible for measuring work has gained confidence from this practical guidance and has applied the method, the work measurement program can be expanded and handled by the firm's own personnel.

The MCD-MOD-I method uses the word *task* to describe an activity performed in the office. For example, in the task, "Prepare Advertising Material," an advertising clerk collates six pages, aligns the six pages in two directions, staples the pages in the corner, places the collated material in a manila envelope, and puts the envelope aside. MCD-MOD-I is used to measure this task as shown in Table 22–3. For each element listed in Table 22–3, the appropriate MCD Code and standard time are obtained from Figure 22–3. For example, the first element,

"Collate six pages of" is identified as MCD Code ACT. In Figure 22–3, we see in Box A, Arrange Papers, that the standard time for ACT is 42. This element occurs once in the task, so "1" is entered in the Frequency column of Table 22–3. The total number of units for each element is obtained by multiplying the standard time by the frequency. The total number of units, 550, in Table 22–3 represents the total time for doing the task. This number of units is equivalent to .33 minutes since each unit is equal to .00001 hours, .0006 minutes, or .036 seconds.

To use this total time as a standard, we must add an allowance for break periods, personal time, and unavoidable delays. The average allowance used is about 15 percent. Adding 15 percent results in a standard time of .38 minutes. This is equivalent to .00633 hours per item, or about 1,263 items in an eight-hour day. If the advertising clerk produced 1,200 items in an eight-hour day, the performance is 95 percent [(1,200 ÷ 1,263) × 100].

PERFORMANCE STANDARDS FOR NONROUTINE OFFICE JOBS

Most measurement of administrative work focuses upon those jobs that are routine and repetitive. However, we should also consider the development of standards for those administrative activities that are classified as nonroutine, varied, or creative. Some examples of such jobs are drafting, designing, editing, proofreading, and processing investment trust portfolios. Many nonroutine office jobs are complex and consist of ever-changing mental activities that affect job performance. Since such jobs are accomplished in a variety of ways, it is extremely difficult, if not impracticable, to measure the work and to develop sound performance standards. However, certain kinds of nonroutine work may be measured in the

---

[5]The time values for each of the elements in the MCD method were developed from the most widely used predetermined time system, Methods Time Measurement (MTM). MTM and its application data are copyrighted by the MTM Association for Standards and Research, Fair Lawn, NJ 07410.

Figure 22-2
MCD-MOD-I
Elements
Used for
Measuring
Office Work

Arrange Papers	This contains the elements needed to collate or sort papers by various methods.
Body Elements	This contains the elements needed for moving from one location to another.
Calculate	This contains elements for measuring machine or mental calculations.
Duplicate	This contains the basic elements needed for measuring photocopying.
Eye Times	This contains the elements needed for reading, looking up information, and making simple decisions.
Fasten/Unfasten	The elements for various fastening and unfastening of papers are in this category, such as rubber bands, paper clips, staples, etc.
Get and Aside	These elements are used for getting and putting aside papers, files, books, etc.; they are the most used category.
Handle Paper	This category contains elements for folding, tearing, aligning, etc., of paper.
Insert	These elements cover placing and removing of material, folders, or cards in files or binders.
Keystrokes	This category provides times for keystrokes located on the various keyboard configurations found on office equipment.
Locate	The basic elements needed for locating folders, cards, pages, etc., are in this category.
Mailing	The elements in this category cover folding letters, inserting them in envelopes, closing the envelope as well as opening envelopes, removing contents, etc.
Open and Close	Covers the elements needed for opening and closing binders, drawers, boxes, etc.
Post	Provides elements for reading information and writing it down.
Read	Provides elements for reading addresses, lines, names, numbers, etc.
Type	Provides elements for all forms of typing.
Write	Provides elements for writing names, numbers or printing them.

Source: Serge A. Birn Company, Division of SABCO, Inc., © 1981, Training Techniques Company, Inc.

aggregate, or as a whole, in order to provide useful standards.

As an example, let's look in on the text/word processing center of a large insurance company. Here we find that no one operator is assigned to any particular keyboarding task on a daily basis. The work load of the center is cyclically repetitive in that each day the same keyboarding tasks—from preparing the initial application form to filling in the completed policy—occur over and over again. The work load of the center is probably

Figure 22-3 Typical MCD-MOD I Elements

A	ARRANGE PAPERS	
Collate		
Two Sheets	ACT	42
Additional Sheets	ACA	27
Sort		
Groups	ASG	47
Pigeonholes	ASP	69
Alphabetically		
0 Thru 19	ASA01	72
20 Thru 29	ASA02	79
Over 30	ASA03	85

G	GET AND PUT ASIDE	
Get Only		
Batch of Papers (Loose)	GGB	31
Jumbled Object	GGJ	27
Medium Object	GGM	18
Sheet of Paper	GGS	21
Aside Only		
To Fixture	GAF	23
To Other Hand	GAH	20
To Pile	GAP	32
To Table	GAT	15
Combined Get and Aside		
Batch to Fixture	GBF	54
Batch to Pile	GBP	63
Batch to Table	GBT	46
Jumbled to Fixture	GJF	50
Jumbled to Other Hand	GJH	47
Jumbled to Table	GJT	42
Medium to Fixture	GMF	41
Medium to Other Hand	GMH	38
Medium to Table	GMT	33
Sheet to Fixture	GSF	44
Sheet to Other Hand	GSH	41
Sheet to Pile	GSP	53
Sheet to Table	GST	36

B	BODY ELEMENTS	
Arise and Sit	BAS	208
Seated Turn	BST	122
Bend and Arise	BBA	61
Walk Per Step	BWS	17

M	MAILING	
Fold		
Insert		
No-Seal		
Regular Envelope	MFIN01	195
Manila Envelope	MFIN02	240
Stringed Envelope	MFIN03	226
Seal		
Regular Envelope	MFIS01	275
Manila Envelope	MFIS02	340
Identify		
Label / Sticker		
Dry	MIL01	49
Wet	MIL02	85
Stamp		
Normal per Time	MIS01	13
Self-Inking	MIS02	56
Date Set	MIS03	49
Open		
Sealed		
Folded		
Regular Envelope	MOSF01	192
Manila Envelope	MOSF02	199
Unfolded		
Regular Envelope	MOSU01	132
Manila Envelope	MOSU02	169
Unsealed		
Folded		
Regular Envelope	MOUF01	101
Manila Envelope	MOUF02	110
Stringed Envelope	MOUF03	148
Unfolded		
Regular Envelope	MOUU01	41
Manila Envelope	MOUU02	80
Stringed Envelope	MOUU03	118
Unfolded		
Insert		
Seal		
Regular Envelope	MUIS01	130
Manila Envelope	MUIS02	258
No-Seal		
Regular Envelope	MUIN01	50
Manila Envelope	MUIN02	158
Stringed Envelope	MUIN03	145

F	FASTEN / UNFASTEN	
Binder		
Duo-Tang		
Fasten	FBDF	125
Unfasten	FBDU	77
Three Ring		
Open	FBTO	31
Close	FBTC	31
Clip		
Paper		
Place	FCPP	75
Remove	FCPR	43
Rubber Band		
Place	FRP	129
Remove	FRR	16
Staple		
Hand		
First	FSHF	77
Additional	FSHA	35
Table		
First	FSTF	37
Additional	FSTA	20
Remove		
First	FSRF	84
Additional	FSRA	52

H	HANDLE PAPER	
Jog		
Cards		
Up to 1" Thick	HJC01	5
Over 1" Thick	HJC02	9
Sheets		
Up to 1" Thick	HJS01	8
Over 1" Thick	HJS02	12
Punch		
Three Hole	HPT	30
Shift		
Flip or Turn	HSF	23
General	HSG	27
Tear		
Care	HTC	32
No-Care	HTN	23

O	OPEN AND CLOSE	
Binder		
Cover		
8 1/2" x 11"	OBC01	48
Drawers and Doors		
Desk Drawer	ODD	62
File Drawer	ODF	78
Tops		
Flaps	OTF	95
Hinged Lid	OTH	35
Loose Lid	OTL	71

measurable in terms of *total production* for the cycle. Such a type of measurement can be used to determine optimum staffing needs or to compare the production of one cycle against another.

When measuring the productivity of managers and supervisors, we may find that an analysis of *goal achievement* is used. First, the mission of a department or a division is defined in terms of measurable goals

Table 22-3
Measuring
the Task,
"Prepare
Advertising
Material,"
by Use of
MCD-MOD-I

Description	MCD Code	Standard Time	Frequency	Total Units
Collate six pages of	ACT	42	1	42
advertising material	ACA	27	4	108
Move material up	GAT	15	1	15
Align end of material	HJSO1	8	3	24
Turn material to side	HSG	27	1	27
Align side of material	HJSO1	8	3	24
Staple corner of material	FSTF	37	1	37
Place material in manila envelope.	MUISO2	258	1	258
Seal and put aside	GAT	15	1	15
				550

Source: Serge A. Birn Company, Division of SABCO, Inc., © 1981, Training Techniques Company, Inc.

that support the overall objectives of the organization. Next, the contributions of the managers or supervisors are measured in terms of how successful they were in achieving the goals. For example, let's say that a departmental goal is to reduce overhead expenses by 12 percent during the next six months. The productivity of that department's manager can be clearly evaluated in terms of the overhead-reduction goal.[6]

In establishing performance standards for administrative personnel, a company may utilize the Program Evaluation and Review Technique (PERT), which was described in an earlier chapter. You may recall that the PERT network is divided into the three aspects of time, cost, and performance to show the sequence, interrelationships, and dependencies of individual tasks in the project. The PERT technique lends itself to use in computerized projects, and most software manufacturers offer PERT programs.

At about the same time the PERT technique was being devised, a similar network control system, the **Critical Path Method (CPM)**, was being developed. In this method, we arrange all the activities of a project in sequence, estimate the time allowance (standard) to complete each activity, and plot all factors on a network diagram. Our objective is to determine the minimum elapsed time for completing the entire project. Finally, we relate the time required to complete each activity to its cost and determine whether the time can be shortened by spending additional funds. Thus, with both CPM and PERT, our aim is to strengthen the cost-effectiveness of programs or projects as part of the goal of office productivity improvement, which we discuss in the following section.

OFFICE PRODUCTIVITY IMPROVEMENT

We hear and read that our country's major economic problem is our miserably slow pace of productivity improvement. During the past 15 years the volume of output from one hour's labor has increased, on the average, only 1 percent each year, compared

[6]For a complete discussion of methods used to measure managerial productivity, see Randy J. Goldfield, *Office Information Technology* (Westport, CT: Greenwood Press, Inc., 1986), pp. 21–23.

with an average annual increase of 2.7 percent during the previous 15 years.[7] We read that productivity among white-collar workers has increased only 4 percent during the last 20 years compared with a 90 percent increase for blue-collar workers.[8] The seemingly endless demand by organizations for information has brought about an expanding number of office employees whose salaries and benefits cause administrative costs to rise as much as 8 to 10 percent each year.

We might expect that, with computerization, service-type companies (banks, brokerage houses, hospitals, health care clinics, hotels, etc.) could easily increase productivity and reduce costs, especially labor costs. We do see that this occurs in some companies, such as the bank that installed a sophisticated computer system which enables human tellers to cash checks at half the cost of automatic teller machines. Further, a computer analysis of the customers waiting in line at the tellers' windows showed that the bank could reduce the number of its part-time tellers.[9] However, we find evidence that the installation of computer systems often falls short of the goal of improving productivity. In fact, despite the huge sums of money spent on computers and office equipment during the past ten years, productivity in service-type firms has not kept pace. There are those who predict that the anticipated productivity gains from the computer revolution will continue to elude the U.S. economy; however, others expect that in the 1990s, "we're going to turn the corner" and realize productivity gains

from the computer revolution.[10] At the International Productivity Symposium in 1988, Secretary of Labor McLaughlin summed it up with her statements: "Clearly, machinery and technology alone don't improve productivity. People do."[11]

Some observers claim that the drop in productivity among service-type firms has dragged down the growth rate for productivity in the overall economy.[12] Some industries find that their new technology increases, rather than decreases, the need for labor. As one human resources executive remarked, "Every time we automate something, there is some new technology that comes into the market that requires more workers."[13] A study by the Rand Corp. shows that when the U.S. Forest Service added computers to handle tasks such as payroll, billing, and mailing, the machines did not reduce work; on the contrary, they increased it. After introducing computers, managers cut back their clerical staffs in anticipation that the hardware would pick up the slack. The Service soon found, however, that they had to rehire the clerical employees. In the end, the number of clerical workers did shrink but by less than other groups.[14]

To handle the ever-expanding work load without a corresponding increase in costs is the goal of programs designed to improve office productivity. At the heart of any productivity improvement program is the

---

[7]Alan S. Blinder, "Want to Boost Productivity? Try Giving Workers a Say," *Business Week* (April 17, 1989), p. 10.

[8]Dianna Booher, "How to Slash the $100 Billion Cost of Paperwork," *Personnel Journal* (December, 1987), p. 55.

[9]David Wessel, "With Labor Scarce, Service Firms Strive to Raise Productivity," *The Wall Street Journal* (June 1, 1989), p. A16.

[10]"The New America: Economic Prospects for the Year 2000," *Business Week* (September 25, 1989), pp. 159 and 162.

[11]Horst Brand, "Productivity and Employment: The 1988 International Symposium," *Monthly Labor Review* (August, 1988), p. 32.

[12]"The Productivity Paradox: Why the Payoff from Automation Is Still So Elusive—and What Corporate America Can Do about It," *Business Week* (June 6, 1988), p. 102.

[13]Ibid.

[14]Amanda Bennett, "When Management Professors Gather, Relevance Sometimes Rears Its Ugly Head," *The Wall Street Journal* (August 15, 1988), p. A17.

organization's acceptance of increased productivity as a philosophy, a basic "value" of the firm. Productivity improvement must be woven into the fabric of the organization so that it becomes an essential element in the overall operations of the enterprise. Any productivity improvement program requires the involvement of *every* employee—from top managers to those at the operative level—in identifying and pursuing opportunities for improving productivity. In the closing sections of this chapter, we describe several techniques designed to improve the productivity of office employees, their managers and supervisors, and, in turn, their organizations.

Quality Circles

As an example of *employee involvement*, consider the **quality circle**, which is a group of workers who voluntarily meet together on a regular basis to identify, analyze, and solve job-related quality problems and to develop employee potential.[15] The proposed solutions, designed to lead to cost reduction and increased productivity, are submitted to management for adoption or rejection. Figure 22–4 shows the typical functioning of a quality circle involved in solving problems

---

[15]Quality circles were conceived in Japan in 1961, where they are known as *quality control circles*. Under the leadership of Dr. Kaoru Ishikawa, the theories of behavioral scientists such as Maslow, Herzberg, and McGregor were tied together with the statistical quality control practices advanced by W. Edwards Deming and other practitioners of productivity improvement. *See* Donald L. Dewar, *Quality Circles: Answers to 100 Frequently Asked Questions* (Red Bluff, CA: Quality Circle Institute, 1979). Some companies and unions refer to their quality circles as *quality-of-work-life programs, self-managed work teams, problem-solving committees,* or *labor-management steering committees.*

Figure 22–4
Problem
Solving in a
Quality
Circle

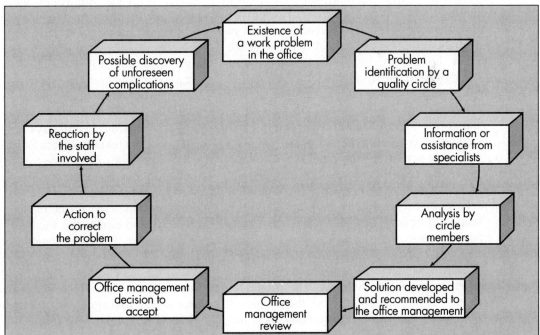

Source: Reprinted, by permission of the publisher, from PROFITABLE OFFICE MANAGEMENT FOR THE GROWING BUSINESS, by Edward N. Rausch, p. 139. © 1984 AMACOM Book Division, American Management Associations, New York. All rights reserved.

The use of quality circles usually results in increased morale and improved productivity.

related to office work. During the problem-solving stages, where the solution to one problem often creates another problem, there is much interaction between office management and the workers.

A 1987 survey by the U.S. General Accounting Office found that 70 percent of 476 large companies had installed quality circles, the most common form of employee involvement.[16] The number of members in a quality circle varies from 3 to 15, with the ideal size being 7 or 8. The members of a circle should be from the same work area or do similar work so that the problems they select will be familiar to all of them. The quality circle teams must be allowed to meet regularly on company-paid time. To help focus the activity of the quality circle, each group has a leader, who may be a supervisor or a person selected by the group. The leader, a key person in each circle, helps keep the team "on course" and acts as spokesperson for the group.

Quality circle members should be trained in statistical methods, group dynamics, and problem-solving techniques. The members should be permitted to choose the problems they will tackle, and where possible, become

involved by implementing the solutions and monitoring the results. To do so, of course, management must share with the circle members all the information they need.

For an example of how quality circles may lead to increased involvement among its office workers, let's examine an eastern credit corporation that provides financial services for customers who lease equipment. The company set up 11 teams, each with 10 to 15 workers, in its division that services small businesses. The three major lease-processing functions (handling applications and checking customers' credit standing, drawing up contracts, and collecting payments) were combined so that each team is responsible for providing full service to each customer. No longer are customers' incoming calls shunted from one department to another; instead, each team works with and establishes a personal relationship with the same customers. Each team largely manages itself, with its members making most decisions on how to deal with customers, schedule time off, reassign work when co-workers are absent, and interview prospective new employees. The payoff for employee involvement such as this? The teams process up to 800 lease applications each day vs. 400 under the old system. And, instead of taking several days to give a final yes or no, the team does it in 24 to 48 hours.[17]

Working with each group is a *facilitator* or *coordinator*, a company employee who serves as a consultant to a number of circles. When a solution to a problem has been developed by the circle, the facilitator arranges to have the solution considered by the appropriate managers and takes part in installing acceptable improvements. The facilitator may report to a steering committee or a senior manager with top-level responsibility for company programs.

---

[16]John Hoerr, "The Payoff from Teamwork," *Business Week* (July 10, 1989), p. 58.

[17]Ibid., p. 59.

Quality circles were first introduced into manufacturing operations, but the concept has grown to include other areas such as engineering, research and development, and clerical.

Nominal Group Technique (NGT)

The **nominal group technique (NGT)**, a variation of the quality circle and the brainstorming techniques, is particularly useful for solving problems related to the improvement of office productivity. This technique is distinguished from other group processes in that individuals work alone in small *noninteraction* groups, where a silent generation of ideas replaces an oral exchange. The nominal groups meet regularly to decide what aspects of their work should be measured and how the measurement should be accomplished. The NGT is applicable to clerical workers as well as to middle managers and is especially successful in determining the effectiveness of new administrative office systems.

Each group consists of five to nine workers having equal status, who are guided in their discussion by a facilitator. One by one, the members of the group are polled in writing to state their ideas about indexes that may be used to measure productivity. After much discussion of the indexes, the group votes to select the most important items, which are weighted and listed in sequential order.

Time Management

As we have seen, the productivity of managers and supervisors cannot be measured by traditional methods such as motion and time study and the setting of production standards. Many managerial functions require weeks or months to complete, with the full effect of the work not being felt for years, if at all. Thus, measurements that are limited by the

element of time do not apply well to the work of managers and supervisors. However, the element of time and how that time is spent are very important considerations in developing yardsticks to measure managerial productivity. For example, a year-long study undertaken by a management consulting firm found that managers and other professionals spend anywhere from 15 percent to more than 40 percent of their time on less productive activities, which they consider wasteful.[18] As discussed in the following paragraphs, there is need for all office employees, but especially managers and supervisors, to develop effective time management programs.

The need for an effective time management program becomes clear when AOMs and supervisors answer the following questions:

1. Do I never seem to get everything done that I had hoped to accomplish? As a result, am I being placed under too much stress?
2. Is my desk cluttered with papers that I constantly reshuffle but never take care of?
3. When making a decision, do I usually have incomplete information?
4. Do the meetings that I schedule to last an hour go on for two hours or more?
5. Do I often work overtime at the office?
6. Do I frequently take work home over the weekend?
7. Am I continually being interrupted by telephone calls, visitors, employees who monopolize my time, and co-workers who want to socialize?
8. By failing to delegate, do I spend most of my time on trivial items, with not enough time left over to tackle the big jobs?

---

[18]Debra L. Haskell, "Emerging from the Fog of Uncertainty," *Modern Office Procedures* (March, 1981), p. 60.

Managers who answer "Yes" to all or most of the questions above probably spend the bulk of their time on projects that produce only minimal benefits. In order to obtain the most out of their working hours, these managers must realize that they may be the chief cause of their own time problems.

The aim of **time management** is to provide for efficient use of all resources, including time, so that individuals become productive in achieving their important professional and personal goals. Therefore, managers must break their old, inefficient habits and establish new routines to overcome the stumbling blocks to time management.

Using a Time Log[19]

A common technique for determining how much time is used on various tasks throughout the workday is to keep a time log, such as that shown in Figure 22–1, page 685. In the log we record what we have done during stated time intervals, such as every 15–20 minutes. After we have listed the activities for several days, we should have a sufficient number of typical observations for analysis. Next, we analyze the time log to determine what could have been done to make better use of our available time. In analyzing the time log, we should answer questions such as these:

1. What are the major activities or events that cause me to use my time ineffectively?
2. Which of these tasks can be performed by me only?
3. What activities can be delegated, better controlled, or eliminated?

Analyzing Time Wasters

After we have developed a list of the time wasters, we can pinpoint those activities that require change or elimination. Some of the most common time wasters appear in the eight questions raised at the beginning of this section.

As a result of analyzing time wasters, we may find that we are spending 80 percent of our time on items that produce only 20 percent of the real benefit. Getting bogged down on low-value activities could be the reason for our inability to do important tasks. Low-value items are generally easy to do and give a sense of accomplishment, but they are often time consuming.

Time wasters may be *internally* generated by ourselves or *externally* created by events or other people. Internally generated time wasters (procrastination, failure to delegate, failure to set priorities, and failure to plan) are the easier ones to resolve because they stem from our own actions or inactions. Thus, we, who are part of the problem, can become part of the solution. Time problems that are externally generated (telephone and fax interruptions, meetings, visitors, and socializing), however, require more imagination and creativity because they are not totally within our control.

Socializing is a time waster that can be internally or externally generated.

[19]The remaining parts of this section are adapted from H. Kent Baker, *Techniques of Time Management*, Management Aid No. 239, U.S. Small Business Administration.

Office managers may find that they are grossly overpaid for some of the tasks they perform. Some people become so involved in work that they lose sight of why they are doing it and how much it really costs. The cost of performing each of the tasks listed in the manager's log should be determined. Thus, managers will find that doing certain tasks themselves simply is not worth the cost. For example, sitting in front of a PC to input one's own correspondence may not be a very efficient use of a manager's time. This does not mean that the task is not important, but rather, that some tasks are worth doing only if done by lower paid individuals.

Setting Goals and Listing Priorities

Having analyzed time wasters, we may find we have failed to make the best use of our time because we lack specific goals. We may become easily sidetracked and waste time due to a lack of direction and focus. To determine what we really want to accomplish, we must set short- and long-range goals and allocate specific blocks of time to each. We should put the goals in writing and review them frequently by ourselves as well as with our immediate superiors.

To make these goals operational, we can use a daily "to-do" list. We should begin each workday with a plan of the tasks to be performed and the priority of each task. In budgeting our time, we should allocate part of each day to those tasks that will lead to the accomplishment of our goals. Thus, by blocking out part of the day or week for major projects, we are assured of having time to do the important tasks.

Using Time Productively

Ten useful tips on effective time management follow.

1. *Consolidate similar tasks*. This step aids in minimizing interruptions and economizes on the use of resources and efforts. For example, instead of making calls sporadically throughout the day, combine and make outgoing calls at specific times each day. Also, inform frequent callers of the best time to reach us. Thus, callers can be helped to develop a habit of calling when we prefer, not when the callers prefer.

2. *Tackle tough jobs first*. We have a tendency to work on the less difficult tasks first with the idea of working up to bigger projects. What often happens, however, is that the tough jobs simply do not get done because we spend too much time doing the less important tasks. By the time the tough jobs are ready to be tackled, we are too tired to work on them. The solution is to reverse the process. Start the day with the important work when the energy level is high; then work down the list of priorities. If time is available at the end of the day, the "low-value" items can be completed.

3. *Delegate work and develop others*. Try to break the "do-it-yourself" habit. Delegate work whenever possible. Delegation does not mean "dumping" a task on someone else. Rather, delegating carries with it the responsibility of making sure that the individual has the requisite skills and knowledge to do the job. The time we devote to training and motivating people to do tasks that customarily we perform will reduce our own time burdens in the future and enrich the jobs of others.

   For example, we can give more work to our secretary or executive assistant, if we have one. A secretary can perform many tasks that are great time savers, such as screening visitors and telephone calls, composing letters, and anticipating problems before they arise.

4. *Learn to use idle time*. Always try to maintain a list of tasks to do during idle periods. Instead of doing nothing while

waiting for an appointment, we could read an article, review a report, or catch up on correspondence. Travel time can also be converted into useful time. For instance, if we have always wanted to take a management improvement course but could not find time during our workday, we can listen to tapes on the way to and from work.

5. *Get control of the paper flow.* To help stem the flood of paperwork, decide what can be streamlined or eliminated. Throw out junk mail, cancel unused subscriptions, and have mail routed directly to subordinates. If possible, handle each piece of paper once and do not pick up a piece of paper unless there is a plan to do something with it. For example, a complaint does not go away simply because the letter has been put aside; so, move the paperwork along to the appropriate person instead of letting it stack up on the desk. Being a paper shuffler wastes time and leads to inefficiencies.

6. *Avoid the cluttered-desk syndrome.* If our desk is piled with paper and we waste time looking for buried items, we should clear the desk of everything except the work to be done during the day.

7. *Get started immediately on important tasks.* Putting things off until tomorrow is easy. Like most people, we generally do the things we enjoy first and procrastinate on the tasks we dislike. Here is where we need self-discipline to overcome that procrastination. First, rather than put off doing a job because it seems overwhelming, poke holes in the task by breaking it down into bite-sized pieces that are more palatable to digest. By following this "Swiss cheese" technique, we will soon find that poking holes in the project makes it less overwhelming. Second, unfinished work is more of a motivator than unstarted work. By having started a job, we have made an

investment of our time and are more likely to complete the task.

8. *Reduce meeting time.* No doubt, many meetings should not take place. Sometimes the only reason for a weekly staff meeting is because a week has passed since the last one. Such meetings disrupt work. Reduce the number and improve the quality of meetings by following an agenda; it saves time and money. If needed meetings are too long, schedule them to precede immediately the lunch hour or quitting time. Thus, most people will be motivated to end the meeting promptly. Also, a stand-up meeting helps to guarantee a short meeting.

9. *Take time to plan.* Sometimes we may be heard saying, "I just don't have the time to plan." No doubt we are very busy but not very effective. Although it appears to be a contradiction, by taking time to plan, we end up saving time. Instead of spending the day "fighting fires," we should develop a schedule for doing the things that must be done in the available time.

10. *Learn to say "no."* Someone is always asking us for a piece of our time. Instead of being honest and saying "no" to requests, we often tend to hedge and end up accepting responsibilities that are neither wanted nor for which we have time to perform. Saying "no" requires some courage and tact, but it is necessary for effective time management.

By applying the ten tips listed above, we can use our time far more productively. This in turn will help us cope with overly stressful situations that place undue physical or psychological demands on us. Along with interpersonal problems, either at home or at work, time management problems have been identified as a major source of stress.[20] By

---

[20]Dr. Farris Jordan, "Taking Control of Your Stress," *Management World* (June-August, 1987), pp. 13–16. In this same issue, see also Manuel A. Tipgos, "The Things That Stress Us," pp. 17–18.

adopting time management strategies, we can learn to control the sources of stress more effectively. Also, for our own increased effectiveness and personal well-being, we should work toward identifying those personal and organizational goals that will provide balance in our daily lives.

SUMMARY

1. The organization that designs an effective program of measuring work and setting standards is able to determine more precisely the true cost of performing many kinds of administrative services and thus budget more realistically the firm's needs for resources.

2. Some of the factors that result from an ongoing program of work measurement and which contribute directly toward improving office productivity are: better control over the scheduling of work, availability of realistic performance goals for employee appraisal, compensation of employees according to their productivity, development of cost and volume information for use in feasibility studies, interdepartment cost comparisons for use in diagnosing wasteful practices, and indicators that show when employees are sufficiently trained for entry onto their jobs or for assignment to new positions.

3. Perhaps two-thirds to three-fourths of all office work can be measured, although for several reasons such work is not commonly measured. One of the arguments advanced against the measurement of office work is that because of its varied, complex nature, the work cannot be measured. However, work whose content is repetitive, consistent, countable, and sufficient in volume can be measured; and standards for such work can be set.

4. The selection of one or more methods to measure administrative work is conditioned by the financial resources, qualified personnel, and time available to the organization.

5. Work measurement methods include historical data, time log, work sampling, motion and time study, and predetermined times. Techniques are also available whereby some types of nonroutine office work may be measured in the aggregate.

6. For the organization that accepts the improvement of office productivity as part of its philosophy, there are many techniques or approaches for improving the quantity and quality of output of its office employees, supervisors, and managers. In addition to the innovative approaches discussed in earlier chapters of this textbook, the firm should consider the establishment of quality circles and the use of the nominal group technique.

7. Regardless of which approach is used by the organization in its productivity improvement program, there is need for all personnel, and in particular the supervisors and managers, to use more effectively all of their resources, including time. Only through the effective use of their resources can all office employees attain their important professional and personal goals and thereby maximize office productivity.

GLOSSARY **Critical path method (CPM)**—a network control system that shows the sequence of activities in a project and the time allowance (standard) for completing each activity, with the objective of determining the minimum elapsed time for completing the project.

Historical data—a work measurement method in which past production records of various office activities are studied to measure what was produced in the past; also known as the *past performance method*.

Micromotion study—the use of motion pictures to study and analyze parts of a given operation with the objective of eliminating wasteful movements.

Motion study—a work measurement method in which work is divided into its most fundamental elements, which are studied and timed in order to eliminate wasteful movement and effort.

Nominal group technique (NGT)—a technique of improving productivity whereby small noninteraction groups of workers meet regularly to decide what aspects of their work should be measured and how the measurement should be accomplished.

Performance rating—the adjustment of individual differences obtained in stopwatch studies in order to obtain a theoretical normal time required by average workers to complete their jobs under standardized conditions; also known as *leveling*.

Predetermined times—the constant time values applied to basic motions of each job element so that the time value for performing the entire job may be read from a table in order to set time standards.

Quality circle—a group of workers who voluntarily meet together on a regular basis to identify, analyze, and solve job-related quality problems and to develop employee potential.

Quality control—a regulatory process in which the quality of performance is measured and compared with standards so that any difference between performance and standards may be acted upon.

Time log—a work measurement method in which workers measure their output by recording the time spent and units of work produced for a stipulated time period; also known as the *time ladder method*.

Time management—the process of efficiently using all resources, including time, so that individuals are productive in achieving their professional and personal goals.

Time study—a work measurement method in which the time required to perform each operation at an average pace is determined.

Tolerance—the degree of accuracy that will be accepted when determining sample size.

Work measurement—a tool of cost control used to determine how much work is completed (a quantitative measure) and how effectively it is completed (a qualitative measure).

Work sampling—a work measurement method based on the statistical law of probability in which findings representative of the universe are obtained by taking valid random samples of work done.

Work standard—a yardstick of performance, or par, which indicates what is expected of workers and how their output can be evaluated.

FOR YOUR REVIEW

1. For what kinds of office activities are work standards most commonly established?

2. Define "100 percent efficiency," the attainment of which is the goal of all work standards.

3. List the benefits available to an organization that establishes a program of work standards.

4. Why are formal programs of work measurement not commonly undertaken in many of today's offices?

5. To be capable of measurement, office tasks should meet certain criteria. What are these criteria?

6. What are the major points to be kept in mind by the administrative office manager when communicating to employees the nature of the planned work measurement program?

7. Describe the role played by first-line supervisors in administering a work measurement program.

8. What are the limitations of the historical data method when used to measure work?

9. Explain how office employees participate in the measurement of their work when the time log method is used.

10. What is the underlying premise upon which work sampling is based? In determining the proper sample size to be used in work sampling, what factors should be considered?

11. A work sampling study is planned with the following specifications: 15 percent tolerance, 9 percent critical percentage, and 95 percent reliability. To meet the requirements of this study, how many observations must be made?

12. What are the disadvantages of using work sampling to set standards?

13. What is the essential difference between motion study and time study?

14. What characteristics should be possessed by office workers selected for observation in a time study?

15. Why must the actual time required by a worker to complete operational elements be leveled?

16. Compare the advantages and disadvantages of using predetermined times in setting standards for office work.

17. Describe how performance standards may be established for nonroutine office jobs.

18. Explain how the use of quality circles aids in improving the productivity of office workers.

19. For what reasons is the nominal group technique (NGT) used by an organization?

20. What is the objective of a time management program?

FOR YOUR DISCUSSION

1. Explain how the 72-stroke par for an 18-hole golf course serves as an excellent example of a standard.

2. With the increasing number of office automation applications designed to speed up information processing and reduce costs, why should we be concerned about white-collar productivity?

3. A management professor made the following statement: "If you can't measure it, you can't improve it."[21] Do you agree with this observation? Discuss the relevance of the statement to productivity improvement in the office.

4. Some managers believe they have a productivity improvement program in place because they have set up quality circles, or revitalized their suggestion systems, or installed "office automation." However, these techniques are not *solutions* to the problem of improving office productivity, but, rather, *approaches* used to solve problems. One management consultant has claimed that America's present low productivity is a *management problem* and that we cannot adequately address the issue of office automation until we have our offices operating at a first-class *managerial* level. Further, it was stated that an organization does not want to bring automation into an operation where labor is only 50 percent effective (where the 4/8 Theory exists).[22]

   Do you support this consultant's claims? What is a first-class managerial level? What evidence can you offer to dispute the validity of the statements?

5. As a result of having set up four quality circles at the Kenyon Business Forms Company, the manager of office services, Lance Charles, has been able to document a savings of 9 percent in administrative costs. At the last weekly meeting of Quality Circle 4, the following questions were raised by several of the members:
   a. How will the 9 percent financial gain that resulted from our greater productivity be shared?
   b. Since we have been in operation for several years, we feel that our group has dealt with at least 95 percent of the obvious problems. What do we do now at our weekly meetings?

   As the facilitator for the company's quality circles, how would you answer these two questions?

6. Maria Hurchick, who manages a small office consisting of 28 employees, has been reading for the past six months about office work measurement. In a discussion with several other office managers at a recent chapter meeting of the Administrative Management Society (AMS), Hurchick remarks, "All of these work measurement programs sound good, but my office is too small to think about bringing in any direct controls. Besides, I know my workers are more than 50 percent productive." How do you react to Hurchick's comments? Are her remarks valid, or is she "way off base" in her thinking?

7. Michael Sherrin, accounting manager for the George Company, was recently asked how many errors he will accept from the accountants he supervises. Right to the point Sherrin stated, "We don't permit any errors." Do you conclude from Sherrin's reply that the performance standard for the error rate of accounts is zero? Explain.

8. The time study analyst at Rubin Manufacturing Company measured the posting work in the accounts receivable department and arrived at a standard of 100 postings per hour. This standard was announced to the supervisor of the accounts receivable

---

[21]D. Keith Denton, "Work Sampling: Increasing Service and White-Collar Productivity," *Management Solutions* (March, 1987), p. 36.
[22]"Coping with White-Collar Waste," *Management Review* (November, 1983), p. 62.

department and then in a separate memo to the posting clerks. Shortly thereafter, a confusing and panicky situation arose, which resulted in more errors, morale problems, and less work done than before.

Assuming that the output of 100 postings per hour is feasible and accurate, discuss the use of this standard and the analyst's method of presenting it to the supervisor and employees.

9. What relationship, if any, do you see between worker productivity and participation in the firm's profit-sharing plan? between employee motivation and productivity?

10. During the coffee break at a recent national office management meeting, you overheard these comments following a seminar on "Workplace Errors in Our Company's Quality Control Program":
    a. I just tell my workers they've got to pay more attention to their tasks and they won't be making all those mistakes!
    b. We just don't allow any errors.
    c. Well, I don't think there is any way to stop errors from occurring.
    d. I think most errors are "situation-caused" rather than "human-caused"—that is, most errors are related to the design of the work environment.

    Evaluate the validity of each of the four comments.

SOLVING CASE PROBLEMS

Case 22-1 Evaluating Productivity Improvement Programs

As supervisor of the records management department, you were selected to serve on your firm's ten-member employee-management committee. One of the areas that the committee has selected for study is your firm's productivity improvement (PI) programs. At this week's meeting, you make the following notes as committee members list the PI programs now in effect:

Group financial incentives	Job redesign
Individual financial incentives	Worker participation
Awards and recognition	Alternative work schedules
Wage and salary increases	Training and development

The committee now wishes to get underway in evaluating the effectiveness of each PI program—to determine those programs that are highly effective and those that are disappointing or ineffective. However, the members are unable to agree on the next step— where to start in the evaluation process.

What input can you provide to spell out the steps your committee should follow in evaluating the company's PI programs?

Case 22–2 Overcoming Resistance to Time and Motion Study

Marlo Manning, director of administrative services for Klicka Controls, has just examined the results of the company's semiannual employee attitude survey. The survey results confirm many of the comments that Manning has heard via the grapevine—too many inequities in the salaries paid newly employed workers and those with years of seniority, and very little relationship between output and salaries earned. Manning firmly believes that if a time and motion study were undertaken, meaningful standards could be set for many of the office tasks. However, before drafting her recommendations for a time and motion study, she has decided "to kick it around" with several employees.

Here is a little of her conversation with Norman Beadley, supervisor of the computer center:

Manning: Your data-entry people are "naturals" for a time and motion study. And you know, Norman, they're the loudest complainers about salaries.

Beadley: That's true, Marlo; they do gripe a lot—I'll grant you that. But just look at the kind of work they do—you can't measure it! They jump around during the day from purchase orders to sales invoices to purchase invoices to time cards. There's just too much variety in their daily work to think about setting a standard that will make any sense. I'm sorry, Marlo, but this time I just can't "buy" your thinking.

Then Manning talks with Betty Moffat and Alvin Perry, two of the data-entry personnel:

Manning: Well, there you have the gist of how a time and motion study will help you in ironing out the salary problems you have described.

Moffat: All of that sounds good in theory. But I don't want anyone standing over me, breathing down my neck while I work. Besides, all they do in the study is try to speed us up so that we can grind out more strokes.

Perry: That's right, Marlo. I heard that after they did a study at Higgins down the road, seven of their workers were let go. You know very well that's what will happen here, and I don't want to be one of them out looking for a new job! Isn't there some other way you can "clean up" this lousy salary structure to guarantee us that we'll be paid for what we produce? You know, I've been with Klicka for 19 years now, and never before have I heard anyone talk about needing a time study. . . .

Prepare a report in which you:

1. Outline the approach you would follow in working with Beadley, the supervisor of the computer center.

2. Include all possible points and factors that will convince Beadley and his workers that the time and motion study will bring favorable results not only to the company but also to them.

23
Budgetary Control

GOALS FOR THIS CHAPTER

After completing this chapter, you should be able to:

1. List the objectives that management seeks to attain through the use of budgets and budget performance reports.
2. Identify the principles that guide administrative office managers in preparing budgets of administrative expenses.
3. Discuss the different kinds of costs to be considered when formulating a budget of administrative expenses.
4. Identify the bases commonly used in allocating indirect expenses.
5. Distinguish between incremental budgeting, zero-base budgeting, and compromise budgeting.
6. Describe the role of budget performance reporting in the overall program of budgetary control.
7. Discuss the contribution made by a work standards program to the analysis of administrative expenses.
8. Describe alternate methods for controlling fluctuations in the volume of office work.

To conduct business operations efficiently, managers must *plan* how the resources of their organization will be acquired and used. Also, they must *control* the acquisition and use of these resources. To obtain financial information quickly about these two very important activities—*planning and controlling*—management relies upon budgeting.

Budgeting is the process of planning future business activities and expressing those plans in a formal manner. The carefully prepared formal statement of plans for the future, expressed in financial terms, is called a **budget**.

We may develop budgets for a short period of time such as a month, a quarter, or a year. In most companies, however, the budget period is one year in length. We often divide the annual budget into quarterly or monthly budgets so that managers and supervisors are able to evaluate performance and take corrective actions promptly over a relatively short period of time. On the other hand, we may find that other budgets are developed for a long time period such as three to five or ten years. Long-range budgets are important in planning major expenditures such as the purchase of buildings, machinery, and equipment. Both short-term and long-range budgets are vital to the organization's program of budgetary control.

Budgetary control, the theme of this chapter, refers to the use of a budget in regulating and guiding those business activities concerned with acquiring and using resources. These activities may relate to developing new products, expanding or contracting product lines, increasing revenues, or decreasing operating expenses. Of great importance in budgetary control is the preparation of periodic **budget performance reports** that compare the actual operating data with the budgeted data. For example, we can compare the $15,000 revenue earned from the sales of Product A during April with the $20,000 sales volume budgeted for April. As a result of this comparison, we are able to identify and explain the causes of any significant **variance**, or difference, between actual operating data and budgeted data. In our example of Product A sales, we might conclude that the $5,000 variance between actual sales and budgeted sales seemed to be caused by a lack of sales promotion in April. As a result, we may plan to advertise Product A more intensively in May.

By means of budgets and budget performance reports, management tries to attain the following objectives:

1. *To establish procedures for planning and studying future revenues and expenses* so the organization's budget may be reviewed and modified when needed.
2. *To coordinate the activities of the various departments of the organization* so that individual department heads may become more aware of the financial problems of others on the management team.
3. *To build a basis for administrative control* by providing managers with factual measures of performance that they have helped to develop and for which they are held responsible.
4. *To communicate formally the plans that have been approved by management* and the actions that management wishes the organization to take during the budget period.
5. *To motivate all individuals by creating a climate of cost consciousness* in which they are stimulated to reach desired performance levels.

In the following section, we describe the role of the administrative office manager in achieving these objectives of budgetary control. As you will see, the responsibilities of AOMs vary among business organizations.

THE AOM'S ROLE IN BUDGETARY CONTROL

In Chapter 1, we pointed out that the differences in responsibilities assigned to

In small companies the AOM's wide range of responsibilities may include accounting functions.

AOMs are due to several factors, the most important of which is the size of the organization. In small and medium-size firms, the AOM may be an accountant who, in addition to regularly assigned duties, has responsibility for all administrative services. In large companies, the person responsible for administrative services may be a top-level executive such as a controller or a vice-president. As the head of administrative services in an organization, the AOM has responsibility for the support services described earlier in this textbook.

The reports prepared by (or for) the AOM typically include the following:

1. *Budgeted expense reports for the various administrative services.* The estimated expense reports are usually supported by detailed schedules of costs, which in large organizations may be prepared by first-line supervisors.
2. *Budget performance reports.* These department reports show in detail the actual costs incurred compared with the budgeted figures, the amount or per-

Dialog on the Firing Line

HOWARD FREEDMAN
Manager, Payroll
Tredegar Industries, Inc.
Richmond, Virginia

BS, Northeastern University
MBA, Suffolk University
CPP (Certified Payroll Professional)

As manager of payroll for Tredegar Industries, Inc., Howard Freedman is responsible for the administration of the corporate payroll function including administration of salary and hourly payroll; accounting for benefit administration plans; federal, state, and local tax reporting; systems development and selection; data administration for all payroll input and transmission; and employee support and communication regarding all payroll issues and services required of the employee. Mr. Freedman was 1987 Payroll Man of the Year for the American Payroll Association.

QUESTION: What role do you, as a manager, play in your company's program of budgetary control? Which budget reports are prepared for you? by you?

RESPONSE: As a manager, I am responsible for assuring that my department achieves its goals and objectives by utilizing "realistic" budgets. Since a budget is only a guideline, I always strive to meet or stay below it by continually trying to save money and improving operating efficiencies. In the event that actual expenses may exceed budget, I am careful to monitor them and justify the variances.

Since management success is based on getting the job done, even if it exceeds budget, there should be enough flexibility to provide funds for opportunities that will contribute to profitability.

Regarding budget reports, the corporate budget department prepares master reports for the finance division at the division and department levels. The reports show current and year-to-date information for the previous and current year's activity and provide space for projecting the new budget based on history and projected expenses.

From the data provided by the corporate budget department, each manager completes worksheets to calculate the new budget amounts. During this stage the following reports are prepared:

1. A statement of organizational purpose.
2. An organization chart that illustrates reporting relationships.
3. Detailed wage projections for each employee and addition to staff. This wage information includes current salary, overtime, bonuses, increases, differentials, etc.
4. A worksheet for all expenses by general ledger account number. The manager posts the prior year's budget and actual amounts, the current year's budget and actual amounts, and the new year's budget amounts. The new budget is then compared with the current year's on a dollar-for-dollar amount and percentage basis. For each account, a full explanation justifying the variance is required for management approval.

Note: During this process, I recommend that you build in any financial requirements that will be necessary to get the job done. By making your budget too tight, you subject yourself to added pressures of trying to get the job done with insufficient resources. Since your initial budgets will also be subject to further cuts by management, a built-in hedge against these cuts is recommended.

centage of variance, and explanations of significant variances.

3. *Analytical reports*. These reports show an analysis of the total costs in each department. For example, the supervisor of text/word processing services may prepare reports showing unit costs such as the cost per page or the cost per line of each letter produced.

4. *Special reports*. Most special reports document studies are prepared at the request of a company officer or initiated by the AOM to improve some phase of the information management function. For example, a report may be prepared to compare the costs of a desk-top dictation-transcription system vs. a central recorder system. Or a study may be undertaken to determine the feasibility of converting from accounting machines to microcomputers for the direct entry of accounts receivable data.

The accountant in the small or medium-size firm, assisted by department heads or supervisors, may prepare the operating budget for general and administrative expenses. In a like fashion, those in charge of the selling and purchasing functions prepare operating budgets. The individual budgets are then submitted to the people whose job it is to study and consolidate all the budgets into one master budget of operating expenses for the entire company.

In large organizations, the executive in charge of administrative services receives reports of budgeted expenses from department heads, such as those in charge of records management, word processing, mailing, and accounting. The administrator analyzes these reports, consolidating and condensing them into one budget covering all the information management expenses, and submits the final budget to the budget committee.

The Budget Committee

The *budget committee* may consist of the budget director and other executives such as the controller, treasurer, production manager, sales manager, and possibly the AOM. After receiving all the various estimates of income and expenses, the budget committee reviews and revises, if necessary, the dollar amounts. If a department head submits estimates that do not accurately relate to the goals of the company, the budget committee usually returns the estimates to the department head with recommendations for change. The originating department then either alters or justifies the amounts first submitted. After agreement has been reached, the figures are finally assembled and consolidated to form the master budget.

The Master Budget

The **master budget** consists of a number of budgets that collectively express the planned activities of the organization. The number and arrangement of the individual budgets included in the master budget depend on the size and complexity of the organization. The individual budgets typically found in a master budget are listed in Figure 23–1.

Some of the budgets listed in this figure cannot be prepared until other budgets have first been completed. For example, in a retail merchandising company, the buyers and other retail personnel cannot prepare the merchandise purchases budget until the sales budget has been completed. The number of units to be sold must be forecast before the buyers can estimate the number of units to be purchased. Thus, the sales department prepares its budget first since the remaining budgets depend upon the information contained in the sales budget.

In preparing the sales budget for a manufacturing company, the sales department or division estimates the quantity of

Figure 23-1
Contents of a
Typical Mas-
ter Budget

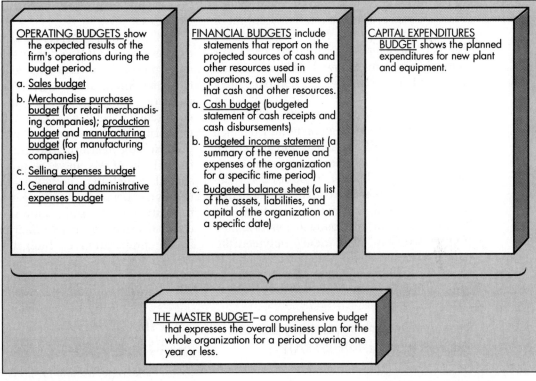

OPERATING BUDGETS show the expected results of the firm's operations during the budget period.

a. Sales budget
b. Merchandise purchases budget (for retail merchandising companies); production budget and manufacturing budget (for manufacturing companies)
c. Selling expenses budget
d. General and administrative expenses budget

FINANCIAL BUDGETS include statements that report on the projected sources of cash and other resources used in operations, as well as uses of that cash and other resources.

a. Cash budget (budgeted statement of cash receipts and cash disbursements)
b. Budgeted income statement (a summary of the revenue and expenses of the organization for a specific time period)
c. Budgeted balance sheet (a list of the assets, liabilities, and capital of the organization on a specific date)

CAPITAL EXPENDITURES BUDGET shows the planned expenditures for new plant and equipment.

THE MASTER BUDGET—a comprehensive budget that expresses the overall business plan for the whole organization for a period covering one year or less.

goods to be sold and the revenue to be derived from those sales. After the sales division has prepared the company's sales budget, the other divisions prepare their operating budgets. The production division prepares its budget before the manufacturing budget is developed since the number of units to be manufactured is affected by the amount of material, labor, and overhead to be budgeted. Generally after the production budget has been prepared, we find that the budgets for manufacturing costs or merchandise costs, selling expenses, and general and administrative expenses may be prepared in any sequence.

The Flexible Budget

The master budget is based on *the one most likely level of activity that will take place.*

Also, the master budget is prepared *before* any activity occurs. However, we often find that many companies prepare one or more **flexible budgets**, which are a prediction of costs at *various levels of activity.* We may prepare a flexible budget *before* the time period begins and indicate what the predicted costs will be for different levels of future activity. In this way, the flexible budgeting process aids managers in their planning for that time period. Having developed flexible budgets shows that managers have done some contingency planning and know what steps should be taken when performance begins to fall short of expectations. On the other hand, we may prepare a flexible budget *after* the period has ended and the actual activity is known. In this case, the flexible budget shows the costs that we might have expected for the actual production.

Let us say that the Roper Company's master budget shows an estimated output of 20,000 units for April. However, a flexible budget showing the *estimated* costs for output above and below 20,000 units might be useful. For example, the company may wish to know how an output of 15,000 or 25,000 units would affect the items listed on its budgeted income statement and balance sheet. After April has ended and the *actual* output and costs are known, we can prepare another flexible budget to be used for the budget performance report. This flexible budget is based on the actual output, say 21,500 units. In the budget performance report, we show the variance between the actual costs and the flexible budget amounts and thus indicate whether the output was produced efficiently.

PRINCIPLES OF PREPARING A BUDGET OF ADMINISTRATIVE EXPENSES

Of the budgets listed in Figure 23-1, the most important ones to the AOM are the operating budgets and more particularly the general and administrative expenses budget. **Administrative expenses** (or *general expenses*)[1] are those expenses incurred in the general operations of the organization. Examples of administrative expenses are office salaries and wages, depreciation of office furniture and equipment, and office supplies used. In medium-size and large firms, some expenses such as rent, insurance, and taxes are partly related to revenue-producing activities and partly related to administrative operations. Such *mixed expenses* may be divided between the two categories—selling expenses and administrative expenses. In small businesses, however, mixed expenses are

commonly reported as administrative expenses.

Well-prepared budgets of administrative expenses help AOMs and their superiors plan and control operations and give them the financial information needed for decision making. Budgets aid in heading off emergencies; they also direct attention to unprofitable office services and provide a yardstick for measuring progress in all areas for which AOMs have responsibility. We should remember, however, that administrative expenses budgets are effective only in relation to the skill, understanding, and effort that have gone into their preparation. In the preparation of budgets of administrative expenses, AOMs should pay close attention to each of the following principles.

PRINCIPLE OF RESPONSIBILITY

Assign initial responsibility for preparing budgets to key employees at the operative level so that budgets flow upward from department heads to the AOM.

Beginning the budget-making process at the operative level (see Figure 2–5, page 41) develops cost consciousness among workers and a common understanding about the budgeting process. Having those who are close to the work participate in the budgeting process also aids in gaining acceptance of the plan, improves morale among employees, and assists in increasing productivity. Participating in the preparation of a budget becomes a form of job enrichment for workers and may serve as a motivator to improve job performance. If, on the other hand, the budget originates at the top-management level and is imposed on the departments from that level, the budget may have a negative impact on the attitudes of employees.

---

[1]Often on income statements the heading "General and Administrative Expenses" is used to identify those expenses incurred in general operations.

PRINCIPLE OF OBJECTIVITY

Be realistic when stating budgeted amounts and show as objectively as possible what each service department is capable of producing.

A sound budget is neither unduly optimistic nor pessimistic about future revenues and costs. Instead, the budget sets forth in an objective fashion what each department is capable of producing along with a realistic statement of the costs to be incurred in producing that volume. We can use records from previous accounting periods as guides, but we should not be bound to the past; for cost factors and their interrelationships do not remain static. To ensure the development of objective, realistic budgets, some organizations use zero-base budgeting, which is discussed later in this chapter.

PRINCIPLE OF TARGET SETTING

Make sure that each budget shows specific targets.

In its long-range planning, an organization sets goals such as a 5 percent increase in the share of the market. After the goal has been set, it must be translated into projected sales dollars and the number of units to be produced to generate the anticipated volume of sales. Specific targets are then set for each department or for the entire office in order to achieve the company's goal. At the operative level, employee performance standards of the past should be reviewed and necessary adjustments made so that the performance of each department is geared to the newly established company goal. For example, a projected growth in sales volume may require that the supervisor of the order processing department modify the department budget to provide for the purchase of two computer terminals, the employment of two data-entry operators, and the additional allocation of 125 square feet of office space.

PRINCIPLE OF FLEXIBILITY

Provide sufficient flexibility in the budget so that in the event of emergencies, action may be taken quickly to adjust the estimates.

A flexible budget provides *safety valves*—measures that can be taken in case the company experiences emergencies such as a sharp reduction in revenue, a strike, or a sudden price-slashing move by competitors. The budget must not be so rigid that it stifles progress and prevents timely decision making. Although budget figures serve as standards, they should never become straitjackets. If, after a budget has been prepared, it is discovered that some targets cannot be realized or that they are impractical, the conflicts must be resolved. For example, the budget amounts will have to be changed to agree with the reality of a prolonged strike that has decreased by 20 percent the estimated annual production.

A common approach to budgeting, known as *tight but attainable*, is based on better than average performance. Any unfavorable variances are critically reviewed since this approach usually includes allowances for less than ideal performance. The *ideal performance* approach to budgeting, on the other hand, presumes that nothing will go wrong in the company's operations; it allows for no alterations in schedules and contains no provisions for contingencies. Following another budgeting method, termed the *suicide approach*, top-level managers set a budget that is practically impossible to meet and push hard enough so that unfavorable variances are kept to a minimum. Often the impossible *is* accomplished, and the budget *is* met. However, when the suicide approach is followed, many department managers soon learn that the budget is an impossible goal and stop trying to achieve it.

■ *PRINCIPLE OF ADHERENCE*

Department managers, supervisors, and their subordinates must accept and adhere to the completed budget of administrative expenses, as adjusted by the master budget.

How the budget is accepted and adhered to at each level depends upon the tone set by top management. If top-level managers are neutral or passive about budget making and "budget following," they cannot expect that department managers, supervisors, and their subordinates will be much concerned about attaining the planned goals.

■ *PRINCIPLE OF REVIEW*

Review the budget frequently in order to determine variances that can be corrected before the budget has lost its effectiveness.

Delay in comparing actual expenses with estimated expenses can be extremely costly. To overcome such delay, a program of reliable measurement and reporting of actual performance must be established. Computers are often used in budget performance reporting to spot favorable and unfavorable variances from the budget. Depending on the individual company, variances of plus or minus 1 to 3 percent are normal. At the department level, managers should require written reports to explain significant deviations from the budget; at the operating level, employees may give oral explanations to their supervisors.

THE ADMINISTRATIVE EXPENSES BUDGET

The administrative expenses budget must be coordinated with the estimates of those who are preparing budgets for other departments or cost centers of the firm. For example, the administrative expenses budget is directly related to the sales volume estimated by the sales department. Also, we find that management policies and economic ups and downs affect the estimates appearing on the administrative expenses budget. As indicated in the following paragraphs, we can control some of the costs that are incurred to earn revenue; on the other hand, we know that certain costs lie outside our control. Some administrative expenses are directly traceable to the operations of a particular department. Other administrative expenses are incurred in order to meet the needs of several user-departments or the entire organization and are charged to the users on some basis. Therefore, we must analyze the nature and behavior of costs when preparing an administrative expenses budget.

Nature and Behavior of Costs

In planning and controlling administrative expenses, one of the most important considerations is an *analysis* of costs. This analysis is especially useful in setting production levels, in budgeting costs, in estimating costs for special projects, and in determining break-even points.

If we have properly planned administrative costs and they are being controlled, each person responsible for carrying on certain activities of the business is identified; and the controllable costs of those activities can be assigned to that person. Generally responsibility assignments are made at the lowest supervisory level since the supervisor or department head nearest the action is in the best position to control costs at that level. For example, the supervisor or department head in charge of receiving and issuing office supplies is assigned the responsibility for safeguarding this asset and monitoring its usage.

Through the design of the firm's accounting systems, internal control procedures aid the supervisor in protecting the firm's assets from theft, waste, and fraud. **Responsibility accounting**—one of these accounting systems—provides means for establishing control over costs and expenses. The accounting system is designed to record and accumulate costs so that timely reports can be made to managers and supervisors of those costs for which they are responsible. The ability to control costs and keep them within the budgeted range is then used as a basis for judging performance. In modern budgeting practice, it is widely held that managers should not be charged with those costs over which they have no control. Thus, an analysis of costs and their behavioral patterns must be undertaken. In such an analysis, costs are usually classified as fixed, variable, and semivariable.

Fixed Costs

Fixed costs, as described in Chapter 15, are usually related to a time period and tend to remain unchanged when the volume of activity changes. As shown on the cost-volume graph in Figure 23–2, fixed costs do not respond to changes in the volume level. Therefore, fixed costs are represented by a horizontal line. Examples of fixed costs are the rent expense for office space and equipment, real estate taxes, property insurance, depreciation expense on buildings and equipment, and administrative and supervisory salaries. Over a period of time, the AOM has little or no control over fixed costs.

Variable Costs

The most important and most controllable costs are known as *variable costs*. As explained in Chapter 15, variable costs change in response to changes in the volume of activity. In Figure 23–2, you see that the variable cost pattern passes through the

origin point "0" since there is zero cost associated with zero volume. In this illustration, the variable costs respond in direct proportion to changes in volume; therefore, the variable costs line slopes upward to the right. The steepness of the slope depends on the amount of cost associated with each unit produced; the greater the unit cost, the steeper the slope. In Figure 23–2, where volume is measured in thousands of units processed, the total variable dollar cost is twice as great for 20,000 units as for 10,000 units.

Examples of variable office costs include direct materials such as stationery and supplies, equipment repair and maintenance expenses, and mailing expenses. To control variable costs, AOMs are continually striving to improve their administrative office systems and procedures.

Semivariable Costs

Another important group of controllable costs, the *semivariable* or *mixed costs*, contains both fixed and variable components. A semivariable cost increases or decreases with changes in activity. At the zero level of activity, the semivariable cost is some positive amount, as shown in Figure 23–2.

Changes in total semivariable costs are not directly proportional to changes in operating volume. Consider as an example of semivariable costs the electric power expense incurred in operating the computer center. If the center were closed for a period of time, the company would still be required to pay a minimum base fee for power. Then, when the center reopened, the cost of the electric power would increase as the processing of data increased. Another example of mixed costs is the *total* payment for office wages and salaries. Earlier we saw that the salaries paid administrators and supervisors are fixed costs since these salaries are paid regardless of the level of activity. However, the wages and salaries paid part-time

Figure 23-2
Graphic
Representa-
tion of Varia-
tions in Cost
Behavior

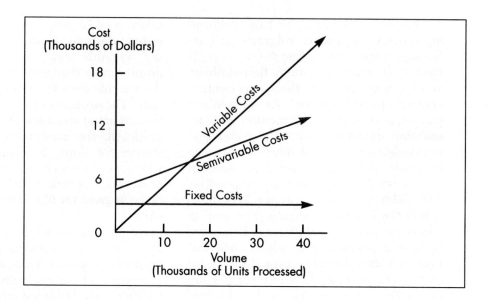

workers and temporary service personnel tend to vary according to the volume of work to be completed.

Allocating Administrative Expenses

To analyze administrative expenses from a budgetary viewpoint, managers prepare department budgets of operating expenses. Some expenses, called **direct expenses**, originate in and are chargeable directly to one department. For example, the direct expenses of the reprographics department include the salaries of the workers and the depreciation expense of the machines and equipment used in that department. Other administrative expenses, known as **indirect expenses**, are general in nature and may benefit several departments or the entire company. Such indirect costs are not directly traceable to any one department and probably could not be eliminated if the operations of a specific department were terminated. Indirect expenses are often allocated or prorated among various user departments. Several indirect expenses and their common

bases of allocation are listed in Figure 23-3. When selecting an appropriate basis for allocating indirect expenses, the AOM must verify that a reasonable relationship exists between the expense and the selected basis.

To control the rapidly rising costs of administrative services, some companies use chargeback accounting systems as a means of directly allocating the costs of office services. In a **chargeback accounting system**, each department or cost center is charged for its actual usage of support services such as text/word processing, reprographics, graphic arts, office supplies, and computing. Included in the amount charged back to the user departments are salaries, supplies, machine expenses, and training costs.

To illustrate the operation of a chargeback accounting system, let's go into the offices of a utility company. Here, every month we find that each department manager receives a monthly accounting statement showing how much was spent by the department on office services. The charge for each work order, as determined by the office services division, depends upon the amount of time required to perform the service and the

Figure 23-3
Indirect
Expenses
and Bases of
Allocation

Indirect Expense	Basis of Allocation
1. Long-distance (toll) telephone services	1. Itemized charges for each user telephone as listed on the telephone bill.
2. Text/word processing	2. Cost-per-page or cost-per-line produced for each user department.
3. Rent or property taxes	3. Square feet of space used by department.
4. Office supplies	4. Items listed on requisitions filled for user department.
5. Filing	5. Number of documents, microforms, etc., filed and retrieved for each user.
6. Data processing in computer center	6. Terminal hours used.
7. Postage	7. Volume of outgoing mail for each user department.
8. Utilities	8. Number of kilowatt-hours of electricity or cubic feet of gas consumed by user department.

complexity of the work. The total amount charged each month is subtracted from the department's budget for office expenses, thus reminding each department head of the cost of such services.

Methods of Budgeting

After we have assigned responsibilities for planning and controlling administrative costs and identified their behavioral patterns, we must determine which method of budgeting will provide the best opportunities for control. In the following paragraphs, two of the many methods of budgeting are briefly described.[2] Because neither of these methods completely meets the needs of managers as

they establish their programs of budgetary control, we shall also discuss a form of compromise budgeting.

Incremental Budgeting

The traditional or conventional approach to budgeting is called **incremental budgeting**. This method involves the addition of a given percentage of increase (the *increment*) to the budgeted amounts of the preceding period to arrive at new figures. Cost data from the prior period are revised upward under the assumption that a given percentage of increase in business activities will bring about a like increase in department expenditures. In many cases, the base to which the increment is added is treated as though it were already authorized and requires little additional review or evaluation. In a similar fashion, if it becomes necessary to reduce the budgeted amounts, all budget items are reduced by a stipulated percentage. Thus,

---

[2]Other methods of budgeting, which are modifications of those presented in this section, are described in accounting principles and financial management textbooks. *Also see*: H. W. Allen Sweeney and Robert Rachlin (editors), *Handbook of Budgeting* (New York: John Wiley & Sons), 1981.

under incremental budgeting, all departments, regardless of their cost effectiveness, share equally in increases or decreases.

Table 23-1 illustrates the use of incremental budgeting in establishing the estimated administrative expenses for 1992. To obtain these estimates, the actual figures for 1991 were simply increased by 20 percent and rounded to cover the company's projected growth in sales and the anticipated rise in the inflation rate.

Incremental budgeting carries forward into each new budgeting period the inefficiencies and wastes of the prior period. Thus, the cost of such waste becomes part of an ever-growing budgeting base. With this type of budgeting, there is little opportunity for managers and supervisors to assess which projects or programs are deserving of special attention and additional funds; and managers have no incentive to control the cost of resource allocations. Also, since requests often exceed the availability of funds, managers and supervisors are obligated to rethink and redo their budgets. Anticipating a lack of funds to cover their budget requests and realizing that their requests will be slashed, managers often inflate the amounts requested. Even cost-conscious managers who have prepared realistic, cost-effective

budgets soon learn that their budgeted amounts will be cut very much the same as those managers who initially inflated their budget requests. Thus, the budgeting process becomes routine. Managers tend to be very complacent about budgetary control, and motivation declines in those departments that are operating profitably.

Zero-Base Budgeting (ZBB)

The objective of any budgeting method is to allocate resources to those operations that contribute most to the goals of the organization. **Zero-base budgeting (ZBB)** is a resource-allocation method that requires budget makers to examine every expenditure anew each budget period and to justify the expenditure in light of current needs and developments. Thus, unlike incremental budgeting, the budget figures are not based on a percentage of increase or decrease related to the previous budgetary period. Instead, each year the budget is reduced to zero. The budget maker starts from the base line (zero) each time an expenditure is examined and justifies the first as well as the last dollar to be spent.

In using ZBB, we assume that each of the current operations and functions is of no

Table 23-1
DEFORE
COMPANY
Administrative
Expenses—
Actual and
Budget
(Thousands
of Dollars)

Expense	Actual 1991	Budget 1992
Salaries	$500	$ 600
Rent	80	100
Supplies	35	40
Telephone	120	140
Travel and meetings	70	80
Maintenance and repairs	15	20
Postage and mailing	50	60
Utilities	60	70
Miscellaneous	25	30
Totals	$955	$1,140

value. Next, we review the cost of every budget program or project (old and new), as well as the output of each program. Then, we rank each program according to its cost effectiveness. Finally, we prepare the master budget to reflect the highest cost-effective programs.

Most of the data collected about a program are presented in a document called a *decision package*. This document describes the program broken down into the smallest decision units that can be defended. A *decision unit* represents the lowest operating level where meaningful cost data can be compiled. Each decision unit is summarized in terms of the reasons for its existence, the benefits the organization gains from the unit, and the consequences for the company if the unit were to be terminated. Also included in the decision package is the manager's evaluation of alternative ways of getting the job done.

As an example of the procedure for preparing a decision package, consider Al Olsen, a records manager who is responsible for both micrographic and reprographic services. In describing the micrographic services, Olsen lists each activity, or decision unit, that can be evaluated for budgetary purposes. Once Olsen has identified the decision units, he develops a decision package for each unit. In the decision package, he summarizes the benefits that the company realizes by retaining each activity. Also, Olsen evaluates the cost effectiveness of other approaches for getting the job done: microfiche versus aperture cards versus computer output microfilm versus the use of outside micrographic services. In a similar fashion, Olsen breaks down the reprographics services into decision units and evaluates each of them. After Olsen has described all the decision packages, he ranks them in their order of importance. As a result of listing all the packages in rank order, Olsen has converted the budget process from primarily a clerical task into a managerial function where he must declare and defend

his administrative priorities. In turn, when the budget committee ranks the decision packages of all departments prior to preparing the master budget, the committee learns what each manager considers important and thus is aided in adjusting the differences in priorities.

The benefits realized from the use of ZBB include:

1. Alternative ways of performing the same job are evaluated so that cost savings may be compared.
2. Managers focus their attention upon analysis and decision making, thus improving the planning process.
3. Each budget request must be justified in relation to the costs and benefits of each program.
4. Top-level managers are enabled to follow up and exercise control over costs and performance.

On the other hand, users of ZBB experience problems such as these:

1. There is difficulty in evaluating and comparing different decision packages because departments differ in both structure and purpose and may use different performance measures.
2. The method requires more time and effort of operating managers who may have had little training in ZBB.
3. There is difficulty in ranking a large number of decision packages.
4. The required cost-performance information may not be available or may be difficult to obtain.

However, some of the problems associated with ZBB are minimized or eliminated by using computers to process information, to rank the decision packages, and to consolidate the packages and assign priorities at the higher level as the master budget is prepared.

Compromise Budgeting

The incremental budgeting and ZBB methods are often modified in order to overcome the disadvantages described earlier and to realize the benefits to be gained from each method. Under a *compromise budgeting approach*, the budget maker does not start from zero but instead accepts the realities of business conditions as they exist and makes the needed adjustments or compromises. That is, the budget maker reduces the amount of funds allocated to those programs or activities that have been evaluated as less beneficial; however, the funds are reduced only to a realistic base.[3] For example, under a compromise budgeting approach known as *modified ZBB*, the budget committee may undertake the preparation of the current budget by accepting 90 percent of last year's budget. Thus, operating managers are asked to submit ZBB decision packages only for the least essential 10 percent of their costs. As a result, operating managers prepare detailed justifications for only those parts of the budget where real decisions are likely to be made.[4]

Budget Performance Reporting

As you read earlier, budgetary control provides a means of comparing estimated expenses with actual expenses and of analyzing variances so that the controllable causes of the variances may be eliminated. Figure 23-4 shows one type of budget performance report prepared monthly by each department of the company for this purpose. Variances that have been defined as significant (such as 5 percent over or

under the budgeted amounts) should be investigated immediately to determine their causes and to seek means of preventing their recurrence. Possibly, corrective action cannot be taken because of a change in economic conditions that occurred after the budget was prepared. In such a case, future budget amounts should be revised accordingly.

The amounts in the Budget column are obtained from the sales department's schedule of estimated operating expenses that accompanied the master budget. The amounts in the Actual column, supplied by the accounting department, represent costs actually incurred during the month. The last two columns show the variances—the amounts by which actual costs were over or under the budgeted figures. At the bottom of the report, the department head has indicated for each line item the reason for the variance if it is more than or less than 5 percent of the amount budgeted.

Year-to-date cumulative figures may be more significant than monthly figures when comparing budgeted and actual expenses. The use of cumulative figures also aids in more effective budgetary control than monthly figures alone. For example, the year-to-date actual expenses tend to smooth out some of the variances caused by events not in existence at the time of preparing the original budget figures. Year-to-date figures also diminish the significance of month-to-month figures, such as when it is unexpectedly decided that an expense planned for one particular month will be carried forward into the following month. A partially completed year-to-date budget performance report is illustrated in Figure 23-5.

COST-ANALYSIS PROBLEMS RELATED TO BUDGETARY CONTROL

Among the various problems arising in cost analysis through the use of budgets, two stand out: (1) the need for developing a work

[3]Carl Joiner and J. Brad Chapman, "Budgeting Strategy: A Meaningful Mean," *S.A.M. Advanced Management Journal* (Summer, 1981), pp. 4–11.

[4]Ray L. Brown, "Beyond Zero-Base Budgeting," *Journal of Accountancy* (March, 1981), pp. 44–52.

Figure 23–4
An Example
of a Monthly
Budget Per-
formance
Report

MONTHLY BUDGET PERFORMANCE REPORT

Sales department   For the month ended May 31, 19--

Expenses	Budget	Actual	Variance Over	Variance Under
Salaries	$ 8,000	$ 8,500	$500	
Rent	200	200		
Property taxes	90	90		
Insurance	60	60		
Depreciation	300	300		
Office supplies	210	200		$10
Word processing	600	750	150	
Data processing	900	940	40	
Filing	140	120		20
Telephone	330	345	15	
Postage and mailing	500	570	70	
Totals	$11,330	$12,075	$775	$30

Variances of 5% Over (+) or Under (-) Budget

Line Item and Percentage of Variance

Salaries	+ 6.3
Word processing	+25.0
Filing	-14.3
Postage and mailing	+14.0

Reasons for Variances

_X_ Change in volume of work (specify): Part-time sales correspondent
      employed; not anticipated in budget.

____ Work postponed or eliminated:

_X_ Procedural changes affecting work: Form letters and form paragraphs
      now held in storage on microcomputer diskettes rather than hard
      copies being filed; brochures keyboarded in May rather than June.

_X_ Special assignments received, not anticipated in budget: End-of-season
      brochures mailed in May rather than in planned month of June.

____ Other reasons:

June 2, 19--
Date

Gloria Le Mas
Department Head

Figure 23–5
A Partially
Completed
Year-to-Date
Budget Per-
formance
Report

YEAR-TO-DATE BUDGET PERFORMANCE REPORT

Sales department   For the month ended May 31, 19--

Expenses	Budget Month	Actual Month	Monthly Variance Over	Monthly Variance Under	Budget Year to Date	Actual Year to Date	Year-to-Date Variance Over	Year-to-Date Variance Under
Salaries	$ 8,000	$ 8,500	$500		$40,000	$40,500	$ 500	
Rent	200	200			1,000	1,000		
Property taxes . . .	90	90			450	450		
Insurance	60	60			300	300		
Depreciation	300	300			1,500	1,500		
Office supplies . .	210	200		$10	1,050	1,180	130	
Word processing . .	600	750	150		3,000	3,220	220	
Data processing . .	900	940	40		4,500	4,800	300	
Filing	140	120		20	700	690		$ 10
Telephone	330	345	15		1,650	1,600		50
Postage and mailing.	500	570	70		2,500	2,390		110
Totals	$11,330	$12,075	$775	$30	$56,650	$57,630	$1,150	$170

standards program and (2) controlling fluctuations in the volume of administrative services as a result of periodic or seasonal factors.

Using Work Standards in Analyzing Costs

In Chapter 22, we described the benefits to be gained from installing a work standards program. One of these benefits relates to the establishment of work targets and the planning of human resources. As a result of a work standards program, the AOM is able to prepare realistic budgets, to plan the number of workers needed to provide administrative services, and to measure the effectiveness of the budgeted amounts.

In the following example, you will see how work standards may be used to calculate the unit cost of administrative support services and to determine the need for additional workers. Consider a firm that has divided its text/word processing function among several cost centers, each of which serves a group of technical writers. Through the use of a daily time log completed by the senior

word processing operator, the supervisor of one cost center has determined the standard production rate to lie within the range of 115 to 134 lines of copy per hour. The midpoint of this range, 125, has been adopted as the standard number of lines to be produced per hour. For the past 52 weeks of 37½ hours each, the standard output was 243,750 lines. The costs allocated to word processing in this center total $33,100 for the year, as shown below:

Salary and benefits.	$28,000
Materials and stationery	2,100
Telephone	400
Depreciation expense	2,600
Total costs	$33,100

The standard unit cost for each line produced during the past year is calculated as follows:

$$\frac{\$33,100 \text{ (total costs)}}{243,750 \text{ (standard lines of output)}} =$$

$$\$ .1358 \text{ standard unit cost per line}$$

Assume that for next year, the sales department projects a sales volume that converts into a 50 percent increase in the number of lines to be produced in the cost center. Thus, the estimated standard output for the following year would be 365,625 lines (243,750 $\times$ 150 percent). The estimated output is then translated into personnel needs as follows:

$$\frac{365,625 \text{ estimated lines to be produced}}{243,750 \text{ standard lines per year}} =$$

1.5 operators

To meet the need for an additional part-time operator in the center, the supervisor has studied several options such as overtime work, part-time help, and temporary office help. Assume that the supervisor has decided to employ a part-time worker next year to meet the increased needs. The total costs of operating the center, taking into consideration the effects of inflation and the purchase of additional equipment, are estimated by the supervisor as:

Full-Time Senior Word Processing Operator

Salary and benefits	$31,000	
Materials and supplies	2,300	
Telephone	450	
Depreciation expense	2,600	$36,350

Part-Time Word Processing Operator

Salary and benefits	$13,000	
Materials and supplies	1,200	
Telephone (shared with full-time operator)	...	
Depreciation expense (new processing unit)	3,000	17,200
Total costs		$53,550

As a result of employing a part-time operator, the standard unit cost per line produced during the following year will increase by a little more than one cent, as calculated below:

$$\frac{\$53,550 \text{ (total costs)}}{365,625 \text{ (standard lines of output)}} =$$

$ .1465 standard unit cost per line

$$\frac{\text{Unit Cost}}{\text{for New Year}} - \frac{\text{Unit Cost}}{\text{for Last Year}} = \frac{\text{Increase in}}{\text{Unit Cost for}}$$
New Year

$$\$.1465 \quad - \quad \$.1358 \quad = \quad \$.0107$$

During the new year the AOM should strive to increase the output of each operator while at the same time searching for means of reducing the variable costs. The present system and its supporting procedures should be analyzed in order to eliminate poor work habits, wasted motions, and unnecessary physical effort. Also, close control should be exercised over the issuance and usage of materials and supplies. If the output of each of the two operators could be increased by about 9.8 lines per hour during the new year, the standard unit cost of production would be reduced to its former level, $.1358.

Controlling the Cost of Peak-Load Fluctuations

In many organizations there are periods of time during which peak-load needs must be considered when preparing and using an administrative expenses budget. For example, during certain periods of each month, the payroll must be prepared. Statements must be completed and sent to customers. Quarterly or annual financial reports and statements must be compiled; inventories must be taken periodically. Although occurring with a certain amount of regularity, these activities complicate the planning, scheduling, and estimating of administrative costs, especially when the tasks must be completed by a definite date.

Management must recognize the problem of peak-load fluctuations and develop efficient means of controlling the costs. Office managers have used some or all of the following means to control the costs of peak-load fluctuations in office work.

Cycle Billing

Firms use cycle billing to overcome peak work loads at the end of the month. A **cycle billing system** distributes evenly throughout the month the work related to preparing and mailing monthly statements of customers' accounts (accounts receivable). Cycle billing is an effective accounting technique used by most utilities, retail stores, banks, stock brokerage houses, and industrial firms.

In firms that use cycle billing, the customers' accounts are divided into groups. There may be as many as 16 to 20 groups, each of which is approximately equal in size in order to balance the work load among the billing department personnel. Each group of customers' accounts covers certain letters of the alphabet and certain days of the month. For example, statements to customers in the alphabetic group A–B may be sent out on the first day of each month; on the fifth day, statements are mailed for the C–D group. The system is continued during the entire month until the last cycle group—W–Z—is completed.

Following the closing day for each cycle group, a single billing operation is performed. Thus, the statements for all active accounts may be printed out in one run on the computer printer. By dividing the accounts receivable ledger into alphabetic groups and closing each of these groups at a different time during the month, we spread the daily work load more evenly throughout the month. In turn, this procedure reduces the need for overtime and part-time workers. As a result, collection schedules, cash intake, and all supporting operations flow more evenly.

Split-Payroll Dates

We find that some payroll accounting systems are designed similar to a cycle billing plan. By having different payroll dates for different departments, peak-load fluctuations in preparing the payroll may be minimized. For example, for many years in one firm all personnel were paid on the 15th and the last day of the month. As part of a study to reduce peak-load activities in the payroll department, the firm decided to pay the office workers and workers in the shipping and packing departments every two weeks; administrative and executive personnel continued to be paid twice a month on the 15th and the last day. Thus, the company was able to smooth out the peak load that formerly occurred at the time of every semimonthly pay; and the firm more effectively used the services of the personnel in the payroll department.

Using Current Personnel on an Overtime Basis

Overtime work is best scheduled where the overload is unexpected or of short duration and is not expected to recur with any degree of regularity. Scheduling work beyond the firm's standard workweek is an expensive method that may increase costs 50 percent or more. In addition to increased labor costs, a firm may find that during the overtime hours, employee productivity continues to decline while the probability of error rises.[5] The major advantage of using current personnel on an overtime basis is that the people doing the work come from the regular skilled staff who are already familiar with the organization's operations and procedures.

Hiring Part-Time Employees

Part-time workers (nonpermanent employees) make up a significant portion of

---

[5]The Bureau of Labor Statistics reports that during the workday, an employee's productivity steadily declines until it is at 50 percent by the eighth hour. By the same hour, the probability of error has risen to 40 percent. During the first hour of overtime, productivity continues to decline while the probability of error climbs. *See* Douglas Finlay, "Temporary Services: Ideal Solutions to Changing Labor Needs," *Administrative Management* (February, 1987), pp. 20–21.

the working population and represent a growth that has stemmed partly from the rising number of women, retired persons, and young people who want to work only a part of each day. The 1988 AMS Contract Labor Survey found that most companies use part-time employees for clerical and secretarial work; the types of business that most often use part-time help are: insurance, banking, finance, and educational and government agencies.[6]

Hiring part-time employees may initially represent an economical move for the organization since the hourly labor costs would be relatively low. However, since all new part-time employees start from a zero-base salary, most, if not all, of their annual salaries would cause the employer's payroll taxes to increase substantially. In addition, the employer may be faced with added costs such as an increased premium for group life insurance coverage. Other factors to consider include the costs facing the human resources department in recruiting, orienting, and training the part-time people and the payroll department's costs of processing additional payroll records.

Using Temporary Office Workers

As indicated in Chapter 6, a company that uses the services of temporary office personnel for varying periods of time realizes significant savings. The only cost to the employer is the fee paid to the temporary help service. The employer is not faced with payroll taxes and costly employee benefits, and the human resources department incurs very little, if any, recruitment and orientation expense.

Often during a recession, a company will lower its variable expenses by reducing the size of its full-time office work force. Shortly thereafter, the firm may find that there is

Hiring temporary workers is one way to handle cyclical work overloads.

more work than the reduced work force can handle. The company may then turn to the use of temporary office help until the return of a stable economy—and the need for hiring additional full-time workers—is indicated. Thus, the firm can fill in with temporary workers as needed without adding to its overhead costs.

Floating Workers

Office workers often "float" from one peak-load area to another as the firm's needs require. Some organizations hire workers whose major function is to float or to "fly" from one department to another during peak workload hours. In other companies, workers leave their regularly assigned workstations and "lend a helping hand" in peak-load areas during rush periods. For example, during the peak hours when the mailing center receives the incoming mail or when it is processing the outgoing mail, the center may temporarily use the services of "floaters" who regularly work in other departments such as order processing, billing, and filing.

---

[6]Jeffrey E. Long, "The State of Contract Labor: 1988," *Management World* (May/June, 1988), p. 15.

Service Bureaus

The increase in the number of service bureaus, or data service centers, indicates that many companies find these sources to be an answer to the periodic overloads of office work.

To illustrate how a service bureau is used to reduce peak loads, let's drop into a typical payroll department. By its very nature, the peak loads in payroll operations occur right before and after a payroll is processed. Depending upon how often employees are paid, we find additional resources required during these peak periods, but not every day. The need for additional resources may be met by using floating workers from other departments, by hiring part-time workers, or by paying overtime to present payroll personnel. However, by taking advantage of the service bureau's services, we can reduce some of the added costs associated with the peak loads. For example, most service bureaus will sign, burst, stuff, and distribute checks according to our instructions. The bureau will also print out reports, such as labor cost analyses, and tax forms. Thus, these services reduce the resources required in the mailing center and the payroll department. As we saw in Chapter 16, the high degree of skill, the confidential nature of their work, and their comparatively low cost have much to recommend service bureaus as a means for establishing cost control over peak-load fluctuations.

SUMMARY

1. Budgets are used by AOMs in acquiring and using resources for the information-processing activities under their supervision and control. By means of periodic budget performance reports, the AOM compares actual operating expenses with budgeted expenses and determines the variances. Thus, the AOM can take steps to improve productivity by reducing or eliminating significant variances.

2. Depending upon the size of the organization, the AOM may prepare budgets; receive budgets from subordinates; or analyze, consolidate, and condense budgets into a final report for the budget committee, which is responsible for preparing the firm's master budget.

3. When preparing a budget of administrative expenses, the AOM is guided by the following principles: (a) assign initial responsibility to key employees for budget preparation, (b) objectively develop budget figures, (c) set realistic targets for each department, (d) provide flexibility in the budget so that timely decision making is not impeded, (e) ensure that the budget is accepted and adhered to, and (f) plan for frequent review of the budget in order to detect and correct variances. While following each of these principles of budget preparation, the AOM must be aware of the nature and behavior of costs and realize which kinds of costs present the greatest opportunity for cost reduction and control.

4. The AOM evaluates various methods of budgeting, such as incremental budgeting and zero-base budgeting. From these methods, the AOM selects one method or a combination of methods that provides the best opportunities for analyzing and controlling costs. With an effective budgeting method, the AOM is also aided in solving cost-related problems, such as relating work standards to budget preparation, estimating future needs for additional employees, and reducing the fluctuating output of office work during peak-load periods.

GLOSSARY **Administrative expenses**—those expenses incurred in the general operations of the organization; also called *general expenses*.

Budget—a formal statement of plans for the future, expressed in financial terms.

Budget performance report—the periodic comparison of actual operating data with budgeted data.

Budgetary control—the use of a budget in regulating and guiding those business activities concerned with acquiring and using resources.

Budgeting—the process of planning future business activities and expressing those plans in a formal manner.

Chargeback accounting system—a plan for directly allocating the costs of support services by charging each department or cost center for its actual use of the services.

Cycle billing system—a plan for evenly distributing throughout the month the work related to preparing and mailing monthly statements of customers' accounts.

Direct expenses—expenses originating in and chargeable directly to one department.

Flexible budget—a prediction of costs at various levels of activity.

Incremental budgeting—a budgeting method in which a given percentage of increase (or decrease) is added to (or subtracted from) the budgeted amounts of the preceding period to arrive at new figures.

Indirect expenses—general expenses that benefit several departments or the entire company but are not directly traceable to any one department.

Master budget—a number of budgets that collectively express the planned activities of the organization.

Responsibility accounting—the system that provides means for establishing control over costs and expenses so that timely reports are made to managers and supervisors of those costs for which they are responsible.

Variance—the difference between actual operating data and budgeted data.

Zero-base budgeting (ZBB)—a budgeting method in which budget makers examine anew and justify each expenditure each budget period.

FOR YOUR REVIEW

1. Of what value are budget performance reports in a program of budgetary control?

2. What objectives is management trying to attain in the use of budgets and budget performance reports?

3. What is the function of a budget committee?

4. What is the main difference between a master budget and a flexible budget?

5. How do well-prepared budgets of administrative expenses aid the AOM in planning and controlling office operations?

6. For what reasons should the budget-making process begin at the operative level?

7. Why should a budget contain safety valves?

8. Explain how control over costs and expenses is provided through the establishment of a responsibility accounting system.

9. Why are variable costs and semivariable costs more controllable than fixed costs?

10. Distinguish between direct expenses and indirect expenses and give examples of each kind.

11. What is a commonly used basis for allocating each of the following indirect expenses: (a) text/word processing, (b) filing, and (c) data processing in the computer center?

12. What disadvantages are associated with incremental budgeting?

13. Describe zero-base budgeting and list the major benefits to be realized from using this budgeting method.

14. Explain how a monthly budget performance report is prepared.

15. Briefly describe how the use of work standards contributes to the preparation of realistic budgets and planning the number of workers needed for a future time period.

16. How does a cycle billing system aid in minimizing peak-load fluctuations?

FOR YOUR DISCUSSION

1. The sales forecast is the starting point in all budgeting. Why?

2. One management consultant observes that in many offices, the "human problems" associated with budgeting require almost as much attention from the manager as do the analytical opportunities that the budgeting data provide.[7] For example, when budgets are used to exert unfair pressures on office employees, some workers may directly retaliate with unnecessarily wasteful actions. What other kinds of human problems would you anticipate when budgetary control is improperly used in the office? What solutions can you offer to solve these problems?

3. When top management demands an explanation for variances, it is not an uncommon practice for someone to manipulate numbers so that the variances are reduced; thus, the expenses appear to be more in line and no explanation of a variance is any longer needed. For example, to alter the amount of variance and present a more favorable picture, we may find that someone has made a journal entry that overstates the amount of income earned. Thus, top management is given a false summary of operating results. What is your reaction to altering the actual operating results to comply with the budget?

4. "An organization must use a budget for a long period of time before it becomes an effective tool of management." Explain the meaning of this statement.

5. The effectiveness of a budgetary control program is measured by making department heads responsible for their department budget figures. Explain.

---

[7]Edward N. Rausch, *Profitable Office Management for the Growing Business* (New York: American Management Association, Inc., 1984), p. 126.

6. In discussing his budgetary needs for the forthcoming year, George Anka remarked to his supervisor of accounting operations, "I really need only eight workers, but those up above always cut my budget by 20 percent. So this year I'll ask for ten." How do you explain this type of attitude on the part of Anka? What is your reaction to Anka's philosophy of budgeting?

7. Most conscientious office managers want to know from time to time how well they are performing. By means of monthly budget performance reports, office managers are informed of how well they are doing. Likewise, all others who receive copies of the monthly reports are informed of the office manager's progress (or lack of progress). As an office manager who has been receiving monthly budget performance reports, how can you use the information in analyzing your performance and in impressing upon others the progress that you have made in "holding the line" on costs?

8. Terry Silverstein, a word processing manager, has been laying out plans to automate some of the procedures that will link all branch offices together with the headquarters office. In discussing her proposed pilot test with Mark Lamar, head of the budgeting committee, she is told: "Take a look around and see what you can get for $50,000." Evaluate Lamar's statement as the first step to be taken in the budgetary process.

9. At Tel-Com Information Services, budgetary control often involves decisions on whether to lease or buy electronic office equipment. Why is it advisable for this organization to appoint a qualified accountant to be part of the initial budgetary process?

SOLVING CASE PROBLEMS

Case 23-1 Spending to Budget

At the first meeting of the budget committee of Fleer Products, the newly appointed budget director, Melissa Krunn, was reviewing the year-to-date performance figures of each department. After Krunn read the budget figures for the office services department, headed by Wesley Hunter, the following conversation took place:

Krunn: Wes, I know some people in this company feel it is common practice to "spend to budget." I know very well that you, like some of the others, feel that if you don't spend all that was budgeted this year, you're going to be cut in next year's allocations.

Hunter: That's true, Melissa. Along with most of the others, I know that if we're to prosper next year, each of us must get more. So, we spend all of our allocated funds each year, knowing very well that next year the amount will be reduced if we don't spend this year's funds.

Krunn: Well, I think it's time we changed that attitude on the part of all of you who prepare department budgets. I don't believe any of you should be penalized for holding the line on costs. Rather, you should be rewarded for not spending needlessly.

Hunter: That sounds good in theory, Melissa, but in all my years with Fleer this hasn't been the case. How are you going to overcome the practice of spending to budget?

Krunn: Let me think about that question. I'm sure there are some steps we can take.

A few days later Krunn calls a department meeting in which problems related to budgeting and spending will be discussed. She indicates she is seeking specific steps that can be taken to halt the practice of spending to budget. Hunter now approaches you, his assistant, for your recommendations.

What specific steps do you recommend that the firm take to reduce the common practice of spending to budget?

Case 23-2 Analyzing the Budget Performance Report for a Text/Word Processing Center

In the Hartwick Company, the budget of administrative expenses is prepared by the office manager, James Loprest. This budget is a composite of all the functional departments under his supervision. Each department head is asked to prepare on a standard form the budget figures for the next fiscal year. The budgeted and actual costs are analyzed on a monthly basis and later on a quarterly basis. Some of the costs submitted are fixed and thus are little affected by the volume of work to be done; other costs vary either directly or proportionately with the volume of work.

The budget of the fixed, variable, and allocated costs for the text/word processing center for the quarter ending March 31, 19-- is shown in Table A. The actual costs of the quarter are shown in Table B.

Prepare a quarterly comparison of the budgeted and the actual figures by completing the following:

1. On the performance report for the period ending March 31, show the budget year-to-date and the actual year-to-date figures.

2. On the March 31 report, show the dollar amount and the percentage of variance between the actual and the budgeted figures.

Table A
Budgeted
Costs for
Three
Months

Item	January	February	March
Salaries of principals and supervisor	$20,000	$20,000	$20,000
Salaries of correspondence secretaries	9,500	9,500	11,000
Postage	5,000	5,000	5,500
Telecommunications	4,000	4,000	4,300
Supplies	3,000	3,000	3,100
Maintenance and repairs	200	200	200
Miscellaneous expense	150	160	180
Share of administrative expense	1,800	1,800	1,800
Share of human resources department costs	900	900	900
Rent	900	900	900
Utilities	800	900	850
Depreciation expense—equipment	2,500	2,500	3,900
Insurance	200	200	200
Payroll taxes and workers' compensation	3,670	3,670	3,860
Totals	$52,620	$52,730	$56,690

Table B
Actual Costs
for Three
Months

Item	January	February	March
Salaries of principals and supervisor	$20,000	$20,400	$20,400
Salaries of correspondence secretaries	9,650	9,700	11,250
Postage	5,300	5,350	6,800
Telecommunications	3,800	4,100	4,200
Supplies	3,200	3,100	4,200
Maintenance and repairs	210	180	180
Miscellaneous expense	160	140	190
Share of administrative expense	1,800	1,800	1,800
Share of human resources department costs	900	900	900
Rent	900	900	900
Utilities	890	1,020	900
Depreciation expense—equipment	2,500	2,500	3,980
Insurance	200	200	200
Payroll taxes and workers' compensation	3,690	3,750	3,940
Totals	$53,200	$54,040	$59,840

3. Indicate the possible causes of any variance of plus or minus 5 percent.

4. Compute the unit cost of each line produced during each month and the quarter, using the following output:

> January: 423,604 lines
> February: 429,780 lines
> March: 459,436 lines

Index

PHOTO CREDITS

For permission to reproduce the photographs on the pages indicated, acknowledgment is made to the following: